Macmillan/McGraw-Hill Edition

McGRAW-HILL READING

Contributors

The Princeton Review, Time Magazine, Accelerated Reader

The Princeton Review is not affiliated with Princeton University or ETS.

McGraw-Hill School Division

A Division of The McGraw-Hill Companies

McGraw-Hill School Division
Two Penn Plaza
New York, New York 10121

Printed in the United States of America

ISBN 0-02-184761-4/3, Bk.1, U.3
4 5 6 7 8 9 043/073 04 03 02 01 00

Selected Quizzes Prepared by Accelerated Reader

McGraw-Hill Reading

Authors

Make the Difference...

Dr. James Flood

Ms. Angela Shelf Medearis

Dr. Jan E. Hasbrouck

Dr. Scott Paris

Dr. James V. Hoffman

Dr. Steven Stahl

Dr. Diane Lapp

Dr. Josefina Villamil Tinajero

Dr. Karen D. Wood

Contributing

Authors

Dr. Barbara Coulter

Ms. Frankie Dungan

Dr. Joseph B. Rubin

Dr. Carl B. Smith

Dr. Shirley Wright

Part 1
START TOGETHER

Focus on Reading and Skills

All students start with the SAME:

- Read Aloud
- Pretaught Skills
  - Phonics
  - Comprehension
- Build Background
- Selection Vocabulary

...Never hold a child back. Never leave a child behind.

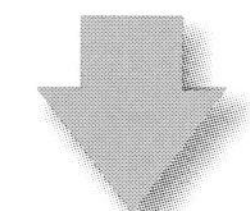

Part 2
MEET INDIVIDUAL NEEDS

Read the Literature

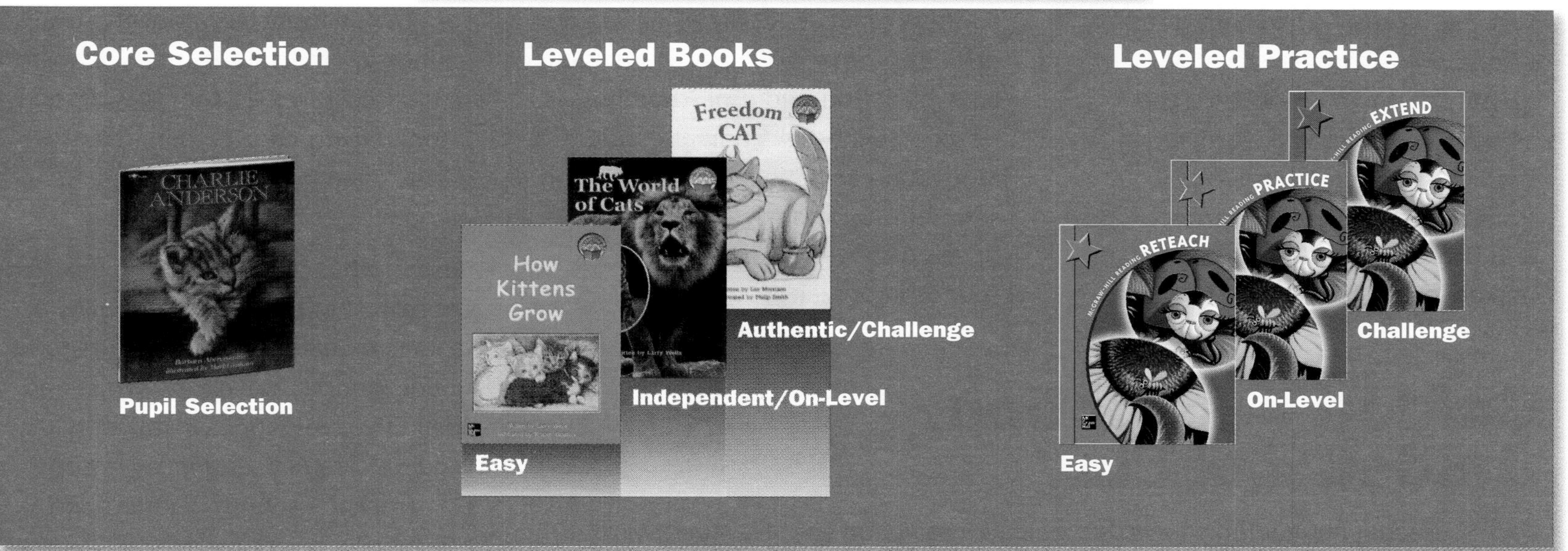

Examples Taken From Grade 2

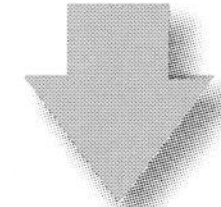

Part 3
FINISH TOGETHER

Build Skills

All students finish with the SAME:

- Phonics
- Comprehension
- Vocabulary
- Study Skills
- Assessment

McGraw-Hill Reading Applying the Research

Phonological Awareness

Phonological awareness is the ability to hear the sounds in spoken language. It includes the ability to separate spoken words into discrete sounds as well as the ability to blend sounds together to make words. A child with good phonological awareness can identify rhyming words, hear the separate syllables in a word, separate the first sound in a word (onset) from the rest of the word (rime), and blend sounds together to make words.

Recent research findings have strongly concluded that children with good phonological awareness skills are more likely to learn to read well. These skills can be improved through systematic, explicit instruction involving auditory practice. McGraw-Hill Reading develops these key skills by providing an explicit Phonological Awareness lesson in every selection at grades K-2. Motivating activities such as blending, segmenting, and rhyming help to develop children's awareness of the sounds in our language.

Guided Instruction/ Guided Reading

Research on reading shows that guided instruction enables students to develop as independent, strategic readers. The *reciprocal-teaching model* of Anne-Marie Palincsar encourages teachers to model strategic-thinking, questioning, clarifying, and problem-solving strategies for students as students read together with the teacher. In McGraw-Hill Reading, guided instruction for all Pupil Edition selections incorporates the Palincsar model by providing interactive questioning prompts. The *guided-reading model* of Gay Su Pinnell is also incorporated into the McGraw-Hill Reading program. Through the guided-reading lessons provided for the leveled books offered with the program, teachers can work with small groups of students of different ability levels, closely observing them as they read and providing support specific to their needs.

By adapting instruction to include successful models of teaching and the appropriate materials to deliver instruction, McGraw-Hill Reading enables teachers to offer the appropriate type of instruction for all students in the classroom.

Phonics

Our language system uses an alphabetic code to communicate meaning from writing. Phonics involves learning the phonemes or sounds that letters make and the symbols or letters that represent those sounds. Children learn to blend the sounds of letters to decode unknown or unfamiliar words. The goal of good phonics instruction is to enable students to read words accurately and automatically.

Research has clearly identified the critical role of phonics in the ability of readers to read fluently and with good understanding, as well as to write and spell. Effective phonics instruction requires carefully sequenced lessons that teach the sounds of letters and how to use these sounds to read words. The McGraw-Hill program provides daily explicit and systematic phonics instruction to teach the letter sounds and blending. There are three explicit Phonics and Decoding lessons for every selection. Daily Phonics Routines are provided for quick reinforcement, in addition to activities in the Phonics/Phonemic Awareness Practice Book and technology components. This combination of direct skills instruction and applied practice leads to reading success.

Curriculum Connections

As in the child's real-world environment, boundaries between disciplines must be dissolved. Recent research emphasizes the need to make connections between and across subject areas. McGraw-Hill Reading is committed to this approach. Each reading selection offers activities that tie in with social studies, language arts, geography, science, mathematics, art, music, health, and physical education. The program threads numerous research and inquiry activities that encourage the child to use the library and the Internet to seek out information. Reading and language skills are applied to a variety of genres, balancing fiction and nonfiction.

Integrated Language Arts

Success in developing communication skills is greatly enhanced by integrating the language arts in connected and purposeful ways. This allows students to understand the need for proper writing, grammar, and spelling. McGraw-Hill Reading sets the stage for meaningful learning. Each week a full writing-process lesson is provided. This lesson is supported by a 5-day spelling plan, emphasizing spelling patterns and spelling rules, and a 5-day grammar plan, focusing on proper grammar, mechanics, and usage.

Meeting Individual Needs

Every classroom is a microcosm of a world composed of diverse individuals with unique needs and abilities. Research points out that such needs must be addressed with frequent intensive opportunities to learn with engaging materials. McGraw-Hill Reading makes reading a successful experience for every child by providing a rich collection of leveled books for easy, independent, and challenging reading. Leveled practice is provided in Reteach, Practice, and Extend skills books. To address various learning styles and language needs, the program offers alternative teaching strategies, prevention/intervention techniques, language support activities, and ESL teaching suggestions.

Assessment

Frequent assessment in the classroom makes it easier for teachers to identify problems and to find remedies for them. McGraw-Hill Reading makes assessment an important component of instruction. Formal and informal opportunities are a part of each lesson. Minilessons, prevention/intervention strategies, and informal checklists, as well as student self-assessments, provide many informal assessment opportunities. Formal assessments, such as weekly selection tests and criterion-referenced unit tests, help to monitor students' knowledge of important skills and concepts. McGraw-Hill Reading also addresses how to adapt instruction based on student performance with resources such as the Alternate Teaching Strategies. Weekly lessons on test preparation, including test preparation practice books, help students to transfer skills to new contexts and to become better test takers.

For information on research that supports this program, visit ***www.mhschool.com/reading***

McGraw-Hill Reading

Theme Chart

GRADE LEVEL	Experience Experiences can tell us about ourselves and our world.	Connections Making connections develops new understandings.
Kindergarten	**My World** We learn a lot from all the things we see and do at home and in school.	**All Kinds of Friends** When we work and play together, we learn more about ourselves.
Subtheme 1	At Home	Working Together
Subtheme 2	School Days	Playing Together
1	**Day by Day** Each day brings new experiences.	**Together Is Better** We like to share ideas and experiences with others.
2	**What's New?** With each day, we learn something new.	**Just Between Us** Family and friends help us see the world in new ways.
3	**Great Adventures** Life is made up of big and small experiences.	**Nature Links** Nature can give us new ideas.
4	**Reflections** Stories let us share the experiences of others.	**Something in Common** Sharing ideas can lead to meaningful cooperation.
5	**Time of My Life** We sometimes find memorable experiences in unexpected places.	**Building Bridges** Knowing what we have in common helps us appreciate our differences.
6	**Pathways** Reflecting on life's experiences can lead to new understandings.	**A Common Thread** A look beneath the surface may uncover hidden connections.

MULTI-AGE Classroom

Using the same global themes at each grade level facilitates the use of materials in multi-age classrooms.

Themes: Kindergarten – Grade 6

Expression	Inquiry	Problem Solving	Making Decisions
There are many styles and forms for expressing ourselves.	By exploring and asking questions, we make discoveries.	Analyzing information can help us solve problems.	Using what we know helps us evaluate situations.
Time to Shine We can use our ideas and our imagination to do many wonderful things.	**I Wonder** We can make discoveries about the wonders of nature in our own backyard.	**Let's Work It Out** Working as part of a team can help me find a way to solve problems.	**Choices** We can make many good choices and decisions every day.
Great Ideas	**In My Backyard**	**Try and Try Again**	**Good Choices**
Let's Pretend	**Wonders of Nature**	**Teamwork**	**Let's Decide**
Stories to Tell Each one of us has a different story to tell.	**Let's Find Out!** Looking for answers is an adventure.	**Think About It!** It takes time to solve problems.	**Many Paths** Each decision opens the door to a new path.
Express Yourself We share our ideas in many ways.	**Look Around** There are surprises all around us.	**Figure It Out** We can solve problems by working together.	**Starting Now** Unexpected events can lead to new decisions.
Be Creative! We can all express ourselves in creative, wonderful ways.	**Tell Me More** Looking and listening closely will help us find out the facts.	**Think It Through** Solutions come in many shapes and sizes.	**Turning Points** We make new judgments based on our experiences.
Our Voices We can each use our talents to communicate ideas.	**Just Curious** We can find answers in surprising places.	**Make a Plan** Often we have to think carefully about a problem in order to solve it.	**Sorting It Out** We make decisions that can lead to new ideas and discoveries.
Imagine That The way we express our thoughts and feelings can take different forms.	**Investigate!** We never know where the search for answers might lead us.	**Bright Ideas** Some problems require unusual approaches.	**Crossroads** Decisions cause changes that can enrich our lives.
With Flying Colors Creative people help us see the world from different perspectives.	**Seek and Discover** To make new discoveries, we must observe and explore.	**Brainstorms** We can meet any challenge with determination and ingenuity.	**All Things Considered** Encountering new places and people can help us make decisions.

UNIT 3

Contents

Be Creative!

We can all express ourselves in creative, wonderful ways.

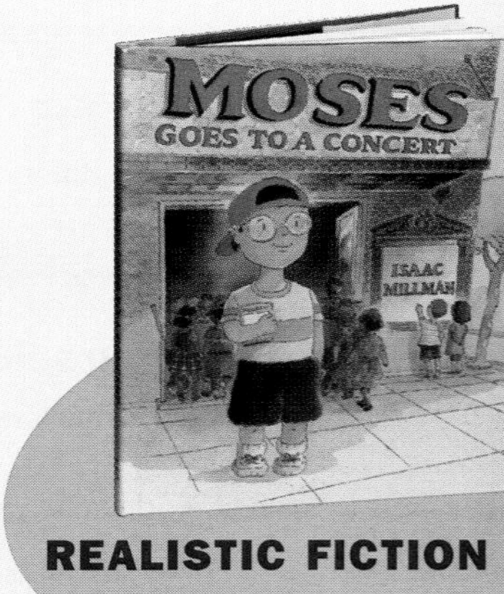

REALISTIC FICTION

SKILLS			
Study Skill	**Comprehension**	**Vocabulary**	**Phonics**
• Using Graphic Aids: Diagram	• **Introduce** Main Idea • **Review** Main Idea • **Introduce** Summarize	• **Review** Context Clues	• Final Consonant Clusters

BIOGRAPHICAL STORY

SKILLS			
Study Skill	**Comprehension**	**Vocabulary**	**Phonics**
• Using Graphic Aids: Map	• **Review** Story Elements • **Review** Summarize	• **Review** Context Clues	• Double Consonants

UNIT 3

Unit Planner

	WEEK 1 Moses Goes to a Concert	WEEK 2 The Little Painter of Sabana Grande
 **Leveled Books**	Easy: *The Night Jazz Came Alive* Independent: *Beethoven: The Man and His Music* Challenge: *All That Jazz*	Easy: *The Barn Raising* Independent: *Rosa's New Home* Challenge: *Aborigines of the Australian Outback*
 **Tested Skills**	Comprehension Main Idea, 260A–260B, 289E–289F Summarize, 289G–289H Vocabulary Context Clues, 289I–289J Study Skills Graphic Aids, 288	Comprehension Story Elements, 292A–292B, 317E–317F Summarize, 317G–317H Vocabulary Context Clues, 317I–317J Study Skills Graphic Aids, 316
Minilessons	**Phonics and Decoding: Final Consonant Clusters,** 279 **Summarize,** 267 **Suffixes,** 273 **Make Inferences,** 275	**Phonics and Decoding: Double Consonants,** 303 **Sequence,** 299 **Summarize,** 301 **Context Clues,** 305 **Make Predictions,** 307 **Draw Conclusions,** 311
Language Arts	**Writing:** Persuasive Writing, 289K **Grammar:** Action Verbs, 289M–289N **Spelling:** Words with Consonant Clusters, 289O–289P	**Writing:** Persuasive Writing, 317K **Grammar:** Present-Tense Verbs, 317M–317N **Spelling:** Words with Double Consonants, 317O–317P

Activities

Curriculum Connections	Week 1	Week 2
Social Studies	Read Aloud: "Take a Bite of Music," 258E	Read Aloud: "The Crow and the Pitcher," 290E
Mathematics	Stories in Art: *Jaws*, 258/259	Stories in Art: In Flanders Field, 290/291
Science	Science: Listen to Your Voice, 268	Social Studies: Map Skills, 294
Music	Social Studies: Careers, 270	Math: Use a Calendar, 298
Art	Science: The Human Ear, 274	Science: Rain Forests, 302
Drama	Math/Music: Find the Beat, 278	Music: Merengue, 308
Language Arts		
CULTURAL PERSPECTIVES	Percussion, 266	Murals, 296

WEEK 3 The Patchwork Quilt	WEEK 4 Pecos Bill	WEEK 5 A Very Cool Place to Visit	WEEK 6 Review, Writing Process, Assessment
Easy: *An Ancient Art* **Independent:** *Recording the Past* **Challenge:** *Buried Treasure*	**Easy:** *Little Fox and Big Coyote* **Independent:** *The King's Oranges* **Challenge:** *Barbara Becomes a Big Sister*	Self-Selected Reading of Leveled Books	Self-Selected Reading
Comprehension Make Inferences, 320A–320B, 349E–349F Main Idea, 349G–349H **Vocabulary** Multiple-Meaning Words, 349I–349J **Study Skills** Graphic Aids, 348	**Comprehension** Story Elements, 352A–352B, 375E–375F Make Inferences, 375G–375H **Vocabulary** Multiple-Meaning Words, 375I–375J **Study Skills** Graphic Aids, 374	**Comprehension** Main Idea, 378A–378B Summarize, 385E–385F **Vocabulary** Multiple-Meaning Words, 385G–385H Review Context Clues, 385I–385J **Study Skills** Graphic Aids, 384	**Assess Skills** Main Idea Summarize Story Elements Make Inferences Context Clues Multiple-Meaning Words Graphic Aids **Assess Grammar and Spelling** Review Verbs, 387G Review Spelling Patterns, 387H **Unit Progress Assessment** **Standardized Test Preparation**
Phonics and Decoding: /ou/ and /oi/, 339 **Character,** 331 **Suffixes,** 333 **Main Idea,** 341	**Main Idea,** 359 **/ou/ and /oi/,** 361 **Context Clues,** 369		
Writing: Persuasive Writing, 349K **Grammar:** Past-Tense Verbs, 349M–349N **Spelling:** Words with /ou/ and /oi/, 349O–349P	**Writing:** Persuasive Writing, 375K **Grammar:** Using Verb Tenses, 375M–375N **Spelling:** Adding *-ed* and *-ing*, 375O–375P	**Writing:** Persuasive Writing, 385K **Grammar:** Sentence Combining with Verbs, 385M–385N **Spelling:** Words from Science, 385O–385P	**Unit Writing Process:** Persuasive Writing, 387A–387F
Read Aloud: "Basket," 318E	**Read Aloud:** "Paul Bunyan, the Mightiest Logger of Them All," 350E	**Read Aloud:** "Ice Cycle," 376E	GROUP **Cooperative Theme Project Research and Inquiry:** Our Special Community, 257
Stories in Art: *African American Kente Cloth Quilt*, 318/319	**Stories in Art:** *Cold Morning on the Range*, 350/351	**Stories in Art:** *Ice Sculpture at Winterlude*, 376/377	
Science: Mixing Colors, 324	**Science:** Desert Life, 360		
Social Studies: What They Wore, 330	**Social Studies:** Wild West, 364		
Math: Patterns and Shapes, 338	**Math:** Measure the Grand Canyon, 366		
Art: Quilting, 340	**Music:** Cowboy Songs, 368		
African Weaving, 332	New Homes, 358		

UNIT 3

Unit Resources

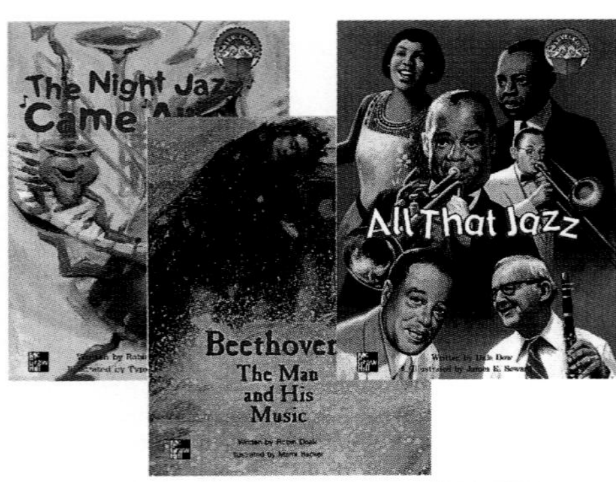

LITERATURE

LEVELED BOOKS

Easy

- ***The Night Jazz Came Alive***
- ***The Barn Raising***
- ***An Ancient Art***
- ***Little Fox and Big Coyote***

Independent

- ***Beethoven: The Man and His Music***
- ***Rosa's New Home***
- ***Recording the Past***
- ***The King's Oranges***

Challenge

- ***All That Jazz***
- ***Aborigines of the Australian Outback***
- ***Buried Treasure***
- ***Barbara Becomes a Big Sister***

THEME BIG BOOK Share *Song and Dance Man* to set the unit theme and make content-area connections.

LISTENING LIBRARY AUDIOCASSETTE Recordings of the student book selections and poetry

SKILLS

LEVELED PRACTICE

Practice Book: Student practice for comprehension, vocabulary, and study skills; plus practice for instructional vocabulary and story comprehension. Take-Home Story included for each lesson.

Reteach: Reteaching opportunities for students who need more help with assessed skills.

Extend: Extension activities for vocabulary, comprehension, story, and study skills.

TEACHING CHARTS Instructional charts for

modeling vocabulary and tested skills. Also available as transparencies.

WORD BUILDING MANIPULATIVE CARDS Cards with words and structural elements for word building and practicing vocabulary.

LANGUAGE SUPPORT BOOK ESL Parallel teaching lessons and appropriate practice activities for students needing language support.

PHONICS/PHONEMIC AWARENESS PRACTICE BOOK Additional practice focusing on vowel sounds, phonograms, blends, digraphs, and key phonetic elements.

LANGUAGE ARTS

GRAMMAR PRACTICE BOOK Provides practice for grammar and mechanics lessons.

SPELLING PRACTICE BOOK Provides practice with the word list and spelling patterns. Includes home involvement activities.

DAILY LANGUAGE ACTIVITIES Sentence activities that provide brief, regular practice and reinforcement of grammar, mechanics, and usage skills. Available as blackline masters and transparencies.

McGraw-Hill School TECHNOLOGY

Phonics CD-ROM provides extra phonics support.

interNET CONNECTION extends lesson activities through Research and Inquiry ideas.

Visit ***www.mhschool.com/reading***

Resources for

Meeting Individual Needs

UNIT 3	EASY	ON-LEVEL	CHALLENGE	LANGUAGE SUPPORT
Moses Goes to a Concert	**Leveled Book:** ***The Night Jazz Came Alive*** **Reteach,** 75–81 **Alternate Teaching Strategies,** T60–T66 **Writing:** Drawing, 289L Phonics **CD-ROM**	**Leveled Book:** ***Beethoven: The Man and His Music*** **Practice,** 75–81 **Alternate Teaching Strategies,** T60–T66 **Writing:** Description, 289L Phonics **CD-ROM**	**Leveled Book:** ***All That Jazz*** **Extend,** 75–81 **Writing:** Sequel, 289L	**Teaching Strategies,** 260C, 261, 263, 269,272, 277, 289M, 289O **Language Support,** 81–88 **Alternate Teaching Strategies,** T60–T66 **Writing:** Write a Letter, 289K–289L Phonics **CD-ROM**
The Little Painter of Sabana Grande	**Leveled Book:** ***The Barn Raising*** **Reteach,** 82–88 **Alternate Teaching Strategies,** T60–T66 **Writing:** Invitation, 317L Phonics **CD-ROM**	**Leveled Book:** ***Rosa's New Home*** **Practice,** 82–88 **Alternate Teaching Strategies,** T60–T66 **Writing:** Mural Idea, 317L Phonics **CD-ROM**	**Leveled Book:** ***Aborigines of the Australian Outback*** **Extend,** 82–88 **Writing:** Dialogue, 317L	**Teaching Strategies,** 292C, 293, 297, 307, 311, 317L **Language Support, 89–96** **Alternate Teaching Strategies,** T60–T66 **Writing:** Write a Letter, 317K–317L Phonics **CD-ROM**
The Patchwork Quilt	**Leveled Book:** ***An Ancient Art*** **Reteach,** 89–95 **Alternate Teaching Strategies,** T60–T66 **Writing:** Greeting Card, 349L Phonics **CD-ROM**	**Leveled Book:** ***Recording the Past*** **Practice,** 89–95 **Alternate Teaching Strategies,** T60–T66 **Writing:** Thank-You Letter, 349L Phonics **CD-ROM**	**Leveled Book:** ***Buried Treasure*** **Extend,** 89–95 **Writing:** Story Scene, 349L	**Teaching Strategies,** 320C, 321, 327, 328, 334, 336, 349L **Language Support,** 97–104 **Alternate Teaching Strategies, T60–T66** **Writing:** Write an Editorial, 349K–349L Phonics **CD-ROM**
Pecos Bill	**Leveled Book:** ***Little Fox and Big Coyote*** **Reteach,** 96–102 **Alternate Teaching Strategies,** T60–T66 **Writing:** Sketch Scenery, 375L Phonics **CD-ROM**	**Leveled Book:** ***The King's Oranges*** **Practice,** 96–102 **Alternate Teaching Strategies,** T60–T66 **Writing:** Comic Characters, 375L Phonics **CD-ROM**	**Leveled Book:** ***Barbara Becomes a Big Sister*** **Extend,** 96–102 **Writing:** Write a Tall Tale, 375L	**Teaching Strategies,** 352C, 353, 355, 357, 375L **Language Support,** 105–112 **Alternate Teaching Strategies,** T60–T66 **Writing:** Write a Play Review, 375K–375L Phonics **CD-ROM**
 ***A Very Cool Place to Visit***	**Review** **Reteach,** 103–109 **Alternate Teaching Strategies,** T60–T66 **Writing:** Winter Skies, 385L	**Review** **Practice,** 103–109 **Alternate Teaching Strategies,** T60–T66 **Writing:** Cool Recreation, 385L	**Review** **Extend,** 103–109 **Writing:** Hot Spots, 385L	**Teaching Strategies,** 378C, 379, 385L **Language Support,** 113–120 **Alternate Teaching Strategies, T60–T66** 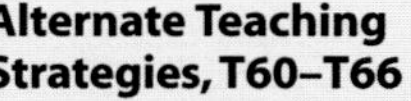 **Writing:** Write a Letter, 385K–385L

UNIT 3

Unit Assessment

INFORMAL

Informal Assessment

- Comprehension, 260B, 284, 285, 289F, 289H; 292B, 312, 313, 317F, 317H; 320B, 344, 345, 349F, 349H; 352B, 370, 371, 375F, 375H; 378B, 380, 381, 385F
- Vocabulary, 289J, 317J, 349J, 375J, 385J

Performance Assessment

- Scoring Rubrics, 289L, 317L, 349L, 375L, 385L
- Research and Inquiry, 257, 387
- Writing Process, 289K, 317K, 349K, 375K, 385K
- Listening, Speaking, Viewing, Representing Activities, 258E, 258–259, 260C, 260–287, 289D; 290E, 290–291, 292C, 292–315, 317D; 318E, 318/319, 320C, 320–347, 349D; 350E, 350/351, 352C, 352–373, 375D, 376E, 376/377, 378C, 378–383, 385D
- Portfolio, 289L, 317L, 349L, 375L, 385L
- Writing, 289K–L, 317K–L, 349K–L, 375K–L, 385K–L, 387A–F
- Cross-Curricular Activities, 260C, 268, 270, 274, 278; 292C, 294, 298, 302, 308; 320C, 324, 330, 338, 340; 352C, 360, 364, 366, 368, 378C

Leveled Practice

Practice, Reteach, Extend

- **Comprehension**
  - Main Idea, 75, 79, 94, 103
  - Summarize, 80, 87, 107
  - Story Elements, 82, 86, 96, 100
  - Make Inferences, 89, 93, 101
- **Vocabulary Strategies**
  - Context Clues, 81, 88, 109
  - Multiple-Meaning Words, 95, 102, 108
- **Study Skills**
  - Graphic Aids, 78, 85, 92, 99, 106

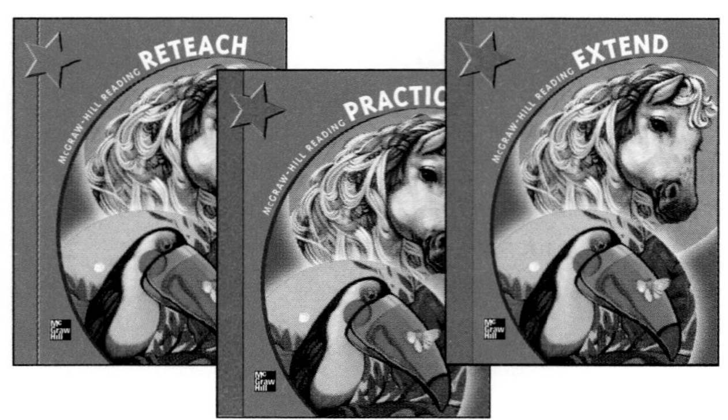

FORMAL

Selection Assessments

- **Skills and Vocabulary Words**
  - *Moses Goes to a Concert,* 21–22
  - *The Little Painter of Sabana Grande,* 23–24
  - *The Patchwork Quilt,* 25–26
  - *Pecos Bill,* 27–28
  - *A Very Cool Place to Visit,* 29–30

Unit 3 Test

- **Comprehension**
  - Main Idea
  - Summarize
  - Story Elements
  - Make Inferences
- **Vocabulary Strategies**
  - Context Clues
  - Multiple-Meaning Words
- **Study Skills**
  - Graphic Aids

Grammar and Spelling Assessment

- **Grammar**
  - Verbs, 69, 75, 81, 87, 93, 95–96
- **Spelling**
  - Words with Consonant Clusters, 70
  - Words with Double Consonants, 76
  - Words with /ou/ and /oi/, 82
  - Adding *-ed* and *-ing*, 88
  - Words from Social Studies, 94
  - Unit 3 Assessment, 95–96

Diagnostic/Placement Evaluation

- Individual Reading Inventory, 31–32
- Running Record, 33–34
- Grade K Diagnostic/Placement
- Grade 1 Diagnostic/Placement
- Grade 2 Diagnostic/Placement
- Grade 3 Diagnostic/Placement

Test Preparation

- TAAS Preparation and Practice Booklet, 40–49
- See also Test Power in Teacher's Edition, 289, 317, 349, 375, 385

Assessment Checklist

Student .... Grade ....

Teacher ....

	Moses Goes to a Concert	The Little Painter of Sabana Grande	The Patchwork Quilt	Pecos Bill	A Very Cool Place to Visit	Assessment Summary
LISTENING/SPEAKING						
Participates in oral language experiences						
Listens and speaks to gain knowledge of culture						
Speaks appropriately to audiences for different purposes						
Communicates clearly						
READING						
Uses a variety of word identification strategies: • Final Consonant Clusters						
• Double Consonants						
• Diphthongs /ou/*ow, ou;* /oi/*oi, oy*						
• Context Clues						
• Multiple-Meaning Words						
Reads with fluency and understanding						
Reads widely for different purposes in varied sources						
Develops an extensive vocabulary						
Uses a variety of strategies to comprehend selections: • Main Idea						
• Summarize						
• Make Inferences						
Responds to various texts						
Analyzes the characteristics of various types of texts: • Story Elements (Character, Setting, Plot)						
Conducts research using various sources: • Graphic Aids						
Reads to increase knowledge						
WRITING						
Writes for a variety of audiences and purposes						
Composes original texts using the conventions of written language such as capitalization and penmanship						
Spells proficiently						
Composes texts applying knowledge of grammar and usage						
Uses writing processes						
Evaluates own writing and writing of others						

+ Observed – Not Observed

Introducing the Theme

Be Creative!

We can all express ourselves in creative, wonderful ways.

PRESENT THE THEME Read the theme statement to students. Ask them how people express themselves creatively, such as through the way they dress or the stories they share. Encourage students to think of songs, books, or movies that they like, and discuss what makes them expressions of creativity. Help students name other ways of being creative—like painting or inventing something new.

READ THE POEM Tell students that writing a poem is one way in which creative people express themselves. Read aloud the lyrics for "Different Drum" by Joe Scruggs. Ask students what they feel the poet is trying to express in his poem. Lead them to see that Scruggs is suggesting that just being yourself can be a creative act.

LISTENING LIBRARY AUDIOCASSETTE

GROUP **MAKE CONNECTIONS** Have students preview the unit by reading the selection titles and looking at the illustrations. Then have them work in small groups to brainstorm a list of ways that the stories, poems, and the *Time for Kids* magazine article relate to the theme Be Creative!

Groups can then compare their lists as they share them with the class.

256

THEME SUMMARY

Each of the selections relates to the unit theme Be Creative! as well as the global theme Expression. These thematic links will help students to make connections across texts.

Moses Goes to a Concert A clever performer helps deaf students enjoy music.

The Little Painter of Sabana Grande A boy in a rural village finds a way to create his own painting materials.

Pecos Bill A play about the legendary Pecos Bill highlights his creativity.

The Patchwork Quilt Tanya helps create a very special quilt.

A Very Cool Place to Visit A resort in Sweden has found a creative solution to entertaining guests in the Arctic.

Be Creative!

UNIT 3

Different Drum

You like to run in sun,
I like to dance in the shade.
I'm marching in my own parade.
You say follow,
But I may not come.
I hear the beat of a different drum.

Some say I'm crazy,
Some say I'm weird.
I'm just marching to the beat I hear.
Sometimes it's hard,
But sometimes it's fun.
I hear the beat of a different drum.

words and music by Joe Scruggs

257

LEARNING ABOUT POETRY

terary Devices: Meter and hythm Read the poem aloud, nphasizing the stressed syllables. ead it again, having students clap ong. Model for students how to ap the loudest at the stressed sylla- es to feel the rhythm. Explain that is rhythm is called *meter*. Have stu- ents read the poem aloud using hat they have learned about meter.

ONE

Poetry Activity Ask students to write a poem that begins with the word *Sing*. Students might want to use "Different Drum" as a model to follow when they write or choose another one.

Activity

Research and Inquiry

GROUP

Theme Project: Our Special Community Have students work in teams to brainstorm features—historical events, landmarks, or products—for which their community is known. They will then choose one feature from the list as the basis for a project that will promote their hometown.

List What They Know Once students have picked a feature, have them list what they already know about it.

Ask Questions and Identify Resources Next ask students to brainstorm some questions they would need to answer in order to prepare their presentations. Have them list possible resources.

QUESTIONS	POSSIBLE RESOURCES
• When was the old trading post built? • Who built it? • Who came to trade? • From how far?	• Records at Town Hall • Talk with a member of the Historical Society • Encyclopedias • Search on the Internet

interNET CONNECTION Have students visit ***www.mhschool.com/reading***.

Create a Presentation When their research is complete, students will present their plan for promoting their community. Encourage students to be creative. They can plan a parade or a festival, make a brochure, or write a song about their town. Encourage students to use visuals in their presentation. See Wrap Up the Theme, page 387.

Moses Goes to a Concert

Selection Summary **Students will read about a deaf boy who goes to a concert and learns about playing percussion instruments from a talented deaf musician.**

Listening Library Audiocassette

INSTRUCTIONAL
Pages 260–289

About the Author/Illustrator Isaac Millman spent many hours doing research before writing *Moses Goes to a Concert*. He worked with deaf teachers to be sure that all of his sign-language drawings were accurate. Millman, who was born in France, came to the United States as a teenager. After serving in the military, he went to art school. He is now living in New York City.

Resources for

Meeting Individual Needs

LEVELED BOOKS

EASY
Pages 289A, 289D

INDEPENDENT
Pages 289B, 289D

Take-Home version available

CHALLENGE
Pages 289C, 289D

LEVELED PRACTICE

Reteach, 75–81
blackline masters with reteaching opportunities for each assessed skill

Practice, 75–81
workbook with Take-Home Stories and practice opportunities for each assessed skill and story comprehension

Extend, 75–81
blackline masters that offer challenge activities for each assessed skill

ADDITIONAL RESOURCES

- **Language Support Book** 81–88
- **Take-Home Story, Practice** p. 76a
- **Alternate Teaching Strategies** T60–T66
- **Selected Quizzes Prepared by** Accelerated Reader

McGraw-Hill School
TECHNOLOGY
Phonics CD-ROM provides extra phonics support.
interNET CONNECTION Research & Inquiry ideas. Visit www.mhschool.com/reading.

Suggested Lesson Planner

Available on CD-ROM

READING AND LANGUAGE ARTS	DAY 1 Focus on Reading and Skills	DAY 2 Read the Literature
• Comprehension • Vocabulary • Phonics/Decoding • Study Skills • Listening, Speaking, Viewing, Representing	Read **Read Aloud and Motivate,** 258E "Take a Bite of Music" **Develop Visual Literacy,** 258/259 ☑ **Introduce Main Idea,** 260A–260B **Teaching Chart,** 61 **Reteach, Practice, Extend,** 75	**Build Background,** 260C Develop Oral Language **Vocabulary,** 260D ***concert ill musician conductor instrument orchestra*** **Teaching Chart 62** **Word Building Manipulative Cards** **Reteach, Practice, Extend,** 76 Read **Read the Selection,** 260–285 Guided Instruction ☑ Main Idea **Minilessons,** 267, 273, 275, 279 **Cultural Perspectives,** 266
• Curriculum Connections	Link **Fine Arts,** 258/259	Link **Music,** 260C
• Writing	**Writing Prompt:** Imagine you are deaf and "hear" vibrations instead of sound. How do you think you would experience something loud like a plane taking off? Write about it.	**Writing Prompt:** You are playing baseball with a deaf girl. She hits the ball and starts running. Describe how you "tell" her to keep running from first base to second base. **Journal Writing,** 285 Quick-Write
• Grammar	**Introduce the Concept: Action Verbs,** 289M Daily Language Activity 1. Mikka _____ the guitar. plays 2. Phil _____ his shoes. ties 3. We _____ our hands. clap **Grammar Practice Book,** 65	**Teach the Concept: Action Verbs,** 289M Daily Language Activity 1. They _____ sign language. use 2. Can we _____ the band? see 3. Moses _____ the music. likes **Grammar Practice Book,** 66
• Spelling	**Pretest: Words with Consonant Clusters,** 289O **Spelling Practice Book,** 65–66	**Explore the Pattern: Words with Consonant Clusters,** 289O **Spelling Practice Book,** 67

Meeting Individual Needs

✓ = **Skill Assessed in Unit Test**

DAY 3 — Read the Literature

Reread for Fluency, 284

Story Questions, 286
Reteach, Practice, Extend, 77
Story Activities, 287

Study Skill, 288
✓ Graphic Aids
Teaching Chart 63
Reteach, Practice, Extend, 78

Test Power, 289

Read the Leveled Books,
Guided Reading
Final Consonant Clusters
✓ Main Idea
✓ Instructional Vocabulary
 **CD-ROM**

 Social Studies, 270

Writing Prompt: Write a story about going to a special concert. Imagine you get to meet the performers and even try their instruments.

Writing Process: Persuasive Writing, 289K
Prewrite, Draft

Review and Practice: Action Verbs, 289N
Daily Language Activity
1. I _____ with my friend. laugh
2. People _____ from all over. come
3. We _____with the music. dance

Grammar Practice Book, 67

Practice and Extend: Words with Consonant Clusters, 289P
Spelling Practice Book, 68

DAY 4 — Build Skills

 **Read the Leveled Books and Self-Selected Books**

✓ **Review Main Idea,** 289E–289F
Teaching Chart 64
Reteach, Practice, Extend, 79
Language Support, 86

✓ **Introduce Summarize,** 289G–289H
Teaching Chart 65
Reteach, Practice, Extend, 80
Language Support, 87

 Science, 274

Writing Prompt: If you could plan a concert series for your school, whom would you like to invite to play? Create a brochure telling who would play and when and where the concert would take place.

Writing Process: Persuasive Writing, 289K
Revise
Meeting Individual Needs for Writing, 289L

Review and Practice: Action Verbs, 289N
Daily Language Activity
1. Steve _____ on stage. walks
2. The teachers _____ to the class. speak
3. Jamiel _____ the clock. watches

Grammar Practice Book, 68

Proofread and Write: Words with Consonant Clusters, 289P
Spelling Practice Book, 69

DAY 5 — Build Skills

 **Read Self-Selected Books**

✓ **Review Context Clues,** 289I–289J
Teaching Chart 66
Reteach, Practice, Extend, 81
Language Support, 88

Listening, Speaking, Viewing, Representing, 289L
Respond to Suggestions
Review the Concert

Minilessons, 267, 273, 275

Phonics Review,
Final Consonant Clusters, 279
Phonics/Phonemic Awareness Practice Book, 12–18
 **CD-ROM**

 Math-Music, 278

Writing Prompt: Why do you think deaf people face each other when they talk and sign? Write a paragraph to explain.

Writing Process: Persuasive Writing, 289K
Edit/Proofread, Publish

Assess and Reteach: Action Verbs, 289N
Daily Language Activity
1. Will you _____ me a program? pass
2. Drums _____ a loud noise. make
3. David _____to the crowd. bows

Grammar Practice Book, 69–70

Assess and Reteach: Words with Consonant Clusters, 289P
Spelling Practice Book, 70

Music

Read Aloud and Motivate

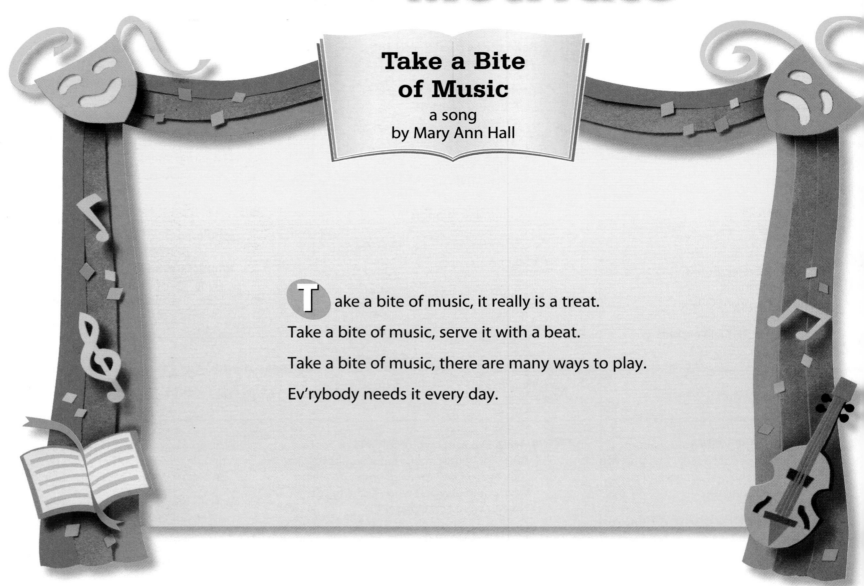

Take a Bite of Music

a song
by Mary Ann Hall

Take a bite of music, it really is a treat.
Take a bite of music, serve it with a beat.
Take a bite of music, there are many ways to play.
Ev'rybody needs it every day.

Oral Comprehension

LISTENING AND SPEAKING Motivate students to draw conclusions as they listen to you read or sing this song about music. Ask them to think about what the songwriter is saying about music. When you have finished, ask: "What conclusions can you draw about how Mary Ann Hall feels about music?" Then read or sing the song again and ask students to join in. Have them tap their feet to the rhythm of the song. Remind students to draw conclusions as they read other stories and poems.

Activity Encourage students to illustrate this song. Ask them to visualize what it might mean to "take a bite of music." Urge students to use their imagination in creating their pictures and not to worry about being realistic.
▶ **Visual/Musical**

Develop Visual Literacy

Works of Art

Anthology pages 258–259

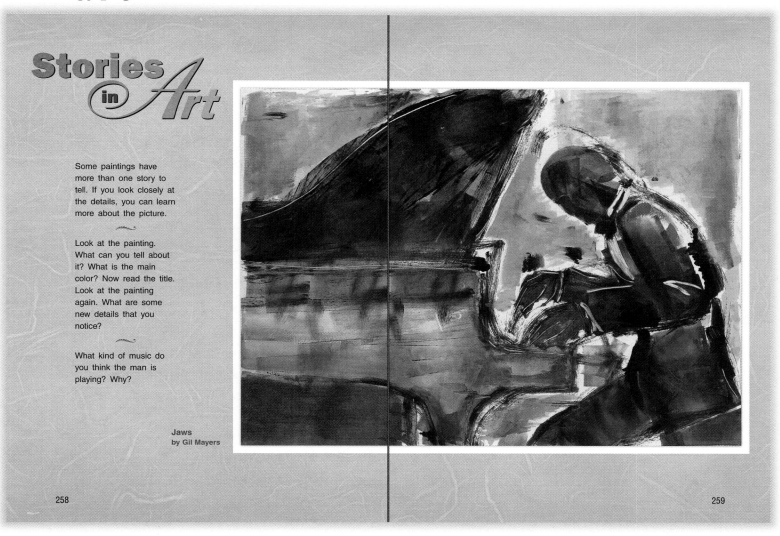

Stories in Art

Some paintings have more than one story to tell. If you look closely at the details, you can learn more about the picture.

Look at the painting. What can you tell about it? What is the main color? Now read the title. Look at the painting again. What are some new details that you notice?

What kind of music do you think the man is playing? Why?

Jaws
by Gil Mayers

258

259

Objective: Identify Main Idea

VIEWING Ask students to describe what is happening in the painting. Do they sense movement? Read the title. Help them see that the shape of the piano looks like the jaws of a shark. Have students close their eyes. What shapes or colors do they recall from the painting?

Help students to identify the painting's main idea. Musicians can become consumed by their playing. Ask students to explain how the painting's title, colors, and details support the main idea. For example:

- Brushstrokes suggest movement and energy that music creates.
- The main color is blue, like the ocean.
- The piano's shape is like a giant shark's head.

REPRESENTING Ask students to make up a dance about the sea. The sea can show many different moods. For example, the water can be stormy or calm.

OBJECTIVES

Students will identify main idea and supporting details.

LANGUAGE SUPPORT

ESL Organize small groups to complete a Main Idea chart. Then have groups retell the story of "Jenna's First Concert" using the completed chart as a guide.

Introduce Main Idea

PREPARE

Discuss How Ideas Are Supported by Details

Invite volunteers to talk about their favorite sport. Ask them to give some details that support why that sport is their favorite. Explain to students that these details help others understand their opinion.

TEACH

Explain Main Ideas and Supporting Details

Tell students that story titles and a sentence at or near the beginning of a paragraph or passage often contain the main idea. Less important events provide details that support the main idea. Supporting details help explain the main idea of a story.

Jenna's First Concert

Today Jenna was going to play the drums in front of lots of people, and she was really excited. When she woke up, the first thing she thought about was the concert. She bounced out of bed. After a quick breakfast, she began to practice her drums. She wanted to be her very best. Finally, it was time to go to the concert hall.

When Jenna got there, she ran onstage and peeked through the curtains. Almost all her friends had come. When the curtains swooshed open, Jenna rushed to her drums and played better than she had ever played before. Everyone cheered.

Teaching Chart 61

Read "Jenna's First Concert" and Model the Skill

Display **Teaching Chart 61**. As you read the story, call students' attention to details that help explain the main idea.

MODEL I'm going to look for what this passage is mostly about. I see details about Jenna playing drums, a concert, doing her best, being onstage. Those all seem related. I think they can help me figure out the main idea. I will look for a sentence that ties them together, that tells the most important thing about the related details.

Identify Main Idea

Ask a volunteer to circle a sentence that gives the main idea and then to restate the main idea in his or her own words.

PRACTICE

Create a Main Idea/Supporting Details Chart

Have volunteers underline the supporting details in "Jenna's First Concert." Then work with students to create a chart with the main idea of the story at the top. Have groups fill in supporting details under the main idea. ▶ **Spatial/Logical**

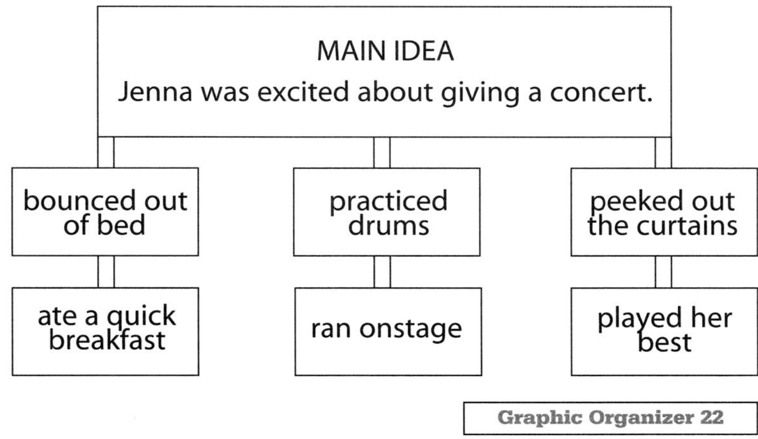

Graphic Organizer 22

ASSESS/CLOSE

Use a Chart to Summarize

Have students create a Main Idea/Supporting Details chart for a favorite story or show. Have them use their chart to write a summary.

SELECTION Connection

Students will identify main idea and supporting details when they read *Moses Goes to a Concert* and the Leveled Books.

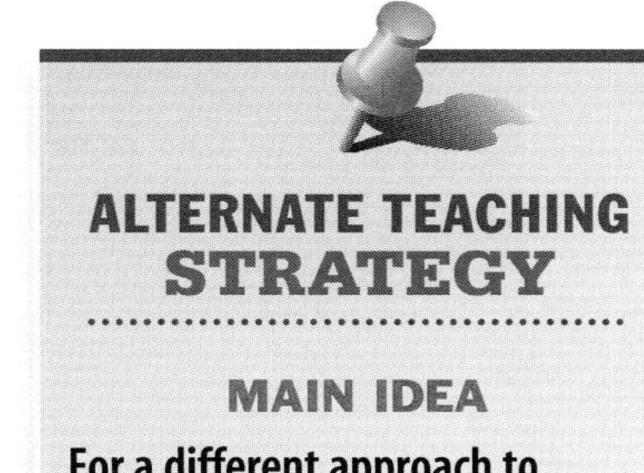

ALTERNATE TEACHING STRATEGY

MAIN IDEA

For a different approach to teaching this skill, see page T60.

Meeting Individual Needs for Comprehension

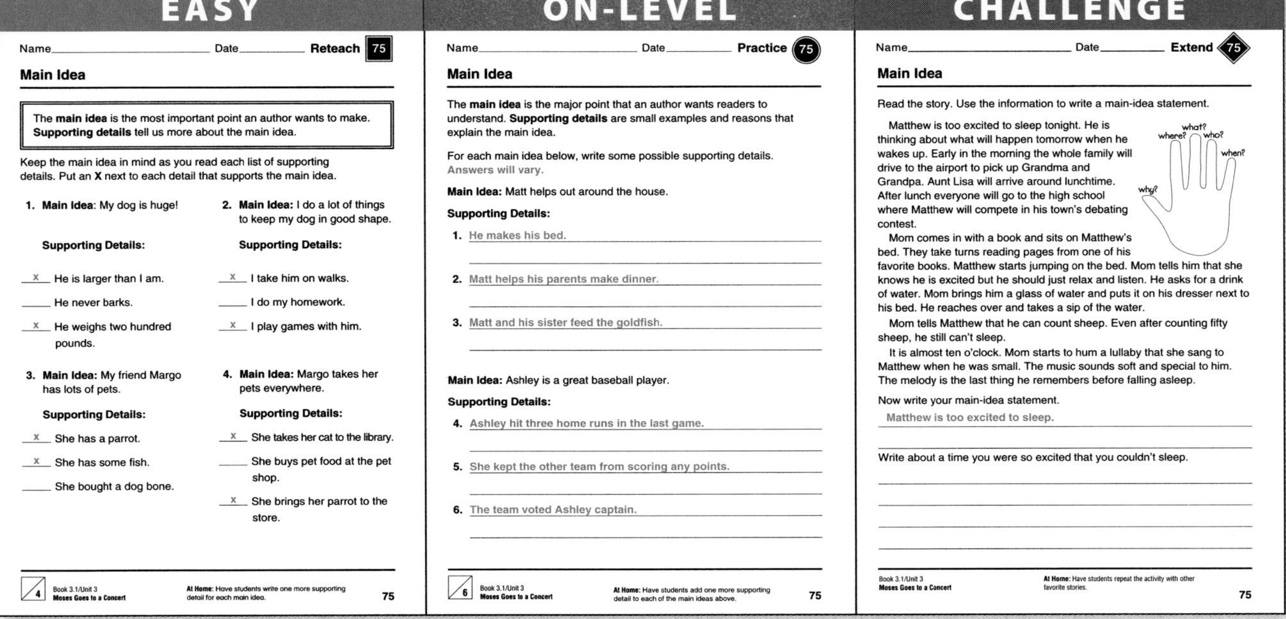

EASY

Name________ Date______ **Reteach 75**

Main Idea

The **main idea** is the most important point an author wants to make. **Supporting details** tell us more about the main idea.

Keep the main idea in mind as you read each list of supporting details. Put an **X** next to each detail that supports the main idea.

1. **Main Idea**: My dog is huge!

   Supporting Details:

   _X_ He is larger than I am.
   ___ He never barks.
   _X_ He weighs two hundred pounds.

2. **Main Idea:** I do a lot of things to keep my dog in good shape.

   Supporting Details:

   _X_ I take him on walks.
   ___ I do my homework.
   _X_ I play games with him.

3. **Main Idea:** My friend Margo has lots of pets.

   Supporting Details:

   _X_ She has a parrot.
   _X_ She has some fish.
   ___ She bought a dog bone.

4. **Main Idea:** Margo takes her pets everywhere.

   Supporting Details:

   _X_ She takes her cat to the library.
   ___ She buys pet food at the pet shop.
   _X_ She brings her parrot to the store.

4 Book 3.1/Unit 3 **Moses Goes to a Concert** **At Home:** Have students write one more supporting detail for each main idea. 75

Reteach, 75

ON-LEVEL

Name________ Date______ **Practice 75**

Main Idea

The **main idea** is the major point that an author wants readers to understand. **Supporting details** are small examples and reasons that explain the main idea.

For each main idea below, write some possible supporting details. Answers will vary.

Main Idea: Matt helps out around the house.

Supporting Details:

1. He makes his bed.
2. Matt helps his parents make dinner.
3. Matt and his sister feed the goldfish.

Main Idea: Ashley is a great baseball player.

Supporting Details:

4. Ashley hit three home runs in the last game.
5. She kept the other team from scoring any points.
6. The team voted Ashley captain.

6 Book 3.1/Unit 3 **Moses Goes to a Concert** **At Home:** Have students add one more supporting detail to each of the main ideas above. 75

Practice, 75

CHALLENGE

Name________ Date______ **Extend 75**

Main Idea

Read the story. Use the information to write a main-idea statement.

Matthew is too excited to sleep tonight. He is thinking about what will happen tomorrow when he wakes up. Early in the morning the whole family will drive to the airport to pick up Grandma and Grandpa. Aunt Lisa will arrive around lunchtime. After lunch everyone will go to the high school where Matthew will compete in his town's debating contest.

Mom comes in with a book and sits on Matthew's bed. They take turns reading pages from one of his favorite books. Matthew starts jumping on the bed. Mom tells him that she knows he is excited but he should just relax and listen. He asks for a drink of water. Mom brings him a glass of water and puts it on his dresser next to his bed. He reaches over and takes a sip of the water.

Mom tells Matthew that he can count sheep. Even after counting fifty sheep, he still can't sleep.

It is almost ten o'clock. Mom starts to hum a lullaby that she sang to Matthew when he was small. The music sounds soft and special to him. The melody is the last thing he remembers before falling asleep.

Now write your main-idea statement.

Matthew is too excited to sleep.

Write about a time you were so excited that you couldn't sleep.

Book 3.1/Unit 3 **Moses Goes to a Concert** **At Home:** Have students repeat the activity with other favorite stories. 75

Extend, 75

Build Background

Anthology and Leveled Books

Music

Evaluate Prior Knowledge

CONCEPT: MUSICAL PERFORMANCES These stories tell about musical performances. Invite students to share what they know about musical performances.

CREATE A MUSIC WEB Invite students to brainstorm words and phrases that describe a musical performance. Help them create a web to organize their responses.

▶ Linguistic/Logical

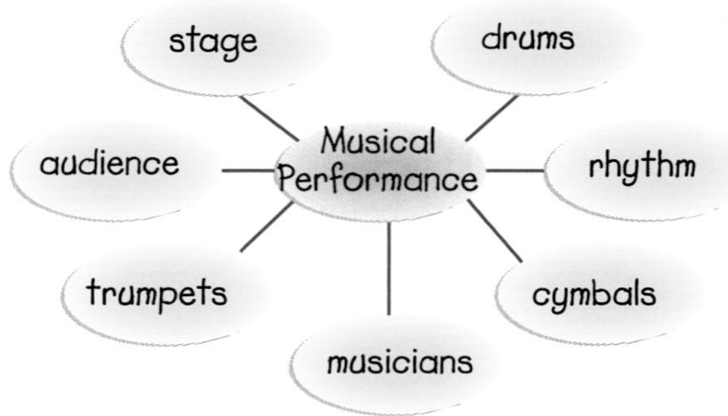

Graphic Organizer 29

DESCRIBE A PERFORMANCE Have students write a short description of a musical performance they have either heard in person or on television. Encourage them to use words and phrases from the completed web in their descriptions. Once they have finished, ask volunteers to share their descriptions with the class.

Develop Oral Language

GET ACQUAINTED WITH MUSICAL INSTRUMENTS ESL Provide different musical instruments, such as bongos, harmonicas, kazoos, and whistles. Help students say the name of each instrument, and then write it on the chalkboard. Invite students to play the instruments and describe the sounds they make.

Encourage students to make homemade percussion instruments from clean containers with lids (such as yogurt cups or coffee cans) filled with dried beans. Tell them that blocks make a great sound when struck together. They can decorate the outside of their instruments with colored paper and markers. Encourage students to perform music and maybe sing along with their instruments.

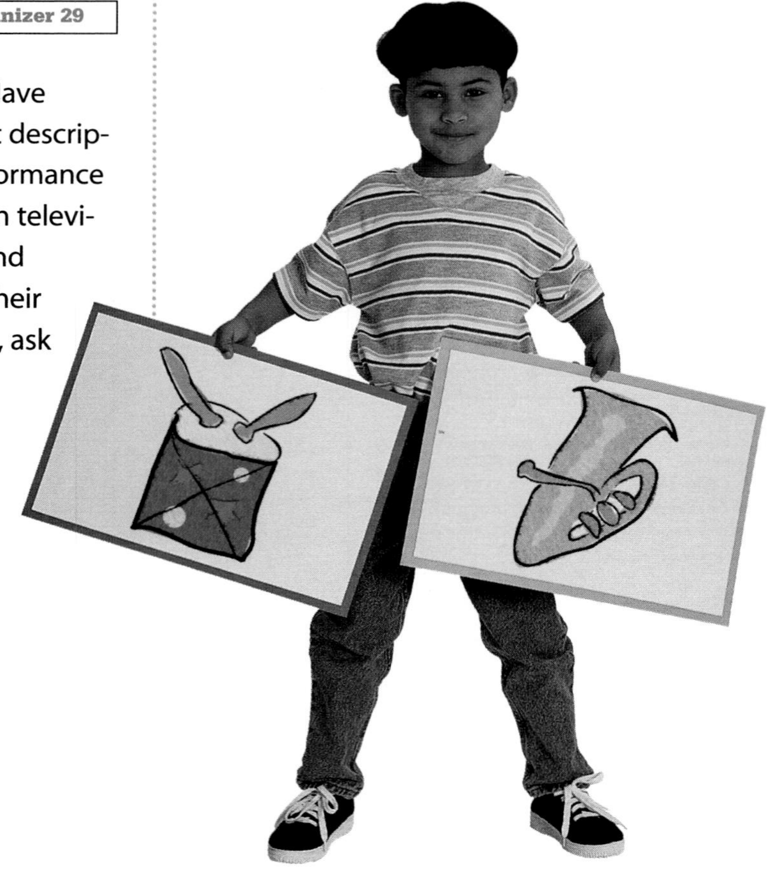

TEACHING TIP

MANAGEMENT While students are working on their paragraphs for the Describe a Performance activity, present the Develop Oral Language activity to students who need help with oral language.

Vocabulary

Key Words

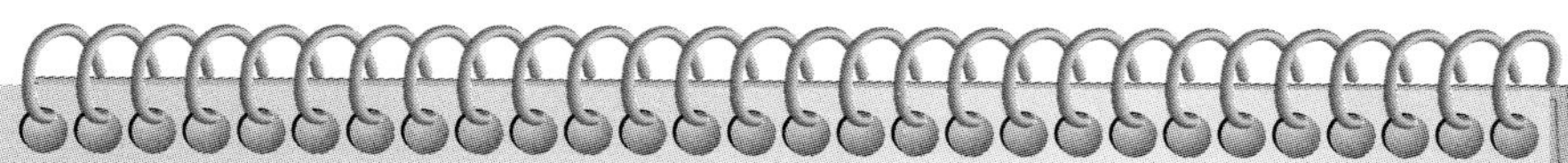

Moses at the Concert

1. Moses could not wait to see all the people playing music onstage at the concert. **2.** He was glad that he had stopped sneezing and coughing and was not ill anymore. **3.** When he got to the concert hall, he saw a big orchestra on the stage. **4.** A musician with a large drum saw Moses and smiled. **5.** Moses wished he could play the drummer's instrument. **6.** Finally, the conductor signaled to the musicians that it was time for the concert to start.

Teaching Chart 62

Definitions

concert (p. 264) a performance or show where music is played

ill (p. 274) sick or not feeling well

orchestra (p. 266) a large group of musicians who work with a conductor

musician (p. 266) a person who plays an instrument or sings

instrument (p. 266) an object used to make music

conductor (p. 273) a person who leads a group of musicians as they play music

SPELLING/VOCABULARY CONNECTIONS

See Spelling Challenge Words, pages 289O–289P.

Vocabulary in Context

IDENTIFY VOCABULARY WORDS Display **Teaching Chart 62** and read the passage with students. Have volunteers circle each vocabulary word and underline other words that are clues to its meaning.

DISCUSS MEANINGS Ask questions like these to help clarify word meanings:

- How is a concert different from a movie?
- Have you ever been ill? Describe how you felt.
- How is an orchestra different from a rock band?
- What kind of music does your favorite musician play?
- Which musical instrument do you play or would you like to play?
- How might a conductor help musicians play together?

Practice

GIVE CLUES TO WORD MEANING One partner can choose a vocabulary card and give the other student a clue to its meaning. After three correct guesses, students can switch roles. ▶ **Linguistic/Interpersonal**

Word Building Manipulative Cards

MATCH DEFINITIONS AND PICTURES

Have partners write definitions of vocabulary words on cards. Have them draw a picture of each word on other cards. Partners can exchange cards and match the pictures to definitions. Have students refer to the Glossary as needed. ▶ **Linguistic/Visual**

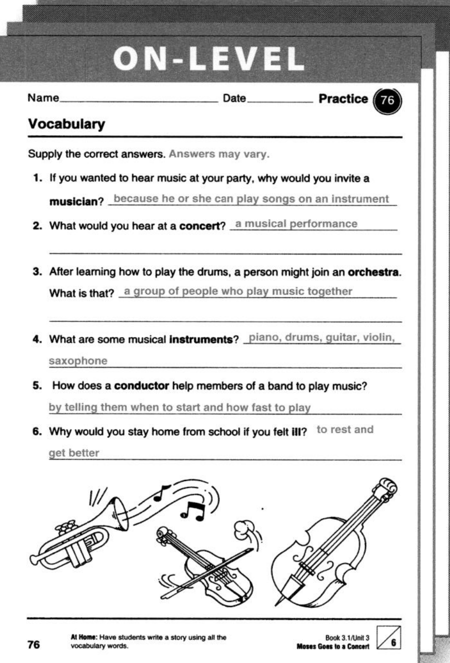

ON-LEVEL

Name______ Date______ **Practice 76**

Vocabulary

Supply the correct answers. Answers may vary.

1. If you wanted to hear music at your party, why would you invite a **musician**? because he or she can play songs on an instrument
2. What would you hear at a **concert**? a musical performance
3. After learning how to play the drums, a person might join an **orchestra**. What is that? a group of people who play music together
4. What are some musical **instruments**? piano, drums, guitar, violin, saxophone
5. How does a **conductor** help members of a band to play music? by telling them when to start and how fast to play
6. Why would you stay home from school if you felt **ill**? to rest and get better

76 **At Home:** Have students write a story using all the vocabulary words. Book 3.1/Unit 3 **Moses Goes to a Concert** 6

Take-Home Story 76a
Reteach 76
Practice 76 • Extend 76

Guided Instruction

Preview and Predict

Have students read the title and preview the illustrations. During their **picture walk**, they should look for clues as to what the story will be about.

- Where does the story take place?
- What is the boy doing in the small pictures?
- What will be the main event?
- Will the story be a realistic one or a fantasy? How can you tell? (Realistic; the characters and surroundings look real.) ***Genre***

Have students record their predictions about the main ideas of the story.

PREDICTIONS	WHAT HAPPENED
The boy in the story makes hand signs.	
He will like the concert.	

Set Purposes

What do students want to find out by reading the story? For example:

- Why are the children holding balloons?
- How did the boy learn sign language?

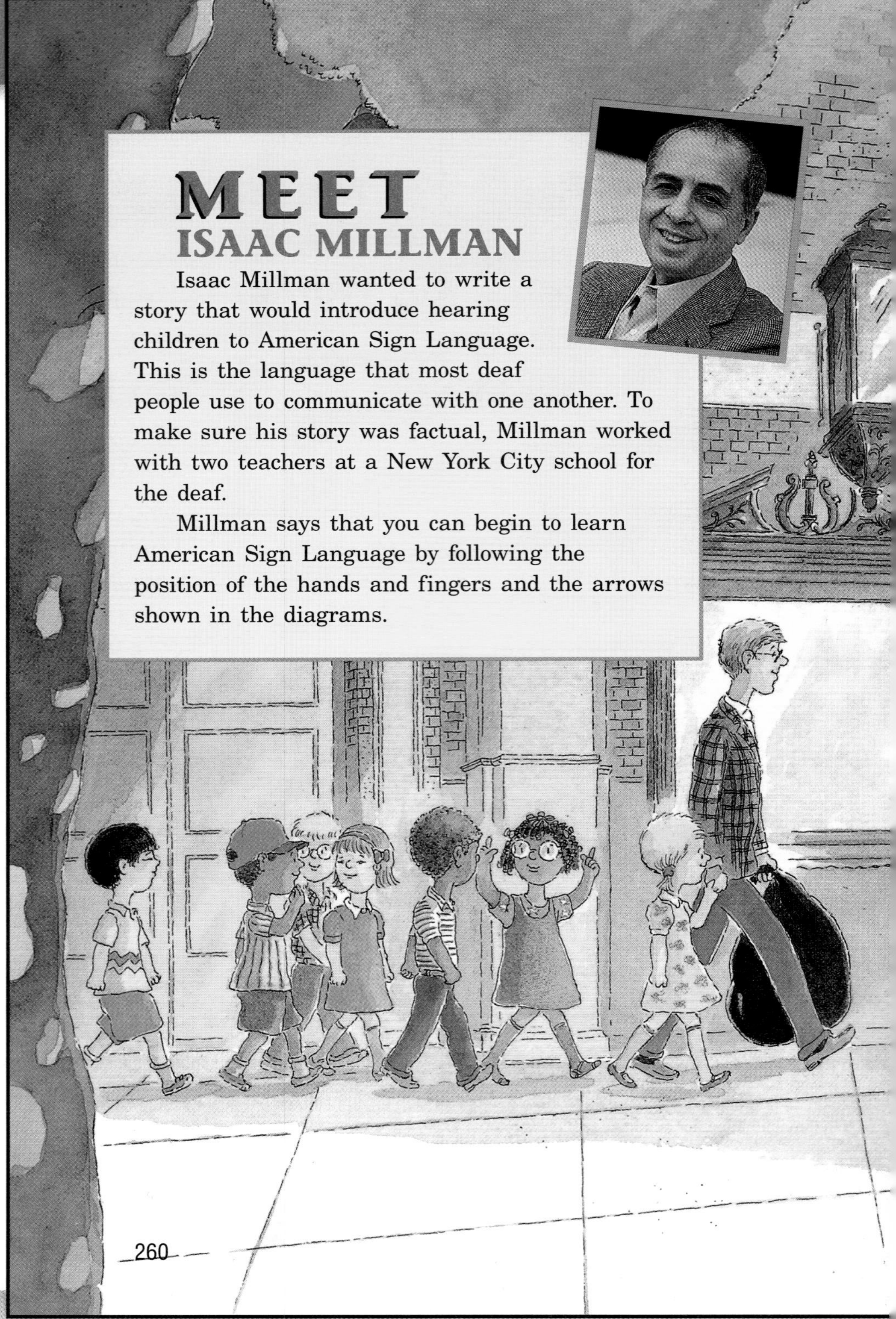

MEET ISAAC MILLMAN

Isaac Millman wanted to write a story that would introduce hearing children to American Sign Language. This is the language that most deaf people use to communicate with one another. To make sure his story was factual, Millman worked with two teachers at a New York City school for the deaf.

Millman says that you can begin to learn American Sign Language by following the position of the hands and fingers and the arrows shown in the diagrams.

260

Meeting Individual Needs • Grouping Suggestions for Strategic Reading

EASY

Read Together Read the story with students or have them use the **Listening Library Audiocassette.** Have students use the Main Idea/Supporting Details chart to record important information about the story elements. Guided Instruction and Intervention prompts offer additional help with decoding, vocabulary, and comprehension.

ON-LEVEL

Guided Reading Preview the story words on page 261. Choose from the Guided Instruction questions as you have students read the story or play the **Listening Library Audiocassette** on their own. Ask them to use the Main Idea/Supporting Details chart to record meaningful information during reading.

CHALLENGE

Read Independently Have students read the story independently. Tell them that deciding which of the story's ideas are most important can help them understand the author's purpose. Have students set up a Main Idea/Supporting Details chart as on page 261.

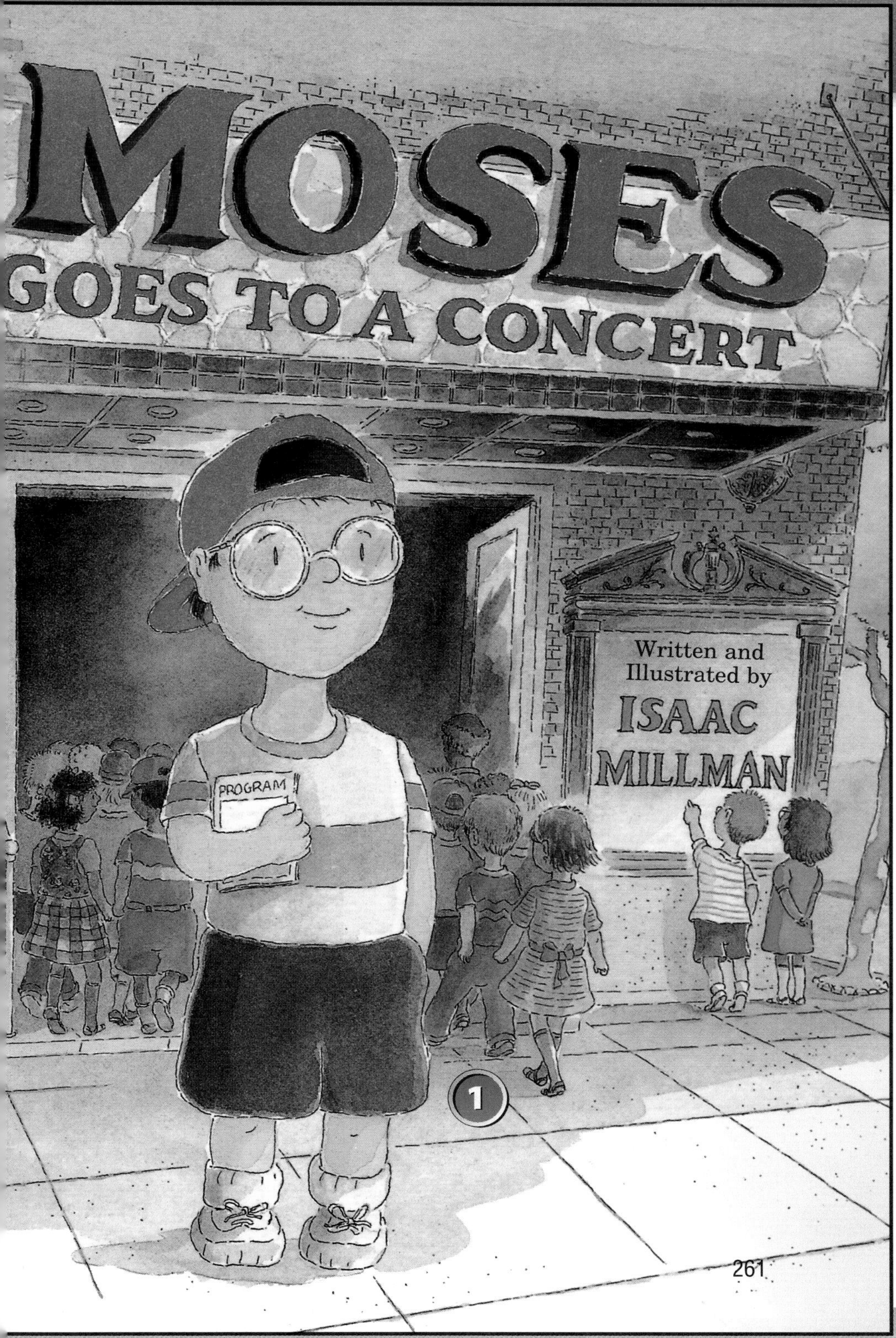

MOSES GOES TO A CONCERT

Written and Illustrated by ISAAC MILLMAN

261

Guided Instruction

 Main Idea

Strategic Reading Paying attention to the main idea and supporting details will help you understand what the story is about.

Before we begin reading, let's prepare Main Idea and Supporting Details charts so we can write down notes on the story. When we know the main idea, or purpose, of a story or page, it helps us to understand what the author is trying to explain. Supporting details are facts that help us to better understand the main idea.

MAIN IDEA	SUPPORTING DETAILS

1 MAIN IDEA/SUPPORTING DETAILS A boy is holding a program. Why might this boy be the main character? What is the program for? What other details are there?

LANGUAGE SUPPORT

A blackline master of the Main Idea and Supporting Details chart is available in the **Language Support Book**. Provide copies to students to help them keep track of main ideas and supporting details as they read the selection with a partner.

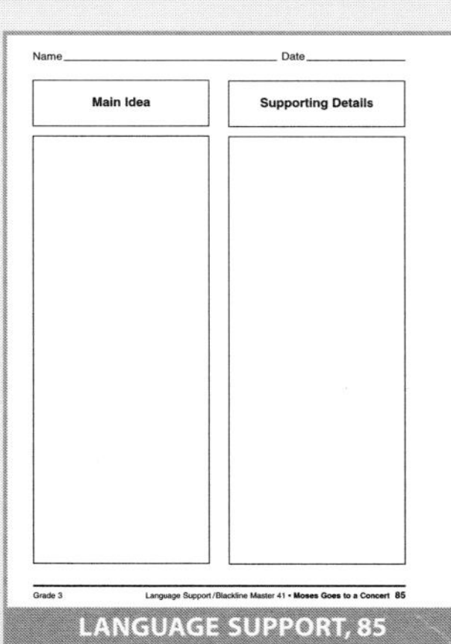
Name_____ Date_____

Main Idea	Supporting Details

Grade 3 Language Support/Blackline Master 41 • Moses Goes to a Concert 85

LANGUAGE SUPPORT, 85

Story Words

The words below may be unfamiliar. Have students check their meanings and pronunciations in the Glossary on page 388.

- deaf, p. 263
- vibration, p. 263
- percussionist, p. 266
- applaud, p. 268
- triangle, p. 279

Guided Instruction

2 **MAIN IDEA/SUPPORTING DETAILS**
Read page 263. What is the main idea, or most important point, in the story so far? What are some supporting details or facts that you learn?

MODEL There is a lot of information in the pictures and the text. What is the main idea? On page 262, a boy is drumming. It is the same boy I saw on the title page. This must be Moses. On page 263, I see Moses making signs with his hands. The picture captions tell me what the signs mean. Let me think. The most important idea in the story so far is that Moses is deaf. A detail I find really interesting is that, nevertheless, he can play the drums. He feels vibrations.

Let's begin filling in our Main Idea and Supporting Details charts.

MAIN IDEA	SUPPORTING DETAILS
Moses is deaf.	He speaks in sign language. He can't hear his drums.

Visual Literacy

VIEWING AND REPRESENTING

Discuss the small boxed pictures of Moses on page 263. Point out that their captions repeat the information in the text about Moses and his drum. Ask students why these pictures are necessary. (The pictures give this information in the same way that a deaf person gives and receives information.) Have students ever seen a person sign, or interpret, a play or lecture for deaf people? Guide students to see that Moses is like the signer at a performance. The pictures of Moses signing the text of the story show how deaf people give and receive information.

262

Moses plays on his new drum.

He can't hear the sounds he is making because he is deaf, but he feels the vibration of the drum through his hands. He has taken off his shoes so he can feel it through his feet, too. 

HOW TO READ THE ARROWS AND SYMBOLS

Hand moves in directon of arrow

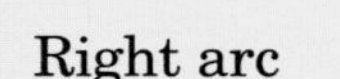 Right arc

Left arc

Swinging movement, back and forth

 Repeated movement, forward, back, forward, or up, down, up

 Slight wiggling motion

 Touching

 One motion 

263

Guided Instruction

3 Look at the arrows and other symbols found in the chart at the bottom of this page. Where else are the arrows and symbols found on the page? (in the pictures) What are the arrows and symbols supposed to be? (hand and finger movements and directions) What does it tell you about the way deaf people communicate? (They use their hands and fingers to make signs that stand for words.) *Critical Thinking*

LANGUAGE SUPPORT

ESL This selection provides a good opportunity for all students to use nonverbal means of communication. To be sure that speakers of other languages understand the ASL signs, translate, or have a bilingual classmate translate, and explain the signs used in the selection. As new signs are introduced, allow time for students to try them out with their classmates.

Guided Instruction

4 **MAIN IDEA/SUPPORTING DETAILS** The main idea of a page is often in the first sentence. What is the first sentence on page 264? (Today, Moses is going on a field trip.) How can we tell that this sentence contains the main idea on the page? If we look at the other information, we find that it all explains or supports the idea that Moses is going on a field trip. For example: Why were the children taking a bus? (to go on a field trip to a concert) For what occasion was Mr. Samuels bringing a surprise? (for the field trip) All the new facts support the idea of going on a field trip to a concert. Let's add to our charts.

MAIN IDEA	SUPPORTING DETAILS
Moses is deaf.	He speaks in sign language. He can't hear his drums.
Moses and his class are going to a concert.	Mr. Samuels, their teacher, is taking them by bus. Moses is excited.

Fluency

READ WITH EXPRESSION

PARTNERS Have partners take turns reading the text on pages 264–265. Afterward, have the entire class read the text while three volunteers sign the dialogue. (Help students use the pictures on page 263 and the diagram on page 288.) Tell students to speak clearly. Remind them:

- to pause at commas, especially during a longer sentence such as the second one on page 264.
- to vary their tone when reading dialogue to make it sound like people talking.

Today, Moses is going on a field trip. His teacher, Mr. Samuels, is taking him and his classmates, who are all deaf, to a young people's concert. 4

As the children climb onto the bus, they wonder what is inside Mr. Samuels's black bag.

"A big surprise," signs Mr. Samuels.

5

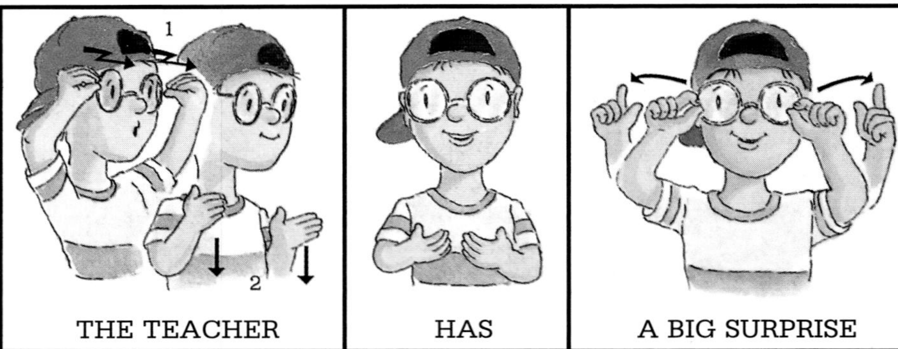

On the bus, Moses signs to his friend. "John! My parents gave me a new drum!"

John signs back. "I got one, too!"

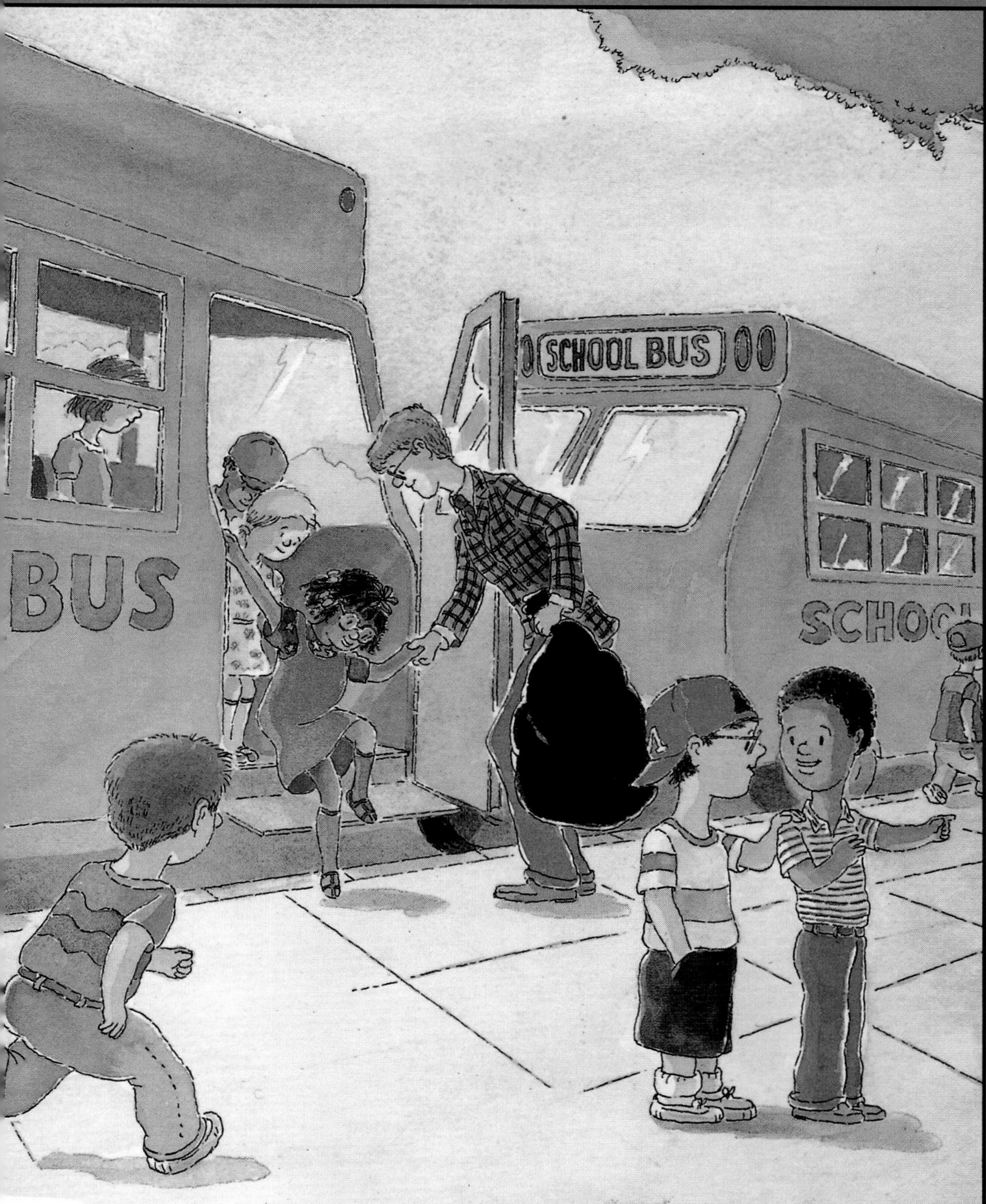

Children from all over the city are coming to the concert. Moses and his friend John wait for their class to get off the bus so they can go inside together.

265

Guided Instruction

5 So far Moses has taught us how to say a few things in sign language. Let's try to make the signs. *Pantomime*

P/I **CONTEXT CLUES** Reread the first sentence on page 264. What do you think the word *field* means in this sentence? Are the students actually going to a green field, such as one you would find in the country or on a farm?

P/I PREVENTION/INTERVENTION

CONTEXT CLUES Ask students to reread pages 264 and 265. Ask them to point to words in the text that give clues about the meaning of *field* as it is used in the story. *(trip, teacher, classmates, concert, bus)* Explain to students that no clues suggest the other meaning of *field*, such as *grass*, *cows*, or *country*. The meaning of *field* in the phrase *field trip* refers to going to an area outside the classroom, where students see what is taught in school. In this story, Moses goes on a trip to a concert, a place where musicians play music.

Guided Instruction

6 Look at the picture. Can you tell which instruments are the percussion instruments? How many can you name? As we read, let's look for each instrument's name.

6 Mr. Samuels leads them to their seats in the first row. Across the stage, in front of the orchestra, are all the percussion instruments.

7 "Children, the percussionist is a friend of mine," signs Mr. Samuels.

"What's a percussionist?" Anna signs back.

"A musician who plays an instrument such as a drum, cymbals, even a piano," replies Mr. Samuels.

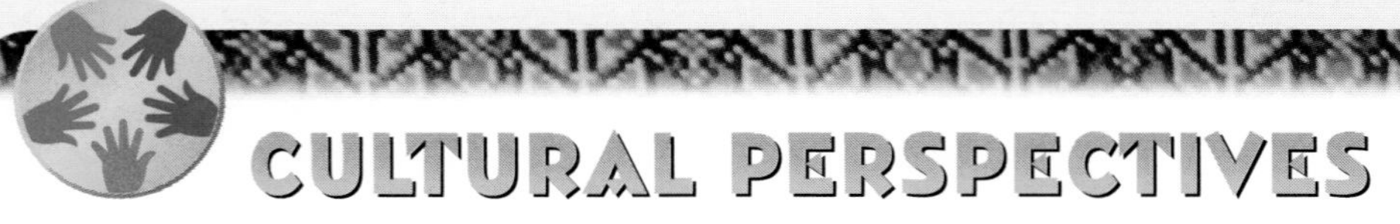

PERCUSSION Point out that the percussion instruments that Ms. Elwyn plays come from all over the world. The marimba is derived from a West African instrument called the *balafon*. Gongs are common in traditional Asian music. Congas are important in Cuban and other Latin musics.

RESEARCH AND INQUIRY Have students research percussion instruments.
▶Auditory/Spatial

*inter***NET** **CONNECTION** Students can learn more about percussion instruments of other cultures by visiting ***www.mhschool.com/reading.***

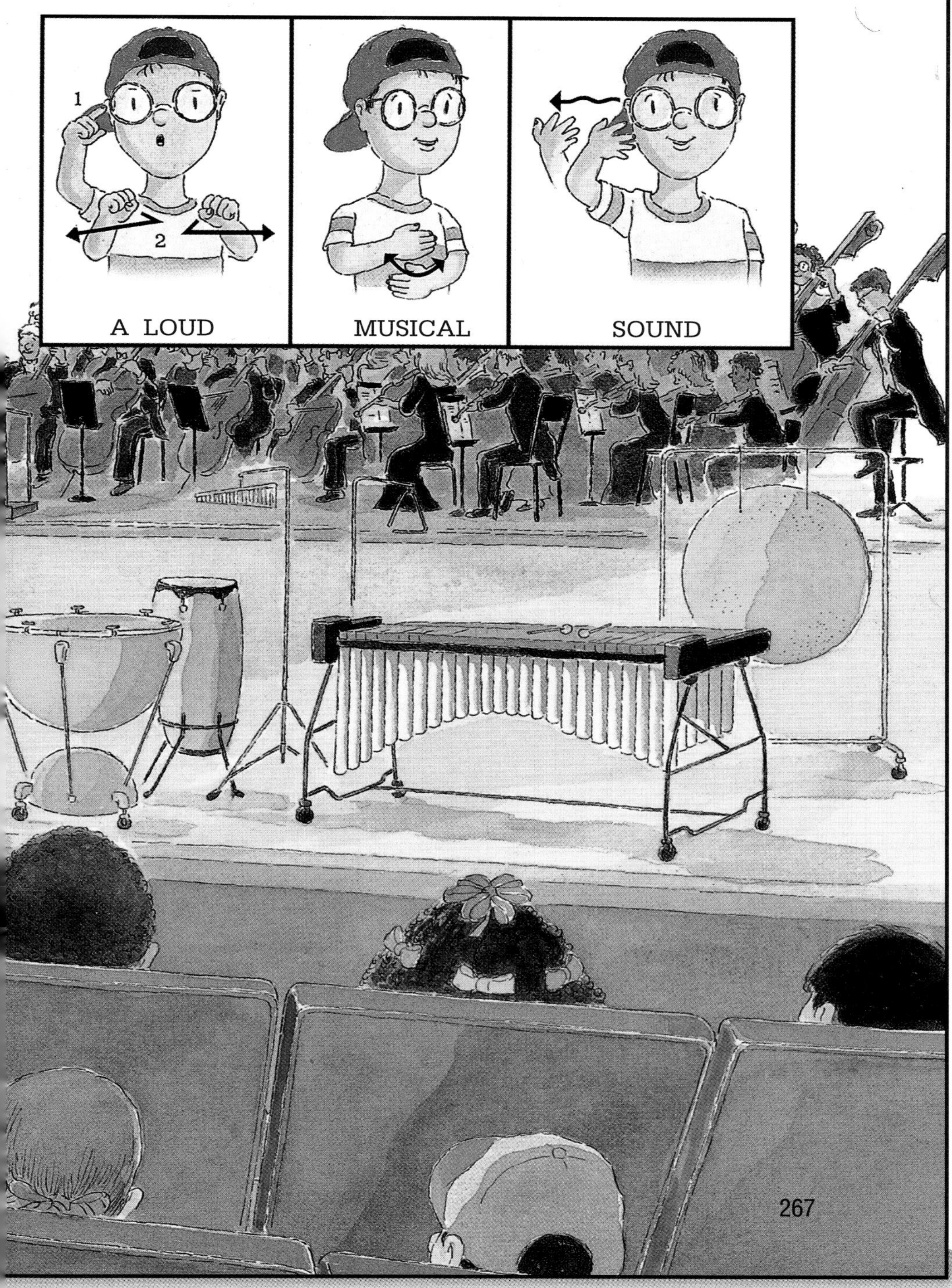

Guided Instruction

7 The percussionist, who plays drums, is a friend of Mr. Samuels. Why might this information interest Moses? (Because Moses plays drums, he will be excited to learn that Mr. Samuels knows a percussionist.) ***Make Inferences***

Minilesson

REVIEW/MAINTAIN

Summarize

Remind students that a summary is a brief statement of the main points or ideas of a story.

- Have students reread the text you have covered so far. Then ask them to give a summary of the story by stating the main ideas in their own words.
- Ask students if they included any supporting details in their summaries. Ask them if someone who has not read the story would know what it was about from listening to their summaries.

Activity Students can take turns summarizing what has happened in their day so far. Remind them to relate only the main, or important, events.

Guided Instruction

8 When the percussionist walks onto the stage, the audience stands up to applaud. What does the excitement of the audience suggest about the percussionist's ability to play her instruments? (She is a really good percussionist.) ***Make Inferences***

8 A young woman walks onto the stage. Everyone stands up to applaud. Some of Moses's classmates wave instead of clapping. The percussionist smiles and bows to the audience.

268

Activity

Cross Curricular: Science

LISTEN TO YOUR VOICE Tell students that people often think their recorded voice sounds higher than their natural voice. This is because sound waves from a recording travel to our ears only through the air. When we speak, we also pick up sound vibrations through our head bones.

Volunteers may want to sing "Row, Row, Row Your Boat" into a tape recorder.
▶**Musical/Interpersonal**

WE

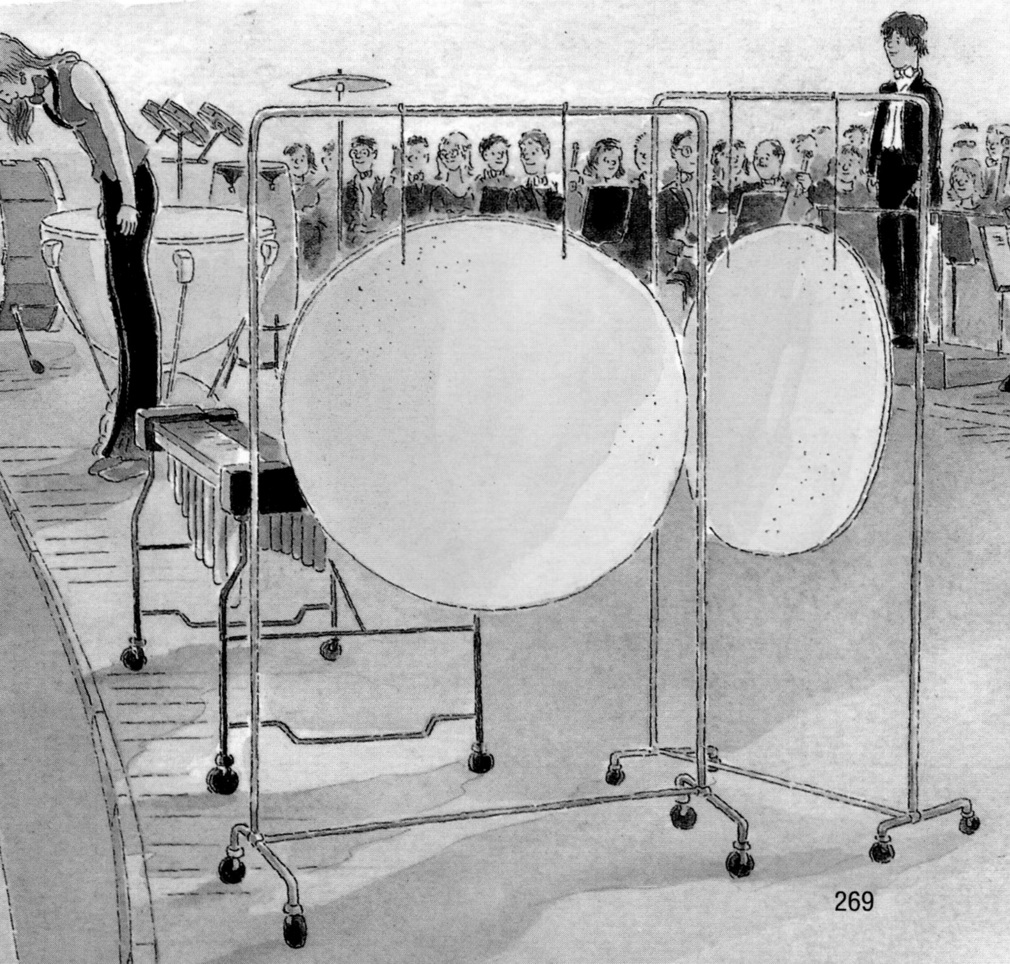

269

Guided Instruction

9 Look at the drawings of the signs for *We wave and applaud* at the top of this page. Do you notice any difference in the signs they illustrate? Which signs are most like the words they stand for? (the signs for *wave* and *applaud*) Which signs might have to be explained to you? (the signs for *we* and *and*) Why might this difference between the signs exists? (Some words are easier to act out than others.) ***Compare and Contrast***

LANGUAGE SUPPORT

ESL Because some of the text of this story appears in the art, some students may have difficulty. Help students needing language support to stay focused on overall comprehension.

- Have students work in pairs. Have partners take turns summarizing each two pages, referring only to the illustrations, not the text.
- Have students pantomine key story events, such as the children holding the balloons and listening to the concert; Marjorie Elwyn playing drums; and the class meeting her and speaking with her in sign language.

Guided Instruction

10 **MAIN IDEA/SUPPORTING DETAILS** What is the main idea on page 270? (The percussionist is deaf.) What are some supporting details about this main idea? (She doesn't wear shoes. She follows the orchestra by feeling the vibrations of the music through her stockinged feet.) Let's add this information to our charts.

MAIN IDEA	SUPPORTING DETAILS
Moses is deaf.	He speaks in sign language. He can't hear his drums.
Moses and his class are going to a concert.	Mr. Samuels, their teacher, is taking them by bus. Moses is excited.
The percussionist with the orchestra is also deaf.	She doesn't wear shoes. She feels the vibrations of the music through her feet.

"She has no shoes!" Moses signs in surprise.

10 The teacher smiles and signs, "She is deaf, too. She follows the orchestra by feeling the vibrations of the music through her stocking feet."

Then Mr. Samuels takes eleven balloons out of his black bag and hands one to each of his students.

"Oh! What beautiful balloons!" Anna signs.

11 "Hold them on your laps," signs Mr. Samuels. "They'll help you feel the music."

270

Activity

Cross Curricular: Social Studies

CAREERS Point out that Mr. Samuels, the teacher, and Ms. Elwyn, the musician, both have jobs that they find rewarding and fun. Invite students to learn about three jobs they themselves might enjoy.

- Have students make fact cards describing the main responsibilities of each job, any special skills or training needed, and what they think the most rewarding part of the job might be.
- Hold a class Career Day and have students present their fact cards.

▶ **Logical/Intrapersonal**

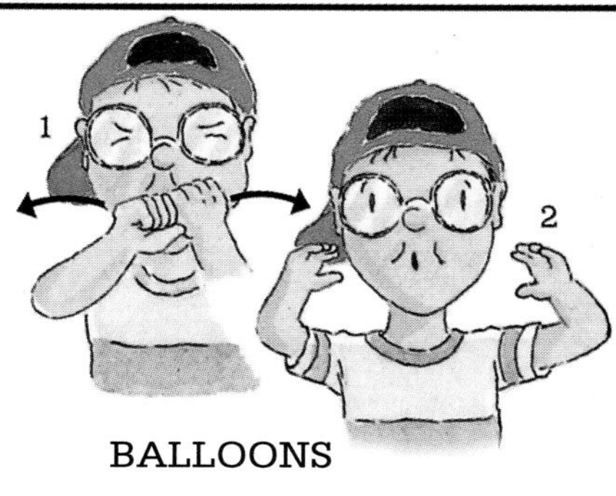

271

Guided Instruction

11 Why did the balloons help the children feel the vibrations from the orchestra? (Because the rubber on blown-up balloons is thin and stiff, it picks up sound vibrations.) What else might the children hold on their laps to feel vibrations? (a piece of paper, a feather) Would they be able to feel the vibrations as well if they were holding a bowling ball? (no) ***Draw Conclusions***

LANGUAGE SUPPORT

ESL Have partners refer to the Main Idea/Supporting Details chart to help them summarize the events that have happened in the story so far. Allow time for partners to discuss any events that they may have found confusing.

Guided Instruction

12 **MAIN IDEA/SUPPORTING DETAILS** What is the main thing happening now? Let's add to our charts.

MAIN IDEA	SUPPORTING DETAILS
Moses is deaf.	He speaks in sign language. He can't hear his drum.
Moses and his class are going to a concert.	Mr. Samuels, their teacher, is taking them by bus. Moses is excited.
The percussionist with the orchestra is also deaf.	She doesn't wear shoes. She feels the vibrations of the music through her feet.
The children "listen" to the concert.	Mr. Samuels gives them balloons to help them feel the music.

TEACHING TIP

MANAGEMENT All students may enjoy taking part in the balloon activity suggested in the Language Support below. Those who understand the word *vibrations* can write a few sentences about what they experienced during the activity while others describe it to you orally.

LANGUAGE SUPPORT

ESL Help students understand the word *vibrations*. Write *vibrations* on the chalkboard and demonstrate how something moves when it vibrates. Provide students with blown-up balloons to hold on their laps. Have students sit in a circle around an audiocassette player while you play a tape of percussive or loud music. Ask them to describe what happens to the balloons in their laps as they listen. Encourage them to tell you what happens using a word other than *vibrations*.

The conductor turns to face the orchestra and raises his baton.  12

The percussionist strikes the huge gong and the concert begins. 13

The percussionist watches the conductor and moves from one instrument to the next, striking each to make a sound. Moses and his classmates hold their balloons in their laps. They can feel the music as their balloons pick up the vibrations.

273

Guided Instruction

13 Just before the concert starts the conductor "raises his baton." What do you think the conductor's action has to do with the beginning of the music? (The players look at him when he raises the baton and start playing when he lowers it on the first beat.) ***Cause and Effect***

Minilesson

REVIEW/MAINTAIN

Suffixes

Suffixes are endings added to words that change their meanings.

- Explain how adding the suffixes *-ist* and *-or* change the meaning of a word.
- Have students find words on this page that end in *-ist* and *-or.* (*percussionist* and *conductor*) Define *percussion* (a drum or other instrument that is struck) and *conduct* (to lead or guide). Explain: A *percussionist* is someone who plays a musical instrument by striking it and a conductor is someone who leads or guides the musicians.

Activity Invite volunteers to think of names of people or things that do a certain activity. Suggest that they come up with names that end in *-ist*, *-or*, or *-er*. Have other students define the words.

Guided Instruction

14 **MAIN IDEA** As you have learned, some main ideas are the most important ideas on a page. Others are the most important ideas of the entire story. Writers have various ways of showing that an idea is important to the entire story. For example, they often mention it more than once. Can you find an idea on this page that has been stated before? (The idea that the percussionist, Ms. Elwyn, is deaf was stated on page 270.) What do you notice about this statement? (It is similar to the main idea that Moses is deaf.)

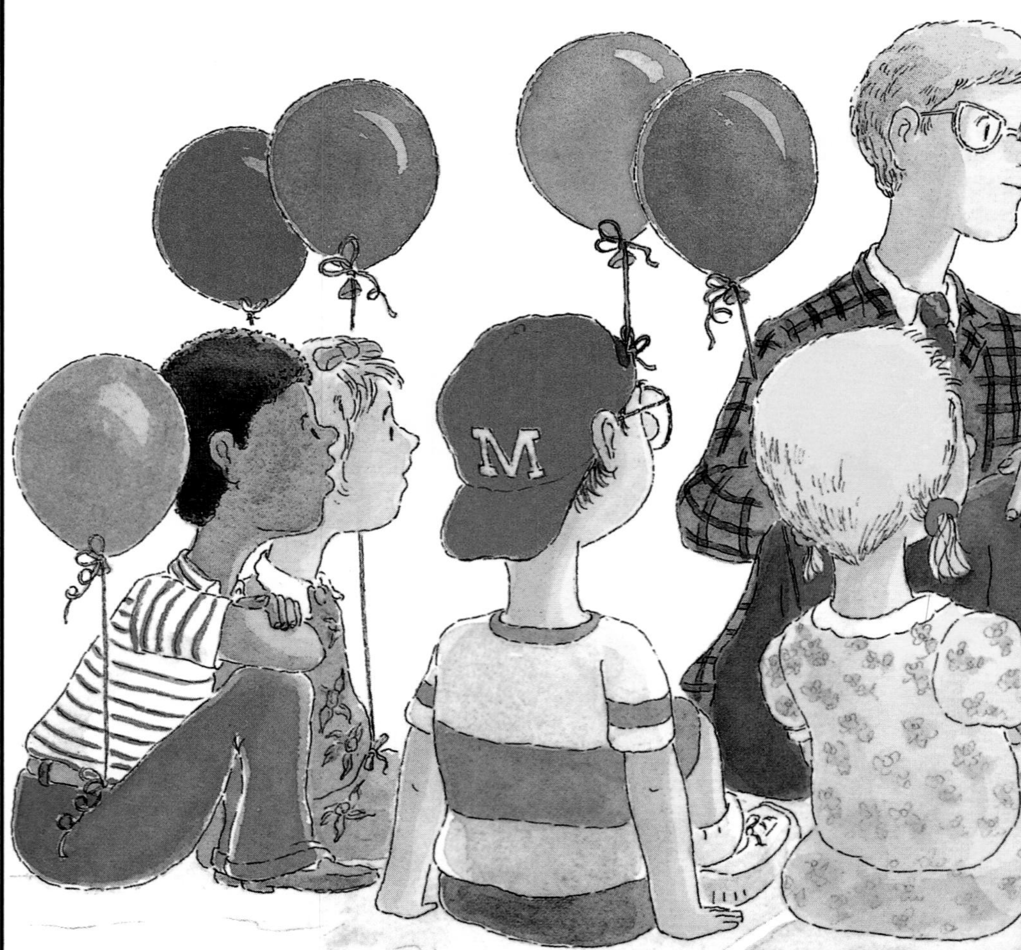

When the concert is over, Mr. Samuels has another surprise. He takes the children onstage to meet his friend, Ms. Marjorie Elwyn. "She will tell you how she became a percussionist," signs Mr. Samuels.

"I became seriously ill at the age of seven," signs Ms. Elwyn. "And when I recovered, I found out that I had lost my

hearing. I was deaf."

"What did you do then?" signs Moses.

274

Activity

Cross Curricular: Science

THE HUMAN EAR Tell students that the human ear consists of three main parts—the outer ear, the middle ear, and the inner ear. Sound vibrations travel through these and enter the brain.

RESEARCH AND INQUIRY Have students research facts about ears and create diagrams illustrating those facts. Ask them to title their diagrams.
▶ **Linguistic/Spatial**

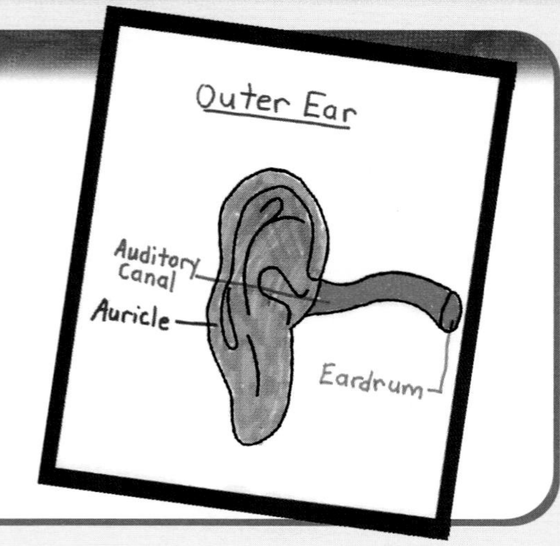

275

Guided Instruction

15 How do you know that Ms. Elwyn had once been able to hear? (She told the children that she had lost her hearing at the age of seven.) What caused her to become deaf? (an illness) ***Cause and Effect***

p/i **SUFFIXES** What is the base word in the word *seriously?* (*serious*) What is the ending *-ly* called when added to a word? (a suffix)

p/i PREVENTION/INTERVENTION

SUFFIXES Write the word *seriously* on the chalkboard. Ask students to underline the suffix. Help them to see that a suffix is a letter or a group of letters, such as *-ly*. Explain that when adjectives (describing words) have the suffix *-ly* added, they become adverbs.

Make a list of adjectives which can be made into adverbs by adding *–ly,* such as *nice, kind, loud,* and *sweet.* Have students brainstorm sentences using each adverb.

Guided Instruction

16 Ms. Elwyn is speaking in sign language. Why did Isaac Millman, the author and illustrator, decide to show her signing the words here? (to give readers a better sense of how deaf people communicate) ***Author's Purpose***

PHONICS AND DECODING

- Read the last word in the first sentence and the second word in the second sentence on this page.
- Slowly sound out each word. Listen to the vowel sound. What consonant seems to be affecting it?

16

I

WORKED HARD.

MY

HEART

WAS SET O

276

PREVENTION/INTERVENTION

PHONICS AND DECODING Write *hard* and *heart* on the chalkboard. Sound out both words with students, and discuss how the letter *r* often changes the sound a vowel makes. Have a volunteer underline the /är/ sound in *hard.*

- Brainstorm a list of other words with *r*-controlled vowels, such as *card, star, car, art,* and *farm.*

Ask volunteers to underline the /är/ sound in each word.

- Have partners write sentences using /är/ words about characters from *Moses Goes to a Concert.*

BECOMING A PERCUSSIONIST

AND I DID. 17

277

Guided Instruction

17 Why do you think Mr. Samuels wanted Ms. Elwyn to talk to the children? (Mr. Samuels probably wanted to show the children that, although they were deaf, they could enjoy and even play music, just like Ms. Elwyn.) ***Make Inferences***

LANGUAGE SUPPORT

ESL Help students understand the meaning of the statement *my heart was set on becoming a percussionist* on pages 276–277. Discuss with students whether or not they have ever heard the expression *my heart was set on it*. Explain that one way to paraphrase this statement is, "I really wanted to do it." Have small groups brainstorm other ways to paraphrase it, such as:

- It was an important goal for me.
- I was determined to do it.

Guided Instruction

18 MAIN IDEA/SUPPORTING DETAILS Ms. Elwyn lets the children play her instruments. Is this a main idea or a detail? Let's fill in our charts.

MAIN IDEA	SUPPORTING DETAILS
Moses is deaf.	He speaks in sign language. He can't hear his drum.
Moses and his class are going to a concert.	Mr. Samuels, their teacher, is taking them by bus. Moses is excited.
The percussionist with the orchestra is also deaf.	She doesn't wear shoes. She feels the vibrations of the music through her feet.
The children "listen" to the concert.	Mr. Samuels gives them balloons to help them feel the music.
The children meet Marjorie Elwyn.	She tells how she became deaf and became a musician. She lets them play on her instruments.

18 "Now you can play on my musical instruments," Ms. Elwyn signs. "Come with me, children."

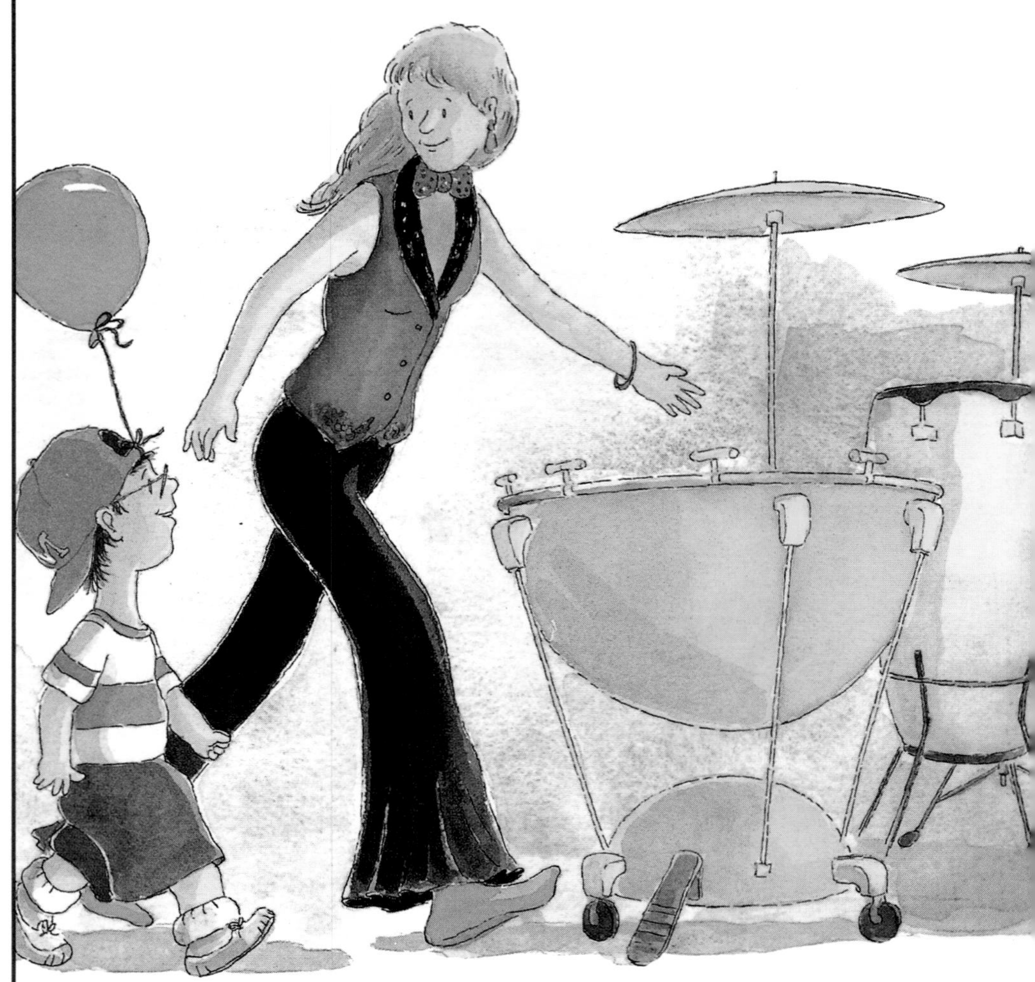

278

Activity

Cross Curricular: Math/Music

FIND THE BEAT Explain to students that rhythm is the way that beats are arranged in a measure of a song. Clap out the rhythm of a familiar song.

- If possible, show students an example of written music. Tell students that the numbers on the left of the staff show how many beats there are in each measure.
- Show them how the beats are divided among the notes. Have students clap out the rhythm of the phrase.

▶Mathematical/Musical

Ann plays on the marimba...
Beverly strikes the triangle...
Mark pounds the floor tom and the cymbal...
Dianne beats the tom-toms...
John hits the snare drum...
and Moses thumps the bass drum...
David strikes the gong...
Tommy and Suzy play on the tubular bells...
while Steve bangs the kettledrum and Maria plays the congas. (19)

279

Guided Instruction

(19) What is the same about the way all these instruments are played? (You have to hit them with your hands or special sticks to make sounds.) What are some details that tell about differences among the instruments? Use the illustrations to help you answer. (Answers will vary.) ***Compare and Contrast***

P/I **WORD STRUCTURE** Read the word *kettledrum* in the last sentence on page 279. What two smaller words are found in *kettledrum*? (*kettle, drum*)

PHONICS KIT
HANDS-ON ACTIVITIES AND PRACTICE

Minilesson

REVIEW/MAINTAIN

Final Consonant Clusters

Have students pronounce the words *pounds* and *thumps* on page 279.

- Write *pound* and *thump* on the chalkboard.
- Ask students what sound (/nd/, /mp/) they hear at the end of each word.
- Ask how the sounds /nd/ and /mp/ are spelled. (*nd* and *mp*)

Tell students that when two or more consonants come together at the end of a word, they are called *final consonant clusters*.

Activity Have students brainstorm and list other words with the final consonant clusters *nd* and *mp*. (*hand, bump*)

Phonics CD-ROM Have students use the interactive phonics activities.

P/I PREVENTION/INTERVENTION

WORD STRUCTURE Review with students that a compound word is made up of two smaller words. Explain that these two smaller words can often give clues to the compound word's meaning. Point out the kettledrum in the illustration. Students should be able to define *kettledrum* as a big drum that looks like a kettle (or pot). Brainstorm other familiar compound words with students, such as *airplane*, *basketball*, and *birthday*. Invite a volunteer to draw a line separating the two small words. Elicit from students the meanings of the small words and how they help give the meanings of their compound words.

Guided Instruction

20 On this page we learn that Ms. Elwyn has to prepare for another concert. Look back at the picture on pages 272 and 273. Why might it take a lot of energy to be a percussionist? (A percussionist has to play many instruments during a concert. Some of these instruments must be struck hard.) What does the fact that Ms. Elwyn plays in more than one concert on a single day tell us about her? (She must be strong and healthy. She must love her work.) ***Character/Draw Conclusions***

SELF-MONITORING

STRATEGY

REREAD Explain: Rereading what you have read can help you identify the supporting details of the main ideas in this story.

MODEL I can't remember all the details I have read so far. I'll glance back at the pages I have read. Once I see a page and read a few words, that will probably remind me of what I have already learned.

20 "Children! We have to go!" Mr. Samuels announces after a while. "Ms. Elwyn has to get ready for another concert."

Moses and his classmates sign thank you, and they wave goodbye to Ms. Elwyn.

280

281

Guided Instruction

21 Look at the sign for *thanks*. Make up a sign for *you're welcome.* To help you think of one, picture the gestures people make when they say that phrase. Do they seem to wave your thanks away as if they had done nothing worthy of thanks? Perhaps they hold their hands spread apart and palms up as if they would like to give you even more. Try to base your sign on a gesture made by people you know when they say "You're welcome." *Pantomime*

Minilesson

REVIEW/MAINTAIN

Make Inferences

Remind students that writers give many clues to help readers understand a character.

- Have students review what they know about Ms. Elwyn. They know that she plays percussion for a living and is good at it. Ask them what qualities it might take for a deaf person to become a musician. Elicit from students the inferences they make about Ms. Elwyn's character.

Activity Invite students to draw a picture of a daydream Moses might have while playing Ms. Elwyn's instruments. For example, he might see himself on stage playing the drum, before a cheering, waving crowd.

Guided Instruction

22 Look at the way Moses signs the words *so much* and *fun*. Make up a new sign for the word *fun*. Now make up signs for the words *boring* and *not enough*. Let's show each other our new signs. *Pantomime*

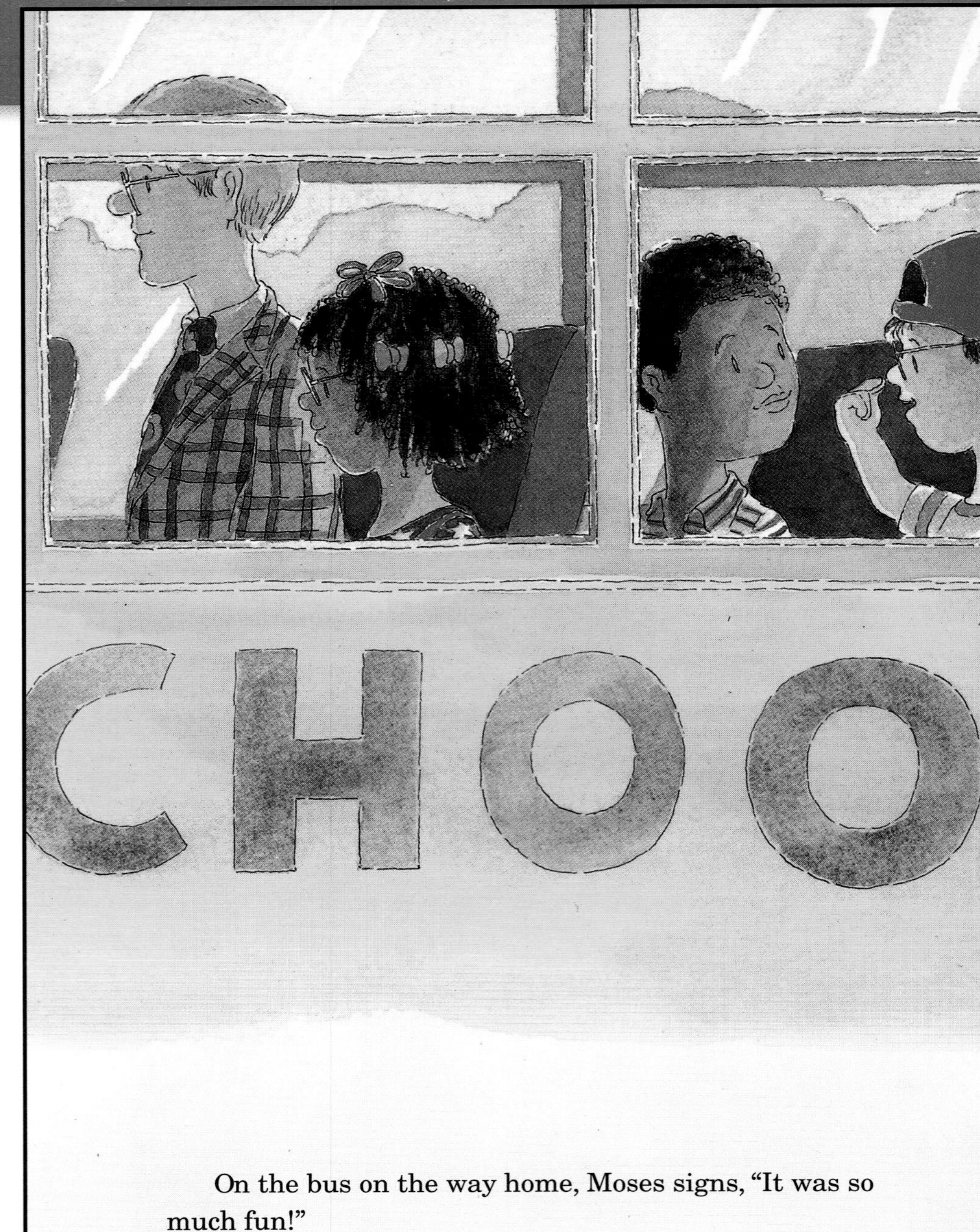

On the bus on the way home, Moses signs, "It was so much fun!"

282

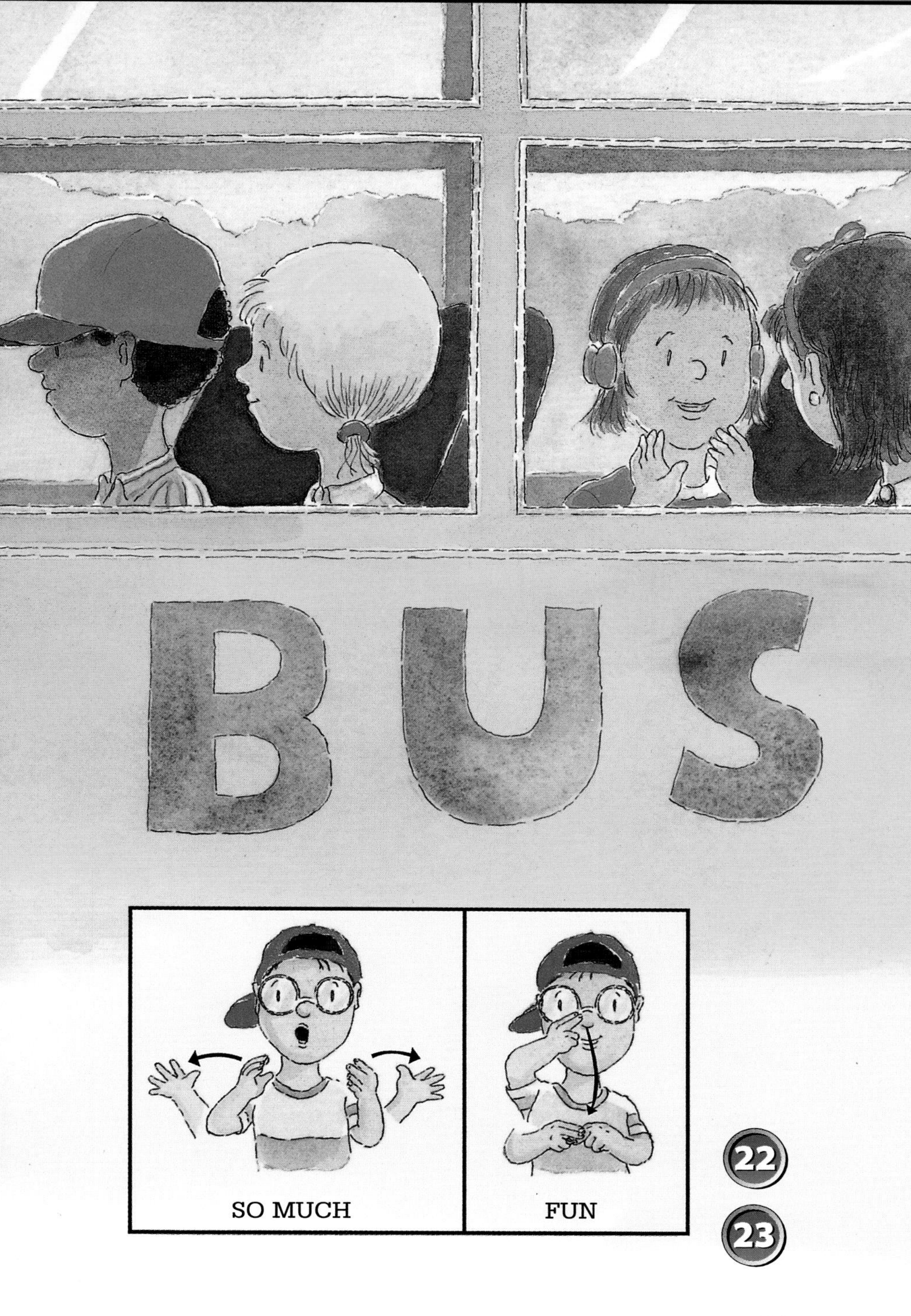

Guided Instruction

23 How is Moses's field trip like a trip you have taken with your class? How is it different? How are Moses and his classmates like you and your classmates? How are they different? *Compare and Contrast*

TEACHING TIP

INSTRUCTIONAL If possible, invite a guest who can demonstrate sign language. Have students learn simple signs, such as "so much" and "fun" or "thanks" and "good-bye."

Guided Instruction

24 MAIN IDEA/SUPPORTING DETAILS

Let's complete our charts.

MAIN IDEA	SUPPORTING DETAILS
Moses is deaf.	He speaks in sign language. He can't hear his drums.
Moses and his class are going to a concert.	Mr. Samuels, their teacher, is taking them by bus. Moses is excited.
The percussionist with the orchestra is also deaf.	She doesn't wear shoes. She feels the vibrations of the music through her feet.
The children "listen" to the concert.	Mr. Samuels gives them balloons to help them feel the music.
The children meet Marjorie Elwyn.	She tells how she became deaf and became a musician. She lets them play on her instruments.
Moses loved the concert.	He says it was fun. Now he wants to be a percussionist, too.

RETELL THE STORY Have volunteers retell the story in their own words. *Summarize*

STUDENT SELF-ASSESSMENT

- How did focusing on main ideas help me to understand the story?
- How did the chart help me?

TRANSFERRING THE STRATEGY

- When might I use this strategy again?
- Would the strategy help me learn another subject?

That night, Moses tells his parents about the concert. Here is what he says:

WHEN YOU

SET YOUR MIND TO IT,

YOU

CAN

BECOME

ANYTHING

YOU

WANT

WHEN

YOU

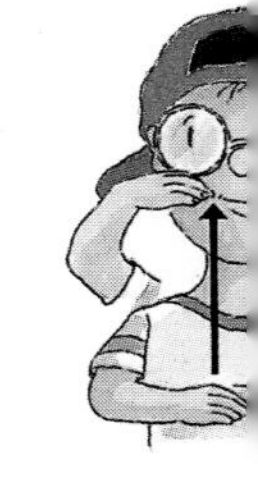

GROW

284

REREADING FOR *Fluency*

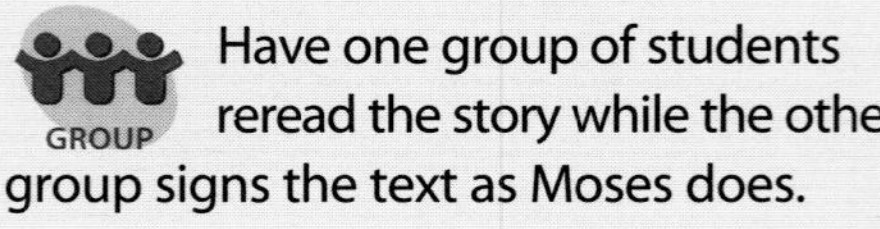

GROUP Have one group of students reread the story while the other group signs the text as Moses does.

READING RATE You may want to evaluate a student's reading rate. Have the student read aloud from *Moses Goes to a Concert* for one minute. Ask the student to place a self-stick note after the last word read. Then count the number of words he or she has read.

Alternatively, you could assess small groups or the whole class together by having students count words and record their own scores.

A Running Record form provided in **Diagnostic/Placement Evaluation** will help you evaluate reading rate(s).

A DOCTOR,

ARTIST,

TEACHER,

LAWYER,

FARMER,

ELECTRICIAN,

OR

ACTOR.

I

WANT

TO BECOME

A PERCUSSIONIST.

285

Guided Instruction

Return to Predictions and Purposes

Review with students their story predictions and reasons for reading the story. Were their predictions correct? Did they find out what they wanted to know?

PREDICTIONS	WHAT HAPPENED
The boy in the story makes hand signs.	Because the boy is deaf, he talks with his hands.
He will like the concert.	He liked the concert so much he wants to be a musician when he grows up.

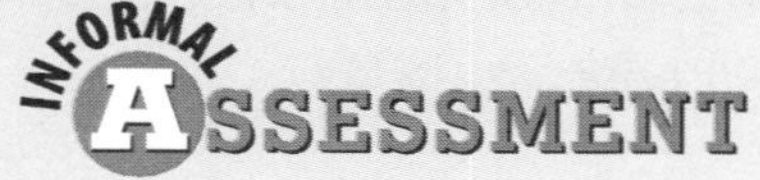

MAIN IDEA

HOW TO ASSESS

- Have students tell the main idea of the whole story in one sentence.
- Ask students to name three details that support the main idea.

Students should recognize that this story mainly tells about how going to a concert featuring a deaf musician affects a deaf boy and his classmates. Their details should relate to the main idea.

FOLLOW UP

If students have trouble distinguishing between main idea and supporting details, have them tell you the main ideas of a familiar fable, such as "The Tortoise and the Hare." Help them to understand that the main idea of a fable is its lesson. Ask them to tell you supporting details found in the familiar fable.

LITERARY RESPONSE

QUICK-WRITE Invite students to record their thoughts about the story. These questions may help them get started:

JOURNAL

- How are Moses and Ms. Elwyn alike?
- What did you learn about people with hearing disabilities?

ORAL RESPONSE Have students share their journal writings and discuss what the story has to teach people who are not physically challenged.

Story Questions

Have students discuss or write answers to the questions on page 286.

Answers:

1. The balloons helped them feel the vibrations of the music. *Literal/Details*
2. It is possible for a deaf person to be a successful percussionist. *Inferential/Main Idea*
3. Because it featured a deaf percussionist, the concert showed the children that they, too, could succeed at whatever work they chose. *Inferential/Draw Conclusions*
4. If you work hard, you can overcome difficulties and become whatever you want. *Critical/Summarize*
5. He might want to ask how she feels about her music, what kind of music she plays. *Critical/Reading Across Texts*

Write a Letter For a full writing process lesson related to this suggestion, see pages 289K–289L.

Story Questions & Activities

1. Why did the children hold balloons at the concert?
2. What did Moses learn from Ms. Elwyn?
3. What made the concert so special for the children?
4. What is this story mainly about?
5. What might the person in the painting on pages 258-259 want to ask Ms. Elwyn?

Write a Letter

Write a letter to the school principal. Try to convince the principal to let your class take a field trip to a concert. Give details about the concert. Tell what the class would learn by going to this concert.

Meeting Individual Needs

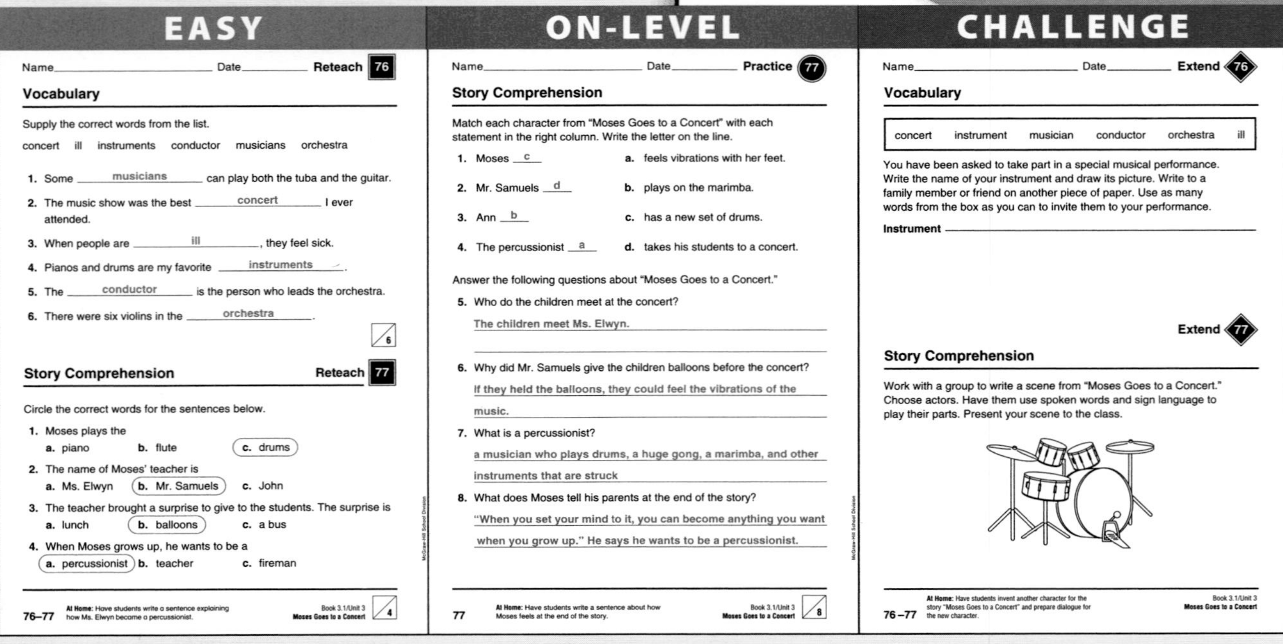

EASY

Name_____ Date_____ Reteach 76

Vocabulary

Supply the correct words from the list.

concert ill instruments conductor musicians orchestra

1. Some musicians can play both the tuba and the guitar.
2. The music show was the best concert I ever attended.
3. When people are ill, they feel sick.
4. Pianos and drums are my favorite instruments.
5. The conductor is the person who leads the orchestra.
6. There were six violins in the orchestra.

Story Comprehension Reteach 77

Circle the correct words for the sentences below.

1. Moses plays the
   a. piano b. flute c. drums
2. The name of Moses' teacher is
   a. Ms. Elwyn b. Mr. Samuels c. John
3. The teacher brought a surprise to give to the students. The surprise is
   a. lunch b. balloons c. a bus
4. When Moses grows up, he wants to be a
   a. percussionist b. teacher c. fireman

76–77 At Home: Have students write a sentence explaining how Ms. Elwyn become a percussionist. Book 3.1/Unit 3 Moses Goes to a Concert

ON-LEVEL

Name_____ Date_____ Practice 77

Story Comprehension

Match each character from "Moses Goes to a Concert" with each statement in the right column. Write the letter on the line.

1. Moses c — a. feels vibrations with her feet.
2. Mr. Samuels d — b. plays on the marimba.
3. Ann b — c. has a new set of drums.
4. The percussionist a — d. takes his students to a concert.

Answer the following questions about "Moses Goes to a Concert."

5. Who do the children meet at the concert?
   The children meet Ms. Elwyn.
6. Why did Mr. Samuels give the children balloons before the concert?
   If they held the balloons, they could feel the vibrations of the music.
7. What is a percussionist?
   a musician who plays drums, a huge gong, a marimba, and other instruments that are struck
8. What does Moses tell his parents at the end of the story?
   "When you set your mind to it, you can become anything you want when you grow up." He says he wants to be a percussionist.

77 At Home: Have students write a sentence about how Moses feels at the end of the story. Book 3.1/Unit 3 Moses Goes to a Concert

CHALLENGE

Name_____ Date_____ Extend 76

Vocabulary

concert instrument musician conductor orchestra ill

You have been asked to take part in a special musical performance. Write the name of your instrument and draw its picture. Write to a family member or friend on another piece of paper. Use as many words from the box as you can to invite them to your performance.

Instrument _____

Extend 77

Story Comprehension

Work with a group to write a scene from "Moses Goes to a Concert." Choose actors. Have them use spoken words and sign language to play their parts. Present your scene to the class.

76–77 At Home: Have students invent another character for the story "Moses Goes to a Concert" and prepare dialogue for the new character. Book 3.1/Unit 3 Moses Goes to a Concert

Reteach, 77 Practice, 77 Extend, 77

Music is found in many different cultures all over the world. Choose a country and find out what kinds of instruments are played there. Create a poster that shows some of the instruments and describes them. Include a paragraph about the country, too.

Make a Drum

Find an empty box or coffee can. Cut a piece of wax paper that is big enough to fit over the opening of the box or the can. Cover the opening with the wax paper and pull it tight. Use a rubber band to hold the paper in place. Then play your drum, using two unsharpened pencils as drum sticks.

Find Out More

The character of Ms. Elwyn is based on a real-life musician named Evelyn Glennie. Find out more about her or another musician you find inspiring. If possible, borrow a recording from the library to share with your class.

287

Story Activities

Create a Poster

Materials: paper, felt-tipped markers, reference books

PARTNERS Provide reference materials. If possible, show students examples of real instruments. Invite students to make sounds with the instruments. If a student has a favorite instrument, he or she may want to research information about its history.

Make a Drum

Materials: empty box or coffee can, wax paper, scissors, rubber bands, pencils

GROUP Help students to make their drums. Then invite them to hold their drums on their laps while they play. Ask them to feel the vibrations. Encourage students to play as a group. A volunteer may enjoy playing the conductor, using a pencil as a baton.

Find Out More

RESEARCH AND INQUIRY

GROUP Suggest students search the Internet for information. Invite students to give oral reports on the musicians they research and play a sample of their music, if possible. If students choose Evelyn Glennie, have them compare her with Ms. Elwyn.

For more information on the topic, have students visit ***www.mhschool.com/reading***.

FORMAL ASSESSMENT

After page 287, see the Selection Assessment.

Study Skills

GRAPHIC AIDS

TESTED OBJECTIVES Students will:

- learn to use a diagram.
- learn the alphabet in American Sign Language.

PREPARE Read the passage with students. Display **Teaching Chart 63.**

TEACH Discuss how to use the diagram and how signing can help the deaf communicate.

PRACTICE Have students answer questions 1–5. Review the answers with them. **1.** a closed fist with the pinkie pointing up **2.** Both signs: the index and middle fingers extend from a closed fist. **3.** Answers will vary. **4.** Answers will vary. **5.** Possible answer: to talk to a deaf person

ASSESS/CLOSE Have students sign to communicate needs, such as the need for water. Invite students to guess each other's needs.

STUDY SKILLS

Use a Diagram

Some hearing-impaired people communicate by using American Sign Language. In this language, words are made with hand shapes, movements, and facial expressions. The **diagram** below shows the hand signs for letters in American Sign Language.

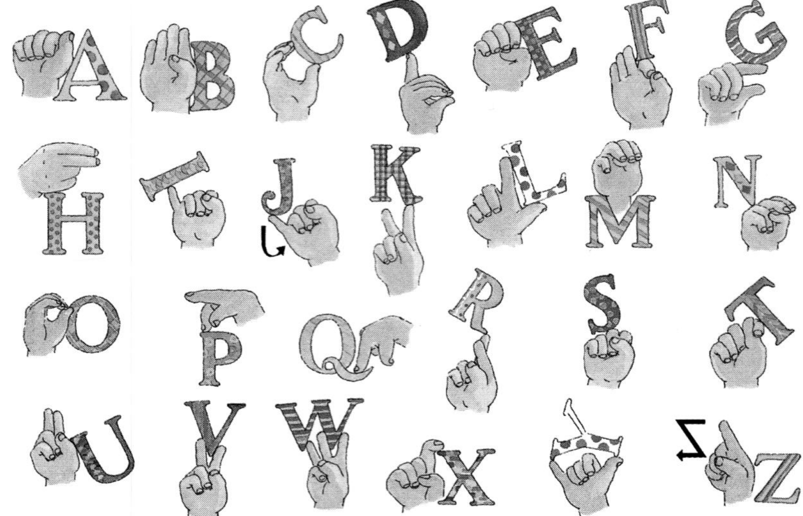

Use the diagram to answer these questions.

1. What is the sign for **I**?
2. How are the signs for **H** and **U** alike?
3. What letter looks the easiest to sign?
4. Sign your name. Was it difficult to do? Why or why not?
5. Why is it good to know something about sign language?

Meeting Individual Needs

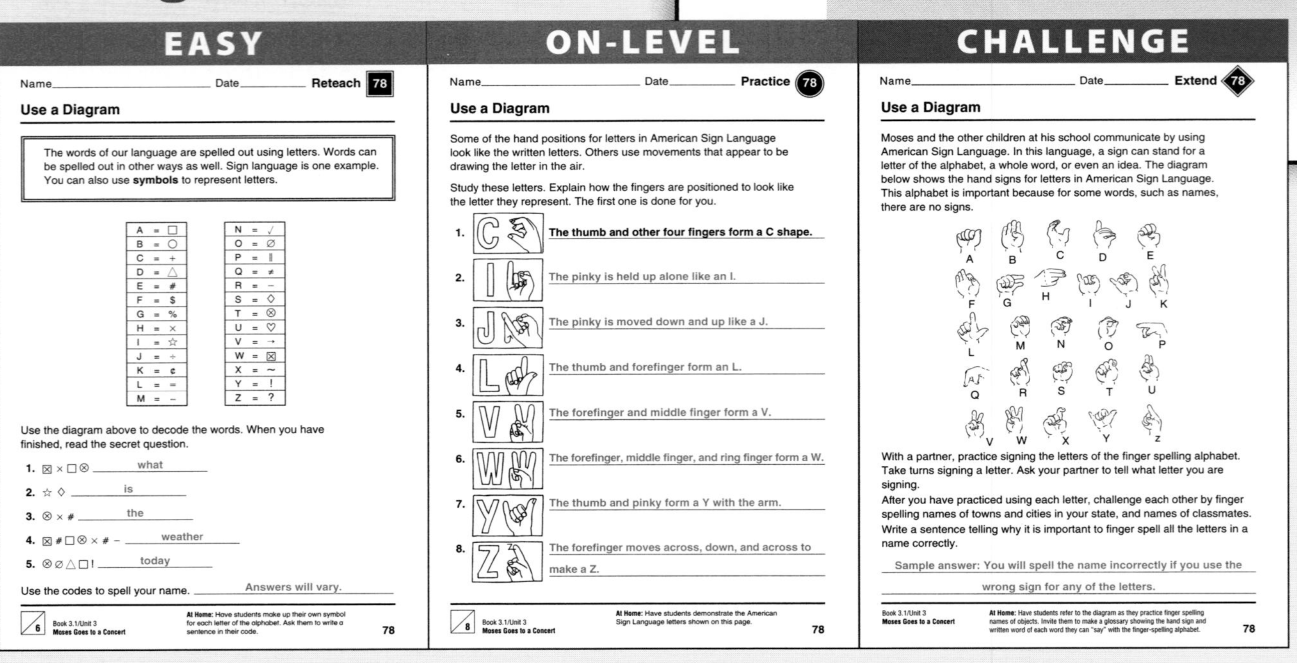

EASY

Name________ Date________ **Reteach 78**

Use a Diagram

The words of our language are spelled out using letters. Words can be spelled out in other ways as well. Sign language is one example. You can also use **symbols** to represent letters.

A	=	□	N	=	√
B	=	○	O	=	∅
C	=	+	P	=	‖
D	=	△	Q	=	≠
E	=	#	R	=	–
F	=	$	S	=	◇
G	=	%	T	=	⊗
H	=	×	U	=	♡
I	=	☆	V	=	→
J	=	÷	W	=	⊠
K	=	¢	X	=	~
L	=	=	Y	=	!
M	=	--	Z	=	?

Use the diagram above to decode the words. When you have finished, read the secret question.

1. ⊠ × □ ⊗ ___what___
2. ☆ ◇ ___is___
3. ⊗ × # ___the___
4. ⊠ # □ ⊗ × # – ___weather___
5. ⊗ ∅ △ □ ! ___today___

Use the codes to spell your name. ___Answers will vary.___

6 Book 3.1/Unit 3 **Moses Goes to a Concert**
At Home: Have students make up their own symbol for each letter of the alphabet. Ask them to write a sentence in their code. 78

Reteach, 78

ON-LEVEL

Name________ Date________ **Practice 78**

Use a Diagram

Some of the hand positions for letters in American Sign Language look like the written letters. Others use movements that appear to be drawing the letter in the air.

Study these letters. Explain how the fingers are positioned to look like the letter they represent. The first one is done for you.

1. C **The thumb and other four fingers form a C shape.**
2. I The pinky is held up alone like an I.
3. J The pinky is moved down and up like a J.
4. L The thumb and forefinger form an L.
5. V The forefinger and middle finger form a V.
6. W The forefinger, middle finger, and ring finger form a W.
7. Y The thumb and pinky form a Y with the arm.
8. Z The forefinger moves across, down, and across to make a Z.

8 Book 3.1/Unit 3 **Moses Goes to a Concert**
At Home: Have students demonstrate the American Sign Language letters shown on this page. 78

Practice, 78

CHALLENGE

Name________ Date________ **Extend 78**

Use a Diagram

Moses and the other children at his school communicate by using American Sign Language. In this language, a sign can stand for a letter of the alphabet, a whole word, or even an idea. The diagram below shows the hand signs for letters in American Sign Language. This alphabet is important because for some words, such as names, there are no signs.

A B C D E
F G H I J K
L M N O P
Q R S T U
V W X Y Z

With a partner, practice signing the letters of the finger spelling alphabet. Take turns signing a letter. Ask your partner to tell what letter you are signing.
After you have practiced using each letter, challenge each other by finger spelling names of towns and cities in your state, and names of classmates. Write a sentence telling why it is important to finger spell all the letters in a name correctly.

Sample answer: You will spell the name incorrectly if you use the wrong sign for any of the letters.

Book 3.1/Unit 3 **Moses Goes to a Concert**
At Home: Have students refer to the diagram as they practice finger spelling names of objects. Invite them to make a glossary showing the hand sign and written word of each word they can "say" with the finger-spelling alphabet. 78

Extend, 78

TEST POWER

Test Tip
Reading the story carefully will make it easier to answer the questions.

DIRECTIONS:
Read the story. Then read each question about the story.

SAMPLE

A Name for Kitten

Heather picked up her kitten and scratched its ears. She looked at Melissa and said, "I haven't picked a name for her yet. Can you think of one?"

Melissa looked at the kitten's striped fur and said, "I think that her orange fur and the stripes make her look like a tiger. What do you think about that name?" she asked.

Heather smiled. "Tiger is a perfect name!" she said. She had read in an encyclopedia that even the smallest house cat is related to a lion. Her tiny kitten was a cousin of the king of the jungle!

Melissa reached out to pet Tiger. "I love kittens," she said. "Maybe I'll get one, too."

"Well, you can't have Tiger," Heather said. "She's all mine." The two friends laughed.

1 This story is mostly about—
- ○ lifting up a kitten
- ○ choosing a kitten
- ● picking a name for a kitten
- ○ two friends laughing

2 Who thought of the name for the kitten?
- ○ Heather's father
- ○ Heather
- ● Melissa
- ○ The encyclopedia

289

ITBS/TEST PREPARATION

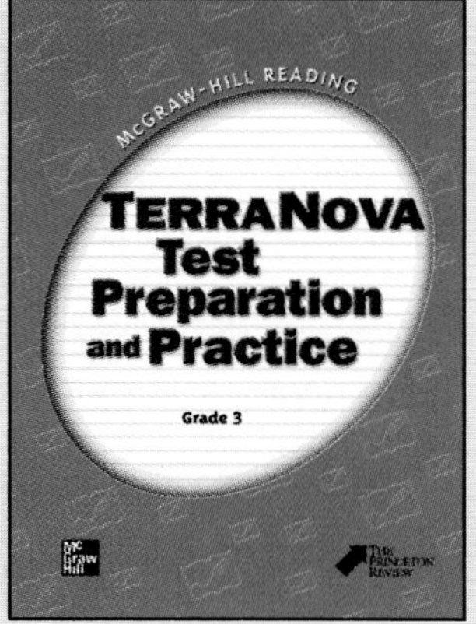

TERRANOVA/TEST PREPARATION

SAT 9/TEST PREPARATION

Test Power

THE PRINCETON REVIEW

Read the Page

Have students read *all* of the information in the story. Instruct students to summarize the story in their own words. This will help students to come up with answers to summary-type questions.

Discuss the Questions

QUESTION 1: Remind students that the word "mostly" is a clue that this is a summary question. Teach students to be cautious with this type of question. Wrong answer choices often give information that is stated in the story but not what the story is mostly about. Students must summarize the whole story.

QUESTION 2: This question requires students to recall a supporting fact. Remind students they should not rely on their memories—this is an *open book test.* They should *always* refer back to the story.

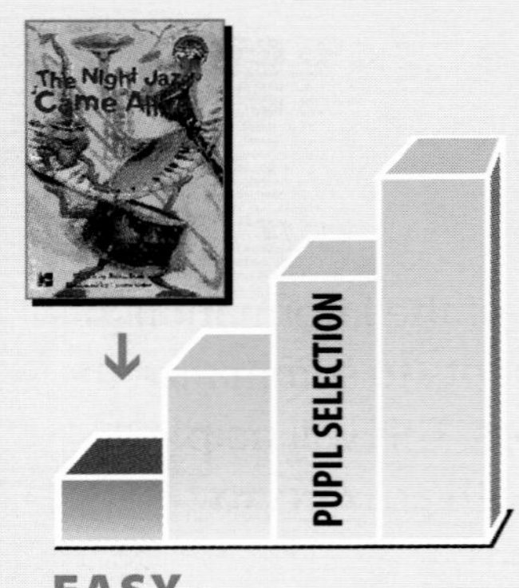

Leveled Books

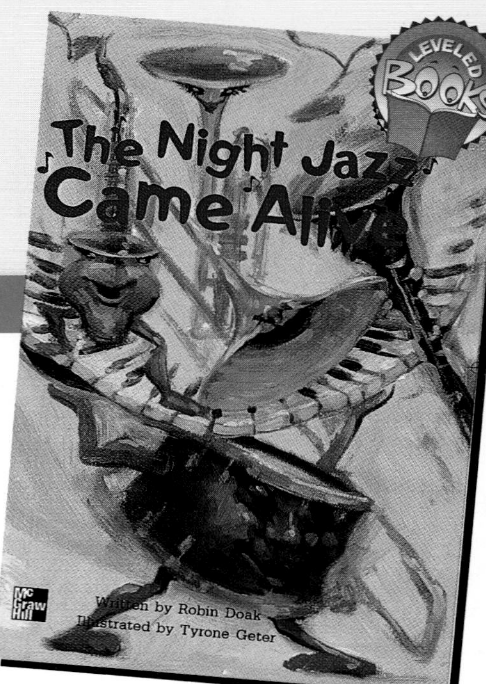

EASY

The Night Jazz Came Alive

Final Consonant Clusters

☑ Main Idea

☑ Instructional Vocabulary: *concert, conductor, ill, instrument, musician, orchestra*

Answers to Story Questions

1. The main character in the story is Joe.
2. Joe wished upon a star and his wish came true.
3. He heard voices talking to him from the stage.
4. The story is mostly about a boy who saves his friends' band by wishing upon a star.
5. Answers will vary.

Story Questions and Writing Activity

1. Who is the main character in the story?
2. What do you think made the instruments come to life? Explain your answer.
3. Why did Joe think someone else was in the Club?
4. What is the story mostly about?
5. What do you think Moses from *Moses Goes to a Concert* might have done if he had been at the Club that Friday night?

Choose a Favorite!

Which jazz band instrument is your favorite? Draw a picture of this instrument. Then write two sentences that tell why you like it.

from *The Night Jazz Came Alive*

Guided Reading

PREVIEW AND PREDICT Conduct a **picture walk**, discussing each illustration up to page 8. Ask: What might the story be about? What might Joe be wishing for?

SET PURPOSES Have students write down five questions they would like to have answered from the story. For example, "Will Joe's wish come true?"

READ THE BOOK Use questions like the following to guide students' reading or after they have read the story independently.

Page 2: What is a musician? (a person who is skilled in playing a musical instrument, composing music, or singing) ***Vocabulary***

Page 3: Find words on this page that end with the consonant clusters *nd* and *nt*. (rent, band) What other words can you think of that end with these clusters? (sent, send, want, hand) ***Phonics and Decoding***

Page 8: Why does Joe get a lump in his throat? (He's holding back tears.) Why is there "nothing to do now but lock up"? (The concert was canceled.) ***Make Inferences***

Pages 12–13: What is the main reason the concert is a success? (The instruments are playing by themselves.) ***Main Idea***

Page 16: Why does Mr. Hicks want the instruments? (perhaps for a club he owns in New Orleans) ***Draw Conclusions***

RETURN TO PREDICTIONS AND PURPOSES Review students' predictions and reasons for reading. Which predictions were correct? Which were not? Which questions were answered? Which were not?

LITERARY RESPONSE Discuss these questions:

- Have you ever listened to jazz before? Based on its description in the story, what might jazz sound like?
- What do you think happened to the jazz band's instruments?

Also see the story questions and activity in *The Night Jazz Came Alive*.

See Phonics **CD-ROM** for practice using consonant cluster words.

Leveled Books

INDEPENDENT

Beethoven: The Man and His Music

☑ Main Idea

☑ Instructional Vocabulary: *concert, conductor, ill, instrument, musician, orchestra*

Guided Reading

PREVIEW AND PREDICT Conduct a **picture walk**, discussing each illustration up to page 14. Ask: What might the story be about? Why might Beethoven be shaking his fist at the sky? Have students record their predictions in a journal.

SET PURPOSES Have students write down three questions they would like to have answered from the story. For example, "What kind of music did Beethoven compose?"

READ THE BOOK Have students read the story themselves. When they finish, return to the text to apply strategies.

Pages 2–3: What is an instrument? (something that produces musical sounds) What instruments did Beethoven play as a young boy? (piano and organ) ***Vocabulary***

Pages 2–3: What important things do you learn about "Young Beethoven"? (He was a great musician at an early age.) ***Main Idea***

Pages 8–9: Why is this chapter titled "A Silent World"? (Beethoven went deaf at the age of 30.) ***Main Idea***

Page 14: Why were Beethoven's last years unhappy? (He did not have many friends and family to visit him.) ***Cause and Effect***

Page 16: What are some of the gifts Beethoven gave to the world? (32 piano sonatas, an opera, 9 symphonies, 6 concertos) What is the main idea of this story? (Beethoven was a gifted composer and overcame a major handicap.) ***Main Idea***

RETURN TO PREDICTIONS AND PURPOSES Review students' predictions and reasons for reading. Which predictions were correct? Which questions were answered? Which were not?

LITERARY RESPONSE Discuss these questions:

- How did Beethoven overcome his loss of hearing?
- How is Beethoven "alive" today?
- What are other possible titles for this book?

Also see the story questions and activity in *Beethoven: The Man and His Music.*

Answers to Story Questions

1. Ludwig van Beethoven was one of the greatest composers who ever lived.
2. He was a famous composer. He may have been embarrassed to tell them. He may have thought people would stop listening to his music.
3. He might not have answered them when they spoke to him.
4. Beethoven was a great composer who continued to create music even after he became deaf.
5. Answers will vary.

Story Questions and Writing Activity

1. Who was Ludwig van Beethoven?
2. What details could you use from the story to explain why you think Beethoven wouldn't tell people at first that he was going deaf?
3. Why do you think some people might have considered Beethoven rude when he was losing his hearing?
4. What is the main idea of the book?
5. If Moses from *Moses Goes to a Concert* had been able to go to one of Beethoven's concerts and spoken to him afterwards, what do you think he might have told him?

Create a Poster

Imagine Ludwig van Beethoven is playing at a concert hall near you. Create a poster to advertise the event. Research the names of some of Beethoven's music and mention the titles of the pieces he will play. Include the date, the time, and the place of the concert.

from *Beethoven: The Man and His Music*

Leveled Books

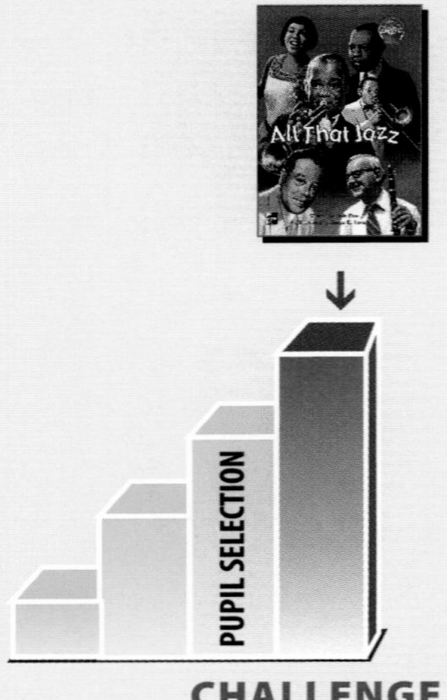

CHALLENGE

All That Jazz

- ☑ Main Idea
- ☑ Instructional Vocabulary: *concert, conductor, ill, instrument, musician, orchestra*

Answers to Story Questions

1. Jazz is a kind of music that has its roots in African American folk music and gospel music.
2. Jazz came into people's homes over the radio. Bands were spoken about and musicians and singers became famous.
3. Mike's great-grandfather, Nicholas, loved Bessie Smith and Louis Armstrong so much he sneaked into a club to see them.
4. Mike's dad explained to him how jazz was born and how it developed.
5. Answers will vary.

Story Questions and Writing Activity

1. What is jazz?
2. How do you think the invention of radio affected jazz?
3. What did Mike's great-grandfather have to do with jazz? Why did Mike's father even mention him?
4. What is the main idea of the book?
5. If Moses's class had gone to see Satchmo and Bessie Smith instead, how might *Moses Goes to a Concert* have ended?

Be a Music Critic

Imagine you are a music critic for a Harlem newspaper long ago. Choose one of the jazz musicians in this book. Then write a review of his or her performance for your paper.

from *All That Jazz*

Guided Reading

PREVIEW AND PREDICT Conduct a **picture walk**, discussing each illustration up to page 9. Ask: What might the story be about? Where did jazz come from? Have students record their predictions.

SET PURPOSES Have students write down five questions they would like to have answered from the story. For example, " Who are some famous jazz musicians?"

READ THE BOOK Have students read the story independently. Then return to the story for teaching opportunities.

Pages 6–7: Why does Mike start tapping his foot? (The music had a bouncy beat and a catchy tune.) ***Make Inferences***

Page 9: Bessie Smith became ill. What is a synonym for *ill*? (sick) What is an antonym for ill? (well, healthy) ***Vocabulary***

Pages 12–13: How does Mike feel about his father's stories? (interested, curious, excited) ***Character***

Pages 14–15: What is the main idea of this story? (Mike's dad passed on his interest in jazz to his son by telling him some of its history and family history in connection with it.) ***Main Idea***

RETURN TO PREDICTIONS AND PURPOSES Review students' predictions and reasons for reading. Which predictions were correct? Which were not? Which questions were answered?

LITERARY RESPONSE Discuss these questions:

- Why does Mike think his dad is "cool"?
- How was jazz "invented"?
- What musical elements mentioned in the story make up jazz?

Also see the story questions and activity in *All That Jazz*.

Connecting Texts

MUSIC CHARTS
Write the story titles on a chart. Discuss with students the role music plays in characters' lives. Call on volunteers and write their suggestions on the chart.

Use the chart to talk about musical performances.

Moses Goes to a Concert	The Night Jazz Came Alive	Beethoven: The Man and His Music	All That Jazz
• Moses, who is deaf, loves to play the drums. • Moses goes to a special concert where the orchestra's percussionist is also deaf. • Moses is happy and inspired.	• Joe's friends' jazz band is in trouble. • Joe wishes upon a star to save the band. • The band's instruments come to life to save the band.	• Beethoven loved and wrote music at a young age. • Even after he went deaf, Beethoven continued to compose. • Beethoven's music is still popular today.	• Mike's dad tells him the history of jazz. • Jazz was invented by African Americans long ago. • Mike's great-grandfather loved jazz, Mike's dad loves jazz, and now Mike does, too!

Viewing/Representing

GROUP PRESENTATIONS Divide the class into groups, one for each of the four books read in the lesson. (For *Moses Goes to a Concert* combine students of different reading levels.) Have each group bring in a piece of music that connects to their book or that all of the group members enjoy. Each group should prepare a dramatic scene or movement to perform for the class as they play the music.

AUDIENCE RESPONSE Ask students to pay attention to each group's presentation. Allow time for questions after each presentation.

Research and Inquiry

MORE ABOUT MUSICAL PERFORMANCES Invite students to:

- find out about an upcoming musical performance (or use the word *concert*) in their area.
- compare the sounds different instruments make.
- go to the library and take out recordings of Beethoven and Duke Ellington. Compare and contrast the sound of drums, piano, strings, woodwinds.

*inter***NET** **CONNECTION** Have students log on to ***www.mhschool.com/reading*** for links to Web pages about music.

OBJECTIVES

Students will identify main ideas and supporting details.

LANGUAGE SUPPORT

Write sets of four sentences on the chalkboard such as these:

- Ms. Elwyn is a successful musician.
- Deaf people can enjoy music, too.
- The class took a bus to the concert.
- Moses and his classmates loved the concert.

As a volunteer reads each sentence aloud, have students raise their hands if they think it is a supporting detail, and stand up if they think it is a main idea.

Review Main Idea

PREPARE

Discuss Main Idea and Supporting Details

Review: Most stories have a main idea that the author wishes to share with the reader. Supporting details help describe the main idea. Ask students how learning more details about a main idea can help them to understand a story.

TEACH

Read "Moses Grows Up" and Model the Skill

Ask students to pay close attention and listen for the main idea in the passage as you read **Teaching Chart 64** with them.

Moses Grows Up

Moses practiced his drumming every day. He remembered what the percussionist had told him after the concert: "You can be anything you want if you set your mind to it." Twice a week, Moses went to a teacher's house to learn how to read music. The teacher taught him how to play music with other people.

When Moses got older, he started his own band, called The Drum People. Everyone in the band played a different kind of drum. Moses and his band practiced a lot. Soon they were performing concerts for people. Everyone loved to listen to Moses's band play. He was glad he listened to the percussionist.

Teaching Chart 64

Discuss how readers can identify the main idea as they read a story.

MODEL Sometimes the main idea of a passage is the message the author wants to share. I wonder if that's true in this case. Let me think about some of the details. Moses remembered what the percussionist had told him. He practiced on his drums, took music lessons, and started his own band. What might the message be?

PRACTICE

Identify Main Idea and Supporting Details

GROUP

Discuss the author's message. Have students underline supporting details in the story. Then have students state the main idea. (Moses set his mind to becoming a musician and worked hard to achieve his goal.)

Have volunteers tell how thinking about the author's message and identifying supporting details helped them figure out the main idea. Then have students tell one or two details from the story that do *not* support the main idea, but just help tell the story.

▶ **Logical/Interpersonal**

ASSESS/CLOSE

Write Supporting Details for a Main Idea

Have partners write supporting details for a story with this main idea: If at first you don't succeed, try and try again. The title of the story is, "Moses Gets a Drum." Brainstorm opening sentences with the class.

ALTERNATE TEACHING STRATEGY

MAIN IDEA

For a different approach to teaching this skill, see page T60.

SELF-SELECTED Reading

Children may choose from the following titles.

ANTHOLOGY

- *Moses Goes to a Concert*

LEVELED BOOKS

- *The Night Jazz Came Alive*
- *Beethoven: The Man and His Music*
- *All That Jazz*

Bibliography, pages T76–T77

Meeting Individual Needs for Comprehension

EASY

Name________________ Date________ **Reteach 79**

Main Idea

If you can identify the main idea and supporting details, you will understand what you read more clearly. The **main idea** tells the major point. **Supporting details** explain the main idea.

Read each main idea from "Moses Goes to a Concert." Then look at the two supporting details that follow. Circle the detail that does **not** support the main idea.

1. **Main Idea:** Moses and the other children in his class go to a concert.
   Supporting Details:
   They travel to the concert on the bus.
   Moses knows how to play many games.
2. **Main Idea:** Mr. Samuels brings balloons for Moses and the other children.
   Supporting Details:
   Drums come in many different sizes.
   The balloons help them to feel the music.
3. **Main Idea:** Moses and his friends are excited about the concert.
   Supporting Details:
   They wave and clap.
   Moses likes school.
4. **Main Idea:** Moses has fun at the concert.
   Supporting Details:
   Moses likes math class.
   Moses likes listening to Ms. Elwyn's story.

McGraw-Hill School Division

79 **At Home:** Have students identify the main idea and supporting details of another story they've read. Book 3.1/Unit 3 **Moses Goes to a Concert** 4

Reteach, 79

ON-LEVEL

Name________________ Date________ **Practice 79**

Main Idea

To understand a passage better, separate the main idea from the details that support it. The **main idea** is the most important point. **Supporting details** are smaller points that explain the main idea.

Read the following sentences about "Moses Goes to a Concert." Write the main idea of the passage and then write the supporting details. Answers will vary.

Moses has a new set of drums. He likes to play with his new drums, but he can't hear the sound they make. Moses is deaf. He can, however, feel the vibration of his drums with his hands. To feel even more of the vibrations, Moses takes off his shoes. Now he can feel his new drums with his hands and his feet!

Main Idea:

1. Moses can play his drums, even though he is deaf.

Supporting Details:

2. Moses has a new set of drums.
3. Moses plays by feeling the vibrations of the drum through his hands.
4. Moses has also taken off his shoes, so he can feel the vibrations through his feet.

McGraw-Hill School Division

79 **At Home:** Have students read a paragraph from an article in a childrens' magazine or newspaper. Then ask them to write down the main idea and supporting details of the paragraph. Book 3.1/Unit 3 **Moses Goes to a Concert** 4

Practice, 79

CHALLENGE

Name________________ Date________ **Extend 79**

Main Idea

Write a main-idea sentence for "Moses Goes to a Concert."

Answers will vary. For example, "When you set your mind to it, you can be anything you want when you grow up."

Develop an idea for another story about Moses and his friends. Write a main idea sentence for this story.

Answers will vary.

Write three or four sentences giving supporting details for your story.

McGraw-Hill School Division

79 **At Home:** Have students draw a picture illustrating the main-idea sentence for their original story. Book 3.1/Unit 3 **Moses Goes to a Concert**

Extend, 79

LANGUAGE SUPPORT

Name________________ Date________

Ways To Hear Music If You Are Deaf

The main idea of the story is

86 **Moses Goes to a Concert** • Language Support/Blackline Master 42 Grade 3

Language Support, 86

Introduce Summarize

OBJECTIVES

Students will summarize a story.

TEACHING TIP

MANAGEMENT You may wish to have students use their summary cards from the Assess/Close activity to create a bulletin board display titled, "Very Creative Stories." Have students make summary cards for other stories they read in the unit and add them to the display.

PREPARE

Discuss Summarizing

Explain: Recognizing main ideas and their supporting details helps you identify the main events of a story. Briefly retelling those main events is called summarizing.

TEACH

Read "Moses Meets a Percussionist" and Model the Skill

Read "Moses Meets a Percussionist" with students. Focus students' attention on the most important things that happen.

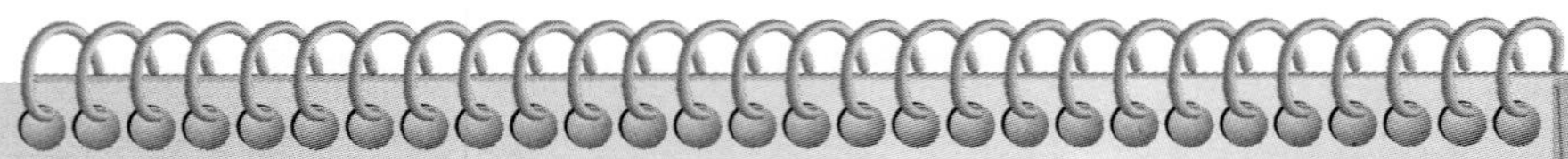

Moses Meets a Percussionist

Moses went with his class to a concert. Since Moses and his classmates were deaf, the teacher gave them balloons so they could feel the vibrations of the music. ~~There were a lot of different musicians in the orchestra.~~ The percussionist also was deaf. She didn't wear any shoes while she played so that she could feel the vibrations of the music.

The whole class loved the concert. Moses was very excited when he met the percussionist. ~~She let him play her bass drum.~~ When Moses got home, he told his parents that he had his heart set on becoming a percussionist.

Teaching Chart 65

Explain that identifying the main ideas or key events is the first step to writing a summary. The next step is to restate those ideas or events in your own words, leaving out any unimportant details.

MODEL If someone who had not read the story asked me what it was about, what would I tell them? I would tell them that it was about a deaf boy named Moses who went to a concert. I would also say that Moses enjoyed the concert and learned something about himself from the percussionist.

Discuss which details are not as important. Have a volunteer cross out two details that are not important and should not be included in a summary.

PRACTICE

Create a Story Summary Chart and Write a Summary

GROUP

Have groups create a Story Summary chart. Help them get started. After they finish, challenge them to use their charts to write a summary of the story. ▶**Linguistic/Spatial**

STORY SUMMARY	
Important Fact 1	Moses and his class went to a concert.
Important Fact 2	Moses is deaf.
Important Fact 3	The class loved the concert.
Important Fact 4	Moses wants to be a percussionist now.

ASSESS/CLOSE

Make a Class Summary File

Distribute index cards to the class. Tell students to write on a card a summary for a story he or she has read. Have them put a tab on each card and write the name of the story on the tab. Then have them write supporting details for the story on other cards and file them behind the appropriate summary card. Help students put the summary cards in alphabetical order.

ALTERNATE TEACHING STRATEGY

SUMMARIZE

For a different approach to teaching this skill, see page T62.

LOOKING AHEAD

Students will apply this skill as they read the next selection, *The Little Painter of Sabana Grande.*

Meeting Individual Needs for Comprehension

EASY

Name________ Date______ **Reteach 80**

Summarize

When you write a **summary**, you give only the most important events or information. You do not include small details when you summarize.

Read each paragraph. Underline the sentence that best summarizes the paragraph.

1. Sarah and her father both felt hungry. Their stomachs growled. They both wanted to eat cheese sandwiches for dinner that night.
   Sarah's stomach growled.
   Sarah's father felt hungry.
   Sarah and her father both felt hungry.
2. Sarah and her father went to the store. They bought cheese and bread. They also bought six plums, a bunch of grapes, and a box of cookies.
   Sarah and her father went to the store.
   Sarah and her father bought cookies.
   Sarah and her father saw a movie.
3. When they got home, it was almost time for dinner. Sarah and her father decided to make cheese sandwiches. Sarah and her father put the cheese on the bread. Then they put the bread in the oven.
   Sarah and her father made dinner.
   Sarah and her father put the cheese on the bread.
   Sarah and her father ate plums.
4. Sarah and her father sat down to eat dinner. Sarah only ate one cheese sandwich, but her father ate four! For dessert, they ate the cookies, plums, and grapes.
   Sarah and her father ate cookies, plums, and grapes for dessert.
   Sarah and her father ate dinner.
   Sarah's father ate four cheese sandwiches.

4 Book 3.1/Unit 3 **Moses Goes to a Concert** **At Home:** Have students use the four paragraphs as one story and summarize it. 80

Reteach, 80

ON-LEVEL

Name________ Date______ **Practice 80**

Summarize

When you **summarize**, you tell only the most important things that happened. Read each passage below. Then write a summary.
Answers may vary.

1. Last summer, Crystal and her parents drove to Florida. On the way, their car broke down. They worried that they might not make it to Florida. However, they got their car fixed and drove there the next morning.
   Summary: Crystal and her parents had car trouble during their drive to Florida.
2. In Florida, they visited Crystal's grandma. Grandma loved to garden. She grew lemon trees, orange trees, and many different types of flowers. She gardened every day.
   Summary: In Florida, they visited Crystal's grandma, who loved to garden.
3. Crystal asked Grandma, "Can I work in the garden, too?" Grandma said yes. First, Crystal chose the kind of flowers she wanted. Crystal chose roses. Then, she planted seeds and watered them every day. Grandma said that Crystal's roses would bloom in the spring.
   Summary: Crystal planted roses in Grandma's garden.
4. After two weeks in Florida, it was time to go home. Crystal and her parents hugged Grandma. Crystal felt sad about leaving, but she knew that they would come back in the spring.
   Summary: After two weeks in Florida, Crystal and her parents headed home.

4 Book 3.1/Unit 3 **Moses Goes to a Concert** **At Home:** Have students write a one-paragraph summary of the story on this page. 80

Practice, 80

CHALLENGE

Name________ Date______ **Extend 80**

Summarize

Read the paragraphs about the planet Earth.

The planet earth is the only planet in the solar system with large amounts of water on its surface and in its atmosphere. Earth is the third planet from the sun. The water in the oceans would boil away if the sun were much closer. If the earth were farther away from the sun, the water would turn to ice. The sun is just the right distance away.

Earth is larger than Mercury, Mars, Venus, and Pluto but smaller than all of the other planets. From space earth looks like a perfectly round ball, but it is really wider in the middle than at the top and bottom.

Earth is tilted a little to one side as it travels around the sun. As it goes around the sun, it spins like a big top. Each spin takes about twenty-four hours and is called a day.

A blanket of air circles the earth to keep the temperature from changing too much. This blanket of air is called the atmosphere. The people on the planet Earth live at the bottom of the atmosphere.

Write a paragraph summarizing the information about planet Earth. Be sure to include important information from each of the paragraphs.

Answers will vary.

Book 3.1/Unit 3 **Moses Goes to a Concert** **At Home:** Have students draw pictures to summarize the paragraphs about planet Earth. 80

Extend, 80

LANGUAGE SUPPORT

Name________ Date______

A Quick Note

orchestra	bass drum	bus trip	percussion

Dear Friends,

I went on a bus trip today.

First, I sat in the first row which was close to the orchestra and instruments.

Second, I heard Marjorie Elwyn play the percussion instruments.

Third, I got to practice on the bass drum.

In summary, I want to be a percussionist, like Ms. Elwyn, when I grow up.

Your friend,

Moses

Grade 3 Language Support / Blackline Master 43 • **Moses Goes to a Concert** 87

Language Support, 87

Review Context Clues

OBJECTIVES

Students will:

- **identify context clues for content-area and specialized vocabulary.**
- **use context clues to determine the meaning of unfamiliar words.**

MATERIALS

- **Teaching Chart 66**
- **music textbooks or reference books about instruments**

> **TEACHING TIP**
>
> **INSTRUCTIONAL** To help students understand what "specialized vocabulary" means, you may wish to start with a simple example. Review the names of tools associated with a teacher's job, such as *chalkboard, textbook,* and *seating plan.*

PREPARE

Discuss the Use of Specialized Vocabulary

Explain: Different types of work require special tools. For example, a doctor uses a stethoscope to listen to your heartbeat. Context clues can help you understand the names of these specialized tools when you are reading a story that includes them.

TEACH

Read the Passage and Model the Skill

Read the passage on **Teaching Chart 66.** Have students listen for musical terms that are unfamiliar.

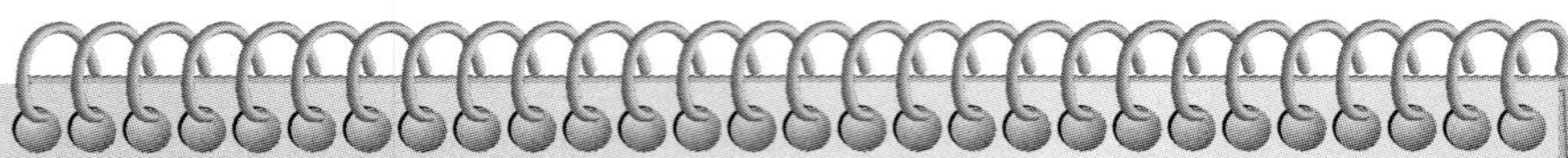

A Percussionist's Instruments

The percussionist talked to Moses and his class about how she learned to play her instruments.

One of her favorite things was using a special stick to strike the huge metal disk called a gong. When she was smaller, she had to climb on a chair to strike the tiny, high-pitched triangle hanging from its tall stand. She would beat on congas with her hands for hours. They are tall bass drums. She would bang on the giant kettledrum until her parents told her to stop making so much noise.

Teaching Chart 66

MODEL I can use clues to help me figure out meanings of special words. The title is "A Percussionist's Instruments." I know that percussionists strike, or beat, their instruments to make sounds. To identify the instruments, I will pick out the objects that the percussionist strikes.

Have students name context clues that could help them find the meaning of the unfamiliar word *gong.* (huge metal disk; special stick)

PRACTICE

Identify and Use Context Clues

Have volunteers circle the specialized vocabulary words that name musical instruments. Then have them underline any context clues that help them define the words. Have groups discuss what they think each instrument looks like and what sounds it might make.

▶ **Logical/Linguistic**

ASSESS/CLOSE

Write Sentences Using Context Clues

Have students work in groups to brainstorm a list of other musical instruments. Ask them to write a sentence for each that includes the name of the instrument and some of the following context clues: what the instrument looks like; the sound it makes; or some clues as to how it is played. Have them check music textbooks or reference books for information about instruments.

ALTERNATE TEACHING STRATEGY

CONTEXT CLUES

For a different approach to teaching this skill, see page T63.

Meeting Individual Needs for Vocabulary

EASY

Name________ Date______ **Reteach 81**

Context Clues

Reading the words and sentences around an unfamiliar word can help you figure out what the word means. Then, you can use a dictionary or glossary to check your meaning or to find a more specific meaning.

Read each passage below. Use the words and phrases in dark type to help you decide what each underlined word means. Then write the meaning of the underlined word on the line.

1. There were **drummers, piano players, and many other musicians** in the orchestra. The children couldn't wait for the **concert** to begin.

   orchestra: a group of musicians playing on different instruments

2. When **Ms. Elwyn comes onto the stage**, people stand up and start to applaud. Some of the children in Moses's class do not **clap**, though. They wave instead.

   applaud: clap

3. I can play the **drums**. She can play the **piano**. Which instrument can you play?

   instrument: something that makes music

4. The musicians rehearsed for many days. They sounded **better each day**. After **practicing** for almost a month, they were ready for the concert.

   rehearsed: practiced

81 **At Home:** Have students write sentences using the underlined words above. Book 3.1/Unit 3 **Moses Goes to a Concert** 4

Reteach, 81

ON-LEVEL

Name________ Date______ **Practice 81**

Context Clues

When you find an unfamiliar word, read the words and sentences around it. They often can help you figure out the word's meaning.

Look at the underlined word in each example. Circle the words and phrases that help you tell what the word means. Then mark an **X** next to the meaning that fits the underlined word.

1. The musicians walked onto the stage. People clapped and waved. The concert was about to begin.

   ___ drums   X musical performance   ___ game

2. The singer sang a very high note. She broke a window.

   ___ red   ___ apple pie   X sound in music

3. She is a percussionist. She plays the piano, the drums, and many other instruments.

   X type of musician   ___ large van   ___ baby duck

4. Mozart is a famous composer. He wrote many beautiful songs.

   ___ cab driver   ___ dog food   X person who creates a musical work

5. He played a pretty melody on the piano. I asked, "What is the name of that song?"

   ___ green   X tune   ___ bat

81 **At Home:** Have students look up each underlined word in a dictionary to check the meaning. Book 3.1/Unit 3 **Moses Goes to a Concert** 10

Practice, 81

CHALLENGE

Name________ Date______ **Extend 81**

Context Clues

Use the words in the box to complete the story.

conductor	orchestra	marimba	kettledrum
snare drum	percussion	cymbal	triangle

Our class went to hear a concert performed by our town's orchestra. The musicians knew exactly when they were supposed to play. The conductor stood in front of them with his baton in his hand, and directed their playing. There were many different percussion instruments that were played by being hit or shaken. There were several kinds of drums, including a small double-headed drum called a snare drum because of the snares across its lower head. It made a sound like a rattle when it was played. I liked the drum that looked like a giant covered soup bowl. It is called a kettledrum.

There were other instruments, too. One of my favorites, the marimba looked a little like a piano keyboard, but you play it with sticks and not your fingers. The brass cymbal is shaped like a plate, but I can't imagine eating my dinner on it! To play it you strike it with a stick or even with another instrument just like it. I think the steel triangle has the funniest name of all. It makes me think of shapes we study in school.

81 **At Home:** Have students underline the context clues in the story that helped them fill in the correct word. Book 3.1/Unit 3 **Moses Goes to a Concert**

Extend, 81

LANGUAGE SUPPORT

Name________ Date______

Word Clues

1. The conductor turns to face the orchestra and raises his baton.
   Circle the conductor in the picture.

2. The percussionist is the word for the musician who strikes the huge gong to begin the concert.
   Make a box around the percussionist.

3. Moses wants to be a percussionist and practices on the big bass drum every chance he gets.
   Put a large X on the bass drum.

88 **Moses Goes to a Concert** • Language Support/Blackline Master 44 Grade 3

Language Support, 88

GRAMMAR/SPELLING CONNECTIONS

See the 5-Day Grammar and Usage Plan on action verbs, pages 289M–289N.

See the 5-Day Spelling Plan on words with consonant clusters, pages 289O–289P.

TECHNOLOGY TIP

Experiment with the different fonts on the class computer to achieve various effects—excitement, importance, artistry, or humor. Use big and bold letters for the most important information.

Persuasive Writing

Prewrite

WRITE A LETTER Assign students to write a letter convincing the school principal to grant a class field trip to a special concert. Give the name of the band or orchestra, and tell what the class could learn by hearing their music.

FOCUS WITH QUESTIONS Have students ask each other questions about the concert. Practical questions should elicit information about place, time, cost, and kind of music. Questions about persuasive strategy should elicit information about methods of persuading the audience to go to the concert.

Strategy: Create a Chart Have students write their practical and persuasive questions in a chart.

Practical	Persuasive
What orchestra or band will play?	What is special about the band?
How much are the tickets?	What will the class learn by attending the concert?
Where and when is the concert?	Why do people like this band's music?

GRAPHIC ORGANIZER 31

Draft

USE THE CHART Have students refer to their charts to make sure that they have included all necessary information in their letters. Urge them to state clear, strong ideas that will make their requests attractive to the principal.

Revise

CREATE CHECKLISTS Have students create a checklist to help revise their letters.

- Where is the concert taking place?
- What is unique about the band?
- What is the best thing about their music?

Edit/Proofread

CHECK FOR ERRORS Students should reread their work to check spelling and punctuation. Explain the use of a colon to help show time, place, and date.

Publish

READ THE LETTERS Students can read their letters aloud. Encourage students to talk about what they think were one another's best arguments. Invite them to offer positive suggestions for improvement.

Dear Ms. Greene:

Next Tuesday, The Blue River Band will play a concert at the stadium. Everyone in our class really wants to see the show. It's at one o'clock, so we need your permission to have a field trip.

We all think this band is great. Their songs are all about good things, like following your dreams in life and being happy. Their music makes people feel positive and strong. Our teacher, Mr. Marks, said we could write a report about the band after the concert.

We hope you'll give us permission to see this special show.

Sincerely,

Tommy Quinn

Presentation Ideas

RESPOND TO SUGGESTIONS Ask students to create posters advertising the concert. Then display the ads in the school hallway. Invite other grades to vote on the most effective ad.
▶ **Viewing/Representing**

REVIEW THE CONCERT Have students pretend they attended the concerts portrayed in the letter. Ask them to tell the class what they expected and what actually happened. ▶ **Speaking/Listening**

COMMUNICATION TIPS

VIEWING Before they vote, encourage students to consider how the text and pictures work together.

LISTENING After "critics" give their reviews, have other students take turns asking for more information.

Consider students' creative efforts, possibly adding a plus (+) for originality, wit, and imagination.

Scoring Rubric

Excellent	Good	Fair	Unsatisfactory
4: The writer • presents a strong argument with convincing details and facts. • has an excellent sense of audience. • presents the argument in a strong personal voice.	**3:** The writer • presents a sound argument with adequate details. • has considered the audience. • shows a sense of personal voice.	**2:** The writer • presents only the basic argument. • has only a vague sense of audience. • shows little personal style.	**1:** The writer • has not understood the purpose. • has not given enough necessary facts and few or no details. • shows little or no personal style.

0: The writer leaves the page blank or fails to respond to the writing task. The student does not address the topic or simply paraphrases the prompt. The response is illegible or incoherent.

PORTFOLIO Invite students to include their letters or another writing project in their portfolios.

Meeting Individual Needs for Writing

EASY

Drawing Have each student draw a picture of an instrument they would like to play in a concert. Encourage them to make their drawings as detailed as possible. Ask them to label their drawings with a few sentences telling what they like about their instruments. They may also wish to tell the type of music they will play with their instruments.

ON-LEVEL

Description Ask students to write a paragraph telling about a concert they have attended. Have them include details about the type of music played, where it was held, who played the music, and whether or not they liked it. They may wish to illustrate their paragraphs.

CHALLENGE

Sequel Invite students to write a sequel to *Moses Goes to a Concert,* titled *Moses Gives a Concert.* Moses is about to give his first concert. Students should include how Moses is feeling, how well he plays, and who attends his concert. Invite students to draw an ad for the concert.

5 Day Grammar and Usage Plan

LANGUAGE SUPPORT

Ask volunteers to act out verbs such as *tap*, *jump*, and *wave*. Have other students say the verb that tells what action each student is performing.

DAILY LANGUAGE ACTIVITIES

Write the Daily Language Activities on the board each day, or use **Transparency 11**. Have students orally add action verbs to the sentences. (Sample answers are given.)

Day 1

1. Mikka______ the guitar. plays
2. Phil __________ his shoes. ties
3. We______ our hands. clap

Day 2

1. They______ sign language. use
2. Can we______ the band? see
3. Moses______ the music. likes

Day 3

1. I______ with my friend. laugh
2. People______ from all over. come
3. We______ with the music. dance

Day 4

1. Steve______ onstage. walks
2. The teachers______ to the class. speak
3. Jamiel______ the clock. watches

Day 5

1. Will you______ me a program? pass
2. Drums______ a loud noise. make
3. David______ to the crowd. bows

Daily Language Transparency 11

DAY 1 Introduce the Concept

Oral Warm-up Read aloud *Janina sings a song*. Ask students what Janina does with the song. Explain that *sing* is an action verb.

Introduce Action Verbs Explain that an action verb tells what the subject does. Present the following:

Action Verbs

An **action verb** is a word that shows action.

Present the Daily Language Activity. Then, write these sentences on the board, asking students to circle the subject, and add an action verb to each. Sample answers are given.

Jeremy ____ the ladder. climbs, carries
The cymbals ____ to the floor. crash, fall

Assign the daily Writing Prompt on page 258C.

LEARN
Name__________ Date______ Grammar 65

What Is an Action Verb?

- An **action verb** is a word that shows action.
  The students clap to the music.
  Moses beats a drum.

Each sentence has an action verb. Find the verb and write it on the line.

1. Mr. Samuels's class rides on a bus. rides
2. Mr. Samuels carries his bag. carries
3. He takes them to a concert. takes
4. Moses sits in the front row. sits
5. A young woman walks onstage. walks
6. The percussionist bows. bows
7. Some of the students wave. wave
8. The conductor raises his baton. raises
9. The percussionist hits the gong. hits
10. The students thank Ms. Elwyn. thank

10 Book 3.1/Unit 3 Moses Goes to a Concert

Extension: Have students work together in pairs. Ask them to list verbs that show the actions of playing instruments. Once they have completed their lists, they can check the story to see if they can find additional musical action verbs. 65

GRAMMAR PRACTICE BOOK, PAGE 65

DAY 2 Teach the Concept

Review Action Verbs Ask students which word in a sentence shows an action done by the subject.

More Action Verbs Explain that some verbs describe actions that can be hard to see. For instance, *jump* is easy to see, but *watch, make, see, like,* and *add* are harder to see.

Action Verbs

Some action verbs tell about actions that are difficult to see.

Present the Daily Language Activity. Have students explain how to identify action verbs. Then, ask students to list three more action verbs and use them in sentences.

Assign the daily Writing Prompt on page 258C.

LEARN AND PRACTICE
Name__________ Date______ Grammar 66

Finding Action Verbs

- An **action verb** is a word that shows action. Some action verbs tell about actions that are hard to see.
  The students listen to the music.
  Moses likes the vibrations.

Circle the action verb in each sentence.

1. The teacher (waits) for the class.
2. The conductor (smiles) at the audience.
3. The students (watch) the conductor carefully.
4. They (enjoy) the concert!
5. Moses (feels) the vibrations in the balloon.
6. The students (learn) the music.
7. The drums (make) a lot of noise.
8. They (practice) their instruments.
9. They (helped) each other.
10. Moses (remembers) that field trip.

Extension: Have the students work in pairs and list four action verbs. Using their list, they should take turns

Book 3.1/Unit 3

GRAMMAR PRACTICE BOOK, PAGE 66

Action Verbs

DAY 3 Review and Practice

Learn from the Literature Review action verbs. Explain that since some subjects do more than one thing, some sentences have more than one action verb. Read the first and second sentences on page 273 of *Moses Goes to a Concert:*

> **The conductor turns to face the orchestra and raises his baton.**
> **The percussionist strikes the huge gong and the concert begins.**

Help students to identify the two action verbs in each sentence.

Use Action Verbs Present the Daily Language Activity. Then, ask students to hunt for action verbs from page 279 of *Moses Goes to a Concert*, and to write new sentences that include those verbs. Ask the class to identify action verbs as volunteers read their sentences aloud.

Assign the daily Writing Prompt on page 258D.

Name________ Date________ PRACTICE AND REVIEW Grammar 67

Using Action Verbs

- An **action verb** is a word that shows action.
- Some action verbs tell about actions that are hard to see.
  Maria plays the congas.
  Moses counts the beats.

Here is a list of action verbs. Choose an action verb to finish each sentence. Write the verb on the line.

bows	meet
climbs	strikes
likes	watches
feel	wonders

1. Mr. Samuels's class __climbs__ into the bus.
2. The class __wonders__ about the surprise.
3. Moses __watches__ his drum.
4. The percussionist __bows__.
5. The members of the orchestra __meet__ the conductor.
6. The percussionist __strikes__ the gong.
7. The deaf students __feel__ the vibrations.
8. The class __likes__ Ms. Elwyn.

8 Book 3.1/Unit 3 **Moses Goes to a Concert** — **Extension:** Ask students to write three sentences telling about a favorite activity. Tell them to use action verbs in their sentences. 67

GRAMMAR PRACTICE BOOK, PAGE 67

DAY 4 Review and Practice

Review Action Verbs Write the sentences from the Daily Language Activities for Days 1 through 3 on the board. Ask students to identify the action verbs in each and to explain how they identified them. Then, present the Daily Language Activity for Day 4.

Mechanics and Usage Before the students begin the daily Writing Prompt on page 258D, review the following:

Capitalization and Commas

- A proper noun begins with a capital letter.
- The name of a day, month, or holiday begins with a capital letter.
- Use a comma between the name of a city and state.
- Use a comma between the day and the year in a date.

Assign the daily Writing Prompt on page 258D.

Name________ Date________ MECHANICS Grammar 68

Using Capital Letters and Commas

- A proper noun begins with a **capital letter**.
- The name of a day, month, or holiday beings with a **capital letter**.
- Use a **comma** between the name of a city and a state.
- Use a **comma** between the day and the year in a date.

Correct each sentence. Write the capital letter over the small letter. Add commas.

1. (M S) mr. samuels teaches deaf students.
2. (M) He was born on march 31,1960.
3. (W) The class went to a concert last wednesday.
4. (M J) On the bus, moses sat next to john.
5. (B M) The conductor is from boston,massachusetts.
6. (M) Many holidays are celebrated on a monday.
7. (D O) The percussionist once played in dayton,ohio.
8. (N) We watched the parade on november 26,1998.
9. (D M S) After the concert, diane, mark, and steve played the drums.
10. (S) One school for the deaf opened on september 4,1964.

68 — **Extension:** Have the students write three sentences about a recent holiday. Ask them to give the date and day of the week that they celebrated the holiday, along with details of what they did. Book 3.1/Unit 3 **Moses Goes to a Concert** 10

McGraw-Hill School Division

GRAMMAR PRACTICE BOOK, PAGE 68

DAY 5 Assess and Reteach

Assess Use the Daily Language Activity and page 69 of the **Grammar Practice Book** for assessment.

Reteach Have students write each rule about action verbs from the lesson's grammar concepts on an index card. Ask students to choose two action verbs from *Moses Goes to a Concert*, and to use these verbs in a new sentence or sentences. Have students act out their sentences, and invite the class to guess what action verbs the volunteer is acting out.

Use page 70 of the **Grammar Practice Book** for additional reteaching.

Assign the daily Writing Prompt on page 258D.

Name________ Date________ TEST Grammar 69

Action Verbs

Read each sentence. Find the action verb and write it on the line.

1. He plays the piano. __plays__
2. The class dances to the vibrations. __dances__
3. Ms. Elwyn takes a bow. __takes__
4. Moses chooses the bass drum. __chooses__
5. She listens to music. __listens__

Find the action verb in the list that best fits each sentence. Write the verb on the line next to the sentence.

gives knows nods pounds shows

6. Moses ____ John his new drum. __shows__
7. Mr. Samuels ____ them balloons. __gives__
8. The conductor ____ to the soloist. __nods__
9. She ____ the tom-toms. __pounds__
10. The player ____ the signal. __knows__

10 Book 3.1/Unit 3 **Moses Goes to a Concert** 69

GRAMMAR PRACTICE BOOK, PAGE 69

GRAMMAR PRACTICE BOOK, PAGE 70

5 Day Spelling Plan

LANGUAGE SUPPORT

To help students spell consonant clusters, write Spelling Words on the chalkboard and highlight the clusters with brightly colored chalk. Be sure to add them to the Word Wall.

DICTATION SENTENCES

Spelling Words

1. He will paint a picture.
2. The young child was silent.
3. Put a stamp on the letter.
4. Say thank you to your mom.
5. Is she your best friend?
6. He likes to draw with ink.
7. He stood behind the tree.
8. The buzz of a bee is very faint.
9. Use a bat to swing at the pitch.
10. There was the sound of a thump on the roof.
11. Does the boat belong to you?
12. The student has a test now.
13. He is my husband.
14. One parent walked with him.
15. Put the trunk in the car.

Challenge Words

16. We went to a concert in the park.
17. The conductor tells us to play music.
18. Can you play an instrument?
19. She is a good musician.
20. The orchestra will play in our school.

DAY 1 Pretest

Assess Prior Knowledge Use the Dictation Sentences at left and **Spelling Practice Book** page 65 for the pretest. Allow students to correct their own papers. If students have trouble, have partners give each other a midweek test on Day 3. Students who require a modified list may be tested on the first eight words.

Spelling Words		Challenge Words
1. paint	9. swing	16. **concert**
2. young	10. **thump**	17. **conductor**
3. stamp	11. belong	18. **instrument**
4. **thank**	12. student	19. **musician**
5. friend	13. husband	20. **orchestra**
6. ink	14. parent	
7. behind	15. trunk	
8. faint		

*Note: Words in **dark type** are from the story.*

Word Study On page 66 of the **Spelling Practice Book** are word study steps and an at-home activity.

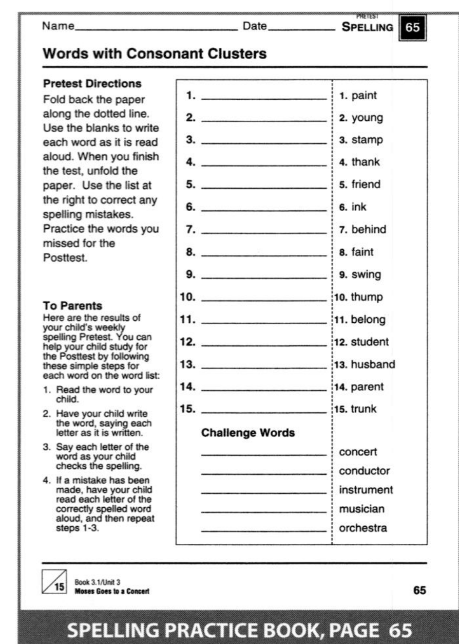

Name_____ Date_____ PRETEST SPELLING 65

Words with Consonant Clusters

Pretest Directions
Fold back the paper along the dotted line. Use the blanks to write each word as it is read aloud. When you finish the test, unfold the paper. Use the list at the right to correct any spelling mistakes. Practice the words you missed for the Posttest.

To Parents
Here are the results of your child's weekly spelling Pretest. You can help your child study for the Posttest by following these simple steps for each word on the word list:
1. Read the word to your child.
2. Have your child write the word, saying each letter as it is written.
3. Say each letter of the word as your child checks the spelling.
4. If a mistake has been made, have your child read each letter of the correctly spelled word aloud, and then repeat steps 1-3.

1. _____ 1. paint
2. _____ 2. young
3. _____ 3. stamp
4. _____ 4. thank
5. _____ 5. friend
6. _____ 6. ink
7. _____ 7. behind
8. _____ 8. faint
9. _____ 9. swing
10. _____ 10. thump
11. _____ 11. belong
12. _____ 12. student
13. _____ 13. husband
14. _____ 14. parent
15. _____ 15. trunk

Challenge Words
_____ concert
_____ conductor
_____ instrument
_____ musician
_____ orchestra

15 Book 3.1/Unit 3 Moses Goes to a Concert 65

SPELLING PRACTICE BOOK, PAGE 65

WORD STUDY STEPS AND ACTIVITY, PAGE 66

DAY 2 Explore the Pattern

Sort and Spell Words Say the words *paint, stamp, friend, swing,* and *ink*. Have students repeat and then identify the final consonant sound. Write the words and circle the final consonant clusters.

Ask students to read aloud the 15 Spelling Words before sorting them according to the spelling patterns below.

nt	mp	nd
paint	stamp	friend
faint	thump	behind
student		husband
parent		

ng	nk
young	thank
swing	ink
belong	trunk

Word Wall As students read other stories and texts, have them look for new words with consonant clusters and add them to a classroom word wall underlining the consonant cluster in each word.

Name_____ Date_____ EXPLORE THE PATTERN SPELLING 67

Words with Consonant Clusters

paint	thank	behind	thump	husband
young	friend	faint	belong	parent
stamp	ink	swing	student	trunk

Pattern Power
Write the spelling words for each of these clusters below.

nk
1. thank
2. ink
3. trunk

mp
4. stamp
5. thump

ng
6. young
7. swing
8. belong

nd
9. friend
10. behind
11. husband

nt
12. paint
13. faint
14. student
15. parent

Guide Words
Dictionary guide words help you find your way. Which spelling words will you find between each pair of words?

than/thunder 16. thank 17. thump
pail/part 18. paint 19. parent
face/front 20. faint 21. friend

Word Hunt
Write the spelling word in which you can find the smaller word.

22. *hum* thump 23. *end* friend
24. *win* swing 25. *rent* parent
26. *long* belong 27. *dent* student
28. *band* husband

28 Book 3.1/Unit 3 Moses Goes to a Concert 67

SPELLING PRACTICE BOOK, PAGE 67

Words with Consonant Clusters

Practice and Extend

Word Meaning: Fill-Ins Ask students to use words from the spelling list to complete sentences such as the following.

The books are mine. They ________ to me. belong

If you stood in back of me, you would be ________ me. behind

Lock the __________ so no one can open it. trunk

The car made a ___________ when it bumped the tree. thump

He was a good __________ to his children. parent

Glossary Have partners write each Challenge Word and divide it into syllables according to the Glossary entry. Have them circle the accented syllable in each word.

Proofread and Write

Proofread Sentences Write these sentences on the chalkboard, including the misspelled words. Ask students to proofread, circling incorrect spellings and writing the correct spellings. There are two spelling errors in each sentence.

She uses piant to draw and inc to write. (paint, ink)

I want to thanc my freind. (thank, friend)

Her husbend packed the trunc. (husband, trunk)

Have students create additional sentences with errors for partners to correct.

WRITING Have students use as many Spelling Words as possible in the daily Writing Prompt on page 258D. Remind students to proofread their writing for errors in spelling, punctuation, and grammar.

Assess and Reteach

Assess Students' Knowledge Use page 70 of the **Spelling Practice Book** or the Dictation Sentences on page 289O for the posttest.

Personal Word List Students may encounter difficulty spelling words with *ie* constructions, such as *friends* and may confuse *ie* and *ei* spellings. Have them begin a list of *ie* troublemakers for their journals.

Students should refer to their lists during future writing activities.

Name________________ Date________ PRACTICE AND EXTEND SPELLING 68

Words with Consonant Clusters

paint	thank	behind	thump	husband
young	friend	faint	belong	parent
stamp	ink	swing	student	trunk

Opposites

An antonym is a word that has the opposite meaning of another word. Write the spelling word that is the antonym of each of the following words.

1. old ___young___ 2. enemy ___friend___
3. ahead ___behind___ 4. wife ___husband___

What's the Word?

Write a spelling word that correctly completes the sentence.

5. The ___student___ studies math in the third grade.
6. This ___parent___ spoke to the principal about her son.
7. I will ___paint___ a picture with watercolors.
8. A ___husband___ is married to his wife.
9. He keeps his spare tire in the ___trunk___ of his car.
10. ___Swing___ your arms left and right to the music.
11. ___Friend___ is the opposite of enemy.
12. The person sitting in back of you is ___behind___ you.

Make a Sentence

Use each word in a sentence.

13. thank ________________
14. faint ________________
15. thump ________________
16. belong ________________

68 **Challenge Extension:** Have students draw and label a picture to illustrate each Challenge Word. Grade 3.1/Unit 3 **Moses Goes to a Concert** 16

SPELLING PRACTICE BOOK, PAGE 68

Name________________ Date________ PROOFREAD AND WRITE SPELLING 69

Words with Consonant Clusters

Proofreading Paragraph

There are six spelling mistakes in this paragraph. Circle the misspelled words. Write the words correctly on the lines below.

"How do the artists draw their cartoons?" Lisa asked.

"Some people use black inck to outline their figures," Mr. Lopez said. "I know other artists who use paynt."

"Who writes the studnt pages in your newspaper?" the girl asked.

"The group is made up of reporters and yung volunteers," the editor answered. "A parrunt is also part of this team."

"Can a frind and I join this group?" she asked.

"Well, you'll both have to take a writing test," he said.

1. ___ink___ 2. ___paint___ 3. ___student___
4. ___young___ 5. ___parent___ 6. ___friend___

Writing Activity

What questions would you like to ask someone who works on a newspaper? Write your interview questions, using at least four spelling words.

10 Book 3.1/Unit 3 **Moses Goes to a Concert** 69

SPELLING PRACTICE BOOK, PAGE 69

Name________________ Date________ POSTTEST SPELLING 70

Words with Consonant Clusters

Look at the words in each set. One word in each set is spelled correctly. Use a pencil to color in the circle in front of that word. Before you begin, look at the sample sets of words. Sample A has been done for you. Do Sample B by yourself. When you are sure you know what to do, you may go on with the rest of the page.

Sample A
Ⓐ tangk
● tank
Ⓒ tanek
Ⓓ tanc

Sample B
Ⓔ thinge
Ⓕ thig
Ⓖ thign
● thing

1. Ⓐ youn Ⓑ yung ● young Ⓓ younk
2. ● ink Ⓕ ingk Ⓖ inck Ⓗ inke
3. Ⓐ studet ● student Ⓒ studen Ⓓ studend
4. Ⓔ pante Ⓕ paynt Ⓖ paink ● paint
5. Ⓐ belone ● belong Ⓒ belawng Ⓓ belon
6. ● behind Ⓕ bahind Ⓖ behined Ⓗ bihine
7. Ⓐ thak Ⓑ thangk Ⓒ thanc ● thank
8. Ⓔ swin Ⓕ swingk ● swing Ⓗ swinge
9. Ⓐ trunc ● trunk Ⓒ trunkk Ⓓ trungk
10. Ⓔ stamb Ⓕ stemp ● stamp Ⓗ stap
11. Ⓐ parunt Ⓑ parrent Ⓒ parind ● parent
12. Ⓔ husban Ⓕ husbend ● husband Ⓗ husbant
13. ● friend Ⓑ frend Ⓒ frened Ⓓ fren
14. Ⓔ thumbp ● thump Ⓖ thup Ⓗ tump
15. Ⓐ faynt Ⓑ fanet ● faint Ⓓ faind

70 Grade 3.1/Unit 3 **Moses Goes to a Concert** 15

SPELLING PRACTICE BOOK, PAGE 70

The Little Painter of Sabana Grande

Selection Summary **Students will read about a country boy who uses his creativity and imagination to solve problems and make his community more beautiful.** TEKS ELA 3.11.E,F

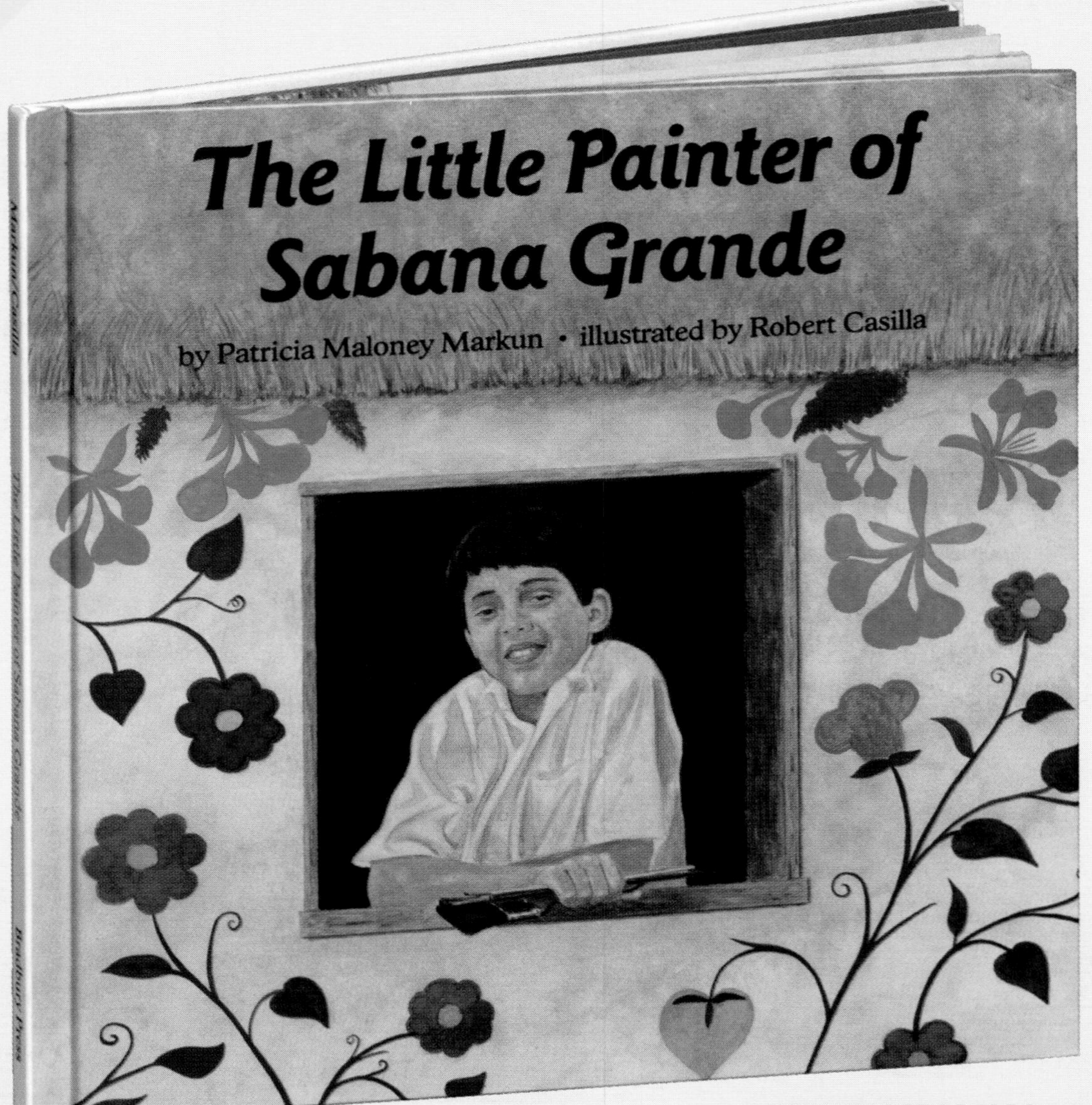

The Little Painter of Sabana Grande
by Patricia Maloney Markun • illustrated by Robert Casilla

Listening Library Audiocassette

INSTRUCTIONAL
Pages 292–317

About the Author Writing has always been a big part of Patricia Maloney Markun's life, and she especially likes writing children's books. She says, "I seem to understand children. I enjoy working with them and writing for them."

About the Illustrator Robert Casilla hopes that *The Little Painter of Sabana Grande* will encourage children to aim high and become whatever they want to be. "I point out that if Fernando could succeed despite the hardships of living in a poor village in Panama, so too can they."

Resources for

Meeting Individual Needs

LEVELED BOOKS

EASY
Pages 317A, 317D

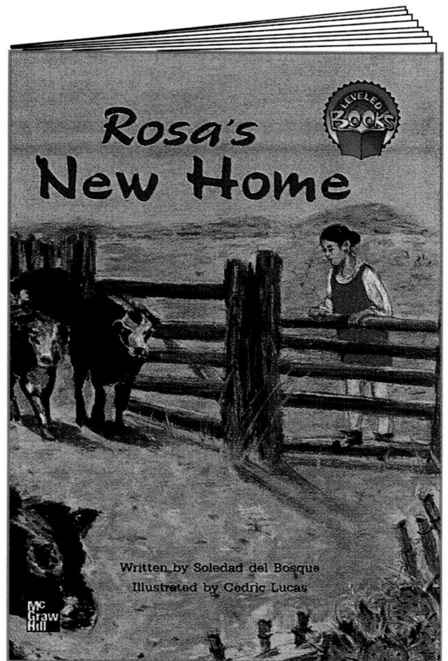

INDEPENDENT
Pages 317B, 317D

Take-Home version available

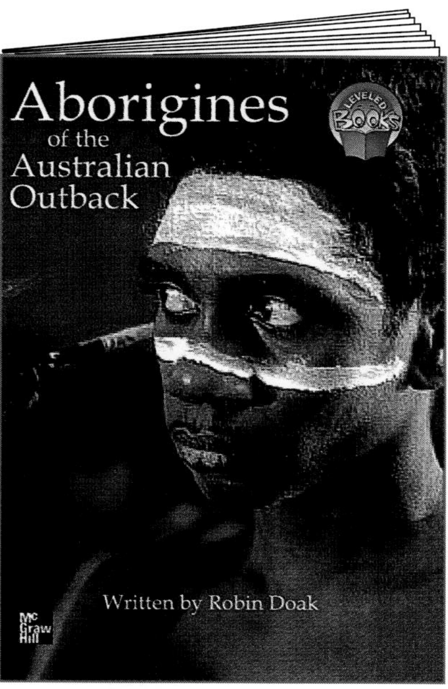

CHALLENGE
Pages 317C, 317D

LEVELED PRACTICE

Reteach, 82-88
blackline masters with reteaching opportunities for each assessed skill

Practice, 82-88
workbook with Take-Home Stories and practice opportunities for each assessed skill and story comprehension

Extend, 82-88
blackline masters that offer challenge activities for each assessed skill

ADDITIONAL RESOURCES

- **Language Support Book** 89-96
- **Take-Home Story, Practice** p. 83a
- **Alternative Teaching Strategies** T60-T66
- **Selected Quizzes Prepared by** Accelerated Reader

McGraw-Hill School
TECHNOLOGY
Phonics CD-ROM provides extra phonics support.
interNET CONNECTION
Research & Inquiry ideas. Visit www.mhschool.com/reading.

Suggested Lesson Planner

Available on CD-ROM

READING AND LANGUAGE ARTS	 DAY 1 Focus on Reading and Skills	 DAY 2 Read the Literature
Comprehension Vocabulary Phonics/Decoding Study Skills Listening, Speaking, Viewing, Representing	Read **Read Aloud and Motivate,** 290E "The Crow and the Pitcher" **Develop Visual Literacy,** 290/291 ☑ **Review Story Elements,** 292A–292B **Teaching Chart 67** **Reteach, Practice, Extend,** 82	**Build Background,** 292C Develop Oral Language **Vocabulary,** 292D ***blossoms*** ***faded*** ***miserable*** ***dawn*** ***imaginary*** ***shallow*** **Teaching Chart 68** **Word Building Manipulative Cards** **Reteach, Practice, Extend,** 83 Read **Read the Selection,** 292–313 Guided Instruction ☑ Story Elements ☑ Summarize **Minilessons,** 299, 301, 303, 305, 307, 311 **Cultural Perspectives,** 296
Curriculum Connections	 **Fine Arts,** 290/291	 **Social Studies,** 292C
Writing	 **Writing Prompt:** Imagine that you live in the village pictured on pages 294–295. Write a short paragraph about the nature around you.	 **Writing Prompt:** You are spending a day in the country. Write a paragraph describing your thoughts as you go for a hike.  **Journal Writing,** 313 Quick-Write
Grammar	**Introduce the Concept: Present-Tense Verbs,** 317M Daily Language Activity 1. The rooster crow at dawn. crows 2. I milks the cow at eight. milk 3. The boys eats tortillas for breakfast. eat **Grammar Practice Book,** 71	**Teach the Concept: Present-Tense Verbs,** 317M Daily Language Activity 1. Every morning, Fernando hurry to the meadow. hurries 2. He mix his paints carefully. mixes 3. You reads very well. read **Grammar Practice Book,** 72
Spelling	**Pretest: Words with Double Consonants,** 317O **Spelling Practice Book,** 71–72	**Explore the Pattern: Words with Double Consonants,** 317O **Spelling Practice Book,** 73

Meeting Individual Needs

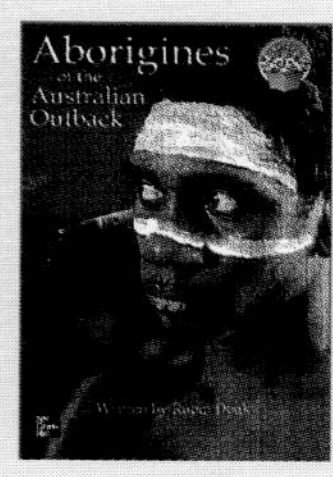

 = **Skill Assessed in Unit Test**

DAY 3 Read the Literature

Reread for Fluency, 312

Story Questions, 314
Reteach, Practice, Extend, 84
Story Activities, 315

Study Skill, 316
 Graphic Aids
Teaching Chart 69
Reteach, Practice, Extend, 85

Test Power, 317

 **Read the Leveled Books,**
Guided Reading
Double Consonants
Story Elements
Instructional Vocabulary
 CD-ROM

 Social Studies, 294; Math, 298

Writing Prompt: Think about an art project you have done. Write a paragraph describing it as if you were creating it now.

Writing Process: Persuasive Writing, 317K
Prewrite, Draft

Review and Practice: Present-Tense Verbs, 317N
Daily Language Activity
1. Fernando carry the paint pots. carries
2. His mother worry about him. worries
3. The girl watch Fernando. watches

Grammar Practice Book, 73

Practice and Extend: Words with Double Consonants, 317P
Spelling Practice Book, 74

DAY 4 Build Skills

 **Read the Leveled Books and Self-Selected Books**

Review Story Elements, 317E–317F
Teaching Chart 70
Reteach, Practice, Extend, 86
Language Support, 94

Review Summarize, 317G-317H
Teaching Chart 71
Reteach, Practice, Extend, 87
Language Support, 95

  Science, 302

Writing Prompt: Write about teachers you have had and special things you have learned from each.

Writing Process: Persuasive Writing, 317K
Revise

Meeting Individual Needs for Writing, 317L

Review and Practice: Present-Tense Verbs, 317N
Daily Language Activity
1. The dog bury the bone. buries
2. You writes well. write
3. Trudy wash the brush. washes

Grammar Practice Book, 74

Proofread and Write: Words with Double Consonants, 317P
Spelling Practice Book, 75

DAY 5 Build Skills

 **Read Self-Selected Books**

Review Context Clues, 317I-317J
Teaching Chart 72
Reteach, Practice, Extend, 88
Language Support, 96

Listening, Speaking, Viewing, Representing, 317L
Illustrate the Plan
Make a Speech

Minilessons, 299, 301, 305, 307, 311

Phonics Review,
Double Consonants, 303
Phonics/Phonemic Awareness Practice Book, 12–18
 CD-ROM

 Music, 308

Writing Prompt: Write a letter from Fernando to a friend describing how he feels after painting his house.

Writing Process: Persuasive Writing, 317K
Edit/Proofread, Publish

Assess and Reteach: Present-Tense Verbs, 317N
Daily Language Activity
1. Fernando's teacher teach him to draw. teaches
2. I likes the painting. like
3. A bee buzz near the flowers. buzzes

Grammar Practice Book, 75–76

Assess and Reteach: Words with Double Consonants, 317P
Spelling Practice Book, 76

Language Arts

Read Aloud and Motivate

The Crow and the Pitcher

a fable by Aesop

A crow perched on a tree branch to rest. He'd been flying for hours and was very thirsty. Looking down, he noticed a fat clay pitcher under the tree. He flew down to take a closer look.

"It has some water in it!" he shouted, amazed at his good luck.

The crow put his beak into the pitcher to take a drink. But he couldn't reach the water with his beak. He tried to stick his head in all the way, only to find that the opening was too small, and his head too big.

"Now what?" he muttered. He glared at the pitcher. "Here I am, dying of thirst, and over there is a pitcher of water. If the pitcher were full, then the water would come right up to the top and I could have all the water I wanted."

The crow looked around. Lots of small rocks lay in the grass. "Rocks and grass, rocks and . . . that's it! I have an idea! A terrific idea, if I say so myself."

The crow picked up a rock and dropped it into the pitcher.

Continued on pages T2-T5

Oral Comprehension

LISTENING AND SPEAKING Encourage students to listen carefully as you read aloud this ancient fable in which a clever crow solves a problem. Ask students to picture the crow's actions as you read. When you have finished, ask: Which words would you use to describe the crow? Lead students in a discussion about other ways the crow could have solved his problem. Then ask students what they think the moral means.

Activity Help students make their own cartoon strip version of *The Crow and the Pitcher.* Have them divide two pieces of paper into four equal squares. Suggest that the first frame set the scene for the action to follow in the seven remaining frames. Ask students to label each frame with a description of the action.

▶ **Visual/Linguistic/Kinesthetic**

Develop Visual Literacy

Works of Art

Anthology pages 290-291

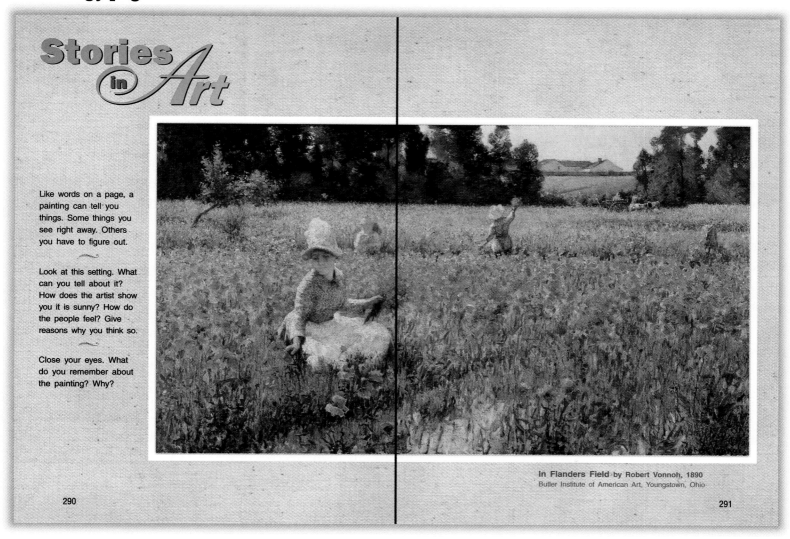

Stories in Art

Like words on a page, a painting can tell you things. Some things you see right away. Others you have to figure out.

Look at this setting. What can you tell about it? How does the artist show you it is sunny? How do the people feel? Give reasons why you think so.

Close your eyes. What do you remember about the painting? Why?

In Flanders Field by Robert Vonnoh, 1890
Butler Institute of American Art, Youngstown, Ohio

290 291

Objective: Analyze Character and Setting

VIEWING In his Impressionist painting, Robert Vannoh captured the effects of light on colors in a country scene. Have students close their eyes and describe the painting. Then ask if the painting's colors helped them remember what they saw. Discuss what they remember in relation to the painting's foreground, middle ground, and background, as well as its color. Read the page with students, encouraging individual interpretations of the painting.

Ask students to support inferences they make about character and setting. For example:

- Dabs of white suggest sunlight hitting objects.
- The people seem to be enjoying the day. One is waving. Another is smiling.

REPRESENTING Have students paint scenes that show how people are affected by setting. Have them consider time, place, and weather.

TESTED OBJECTIVES

Students will:

- **make inferences about character.**
- **analyze setting and plot.**

LANGUAGE SUPPORT

ESL Write the words *Character—Who, Plot—What,* and *Setting—Where* as chart headings on the chalkboard. Then show the covers of fairy tales such as "Cinderella" and "Jack and the Beanstalk." Encourage students to discuss the plot of each book. Have volunteers come to the board to fill in portions of the chart.

Review Story Elements

PREPARE

Discuss a Plot Have students think of a favorite book or movie. Ask: What happened in the beginning? In the middle? In the end?

TEACH

Define Characters, Setting, and Plot Tell students: The characters are the people in the story. The setting is where and when the story takes place. The plot of the story is what happens in the story. The characters and the setting are part of the plot.

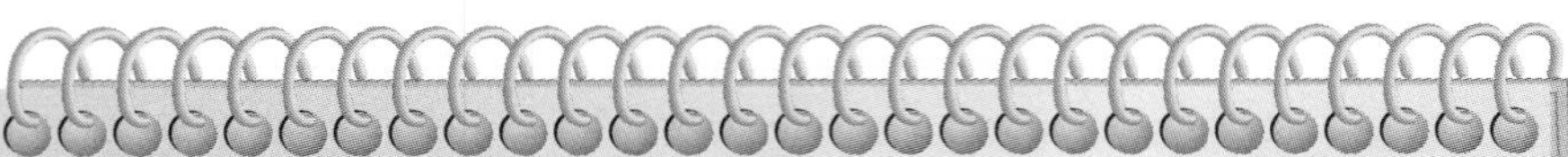

Grandmother's Farm

Hannah snapped off the ends from the beans and added them to the bowl. She was happy to be back on her grandmother's farm for the summer. She leaned back against the trunk of her favorite pecan tree. After helping with farm chores all day, she enjoyed sitting in the shade. She looked at the fields and hills around her. She felt calm and peaceful. She snapped some more beans.

That night Grandma was so surprised. Hannah and Grandma sat down for a lovely meal in the kitchen. She never thought Hannah knew so much about cooking! What a wonderful meal Hannah made from those beans.

Teaching Chart 67

Read the Story and Model the Skill Display **Teaching Chart 67**. Have students pay attention to the plot and clue words about character and setting as they read the story.

MODEL The title of the story tells me right away that the setting is a farm. The main character seems to be Hannah because she is the focus of the story. As I read, I can learn more about how Hannah feels and what she does by paying attention to the clues the writer gives.

Have students underline clues that help them make inferences about Hannah and her feelings, and have them circle clues about setting.

PRACTICE

Create a Character/ Setting/Plot Chart

Using a chart, have students record the plot and describe the characters and setting at each part of the plot. Help them to begin filling in the chart and have volunteers complete it. ▶ **Visual/Logical**

SETTING (WHEN,WHERE)	CHARACTER (WHO)/ PLOT (WHAT HAPPENED)
on Grandma's farm in the summer	Hannah is happy to be back on her grandmother's farm.
under the pecan tree	Hannah is snapping beans.
in the kitchen	Hannah cooks the beans for supper for Grandma.

ASSESS/CLOSE

Make Inferences About Characters, Setting, and Plot

Ask students to think of words they might use to describe Hannah. *(quiet, hardworking, helpful)* What settings might Hannah dislike? (big cities; noisy, crowded places) What might have happened if Hannah wasn't such a good cook? (Grandma might cook dinner; Hannah might burn the beans.)

SELECTION Connection

Students will apply story elements when they read *The Little Painter of Sabana Grande* and the Leveled Books.

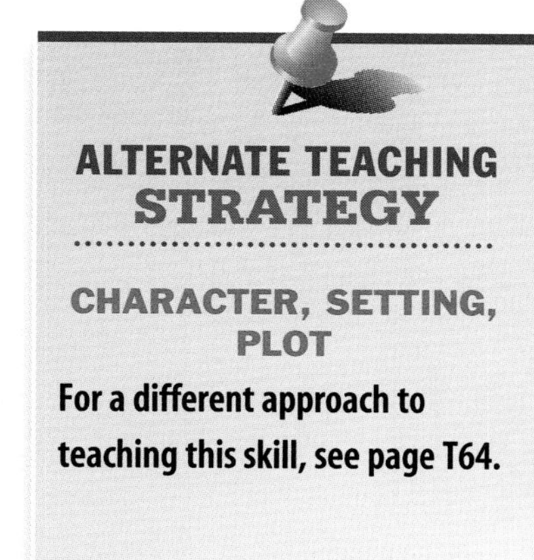

ALTERNATE TEACHING STRATEGY

CHARACTER, SETTING, PLOT

For a different approach to teaching this skill, see page T64.

Meeting Individual Needs for Comprehension

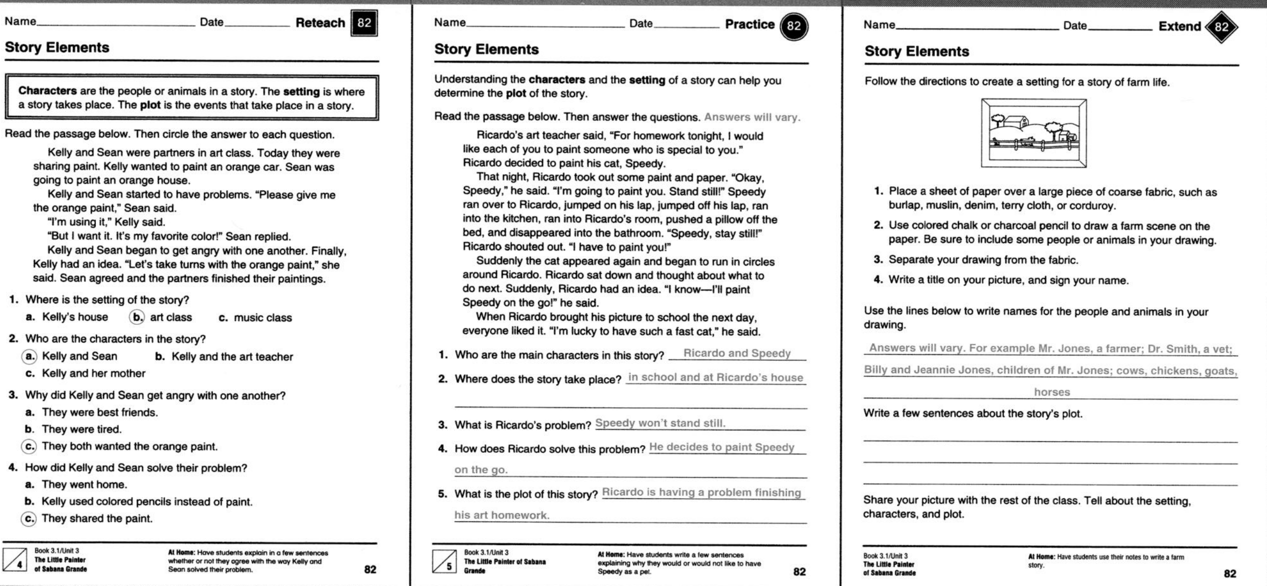

EASY

Name____________ Date________ **Reteach 82**

Story Elements

Characters are the people or animals in a story. The **setting** is where a story takes place. The **plot** is the events that take place in a story.

Read the passage below. Then circle the answer to each question.

Kelly and Sean were partners in art class. Today they were sharing paint. Kelly wanted to paint an orange car. Sean was going to paint an orange house.

Kelly and Sean started to have problems. "Please give me the orange paint," Sean said.

"I'm using it," Kelly said.

"But I want it. It's my favorite color!" Sean replied.

Kelly and Sean began to get angry with one another. Finally, Kelly had an idea. "Let's take turns with the orange paint," she said. Sean agreed and the partners finished their paintings.

1. Where is the setting of the story?
   a. Kelly's house (b.) art class c. music class
2. Who are the characters in the story?
   (a.) Kelly and Sean b. Kelly and the art teacher
   c. Kelly and her mother
3. Why did Kelly and Sean get angry with one another?
   a. They were best friends.
   b. They were tired.
   (c.) They both wanted the orange paint.
4. How did Kelly and Sean solve their problem?
   a. They went home.
   b. Kelly used colored pencils instead of paint.
   (c.) They shared the paint.

4 Book 3.1/Unit 3 **The Little Painter of Sabana Grande**

At Home: Have students explain in a few sentences whether or not they agree with the way Kelly and Sean solved their problem. 82

Reteach, 82

ON-LEVEL

Name____________ Date________ **Practice 82**

Story Elements

Understanding the **characters** and the **setting** of a story can help you determine the **plot** of the story.

Read the passage below. Then answer the questions. Answers will vary.

Ricardo's art teacher said, "For homework tonight, I would like each of you to paint someone who is special to you." Ricardo decided to paint his cat, Speedy.

That night, Ricardo took out some paint and paper. "Okay, Speedy," he said. "I'm going to paint you. Stand still!" Speedy ran over to Ricardo, jumped on his lap, jumped off his lap, ran into the kitchen, ran into Ricardo's room, pushed a pillow off the bed, and disappeared into the bathroom. "Speedy, stay still!" Ricardo shouted out. "I have to paint you!"

Suddenly the cat appeared again and began to run in circles around Ricardo. Ricardo sat down and thought about what to do next. Suddenly, Ricardo had an idea. "I know—I'll paint Speedy on the go!" he said.

When Ricardo brought his picture to school the next day, everyone liked it. "I'm lucky to have such a fast cat," he said.

1. Who are the main characters in this story? Ricardo and Speedy
2. Where does the story take place? in school and at Ricardo's house
3. What is Ricardo's problem? Speedy won't stand still.
4. How does Ricardo solve this problem? He decides to paint Speedy on the go.
5. What is the plot of this story? Ricardo is having a problem finishing his art homework.

5 Book 3.1/Unit 3 **The Little Painter of Sabana Grande**

At Home: Have students write a few sentences explaining why they would or would not like to have Speedy as a pet. 82

Practice, 82

CHALLENGE

Name____________ Date________ **Extend 82**

Story Elements

Follow the directions to create a setting for a story of farm life.

1. Place a sheet of paper over a large piece of coarse fabric, such as burlap, muslin, denim, terry cloth, or corduroy.
2. Use colored chalk or charcoal pencil to draw a farm scene on the paper. Be sure to include some people or animals in your drawing.
3. Separate your drawing from the fabric.
4. Write a title on your picture, and sign your name.

Use the lines below to write names for the people and animals in your drawing.

Answers will vary. For example Mr. Jones, a farmer; Dr. Smith, a vet; Billy and Jeannie Jones, children of Mr. Jones; cows, chickens, goats, horses

Write a few sentences about the story's plot.

Share your picture with the rest of the class. Tell about the setting, characters, and plot.

Book 3.1/Unit 3 **The Little Painter of Sabana Grande**

At Home: Have students use their notes to write a farm story. 82

Extend, 82

Build Background

Anthology and Leveled Books

Social Studies

Evaluate Prior Knowledge

CONCEPT: RURAL SETTINGS The characters in these stories are affected by the rural settings. Have students share experiences or knowledge they may have of a rural, or country, setting.

COMPARE SETTINGS Have students list ways in which a country setting is the same as, or different from, a city or large town.

▶ Logical/Visual

COUNTRY Different	Alike	CITY Different
lots of trees	school	tall buildings
few stores	friends	many stores
few people	pets	lots of people
farms		apartments
quiet, peaceful		noisy, bustling

Graphic Organizer 14

PLAN A DAY GROUP WRITING Have students write a schedule of what they would do on a day in the country. For example, they might begin their day by eating breakfast at five o'clock in the morning and milking the cows at five-thirty.

Develop Oral Language

DISCUSS COUNTRY SIGHTS ESL Ask students to brainstorm a list of things that they might see in the country. Bring in magazine pictures or photos of rural settings as visual cues.

- Write a list of words on the chalkboard suggested by the pictures, such as *farm*, *cows*, *fields*, *barn*, and *hay*.
- Check comprehension through questions that require students to give short answers or point to objects in the pictures or photos.
- Have students create a mural of country sights on butcher paper with crayons, colored pencils, or markers.
- Encourage partners to use words from the list.
- Display students' work and initiate a class discussion. Congratulate the artists on their efforts.

TEACHING TIP

INSTRUCTIONAL Write the word *setting* on the chalkboard. Have students look around the room and describe their surroundings or setting. Now have volunteers describe what the settings are like in their homes.

LANGUAGE SUPPORT

See **Language Support Book, pages 89–92,** for teaching suggestions for Build Background and Vocabulary.

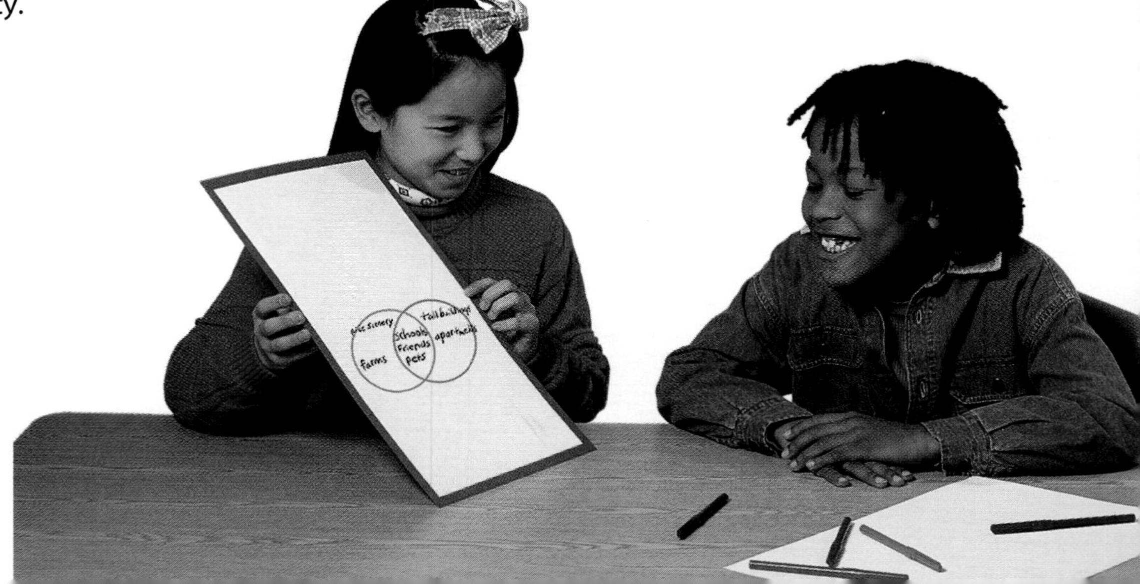

Vocabulary

Key Words

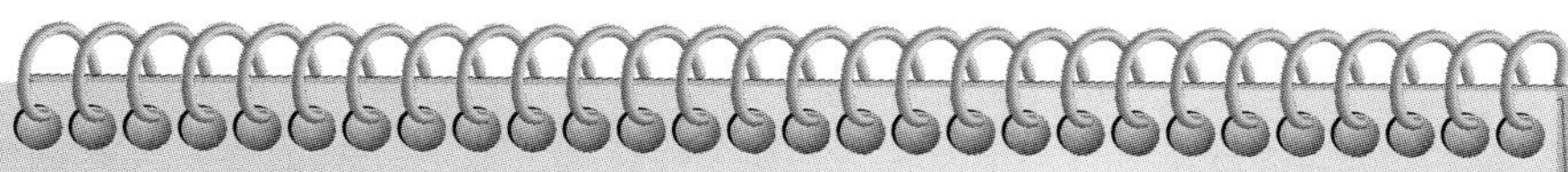

Fernando the Painter

1. Fernando wakes up at (dawn) each morning to watch the sun rise. **2.** Today he will paint the pretty (blossoms) on the flowering trees that smell so sweet. **3.** Fernando needs red clay to make his paint and finds it in a stream (shallow) enough to wade through. **4.** He thinks it is more fun to paint pictures of real plants and animals than (imaginary) ones. **5.** Even after the real flowers have (faded,) the color of the flowers in his picture will remain bright. **6.** Fernando loves to paint and would be (miserable) if he could not.

Teaching Chart 68

Definitions

dawn (p. 295) the first light in the morning; daybreak

blossoms (p. 307) flowers on a tree or plant

shallow (p. 296) not deep

imaginary (p. 307) made up in the mind

faded (p. 304) having lost color or brightness

miserable (p. 302) very unhappy

SPELLING/VOCABULARY CONNECTIONS

See Spelling Challenge Words, page 3170.

Vocabulary in Context

IDENTIFY VOCABULARY WORDS Display **Teaching Chart 68** and read the passage with students. Have volunteers circle each vocabulary word and underline other words that are clues to its meaning.

DISCUSS MEANINGS Ask questions like these to help clarify word meanings:

- What time of day is dawn?
- Where have you seen blossoms?
- Where can you find shallow water?
- What is an *image*? Is a flying dragon a real animal or an imaginary one?
- What color are your jeans when they are new? What color are they when they are old and faded?
- In sentence 6 on the chart, after replacing Fernando's name with your own, how will you change the words *to paint* to something that you love to do?

Practice

DEMONSTRATE WORD MEANING Have partners choose Vocabulary Cards from a pile. They can demonstrate each word meaning by pantomiming while the partner guesses the word.

PARTNERS

▶ **Kinesthetic/Linguistic**

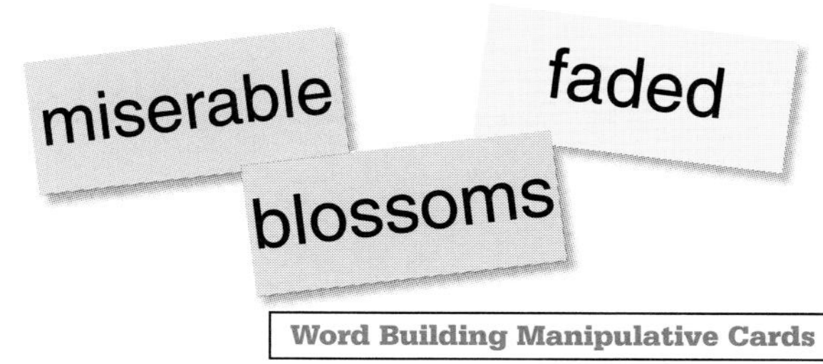

Word Building Manipulative Cards

WRITE CONTEXT SENTENCES Have partners write context sentences, leaving a blank for each vocabulary word. Have them exchange papers and fill in the blanks or use vocabulary cards to show answers. Have students refer to the Glossary as needed. ▶ **Linguistic**

WRITING

ON-LEVEL

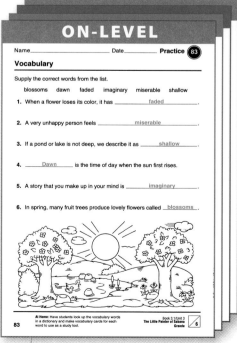

Name________ Date______ Practice 83

Vocabulary

Supply the correct words from the list.

blossoms dawn faded imaginary miserable shallow

1. When a flower loses its color, it has faded.
2. A very unhappy person feels miserable.
3. If a pond or lake is not deep, we describe it as shallow.
4. Dawn is the time of day when the sun first rises.
5. A story that you make up in your mind is imaginary.
6. In spring, many fruit trees produce lovely flowers called blossoms.

83 At Home: Have students look up the vocabulary words in a dictionary and make vocabulary cards for each word to use as a study tool. Book 3.1/Unit 3 The Little Painter of Sabana Grande 6

Take-Home Story 83a
Reteach 83
Practice 83 • Extend 83

Guided Instruction

Preview and Predict

Have students read the title and preview the story, looking for pictures that give strong clues about the setting and characters.

- Where might this story take place?
- What clues about the main character do the title and the pictures give?
- What will the story most likely be about?
- Will the story be a realistic one or a fantasy? How can you tell? (The characters and surroundings look real. Characters' actions seem real.) ***Genre***

Have students record their predictions about the setting and the main character.

PREDICTIONS	WHAT HAPPENED
This story takes place in a village.	
The main character is a boy who paints.	

Set Purposes

What do students want to find out by reading the story? For example:

- Why does the boy paint on houses?
- What is life like in his community?

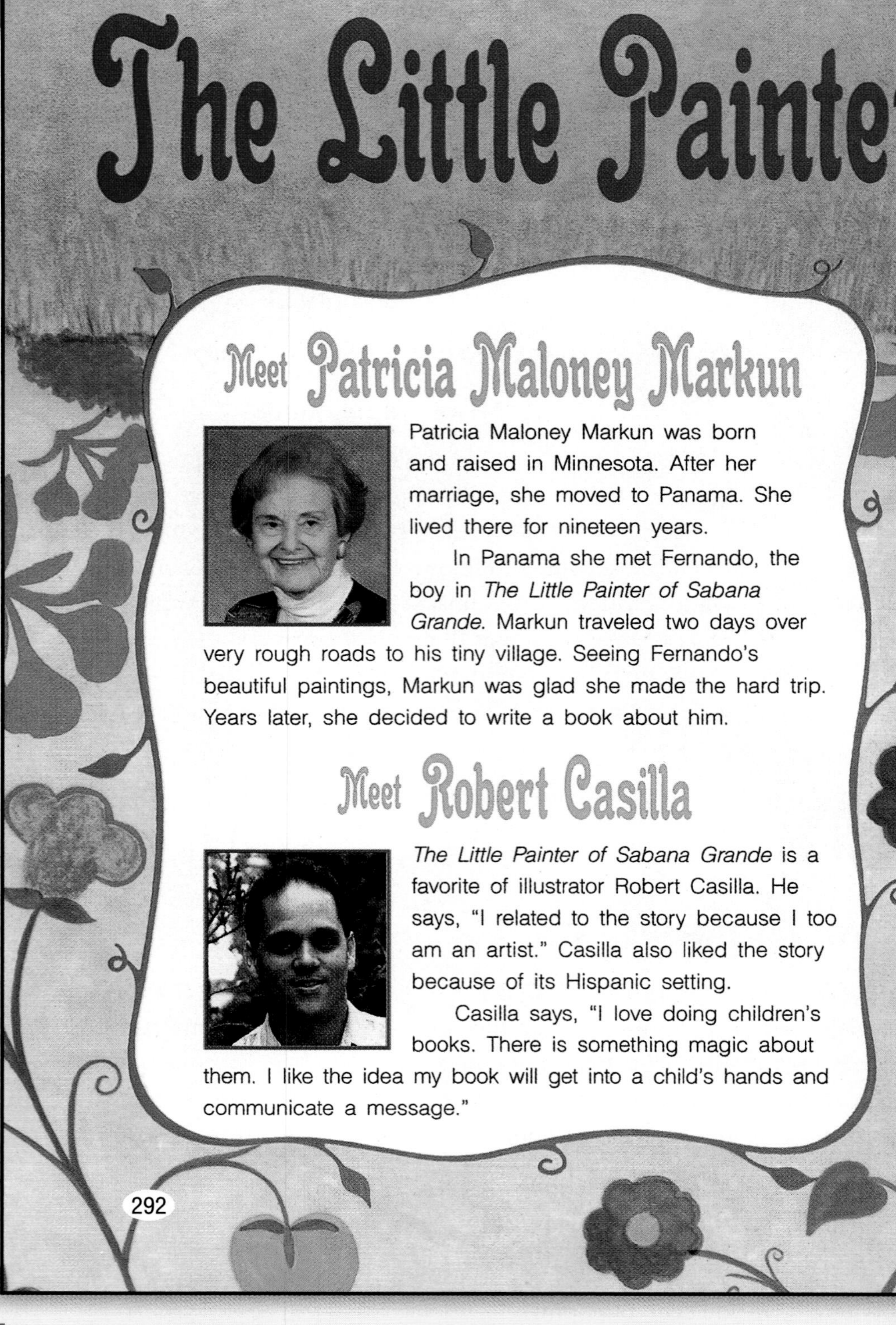

The Little Painter

Meet Patricia Maloney Markun

Patricia Maloney Markun was born and raised in Minnesota. After her marriage, she moved to Panama. She lived there for nineteen years.

In Panama she met Fernando, the boy in *The Little Painter of Sabana Grande.* Markun traveled two days over very rough roads to his tiny village. Seeing Fernando's beautiful paintings, Markun was glad she made the hard trip. Years later, she decided to write a book about him.

Meet Robert Casilla

The Little Painter of Sabana Grande is a favorite of illustrator Robert Casilla. He says, "I related to the story because I too am an artist." Casilla also liked the story because of its Hispanic setting.

Casilla says, "I love doing children's books. There is something magic about them. I like the idea my book will get into a child's hands and communicate a message."

292

Meeting Individual Needs • Grouping Suggestions for Strategic Reading

EASY

Read Together Read the story with students or have them use the **Listening Library Audiocassette**. Have students use the Setting/Character/Plot chart to record important information about the characters and setting. Guided Instruction and Intervention prompts offer additional help with decoding, vocabulary, and comprehension.

ON-LEVEL

Guided Reading Preview the story words listed on page 293. Then choose from the Guided Instruction questions as you read the story with students, or after they have played the **Listening Library Audiocassette**. Have them use the Setting/Character/Plot chart to record meaningful information during reading.

CHALLENGE

Read Independently Remind students that making inferences about the characters and setting will help them understand the story. Have students set up a Setting/Character/Plot chart as on page 293. After reading, they can use their charts to summarize the story.

# of Sabana Grande

ritten by Patricia Maloney Markun Illustrated by Robert Casilla

1

293

Guided Instruction

 Story Elements

 Summarize

Strategic Reading Understanding how the setting and characters affect the plot will help you understand the story better.

Before we begin reading, let's prepare Setting/Character/Plot charts so we can write down story notes.

SETTING	CHARACTER/PLOT

1 PLOT What clues about the plot can you find on this page? (The title is about "a little painter," and the boy is holding a paintbrush. The story must have something to do with the boy painting.)

Story Words

The words below may be unfamiliar to students. Have students check their meanings and pronunciations in the Glossary on page 388.

- adobe, p. 295
- Fernando Espino, pp. 295–296
- Panama, p. 295
- Sabana Grande, p. 295
- sloth, p. 304
- toucan, p. 304

LANGUAGE SUPPORT

This chart is available as a blackline master in the **Language Support Book.**

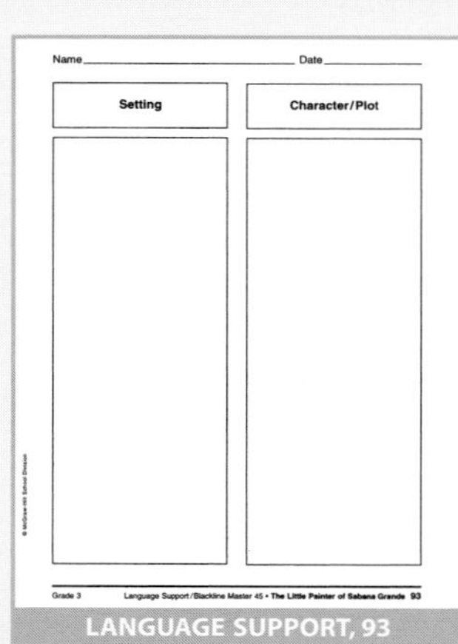

Setting	Character/Plot

LANGUAGE SUPPORT, 93

Guided Instruction

2 **SETTING** When readers begin a story, they should pay special attention to the setting. What does *setting* mean? (the time and place of the story) Use the details in the picture to find clues about the setting. Is the setting a city or somewhere in the country? What picture clues help you know? (The setting is probably a village in the country. The buildings are small, and there is open space all around. There are green plants and no tall buildings, streets, or sidewalks.)

294

Cross Curricular: Social Studies

MAP SKILLS Display a world map. Have students:

- locate North America, the United States, and then the state and area in which they live.
- locate Central America and the country of Panama.
- identify the scale of miles and estimate whether Panama is about 200; 2,000; or 20,000 miles away from your community.
- name the countries and oceans that border Panama.

▶ **Mathematical/Spatial**

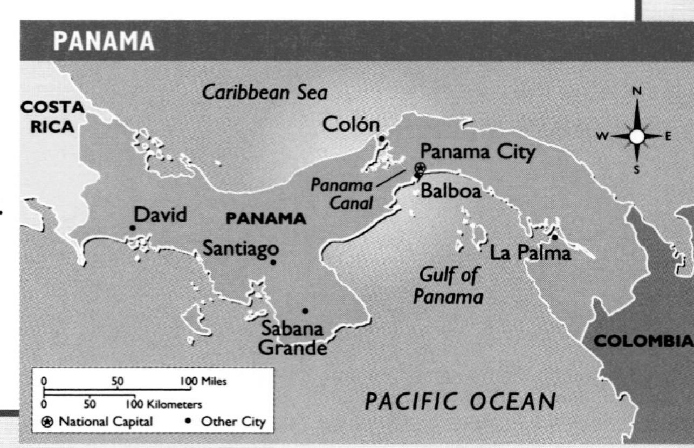

High in the mountains of Panama lies the village of Sabana Grande. It is very small. Just seven houses of clay adobe stand alongside a brook in a grassy meadow. In the middle house lives the Espino family. 3

At dawn one cool purple morning, the rooster next door crowed. The Espinos woke up.

Papa went off to the meadow to milk the cow.

Mama stirred up the fire in the open-air kitchen and fried golden breakfast tortillas. 4

295

Guided Instruction

3 **SETTING** Sabana Grande is in the story title. What do we learn about it? (It is a small village in Panama, and it is surrounded by mountains and a brook in a meadow.)

4 **CHARACTER** What story characters are introduced? (Mama and Papa Espino) Do you think they live alone? Explain. (No, they have a child or children, because they are called *Mama* and *Papa*.)

P/I **DECODING/CONTEXT CLUES** Look at the second paragraph. What's the last word in the first sentence? (*crowed*) Let's sound it out. Can you find any clues to the word's meaning?

PREVENTION/INTERVENTION

DECODING/CONTEXT CLUES Write *crow* on the chalkboard. Elicit that the letters *ow* can make two sounds: /ou/ or /ō/. Have students try saying the word with each sound. Which way do they think is right?

Ask what ending *crowed* has. Discuss how an *-ed* ending usually signals a verb. Help students use context clues to figure out the word's meaning.

For example: *Crowed* is something a rooster does at dawn. *When the rooster crowed, the Espinos woke up. Crowed* means to make a certain sound.

Guided Instruction

5 **CHARACTER, SETTING, PLOT** Who is the character on this page? (Fernando) What is happening on this page? (Fernando is making paints from berries, grass, charcoal, and clay.) What clues can you find about the setting that tell you why Fernando doesn't buy his paints from a store or borrow the paints from school?

MODEL The plot begins with Fernando collecting paints. As I think about the setting, I see that the village is very small and maybe there aren't any stores there. This setting affects the way Fernando gets his paints. I think Fernando must be very interested in painting to go through all of this trouble. I can see how the setting and Fernando's personality affect the plot so far.

Fernando rolled up his straw sleeping mat and put it in the corner. He hurried to the kitchen to eat his tortilla right away.

This was an important day. At school Fernando had learned to draw colored pictures with crayons. Now school was out for dry-season vacation, and Fernando was going to paint for the first time.

His teacher, Señora Arias, had told him exactly how the country people of Panama made their paints. She said:

"Black from the charcoal of a burned tree stump.
Blue of certain berries that grow deep in the jungle.
Yellow from dried grasses in the meadow.
And red from the clay on the bottom of the brook."

It took him a long time to make the paints. Black was easy, because the burned stump of a big tree lay right next to the Espinos' adobe house.

But Fernando had to look and look before he found those certain berries deep in the jungle, to make the blue paint.

In the corner of the meadow he found a patch of very dry grass, and from that he made a large pot of yellow.

He wandered up and down alongside the brook, looking for clay. The fast-flowing water was too deep for him to reach down

to the bottom. At last he came to a bend in the brook where

the water was shallow. He reached down and dug up a fistful of clay. It was red, just the way Señora Arias had said.

296

CULTURAL PERSPECTIVES

MURALS Explain that artists of many civilizations, including ancient Egyptians and Romans, have painted murals to express political or religious beliefs or to tell stories.

RESEARCH AND INQUIRY Have students write a report about a specific mural artist from another country, such as Giotto or Diego Rivera.

▶ **Linguisitic/Visual**

*inter***NET CONNECTION** Students can find more information about mural artists by visiting ***www.mhschool.com/reading.***

Guided Instruction

6 **CHARACTER, SETTING, PLOT** Let's write down what we know about the setting of the story and how it has affected the main character, Fernando, and the events of the plot so far.

SETTING	CHARACTER/PLOT
small village in Panama	He can't buy any paints.
dry-season vacation	His teacher can't help him.
the countryside	Fernando makes his paints.

LANGUAGE SUPPORT

ESL Have your second-language learners work in groups of four. To each group, assign one of the colors of paint that Fernando made: red, yellow, blue, and black. Ask students to draw pictures explaining how Fernando made that specific color paint. Circulate to assist students as needed.

Guided Instruction

7 CHARACTER From what you know about Fernando, do you think he will give up easily? Why or why not?

MODEL I know that Fernando is hard-working and determined because of what he did to make the paints. So I don't think he'll give up now, because he really wants to paint. He'll find a way to use the paints he made.

> ### TEACHING TIP
> **INSTRUCTIONAL** As students read, point out that one way to understand what a character is going through or feeling is to compare that character's life with their own lives. Like Fernando, have they been in a situation in which they wanted something they couldn't get right away? Did they continue to try? How did they feel? What did they decide to do to solve the problem?

Now his paints were stirred up and waiting—black, blue, yellow, and red, in four bowls. Next he got out the three paintbrushes his teacher had given him—one very small, one medium-sized, and one especially large.

I'm ready to paint pictures, Fernando said to himself. He picked up the small brush and dipped it into the pot of red. Then he had a terrible thought.

7 He had nothing to paint a picture on! An artist needs paper.

He looked in both rooms of the house. He could find no
8 paper at all.

He ran from house to house asking everyone in Sabana Grande for paper to paint on. None of the neighbors had any. Not a scrap.

Fernando was sad. After all his work he wouldn't be able to paint pictures—the colored pictures he could almost see, he wanted to make them so badly. Paints and brushes weren't enough. He needed paper, too.

298

Activity

Cross Curricular: Math

USE A CALENDAR During the dry season, Fernando doesn't go to school.

- Ask students to name the months of their summer vacation, and write their responses on the chalkboard.
- Display a 12-month calendar. Hide the names of the months with masking tape. Have volunteers fill in the months and cross off the summer-vacation months.
- Have students note the remaining vacations, holidays, students' birthdays, and other special school events on their calendar.

▶ **Mathematical/Visual**

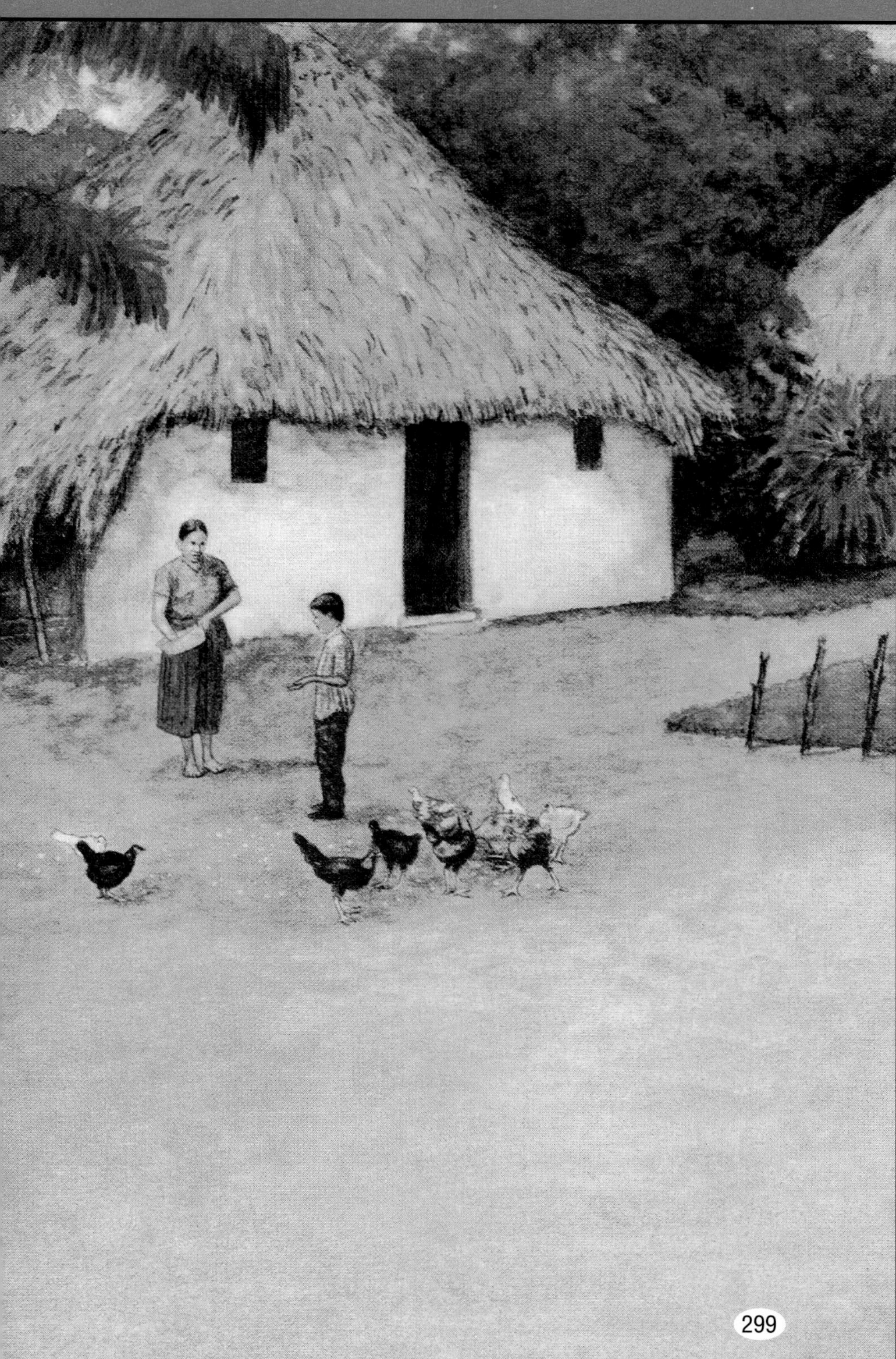

Guided Instruction

8 PLOT, CHARACTER, SETTING An important part of a plot is the problem the characters face. Let's add the problem Fernando now is faced with to our chart. How are the characters and setting part of this problem?

SETTING	CHARACTER/PLOT
small village in Panama	He can't buy any paints.
dry-season vacation	His teacher can't help him.
the countryside	Fernando makes his paints.
village of Sabana Grande	Fernando can't find any paper.

Minilesson

REVIEW/MAINTAIN

Sequence

Review that events in a story are told in order, or sequence.

- Have students look back at pages 296 and 298 to find the order in which Fernando gets ready to paint. (He makes the paints, gets brushes, and dips a brush in paint.)
- Point out the sequence clue words *next* and *then*.

Activity Have partners create a chart, using sequence clue words, to show the sequence of Fernando's actions.

Guided Instruction

9 **CHARACTER, SETTING** Fernando has been drawing in the wet dirt with a stick since he was very little. What does that tell you about him? (He has wanted to be an artist since he was very young. He uses what he finds in his environment.)

P/i **MULTIPLE-MEANING WORDS** Read the sentence that contains the word *comb* in the second paragraph. What is one meaning for the word *comb*? (a piece of plastic or metal that has a row of teeth used to smooth the hair) What do you think the word *comb* means in this sentence?

His fingers itched to draw something—anything. He put down the paintbrush and went over to the mud by the brook.
9 He picked up a stick and drew in the wet dirt, the way he had ever since he was a very little boy.

The big rooster who woke him every morning came out of the chicken yard next door. Fernando looked at him and drew the shape of a rooster. He sighed. He couldn't use his new red and yellow paints to make a bright rooster. He couldn't make the
10 rooster's comb red. He could only scratch out a mud-colored rooster. It wasn't the same as painting would be. It didn't have any color.

300

PREVENTION/INTERVENTION

MULTIPLE-MEANING WORDS Have students reread the sentence that contains *comb*. Explain that the sentence tells them that the *comb* is red, and that it is part of a rooster.

Have students look at the picture of the rooster. Point out the red parts of the rooster. Ask students what part might be the comb. Lead them to see that the red part on top of the rooster's head is the comb. Have students discuss why the top part of the rooster's head is called its comb.

Guided Instruction

10 Fernando has not actually spoken a word so far in the story, yet we've learned a lot about his character. How has the author shown us what Fernando is like and how he is feeling? (through his actions and thoughts) ***Author's Purpose***

Minilesson

REVIEW/MAINTAIN

Summarize

Remind students that summarizing is telling the main events of a story. It can help keep a story's action clear.

- Ask students to summarize the events of this story up to the end of page 301.

Activity Have students:

- work in groups to create a series of cartoons with simple captions to describe the important action.
- display their finished work and discuss how each group chose to summarize the story.

Guided Instruction

11 **CHARACTER, SETTING, PLOT** What happened in this part of the plot? (Fernando's parents told him he could paint on their house.) How do you think Fernando felt when this happened? (happy) Can you show us how Fernando might have looked?

SELF-MONITORING

STRATEGY

REREADING Rereading a part of the story can help a reader to understand why the characters behave as they do.

MODEL I'm not sure why Fernando's parents changed their minds and agreed to let him paint on their house. I'll reread this part aloud. Now I see the problem; I skipped the sentence "I can't stand to see my boy so miserable." Papa changed his mind because he didn't want Fernando to be sad. Mama must have felt the same way.

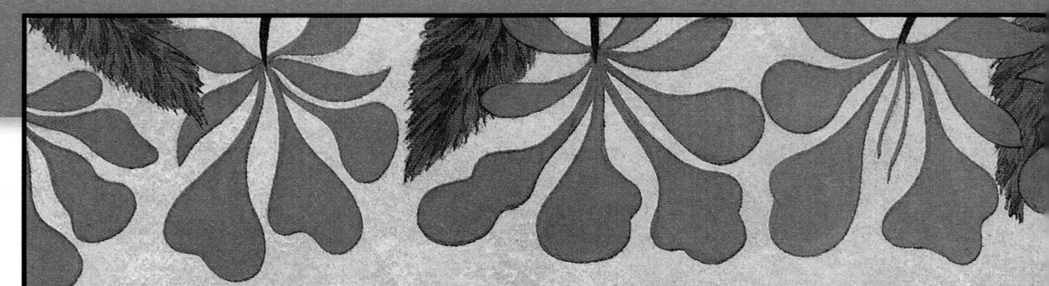

Fernando looked around at the adobe houses of his village. Suddenly he got an idea. Adobe was smooth and white—almost like paper. Why couldn't he paint on the outside of his family's adobe house?

"No!" Papa said. "Who ever saw pictures on the outside of a house?"

"No!" Mama agreed. "What would the neighbors say?"

Fernando looked at his pots of paint and was very unhappy. He wanted to paint pictures more than anything else he could think of.

11 At last Papa said, "I can't stand to see my boy so miserable. All right, Fernando. Go ahead and paint on the
12 house!"

Mama said, "Do your best, Fernando. Remember, the neighbors will have to look at your pictures for a very long time."

First Fernando made a tiny plan of the pictures he was going to paint, painting it with his smallest brush on one corner of the house.

"Your plan looks good to me, Fernando," Papa said. "If you can paint pictures small, you should be able to paint them big."

Fernando picked up his bigger brushes and started to paint a huge picture of the most beautiful tree in Panama, the flowering poinciana, on the left side of the front door. As he painted, he could look up and see the red flowers of a poinciana tree, just beginning its dry season, blooming on the mountainside.

302

Cross Curricular: Science

RAIN FORESTS Much of Panama is rain forest. Discuss what students know about rain forests.

RESEARCH AND INQUIRY Have students create a bulletin board display showing plant and animal life in the rain forests. Suggest they find pictures of rain forests in nature magazines or books.

▶ **Spatial/Interpersonal**

Guided Instruction

12 We need two volunteers to role-play Mama and Papa as they discuss Fernando's plan to paint on the house. Talk about the reasons why he should or should not be allowed to paint on the house. Show us how you came to your final decision.
Role-Play/Judgments and Decisions

303

PHONICS KIT
HANDS-ON ACTIVITIES AND PRACTICE

Minilesson

REVIEW/MAINTAIN

Double Consonants

Write the words *bigger* and *village* from page 302 on the chalkboard.

- Ask a volunteer what these two words have in common. (double consonants)
- Tell students that even though there are two letters, together they sound like only one.

Activity Have students find other words on page 302 with double consonants and write them on the chalkboard, circling the double consonant. (*suddenly, unhappy, all, will, smallest, small, beginning*)

CD-ROM

Guided Instruction

13 **PLOT** What important event do we learn about on this page? (As Fernando paints on his house, all of the neighbors come to watch him.)

14 **CHARACTER** Do you think Fernando will stop painting because of the neighbors' remarks? Explain. (No; because he believes in himself and has his parents' permission.) ***Make Predictions***

PHONICS AND DECODING

- Read the second word on page 304. (*neighbors*)
- Slowly sound out the word. Do you hear sounds for all the letters?

The neighbors were very surprised.

Señora Endara called out, "Come and see what Fernando is doing!"

Señor Remon said, "Who ever saw a house with pictures on the outside?"

13 Pepita, the little girl next door, asked, "Does your mother know you're painting on your house?"

14 Fernando nodded and smiled and kept on painting. Now and then he would look up at the mountain to see the real poinciana. After a week its flowers faded and died. Fernando's tree grew bigger and brighter and redder.

On one branch he added a black toucan with a flat, yellow bill. On another branch a lazy, brown sloth hung by its three toes.

15

304

PREVENTION/INTERVENTION

PHONICS AND DECODING Remind students that they can use words they know to help them read other words.

- Write *neighbors* on chart paper. With self-stick notes, mask all the letters but *eigh*.
- Write the word *eight* below *neighbors*. Help students realize that *eigh* in the word *eight* makes the /ā/ sound.
- Remove the self-stick notes from *neighbors*. Have students read the word.

If necessary, help students blend sounds of the word together.

Guided Instruction

15 **CHARACTER, SETTING, PLOT** Now that we are at the middle of the story, let's add to our chart. What has happened in the plot? How do the characters and setting relate to the plot?

SETTING	CHARACTER/PLOT
small village in Panama	He can't buy any paints.
dry-season vacation	His teacher can't help him.
the countryside	Fernando makes his paints.
village of Sabana Grande	Fernando can't find any paper.
Fernando's white adobe house	Fernando's parents let him paint on the house.

Minilesson

REVIEW/MAINTAIN

Context Clues

Remind students that clues to the meaning of an unfamiliar word can be found in both words and pictures.

- Have students reread the last two sentences on page 304 and discuss how the details help them to find the toucan and sloth in the picture.

Activity Assign students a rain forest animal (boa constrictor, jaguar, macaw) to look up. Have them write two context sentences and illustrate them. Have partners exchange papers and identify the animals.

Guided Instruction

16 **CHARACTER** Do you think Fernando minds that the neighbors are watching him while he paints? Does it make him uncomfortable? (No; because he keeps painting.)

Visual Literacy

VIEWING AND REPRESENTING

Discuss the illustration on page 306: Does it show the front or the back of Fernando? What view do you get of the people watching him? Explain. (The illustrator painted this picture from a point of view that shows Fernando's painting, but it does not show his face very well.)

Compare the illustration on page 309. Ask: What is different about it? (You can see Fernando's face.) Explain: This time the wall is like a window. We see Fernando through it. Ask: Why do you think the illustrator painted the picture this way? (So the viewer can see how happy Fernando is.)

The neighbors brought out chairs. While Fernando worked, they drank coffee and watched him paint. 16

Next he painted the wall on the other side of the door. An imaginary vine with flat, green leaves and huge, purple blossoms crept up the wall.

Word spread about the little painter of Sabana Grande. Even people from Santa Marta, the village around the mountain, hiked into town to watch him paint. The purple vine now reached almost to the thatched roof.

17

307

Guided Instruction

17 The author chose to show us Fernando's character through his actions, not his words. Which of Fernando's actions so far in the story have given you important information about his character? *Author's Purpose*

TEACHING TIP

MANAGEMENT **Have a save-a-tree day in your classroom by taking a day off from using paper. On a designated day, have students do all their work orally or on the chalkboard. At the end of the day, talk about how much paper the class saved and brainstorm other ways to save paper—and trees.**

LANGUAGE SUPPORT

ESL Help students understand the expression *word spread* (page 307). First, to illustrate *spread,* have them drop a blob of glue on a piece of paper and spread it over the paper. Explain that in this expression, *word* means "news" or "information." When you put *word* and *spread* together, it means that "the news has spread."

Play a game in which you say a short sentence to one student, who then repeats it to two classmates. Each of them tells two other classmates. Ask students to listen and notice how long it takes for the information to spread to the entire class. Have some students time how long it takes.

Minilesson

REVIEW/MAINTAIN

Make Predictions

Review that good readers use story clues and their own knowledge to predict events, and then confirm or revise predictions as they get more information.

- Ask students to look back at the predictions they made on page 292. Does the information on pages 292–307 confirm the predictions or make them want to revise them?

Activity Have students revise their predictions if necessary, and then predict what will happen next.

Guided Instruction

18 **PLOT** What is happening as Fernando paints his house? Do you think this is an important event in the story? Why or why not? (Everyone is coming to watch him, even his teacher and people from other towns. This is important because he is becoming famous in his own way.)

19 **CHARACTER** Who wants to role-play Señora Arias for us? Señora Arias, you had to walk very far to see Fernando. Can you tell us why he is so important to you?

Now, who will role-play Fernando? Fernando, how do you feel when your teacher says nice things about your work? What do you want to say to her? *Role-Play*

18 One day Señora Arias came from the school in Santa Marta. Why was his teacher looking for him, Fernando wondered. It was still dry season, when there wasn't any school. It hadn't rained for a month.

19 "School's not starting yet," his teacher said. "I came to see your painted adobe house that everyone in Santa Marta is talking about. Fernando, you did very well with those paintbrushes. I like it!"

She turned to the neighbors. "Don't you?"

20 "We certainly do!" the neighbors agreed.

They poured some coffee for the visiting teacher.

21

308

Activity

Cross Curricular: Music

MERENGUE Point out that Fernando's idea for painting on his house turned into a social occasion for his neighbors. Explain that in Panama, as in other countries, parties are often held to celebrate special occasions. There are sometimes special foods and dancing. A popular form of dance music in Central America is merengue (mə reng′ gā).

Obtain recordings of merengue music and play them for your students. Ask volunteers who can dance the merengue to demonstrate for the rest of the class.
▶ **Auditory/Kinesthetic**

Guided Instruction

20 **CHARACTER** How do people seem to feel about Fernando's painting now? (Since people outside the village are talking about Fernando's paintings, they must be impressed.)

21 How do the neighbors' reactions help you predict what might happen to their houses? (The fact that the neighbors like Fernando's painting so much makes me think they might want their houses painted, too.) ***Make Predictions***

Guided Instruction

22 **SUMMARIZE** Here the neighbors ask Fernando to paint on their houses. Summarize the events that lead to their decision. (Fernando had no paper to paint on, so he painted on his house. People from all over came to watch. They liked his paintings so they asked him to do the same for their houses.)

23 Do you think the neighbors are making the right decision when they ask Fernando to paint on their houses? Give reasons to support your judgments.
Judgments and Decisions

Fluency

READ DIALOGUE

Have students point out the punctuation marks in the dialogue on pages 308–311. Remind them that exclamation points indicate emphasis, and question marks indicate an interrogative rising tone. Suggest that they read aloud the dialogue. Then ask them to turn back to page 304 and read the dialogue aloud with a partner, using expression and feeling.

"Fernando, will you paint pictures on my house?" asked Señora Alfaro.

"And mine, too?" asked Señor Remon.

Fernando nodded yes, but he kept on painting.

For fun he added a black, white-faced monkey looking down at the people through purple flowers. 

Next to the door he painted a big red-and-yellow rooster, flopping its red comb as it crowed a loud "cock-a-doodle-doo!" 

Above the door he painted the words CASA FAMILIA ESPINO, so people would know that this was the home of the Espino family. 

311

Guided Instruction

24 CHARACTER Why is it important to Fernando that he paint his family's name over the door? (Possible answers: He wants everyone to know whose house it is. He is proud of his family.)

LANGUAGE SUPPORT

ESL Ask students to review the events that have led to the neighbors' asking Fernando to paint on their houses. Suggest that they skim the pages they have already read, looking for key events. Then ask them to report what they have found.

Their lists might include:

- Fernando's teacher tells him how to make paints.
- He makes four colors of paint.
- He can't find any paper to use.
- His parents let him paint pictures on the outside of their house.

Minilesson

REVIEW/MAINTAIN

Draw Conclusions

Review that conclusions are decisions readers make based on information in the story.

- Ask students what conclusions they can draw from the information on page 311. Lead students to see that by the end of the story, the villagers are pleased with Fernando's work.

Activity Have students write their conclusions about how Fernando feels about painting and how his parents feel about his pictures at the end of the story. Remind them to provide examples to show how they reached their conclusions.

Guided Instruction

25 **CHARACTER, SETTING, PLOT** Finish your chart by telling about the ending of the story.

SETTING	CHARACTER/PLOT
small village in Panama	He can't buy any paints.
dry-season vacation	His teacher can't help him.
the countryside	Fernando makes his paints.
village of Sabana Grande	Fernando can't find any paper.
Fernando's white adobe house	Fernando's parents let him paint on the house.
village of Sabana Grande	The neighbors ask Fernando to paint their houses, too.

RETELL THE STORY Ask volunteers to tell the major events of the story. Students may refer to their charts. Then have partners write one or two sentences that summarize the story. Have them focus on the main character's problem and how it is solved. *Summarize*

STUDENT SELF-ASSESSMENT

- How did analyzing character and setting help me to understand the plot of the story?
- How did the chart help me?

TRANSFERRING THE STRATEGY

- When might I try using this strategy again? In what other reading could the chart help me?

REREADING FOR *Fluency*

Have students choose a favorite section of the story to read to a partner. Encourage students to read with feeling and expression.

READING RATE You may want to evaluate an individual student's reading rate. Have the student read aloud from *The Little Painter of Sabana Grande* for one minute. Ask the student to place a self-stick note after the last word read. Then count the number of words he or she has read.

Alternatively, you could assess small groups or the whole class together by having students count words and record their own scores.

A Running Record form provided in **Diagnostic/Placement Evaluation** will help you evaluate reading rate(s).

Now his pictures were finished. Fernando sat down with his teacher and the neighbors. Everyone said kind words about his paintings.

Fernando said nothing. He just smiled and thought to himself, there are still six adobe houses left to paint in Sabana Grande.

25

313

Guided Instruction

Return to Predictions and Purposes

Review with students their story predictions and reasons for reading the story. Were their predictions correct? Did they find out what they wanted to know?

PREDICTIONS	WHAT HAPPENED
This story takes place in a village.	The story takes place in Sabana Grande, Panama.
The main character is a boy who paints.	Fernando wants to paint. He makes his own paints. His parents let him paint on their house.

INFORMAL ASSESSMENT

STORY ELEMENTS

HOW TO ASSESS

- Ask students to describe how Fernando's personality and the setting affected the plot.

Students should realize that Fernando's resourcefulness, along with the rural setting, affects the plot by causing him to make his own paints and paint on houses.

FOLLOW UP If students have trouble relating to the characters, have students brainstorm words to describe Fernando.

If students have difficulty seeing the importance of setting, ask them why Fernando couldn't buy paper.

If students have trouble understanding the importance of plot, have them retell what happened in the story, including the setting.

LITERARY RESPONSE

QUICK-WRITE Invite students to record their thoughts about the story. These questions may help them get started:

JOURNAL

- How would you like to be Fernando?
- What did you think of the way Fernando solved his problem?

ORAL RESPONSE Have students share their journal writings and discuss what part of the story they enjoyed most.

Story Questions

Have students discuss or write answers to the questions on page 314.

Answers:

1. The story takes place in Sabana Grande, Panama. *Literal/Setting*
2. The setting provides materials to make paints and adobe to paint on. *Inferential/Setting, Character*
3. Señora Arias; she gave him brushes and taught him to make paints. *Inferential/Judgments and Decisions*
4. A boy who has no paper paints on his family's house instead. *Critical/Summarize*
5. Answers will vary. Possible answer: He would talk to them about the flowers. *Critical/Reading Across Texts*

Write a Letter For a full writing process lesson on persuasive writing, see pages 317K–317L.

Story Questions & Activities

1. Where does the story take place?
2. How is the setting important to the story?
3. Who do you think gave Fernando the most help? Explain.
4. What is this story mainly about?
5. Imagine that Fernando became part of the painting on pages 290-291. What do you think he would say to the other people in the painting?

Pretend you are Fernando. Write a letter to a family in Santa Marta to persuade them to let you paint their house. Give three good reasons.

Meeting Individual Needs

EASY

Name________ Date______ **Reteach 83**

Vocabulary

Match each word below with its definition.

1. blossoms — f. flowers
2. dawn — a. when the sun first comes up
3. faded — d. lost color
4. imaginary — e. make-believe
5. miserable — c. very unhappy
6. shallow — b. not deep

/6

Story Comprehension **Reteach 84**

Write an answer to each question below.

1. When Fernando couldn't find any paper to paint on, what did he ask his parents if he could do? Fernando asked his parents if he could paint the outside of their house.
2. How did the people in Fernando's village react to his painting? They asked him to paint their houses, too.

83–84 **At Home:** Have students identify one problem and the solution to that problem in the story. Book 3.1/Unit 3 **The Little Painter of Sabana Grande** /2

Reteach, 84

ON-LEVEL

Name________ Date______ **Practice 84**

Story Comprehension

Think about the story of Fernando, the little painter. Then finish each sentence by writing the missing word on the blank line. Write that word on the crossword puzzle.

ACROSS

1. The smooth and white adobe houses reminded Fernando of paper.
4. Fernando lived in the village of Sabana Grande.
6. Everyone said kind words about Fernando's paintings.
8. The color yellow is made from dried grasses in the meadow.
9. Soon all the neighbors asked Fernando if he would paint their houses.
10. Above the door Fernando painted the words Casa Familia Espino.

DOWN

2. The color black is made from the charcoal of a burned tree stump.
3. Fernando's teacher taught him how the country people of Panama made their paints.
5. The color blue is made from berries that grow deep in the jungle.
7. The neighbors brought out chairs and watched Fernando paint.

84 **At Home:** Have students think of two more clues and words to add to the puzzle. Book 3.1/Unit 3 **The Little Painter of Sabana Grande** /10

Practice, 84

CHALLENGE

Name________ Date______ **Extend 83**

Vocabulary

blossoms	dawn	faded
imaginary	miserable	shallow

Work with a partner to make up a newspaper story. Use the words in the box to answer these questions: Who is the story about? What happened? When did it happen? Where did it happen? Why did it happen? Write your story on another piece of paper.

Answers will vary.

Extend 84

Story Comprehension

Write a new ending for "The Little Painter of Sabana Grande." Try to imagine what might have happened if Fernando had plenty of paper to paint on.

Answers will vary.

83–84 **At Home:** Have students draw a picture of an adobe house painted by Fernando. Book 3.1/Unit 3 **The Little Painter of Sabana Grande**

Extend, 84

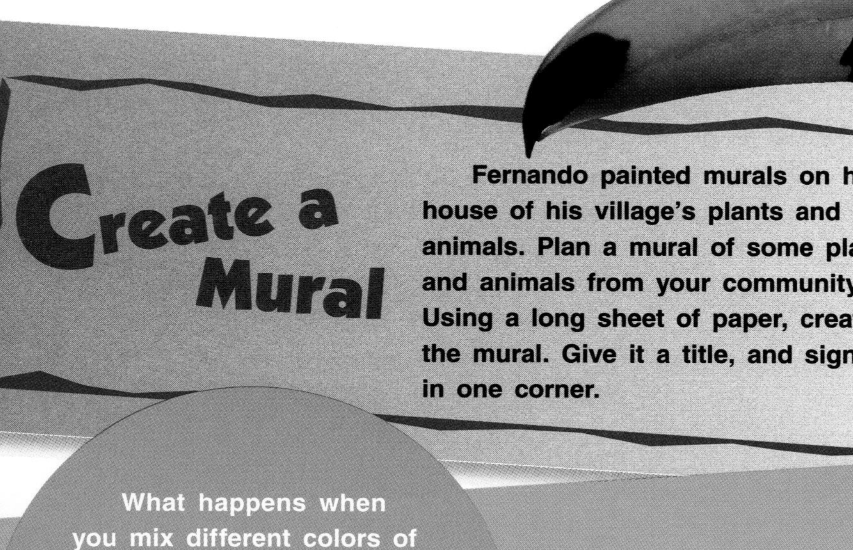

Create a Mural

Fernando painted murals on his house of his village's plants and animals. Plan a mural of some plants and animals from your community. Using a long sheet of paper, create the mural. Give it a title, and sign it in one corner.

Mix Colors of Paint

What happens when you mix different colors of paint? Create a poster to show what happens. Use some red, blue, and yellow paint. Mix red and blue paint. What color do you get? Try mixing other colors.

Find Out More

Fernando's school is closed for the dry season. What months are schools open in Panama? What is a school day like? Start by checking an encyclopedia. Then compare schools there with your school.

315

Story Activities

Create a Mural

Materials: large sheets of paper, paint, paint-brushes

GROUP Have groups brainstorm a list of local plants and animals to include in their murals. Suggest they make a sketch, or blue-print, of what their mural will look like.

Mix Colors of Paint

Materials: paint, paintbrushes, poster board

GROUP Have students mix the colors and record their results as shown:

red + blue = purple

red + yellow = orange

blue + yellow = green

red + blue + yellow = black

Explain that these three primary colors can be mixed in different proportions to make all other secondary colors.

Find Out More

RESEARCH AND INQUIRY Have partners write a report about schools in Panama. They may use an encyclopedia, books on Panama, or the Internet.

PARTNERS

*inter*NET CONNECTION For more information on Panama, have students visit ***www.mhschool.com/reading***.

FORMAL ASSESSMENT

After page 315, see Selection Assessment.

Study Skills

GRAPHIC AIDS

Students will:

- identify cities and countries on a map.
- use a map key and compass rose.

PREPARE Read the passage with students. Display **Teaching Chart 69**.

TEACH Review how to use the compass rose and the map key. Have a student estimate the distance between the capital city and Sabana Grande. Have a volunteer tell the direction of travel from Costa Rica to Sabana Grande.

PRACTICE Have students answer questions 1–5. Review the answers with them.
1. Panama City **2.** Costa Rica **3.** Colon, Panama City, Balboa **4.** southeast **5.** It links North America and South America.

ASSESS/CLOSE Have students write detailed directions from Colombia to Costa Rica.

STUDY SKILLS

Read a Map

The country of Panama lies in Central America. It is home to a great many plants and animals. Sabana Grande is a village in central Panama. Like many other villages in Panama, Sabana Grande is a rural community—a place of farms or open country.

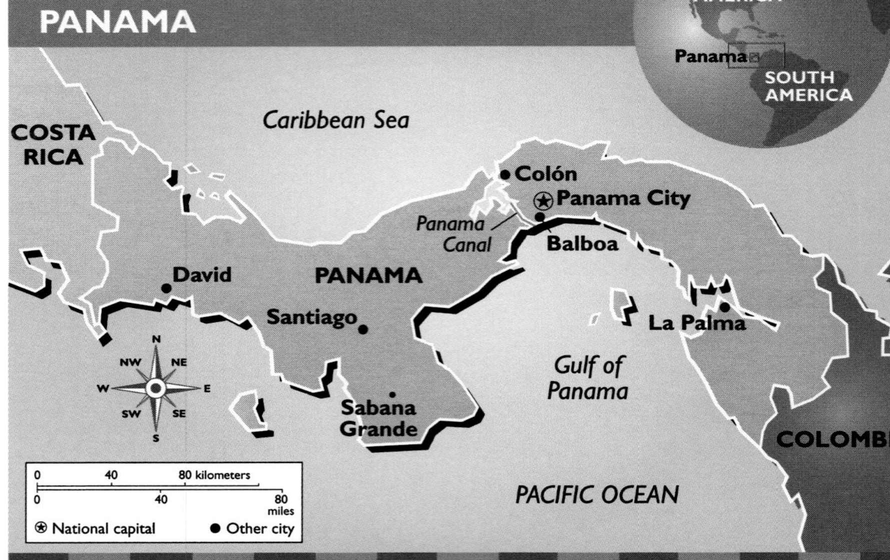

Use the map to answer these questions.

1. What is the capital of Panama?
2. What country is on the western border of Panama?
3. What are the three cities closest to the Panama Canal?
4. In which direction is Sabana Grande from David?
5. Why do you think Panama has been called the "crossroads of the Americas"?

Meeting Individual Needs

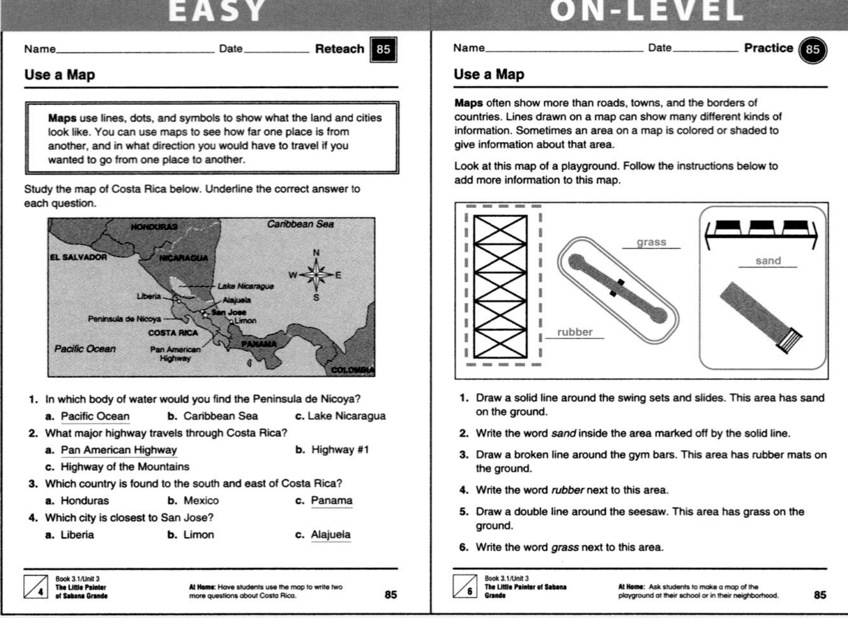

EASY

Name________ Date______ **Reteach 85**

Use a Map

Maps use lines, dots, and symbols to show what the land and cities look like. You can use maps to see how far one place is from another, and in what direction you would have to travel if you wanted to go from one place to another.

Study the map of Costa Rica below. Underline the correct answer to each question.

1. In which body of water would you find the Peninsula de Nicoya?
   a. Pacific Ocean b. Caribbean Sea c. Lake Nicaragua
2. What major highway travels through Costa Rica?
   a. Pan American Highway b. Highway #1 c. Highway of the Mountains
3. Which country is found to the south and east of Costa Rica?
   a. Honduras b. Mexico c. Panama
4. Which city is closest to San Jose?
   a. Liberia b. Limon c. Alajuela

4 Book 3.1/Unit 3 **The Little Painter of Sabana Grande** — **At Home:** Have students use the map to write two more questions about Costa Rica. 85

Reteach, 85

ON-LEVEL

Name________ Date______ **Practice 85**

Use a Map

Maps often show more than roads, towns, and the borders of countries. Lines drawn on a map can show many different kinds of information. Sometimes an area on a map is colored or shaded to give information about that area.

Look at this map of a playground. Follow the instructions below to add more information to this map.

1. Draw a solid line around the swing sets and slides. This area has sand on the ground.
2. Write the word *sand* inside the area marked off by the solid line.
3. Draw a broken line around the gym bars. This area has rubber mats on the ground.
4. Write the word *rubber* next to this area.
5. Draw a double line around the seesaw. This area has grass on the ground.
6. Write the word *grass* next to this area.

6 Book 3.1/Unit 3 **The Little Painter of Sabana Grande** — **At Home:** Ask students to make a map of the playground at their school or in their neighborhood. 85

Practice, 85

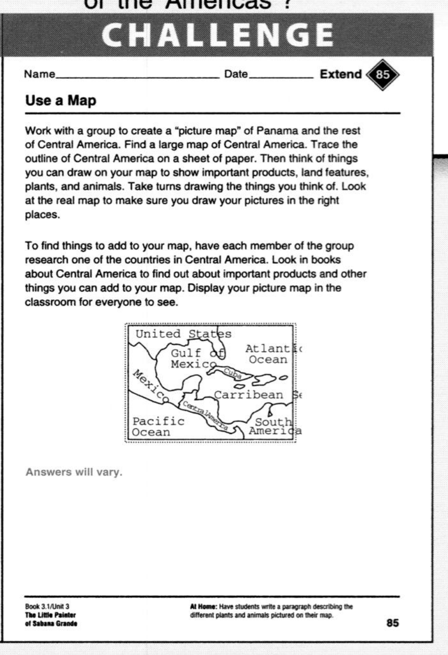

CHALLENGE

Name________ Date______ **Extend 85**

Use a Map

Work with a group to create a "picture map" of Panama and the rest of Central America. Find a large map of Central America. Trace the outline of Central America on a sheet of paper. Then think of things you can draw on your map to show important products, land features, plants, and animals. Take turns drawing the things you think of. Look at the real map to make sure you draw your pictures in the right places.

To find things to add to your map, have each member of the group research one of the countries in Central America. Look in books about Central America to find out about important products and other things you can add to your map. Display your picture map in the classroom for everyone to see.

Answers will vary.

Book 3.1/Unit 3 **The Little Painter of Sabana Grande** — **At Home:** Have students write a paragraph describing the different plants and animals pictured on their map. 85

Extend, 85

TEST POWER

Test Tip

As you read, ask yourself: Is this an important part of the story?

DIRECTIONS:

Read the story. Then read each question about the story.

SAMPLE

October 16

Dear Diary,

Remember when I told you that my friend Ralph has trouble with math? Last night I helped him with some homework problems. Ralph is very smart, but math is his least favorite subject. I showed him how to do long division. It took him a while, but he finally got it. He did all twenty of the practice problems correctly.

Today, Mr. Deevers gave us a surprise math quiz. I looked at Ralph and knew he was nervous.

Mr. Deevers gave us back our tests at the end of class. Ralph got a perfect score and so did I. It made me very happy to have helped out my friend.

—Damon

1 How did Ralph feel when he had to take the surprise quiz?

- ● Nervous
- ○ Excited
- ○ Bored
- ○ Happy

2 This story is mostly about—

- ○ two friends who have trouble with math
- ○ Mr. Deevers' surprise quiz
- ○ why Damon likes math
- ● how Damon helped Ralph with math

317

ITBS/TEST PREPARATION

TERRANOVA/TEST PREPARATION

SAT 9/TEST PREPARATION

Test Power

THE PRINCETON REVIEW

Read the Page

Remind students that after reading the story they should summarize the story in their own words. Instruct them to read through all of the answer choices.

Discuss the Questions

QUESTION 1: This question requires students to understand the feelings of a character. Ask: what facts in the story are clues about how Ralph might feel? The story provides a clue: "Math is his least favorite subject."

QUESTION 2: This question asks students to decide the best summary for the story. Work through all of the answer choices as a group. As you discuss each answer choice, point out why a choice is incorrect even if the fact is stated. A correct answer must summarize the whole story.

Leveled Books

The Barn Raising
LEVELED BOOKS
Written by Soledad del Bosque
Illustrated by Craig Spearing

EASY

The Barn Raising

Double Consonants

☑ Story Elements

☑ Instructional Vocabulary: *blossoms, dawn, faded, imaginary, miserable, shallow*

Guided Reading

PREVIEW AND PREDICT Conduct a **picture walk** up to page 12. Have students discuss illustrations. Ask: What do you think is going to happen by the end of the story?

SET PURPOSES Have students write down questions they would like to have answered by the story. For example, one question might be: How will John help with the barn raising?

READ THE BOOK Have students read the story independently. After they have read the story, return to the text to apply strategies.

Page 2: Find a word with a double consonant on page 2. *(fretting)* Identify the double consonant. *(tt)* ***Phonics and Decoding***

Pages 4–6: What does John want to help do? (He wants to help build the new barn.) Why does his father say no? (He feels that John is too little to help.) ***Plot***

Page 8: What does the word *miserable* mean? (unhappy) How does John's mother know her son is miserable? (He appears unhappy.) ***Vocabulary***

Pages 13–14: How did John feel after he saved Will? (happy and proud) ***Character***

Page 16: Is the story set in the past or the present? (past) ***Setting***

RETURN TO PREDICTIONS AND PURPOSES Review students' predictions and reasons for reading.

LITERARY RESPONSE Discuss these questions:

- All the people in the story worked together to build a barn in only one day. What were some of the jobs?
- When have you worked with other people to complete a project?

Also see the questions and activity in *The Barn Raising*.

See Phonics **CD-ROM** for practice using double-consonant words.

Answers to Story Questions

1. The main character is John.
2. They might have been afraid John would get hurt.
3. Proud, happy, responsible.
4. The story is about John wanting to help out at the barn raising and doing a lot more than anyone had expected.
5. Answers will vary.

Story Questions and Writing Activity

1. Who is the main character of the story?
2. Why do you think Will and Father didn't want John to help?
3. How do you think John felt at the end of the story?
4. What is the story mostly about?
5. Compare John with Fernando from *The Little Painter of Sabana Grande.* What do they have in common?

Come to a Barn Raising

Imagine that you are holding a barn raising. You want to invite your friends and neighbors to come help. Create an invitation to the barn raising.

from *The Barn Raising*

Leveled Books

INDEPENDENT

Rosa's New Home

- ☑ Story Elements
- ☑ Instructional Vocabulary: ***blossoms, dawn, faded, imaginary, miserable, shallow***

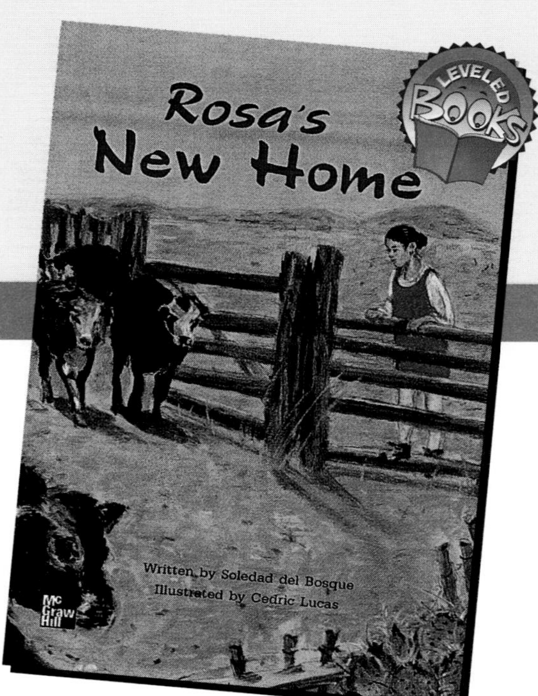

Guided Reading

PREVIEW AND PREDICT Conduct a **picture walk** to page 9. Have students discuss illustrations. Ask: What might this story be about? What can you tell from the title?

SET PURPOSES Have students decide what they would like to have answered by the story. For example, one question might be: What does Rosa think of her new home?

READ THE BOOK Have students read the story independently. After they have read the story, use the questions below to apply strategies.

Pages 2–3: Where does the story take place? (on a ranch) ***Setting***

Pages 4–5: What happened that caused the family to move to Texas? (Grandma's cousin died and left the ranch in Texas to Grandma.) ***Plot***

Pages 6–7: What does Elena try to do for Rosa when Rosa sees her new room? What does this tell you about Elena? (She is caring and warm-hearted; she is fond of her sister.) ***Character***

Page 14: What does the word *shallow* mean? (not deep) What animal did Rosa see near the shallow stream? (She saw an armadillo.) ***Vocabulary***

Pages 15–16: What did Rosa's mother and sister do to help make Rosa happier in their new home? (They painted the walls in her room pink.) ***Cause and Effect***

RETURN TO PREDICTIONS AND PURPOSES Review students' predictions and reasons for reading.

LITERARY RESPONSE Discuss these questions:

- Everybody on the ranch worked hard. Which job would you like to have on a ranch?
- Rosa missed her friends back in the city. What would you do if you moved and missed your friends?

Also see the questions and activity in *Rosa's New Home.*

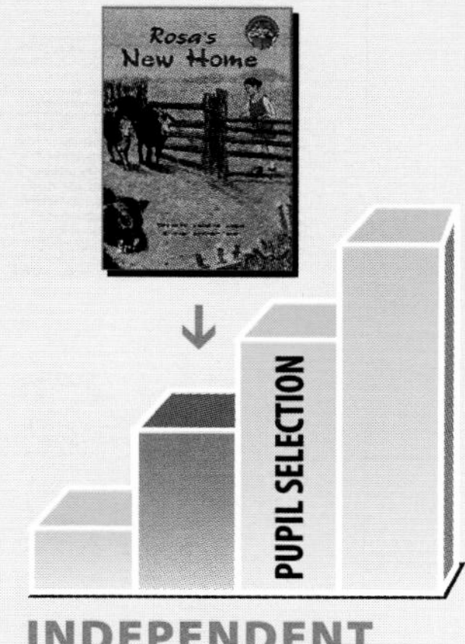

INDEPENDENT

Answers to Story Questions

1. Rosa and her family moved to a ranch in Texas.
2. Rosa was unhappy because she left behind her friends and everything she felt comfortable with. Rosa might have been afraid or worried about the move to the ranch.
3. Grandma probably couldn't believe they would all be living together on the same ranch where she grew up. She felt moved by this.
4. The story is about Rosa adjusting to life in a new environment.
5. Answers will vary.

Story Questions and Writing Activity

1. Where did Rosa and her family go?
2. Why do you think Rosa was unhappy to leave her old home?
3. Why do you think everyone smiled when Grandma looked out the window?
4. What is the story mostly about?
5. What advice might Rosa have for Fernando if he ever had to move from *Sabana Grande*?

How Big Is It?

Rosa's new room is 10 feet long and 6 feet wide. Measure your room at home. Now, use your math skills to figure the area of her new room and that of your room. Write a sentence comparing the two.

from *Rosa's New Home*

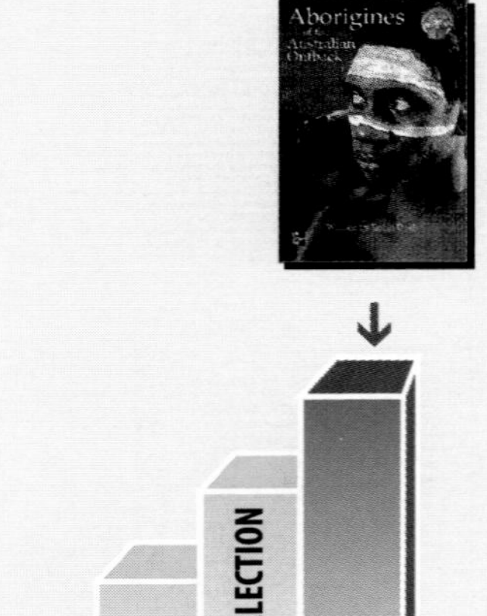

Leveled Books

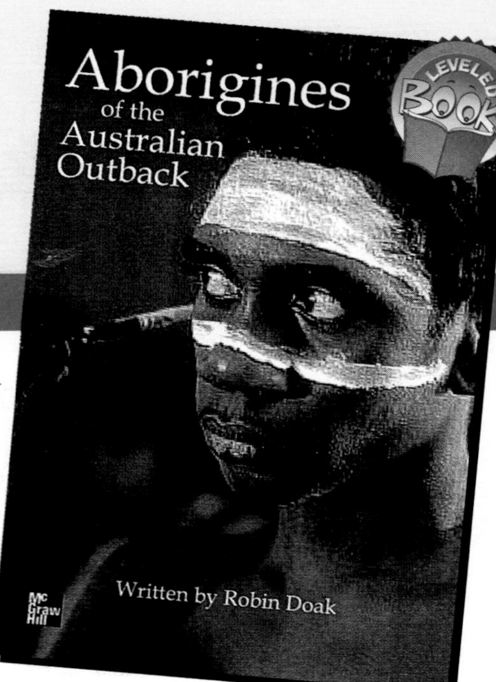

CHALLENGE

Aborigines of the Australian Outback

- ☑ Story Elements
- ☑ Instructional Vocabulary: *blossoms, dawn, faded, imaginary, miserable, shallow*

Answers to Story Questions

1. For 60,000 years.
2. The settlers thought their ways were better than those of the Aborigines and tried to make the Aborigines follow their customs.
3. The Koori feel that they are one with their ancestors, nature, and the land.
4. The book tells about the history and the culture of the Koori of Australia, who have had to struggle over the last two hundred years so that their way of life would not be lost.
5. Answers will vary.

Story Questions and Writing Activity

1. How long have the Koori lived in Australia?
2. Why do you think the settlers made the "Aborigines" speak English?
3. Why do some Koori continue to live as their ancestors did?
4. What is the main idea of the book?
5. If the Koori were to paint a mural like *The Little Painter of Sabana Grande*, what do you think would be in it?

Make a Sign

The Koori ask visitors not to climb Uluru. Why do you think this is? Design a sign to be posted at Uluru. Tell visitors why they should not climb this sacred rock.

from *Aborigines of the Australian Outback*

Guided Reading

PREVIEW AND PREDICT Conduct a **picture walk**. Have students discuss illustrations. Ask: Where do aborigines live?

SET PURPOSES Have students think of questions they would like to have answered by the story. For example, one question might be, "How do aborigines today live differently from aborigines of the past?"

READ THE BOOK Have students read the story independently. After they have read the story, use the questions below to apply strategies.

Pages 2–3: What does the word *aborigines* mean? (from the beginning) Why did British settlers give this name to the people of Australia? (The aborigines were there when the British first set foot in Australia.) *Cause and Effect*

Pages 4–5: How did the tribes help each other? (They traded goods, shared what they had learned, and protected each other.) *Main Idea*

Page 7: What does the word *shallow* mean? (not deep) *Vocabulary*

Page 12: What happened to the native people of Australia after the British arrived? (The British took over the land; the Koori could live only on special reserves.) *Sequence of Events*

Page 13: How would you describe the Outback? (a huge, dry area) *Setting*

RETURN TO PREDICTIONS AND PURPOSES Review students' predictions and reasons for reading.

LITERARY RESPONSE Discuss these questions:

- What was the author's purpose for writing this book?
- How would you have felt about the British if you were a member of a Koori tribe?

Also see the questions and activity in *Aborigines of the Australian Outback*.

Connecting Texts

CLASS DISCUSSION Write the story titles on a chart. Discuss with students the effect that the setting of each story has on the story. Call on volunteers from each reading level and write their suggestions on the chart.

The Little Painter of Sabana Grande	The Barn Raising	Rosa's New Home	Aborigines of the Australian Outback
• Fernando found the berries deep in the jungle, the grass in the corner of the meadow, and the clay in the brook.	• A line of carriages pulls up to the little farmhouse and families pile out to help raise the barn.	• Rosa's new home was a big, run-down house.	• The Koori traveled around Australia, hunting, gathering food, and fishing in streams.

Viewing/Representing

GROUP PRESENTATIONS Divide the class into groups, one for each of the four books read in the lesson. (For *The Little Painter of Sabana Grande,* combine students of different reading levels.) Have each group create story charts with columns labeled: Who (character), What (plot), When (setting), and Where (setting). Allow students to use the bulletin board to present their charts to the class.

AUDIENCE RESPONSE Ask students to pay attention to each group's presentation. Allow time for questions after each presentation.

Research and Inquiry

MORE ABOUT RURAL COMMUNITIES: Have students ask themselves: How would living in the country be different from living in the city? Name five ways that living conditions long ago were different from daily life today. Invite students to do the following:

- Look up New Jersey and Texas in an atlas or almanac to learn more about each state.
- Locate Panama and Australia on a map.
- How did living in a rural country affect Fernando in *The Little Painter of Sabana Grande?* How might this story have been different if he had lived in a city?

*inter*NET CONNECTION Have students log on to ***www.mhschool. com/reading*** for links to Web sites about rural communities.

Students will:

- make inferences about and analyze character and setting.
- understand the plot.

TEACHING TIP

MANAGEMENT When you are working with a small group, sometimes the rest of the class falls off task. Don't sit down. Arrange the small group in such a way that you can stand and move between the group and the whole class.

Review Story Elements

PREPARE

Discuss Character, Setting, and Plot

Review: You can make inferences about story characters by noticing their actions, thoughts, and words. The setting (when and where the story takes place) along with the characters can affect what happens in the plot. The plot consists of the important events in the beginning, middle, and end of the story. Ask students how the characters and setting affected the plot in the story they just read.

TEACH

Read "The Walk" and Model the Skill

Ask students to pay close attention to the character, setting, and plot as you read the **Teaching Chart 70** passage with them.

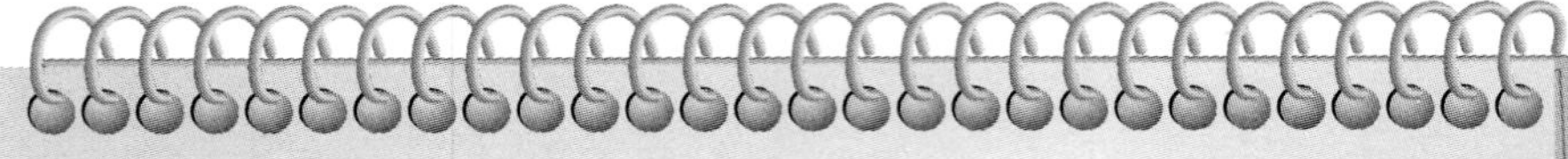

The Walk

Walking through the meadow, Fernando saw a colorful butterfly land on a leaf. Fernando looked carefully at the blue stripes and white dots on the butterfly's wings. His mother loved butterflies. He would paint her a picture of this one for her birthday.

Now Fernando tried to think of what pictures to paint on Señor Remon's house. He looked around. He saw a sunny green meadow, white adobe houses, and mountains in the distance. Fernando decided to paint this scene on Señor Remon's house. He hurried back home, eager to get started.

Teaching Chart 70

Discuss clues in the passage that help readers relate how the character and setting affect the plot.

MODEL I can tell Fernando enjoys nature because he stops during his walk in the meadow to watch a butterfly. The setting of the meadow and Fernando's personality have an effect on the events of the story.

PRACTICE

Make Inferences About Character and Setting and Summarize Plot

Have students underline clues in "The Walk" that help them make inferences about Fernando's character and circle clues about the setting. ▶ **Logical/Interpersonal**

Ask students to summarize the plot by telling the events that were affected by the character and setting. (Fernando sees a butterfly in the meadow. Because he loves nature and his mother, he decides he will paint her a butterfly for her birthday. Fernando then looks around and sees the beautiful scene he will paint for Señor Remon.)

▶ **Linguistic/Oral**

ASSESS/CLOSE

Rewrite a Familiar Tale with a New Setting and Plot

Have students create a new setting for a favorite tale or fable, such as "The Three Little Pigs" or "The Tortoise and the Hare." Ask them how the new setting will affect the characters and the plot. Have each group write their version of the story with a new setting and share it with the class.

ALTERNATE TEACHING STRATEGY

STORY ELEMENTS

For a different approach to teaching this skill, see page T64.

SELF-SELECTED Reading

Students may choose from following titles.

ANTHOLOGY

- *The Little Painter of Sabana Grande*

LEVELED BOOKS

- *The Barn Raising*
- *Rosa's New Home*
- *Aborigines of the Australian Outback*

Bibliography, pages T76–T77

Meeting Individual Needs for Comprehension

EASY

Name_____ Date_____ **Reteach 86**

Story Elements

Every story has **characters** and a **plot**. Thinking about the characters and the plot will help you understand what is important in the story.

Write an answer to each question about "The Little Painter of Sabana Grande."

1. Who are the main characters in the story? Papa, Mama, Fernando, Señora Arias
2. What does Fernando decide to do on his vacation? He wishes to paint a picture.
3. What problem does Fernando face before he can start his project? He has no paper.
4. Who does Fernando ask for help in solving this problem? Papa and Mama
5. Who has to agree to his solution before he can carry out his project? Papa and Mama
6. How do Fernando's parents and the villagers react to his project? At first Papa and Mama say, "No." The neighbors are surprised to see the painting. But soon the villagers say kind words about Fernando's paintings.

86 **At Home:** Have students draw a picture of one of the characters in the story. Book 3.1/Unit 3 **The Little Painter of Sabana Grande** 6

Reteach, 86

ON-LEVEL

Name_____ Date_____ **Practice 86**

Story Elements

Choose a word from the list that describes Fernando, and write it on the line. Answers may vary.

happy bored busy tired sad talented

1. Fernando is busy.
2. Explain your word choice. Possible answer: In the story, Fernando is always doing something. He is busy making paint, searching for paper, and painting the outside of his house.
3. Where does the story take place? The story takes place in the village of Sabana Grande in Panama.
4. What is Fernando's problem in the story? He doesn't have paper to paint on.
5. How does Fernando solve his problem? Fernando solves his problem by painting his house.
6. What do people from the village ask Fernando to do at the end of the story? People ask Fernando to paint their houses, too.

86 **At Home:** Have students choose a different word from the list to describe Fernando, and explain their choice. Book 3.1/Unit 3 **The Little Painter of Sabana Grande** 6

Practice, 86

CHALLENGE

Name_____ Date_____ **Extend 86**

Story Elements

Imagine what it might be like to spend the day with Fernando, the main character in "The Little Painter of Sabana Grande." Write a paragraph telling about your imagined day.

Answers will vary.

Illustrate the setting of your imagined day with Fernando.

Share your paragraph and illustration with the rest of the class. Tell about the setting, characters, and plot.

86 **At Home:** Have students make up a simple plot for a story about something Fernando might do when he grows up. Book 3.1/Unit 3 **The Little Painter of Sabana Grande**

Extend, 86

LANGUAGE SUPPORT

Name_____ Date_____

Story Map

village	artist	parents	excited	flowers
paper	mountains	paints	houses	walls
adobe	Panama	painting	animals	plants
	hard worker		tiny plan	

Setting	Character
village mountains Panama houses plants flowers animals	artist excited hard worker
Problem	**Solution**
paper parents paints	adobe painting tiny plan

94 **The Little Painter of Sabana Grande** • Language Support/Blackline Master 46 Grade 3

Language Support, 94

Students will summarize a story or passage.

TEACHING TIP

INSTRUCTIONAL Have students summarize what they did yesterday. Focus their attention on telling only important events, in order, and omitting minor details.

Review Summarize

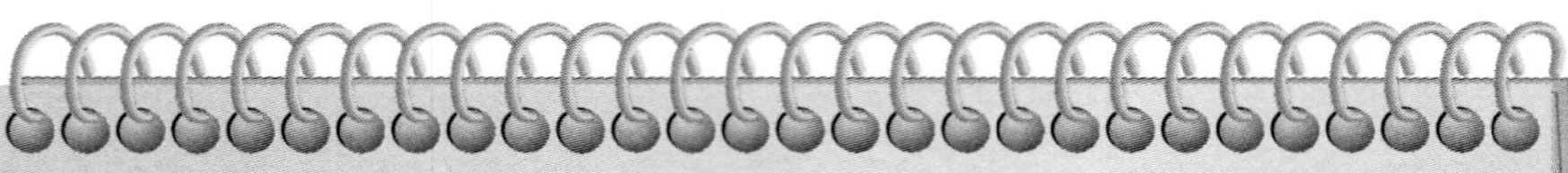

PREPARE

Discuss Summarizing

Explain: To summarize a story or passage, tell the main events in the order in which they occurred. Try to be as brief as possible. Do not include unimportant details in a summary. Be sure to use your own words when summarizing.

TEACH

Read "Boy Paints on Houses" and Model the Skill

Read the newspaper article "Boy Paints on Houses." Focus students' attention on the main events described in the article.

Boy Paints on Houses

Fernando Espino, a boy from a small town in Panama, loved to paint. However, he did not have paints or paper.

Luckily, a teacher taught Fernando how to make paints from charcoal, berries, grass, and clay. After making his paints, Fernando then had to find something to paint on.

Fernando had an idea. Since he couldn't find any paper, he persuaded his parents to let him paint pictures on their house. His neighbors liked the results so much, they asked him to paint on their houses, too.

Teaching Chart 71

Model how to identify important events. Then ask volunteers to underline the important events in the passage.

MODEL The main idea or event can often be found in the title of a story or an article. I can tell from the title that the main idea is that a boy is painting pictures on houses. As I read the article, I will look for the other important information about the boy and what he does.

PRACTICE

Create a Summary Flowchart

GROUP

Work together with students to create and complete a Summary flowchart showing the main events of the story.

▶ **Logical/Interpersonal**

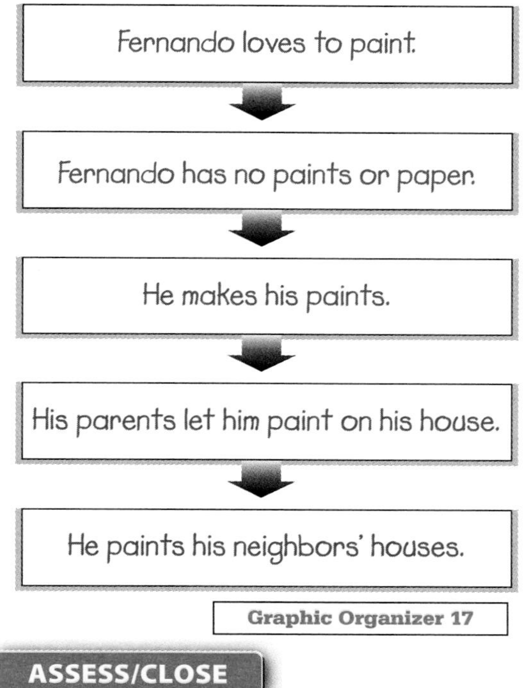

Fernando loves to paint.
Fernando has no paints or paper.
He makes his paints.
His parents let him paint on his house.
He paints his neighbors' houses.

Graphic Organizer 17

ASSESS/CLOSE

Use a Flowchart to Summarize

Have students create a summary flowchart listing events from a familiar story or show. Then have them summarize the story or event.

ALTERNATE TEACHING STRATEGY

SUMMARIZE

For a different approach to teaching this skill, see page T62.

LOOKING AHEAD

Students will apply this skill as they read the next selection, *The Patchwork Quilt*.

Meeting Individual Needs for Comprehension

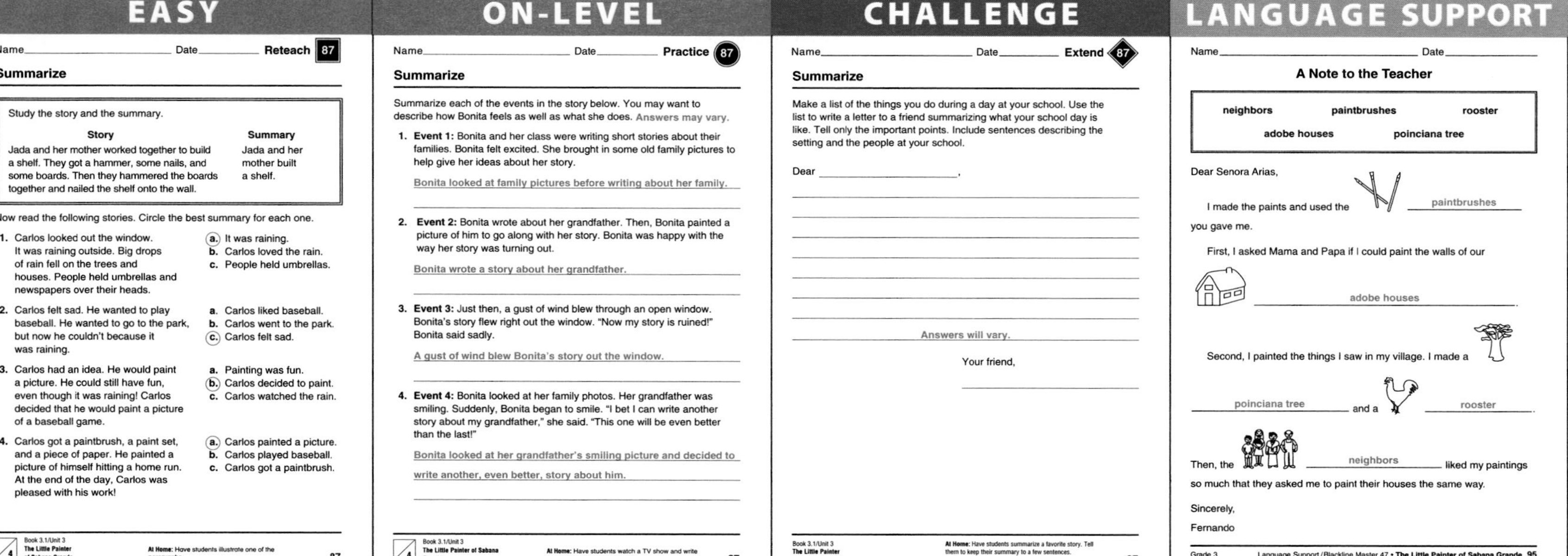

EASY

Name________________ Date__________ **Reteach 87**

Summarize

Study the story and the summary.

Story	Summary
Jada and her mother worked together to build a shelf. They got a hammer, some nails, and some boards. Then they hammered the boards together and nailed the shelf onto the wall.	Jada and her mother built a shelf.

Now read the following stories. Circle the best summary for each one.

1. Carlos looked out the window. It was raining outside. Big drops of rain fell on the trees and houses. People held umbrellas and newspapers over their heads.
   - (a.) It was raining.
   - b. Carlos loved the rain.
   - c. People held umbrellas.
2. Carlos felt sad. He wanted to play baseball. He wanted to go to the park, but now he couldn't because it was raining.
   - a. Carlos liked baseball.
   - b. Carlos went to the park.
   - (c.) Carlos felt sad.
3. Carlos had an idea. He would paint a picture. He could still have fun, even though it was raining! Carlos decided that he would paint a picture of a baseball game.
   - a. Painting was fun.
   - (b.) Carlos decided to paint.
   - c. Carlos watched the rain.
4. Carlos got a paintbrush, a paint set, and a piece of paper. He painted a picture of himself hitting a home run. At the end of the day, Carlos was pleased with his work!
   - (a.) Carlos painted a picture.
   - b. Carlos played baseball.
   - c. Carlos got a paintbrush.

4 Book 3.1/Unit 3 **The Little Painter of Sabana Grande** — **At Home:** Have students illustrate one of the paragraphs. 87

Reteach, 87

ON-LEVEL

Name________________ Date__________ **Practice 87**

Summarize

Summarize each of the events in the story below. You may want to describe how Bonita feels as well as what she does. Answers may vary.

1. **Event 1:** Bonita and her class were writing short stories about their families. Bonita felt excited. She brought in some old family pictures to help give her ideas about her story.
   Bonita looked at family pictures before writing about her family.
2. **Event 2:** Bonita wrote about her grandfather. Then, Bonita painted a picture of him to go along with her story. Bonita was happy with the way her story was turning out.
   Bonita wrote a story about her grandfather.
3. **Event 3:** Just then, a gust of wind blew through an open window. Bonita's story flew right out the window. "Now my story is ruined!" Bonita said sadly.
   A gust of wind blew Bonita's story out the window.
4. **Event 4:** Bonita looked at her family photos. Her grandfather was smiling. Suddenly, Bonita began to smile. "I bet I can write another story about my grandfather," she said. "This one will be even better than the last!"
   Bonita looked at her grandfather's smiling picture and decided to write another, even better, story about him.

4 Book 3.1/Unit 3 **The Little Painter of Sabana Grande** — **At Home:** Have students watch a TV show and write a one-paragraph summary of it. 87

Practice, 87

CHALLENGE

Name________________ Date__________ **Extend 87**

Summarize

Make a list of the things you do during a day at your school. Use the list to write a letter to a friend summarizing what your school day is like. Tell only the important points. Include sentences describing the setting and the people at your school.

Dear ________________,

Answers will vary.

Your friend,

Book 3.1/Unit 3 **The Little Painter of Sabana Grande** — **At Home:** Have students summarize a favorite story. Tell them to keep their summary to a few sentences. 87

Extend, 87

LANGUAGE SUPPORT

Name________________ Date__________

A Note to the Teacher

neighbors **paintbrushes** **rooster** **adobe houses** **poinciana tree**

Dear Senora Arias,

I made the paints and used the paintbrushes you gave me.

First, I asked Mama and Papa if I could paint the walls of our adobe houses.

Second, I painted the things I saw in my village. I made a poinciana tree and a rooster.

Then, the neighbors liked my paintings so much that they asked me to paint their houses the same way.

Sincerely,
Fernando

Grade 3 Language Support/Blackline Master 47 • **The Little Painter of Sabana Grande** 95

Language Support, 95

Review Context Clues

OBJECTIVES

Students will learn how to use context clues to figure out the meaning of content area and specialized vocabulary.

MATERIALS

- **Teaching Chart 72**
- **dictionary**

TEACHING TIP

INSTRUCTIONAL Some of the social studies-related words in this selection are Spanish words. Encourage students who speak Spanish as their native language to participate in explaining the meanings of these words.

PREPARE

Discuss Meaning of Context Clues Explain: Using context clues while you read can help you figure out the meaning of words you do not know. Context clues can be the other words in the sentence, or the sentences before or after the unfamiliar words that give the reader clues to the word's meaning.

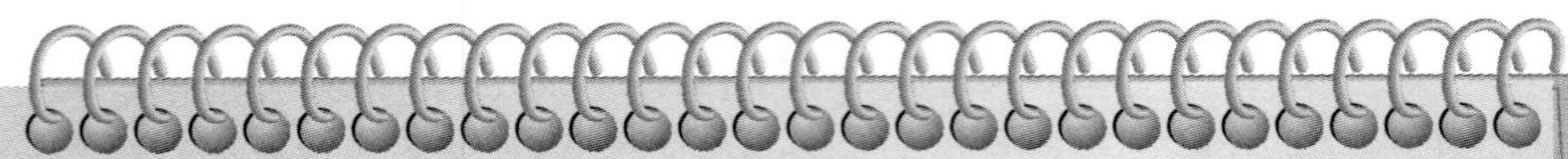

TEACH

Read the Passage and Model the Skill Have students read "Fernando's Home" on **Teaching Chart 72.**

Fernando's Home

There are only seven clay adobe houses in the village of Sabana Grande. The families who live in the village form a community. In other words, they all live in the same area. Sabana Grande is called a rural area because it is in the country, far from any large city.

The Espinos live in the village. Every morning Fernando's mama cooks her family flat, golden, flour tortillas for breakfast. Then Fernando goes to school. Señora Remon, the woman who lives next door to the Espinos, says Fernando's mother is the best cook in the village.

Teaching Chart 72

MODEL I am not sure what *adobe* means. The words that surround *adobe*, "clay" and "houses", give me some clues to the meaning. This helps me understand that *adobe* means "a house made of clay."

Have students explain what a *community* means. Ask them to identify any context clues that can help them better understand its meaning.

PRACTICE

Identify Context Clues for Content-Area Words

First have students circle the following words: *adobe, community, rural, tortillas,* and *Señora*. Next have students underline the context clues that help with word meaning. Ask volunteers to define the words based on the clues. ▶ **Linguistic/Spatial**

ASSESS/CLOSE

Create and Use Context Clues for Unfamiliar Words

Have students write a sentence for each of the following words, using context clues. Then have students exchange papers and underline the context clues in each classmate's sentences. Students may use a dictionary if needed. Have them illustrate one of their classmate's sentences.

mural **palette** **easel** **landscape**

ALTERNATE TEACHING STRATEGY

CONTEXT CLUES

For a different approach to teaching this skill, see page T63.

Meeting Individual Needs for Vocabulary

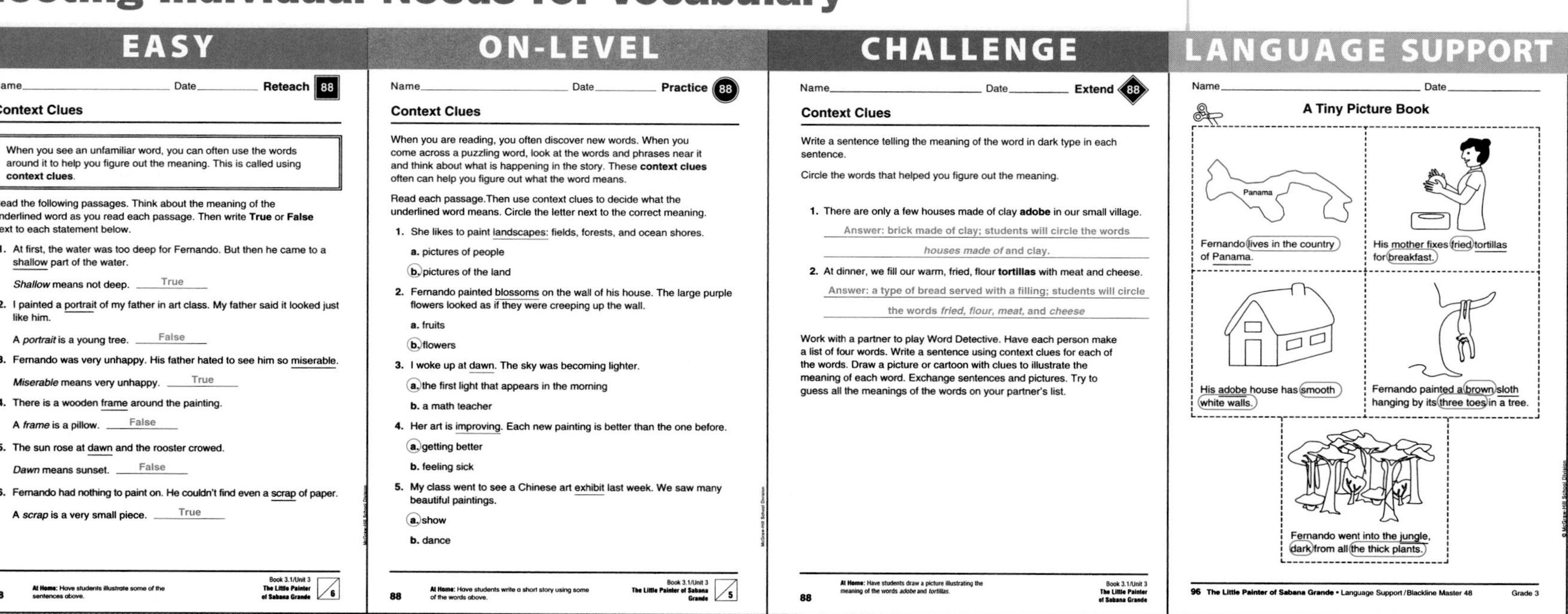

EASY

Name________ Date________ Reteach 88

Context Clues

When you see an unfamiliar word, you can often use the words around it to help you figure out the meaning. This is called using **context clues**.

Read the following passages. Think about the meaning of the underlined word as you read each passage. Then write **True** or **False** next to each statement below.

1. At first, the water was too deep for Fernando. But then he came to a shallow part of the water.
   Shallow means not deep. True
2. I painted a portrait of my father in art class. My father said it looked just like him.
   A *portrait* is a young tree. False
3. Fernando was very unhappy. His father hated to see him so miserable.
   Miserable means very unhappy. True
4. There is a wooden frame around the painting.
   A *frame* is a pillow. False
5. The sun rose at dawn and the rooster crowed.
   Dawn means sunset. False
6. Fernando had nothing to paint on. He couldn't find even a scrap of paper.
   A *scrap* is a very small piece. True

88 **At Home:** Have students illustrate some of the sentences above. Book 3.1/Unit 3 The Little Painter of Sabana Grande 6

ON-LEVEL

Name________ Date________ Practice 88

Context Clues

When you are reading, you often discover new words. When you come across a puzzling word, look at the words and phrases near it and think about what is happening in the story. These **context clues** often can help you figure out what the word means.

Read each passage. Then use context clues to decide what the underlined word means. Circle the letter next to the correct meaning.

1. She likes to paint landscapes: fields, forests, and ocean shores.
   a. pictures of people
   (b.) pictures of the land
2. Fernando painted blossoms on the wall of his house. The large purple flowers looked as if they were creeping up the wall.
   a. fruits
   (b.) flowers
3. I woke up at dawn. The sky was becoming lighter.
   (a.) the first light that appears in the morning
   b. a math teacher
4. Her art is improving. Each new painting is better than the one before.
   (a.) getting better
   b. feeling sick
5. My class went to see a Chinese art exhibit last week. We saw many beautiful paintings.
   (a.) show
   b. dance

88 **At Home:** Have students write a short story using some of the words above. Book 3.1/Unit 3 The Little Painter of Sabana Grande 5

CHALLENGE

Name________ Date________ Extend 88

Context Clues

Write a sentence telling the meaning of the word in dark type in each sentence.

Circle the words that helped you figure out the meaning.

1. There are only a few houses made of clay **adobe** in our small village.
   Answer: brick made of clay; students will circle the words *houses made of* and *clay*.
2. At dinner, we fill our warm, fried, flour **tortillas** with meat and cheese.
   Answer: a type of bread served with a filling; students will circle the words *fried, flour, meat,* and *cheese*

Work with a partner to play Word Detective. Have each person make a list of four words. Write a sentence using context clues for each of the words. Draw a picture or cartoon with clues to illustrate the meaning of each word. Exchange sentences and pictures. Try to guess all the meanings of the words on your partner's list.

88 **At Home:** Have students draw a picture illustrating the meaning of the words *adobe* and *tortillas*. Book 3.1/Unit 3 The Little Painter of Sabana Grande

LANGUAGE SUPPORT

Name________ Date________

A Tiny Picture Book

Panama

Fernando lives in the country of Panama.

His mother fixes fried tortillas for breakfast.

His adobe house has smooth white walls.

Fernando painted a brown sloth hanging by its three toes in a tree.

Fernando went into the jungle, dark from all the thick plants.

96 The Little Painter of Sabana Grande • Language Support/Blackline Master 48 Grade 3

Reteach, 88 | Practice, 88 | Extend, 88 | Language Support, 96

GRAMMAR/SPELLING CONNECTIONS

See the 5-Day Grammar and Usage Plan on present-tense verbs, pages 317M–317N.

See the 5-Day Spelling Plan on words with double consonants, pages 317O–317P.

TECHNOLOGY TIP

A spell-checker won't always find a word that has been used incorrectly, such as a homophone. Use the spell-checker and read over the letter yourself.

Persuasive Writing

Prewrite

WRITE A LETTER Assign students to pretend they are Fernando, and write a letter to a family in Santa Marta to persuade them to let Fernando paint their house. Give three good reasons.

BRAINSTORM IDEAS Have students brainstorm reasons why the family should agree to Fernando's proposal. They will also need to predict the concerns or questions the family might have and address those in their letters.

Strategy: Make a List Have students list good and bad things about having a mural on one's house. Suggest the following:

- List benefits of having one's house painted by Fernando.
- List worries or questions and provide an answer for each one.
- Prioritize the lists ranging from strongest to least strong.

Draft

USE THE LIST In their letters, students should develop the strongest ideas from their prewriting lists. Urge them to use rich descriptions of what they would paint on the house. Give good reasons to convince the family of the beauty that art will add to their home. Letters should include a heading with the writer's address and date, a greeting, and a closing signature.

Revise

SELF-QUESTIONING Ask students to assess their drafts.

- Did I give strong reasons that support Fernando's talent?
- Have I answered potential questions the family might have asked?
- What would improve my letter?

PARTNERS

Have students trade letters with a peer to get another point of view.

Edit/Proofread

CHECK FOR ERRORS Students should reread their letters for spelling, grammar, letter format, and punctuation.

Publish

SHARE THE LETTERS Students can "mail" their letters to one another. Encourage recipients to tell the writers what was most convincing about their letters.

Casa Familia Espino
Sabana Grande
January 8, 20__

Dear Señor and Señora Rosario,

My name is Fernando. I am the boy who painted the houses in Sabana Grande.

I would very much like to paint the houses of Santa Marta. The people in my village think I am a good painter. They say my paintings have made the village brighter.

I hope I can help to brighten your village. My paintings will make your house look special. I will show you sketches of everything before I begin.

Please let me know what you think.

Sincerely,
Fernando Espino
Fernando Espino

Presentation Ideas

ILLUSTRATE THE PLAN Have students make a group model of Sabana Grande's painted homes. Display the model in the school library. ▶ **Viewing/Representing**

MAKE A SPEECH Have students imagine they are presenting their letters at a town meeting. Encourage the audience to ask questions. ▶ **Speaking/Listening**

Consider students' creative efforts, possibly adding a plus (+) for originality, wit, and imagination.

Scoring Rubric

Excellent	Good	Fair	Unsatisfactory
4: The writer • clearly presents benefits of the proposal. • provides supporting details. • presents potential concerns and answers them appropriately.	**3:** The writer • states one or more reasons why the proposal would be a good idea. • adequately organizes supporting details. • addresses potential concerns.	**2:** The writer • presents a proposal, but ideas are not elaborated on. • presents few supporting details. • presents few potential concerns or presents them with unsatisfactory answers.	**1:** The writer • has not clearly presented a proposal. • has provided incomplete or unclear details. • presents no potential concerns.

0: The writer leaves the page blank or fails to respond to the writing task. The student does not address the topic or simply paraphrases the prompt. The response is illegible or incoherent.

COMMUNICATION TIPS

SPEAKING Students should speak loudly enough to be heard and should look at different members of their audience as they speak.

REPRESENTING Have students first close their eyes and visualize how their pictures will look.

LANGUAGE SUPPORT

ESL Pair ESL students with English-fluent partners. Together have them brainstorm reasons for wanting to paint the house in Santa Marta. Suggest they help each other come up with a convincing list of reasons.

PORTFOLIO Invite students to include their letters or another writing project in their portfolios.

Meeting Individual Needs for Writing

EASY

Invitation Have students write an invitation from Fernando asking friends to see his work. Remind them to include place, date, and time.

Talk about what kind of paintings will be seen.

ON-LEVEL

Mural Idea If students could paint a mural to hang at home or in a public building, what would they paint? Have them write a plan to explain the idea and why they chose it. They can make a thumbnail sketch to accompany the written plan.

CHALLENGE

Dialogue Have students write a dialogue in which Fernando persuades his parents to allow him to paint on the house. Fernando's parents should give two or three reasons why he should not paint on the house. Fernando should respond with clear, convincing ideas.

5 Day Grammar and Usage Plan

LANGUAGE SUPPORT

In a group, have each student act out a verb, such as *clap* or *jump*. The rest of the group should say what he or she is doing. Tell students they are using present-tense verbs.

DAILY LANGUAGE ACTIVITIES

Write the Daily Language Activities on the chalkboard each day or use **Transparency 12**. Have students correct the sentences orally, using a verb in the present tense.

Day 1

1. The rooster crow at dawn. crows
2. I milks the cow at eight. milk
3. The boys eats tortillas for breakfast. eat

Day 2

1. Every morning, Fernando hurry to the meadow. hurries
2. He mix his paints carefully. mixes
3. You reads very well. read

Day 3

1. Fernando carry the paint pots. carries
2. His mother worry about him. worries
3. The girl watch Fernando. watches

Day 4

1. The dog bury the bone. buries
2. You writes well. write
3. Trudy wash the brush. washes

Day 5

1. Fernando's teacher teach him to draw. teaches
2. I likes the painting. like
3. A bee buzz near the flowers. buzzes

Daily Language Transparency 12

DAY 1 Introduce the Concept

Oral Warm-Up Read this sentence aloud: He walks by the brook. Ask if it tells about something happening now.

Introduce Present-Tense Verbs The tense of a verb tells when the action takes place. Present the following:

Present-Tense Verbs

- A verb in the **present tense** tells what happens now.
- A present-tense verb must match its subject. This is called **subject-verb agreement**.

Subject	Verb	Example
Singular	Add *-s*	*He* walks
Plural	Do not add *-s*	*They* walk
I or *you*	Do not add *-s*	*I* walk

Present the Daily Language Activity. Then have students make charts like the one above for the verbs *paint* and *sigh*.

Assign the daily Writing Prompt on page 290C.

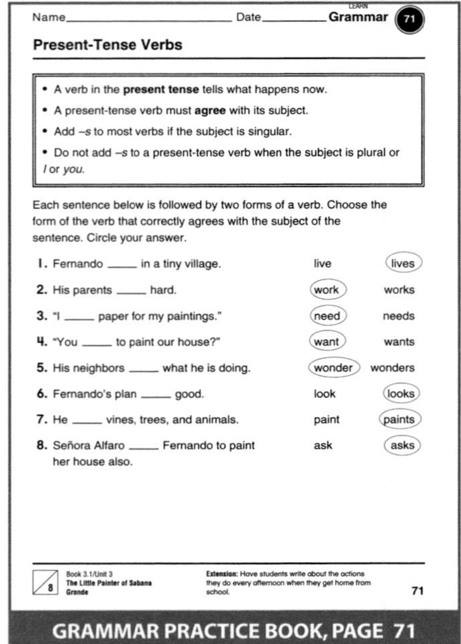

Name________ Date________ LEARN Grammar 71

Present-Tense Verbs

- A verb in the **present tense** tells what happens now.
- A present-tense verb must **agree** with its subject.
- Add –*s* to most verbs if the subject is singular.
- Do not add –*s* to a present-tense verb when the subject is plural or *I* or *you*.

Each sentence below is followed by two forms of a verb. Choose the form of the verb that correctly agrees with the subject of the sentence. Circle your answer.

1. Fernando ____ in a tiny village. live (lives)
2. His parents ____ hard. (work) works
3. "I ____ paper for my paintings." (need) needs
4. "You ____ to paint our house?" (want) wants
5. His neighbors ____ what he is doing. (wonder) wonders
6. Fernando's plan ____ good. look (looks)
7. He ____ vines, trees, and animals. paint (paints)
8. Señora Alfaro ____ Fernando to paint her house also. ask (asks)

8 Book 3.1/Unit 3 The Little Painter of Sabana Grande

Extension: Have students write about the actions they do every afternoon when they get home from school.

71

GRAMMAR PRACTICE BOOK, PAGE 71

DAY 2 Teach the Concept

Review Present-Tense Verbs Ask students what kind of verb is used to tell about something happening now. Have them say sentences using present-tense verbs. Point out when a present-tense verb ends in *-s* and when it does not.

Introduce the *-es* Ending For some verbs *-es* must be added instead of *-s*.

Present-Tense Verbs

- Add *-es* to verbs that end in *s, ch, sh, x,* or *z* if the subject is singular.
- If a verb ends with a consonant and *y*, change the *y* to *i* and add *-es*.

Present the Daily Language Activity. Then have students write four sentences, each with the subject *Fernando* and one of these verbs in singular form: *watch, wish, carry, fix*.

Assign the daily Writing Prompt on page 290C.

Name________ Date________ LEARN AND PRACTICE Grammar 72

Present-Tense Verbs

- A verb in the **present tense** tells what happens now.
- A present-tense verb must **agree** with its subject.
- Add –*es* to verbs that end in *s, ch, sh, x,* or *z* if the subject is singular.
- Change *y* to *i* and add –*es* to verbs that end with a consonant and *y*.
- Do not add –*es* to a present-tense verb when the subject is plural or *I* or *you*.
  He fishes. The paint dries.
  They fish. The dishes dry.

For each verb below, write the form that agrees with the subject given.

1. hurry Fernando hurries.
2. catch We catch.
3. brush They brush.
4. fix Señor Espino fixes.
5. carry You carry.
6. bless Señora Arias blesses.
7. wax The painter waxes.
8. search I search.

72

Extension: Have students write three or four sentences telling the story of the little painter in the present tense.

Book 3.1/Unit 3 The Little Painter of Sabana Grande 8

GRAMMAR PRACTICE BOOK, PAGE 72

Present-Tense Verbs

DAY 3 Review and Practice

Learn from the Literature Review present-tense verbs. Read the first sentence on page 295 of *The Little Painter of Sabana Grande*:

> **High in the mountains of Panama lies the village of Sabana Grande.**

Point out that in this sentence the subject comes after the verb, and help students identify the subject, *village*. Then have them identify the verb and explain its agreement with the subject. (It ends in *-s* to match the singular noun subject.)

Form Present-Tense Verbs Present the Daily Language Activity and have students correct the sentences orally.

Have students suggest verbs that end in *s*, *ch*, *sh*, *x*, and *z*. Then help them to make a chart showing how these verbs change to agree with their subjects.

Assign the daily Writing Prompt on page 290D.

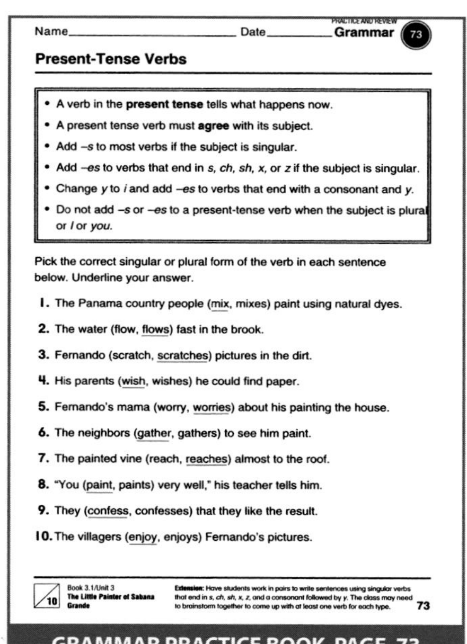

Name________________ Date________ PRACTICE AND REVIEW Grammar 73

Present-Tense Verbs

- A verb in the **present tense** tells what happens now.
- A present tense verb must **agree** with its subject.
- Add *–s* to most verbs if the subject is singular.
- Add *–es* to verbs that end in *s, ch, sh, x,* or *z* if the subject is singular.
- Change *y* to *i* and add *–es* to verbs that end with a consonant and *y*.
- Do not add *–s* or *–es* to a present-tense verb when the subject is plural or *I* or *you*.

Pick the correct singular or plural form of the verb in each sentence below. Underline your answer.

1. The Panama country people (mix, mixes) paint using natural dyes.
2. The water (flow, flows) fast in the brook.
3. Fernando (scratch, scratches) pictures in the dirt.
4. His parents (wish, wishes) he could find paper.
5. Fernando's mama (worry, worries) about his painting the house.
6. The neighbors (gather, gathers) to see him paint.
7. The painted vine (reach, reaches) almost to the roof.
8. "You (paint, paints) very well," his teacher tells him.
9. They (confess, confesses) that they like the result.
10. The villagers (enjoy, enjoys) Fernando's pictures.

10 Book 3.1/Unit 3 The Little Painter of Sabana Grande — **Extension:** Have students work in pairs to write sentences using singular verbs that end in *s, ch, sh, x, z,* and a consonant followed by *y*. The class may need to brainstorm together to come up with at least one verb for each type. 73

GRAMMAR PRACTICE BOOK, PAGE 73

DAY 4 Review and Practice

Review Present-Tense Verbs Write the verbs from the Daily Language Activity for Days 1 through 3 on the chalkboard in infinitive form (with no endings). Ask students to explain how to make each verb agree with a singular noun subject. Then present the Daily Language Activity for Day 4.

Mechanics and Usage Before students begin the daily Writing Prompt on page 290D, review abbreviations. Display and discuss:

Abbreviations

- An **abbreviation** is a shortened form of a word.
- An abbreviation begins with a capital letter and ends with a period.
- Abbreviate most titles of people before names.

Assign the daily Writing Prompt on page 290D.

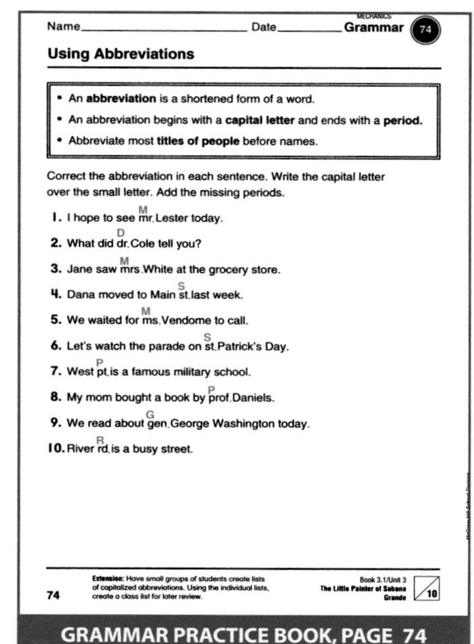

Name________________ Date________ MECHANICS Grammar 74

Using Abbreviations

- An **abbreviation** is a shortened form of a word.
- An abbreviation begins with a **capital letter** and ends with a **period.**
- Abbreviate most **titles of people** before names.

Correct the abbreviation in each sentence. Write the capital letter over the small letter. Add the missing periods.

1. I hope to see mr.Lester today. (M)
2. What did dr.Cole tell you? (D)
3. Jane saw mrs.White at the grocery store. (M)
4. Dana moved to Main st.last week. (S)
5. We waited for ms.Vendome to call. (M)
6. Let's watch the parade on st.Patrick's Day. (S)
7. West pt.is a famous military school. (P)
8. My mom bought a book by prof.Daniels. (P)
9. We read about gen.George Washington today. (G)
10. River rd.is a busy street. (R)

74 **Extension:** Have small groups of students create lists of capitalized abbreviations. Using the individual lists, create a class list for later review. — Book 3.1/Unit 3 The Little Painter of Sabana Grande 10

GRAMMAR PRACTICE BOOK, PAGE 74

DAY 5 Assess and Reteach

Assess Use the Daily Language Activity and page 75 of the **Grammar Practice Book** for assessment.

Reteach Have students write each rule about present-tense verbs from the grammar concepts lesson on an index card.

For each verb in the Daily Language Activity sentences, have students find the rule that it matches. Then ask students to use these verbs in new sentences. Have them write the new sentences on the index card with the rule they are illustrating and then pin the cards to the bulletin board.

Use page 76 of the **Grammar Practice Book** for additional reteaching.

Assign the daily Writing Prompt on page 290D.

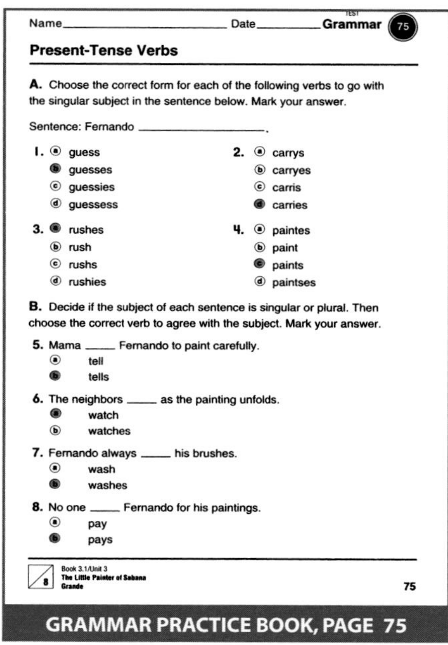

Name________________ Date________ TEST Grammar 75

Present-Tense Verbs

A. Choose the correct form for each of the following verbs to go with the singular subject in the sentence below. Mark your answer.

Sentence: Fernando ______________.

1. ⓐ guess ● guesses ⓒ guessies ⓓ guessess
2. ⓐ carrys ⓑ carryes ⓒ carris ● carries
3. ● rushes ⓑ rush ⓒ rushs ⓓ rushies
4. ⓐ paintes ⓑ paint ● paints ⓓ paintses

B. Decide if the subject of each sentence is singular or plural. Then choose the correct verb to agree with the subject. Mark your answer.

5. Mama ____ Fernando to paint carefully. ⓐ tell ● tells
6. The neighbors ____ as the painting unfolds. ● watch ⓑ watches
7. Fernando always ____ his brushes. ⓐ wash ● washes
8. No one ____ Fernando for his paintings. ⓐ pay ● pays

8 Book 3.1/Unit 3 The Little Painter of Sabana Grande 75

GRAMMAR PRACTICE BOOK, PAGE 75

GRAMMAR PRACTICE BOOK, PAGE 76

5 Day Spelling Plan

LANGUAGE SUPPORT

Ask students to explain how the way they form their mouth and lips to make each consonant sound enables them to tell the difference between similar sounds.

DICTATION SENTENCES

Spelling Words

1. That new car is very small.
2. Use a ladder to go up to the window.
3. A little bird walked on the shore.
4. No one knows what could happen.
5. The wheels on the toy car are made of rubber.
6. When does your father cut the grass?
7. Tie a ribbon on the birthday bike.
8. There could be a test on that lesson.
9. Her jokes are silly.
10. I like butter on my toast.
11. I have to go eat my supper.
12. I am awake in the middle of the night.
13. Is it possible for you to carry my books?
14. Her hobby is playing music with her friends.
15. She was unhappy because her grades were not high.

Challenge Words

16. The plant has pretty blossoms.
17. The sky at dawn was pretty.
18. He had an imaginary friend.
19. Her cold made her miserable.
20. The creek is very shallow.

DAY 1 Pretest

Assess Prior Knowledge Use the Dictation Sentences at left and **Spelling Practice Book** page 71 for the pretest. Allow students to correct their own papers. If students have trouble, have partners give each other a midweek test on Day 3. Students who require a modified list may be tested on the first eight words.

Spelling Words		Challenge Words
1. **small**	9. silly	16. **blossoms**
2. ladder	10. butter	17. **dawn**
3. **little**	11. supper	18. **imaginary**
4. happen	12. **middle**	19. **miserable**
5. rubber	13. possible	20. **shallow**
6. **grass**	14. hobby	
7. ribbon	15. **unhappy**	
8. lesson		

*Note: Words in **dark type** are from the story.*

Word Study On page 72 of the **Spelling Practice Book** are word study steps and an at-home activity.

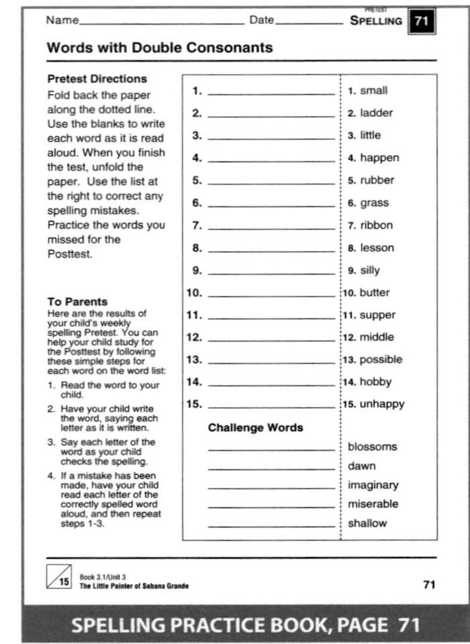

Name________ Date______ PRETEST SPELLING 71

Words with Double Consonants

Pretest Directions
Fold back the paper along the dotted line. Use the blanks to write each word as it is read aloud. When you finish the test, unfold the paper. Use the list at the right to correct any spelling mistakes. Practice the words you missed for the Posttest.

To Parents
Here are the results of your child's weekly spelling Pretest. You can help your child study for the Posttest by following these simple steps for each word on the word list:
1. Read the word to your child.
2. Have your child write the word, saying each letter as it is written.
3. Say each letter of the word as your child checks the spelling.
4. If a mistake has been made, have your child read each letter of the correctly spelled word aloud, and then repeat steps 1-3.

1. ______ 1. small
2. ______ 2. ladder
3. ______ 3. little
4. ______ 4. happen
5. ______ 5. rubber
6. ______ 6. grass
7. ______ 7. ribbon
8. ______ 8. lesson
9. ______ 9. silly
10. ______ 10. butter
11. ______ 11. supper
12. ______ 12. middle
13. ______ 13. possible
14. ______ 14. hobby
15. ______ 15. unhappy

Challenge Words
______ blossoms
______ dawn
______ imaginary
______ miserable
______ shallow

15 Book 3.1/Unit 3 The Little Painter of Sabana Grande 71

SPELLING PRACTICE BOOK, PAGE 71

WORD STUDY STEPS AND ACTIVITY, PAGE 72

DAY 2 Explore the Pattern

Sort and Spell Words Explain that each Spelling Word contains a consonant sound spelled by two of the same letter, either in the middle or at the end of the word. Have students read the Spelling Words aloud and sort them, according to the double consonants they contain.

Syllable Patterns Ask students to divide the two-syllable words on the list into syllables. Remind them that words with double consonants in the middle are divided between the two consonants.

tt	bb	pp
little	rubber	happen
butter	ribbon	supper
	hobby	unhappy

ll	dd	ss
small	ladder	grass
silly	middle	lesson
		possible

Name________ Date______ EXPLORE THE PATTERN SPELLING 73

Words with Double Consonants

small	happen	ribbon	butter	possible
ladder	rubber	lesson	supper	hobby
little	grass	silly	middle	unhappy

Pattern Power
Write the spelling words that have these spelling patterns.

tt
1. little
2. butter

ll
3. small
4. silly

bb
5. rubber
6. ribbon
7. hobby

dd
8. ladder
9. middle

pp
10. happen
11. supper
12. unhappy

ss
13. grass
14. lesson
15. possible

Rhyme Time
Write the spelling word that rhymes with each word.

16. brass grass
17. tall small
18. chilly silly
19. upper supper
20. lobby hobby
21. fiddle middle
22. whittle little
23. sadder ladder
24. flutter butter

24 Book 3.1/Unit 3 The Little Painter of Sabana Grande 73

SPELLING PRACTICE BOOK, PAGE 73

CD-ROM

Words with Double Consonants

DAY 3 Practice and Extend

Word Meaning: Prefixes Remind students that a prefix is a word part added to the beginning of a word that changes the meaning of the word. Ask students which spelling word contains a prefix. (*unhappy*) Ask students to recall what the prefix *un-* means. (not) What does *unhappy* mean? (not happy) Have students add *un-* to these words: *clear, hurt, easy, lucky, sure*. Ask them what each new word means.

Glossary Have students:

- look up each Challenge Word in the Glossary and find which ones have synonyms listed.
- write each synonym they found in the Glossary next to the appropriate Challenge Word.

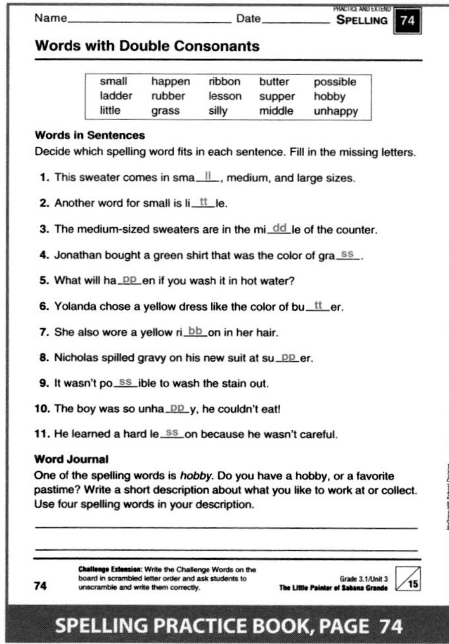

Name________________ Date________ PRACTICE AND EXTEND **SPELLING 74**

Words with Double Consonants

small	happen	ribbon	butter	possible
ladder	rubber	lesson	supper	hobby
little	grass	silly	middle	unhappy

Words in Sentences

Decide which spelling word fits in each sentence. Fill in the missing letters.

1. This sweater comes in sma_ll_, medium, and large sizes.
2. Another word for small is li_tt_le.
3. The medium-sized sweaters are in the mi_dd_le of the counter.
4. Jonathan bought a green shirt that was the color of gra_ss_.
5. What will ha_pp_en if you wash it in hot water?
6. Yolanda chose a yellow dress like the color of bu_tt_er.
7. She also wore a yellow ri_bb_on in her hair.
8. Nicholas spilled gravy on his new suit at su_pp_er.
9. It wasn't po_ss_ible to wash the stain out.
10. The boy was so unha_pp_y, he couldn't eat!
11. He learned a hard le_ss_on because he wasn't careful.

Word Journal

One of the spelling words is *hobby*. Do you have a hobby, or a favorite pastime? Write a short description about what you like to work at or collect. Use four spelling words in your description.

Challenge Extension: Write the Challenge Words on the board in scrambled letter order and ask students to unscramble and write them correctly.

74 Grade 3.1/Unit 3 The Little Painter of Sabana Grande 15

SPELLING PRACTICE BOOK, PAGE 74

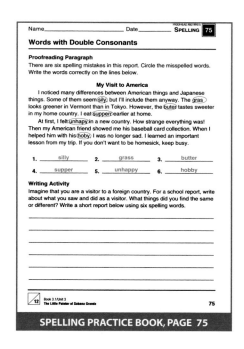

DAY 4 Proofread and Write

Proofread Sentences Write these sentences on the chalkboard, including the misspelled words. Ask students to proofread, circling incorrect spellings and writing the correct spellings. There are two spelling errors in each sentence.

Is it posible to eat fruit for super? (possible, supper)

He used a littel lader to reach the roof. (little, ladder)

She tied a smal ribbin on the toy. (small, ribbon)

Have students create additional sentences with errors for partners to correct.

WRITING Have students use as many Spelling Words as possible in the daily Writing Prompt on page 290D. Remind students to proofread their writing for errors in spelling, punctuation, and grammar.

Name________________ Date________ PROOFREAD AND WRITE **SPELLING 75**

Words with Double Consonants

Proofreading Paragraph

There are six spelling mistakes in this report. Circle the misspelled words. Write the words correctly on the lines below.

My Visit to America

I noticed many differences between American things and Japanese things. Some of them seem sily, but I'll include them anyway. The gras looks greener in Vermont than in Tokyo. However, the buter tastes sweeter in my home country. I eat superr earlier at home.

At first, I felt unhapy in a new country. How strange everything was! Then my American friend showed me his baseball card collection. When I helped him with his hoby, I was no longer sad. I learned an important lesson from my trip. If you don't want to be homesick, keep busy.

1. silly 2. grass 3. butter
4. supper 5. unhappy 6. hobby

Writing Activity

Imagine that you are a visitor to a foreign country. For a school report, write about what you saw and did as a visitor. What things did you find the same or different? Write a short report below using six spelling words.

12 Book 3.1/Unit 3 The Little Painter of Sabana Grande 75

SPELLING PRACTICE BOOK, PAGE 75

DAY 5 Assess and Reteach

Assess Students' Knowledge Use page 76 of the **Spelling Practice Book** or the Dictation Sentences on page 317O for the posttest.

Personal Word List Have students JOURNAL keep a list of "middle" words—those with double consonants in the middle—in their journals. Have them review previous lessons to find words that may fit in the category. Students should refer to their lists during future writing activities.

Name________________ Date________ POSTTEST **SPELLING 76**

Words with Double Consonants

Look at the words in each set. One word in each set is spelled correctly. Use a pencil to color in the circle in front of that word. Before you begin, look at the sample sets of words. Sample A has been done for you. Do Sample B by yourself. When you are sure you know what to do, you may go on with the rest of the page.

Sample A: (A) peble (B) pebble (C) pebbal (D) pebul

Sample B: (E) slipper (F) sliper (G) slippur (H) slyper

1. (A) unhappy (B) unhappey (C) unnhapy (D) unhapey
2. (E) ruber (F) rubbur (G) rubbor (H) rubber
3. (A) sily (B) siley (C) silley (D) silly
4. (E) midle (F) middel (G) middle (H) mittle
5. (A) gras (B) grasss (C) grasse (D) grass
6. (E) ribin (F) ribbon (G) ribben (H) ribban
7. (A) butter (B) budder (C) buttar (D) buttor
8. (E) hobey (F) hobby (G) hobbey (H) hobbie
9. (A) suppre (B) suppor (C) supar (D) supper
10. (E) smaul (F) smawll (G) smal (H) small
11. (A) lader (B) ladder (C) lattar (D) laddar
12. (E) leson (F) lesson (G) lescon (H) lesun
13. (A) posible (B) possibul (C) possible (D) possuble
14. (E) happun (F) hapin (G) happn (H) happen
15. (A) litel (B) littul (C) little (D) litle

76 Grade 3.1/Unit 3 The Little Painter of Sabana Grande 15

SPELLING PRACTICE BOOK, PAGE 76

Lesson Overview

The Patchwork Quilt

Selection Summary Students will read about how Grandma makes a patchwork quilt and why this quilt becomes a family treasure.

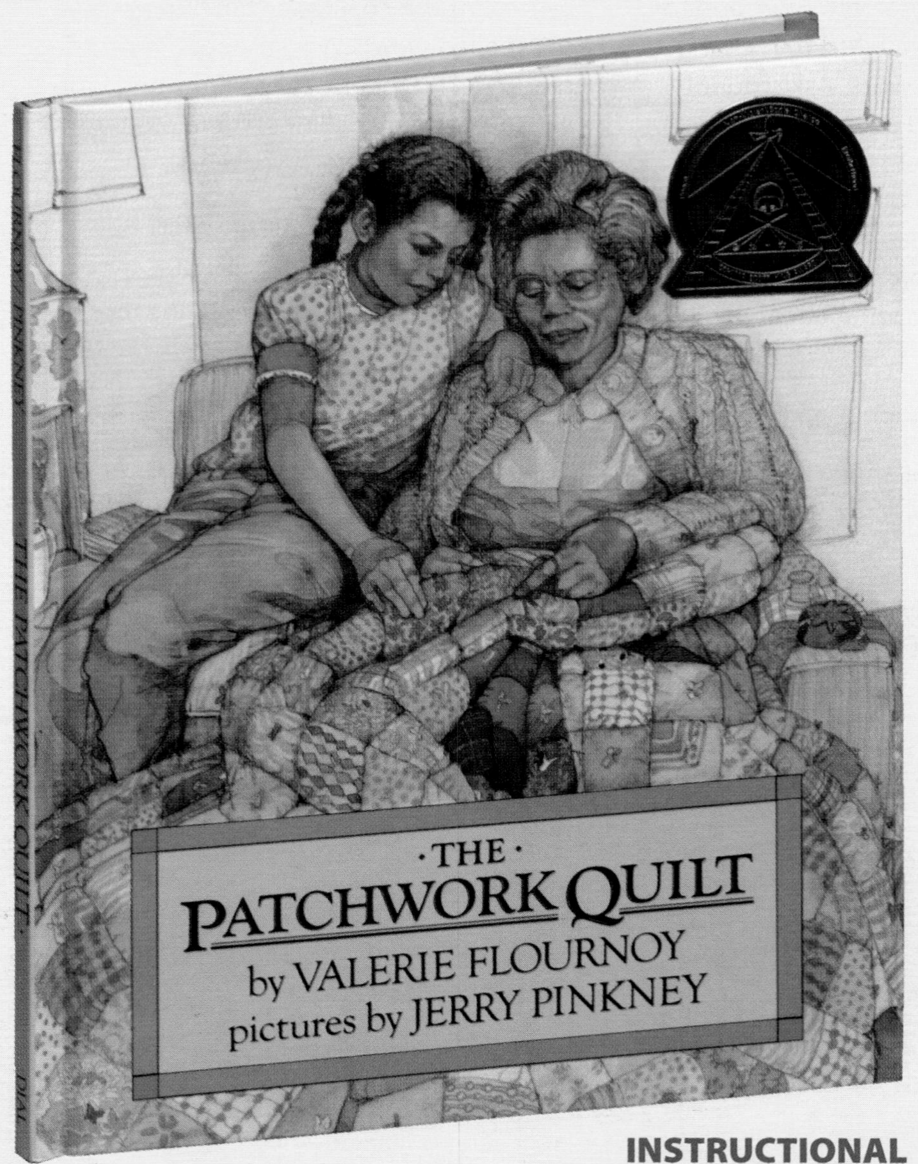

Listening Library Audiocassette

INSTRUCTIONAL
Pages 320–345

About the Author Valerie Flournoy says that her memories of the fun times she had with her grandma while she was growing up motivated her to write *The Patchwork Quilt*. She hopes that this tribute to her Grandma will help children to develop a deeper respect for their own family histories.

About the Illustrator Jerry Pinkney won the Coretta Scott King Award for his illustrations in *The Patchwork Quilt*. Jerry Pinkney says that he always challenges himself in his art. He adds that facing and resolving artistic problems helps bring a freshness to his work.

Resources for
Meeting Individual Needs

LEVELED BOOKS

EASY
Pages 349A, 349D

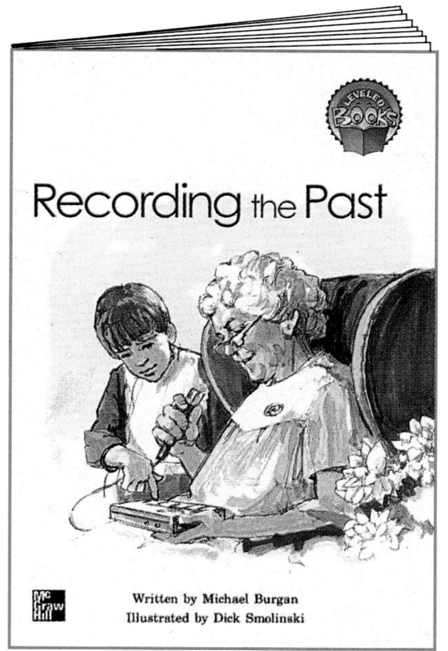

INDEPENDENT
Pages 349B, 349D

Take-Home version available

CHALLENGE
Pages 349C, 349D

LEVELED PRACTICE

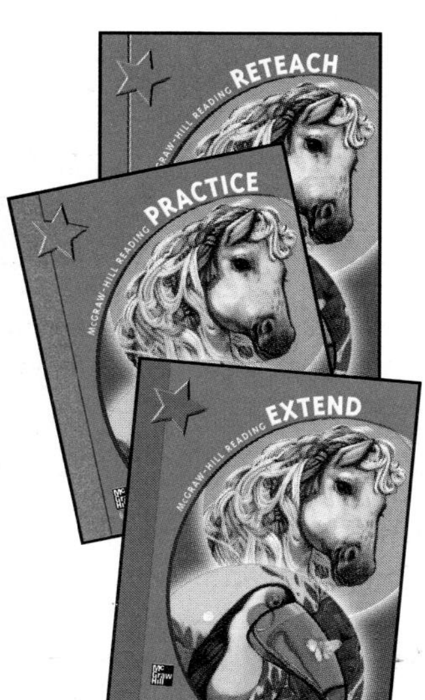

Reteach, 89–95
blackline masters with reteaching opportunities for each assessed skill

Practice, 89–95
workbook with Take-Home stories and practice opportunites for each assessed skill and story comprehension

Extend, 89–95
blackline masters that offer challenge activities for each assessed skill

ADDITIONAL RESOURCES

- **Language Support Book** 97–104
- **Take-Home Story, Practice** p. 90a
- **Alternate Teaching Strategies** T60–T66
- **Selected Quizzes Prepared by** 

Phonics CD-ROM Provides extra phonics support.

interNET CONNECTION Research & Inquiry ideas. Visit *www.mhschool.com/reading.*

Suggested Lesson Planner

Available on CD-ROM

READING AND LANGUAGE ARTS	 DAY 1  *Focus on Reading and Skills*	 DAY 2 *Read the Literature*
• Comprehension • Vocabulary • Phonics/Decoding • Study Skills • Listening, Speaking, Viewing, Representing	**Read Aloud and Motivate,** 318E "Basket" **Develop Visual Literacy,** 318/319 ☑ **Introduce Make Inferences,** 320A–320B **Teaching Chart 73** **Reteach, Practice, Extend,** 89	**Build Background,** 320C Develop Oral Language **Vocabulary,** 320D ***anxious*** ***costume*** ***gazed*** ***attic*** ***examined*** ***pattern*** **Teaching Chart 74** **Word Building Manipulative Cards** **Reteach, Practice, Extend,** 90  **Read the Selection,** 320–345 Guided Instruction ☑ Make Inferences ☑ Summarize **Minilessons,** 331, 333, 339, 341 **Cultural Perspectives,** 332
• Curriculum Connections	 **Fine Arts,** 318/319	 **Social Studies,** 320C
• Writing	 **Writing Prompt:** Write a short paragraph about a tradition in your family or a family that you know. Tell how the tradition started. Be sure to write your paragraph in the past tense.	 **Writing Prompt:** Think of a beautiful piece of art you have seen, such as a painting, sculpture, or photograph. Write a poem telling how the art made you feel.  **Journal Writing,** 345 Quick-Write
• Grammar	**Introduce the Concept: Past-Tense Verbs,** 349M Daily Language Activity 1. Tanya talk with Grandma earlier. talked 2. Grandma rest in her chair yesterday. rested 3. She look for patches before Tanya came. looked **Grammar Practice Book,** 77	**Teach the Concept: Past-Tense Verbs,** 349M Daily Language Activity 1. Mama hurryed to make breakfast. hurried 2. Then she plan the rest of the day. planned 3. She love seeing Tanya with Grandma. loved **Grammar Practice Book,** 78
• Spelling	**Pretest: Words with /ou/ and /oi/,** 349O **Spelling Practice Book,** 77–78	**Explore the Pattern: Words with /ou/ and /oi/,** 349O **Spelling Practice Book,** 79

leeting
ndividual
eeds

 = **Skill Assessed in Unit Test**

DAY 3 Read the Literature

Reread for Fluency, 344

Story Questions, 346
Reteach, Practice, Extend, 91
Story Activities, 347

Study Skill, 348
Graphic Aids
Teaching Chart 75
Reteach, Practice, Extend, 92

Test Power, 349

Read the Leveled Books,
Guided Reading
/ou/ and /oi/
Make Inferences
Instructional Vocabulary
 CD-ROM

Activity: Science, 324; Social Studies, 330

Writing Prompt: Write a short story about a time when an older person and young person worked together on a project.

Writing Process: Persuasive Writing, 349K
Prewrite, Draft

Review and Practice: Past-Tense Verbs, 349N
Daily Language Activity
1. Tanya carryed the material. carried
2. Grandma reach for the cloth. reached
3. Each one grabed a pair of scissors. grabbed

Grammar Practice Book, 79

Practice and Extend: Words with /ou/ and /oi/, 349P
Spelling Practice Book, 80

DAY 4 Build Skills

 **Read the Leveled Books and Self-Selected Books**

Review Make Inferences, 349E–349F
Teaching Chart 76
Reteach, Practice, Extend, 93
Language Support, 102

Review Main Idea, 349G–349H
Teaching Chart 77
Reteach, Practice, Extend, 94
Language Support, 103

 Math, 338

Writing Prompt: Choose three people in your family or three of your friends. Tell how they are alike and how they are different.

Writing Process: Persuasive Writing, 349K
Revise

Meeting Individual Needs for Writing, 349L

Review and Practice: Past-Tense Verbs, 349N
Daily Language Activity
1. Mama join in the work last night. joined
2. They add to the pile of patches. added
3. Tanya like watching the pile grow. liked

Grammar Practice Book, 80

Proofread and Write: Words with /ou/ and /oi/, 349P
Spelling Practice Book, 81

DAY 5 Build Skills

 **Read Self-Selected Books**

Introduce Multiple-Meaning Words, 349I–349J
Teaching Chart 78
Reteach, Practice, Extend, 95
Language Support, 104

Listening, Speaking, Viewing, Representing, 349L
Create a Collage
Have a Debate

Minilessons, 331, 333, 341

Phonics Review,
/ou/ and /oi/, 339
Phonics/Phonemic Awareness
Practice Book, 61–64
 CD-ROM

 Art, 340

Writing Prompt: Think of the best costume you have ever seen, either for a holiday such as Halloween, or for a play. Write a short paragraph describing it. Use past-tense verbs.

Writing Process: Persuasive Writing, 349K
Edit/Proofread, Publish

Assess and Reteach: Past-Tense Verbs, 349N
Daily Language Activity
1. Tanya hope they would finish the quilt soon. hoped
2. Mama tryed to work faster. tried
3. Tanya smile when they were done. smiled

Grammar Practice Book, 81–82

Assess and Reteach: Words with /ou/ and /oi/, 349P
Spelling Practice Book, 82

Language Arts

Read Aloud and Motivate

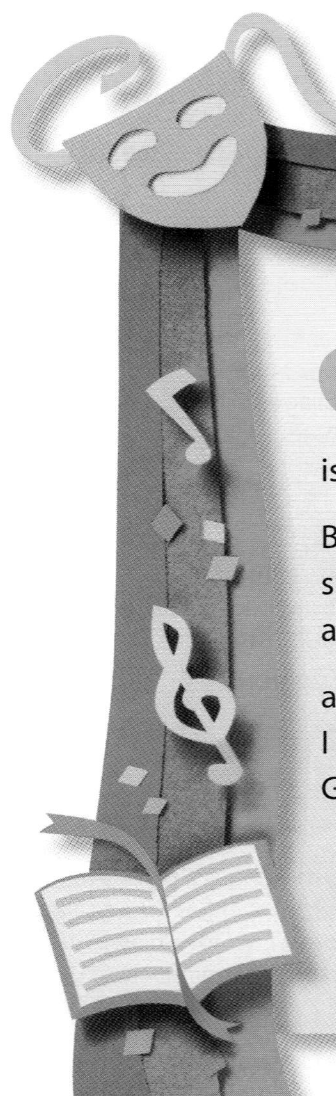

Basket

a poem by
Myra Cohn Livingston

Grandmother's basket
of ribbon and lace
is kept in a high-up closet place.

But when I go over
she'll take it out
and let me rummage all about

and find materials.
I can choose whatever
Grandmother doesn't use

when she knits an afghan
or sews a gown.
So, whenever I see her take it down

I think of the things
my dolls could wear
of whatever my grandmother has
to spare.

Oral Comprehension

LISTENING AND SPEAKING Ask students to think about the characters in the poem as you read aloud. When you have finished, ask, "How would you describe the character of the grandmother?" Then ask, "How would you describe the grandchild in the poem? What clues in the text helped you understand these characters?" Ask students to say what they liked about the poem.

Activity Have students make pictures using yarn. Encourage them to draw simple outlines on a piece of oaktag. Help them put glue on the outline and press yarn onto the glue to create a shape. Invite students to experiment by pulling yarn apart to make wider lines or to fill in areas.

▶ **Visual/Kinesthetic**

Develop Visual Literacy

Works of Art

Anthology pages 318–319

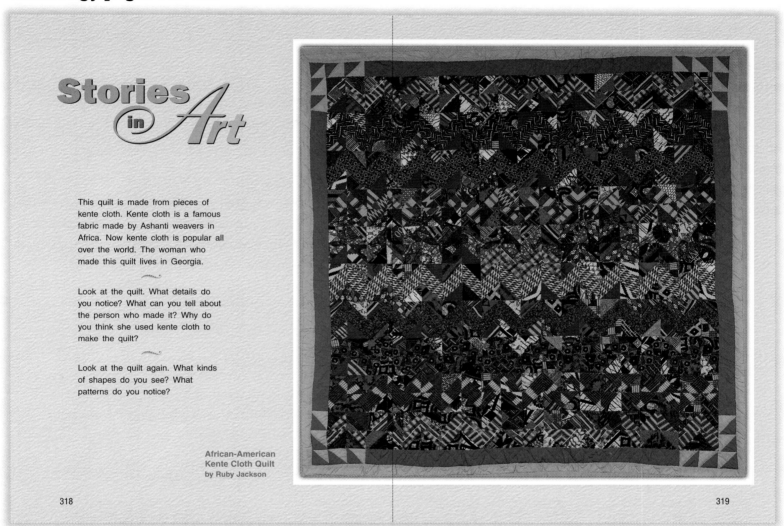

Stories in Art

This quilt is made from pieces of kente cloth. Kente cloth is a famous fabric made by Ashanti weavers in Africa. Now kente cloth is popular all over the world. The woman who made this quilt lives in Georgia.

Look at the quilt. What details do you notice? What can you tell about the person who made it? Why do you think she used kente cloth to make the quilt?

Look at the quilt again. What kinds of shapes do you see? What patterns do you notice?

African-American Kente Cloth Quilt
by Ruby Jackson

318

319

Objective: Make Inferences

VIEWING This quilt reflects African American heritage with the use of Kente cloth made famous by Ashanti weavers in Africa. Have students note the border pattern and internal patterns. What do these patterns suggest? Ask students to close their eyes and try to recall the colors of the quilt. Read the page with students, encouraging individual interpretations of the quilt.

Ask students to support the inferences they make. For example:

- The zigzag pattern suggests movement.
- The bold colors suggest a celebration.

REPRESENTING Have students create their own quilts by cutting and pasting colored construction-paper shapes to background squares. Have students make up names for their quilts that go with the colors and patterns they use.

OBJECTIVES

Students will make and explain inferences about characters.

Introduce Make Inferences

TEACHING TIP

INSTRUCTIONAL Provide examples of drawings, fabric cutouts, and photo transfers from various patchwork quilts. Have each student create something for a class patchwork quilt. Discuss what each item for the quilt tells about.

PREPARE

Discuss Clues to Character Ask students to imagine they see a girl with ice skates over her shoulder. Ask: Where might she be going? What makes you think that?

TEACH

Define Making Inferences State: An author does not always tell you directly how characters feel or what they are thinking. But you can use what the author does tell you, the illustrations, and what you know from your own experiences to discover this information. This is called making inferences.

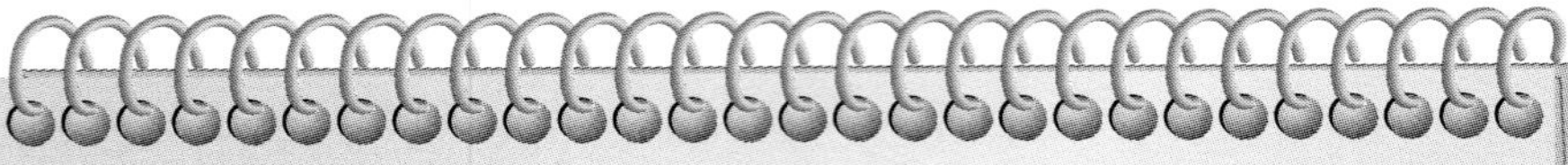

The Photo Album

Tracy was looking for some wrapping paper in the hall closet when she found a photo album. It was a big green book with worn leather covers. What could it be? She was thrilled. "What's this?" she asked her mother.

"Oh, nothing," her mother yawned. "Just an old book with some photographs in it."

"Photographs?" said Tracy. She opened the book. Inside were pages and pages of old black-and-white photographs. She pointed to one of a young girl. "Is that you, Mom?" she asked, amazed.

Teaching Chart 73

Read "The Photo Album" and Model the Skill Display **Teaching Chart 73**. Have students pay attention to clues about the characters as the story is read.

MODEL The title tells me right away that the story will be about a photo album. The author doesn't say so directly, but Tracy and her mother seem to have different feelings about the photo album.

Make Inferences Have students underline clues that help them make inferences about the different feelings Tracy and her mother have about the photo album.

PRACTICE

Create a Make and Explain Inferences Chart

Start a Make and Explain Inferences chart. Have students make inferences about the different feelings Tracy and her mother have about the photo album. Help them begin filling in the chart and have partners finish it. ▶ **Interpersonal/Logical**

MAKE INFERENCE	EXPLAIN INFERENCE
Tracy is excited about the photo album.	She wonders what it is and opens it up.
Her mother is not interested in the photo album.	She tells Tracy it is "nothing." She is bored by it.

ASSESS/CLOSE

Make Inferences About Characters

Ask students what other inferences they might make about either character. (Tracy is curious. She is interested to discover more about her family's history. She is excitable.)

Ask: Suppose Tracy visited her grandfather. What questions might she ask him? (Where was he born? When was he born? What was his childhood like?)

Meeting Individual Needs for Comprehension

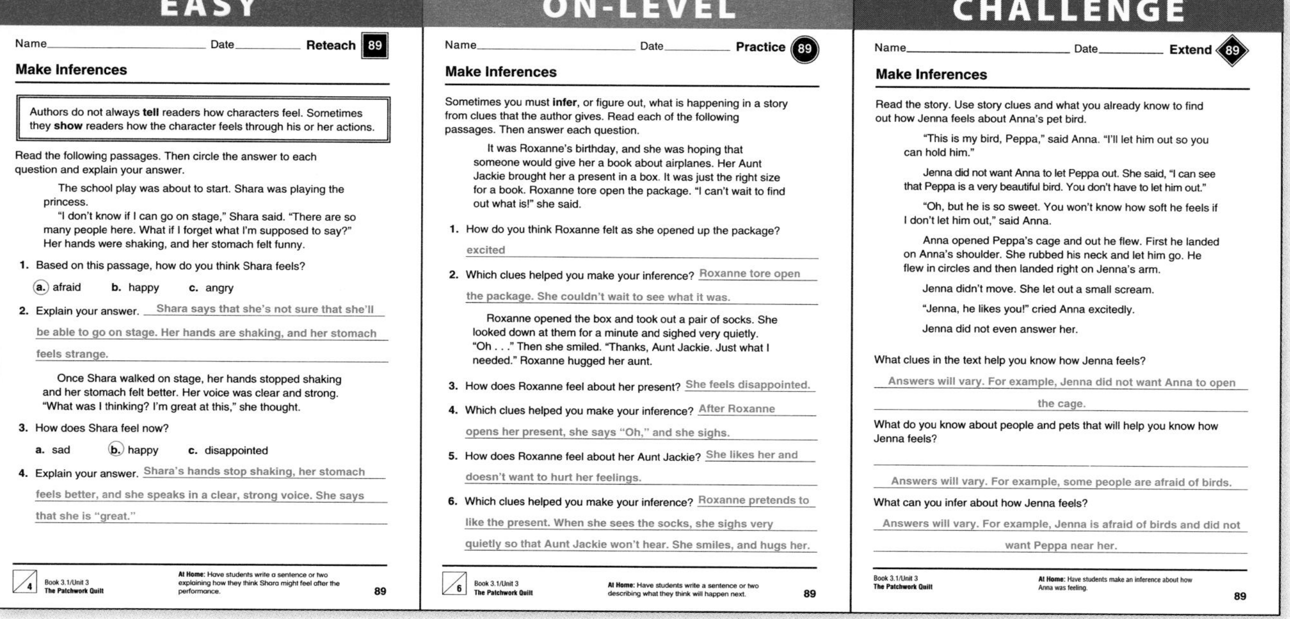

EASY

Name________ Date______ Reteach 89

Make Inferences

Authors do not always **tell** readers how characters feel. Sometimes they **show** readers how the character feels through his or her actions.

Read the following passages. Then circle the answer to each question and explain your answer.

The school play was about to start. Shara was playing the princess.

"I don't know if I can go on stage," Shara said. "There are so many people here. What if I forget what I'm supposed to say?" Her hands were shaking, and her stomach felt funny.

1. Based on this passage, how do you think Shara feels?
   (a.) afraid b. happy c. angry
2. Explain your answer. Shara says that she's not sure that she'll be able to go on stage. Her hands are shaking, and her stomach feels strange.

Once Shara walked on stage, her hands stopped shaking and her stomach felt better. Her voice was clear and strong. "What was I thinking? I'm great at this," she thought.

3. How does Shara feel now?
   a. sad (b.) happy c. disappointed
4. Explain your answer. Shara's hands stop shaking, her stomach feels better, and she speaks in a clear, strong voice. She says that she is "great."

4 Book 3.1/Unit 3 The Patchwork Quilt

At Home: Have students write a sentence or two explaining how they think Shara might feel after the performance.

89

Reteach, 89

ON-LEVEL

Name________ Date______ Practice 89

Make Inferences

Sometimes you must **infer**, or figure out, what is happening in a story from clues that the author gives. Read each of the following passages. Then answer each question.

It was Roxanne's birthday, and she was hoping that someone would give her a book about airplanes. Her Aunt Jackie brought her a present in a box. It was just the right size for a book. Roxanne tore open the package. "I can't wait to find out what is!" she said.

1. How do you think Roxanne felt as she opened up the package? excited
2. Which clues helped you make your inference? Roxanne tore open the package. She couldn't wait to see what it was.

Roxanne opened the box and took out a pair of socks. She looked down at them for a minute and sighed very quietly. "Oh . . ." Then she smiled. "Thanks, Aunt Jackie. Just what I needed." Roxanne hugged her aunt.

3. How does Roxanne feel about her present? She feels disappointed.
4. Which clues helped you make your inference? After Roxanne opens her present, she says "Oh," and she sighs.
5. How does Roxanne feel about her Aunt Jackie? She likes her and doesn't want to hurt her feelings.
6. Which clues helped you make your inference? Roxanne pretends to like the present. When she sees the socks, she sighs very quietly so that Aunt Jackie won't hear. She smiles, and hugs her.

6 Book 3.1/Unit 3 The Patchwork Quilt

At Home: Have students write a sentence or two describing what they think will happen next.

89

Practice, 89

CHALLENGE

Name________ Date______ Extend 89

Make Inferences

Read the story. Use story clues and what you already know to find out how Jenna feels about Anna's pet bird.

"This is my bird, Peppa," said Anna. "I'll let him out so you can hold him."

Jenna did not want Anna to let Peppa out. She said, "I can see that Peppa is a very beautiful bird. You don't have to let him out."

"Oh, but he is so sweet. You won't know how soft he feels if I don't let him out," said Anna.

Anna opened Peppa's cage and out he flew. First he landed on Anna's shoulder. She rubbed his neck and let him go. He flew in circles and then landed right on Jenna's arm.

Jenna didn't move. She let out a small scream.

"Jenna, he likes you!" cried Anna excitedly.

Jenna did not even answer her.

What clues in the text help you know how Jenna feels?
Answers will vary. For example, Jenna did not want Anna to open the cage.

What do you know about people and pets that will help you know how Jenna feels?
Answers will vary. For example, some people are afraid of birds.

What can you infer about how Jenna feels?
Answers will vary. For example, Jenna is afraid of birds and did not want Peppa near her.

Book 3.1/Unit 3 The Patchwork Quilt

At Home: Have students make an inference about how Anna was feeling.

89

Extend, 89

SELECTION Connection

Students will make and explain inferences when they read *The Patchwork Quilt* and the Leveled Books.

ALTERNATE TEACHING STRATEGY

MAKE INFERENCES

For a different approach to teaching this skill, see page T66.

Build Background

Social Studies

Anthology and Leveled Books

Evaluate Prior Knowledge

CONCEPT: SHARING MEMORIES The characters in these stories have objects that help them share family memories. Ask volunteers to talk about what kind of objects help them share memories.

BRAINSTORM KEEPSAKES Have students brainstorm objects that might be kept as reminders of special people, places, or events. Encourage students to think of some of the objects in their homes that are kept as mementos. ▶ **Interpersonal/Logical**

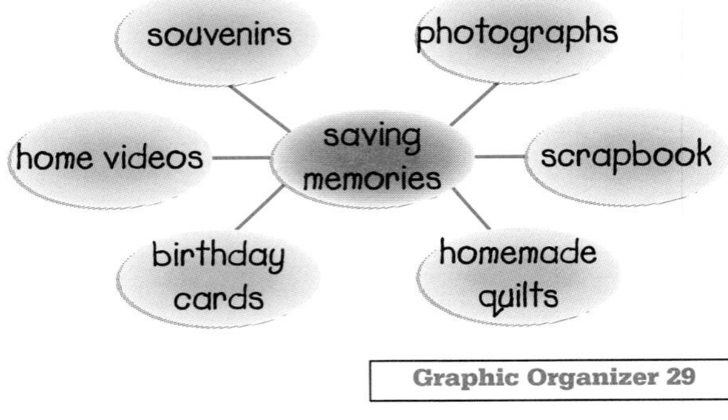

Graphic Organizer 29

PLAN A PARTY Have students write a schedule of what they will need to do to make a surprise party for a friend or family member. For example, they may begin by sending out invitations two weeks in advance.

ONE WRITING

Develop Oral Language

ESL **CAPTIONS** Ask students to think of special memories. Then ask each student to:

- list their favorite memories such as: birthdays, holidays, vacations, and so on.
- choose one memory and draw a picture of it. Help students write captions for their drawings.
- orally present each illustration and talk about what makes that particular memory special for the student.

TEACHING TIP

MANAGEMENT Start a bulletin-board display or learning center to share class memories. Include samples of students' work and photos of students at work. Students may suggest additions for the display.

LANGUAGE SUPPORT

See **Language Support Book, pages 97–100,** for teaching suggestions for Build Background and Vocabulary.

Vocabulary

Key Words

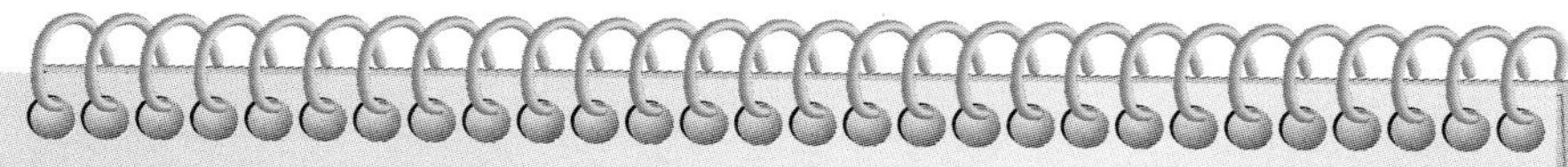

A Special Find

1. Tanya eagerly climbed the stairs all the way up to the attic of her house. 2. She was anxious and could hardly wait to hunt for something special there. 3. Then she found what she was looking for—a princess costume she had once worn to a Halloween party. 4. For a long time she stood and just gazed at the dress. 5. She held the dress up to her face and examined it closely. 6. She loved the dress's pattern of red and orange flowers.

Teaching Chart 74

Vocabulary in Context

IDENTIFY VOCABULARY WORDS
Display **Teaching Chart 74** and read the passage with students. Have volunteers circle each vocabulary word and underline other words that are clues to its meaning.

DISCUSS MEANINGS Ask questions like these to help clarify word meanings:

- Would you go up or down the stairs to get to the attic?
- Are you anxious for summer vacation?
- What costume do you like to wear for Halloween?
- If you gazed at something, was it a quick look or a long look?
- How does a magnifying glass help you examine something?
- Does your clothing have any pattern on it?

Practice

DEMONSTRATE WORD MEANING
Organize students into groups. Each student pantomimes the meaning of a vocabulary word for his/her group and the group identifies it. ▶ Kinesthetic/Linguistic

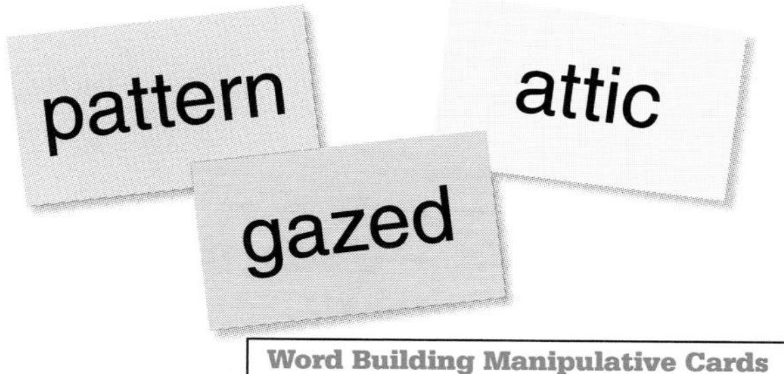

Word Building Manipulative Cards

WRITE CONTEXT SENTENCES Have partners write context sentences, leaving a blank for each vocabulary word. Have them exchange papers to fill in the blanks. Have students refer to the Glossary as needed.

WRITING

▶ Linguistic/Interpersonal

Definitions

attic (p. 329) the space just below the roof of a house

anxious (p. 323) eager

costume (p. 342) clothes worn in order to look like someone or something else

gazed (p. 323) looked at something for a long time

examined (p. 337) looked at closely and carefully; checked

pattern (p. 332) how colors, shapes, or lines are arranged or repeated in some order or design

SPELLING/VOCABULARY CONNECTIONS

See Spelling Challenge Words, pages 349O–349P.

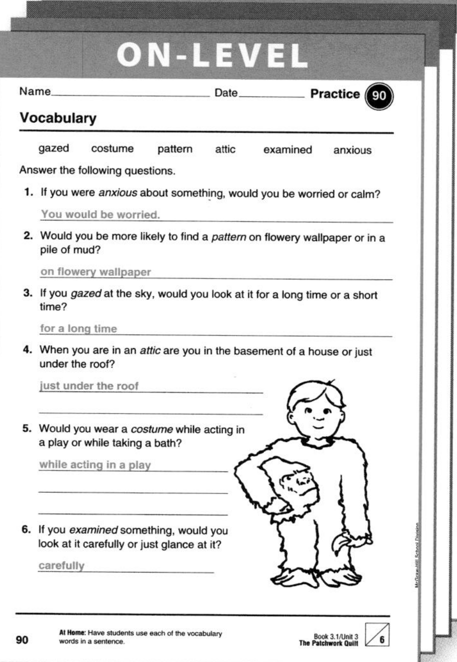

ON-LEVEL

Name________ Date________ Practice 90

Vocabulary

gazed costume pattern attic examined anxious

Answer the following questions.

1. If you were *anxious* about something, would you be worried or calm?
You would be worried.
2. Would you be more likely to find a *pattern* on flowery wallpaper or in a pile of mud?
on flowery wallpaper
3. If you *gazed* at the sky, would you look at it for a long time or a short time?
for a long time
4. When you are in an *attic* are you in the basement of a house or just under the roof?
just under the roof
5. Would you wear a *costume* while acting in a play or while taking a bath?
while acting in a play
6. If you *examined* something, would you look at it carefully or just glance at it?
carefully

90 At Home: Have students use each of the vocabulary words in a sentence. Book 3.1/Unit 3 The Patchwork Quilt 6

Take-Home Story 90a
Reteach 90
Practice 90 • Extend 90

Guided Instruction

Preview and Predict

Have students read the title and take a **picture walk**, looking for pictures that give strong clues about the plot and characters.

- What clues about the selection do the title and pictures give?
- Who might the main character be?
- What will the selection most likely be about?
- Will the selection be a realistic one or a fantasy? How can you tell? (The characters and surroundings look real.) ***Genre***

Have students record their predictions about the story and its main character.

PREDICTIONS	WHAT HAPPENED
The story is about a patchwork quilt.	
The main character is an African American girl.	

Set Purposes

What do students want to find out by reading the story? For example:

- Why are the characters making a quilt?
- Why is the quilt important to the characters?

◆MEET◆
VALERIE FLOURNOY

Valerie Flournoy was thinking about the members of her own family when she wrote *The Patchwork Quilt*. She was especially remembering her Grandma Buchanan and how much fun they had had together when Valerie was growing up.

Flournoy hopes children who read her story will have respect "not only for their own parents and grandparents but for all of their 'family'—their ancestors—who have gone before them."

320

Meeting Individual Needs • Grouping Suggestions for Strategic Reading

EASY

Read Together Read the story with students or have them use the **Listening Library Audiocassette**. Have students use the Make Inferences chart to record important information about the story. Guided Instruction and Intervention prompts offer additional help with decoding, vocabulary, and comprehension.

ON-LEVEL

Guided Reading Use the Guided Instruction questions as you read with students or after they have played the Listening Library Audiocassette. You may want to have students read the story first on their own. Have them use the Make Inferences chart to record important information about the story during reading.

CHALLENGE

Read Independently Direct students to read independently. Remind them that making inferences about the characters will help them to better understand and enjoy the story. Have students set up a Make Inferences chart as on page 321. After reading, they can use their charts to summarize the story.

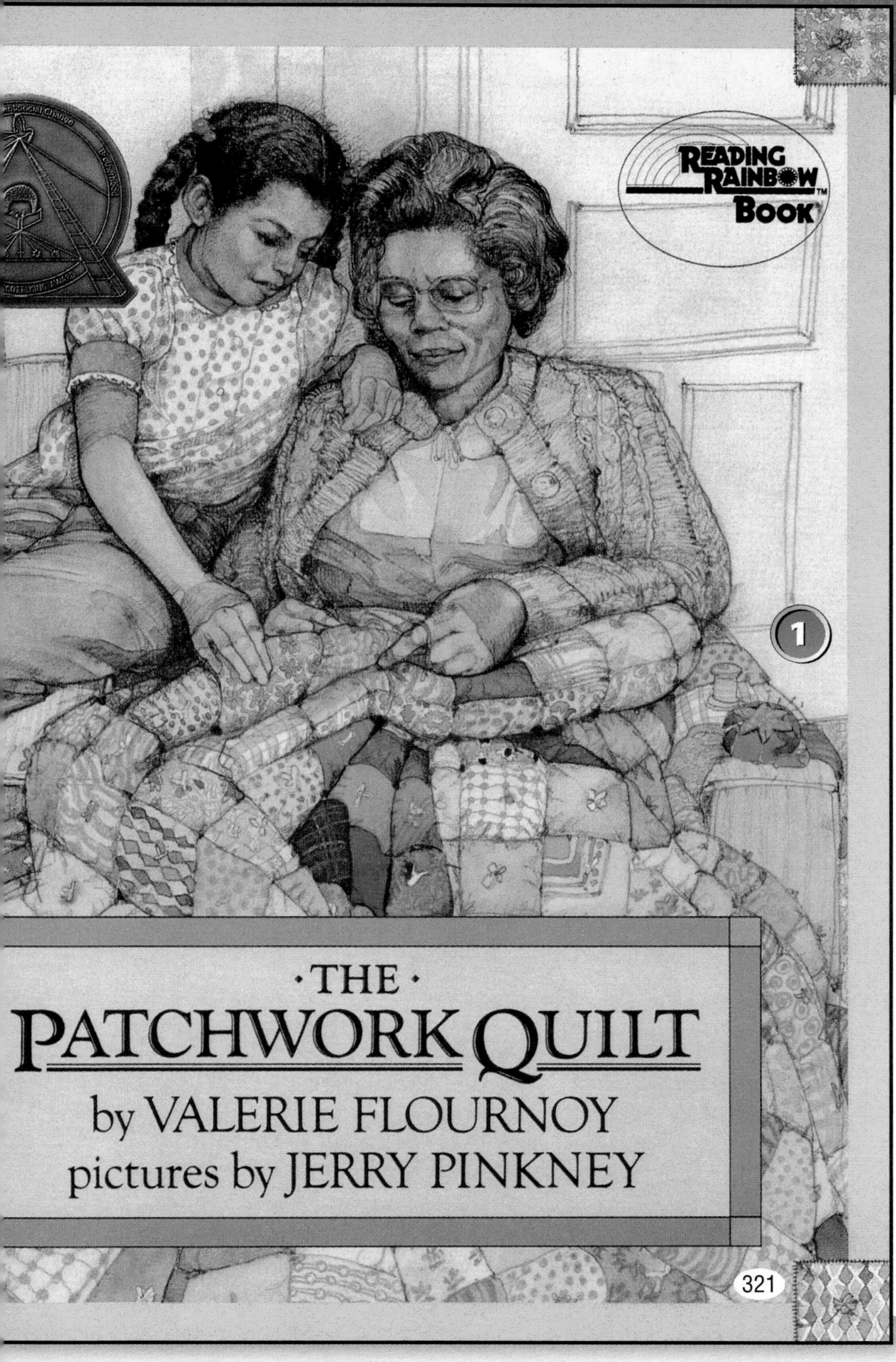

READING RAINBOW BOOK
1
·THE·
PATCHWORK QUILT
by VALERIE FLOURNOY
pictures by JERRY PINKNEY
321

Guided Instruction

☑ Make Inferences
☑ Summarize

Strategic Reading Making inferences will help you understand the characters and plot as you read the story. Let's recall that we can make inferences in order to learn more about a story's characters. Before we begin reading, let's prepare our Make Inferences charts so we can write down notes about the story's characters.

MAKE INFERENCES	EXPLAIN INFERENCES

(1) **MAKE INFERENCES** Remember that you can make inferences about characters just from looking at a story's pictures. Take a look at the picture on this page. What can we infer about the two people in the picture? (They care about each other; they feel comfortable with each other. They are both interested in patchwork quilts.)

Story Words

The words below may be unfamiliar. Have students check their meaning and pronunciation in the Glossary on page 388.

- flexed, p. 324
- jingled, p. 329
- mischievous, p. 332
- snipping, p. 339
- trimmed, p. 339

LANGUAGE SUPPORT

A blackline master of the Make Inferences chart is available in the **Language Support Book**.

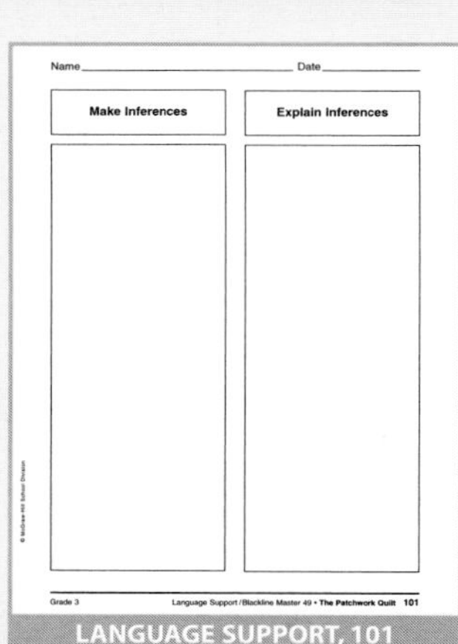

Name_______ Date_______

Make Inferences	Explain Inferences

Grade 3 Language Support/Blackline Master 49 • The Patchwork Quilt 101

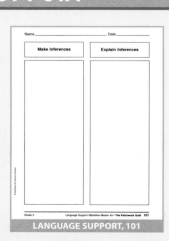

LANGUAGE SUPPORT, 101

Guided Instruction

2 **MAKE INFERENCES** What can you infer about the characters in this picture?

MODEL The way the girl is smiling at the woman makes me think she is happy to be in the kitchen with her. I think the woman is probably the girl's mother. I think the mother likes things to be neat and orderly, because the kitchen looks very neat.

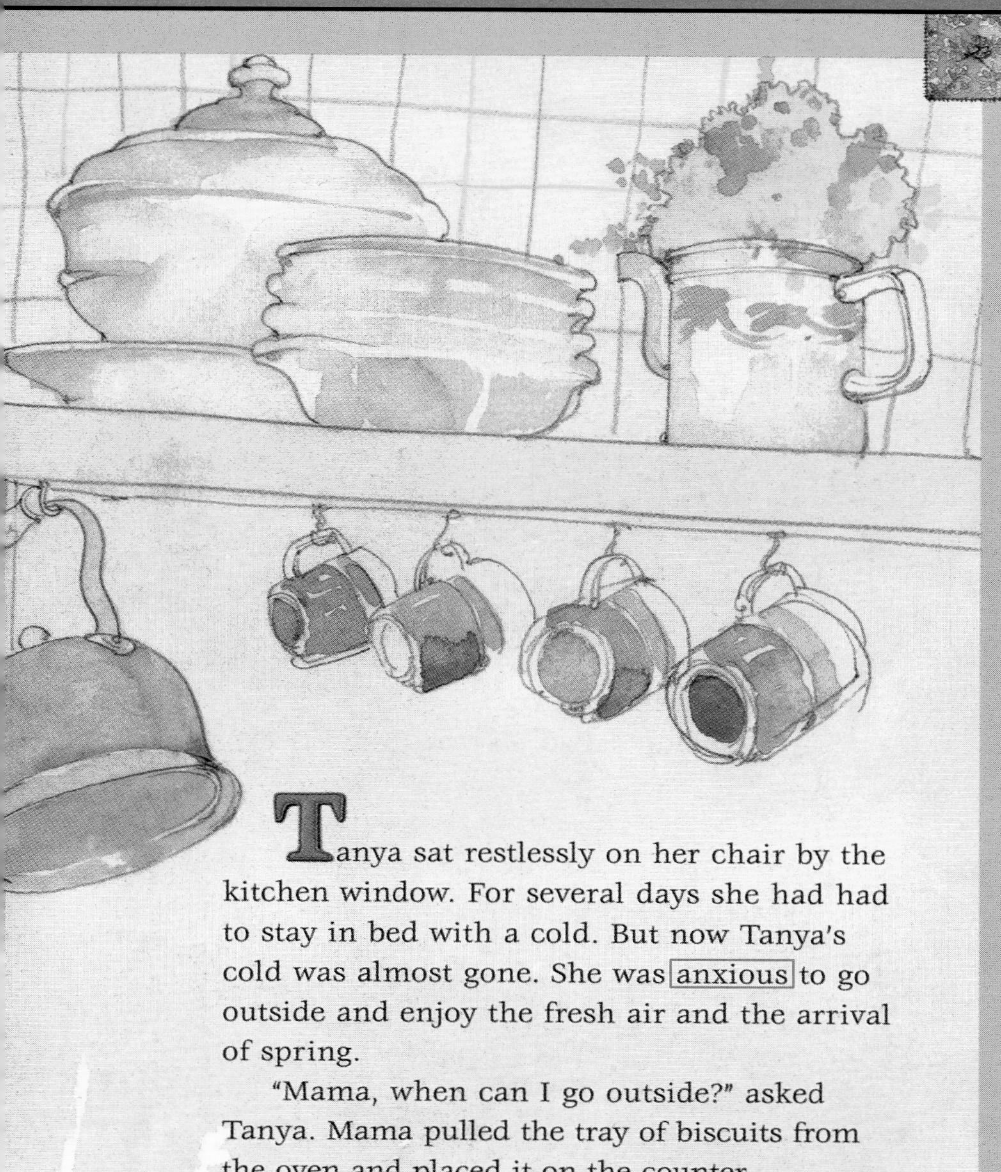

Tanya sat restlessly on her chair by the kitchen window. For several days she had had to stay in bed with a cold. But now Tanya's cold was almost gone. She was anxious to go outside and enjoy the fresh air and the arrival of spring.

"Mama, when can I go outside?" asked Tanya. Mama pulled the tray of biscuits from the oven and placed it on the counter.

"In time," she murmured. "All in good time."

Tanya gazed through the window and saw her two brothers, Ted and Jim, and Papa building the new backyard fence.

"I'm gonna talk to Grandma," she said. 3

323

Guided Instruction

3 Why do you think the author has mentioned all the members of the family on this page? (Authors often introduce the characters of a story early on, so that readers know whom the story will be about.) ***Author's Purpose***

P/I **MULTIPLE-MEANING WORDS** Read the last word of the first paragraph on page 323. *(spring)* *Spring* can have several meanings. What is the meaning here? How do you know?

P/I PREVENTION/INTERVENTION

MULTIPLE MEANING WORDS

- Write *spring* on the chalkboard. Remind students that the word has more than one meaning.
- Write these sentences on the chalkboard and have students explain what *spring* means in each one.

Many flowers bloom during *spring*.
The jack-in-the-box *springs* out of the box.

- Ask students to look up the word *spring* in the dictionary and challenge them to write context sentences for the different meaning of *spring*.

Guided Instruction

4 MAKE INFERENCES What can you infer about Mama from what she says on page 324?

MODEL We can learn a lot about characters from what they say. When Mama says, "I just cleaned this room, and now it's a mess," I can tell that she likes things to be neat. Later, when she offers to buy a quilt from a store, I can tell she does not think it is necessary to make a quilt.

TEACHING TIP

INSTRUCTIONAL Point out to students that sometimes an author will use *dialect*—language that is a variation on standard usage—in order to better express a character's speaking voice.

Point out that on this page, ***whatcha*** is dialect for "what are you," ***gonna*** is dialect for "going to," and ***ain't*** is dialect for "is not."

Grandma was sitting in her favorite spot—the big soft chair in front of the picture window. In her lap were scraps of materials of all textures and colors. Tanya recognized some of them. The plaid was from Papa's old work shirt, and the red scraps were from the shirt Ted had torn that winter.

"Whatcha gonna do with all that stuff?" Tanya asked.

"Stuff? These ain't stuff. These little pieces gonna make me a quilt, a patchwork quilt."

Tanya tilted her head. "I know what a quilt is, Grandma. There's one on your bed, but it's old and dirty and Mama can never get it clean."

Grandma sighed. "It ain't dirty, honey. It's worn, the way it's supposed to be."

Grandma flexed her fingers to keep them from stiffening. She sucked in some air and said, "My mother made me a quilt when I wasn't any older than you. But sometimes the old ways are forgotten."

Tanya leaned against the chair and rested her head on her grandmother's shoulder.

Just then Mama walked in with two glasses of milk and some biscuits. Mama looked at the scraps of material that were scattered all over.

"Grandma," she said, "I just cleaned this room, and now it's a mess."

"It's not a mess, Mama," Tanya said through a mouthful of biscuit. "It's a quilt."

"A quilt! You don't need these scraps. I can get you a quilt," Mama said.

324

Activity

Cross Curricular: Science

MIXING COLORS Grandma uses scraps of different colors in her quilt. Explain to students:

- Pictures in books are made by combining the three primary colors—red, blue, and yellow—and black ink.

 Have students cut 2-inch squares from clear red, blue, and yellow cellophane wrapping paper. On white paper, have students combine color "patches" to create new colors. Students may tape and label their color "patches."
▶ **Spatial/Intrapersonal**

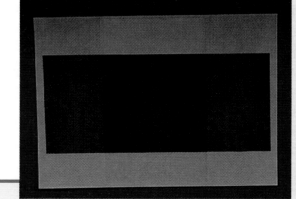

Guided Instruction

5 Mama calls the scraps of material *a mess*. Is this a fact or nonfact? (This is a nonfact because it is Mama's opinion. Grandma and Tanya don't think it's a mess, they call it a "patchwork quilt.") ***Fact and Nonfact***

COMPOUND WORDS Look at the word *patchwork* on page 324. Can you see that it is made up of two separate words? What are they? (*patch* and *work*)

PREVENTION/INTERVENTION

COMPOUND WORDS Remind students that a compound word is made up of two or more words. Explain that the meaning of a compound word is often a combination of the meaning of the smaller words it contains.

Have students define the compound word *patchwork*. Remind them to look for the smaller words it contains.

Invite students to create compound words by writing words on cards and then putting the cards together—like squares of a patchwork quilt!

Guided Instruction

6 **MAKE INFERENCES** Read the first paragraph on page 327. Why does Grandma say that a store-bought quilt "won't be like her patchwork quilt"? (Since her quilt is made by hand and with much care, Grandma knows a store-bought quilt won't be as special.)

7 **SUMMARIZE** Good readers often stop while reading a story to think about the important information they have read. Can you write down the most important events of the story so far? Remember to be as brief as possible. An important event is an event that cannot be left out in retelling a story. (Answers may vary: Tanya lives with her mother, father, two brothers, and her grandmother. Grandma is making a quilt.)

Visual Literacy

VIEWING AND REPRESENTING

Discuss the illustration on page 326. How do Tanya and Grandma feel about each other? Explain your answer. (Grandma and Tanya love and care for each other. Their faces express their love for each other as they hug.) Compare this illustration with the one on the front cover. Does this picture support what you think about their relationship? (Yes, they seem very close.)

Grandma looked at her daughter and then turned to her grandchild. "Yes, your mama can get you a quilt from any department store. But it won't be like my patchwork quilt, and it won't last as long either."

Mama looked at Grandma, then picked up Tanya's empty glass and went to make lunch.

Grandma's eyes grew dark and distant. She turned away from Tanya and gazed out the window, absent-mindedly rubbing the pieces of material through her fingers.

"Grandma, I'll help you make your quilt," Tanya said.

"Thank you, honey."

"Let's start right now. We'll be finished in no time."

Grandma held Tanya close and patted her head. "It's gonna take quite a while to make this quilt, not a couple of days or a week—not even a month. A good quilt, a masterpiece . . ." Grandma's eyes shone at the thought. "Why I need more material. More gold and blue, some red and green. And I'll need the time to do it right. It'll take me a year at least."

"A year," shouted Tanya. "That's too long. I can't wait that long, Grandma."

Grandma laughed. "A year ain't that long, honey. Makin' this quilt gonna be a joy. Now run along and let Grandma rest." Grandma turned her head toward the sunlight and closed her eyes.

"I'm gonna make a masterpiece," she murmured, clutching a scrap of cloth in her hand, just before she fell asleep.

327

Guided Instruction

8 **MAKE INFERENCES** When Grandma's eyes grow "dark and distant," what do you think she might be thinking about? (She is probably remembering the other patchwork quilts and other events that took place in her life. She may also be thinking about how she wants to make this one.)

9 **MAKE INFERENCES** What does Tanya's attitude about making the quilt tell you about her? (Tanya wants things to happen quickly. She doesn't know yet what goes into making a quilt.)

Let's add this information to our Make Inferences chart.

MAKE INFERENCE	EXPLAIN INFERENCE
Tanya wants things to happen quickly.	She doesn't want to wait a year to finish the quilt.

LANGUAGE SUPPORT

ESL Bring in a picture of a handmade quilt and a picture of a store-bought quilt. Initiate a discussion about quilts. Then have the students work in small groups to compare and contrast homemade quilts and store-bought quilts. Allow students to refer back to the pictures when necessary. When students have finished their lists, have them complete a Venn diagram.

Guided Instruction

10 Who would like to role-play Jim for us? Jim, you can no longer wear your favorite pants. How do you feel about that? When Grandma suggests sewing squares from the pants into the quilt, how does it change your feelings? ***Role-play***

11 **MAKE INFERENCES** Grandma says, "A quilt won't forget. It can tell your life story." What do you think she means by that?

MODEL I think Grandma means that all the scraps that make up a patchwork quilt remind her of important people and events that happened in their lives.

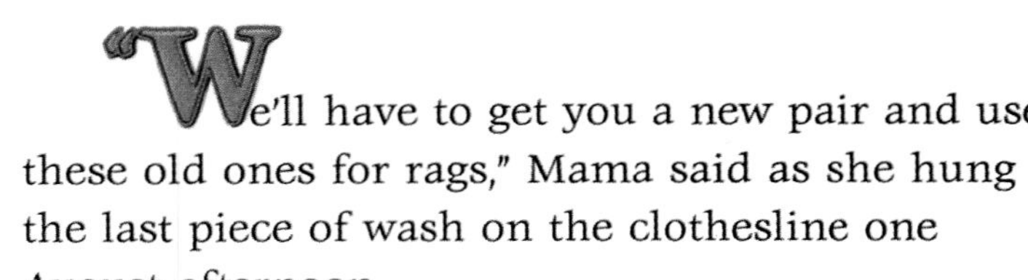

"We'll have to get you a new pair and use these old ones for rags," Mama said as she hung the last piece of wash on the clothesline one August afternoon.

Jim was miserable. His favorite blue corduroy pants had been held together with patches; now they were beyond repair.

"Bring them here," Grandma said.

Grandma took part of the pant leg and cut a few
10 blue squares. Jim gave her a hug and watched her add his patches to the others.
11 "A quilt won't forget. It can tell your life story," she said.

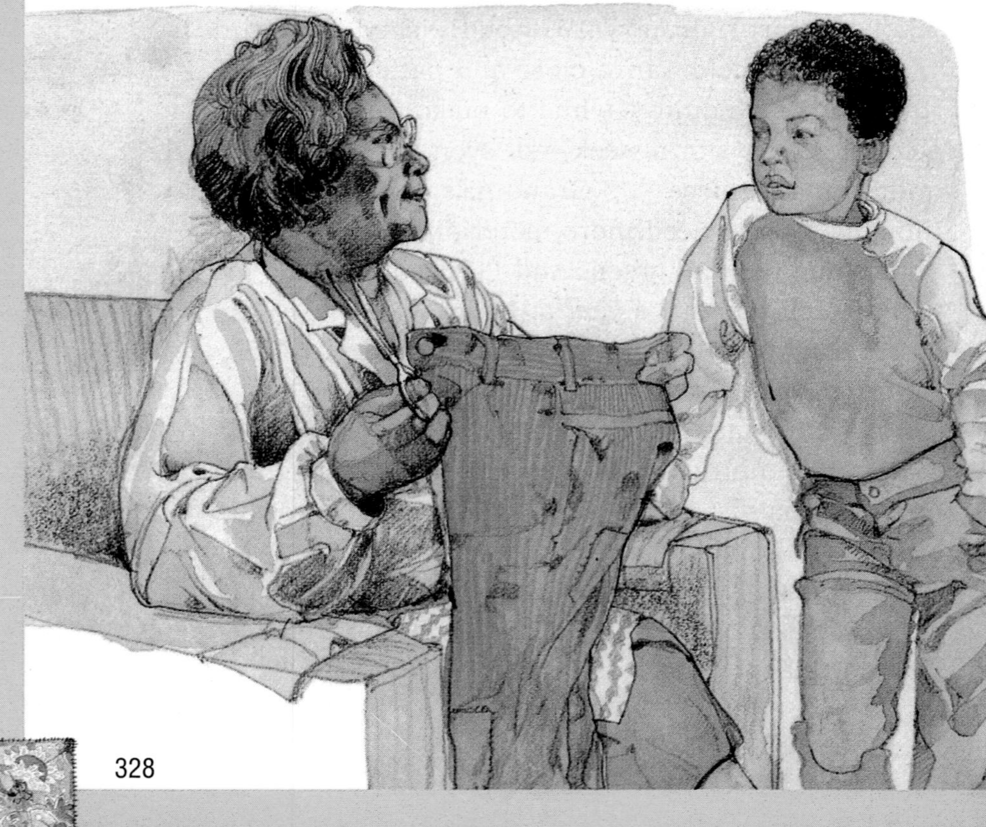

LANGUAGE SUPPORT

ESL Some ESL students may be confused by some things Grandma says. For example, on page 324 she says, "These ain't stuff. These little pieces gonna make me a quilt . . ." On page 327 she says, "Makin' this quilt gonna be a joy." Explain that some people use *ain't* in place of *isn't* and *aren't* and *am not* in spoken English. Help students see that *gonna* means *going to.* When you encounter nonstandard usages like these, help students rephrase the sentences in their own words.

The arrival of autumn meant school and Halloween. This year Tanya would be an African princess. She danced around in the long, flowing robes Mama had made from several yards of colorful material. The old bracelets and earrings Tanya had found in a trunk in the attic jingled noisily as she moved. Grandma cut some squares out of the leftover scraps and added Tanya to the quilt too! 12

329

Guided Instruction

12 **MAKE INFERENCES** When Grandma adds leftover scraps from Tanya's costume to the quilt, how do you think Tanya feels? (She probably feels happy and important because she has been added to the family quilt.)

TEACHING TIP

MANAGEMENT **To create quick and inexpensive transparencies, set a roll of plastic wrap on one side of an overhead projector. Use a permanent felt-tipped marker and pull the roll for clean writing space when necessary.**

Guided Instruction

13 **SUMMARIZE** Let's summarize the events from pages 326–331. Remember to use your own words and include only main events. (Answers may vary: Grandma's masterpiece will take a year to make. The quilt has scraps of the family's clothing in it. In winter, Grandma continues working on the quilt.)

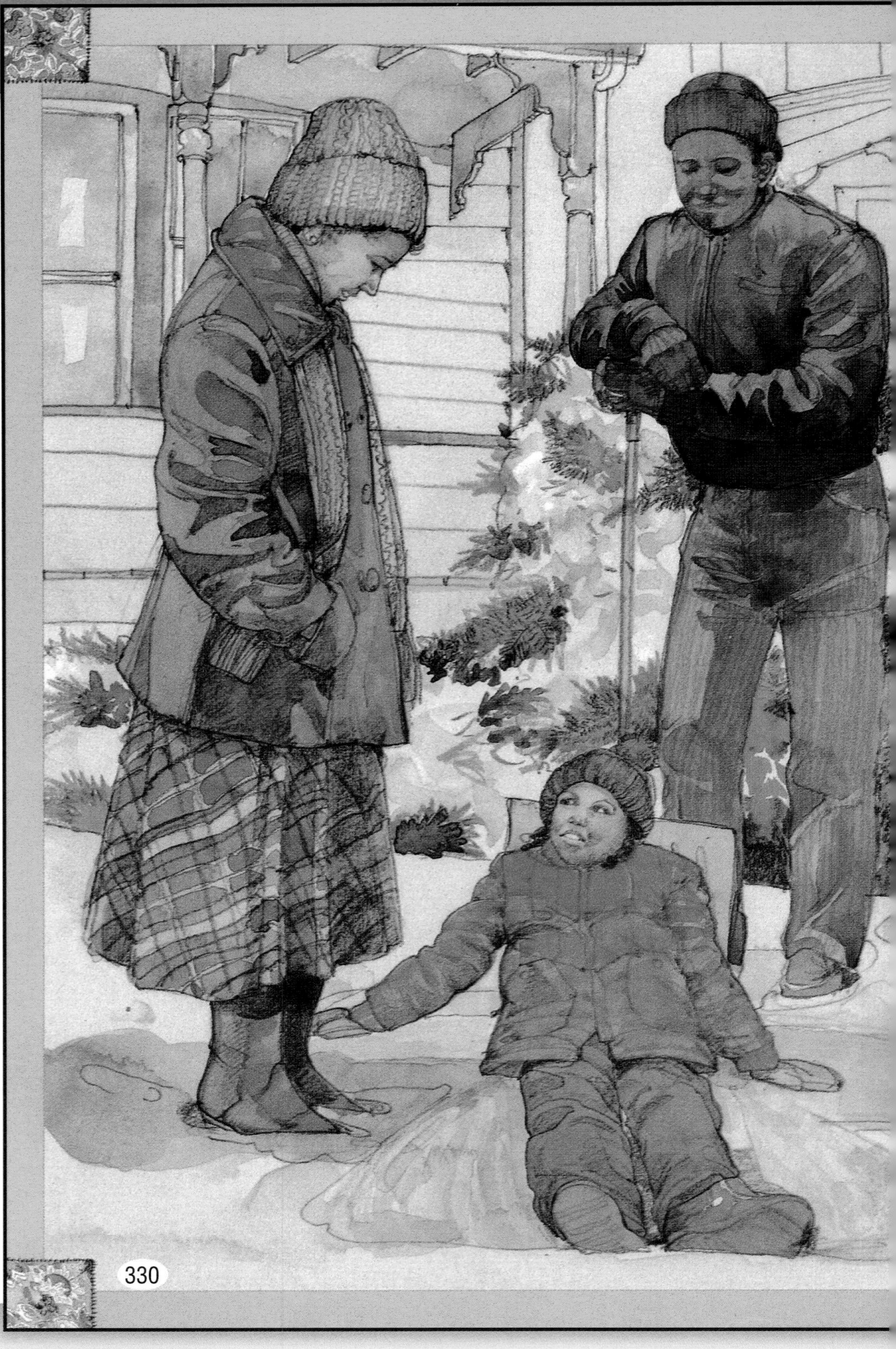

Cross Curricular: Social Studies

WHAT THEY WORE The robe Tanya wore is similar to traditional garments worn by an African princess. Have students choose a country and draw the traditional clothing worn in that country.

RESEARCH AND INQUIRY Have students create a display of their pictures.

▶ **Spatial/Intrapersonal**

interNET CONNECTION Students can learn more about this topic by visiting ***www.mhschool.com/reading.***

The days grew colder but Tanya and her brothers didn't mind. They knew snow wasn't far away. Mama dreaded winter's coming. Every year she would plead with Grandma to move away from the drafty window, but Grandma wouldn't budge. 13

"Grandma, please," Mama scolded. "You can sit here by the heater."

"I'm not your grandmother, I'm your mother," Grandma said. "And I'm gonna sit here in the Lord's light and make my masterpiece."

It was the end of November when Ted, Jim, and Tanya got their wish. They awoke one morning to find everything in sight covered with snow. Tanya got dressed and flew down the stairs. Ted and Jim, and even Mama and Papa, were already outside.

"I don't like leaving Grandma in that house by herself," Mama said. "I know she's lonely."

Tanya pulled herself out of the snow being careful not to ruin her angel. "Grandma isn't lonely," Tanya said happily. "She and the quilt are telling each other stories."

Mama glanced questioningly at Tanya, "Telling each other stories?"

"Yes, Grandma says a quilt never forgets!"

The family spent the morning and most of the afternoon sledding down the hill. Finally, when they were all numb from the cold, they went inside for hot chocolate and sandwiches.

Guided Instruction

14 MAKE INFERENCES Take a look at the conversation between Mama and Tanya on this page. Which family member understands Grandma the best? (Tanya understands Grandma the best, because she knows that Grandma is not lonely when she is with the quilt.)

Let's add this information to our Make Inferences chart.

MAKE INFERENCE	EXPLAIN INFERENCE
Tanya wants things to happen quickly.	She doesn't want to wait a year to finish the quilt.
Tanya understands Grandma the best.	Mama thinks Grandma is lonely, but Tanya knows that she is happy to be with the quilt.

Minilesson

REVIEW/MAINTAIN

Character

Review that readers can learn a lot about characters by paying careful attention to what they do and say.

- Direct students to reread page 331. Ask: what can you tell about Grandma from what she does and says on this page? (She is strong-minded. She cares deeply about her quilt.)

Activity Have students choose one character from the story and write a brief paragraph describing that character. Have them use examples from the story to make their points.

Guided Instruction

15 **MAKE INFERENCES** What can we infer from what Grandma tells Mama about the quilt?

MODEL I can make inferences by looking at a character's actions. Grandma is talking to Mama. Then Mama picks up a piece of fabric, rubs it, and smiles. I think that Grandma is telling Mama the story of each scrap of cloth. I think that when Mama picks up the piece of fabric and smiles, she is probably remembering where it came from.

16 **MAKE INFERENCES** How do you think Tanya knew, without asking, that the gold scraps would be in the quilt? (Tanya knew because Grandma is using scraps from the family's special clothing for the quilt. The gold dress is special to Mama, so scraps from it will be in the quilt.)

"I think I'll go sit and talk to Grandma," Mama said.

"Then she can explain to you about our quilt—our very own family quilt," Tanya said.

Mama saw the mischievous glint in her youngest child's eyes.

"Why, I may just have her do that, young lady," Mama said as she walked out of the kitchen.

Tanya leaned over the table to see into the living room. Grandma was hunched over, her eyes close to the fabric as she made tiny stitches. Mama sat at the old woman's feet. Tanya couldn't hear what was said but she knew Grandma was telling Mama all about quilts and how *this* quilt would be very special. Tanya sipped her chocolate slowly, then she saw Mama pick up a piece of fabric, rub it
15 with her fingers, and smile.

From that moment on both women spent their winter evenings working on the quilt. Mama did the sewing while Grandma cut the fabrics and placed the scraps in a pattern of colors. Even while they were cooking and baking all their Christmas specialties during the day, at night they still worked on the quilt. Only once did Mama put it aside. She wanted to wear something special Christmas night,
16 so she bought some gold material and made a beautiful dress. Tanya knew without asking that the
17 gold scraps would be in the quilt too.

332

CULTURAL PERSPECTIVES

AFRICAN WEAVING Display for the class some photographs of *Kente* cloth. Explain that:

- *Kente* is a beautiful fabric made in Ghana, Africa. The weaving of *kente* began about 250 years ago.
- Narrow strips of *kente* are stitched together to give the garments a quilt-like appearance.

▶ **Interpersonal/Spatial**

Activity Have students draw patterns on strips of colored paper. Tape them together to make a *kente*-style paper quilt.

Guided Instruction

17 **MAKE INFERENCES** What do you think Mama's attitude toward the quilt is now? (She thinks it is important.) How can you tell that her attitude has changed? (A piece of fabric makes her smile. She starts to help Grandma with the quilt.)

Let's add this new information to our Make Inferences chart.

MAKE INFERENCE	EXPLAIN INFERENCE
Tanya wants things to happen quickly.	She doesn't want to wait a year to finish the quilt.
Tanya understands Grandma the best.	Mama thinks Grandma is lonely, but Tanya knows that she is happy to be with the quilt.
Mama thinks the quilt is important.	She smiles and helps Grandma with the quilt.

Minilesson

REVIEW/MAINTAIN

Suffixes

Review that a *suffix* is a word part added to the end of a base word that changes the word's meaning. The suffix *-est* means "most". Added to a word such as *old*, *-est* changes its meaning to one of comparison ("most old"). Read a sentence aloud. Find a word ending with *-est* on page 332. (*youngest*) Discuss the example.

Activity Ask students to write two context sentences that include examples of words with the ending *-est*. Circle and discuss examples.

Guided Instruction

18 Explain that the *mood* of a passage is the feeling that the author wants to convey to the reader. The mood can be created through characters' actions and words, or by descriptions of setting. Read over the paragraph on this page. What kind of mood has been created? How do you think the author conveyed this? (The author conveys a happy mood through the characters' actions—singing and laughing—and through descriptions using phrases such as "shone brightly" and "sparkling colors.") ***Analyze Moods***

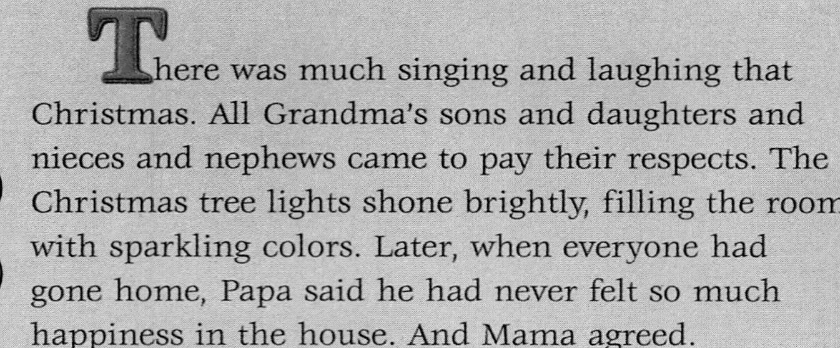

There was much singing and laughing that
Christmas. All Grandma's sons and daughters and
18 nieces and nephews came to pay their respects. The
Christmas tree lights shone brightly, filling the room
19 with sparkling colors. Later, when everyone had
gone home, Papa said he had never felt so much
20 happiness in the house. And Mama agreed.

334

LANGUAGE SUPPORT

ESL Discuss with students family-member words such as *niece, nephew, son,* and *daughter*. These words may be unfamiliar to non-English speakers. Using the illustration, point out some of these family members. Non-English speakers can share names of family members in their own language.

Encourage students to draw a family tree of their own family, including family-member words.

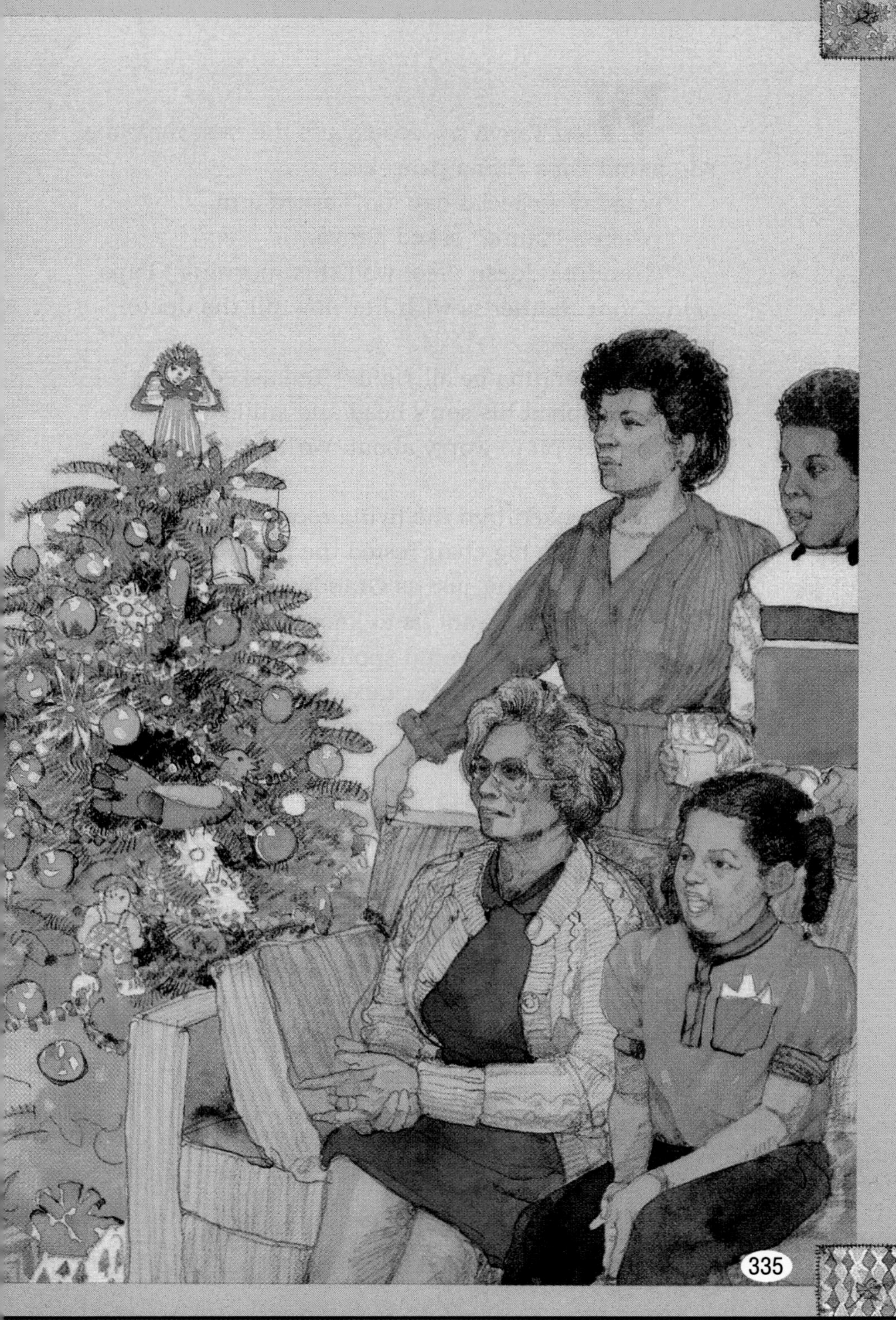

Guided Instruction

19 Remember that setting deals with time as well as place. The setting of this story has changed many times. What major change in the setting has occurred on pages 334-335? (The setting is Christmas time.) ***Setting***

20 What do you think the main idea is on page 334? (There was a lot of happiness in the house at Christmas.) Name a few of the supporting details to the main idea. (Everyone was singing and laughing. The tree filled the room with sparkling colors.) ***Main Idea and Details***

TEACHING TIP

INSTRUCTIONAL You may want to discuss with students how holidays and traditions help bring families closer together. Have volunteers share information about holidays and traditions that are important to their own families.

Guided Instruction

21 **MAKE INFERENCES** What can you infer about Mama's feelings from the description of her on this page? (She is very unhappy. Her face is "drawn and tired," so she probably has not slept well. Her eyes are red and puffy, so she has probably been crying.)

22 What kind of person do you think Papa is? What makes you say that? (He seems to be a very kind and concerned person. He makes pancakes for the family. He reassures his son. He wants Grandma to get better.) *Draw Conclusions*

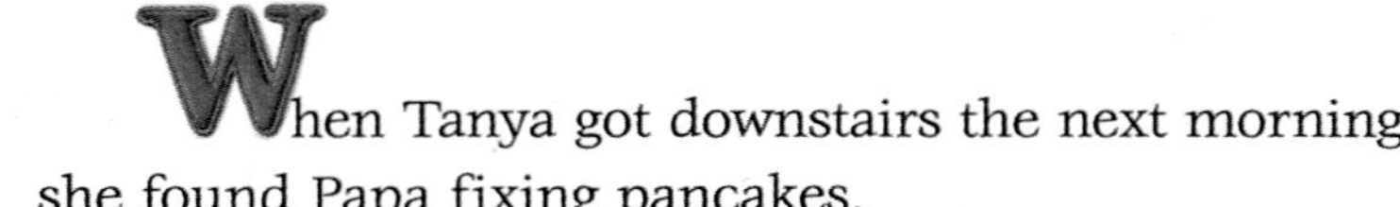

When Tanya got downstairs the next morning, she found Papa fixing pancakes.

"Is today a special day too?" asked Jim.

"Where's Mama?" asked Tanya.

"Grandma doesn't feel well this morning," Papa said. "Your mother is with her now till the doctor gets here."

"Will Grandma be all right?" Ted asked.

Papa rubbed his son's head and smiled. "There's nothing for you to worry about. We'll take care of Grandma."

Tanya looked into the living room. There on the back of the big chair rested the patchwork quilt. It was folded neatly, just as Grandma had left it.

"Mother didn't want us to know she wasn't feeling well. She thought it would spoil our Christmas,"
21 Mama told them later, her face drawn and tired, her eyes a puffy red. "Now it's up to all of us to be quiet and make her as comfortable as possible." Papa put
22 an arm around Mama's shoulder.

"Can we see Grandma?" Tanya asked.

"No, not tonight," Papa said. "Grandma needs plenty of rest."

It was nearly a week, the day before New Year's, before the children were permitted to see their grandmother. She looked tired and spoke in whispers.

336

Fluency

READING DIALOGUE

Ask for volunteers, and then assign roles to read aloud on pages 336–337. Individual students can read the parts of Ted, Jim, Tanya, Papa, Mama, and Grandma. Either you or another student can read the narration. Alternatively, students can stand and role-play the actions as they read the text.

Remind students to think about how the characters are feeling and to read with expression.

LANGUAGE SUPPORT

ESL On these pages there are no illustrations to aid comprehension. Chunk the text into manageable pieces, ask questions that require specific information from a chunked passage, and then discuss with students the meaning of the passage.

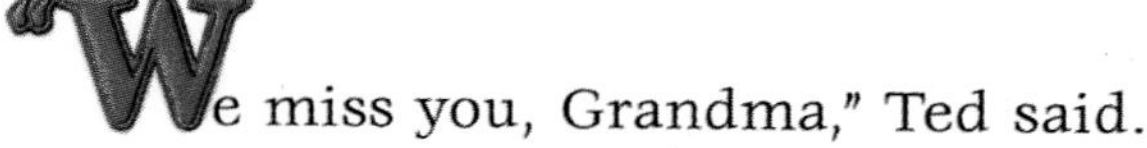

"We miss you, Grandma," Ted said.

"And your muffins and hot chocolate," added Jim. Grandma smiled.

"Your quilt misses you too, Grandma," Tanya said. Grandma's smile faded from her lips. Her eyes grew cloudy.

"My masterpiece," Grandma sighed. "It would have been beautiful. Almost half finished." The old woman closed her eyes and turned away from her grandchildren. Papa whispered it was time to leave. Ted, Jim, and Tanya crept from the room. 

Tanya walked slowly to where the quilt lay. She had seen Grandma and Mama work on it. Tanya thought real hard. She knew how to cut the scraps, but she wasn't certain of the rest. Just then Tanya felt a hand resting on her shoulder. She looked up and saw Mama.

"Tomorrow," Mama said.

New Year's Day was the beginning. After the dishes were washed and put away, Tanya and Mama examined the quilt.

"You cut more squares, Tanya, while I stitch some patches together," Mama said. 

337

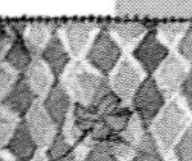

Guided Instruction

23 **MAKE INFERENCES** Grandma says of the quilt, "It would have been beautiful." Why do you think she says this? (Grandma is afraid that she will be too sick to continue working on the quilt.)

24 **MAKE INFERENCES** What does Tanya decide to do? Why do you think this? (Tanya decides to work on the quilt. She goes to the quilt and thinks about how to work on it. Then her mother tells her to cut more squares.) What do you think has caused the decision? (Tanya is concerned about Grandma and wants to help finish the quilt for her.)

P/I **PHONICS AND DECODING** Read the sentence beginning with "She knew how..." in the fifth paragraph on page 337.

- What words begin with the letter *c*? (*cut, certain*)
- What are the two sounds that the letter *c* makes here? (/k/, /s/)

P/I PREVENTION/INTERVENTION

PHONICS AND DECODING
Remind students that sometimes the same letter can make different sounds. Explain that at the beginning of a word:

- the letter c makes the sound /k/ when followed by the vowel *a, o,* or *u.*
- the letter c makes the sound /s/ when it is followed by the vowel *e* or *i.*

Have students give examples of words for each rule.

Guided Instruction

25 **SUMMARIZE** Reread pages 332-339. How would you summarize the events occurring on these pages? (Answers will vary. After Grandma told Mama why this quilt would be special, Mama helped with the quilt. Grandma got sick, so Tanya and Mama worked on the quilt together. They worked very hard.)

Self-Monitoring

STRATEGY

ASK QUESTIONS Asking questions can help a reader to better understand a story.

MODEL After I read page 337, I wasn't sure how Tanya felt about Grandma's illness. Tanya doesn't talk about it in the story. So I asked myself how I have felt when someone close to me was sick. I was sad and worried and I wanted to help. I think that's how Tanya feels.

Activity

Cross Curricular: Math

PATTERNS AND SHAPES Explain to students that a quilt is made up of many squares of fabric.

- Have each student use a ruler to draw a one-foot square and then cut it out.
- Help students fold their squares, making four smaller squares.
- Have students use colored markers to create other shapes and patterns within the squares.
- Combine all squares to make a class quilt.

Determine the number of total squares in the class quilt. ▶ **Mathematical/Spatial**

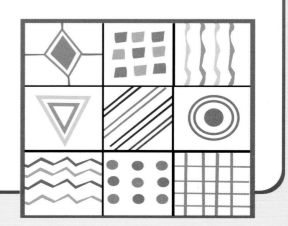

Tanya snipped and trimmed the scraps of material till her hands hurt from the scissors. Mama watched her carefully, making sure the squares were all the same size. The next day was the same as the last. More snipping and cutting. But Mama couldn't always be around to watch Tanya work. Grandma had to be looked after. So Tanya worked by herself. Then one night, as Papa read them stories, Jim walked over and looked at the quilt. In it he saw patches of blue. His blue. Without saying a word Jim picked up the scissors and some scraps and started to make squares. Ted helped Jim put the squares in piles while Mama showed Tanya how to join them. 25

Every day, as soon as she got home from school, Tanya worked on the quilt. Ted and Jim were too busy with sports, and Mama was looking after Grandma, so Tanya worked alone. But after a few weeks she stopped. Something was wrong—something was missing, Tanya thought. For days the quilt lay on the back of the chair. No one knew why Tanya had stopped working. Tanya would sit and look at the quilt. Finally she knew. Some*thing* wasn't missing. Some*one* was missing from the quilt.

That evening before she went to bed Tanya tiptoed into Grandma's room, a pair of scissors in her hand. She quietly lifted the end of Grandma's old quilt and carefully removed a few squares.

339

Guided Instruction

26 MAKE INFERENCES What do you think caused Jim to start working on the quilt? (He was pleased that something of his was in the quilt. He has come to see that the quilt is important for the family and wants to be a part of it.)

27 What was Tanya doing in Grandma's room? (Tanya was cutting patches from Grandma's old quilt.) **What do you think Tanya will do now?** (Tanya will sew Grandma's old patches into the new quilt.) **Why?** (Grandma will be represented in the new quilt now.) ***Make Predictions***

PHONICS KIT
HANDS-ON ACTIVITIES AND PRACTICE

Minilesson

REVIEW/MAINTAIN

/ou/ and /oi/

Write the words *without* and *join* on the chalkboard. Use different colored chalk for the diphthongs /ou/ and /oi/. Have students:

- Pronounce each diphthong from the words.
- Notice how each sound is spelled in the words.

Activity Have students brainstorm other words using these spellings for the diphthongs /ou/ and /oi/. Have students record their words in a two-column chart.

Phonics CD-ROM Have students use the interactive phonics activities on the CD-ROM for more reinforcement.

Guided Instruction

28 The family had to work very hard to make the quilt. Yet Grandma says that the quilt is "nothin' but a joy." What do you think she means? (She thinks about how the family worked on it together and how it is made up of scraps of material from the whole family, and this makes her feel joyful.) ***Draw Conclusions***

29 How did Tanya solve the problem of Grandma being too ill to finish her quilt? (She worked on it herself) ***Problem and Solution***

February and March came and went as Mama proudly watched her daughter work on the last few rows of patches. Tanya always found time for the quilt. Grandma had been watching too. The old woman had been getting stronger and stronger as the months passed. Once she was able, Papa would carry Grandma to her chair by the window. "I needs the Lord's light," Grandma said. Then she would sit and hum softly to herself and watch Tanya work.

28 "Yes, honey, this quilt is nothin' but a joy," Grandma said.

29 Summer vacation was almost here. One June day Tanya came home to find Grandma working on the quilt again! She had finished sewing the last few squares together; the stuffing was in place, and she was already pinning on the backing.

"Grandma!" Tanya shouted.

Grandma looked up. "Hush, child. It's almost time to do the quilting on these patches. But first I have some special finishing touches . . ."

The next night Grandma cut the final thread with her teeth. "There. It's done," she said. Mama helped Grandma spread the quilt full length.

Nobody had realized how big it had gotten or how beautiful. Reds, greens, blues, and golds, light shades and dark, blended in and out throughout the quilt.

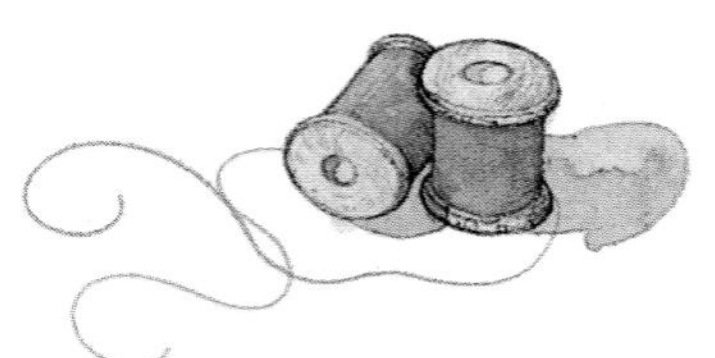

340

Activity

Cross Curricular: Art

QUILTING Encourage students to make patchwork-quilts of their own.

- Have students bring in four fabric scraps and cut each into a two-inch square.
- Help them sew or glue their two-inch squares together to form a four-inch square.
- Cut a four-inch square for the back. Sew the squares together to make a pillow, leaving an opening in one side.
- Help students fill and close their pillows.

▶ **Spatial/Intrapersonal**

Guided Instruction

30 The setting continues to change throughout the story. Reread the first paragraph of page 323. What time of the year was it when the story began? (almost spring) Read the third paragraph of page 340. What time of year is it now? (It is almost summertime; June, a year later.) Was Grandma right about how long it would take to finish the quilt? (Yes, over a year has passed.) ***Setting***

Minilesson

REVIEW/MAINTAIN

Main Idea

Review that the *main idea* tells the theme or purpose of the story.

- Ask students to summarize the events. Have students identify the main idea of *The Patchwork Quilt* up to the end of page 341.
- Ask students to find a few supporting details for the main idea.

Activity Read aloud a short story to students. Organize students into groups and have each group make a story map that shows the most important events of the story. Ask groups to write the main idea at the bottom of their story maps. Have the groups share their story maps.

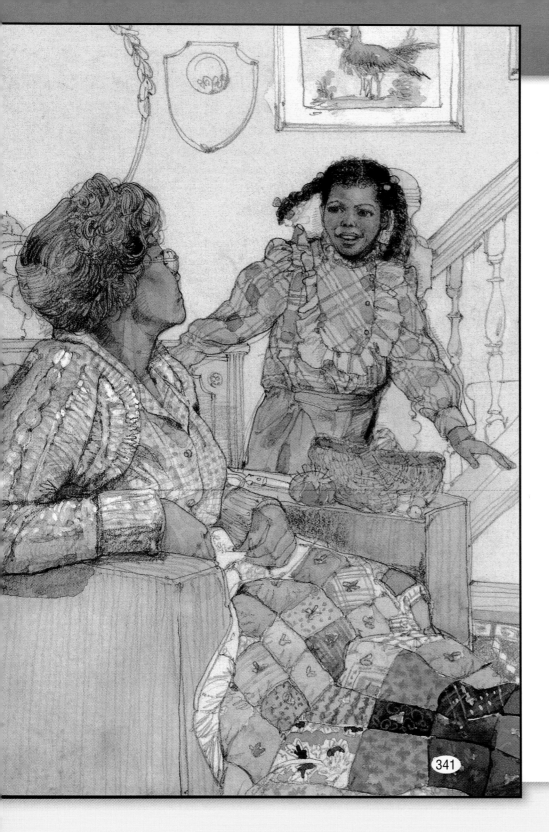

Guided Instruction

31 **MAKE INFERENCES** When Papa touches the gold patch and looks at Mama, what do you think he is remembering? (He is probably remembering the gold dress that Mama wore on Christmas night.)

TEACHING TIP

MANAGEMENT Assign a number to each book in your class library. Hold the book closed and write the number across the top of the book. Arrange the books in numerical order. Record all necessary information, like author and title, on index cards. Now you only have to scan the tops of the books to see what's missing.

31 "It's beautiful," Papa said. He touched the gold patch, looked at Mama, and remembered. Jim remembered too. There was his blue and the red from Ted's shirt. There was Tanya's Halloween costume. And there was Grandma. Even though her

32 patch was old, it fit right in.

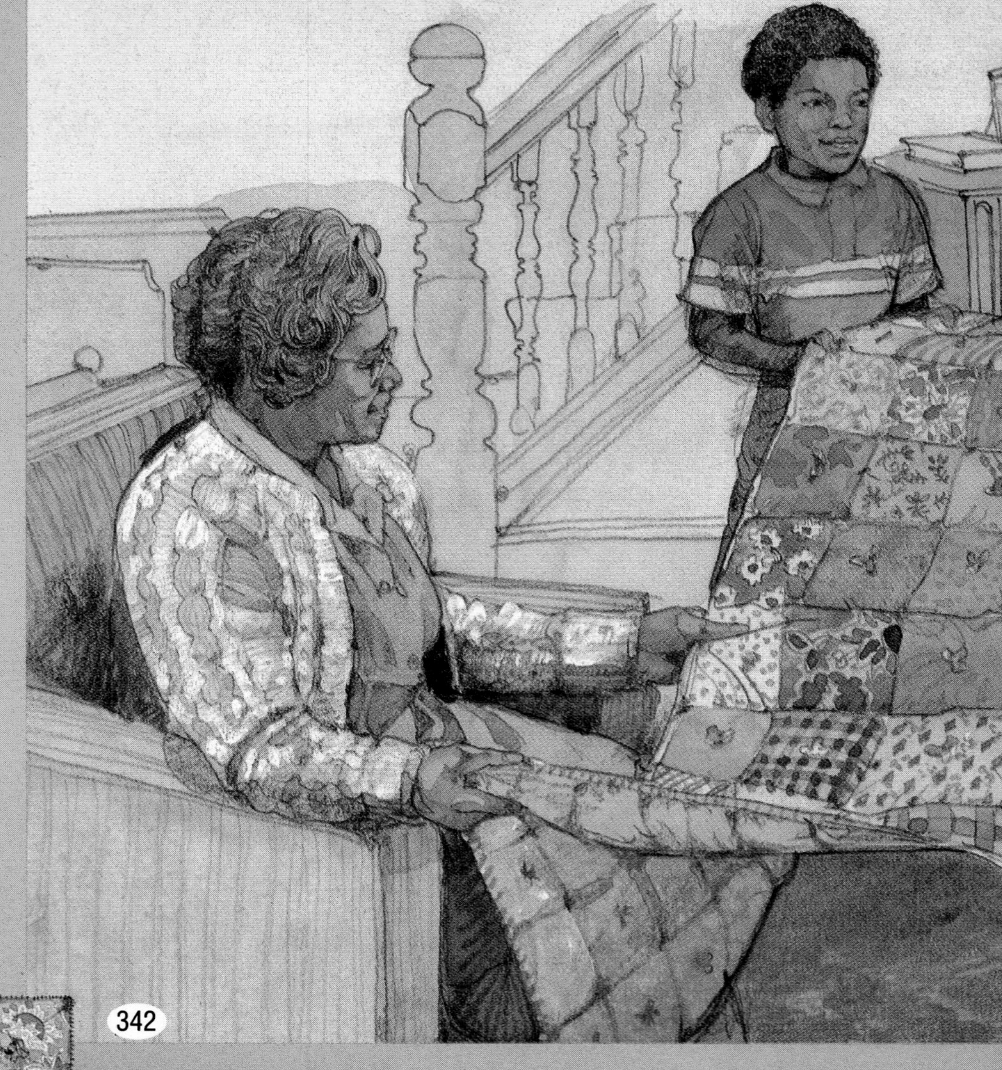

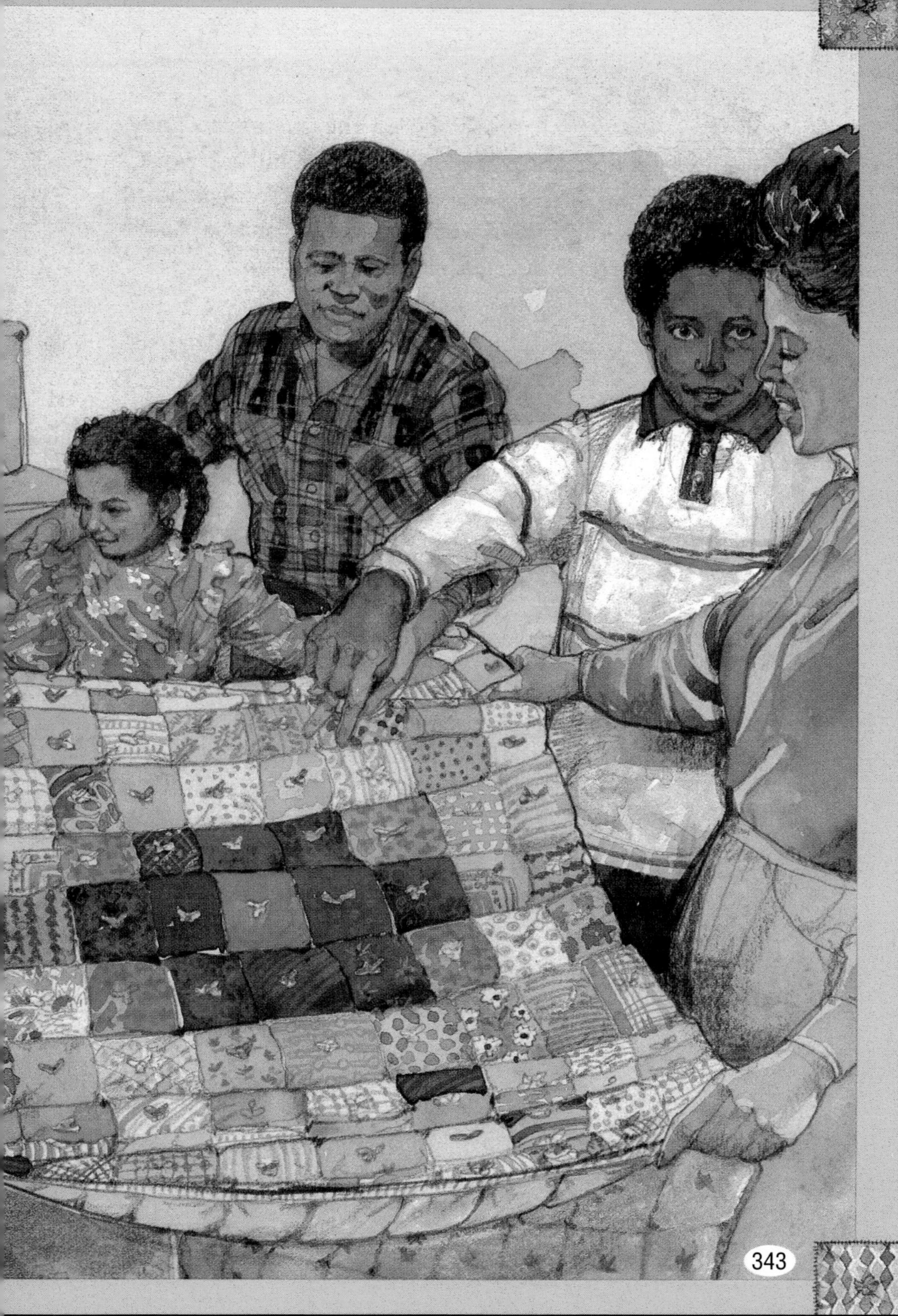

Guided Instruction

32 **MAKE INFERENCES** The quilt is done! How do you think the family feels about having worked together on the quilt? Why do you think this?

MODEL I can tell by looking at the illustration that everyone thinks the quilt is beautiful. Everyone is holding it or pointing to a particular patch. I think that the family is glad that they all took part in making the quilt.

Guided Instruction

33 MAKE INFERENCES The quilt is for Tanya. What does this tell you about Grandma's and Mama's feelings? (They appreciate all the work Tanya did and want the quilt to be passed down in the family.)

MAKE INFERENCE	EXPLAIN INFERENCE
Tanya wants things to happen quickly.	She doesn't want to wait a year to finish the quilt.
Tanya understands Grandma the best.	Mama thinks Grandma is lonely, but Tanya knows that she is happy to be with the quilt.
Mama thinks the quilt is important.	She smiles and helps Grandma with the quilt.
Grandma and Mama appreciate the work Tanya did.	They give the quilt to Tanya.

RETELL THE STORY Ask volunteers to tell the major events of the story. Students may refer to their charts. Then have partners write one or two sentences that summarize the story.

STUDENT SELF-ASSESSMENT

- How did making inferences help me to understand the story?
- How did the chart help me?

TRANSFERRING THE STRATEGY

- When might I try using this strategy again? In what other reading might the chart help me?

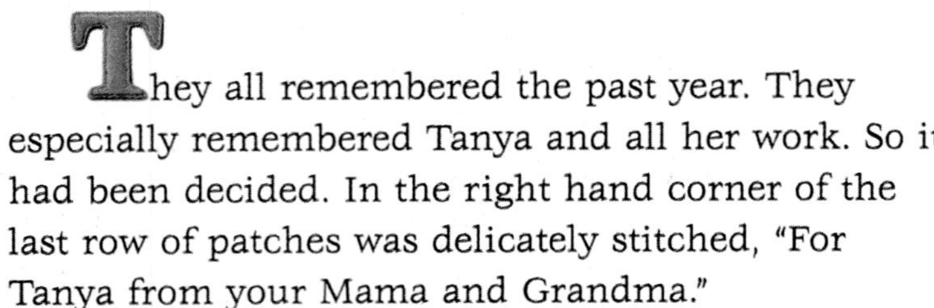
They all remembered the past year. They especially remembered Tanya and all her work. So it had been decided. In the right hand corner of the last row of patches was delicately stitched, "For Tanya from your Mama and Grandma."

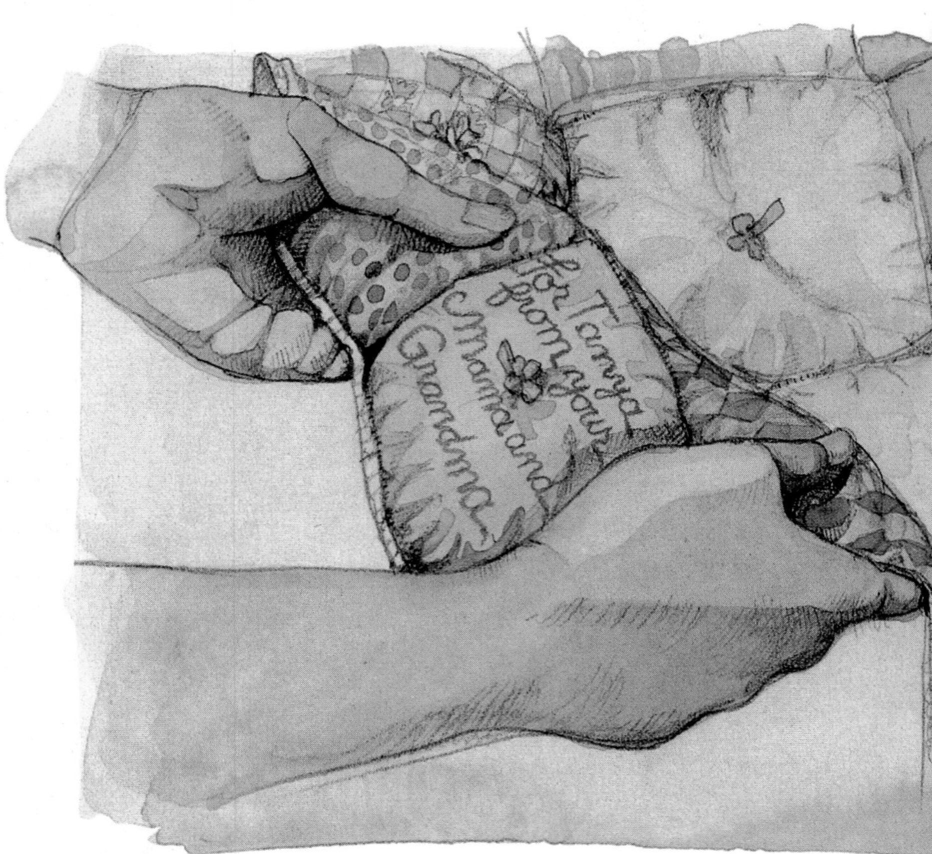

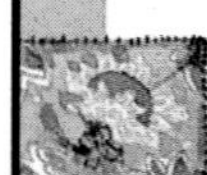
344

REREADING FOR *Fluency*

PARTNERS Have students role-play their favorite characters in the story with partners. Encourage students to read with feeling and expression as they read different sections of the story.

READING RATE You may want to evaluate an individual student's reading rate. Have the student read aloud from *The Patchwork Quilt* for one minute. Ask the student to place a self-stick note after the last word read. Then count the number of words he or she has read.

A Running Record form provided in **Diagnostic/Placement Evaluation** will help you evaluate reading rate(s).

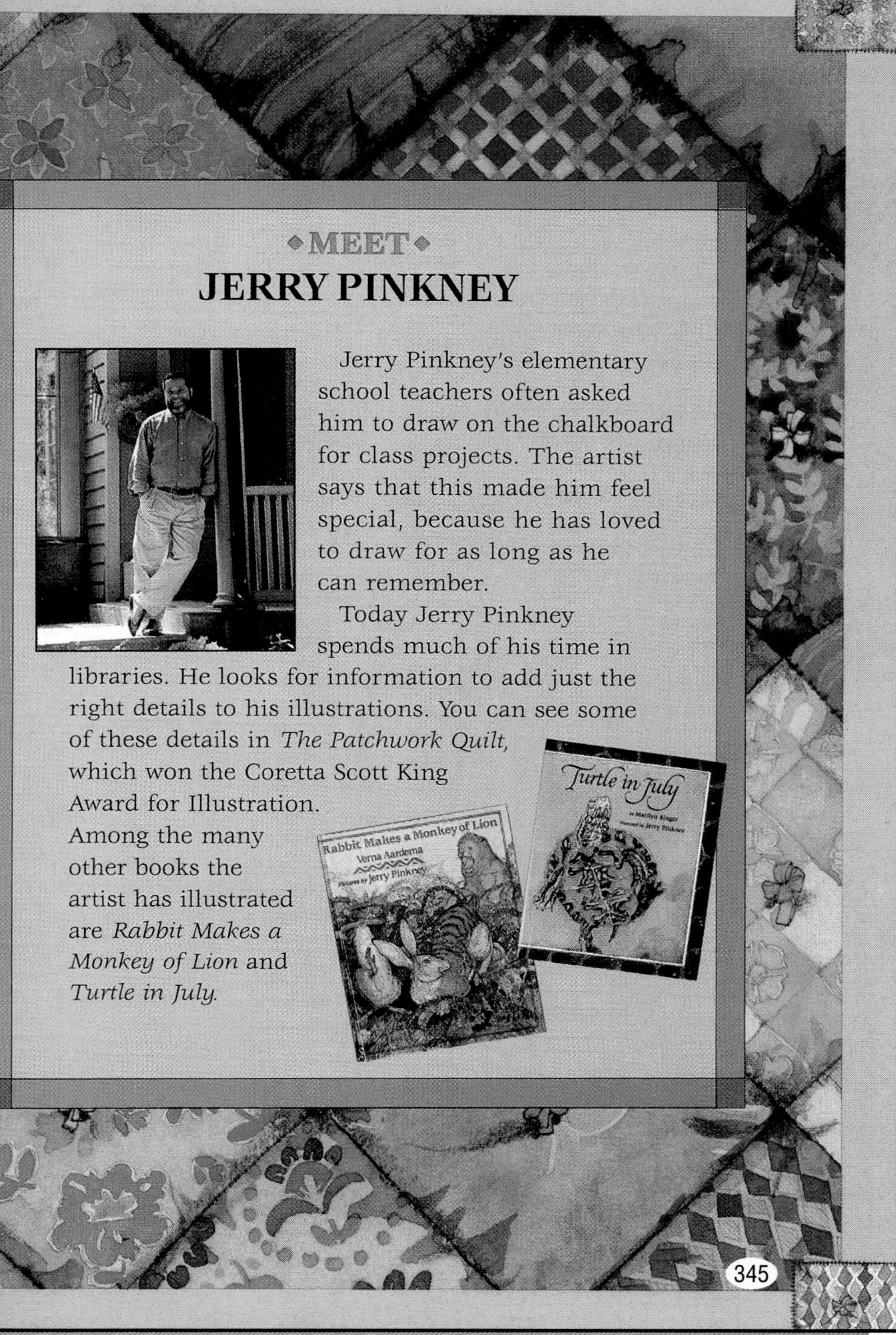

◆MEET◆
JERRY PINKNEY
Jerry Pinkney's elementary school teachers often asked him to draw on the chalkboard for class projects. The artist says that this made him feel special, because he has loved to draw for as long as he can remember.
Today Jerry Pinkney spends much of his time in libraries. He looks for information to add just the right details to his illustrations. You can see some of these details in *The Patchwork Quilt,* which won the Coretta Scott King Award for Illustration. Among the many other books the artist has illustrated are *Rabbit Makes a Monkey of Lion* and *Turtle in July.*
Rabbit Makes a Monkey of Lion
Verna Aardema
Pictures by Jerry Pinkney
Turtle in July
345

Guided Instruction

Return to Predictions and Purposes

Review with students their story predictions and reasons for reading the story. Were their predictions correct? Did they find out what they wanted to know?

PREDICTIONS	WHAT HAPPENED
The story is about a patchwork quilt.	The story is about a family who makes a patchwork quilt.
The main character is an African American girl.	The main character is Tanya, an African American girl.

INFORMAL ASSESSMENT

MAKE INFERENCES

- Have students make inferences about Tanya's character from her actions.
- Ask them to explain the inferences that they make.

HOW TO ASSESS Students should recognize that making inferences can help them understand a character's feelings, thoughts, and motivation.

FOLLOW UP If students have trouble making inferences about Tanya's character, help them list her actions. Ask them: What kind of person would do this?

If students have trouble explaining their inferences, ask them to list an action of Tanya's that would support each inference.

LITERARY RESPONSE

QUICK-WRITE Invite students to record their thoughts about the story. These questions may help them get started:

JOURNAL

- What do you think of Tanya? Of Grandma? Would you like to have either of them as friends? Why?
- Would you like to make a family patchwork quilt? What might you include in it?

ORAL RESPONSE Have students share their journal writing and discuss what part of the story they enjoyed most.

Story Questions

Have students discuss or write answers to the questions on page 346.

Answers:

1. Grandma used leftover scraps. *Literal/Plot*
2. Sometimes people forget to keep up old family traditions. *Inferential/Make Inferences*
3. Tanya will probably make another quilt; she has learned the value of keeping and sharing family memories. *Inferential/Make Predictions*
4. This story is about a girl who makes a patchwork quilt with her family. *Critical/Summarize*
5. Possible answer: It would have pictures of their community painted on the patches. *Critical/Reading Across Texts*

Write an Editorial For a full writing process lesson related to this suggestion, see pages 349K–349L.

Story Questions & Activities

1. Where did Grandma get the cloth for the squares on her quilt?
2. What do you think Grandma meant when she said, "Sometimes the old ways are forgotten"?
3. Do you think Tanya will make another quilt some day? Why or why not?
4. What is this story mostly about?
5. Pretend Tanya and Fernando Espino are working together on a quilt. What do you think the quilt would look like?

Write an Editorial

Write an editorial for your school paper. Explain why it is important for young people and older people to work together. Tell what they might learn from each other. Support your ideas with examples.

Meeting Individual Needs

EASY

Name________________ Date__________ **Reteach 90**

Vocabulary

costume attic gaze pattern examined anxious

Choose the vocabulary word that matches each meaning. Then complete the puzzle.

Across

3. excited anxious
5. looked at examined
6. the space just below the roof of a house attic

Down

1. to look at something for a long time gaze
2. clothes worn to look like someone or something else costume
4. a design pattern

6

Story Comprehension **Reteach 91**

Put an **X** next to the sentences that describe "The Patchwork Quilt."

x Tanya agrees to help Grandma make the quilt.
x Grandma sews the last pieces of the quilt together.
x Everyone works on the quilt when Grandma gets sick.
___ Grandma sells the finished quilt.
x Grandma makes the quilt patches from old clothes.

90–91 **At Home:** Have students write a sentence explaining why the patchwork quilt is important to Tanya and her family. Book 3.1/Unit 3 **The Patchwork Quilt** 5

Reteach, 91

ON-LEVEL

Name________________ Date__________ **Practice 91**

Story Comprehension

Look back over "The Patchwork Quilt." Then complete the chart below. Answers may vary.

1. Setting of story	Tanya's house
2. Main characters	Tanya, Grandma, Mama, Papa, Ted, and Jim
3. Beginning of story	Grandma tells Tanya about the patchwork quilt she wants to make. Tanya says that she will help her.
4. Middle of story	Grandma gathers patches for her quilt from the family's clothes. Mama decides to help. After Grandma gets sick, the whole family helps cut and prepare patches for the quilt.
5. End of story	Grandma feels better and sews the patches of the quilt together.

Now match each patch of clothing or fabric with the person it belonged to in the story.

b 6. gold dress — a. Grandma
a 7. piece of old quilt — b. Mama
e 8. red shirt — c. Tanya
c 9. African princess costume — d. Jim
d 10. blue corduroy pants — e. Ted

91 **At Home:** Have students write a sentence explaining why the patchwork quilt was important to Tanya and her family. Book 3.1/Unit 3 **The Patchwork Quilt** 10

Practice, 91

CHALLENGE

Name________________ Date__________ **Extend 90**

Vocabulary

anxious attic costume examined gazed pattern

Make up a story with a partner. First make a list of the events that will happen in the story. Then use words in the box to tell how the characters feel or what they will do. Write your story on another piece of paper.
Answers will vary.

Extend 91

Story Comprehension

Work with a group to make a patchwork quilt "drawing" about your class that you "won't forget." Group members can include a drawing that tells something special about themselves. Write a sentence under each picture that tells what is important about it.

90–91 **At Home:** Have students write a paragraph about other ways besides quilting that families might use to record special memories. Book 3.1/Unit 3 **The Patchwork Quilt**

Extend, 91

Design a Geometric Quilt

With a pencil, divide a piece of paper into four equal rectangles or triangles. Using only triangles and rectangles, create a different design for each of the four sections. Use markers to color in your designs.

Create a Scrapbook

Make a scrapbook to record special memories. Take several sheets of paper. Cut two pieces of poster board the same size as your paper. Use the poster board to form the cover of your book. Staple the cover and pages in place. Decorate the cover with colored markers.

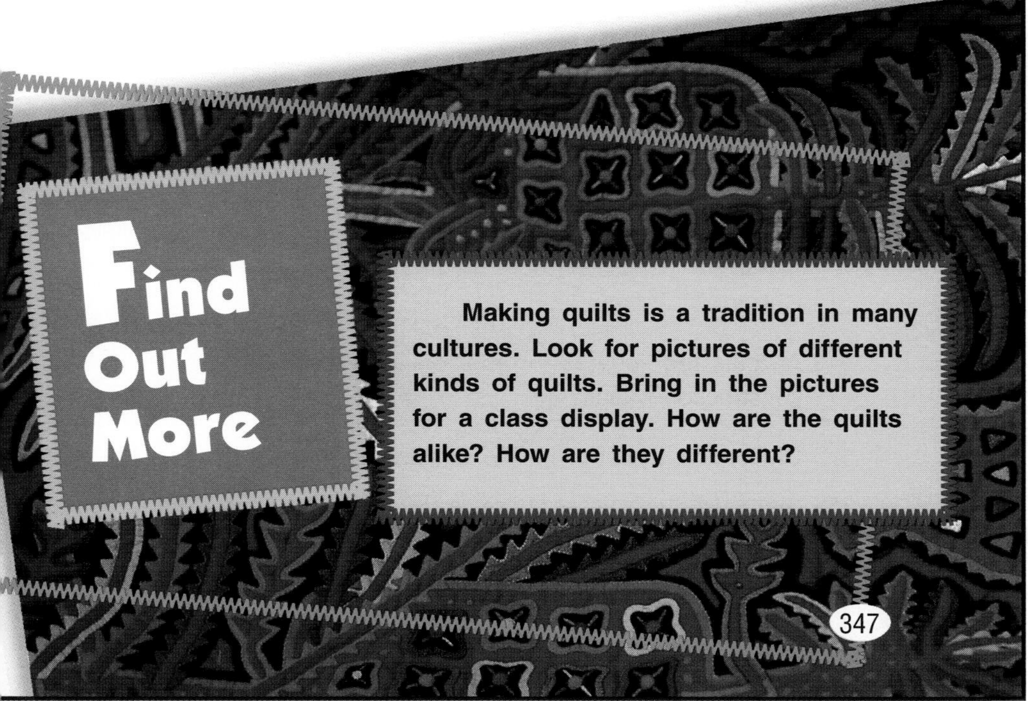

Find Out More

Making quilts is a tradition in many cultures. Look for pictures of different kinds of quilts. Bring in the pictures for a class display. How are the quilts alike? How are they different?

347

Story Activities

Design a Geometric Quilt

Materials: paper, pencil, felt-tipped markers

ONE Encourage students to create colorful patterns with their geometric shapes. When finished, attach each student's squares to form a geometric quilt.

Create a Scrapbook

Materials: paper, poster board, felt-tipped markers

ONE Help students make their own scrapbooks. After they finish, have them fill their scrapbooks with memorabilia (photographs, party invitations, and so on).

Find Out More

GROUP **RESEARCH AND INQUIRY** Tell groups of students that each group is going to choose a picture of a quilt and give a presentation about it. Guide students to use encyclopedias, books on quilting, and the Internet.

interNET CONNECTION Go to ***www.mhschool.com/reading*** for more information on patchwork quilts.

FORMAL ASSESSMENT

After page 347, see Selection Assessment.

GRAPHIC AIDS

Students will:

- use a diagram.
- follow directions to make a paper quilt.

PREPARE Preview the diagram with students. Display **Teaching Chart 75.**

TEACH Review that diagrams can help keep ideas organized in the way they show information. Review that rows run horizontally and columns run vertically. Have a student circle the second row. Have a student circle the first column. Have a student identify the square in the third row, first column.

PRACTICE Have students follow directions 1–4. Review each step with them as it is completed.

ASSESS/CLOSE Have students choose a single color and identify, by row and column, which squares in the quilt are that color.

STUDY SKILLS

Use a Diagram

A diagram is a picture that shows the parts of something. The diagram below shows a pattern for making a quilt. You will need paper, scissors, glue, crayons, and construction paper to make a paper quilt.

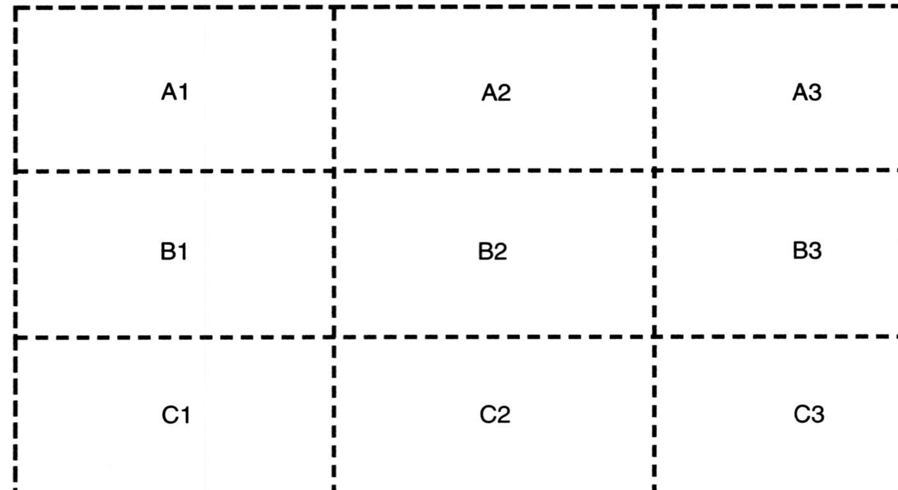

Follow directions 1–4. Then answer question 5.

1. Trace the diagram onto a sheet of paper. Color each square a different color, but don't cover up the numbers and letters.
2. Cut out the squares.
3. Arrange the squares in order on a piece of construction paper.
4. Glue each square onto the construction paper.
5. What colors are in Row 2? Row 3?

Meeting Individual Needs

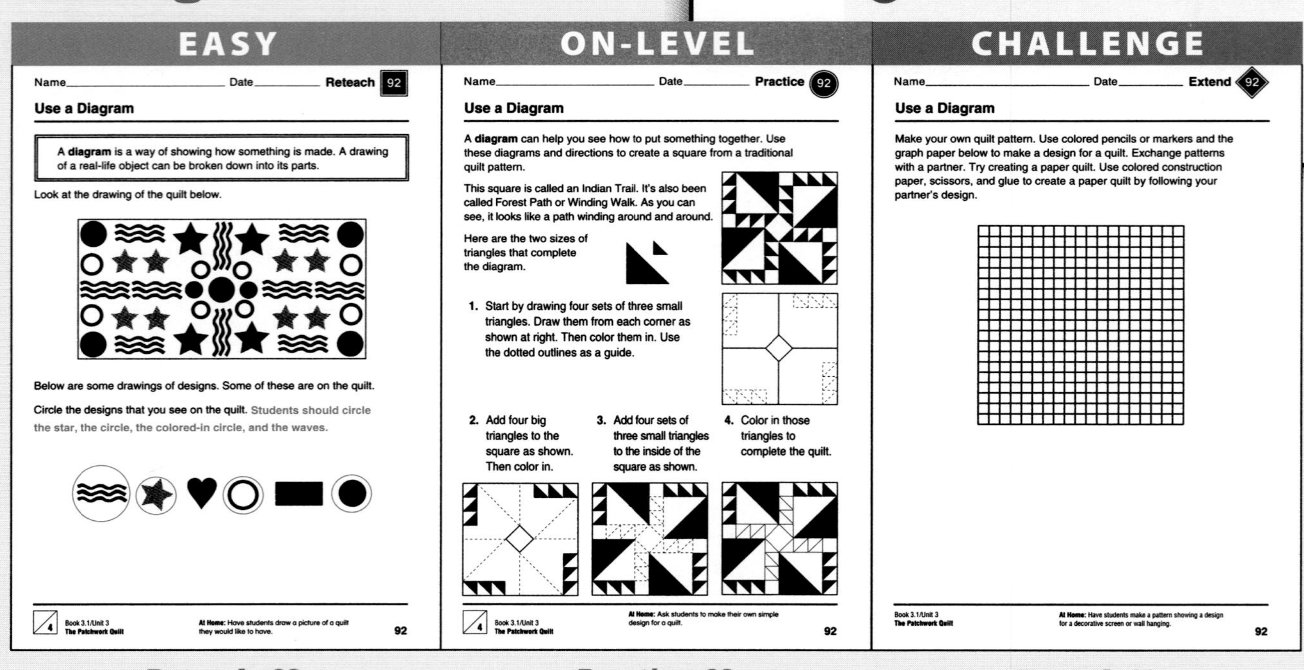

EASY

Name________ Date______ Reteach 92

Use a Diagram

A **diagram** is a way of showing how something is made. A drawing of a real-life object can be broken down into its parts.

Look at the drawing of the quilt below.

Below are some drawings of designs. Some of these are on the quilt.

Circle the designs that you see on the quilt. Students should circle the star, the circle, the colored-in circle, and the waves.

4 Book 3.1/Unit 3 The Patchwork Quilt — At Home: Have students draw a picture of a quilt they would like to have. 92

ON-LEVEL

Name________ Date______ Practice 92

Use a Diagram

A **diagram** can help you see how to put something together. Use these diagrams and directions to create a square from a traditional quilt pattern.

This square is called an Indian Trail. It's also been called Forest Path or Winding Walk. As you can see, it looks like a path winding around and around.

Here are the two sizes of triangles that complete the diagram.

1. Start by drawing four sets of three small triangles. Draw them from each corner as shown at right. Then color them in. Use the dotted outlines as a guide.
2. Add four big triangles to the square as shown. Then color in.
3. Add four sets of three small triangles to the inside of the square as shown.
4. Color in those triangles to complete the quilt.

4 Book 3.1/Unit 3 The Patchwork Quilt — At Home: Ask students to make their own simple design for a quilt. 92

CHALLENGE

Name________ Date______ Extend 92

Use a Diagram

Make your own quilt pattern. Use colored pencils or markers and the graph paper below to make a design for a quilt. Exchange patterns with a partner. Try creating a paper quilt. Use colored construction paper, scissors, and glue to create a paper quilt by following your partner's design.

Book 3.1/Unit 3 The Patchwork Quilt — At Home: Have students make a pattern showing a design for a decorative screen or wall hanging. 92

Reteach, 92 — Practice, 92 — Extend, 92

TEST POWER

Test Tip

Take your time and do your work carefully.

DIRECTIONS:

Read the story. Then read each question about the story.

SAMPLE

Randy and the Beaver

One day, Randy the park ranger was walking near the pond. He saw a baby beaver chewing on a log. Winter was coming soon and so Randy decided that he would make a house for the little beaver.

He went home and came back with some old wood, nails, and a hammer. When Randy was finished building the house, he hid behind a tree to see if the beaver would use the house.

Soon the beaver came up to the house. But instead of going inside, he started to chew on the wood.

Randy chuckled and said, "Next time, I'll know better. You're the best one to build a house for yourself. You can only be what you are—a beaver."

1 How did Randy feel about the beaver at the end of the story?

- ● Happy
- ○ Upset
- ○ Worried
- ○ Angry

2 The main idea of this story is that Randy—

- ● learned that animals will be themselves
- ○ should make another house for the beaver
- ○ has too many pets
- ○ will need to get more nails

349

ITBS/TEST PREPARATION

TERRANOVA/TEST PREPARATION

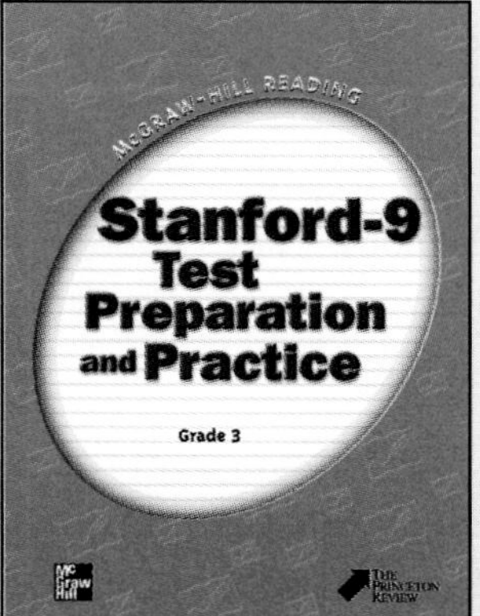

SAT 9/TEST PREPARATION

Test Power

THE PRINCETON REVIEW

Read the Page

Have students read the story. As a group, discuss how the ranger's feelings change from the beginning of the story to the end.

Discuss the Questions

QUESTION 1: This question requires students to understand the feelings of a character at the end of the story. Ask: Why do you think that Randy chuckled? (He is happy that the beaver knows how to build his own house.)

QUESTION 2: This question asks students to find the main idea. It is found in the final sentence. Work through the answer choices as a group. As you discuss each choice, point out why each choice is incorrect *even* if some of the facts are stated in the story. The main idea paraphrases the *whole* story in a few words. Refer back to the story.

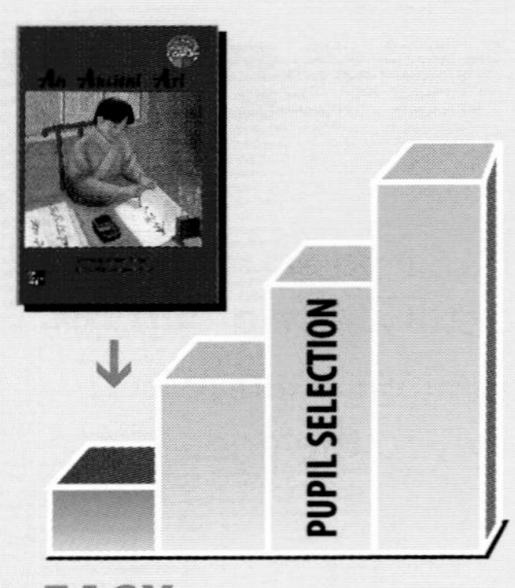

Answers to Story Questions

1. The boys were waiting for it to stop raining.
2. David learned calligraphy to please his grandfather.
3. David's grandfather was an expert, so he must have studied for many years.
4. The story is about how David learned Japanese arts from his grandfather and how he came to appreciate them.
5. Answers will vary.

Story Questions and Writing Activity

1. What were the boys doing at the beginning of the story?
2. Why did David decide to learn calligraphy?
3. How long did David's grandfather study calligraphy?
4. What is the story mostly about?
5. If David happened to meet Tanya from *The Patchwork Quilt,* what do you think they might talk about?

Write a Haiku

David wrote a haiku. You can, too. A haiku is a short poem. It does not have any rhymes. It has seventeen syllables: five in the first line, seven in the second line, and five in the last line. It usually describes something in an unusual way. Write a haiku about a member of your family or a friend.

from *An Ancient Art*

Leveled Books

EASY

An Ancient Art

/ou/ and /oi/

☑ Make Inferences

☑ Instructional Vocabulary
anxious, attic, costume, examined, gazed, pattern

Guided Reading

PREVIEW AND PREDICT Conduct a **picture walk**, discussing each illustration up to page 6. Ask: What might the story be about?

SET PURPOSES Students should decide what they want to find out as they read the story. Have students write down questions they would like to have answered from the story. For example, What did David's grandfather show him how to do?

READ THE BOOK Use questions like the following to guide students' reading or after they have read the story independently.

Page 2: What does the word *gazed* mean? (to look at something a long time) ***Vocabulary***

Page 4: What might have happened to David's grandfather? Explain. (He may have died. Jimmy refers to his grandfather in the past tense.) ***Draw Conclusion***

Page 7: Reread page 7. What word on this page has the same vowel sound as *spoil*? (joined) How is the /oi/ sound spelled? *(oi)* ***Phonics and Decoding***

Page 12: What might David's grandfather have been saving the kimono for? (He might have been saving it for future generations of his family.) ***Make Inferences***

Page 16: After Jimmy tells David that he thinks that his grandfather would've really liked his poem, how does David feel? How do you know? (David is thrilled. "His eyes shone with joy.") ***Character***

RETURN TO PREDICTIONS AND PURPOSES Review students' predictions and reasons for reading.

LITERARY RESPONSE Discuss these questions:

- Why did David wear a kimono while practicing his calligraphy?
- Other than calligraphy, what did David learn from his grandfather?

Also see the story questions and activity in *An Ancient Art*.

See the Phonics **CD-ROM** for practice using /ou/ and /oi/ words.

Leveled Books

INDEPENDENT

Recording the Past

- ☑ Make Inferences
- ☑ Instructional Vocabulary: *anxious, attic, costume, examined, gazed, pattern*

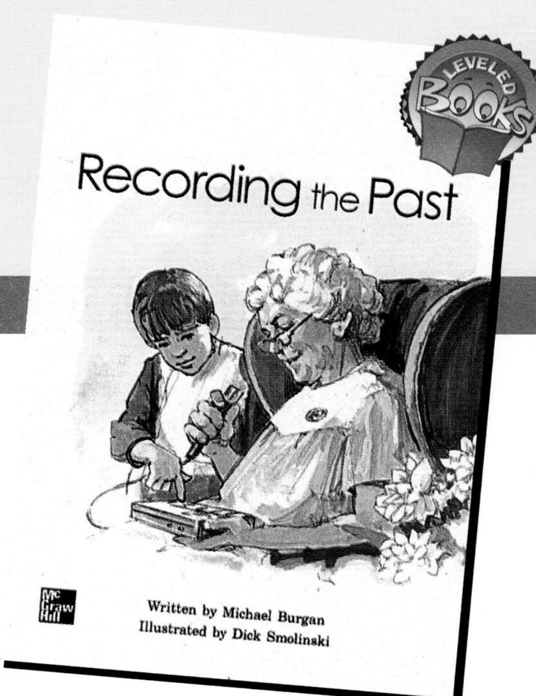

Guided Reading

PREVIEW AND PREDICT Conduct a **picture walk**, discussing each illustration up to page 8. Ask: What might the story be about?

SET PURPOSES Students should decide what they want to find out as they read the story. For example, what Babci is telling her grandchildren.

READ THE BOOK Use questions like the following to guide students' reading or after they have read the story independently.

Page 6: What does the word *examined* mean? (look closely) ***Vocabulary***

Page 10: What was Babci's life like in Poland? (It was hard. She worked on the farm with her family.) ***Draw Conclusions***

Page 12–13: Why did Babci and her siblings have to make their own clothes for the Bransk festival? (They could not buy the clothes or costumes.) ***Cause and Effect***

Page 14: What might Babci think of when she looks at her silver pin? (She thinks about her ancestors who wore it.) ***Make Inferences***

Page 16: What can you tell about Billy? (He cares about his family's history.) ***Character***

RETURN TO PREDICTIONS AND PURPOSES Review students' predictions and reasons for reading. Which predictions were correct? Which were not? Which questions were answered? Which were not?

LITERARY RESPONSE Discuss these questions:

- How does Babci's childhood differ from that of her grandchildren's?
- Why did Babci's mother share her only piece of jewelry with her daughter?

Also see the story questions and activity in *Recording the Past*.

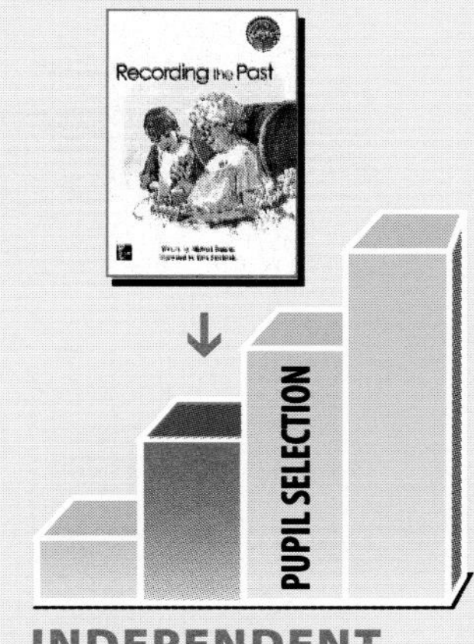

Answers to Story Questions

1. Babci lived in Poland.
2. He was afraid for his family's safety in the coming war.
3. The family was poor and could not hire workers.
4. The story is mostly about Babci's memories of her life as a girl in Poland.
5. Answers will vary.

Story Questions and Writing Activity

1. What country did Babci live in before she came to America?
2. Why did Babci's father want to leave their farm?
3. Why did Babci and her brothers and sisters have to work on the farm?
4. What is the story mostly about?
5. How is Babci's silver pin like Tanya's quilt in *The Patchwork Quilt*?

Record a Memory

Ask an older relative to describe something he or she enjoyed doing as a child. If you want, you can tape record this memory. Then draw a picture showing your relative doing this activity. Finally, write a short description of the activity in your drawing.

from *Recording the Past*

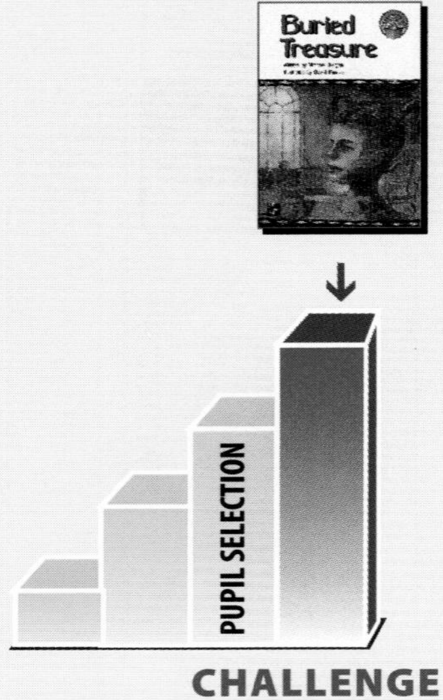

Answers to Story Questions

1. María's relatives lived in New Mexico and Mexico.
2. María was scared to be in the dark and didn't know what was there.
3. Because they were important to her and the rest of the family.
4. María guessed they might be relatives because their pictures were in a box of old family photographs.
5. Answers will vary.

Story Questions and Writing Activity

1. Where did María's relatives live before they came to California?
2. Why did María scream when she walked into the dark corner of the attic?
3. How did María know she had Native American relatives?
4. What is the story mostly about?
5. If Tanya's mom from *The Patchwork Quilt* met María's mom, what do you think they might talk about?

Can You Do It?

In the story, María puts the photos into three piles. If there were seventy-five photos and the piles were equal, how many photos would be in each pile? Write two or three sentences explaining how you determined the answer.

from *Buried Treasure*

Leveled Books

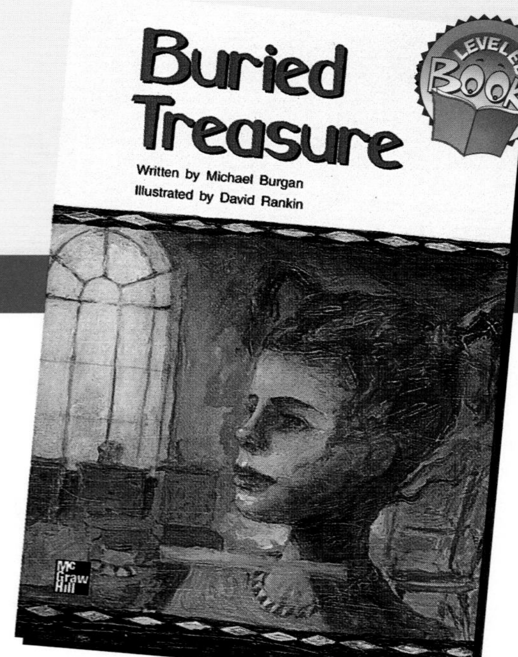

CHALLENGE

Buried Treasure

☑ Make Inferences

☑ Instructional Vocabulary: *anxious, attic, costume, examined, gazed, pattern*

Guided Reading

PREVIEW AND PREDICT Conduct a **picture walk**, discussing each illustration up to page 7. Ask: What might the story be about?

SET PURPOSES Students should decide what they want to find out as they read the story. For example, they may want to know who the people are in the old photos.

READ THE BOOK Use questions like the following to guide students' reading or to discuss after they have read the story independently.

Page 3: What does the word *anxious* mean in the last sentence on this page? (eager) Why does Maria feel anxious? (She is excited about what she might discover.) ***Vocabulary***

Page 6: When was the box Maria discovered packed? (1926) How do you know? (The paper packing was newspaper dated September 7, 1926.) ***Draw Conclusions***

Page 7: Why did Maria think the photos were taken on a farm? (There was a horse-drawn plow and some farm animals in the background of the photo.) ***Setting***

Page 10: Why does Maria think she may be part Native American? (She found a photo showing a group of Native Americans.) ***Cause and Effect***

Page 11: How does Maria's mother feel about the photographs that Maria found? (She is happy to see them.) ***Make Inferences***

RETURN TO PREDICTIONS AND PURPOSES Review students' predictions and reasons for reading. Which predictions were correct? Which were not? Which questions were answered? Which were not?

LITERARY RESPONSE Discuss these questions:

- Why do Mrs. Ayala's eyes well up with tears when she sees the old photographs?
- Why does Mrs. Ayala think the old photos are better than gold and jewels?
- Why is the story titled *Buried Treasure?*

Also see the story questions and activity in *Buried Treasure*.

Connecting Texts

CLASS DISCUSSION
Create a Sharing Memories chart. Write the story titles on a chart. Discuss with students the importance of memories in characters' lives and how memories are shared. Why might it be important to know where you come from? Call on volunteers from each reading level and write their suggestions on the chart.

SHARING MEMORIES

The Patchwork Quilt	An Ancient Art	Recording the Past	Buried Treasure
• Tanya's grandmother is making a quilt made up of patches that bring to mind special people and events in her life. • The quilt is finished and brings memories to mind for the entire family.	• David shares his memories of his grandfather with his friend Jimmy. • David's grandfather taught him the Japanese art of calligraphy.	• Babci shares with her grandchildren memories of her life growing up in Poland. • Jean and Billy use a tape recorder to record their grandmother's recollections.	• Maria finds old family photographs while exploring in the attic. • Maria shows the photos to her mom who happily shares with Maria their family history.

Viewing/Representing

GROUP PRESENTATIONS Divide the class into groups, one for each of the four books read in the lesson. (For *The Patchwork Quilt* combine students of different reading levels.) Have each group create a skit for two or three scenes from their book. Have each group present its skit to the class.

AUDIENCE RESPONSE Ask students to pay attention to each group's presentation. Have the audience tell what they found interesting about each performance. Allow time for questions after each presentation.

Research and Inquiry

MORE ABOUT SHARING MEMORIES Have students ask themselves: Why is it important to share memories? Invite students to do the following:

- Ask your parents to share a story with you that their parents told them.
- Work with your parents or grandparents on your own family tree.
- What memories do you want to share? Create a family scrapbook.

*inter***NET** **CONNECTION** Students can log on to ***www.mhschool.com/reading*** to learn more about family trees.

Students will make and explain inferences about characters.

LANGUAGE SUPPORT

ESL Hold up a photo of a child and ask students to make statements about him or her. On the board write each factual statement under the word *Fact* and each inference under the word *Inference*.

Review Make Inferences

PREPARE

Define Making Inferences Review: Even when an author doesn't state directly how characters feel or what they are thinking, a reader can use what the author says, what the illustrations show, and personal experience to discover this information. This is called *making inferences*. Ask students about some of the inferences they have made about the characters in the selection they have just read.

TEACH

Read "The Masterpiece" and Model the Skill Ask students to pay close attention to what the author states and does not state directly as you read the **Teaching Chart 76** passage.

The Masterpiece

Tanya brushed away a tear as she thought about her grandmother. Grandma lay sick in her bed behind a closed door. Tanya worried about whether Grandma was ever going to get better. Then she wondered whether Grandma would ever be strong enough to finish her patchwork quilt—her masterpiece. If not, what would happen to it?

Picking up an edge of the quilt, Tanya looked closely at the work Grandma had done on it. The stitches were small and close together, but Tanya was sure that she could sew like that, too.

Teaching Chart 76

Discuss clues in the passage that help readers to make inferences about the character.

MODEL I can tell that Tanya feels sad, because she brushes away a tear. Plus, I know that you feel sad when someone you care about is sick. I can also tell Tanya is confident, because she knows she could sew like her grandmother.

PRACTICE

Make Inferences About Character

Have students make inferences about what Tanya is like based on clues in "The Masterpiece." First have them underline clues in the passage that help them to make their inferences. Then have them explain why they made those inferences. ▶ **Linguistic/Interpersonal**

ASSESS/CLOSE

Make and Explain Inferences Chart

Assign partners. Have one student write a paragraph about a character, giving hints about what the person is like but not stating it directly. The other student can make and explain inferences about this character based on the description.

ALTERNATE TEACHING STRATEGY

MAKE INFERENCES

For a different approach to teaching this skill, see page T66.

SELF-SELECTED Reading

Students may choose from the following titles.

ANTHOLOGY

- *The Patchwork Quilt*

LEVELED BOOKS

- *An Ancient Art*
- *Recording the Past*
- *Buried Treasure*

Bibliography, pages T76–T77

Meeting Individual Needs for Comprehension

EASY

Name__________ Date______ **Reteach 93**

Make Inferences

Good authors do not always **tell** readers how characters feel or why they act as they do. They **show** readers how a character feels through what the characters do.

Read the following passages about "The Patchwork Quilt." Then answer each question.

"Yes, your mother can find a quilt in most big stores. However, it won't look like my quilt. I'm sure it won't last very long either . . ."

Grandma grew silent. Suddenly she looked away from Tanya and stared out the window for a long time. Then she began to rub the pieces of material between her fingers.

1. Based on this passage, how do you think Grandma feels when Mama offers to buy a quilt? Grandma's feelings are hurt.
2. Why do you think Grandma turns away from Tanya? She is remembering the quilt her mother made.
3. Why does Grandma rub the pieces of material between her fingers? She is thinking about what the pieces mean to her.

"Grandma didn't want to tell us that she was feeling sick. She thought it would ruin our Christmas," Mama said later, her face tired, her eyes red and puffy.

4. Why is Mama tired? She is worried about Grandma.
5. Why are Mama's eyes puffy and red? Mama has probably been crying.

93 **At Home:** Have students make another inference based on the story. Book 3.1/Unit 3 **The Patchwork Quilt** 5

McGraw-Hill School Division

Reteach, 93

ON-LEVEL

Name__________ Date______ **Practice 93**

Make Inferences

An **inference** is very much like a conclusion. A conclusion is almost certainly true. An inference is probably true.

Read each of the following passages about "The Patchwork Quilt." Then answer each question. Answers will vary.

Grandma's eyes grew distant and dark. She turned away from Tanya and looked out the window for a long time, rubbing the material between her fingers.

1. What do you think Grandma was thinking about? the past and the old ways
2. How do you think she felt as she looked out the window? sad; longing for the past
3. What information helped you make your inferences? Grandma's eyes grew dark, so she was probably feeling sad. Rubbing the cloth helped her remember the past.

Finally, Grandma was ready to do the quilting, but she had one very important thing to add.

4. What "very important thing" did Grandma add to the quilt? She stitched "For Tanya from your Mama and Grandma" on one of the patches.
5. When did you learn about the very important thing Grandma wanted to add? at the end of the story
6. Why do you think Grandma didn't tell Tanya what she was going to do? She wanted to surprise Tanya.

93 **At Home:** Have students write a sentence or two explaining whether they think Tanya will teach her children about quiltmaking. Book 3.1/Unit 3 **The Patchwork Quilt** 6

McGraw-Hill School Division

Practice, 93

CHALLENGE

Name__________ Date______ **Extend 93**

Make Inferences

Write a sentence or two about "The Patchwork Quilt" telling how you think Grandma feels about the past.

Answers will vary. For example, She longs for the past. She wants to remember the past and the old ways of doing things.

What clues in the story helped you infer this?

Answers will vary. For example, Grandma tells Tanya about the quilt her own mother made.

Work with a partner to write interview questions to ask Grandma about her past. Act out the interview.

93 **At Home:** Have students write a sentence telling why they think Tanya removed a few squares from Grandma's old quilt. Book 3.1/Unit 3 **The Patchwork Quilt**

McGraw-Hill School Division

Extend, 93

LANGUAGE SUPPORT

Name__________ Date__________

Story Patches

The Patch	What this tells you about...
	Tanya
	Jim
	Grandmother
	Father

102 **The Patchwork Quilt** • Language Support/Blackline Master 50 Grade 3

Language Support, 102

Students will identify the main idea and supporting details.

TEACHING TIP

MANAGEMENT Save projects, papers, and other assignments your students do throughout the year. Next September, use them to create a "See What You'll Do" bulletin board highlighting what awaits your new class.

Review Main Idea

PREPARE

Discuss Main Idea and Supporting Details

Explain: Finding the main idea is a useful way to understand what the author is trying to say. You can also look for supporting details to decide if the author has explained or supported the main point.

TEACH

Read "Family Makes Patchwork Quilt" and Model the Skill

Read the newspaper article "Family Makes Patchwork Quilt" on **Teaching Chart 77.** Focus students' attention on the article's main idea and supporting details.

Family Makes Patchwork Quilt

This weekend, our public library will present something very special. The library will display a patchwork quilt made by all the members of one local family.

The family members include a grandmother, a mother and father, and three children. "We all worked together on the quilt," said Tanya, one of the family's children. "It was hard, but it was also fun."

They spent a full year working on it. In making the quilt, the family used scraps of material representing all the special moments of that year.

Teaching Chart 77

Help students to think about what the main idea is and why. Ask a volunteer to find and underline the sentence that contains the main idea of the article.

MODEL Often, the title of a newspaper article can give me a clue to the main idea. From this title I know that the article is about a family who has made a patchwork quilt. When I read the second sentence, I found that it contained all the important information that would be discussed in the rest of the article.

PRACTICE

Create a Main Idea/Supporting Details Chart

GROUP

Have students create a Main Idea/Supporting Details chart for the article. Help them get started. ▶ **Spatial/Interpersonal**

Main Idea	Supporting Details
The library will display a patchwork quilt made by all the members of one local family.	Family members include a grandmother, mother and father, and three children.
	The family used scraps of material representing special moments of the year.

Graphic Organizer 31

ASSESS/CLOSE

Identify Main Ideas and Supporting Details

Have students create a Main Idea/Supporting Details chart for a familiar story or show. Have them use their charts to summarize the story or event.

ALTERNATE TEACHING STRATEGY

MAIN IDEA

For a different approach to teaching this skill, see page T60.

LOOKING AHEAD

Students will apply this skill as they read the next selection, *Pecos Bill*.

Meeting Individual Needs for Comprehension

EASY

Name______ Date______ Reteach 94

Main Idea

You can better understand what you read if you notice the **main idea** and **supporting details**. The main idea tells the most important point the author wants to make. The supporting details are smaller points that explain the main idea.

Read the story below. First write the main idea of the story. Then write the supporting details.

When it was time to make lunch, the whole family helped out. Dad cut the bread. I set the table. My sister, Betty, folded the napkins. Mom made sandwiches. Our dog, Lenny, didn't help. He just waited for the leftovers.

Main Idea:

1. The whole family helped prepare lunch.

Supporting Details:

2. I set the table.
3. Betty folded the napkins.
4. Dad cut the bread.
5. Mom made sandwiches.

5 Book 3.1/Unit 3 The Patchwork Quilt — **At Home:** Encourage students to add two more supporting details to the story. 94

Reteach, 94

ON-LEVEL

Name______ Date______ Practice 94

Main Idea

Read the following paragraphs. Then fill in the details that support the main ideas. Answers will vary.

Yesterday, Carl went to the store. His mom and dad are fixing up his room. Carl bought green, brown, and orange paint for the walls and ceiling. Carl asked his mom to order a white shade for the window. For the floor, Carl hopes to find a red rug. Carl's mom thinks that his room will look like a rainbow.

Main Idea: Carl's mom and dad are fixing up his room.

Supporting details:

1. Carl bought paint for the walls and ceiling.
2. Carl asked his mom to order a shade.
3. Carl wants a red rug.

Gina went out to lunch with her friend, Wendy. Both girls had hamburgers. For dessert, Gina had a banana split. Wendy had fresh fruit. After lunch, the two friends went shopping.

Main Idea: Gina went out to lunch with her friend, Wendy.

Supporting details:

1. Both girls had hamburgers.
2. Gina had a banana split for dessert.
3. Wendy had fresh fruit.

6 Book 3.1/Unit 3 The Patchwork Quilt — **At Home:** Have students read a short magazine or newspaper article and identify a main idea and two supporting details. 94

Practice, 94

CHALLENGE

Name______ Date______ Extend 94

Main Idea

Work with a group to read copies of a short newspaper article. Write a sentence stating the main idea of the article. List the supporting details from the article. List any details from the article that do not support the main idea. Answers will vary.

MAIN IDEA:

SUPPORTING DETAILS:

OTHER DETAILS:

Write a sentence telling why you think the article might have included details that do not support the main idea.

Answers may vary. For example, the author wanted to include an interesting fact.

Book 3.1/Unit 3 The Patchwork Quilt — **At Home:** Have students read a short magazine or newspaper article and identify the main idea and two supporting details. 94

Extend, 94

LANGUAGE SUPPORT

Name______ Date______

What Is It All About?

Main Idea	
Who?	Grandmother, Tanya and family
What?	Make patchwork quilt
Where?	at home
How?	by using patches of fabric from old clothes
When?	over many months
Why?	Grandmother wanted to leave a memory

Grade 3 — Language Support/Blackline Master 51 • The Patchwork Quilt 103

Language Support, 103

Students will:

- recognize that some words have more than one meaning.
- identify and use contrast clues for multiple-meaning words.

MATERIALS

- **Teaching Chart 78**
- dictionary

TEACHING TIP
INSTRUCTIONAL

- Although some multiple-meaning words are spelled the same, they are often pronounced differently (*minute, lead*).
- Multiple-meaning words often can be used as different parts of speech. (*Stick* and *light* can be nouns or verbs.)

Introduce Multiple-Meaning Words

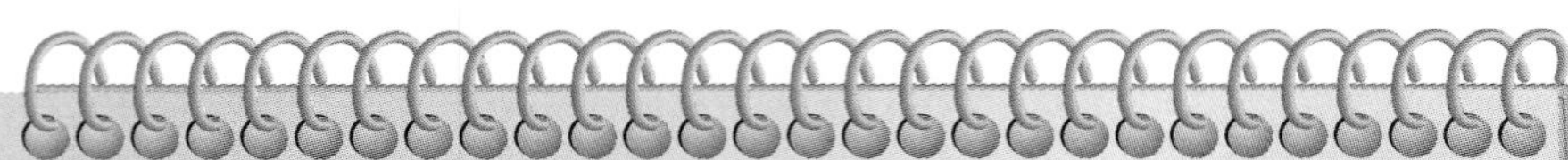

PREPARE

Discuss Multiple-Meaning Words Explain: Many words have more than one meaning. A reader can often determine a word's correct meaning by looking for context clues—clues in the words around it.

TEACH

Read the Passage and Model the Skill Have students read the passage on **Teaching Chart 78.**

The Prettiest Quilt

Tanya looked at the quilt her family had made. She felt very pleased and content about what she saw.

The quilt was heavy and soft, with lots of pretty light colors. They had washed the quilt with a special soap to make sure the colors wouldn't run. The carefully sewn stitches were so minute you could barely see them. She thought it must be the prettiest quilt in the whole country!

Teaching Chart 78

Help students to determine what *content* means.

MODEL I know the word *content* can mean two different things. As an adjective, it means to be satisfied with something. As a noun, it's pronounced differently and means something that is contained inside, like the content of a book. If I try to apply both meanings to the sentence, I can see that the first meaning—to be satisfied—must be correct, since that is how Tanya is feeling about her quilt.

Have students define the meanings of the word *light*. Ask them which meaning makes sense in the third sentence of the passage.

PRACTICE

Identify Multiple-Meaning Words and Use Context Clues

GROUP

Have students circle each multiple-meaning word in "The Prettiest Quilt." Have students discuss the meanings of each word and use context clues to decide which is the appropriate meaning in the passage.
▶ **Visual/Logical**

ASSESS/CLOSE

Form Sentences with Multiple-Meaning Words

Have students write down each of the words listed below. Then have them write down at least two meanings for each word, using a dictionary if necessary. Ask them to work with a partner to write two sentences for each word, using the two different meanings. They may want to draw pictures to go along with their sentences.

stick **lead** **saw** **safe**

ALTERNATE TEACHING STRATEGY
MULTIPLE-MEANING WORDS
For a different approach to teaching this skill, see page T65.

Meeting Individual Needs for Vocabulary

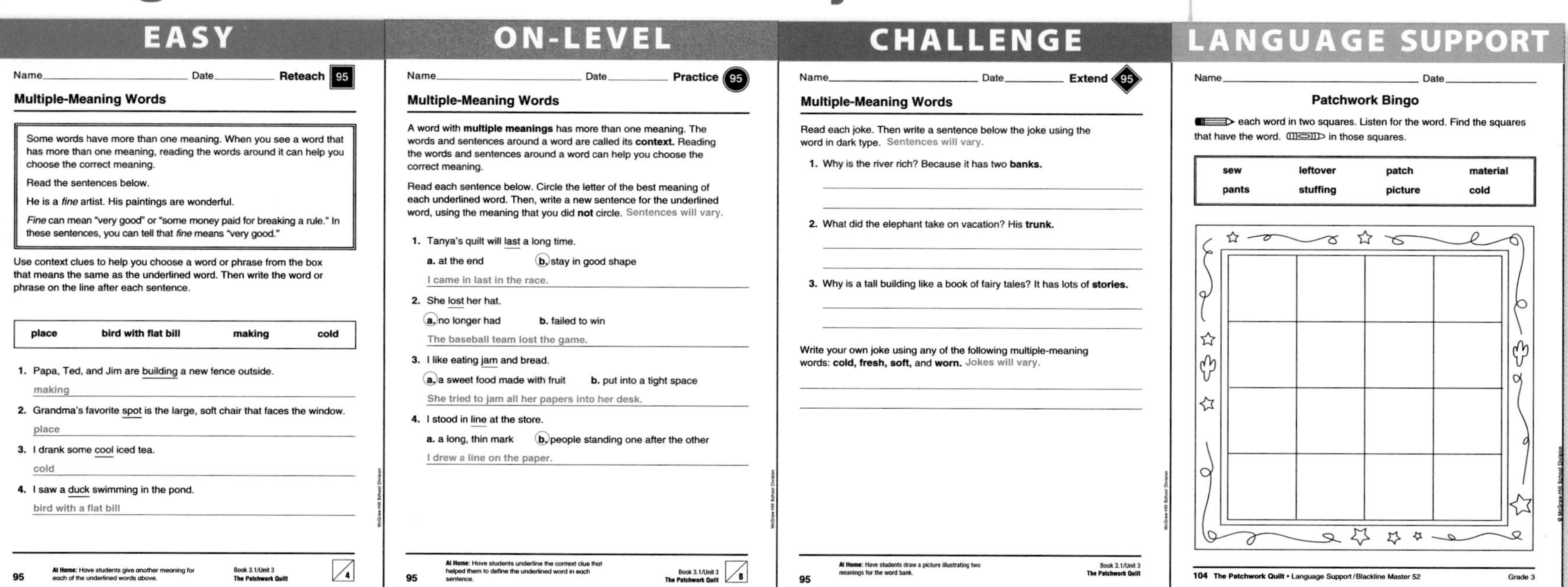

EASY

Name________ Date________ Reteach 95

Multiple-Meaning Words

Some words have more than one meaning. When you see a word that has more than one meaning, reading the words around it can help you choose the correct meaning.

Read the sentences below.

He is a *fine* artist. His paintings are wonderful.

Fine can mean "very good" or "some money paid for breaking a rule." In these sentences, you can tell that *fine* means "very good."

Use context clues to help you choose a word or phrase from the box that means the same as the underlined word. Then write the word or phrase on the line after each sentence.

place	bird with flat bill	making	cold

1. Papa, Ted, and Jim are building a new fence outside. making
2. Grandma's favorite spot is the large, soft chair that faces the window. place
3. I drank some cool iced tea. cold
4. I saw a duck swimming in the pond. bird with a flat bill

95 At Home: Have students give another meaning for each of the underlined words above. Book 3.1/Unit 3 The Patchwork Quilt 4

ON-LEVEL

Name________ Date________ Practice 95

Multiple-Meaning Words

A word with **multiple meanings** has more than one meaning. The words and sentences around a word are called its **context.** Reading the words and sentences around a word can help you choose the correct meaning.

Read each sentence below. Circle the letter of the best meaning of each underlined word. Then, write a new sentence for the underlined word, using the meaning that you did **not** circle. Sentences will vary.

1. Tanya's quilt will last a long time.
   a. at the end b. stay in good shape
   I came in last in the race.
2. She lost her hat.
   a. no longer had b. failed to win
   The baseball team lost the game.
3. I like eating jam and bread.
   a. a sweet food made with fruit b. put into a tight space
   She tried to jam all her papers into her desk.
4. I stood in line at the store.
   a. a long, thin mark b. people standing one after the other
   I drew a line on the paper.

95 At Home: Have students underline the context clue that helped them to define the underlined word in each sentence. Book 3.1/Unit 3 The Patchwork Quilt 8

CHALLENGE

Name________ Date________ Extend 95

Multiple-Meaning Words

Read each joke. Then write a sentence below the joke using the word in dark type. Sentences will vary.

1. Why is the river rich? Because it has two **banks.**
2. What did the elephant take on vacation? His **trunk.**
3. Why is a tall building like a book of fairy tales? It has lots of **stories.**

Write your own joke using any of the following multiple-meaning words: **cold, fresh, soft,** and **worn.** Jokes will vary.

95 At Home: Have students draw a picture illustrating two meanings for the word bank. Book 3.1/Unit 3 The Patchwork Quilt

LANGUAGE SUPPORT

Name________ Date________

Patchwork Bingo

each word in two squares. Listen for the word. Find the squares that have the word. in those squares.

sew	leftover	patch	material
pants	stuffing	picture	cold

104 The Patchwork Quilt • Language Support/Blackline Master 52 Grade 3

Reteach, 95 | Practice, 95 | Extend, 95 | Language Support, 104

GRAMMAR/SPELLING CONNECTIONS

See the 5-Day Grammar and Usage Plan on past-tense verbs, pages 349M–349N.

See the 5-Day Spelling Plan on words with /ou/ and /oi/, pages 349O–349P.

TECHNOLOGY TIP

Repetition of words can become boring. If you find yourself using the same word over and over, use the thesaurus on your computer to find alternatives.

Persuasive Writing

Prewrite

WRITE AN EDITORIAL Present this writing assignment: Tanya and her grandmother worked together to make their quilt. Write an editorial stating why it is, or is not, important for young people and older people to work together. Support your ideas with examples.

BRAINSTORM IDEAS Discuss the pros and cons of this issue. Ask students: What can older and younger people learn from each other? What might prevent them from working well together?

Strategy: Make a Pro and Con Chart. Have students list arguments for and against young and older people working together. Suggest the following:

- In one column, list benefits of young and older people working together.
- In the other column, list possible reasons why it is not important for them to work together.
- Rank the arguments on each side of the chart from strongest to weakest.

Draft

USE THE PRO AND CON CHART In their editorials, students should include the strongest ideas from their prewriting charts and develop them with examples, facts, quotations, or comparisons. Editorials should also contain a title, as well as strong opening and closing statements that summarize the writer's position.

Revise

SELF-QUESTIONING Ask students to assess their drafts.

- Did I make clear and effective opening and closing statements?
- Did I support my position with strong reasons?
- Have I responded to possible arguments against my position?

ONE Have students leave their editorials alone for a while and then come back to them. A fresh eye will often lead to improvement.

Edit/Proofread

CHECK FOR ERRORS Students should reread their editorials for spelling, grammar, and punctuation.

Publish

SHARE THE EDITORIALS Students can display their editorials on two bulletin boards labeled "Pro" and "Con." Encourage readers to tell the writers what was most convincing about their editorials.

Making the World a Better Place

Older people know a lot of history and traditions. They can share what they have learned with younger people. Young people often know a lot about computers. They can share this knowledge with older people. Young people and older people have a lot to learn from one another. If they do, the world might become a better place.

Presentation Ideas

CREATE A COLLAGE Have students find magazine photos of younger and older people working together or with their own peers. Display collages on the bulletin board.

▶ **Viewing/Representing**

HAVE A DEBATE Have students participate in a debate. Be sure to have some take the pro side and some take the con side. Others may play reporters asking questions.

▶ **Speaking/Listening**

COMMUNICATION TIPS

REPRESENTING Remind students to look for collage photographs that show specific feelings and activity.

SPEAKING Remind students that speaking calmly and confidently in a debate can help persuade others.

Consider students' creative efforts, possibly adding a plus (+) for originality, wit, and imagination.

Scoring Rubric

Excellent	Good	Fair	Unsatisfactory
4: The writer • clearly states main idea in his/her editorial. • provides supporting information and examples. • presents potential oppositions and answers them appropriately.	**3**: The writer • states one or more reasons for the main idea in his/her editorial. • adequately organizes supporting details. • raises potential oppositions.	**2**: The writer • states main idea, but idea is not elaborated on in his/her editorial. • presents few supporting details. • presents no potential oppositions or presents them with unsatisfactory answers.	**1**: The writer • has not stated main idea in his/her editorial. • has provided incomplete or unclear details. • shows no awareness of potential oppositions.

0: The writer leaves the page blank or fails to respond to the writing task. The student does not address the topic or simply paraphrases the prompt. The response is illegible or incoherent.

LANGUAGE SUPPORT

ESL Ask students to role-play an example of how young people interact with older people in their native culture. Have students work with a partner who is a native English speaker.

PORTFOLIO Invite students to include their editorials or another writing project in their portfolios.

Meeting Individual Needs for Writing

EASY

Greeting Card Help students design, draw, and write a greeting card from Grandma and Mama congratulating Tanya for her work on the quilt. If possible, provide students with examples of different cards to use as models.

ON-LEVEL

Thank-You Letter Direct students to write a letter from Tanya thanking her mother and grandmother for the quilt. Remind them to think about how Tanya feels about the quilt and include specific details from the story.

CHALLENGE

Story Scene Ask students to write a scene that takes place after the end of the story, in which Tanya decides to work on a new quilt. If students wish, they may add illustrations to the scene.

LANGUAGE SUPPORT

ESL **In a group, have each student act out a verb, such as *jump* or *walk*. Others in the group should describe the action, using the past tense.**

DAILY LANGUAGE ACTIVITIES

Write the Daily Language Activities on the chalkboard each day or use **Transparency 13**. Have students correct the sentences orally, using a verb in the past tense.

Day 1

1. Tanya talk with Grandma earlier. talked
2. Grandma rest in her chair yesterday. rested
3. She look for patches before Tanya came. looked

Day 2

1. Mama hurryed to make breakfast. hurried
2. Then she plan the rest of the day. planned
3. She love seeing Tanya with Grandma. loved

Day 3

1. Tanya carryed the material. carried
2. Grandma reach for the cloth. reached
3. Each one grabed a pair of scissors. grabbed

Day 4

1. Mama join in the work last night. joined
2. They add to the pile of patches. added
3. Tanya like watching the pile grow. liked

Day 5

1. Tanya hope they would finish the quilt soon. hoped
2. Mama tryed to work faster. tried
3. Tanya smile when they were done. smiled

Daily Language Transparency 13

DAY 1 Introduce the Concept

Oral Warm-Up Read aloud: *The man looked for some thread.* Ask students whether the sentence tells what is happening now or what happened in the past. Point out the verb ending with *-ed*.

Introduce Past-Tense Verbs Present the following:

> **Past-Tense Verbs**
>
> - A verb in the **past tense** tells about an action that already happened.
> - Add *-ed* to most verbs to show past tense.

Present the Daily Language Activity and have students correct them orally. Then have students form the past-tense form of *sew* (*sewed*), *help* (*helped*), and *paint* (*painted*). Have each student write a sentence using one or more of those past-tense verbs.

WRITING

Assign the daily Writing Prompt on page 318C.

Name________ Date________ LEARN **Grammar** 77

Past-Tense Verbs

- A verb in the **past tense** tells about an action that already happened.
- Add *–ed* to most verbs to show past tense.
  Grandma waited for the scraps.

Find the past-tense verb in each sentence. Write it on the line.

1. Tanya wanted to go outside. wanted
2. She looked longingly out the window. looked
3. Grandma flexed her fingers. flexed
4. Tanya remembered some of the fabrics in the scraps. remembered
5. Mama complained about the mess. complained
6. "A year," shouted Tanya. shouted
7. One by one, Grandma added each person to the quilt. added
8. Tanya and her family romped in the snow. romped
9. Grandma grouped the scraps in a pattern of colors. grouped
10. Mama helped Grandma with the quilt. helped

10 Book 3.1/Unit 3 **The Patchwork Quilt**

Extension: Have students write present-tense verbs on scraps of paper, and shuffle the scraps for them to pick. Have each student spell the past-tense form of his or her verb and use it in a sentence. 77

GRAMMAR PRACTICE BOOK, PAGE 77

DAY 2 Teach the Concept

Review Past-Tense Verbs Ask students when the past tense is used, and how most past-tense verbs end.

Introduce Spelling Changes Some words change their spelling when the ending *-ed* is added. Present:

> **Past-Tense Verbs**
>
> - If a verb ends with *e*, drop the *e* and add -*ed*.
> - If a verb ends with a consonant and *y*, change *y* to *i* and add *-ed*.
> - If a verb ends with one vowel and one consonant, double the consonant and add *-ed*.

Present the Daily Language Activity. Then have students write the past-tense form of *hurry* (*hurried*), *plan* (*planned*), and *love* (*loved*) in sentences.

WRITING

Assign the daily Writing Prompt on page 318C.

Name________ Date________ LEARN AND PRACTICE **Grammar** 78

Past-Tense Verbs

- If a verb ends with *e*, drop the *e* and add *–ed* to show past tense.
- If a verb ends with a consonant and *y*, change *y* to *i* and add *–ed*.
- If a verb ends with one vowel and one consonant, double the consonant and add *–ed*.
  pull, **pulled** carry, **carried**
  arrive, **arrived** clap, **clapped**

Change each underlined verb to past tense. Write the past-tense verb on the line.

1. All last year, Grandma trim scraps for the quilt. trimmed
2. That December, Mama cook for Christmas all day. cooked
3. At that time, Grandma join her in the kitchen. joined
4. Last night, she fold the quilt neatly. folded
5. A week ago, Mama and Papa permit them to see Grandma. permitted
6. Last night, Grandma smile at Ted, Jim, and Tanya. smiled
7. That spring, Tanya hurry home each day to work on the quilt. hurried
8. Last week, Tanya stop working on the quilt. stopped
9. Yesterday, she tiptoe into Grandma's room. tiptoed
10. Starting last month, Papa carry Grandma to her chair. carried

78 **Extension:** Have students work in pairs to list ten past-tense verbs that describe the actions of making a quilt. Develop a glossary page, giving their own definition for each verb. Encourage them to illustrate their glossary pages.

Book 3.1/Unit 3 **The Patchwork Quilt** 10

GRAMMAR PRACTICE BOOK, PAGE 78

Past-Tense Verbs

DAY 3 Review and Practice

Learn from the Literature Review past-tense verbs. Read the first sentence on page 339 of *The Patchwork Quilt*:

> **Tanya snipped and trimmed the scraps of material till her hands hurt from the scissors.**

Ask students to identify the past-tense verbs, and the base words *snip* and *trim.* Have students explain how the past tense of each verb was formed.

Form Past-Tense Verbs Present the Daily Language Activity and have students correct the sentences orally.

Have students make a 4-column chart and write one of the rules from Days 1 and 2 at the top of each column. Ask them to list each past-tense verbs in the column that has the appropriate rule.

Assign the daily Writing Prompt on page 318D.

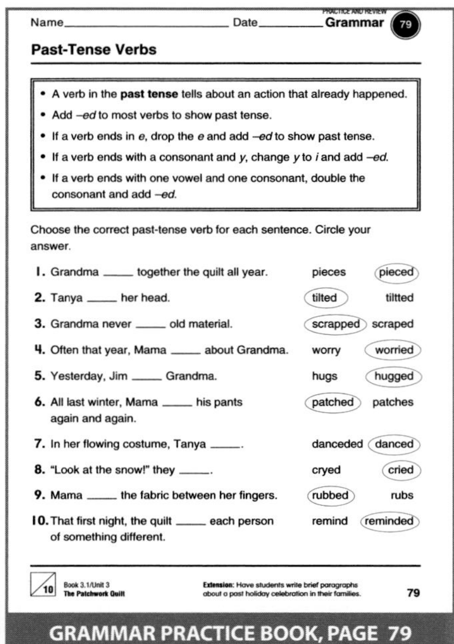

PRACTICE AND REVIEW

Name__________ Date________ **Grammar 79**

Past-Tense Verbs

- A verb in the **past tense** tells about an action that already happened.
- Add *–ed* to most verbs to show past tense.
- If a verb ends in *e*, drop the *e* and add *–ed* to show past tense.
- If a verb ends with a consonant and *y*, change *y* to *i* and add *–ed.*
- If a verb ends with one vowel and one consonant, double the consonant and add *–ed.*

Choose the correct past-tense verb for each sentence. Circle your answer.

1.	Grandma ____ together the quilt all year.	pieces	(pieced)
2.	Tanya ____ her head.	(tilted)	tiltted
3.	Grandma never ____ old material.	(scrapped)	scraped
4.	Often that year, Mama ____ about Grandma.	worry	(worried)
5.	Yesterday, Jim ____ Grandma.	hugs	(hugged)
6.	All last winter, Mama ____ his pants again and again.	(patched)	patches
7.	In her flowing costume, Tanya ____.	danceded	(danced)
8.	"Look at the snow!" they ____.	cryed	(cried)
9.	Mama ____ the fabric between her fingers.	(rubbed)	rubs
10.	That first night, the quilt ____ each person of something different.	remind	(reminded)

10 Book 3.1/Unit 3 **The Patchwork Quilt**

Extension: Have students write brief paragraphs about a past holiday celebration in their families. 79

GRAMMAR PRACTICE BOOK, PAGE 79

DAY 4 Review and Practice

Review Past-Tense Verbs Write the present-tense verbs from the Daily Language Activity for Days 1 through 3 on the chalkboard. Ask students to name the rule that is used to create each past-tense form, say the correct past-tense form, and use it in a sentence. Then present the Daily Language Activity for Day 4.

Mechanics and Usage Before the students begin the daily Writing Prompt on page 318D, review the following:

> **Commas**
>
> Use *commas* to separate three or more words in a series.

Discuss the following example: *The girl cut, trimmed, and stitched the materials.*

Assign the daily Writing Prompt on page 318D.

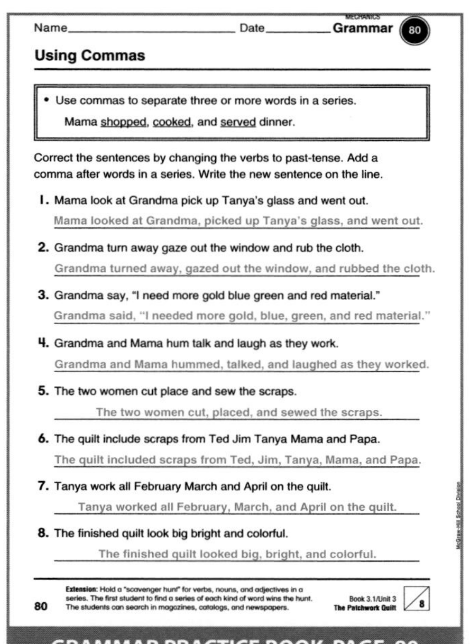

MECHANICS

Name__________ Date________ **Grammar 80**

Using Commas

- Use commas to separate three or more words in a series.
  Mama shopped, cooked, and served dinner.

Correct the sentences by changing the verbs to past-tense. Add a comma after words in a series. Write the new sentence on the line.

1. Mama look at Grandma pick up Tanya's glass and went out.
Mama looked at Grandma, picked up Tanya's glass, and went out.

2. Grandma turn away gaze out the window and rub the cloth.
Grandma turned away, gazed out the window, and rubbed the cloth.

3. Grandma say, "I need more gold blue green and red material."
Grandma said, "I needed more gold, blue, green, and red material."

4. Grandma and Mama hum talk and laugh as they work.
Grandma and Mama hummed, talked, and laughed as they worked.

5. The two women cut place and sew the scraps.
The two women cut, placed, and sewed the scraps.

6. The quilt include scraps from Ted Jim Tanya Mama and Papa.
The quilt included scraps from Ted, Jim, Tanya, Mama, and Papa.

7. Tanya work all February March and April on the quilt.
Tanya worked all February, March, and April on the quilt.

8. The finished quilt look big bright and colorful.
The finished quilt looked big, bright, and colorful.

80 **Extension:** Hold a "scavenger hunt" for verbs, nouns, and adjectives in a series. The first student to find a series of each kind of word wins the hunt. The students can search in magazines, catalogs, and newspapers.

Book 3.1/Unit 3 **The Patchwork Quilt** 8

GRAMMAR PRACTICE BOOK, PAGE 80

DAY 5 Assess and Reteach

Assess Use the Daily Language Activity and page 81of the **Grammar Practice Book** for assessment.

Reteach Have students write each rule about past-tense verbs from the lesson grammar concepts on an index card.

For each verb in Daily Language Activity sentences, have students find the rule that the verb matches and note what the rule tells them to do. Then they should write the verb and its correct past-tense form on the appropriate index card.

Have students create a word wall with lists of verbs that follow each pattern.

Use page 82 of the **Grammar Practice Book** for additional reteaching.

Assign the daily Writing Prompt on page 318D.

TEST

Name__________ Date________ **Grammar 81**

Past-Tense Verbs

Read each sentence. Find the past-tense verb and write it on the line.

1. Tanya hoped to go outside. hoped

2. She leaned against Grandma's chair. leaned

3. Grandma patted Tanya's head. patted

4. The students scurried outside to enjoy the snow. scurried

Spell the past-tense form of the action verb in each sentence. Write the answer on the line.

5. "A whole year!" Tanya (cry) last spring. cried

6. Beginning that day, Grandma (plan) her quilt. planned

7. Tanya (amaze) her family that year. amazed

8. All that spring, they (watch) her working on the quilt. watched

9. That day, Grandma (pin) some scraps together. pinned

10. Back then, nobody (imagine) the quilt's final size. imagined

10 Book 3.1/Unit 3 **The Patchwork Quilt** 81

GRAMMAR PRACTICE BOOK, PAGE 81

GRAMMAR PRACTICE BOOK, PAGE 82

LANGUAGE SUPPORT

ESL **To help students distinguish between the /ou/ and /oi/ sounds, say each spelling word. Whenever you pronounce an *ow* sound, have students say "Ow!" as if expressing pain.**

DICTATION SENTENCES

Spelling Words

1. She found her shoe behind the sofa.
2. Butter can spoil in hot weather.
3. The clock blinked when the power went out.
4. My parents enjoy eating breakfast.
5. Put foil in the pan when you bake.
6. The clown told silly jokes.
7. The boat went on a voyage over the sea.
8. The sky is dark and cloudy.
9. Mice are not noisy animals.
10. Can you count the money?
11. The bite of a snake could poison you.
12. The pet is loyal to the child.
13. My parents might allow me to sleep over.
14. To go or stay can be a hard choice.
15. The boys at the beach like to shout.

Challenge Words

16. He was anxious after the test.
17. She kept the old trunk in the attic.
18. He picked out a cowboy costume for the party.
19. The boy examined the shiny rocks he found.
20. The dress had a pretty pattern.

DAY 1 Pretest

Assess Prior Knowledge Use the Dictation Sentences at left and **Spelling Practice Book** page 77 for the pretest. Allow students to correct their own papers. If students have trouble, have partners give each other a midweek test on Day 3. Students who require a modified list may be tested on the first eight words.

Spelling Words		Challenge Words
1. **found**	9. noisy	16. **anxious**
2. **spoil**	10. count	17. **attic**
3. power	11. poison	18. **costume**
4. **enjoy**	12. loyal	19. **examined**
5. foil	13. allow	20. **pattern**
6. clown	14. choice	
7. voyage	15. shout	
8. **cloudy**		

*Note: Words in **dark type** are from the story.*

Word Study On page 78 of the **Spelling Practice Book** are word study steps and an at-home activity.

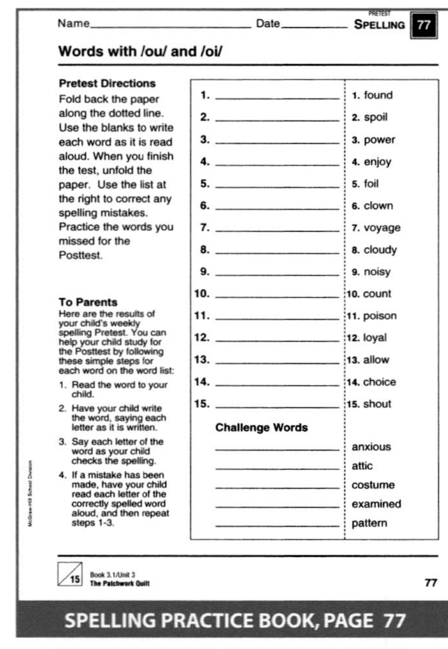

Name__________ Date_______ PRETEST SPELLING 77

Words with /ou/ and /oi/

Pretest Directions
Fold back the paper along the dotted line. Use the blanks to write each word as it is read aloud. When you finish the test, unfold the paper. Use the list at the right to correct any spelling mistakes. Practice the words you missed for the Posttest.

1. ______	1. found
2. ______	2. spoil
3. ______	3. power
4. ______	4. enjoy
5. ______	5. foil
6. ______	6. clown
7. ______	7. voyage
8. ______	8. cloudy
9. ______	9. noisy
10. ______	10. count
11. ______	11. poison
12. ______	12. loyal
13. ______	13. allow
14. ______	14. choice
15. ______	15. shout
Challenge Words	
______	anxious
______	attic
______	costume
______	examined
______	pattern

To Parents
Here are the results of your child's weekly spelling Pretest. You can help your child study for the Posttest by following these simple steps for each word on the word list:
1. Read the word to your child.
2. Have your child write the word, saying each letter as it is written.
3. Say each letter of the word as your child checks the spelling.
4. If a mistake has been made, have your child read each letter of the correctly spelled word aloud, and then repeat steps 1-3.

15 Book 3.1/Unit 3 The Patchwork Quilt 77

SPELLING PRACTICE BOOK, PAGE 77

WORD STUDY STEPS AND ACTIVITY, PAGE 78

DAY 2 Explore the Pattern

Sort and Spell Words Say *loyal* and *found*. Ask students what vowel sound they hear in each word. Those words contain the sounds /oi/ and /ou/. Ask students to read aloud the 15 Spelling Words and sort them according to the sounds and spelling below.

Spelling Patterns Have students generalize about where the spelling of /oi/ and /ou/ appears in words. Usually *oy* appears at the end of a word or syllable and *oi* in the middle; *ow* may appear at the end of a word but *ou* may not.

/ow/ spelled ow	/oi/ spelled oi
power	spoil
clown	foil
allow	noisy
	poison
	choice
/ow/ spelled ou	**/oi/ spelled oy**
found	enjoy
cloudy	voyage
count	loyal
shout	

Name__________ Date_______ EXPLORE THE PATTERN SPELLING 79

Words with /ou/ and /oi/

found	enjoy	voyage	count	allow
spoil	foil	cloudy	poison	choice
power	clown	noisy	loyal	shout

Pattern Power
Write the spelling words with the /ou/ sound spelled:

ou
1. found
2. cloudy
3. count
4. shout

ow
5. power
6. clown
7. allow

Write the spelling words with the /oi/ sound spelled:

oi
8. spoil
9. foil
10. noisy
11. poison
12. choice

oy
13. enjoy
14. voyage
15. loyal

Syllable Stuff
Write the spelling words that have one syllable:
16. found 17. spoil 18. foil
19. clown 20. count 21. choice
22. shout

Write the spelling words that have two syllables:
23. power 24. enjoy 25. voyage
26. cloudy 27. noisy 28. poison
29. loyal 30. allow

30 Book 3.1/Unit 3 The Patchwork Quilt 79

SPELLING PRACTICE BOOK, PAGE 79

Words with /ou/ and /oi/

DAY 3 Practice and Extend

Word Meaning: Antonyms Remind students that an antonym has the opposite meaning of another word. Ask them to think of antonyms for *found*, *enjoy*, *cloudy*, *noisy*, *allow*, and *shout*.

Glossary Have students:

- find the definition of each Challenge Word in the Glossary.
- write a sentence for each each Challenge Word.
- rewrite each sentence substituting the definition for the word. Example: I was nervous about the test.
- exchange sentences with a partner and replace the definition with the Challenge Words.

PRACTICE AND EXTEND
Name________________ Date__________ SPELLING **80**

Words with /ou/ and /oi/

found	enjoy	voyage	count	allow
spoil	foil	cloudy	poison	choice
power	clown	noisy	loyal	shout

Analogies

An **analogy** is a statement that compares sets of words that are alike in some way. Use spelling words to complete the analogies below.

1. *Dark* is to *light* as *silent* is to ____noisy____.
2. *Jolly* is to *merry* as *let* is to ____allow____.
3. *Ship* is to *boat* as *trip* is to ____voyage____.
4. *Night* is to *day* as *lost* is to ____found____.
5. *Up* is to *down* as *whisper* is to ____shout____.
6. *Dull* is to *shiny* as *sunny* is to ____cloudy____.

A Fine Definition

Fill in the spelling word that matches the definition.

7. be happy with ____enjoy____
8. thin metal sheet ____foil____
9. say numbers in order ____count____
10. faithful ____loyal____
11. a silly performer ____clown____
12. a chance to decide ____choice____
13. strength or force ____power____
14. a harmful or deadly drink ____poison____
15. to ruin or damage ____spoil____

80 **Challenge Extension:** Have students write a fill in the blank sentence for each Challenge Word, then exchange papers with a partner and complete each other's sentences.

Book 3.1/Unit 3 **The Patchwork Quilt** 15

SPELLING PRACTICE BOOK, PAGE 80

DAY 4 Proofread and Write

Write these sentences on the chalkboard, including the misspelled words. Ask students to proofread, circling incorrect spellings and writing the correct spellings. There are two spelling errors in each sentence.

The cloun did tricks on a clowdy day. (clown, cloudy)

The loyle dog was very noysy. (loyal, noisy)

His parents would not allou him to make a choyce. (allow, choice)

Have students create additional sentences with errors for partners to correct.

WRITING Have students use as many spelling words as possible in the daily Writing Prompt on page 318D. Remind students to proofread their writing for errors in spelling, punctuation, and grammar.

PROOFREAD AND WRITE
Name________________ Date__________ SPELLING **81**

Words with /ou/ and /oi/

Proofreading Paragraph

There are six spelling mistakes in this letter. Circle the misspelled words. Write the words correctly on the lines below.

Dear President:

I am writing this letter to let you know about your toy cloun. I bought a Happy Face toy yesterday. But when I took the toy out of the box, I saw that it was broken. Boy, did it ever spoyle my day!

I used to be a loyle customer of Happy Face toys. However, now my Mom and Dad won't alow me to buy another one of your toys.

Now all I want is my money back. I hope I can counte on you to do the right thing. Since you are the president of the company, I know you have the powre to do it. Thank you.

Sincerely,
Marcy Shore

1. clown 2. spoil 3. loyal
4. allow 5. count 6. power

Writing Activity

Did you ever have a toy spoil your day? What went wrong? Write several sentences explaining what happened. Use six spelling words and circle them.

12 Book 3.1/Unit 3 **The Patchwork Quilt** 81

SPELLING PRACTICE BOOK, PAGE 81

DAY 5 Assess and Reteach

Assess Students' Knowledge Use page 82 of the **Spelling Practice Book** or the Dictation Sentences on page 349O for the posttest.

Personal Word List If student's have trouble with any words in the lesson, have them add the words to their personal word lists in their journals. Ask them to think of hints to help themselves remember the spelling.

JOURNAL

Students should refer to their lists during future writing activities.

POSTTEST
Name________________ Date__________ SPELLING **82**

Words with /ou/ and /oi/

Look at the words in each set. One word in each set is spelled correctly. Use a pencil to color in the circle in front of that word. Before you begin, look at the sample sets of words. Sample A has been done for you. Do Sample B by yourself. When you are sure you know what to do, you may go on with the rest of the page.

Sample A
(A) boyle
(B) boile
(C) boyalt
(D) boil

Sample B
(E) toun
(F) toune
(G) town
(H) towne

1. (A) spoyl (B) spoil (C) spole (D) spoyal
2. (E) noyzy (F) nousy (G) noisy (H) noizee
3. (A) loiyal (B) loyle (C) loyel (D) loyal
4. (E) choice (F) choyce (G) choyse (H) choise
5. (A) fole (B) foil (C) foyal (D) foile
6. (E) foud (F) found (G) fown (H) fownd
7. (A) posin (B) poizon (C) poisun (D) poison
8. (E) voiage (F) voyaj (G) voyage (H) voiag
9. (A) shout (B) shhout (C) showt (D) sout
10. (E) alow (F) allow (G) alou (H) allou
11. (A) cout (B) cownt (C) count (D) counte
12. (E) powa (F) poure (G) power (H) powor
13. (A) kloudy (B) cloudy (C) clody (D) cloude
14. (E) clown (F) klown (G) clon (H) kloun
15. (A) enjoy (B) injoy (C) enjoe (D) engoy

82 Book 3.1/Unit 3 **The Patchwork Quilt** 15

SPELLING PRACTICE BOOK, PAGE 82

Pecos Bill

Selection Summary: In this play, students will join cowgirls and boys as they listen to or act out the tale of Pecos Bill, a lost boy who survives in the wild, finally finding his family, and even a wife.

Listening Library Audiocassette

INSTRUCTIONAL
Pages 352–375

About the Author Angela Shelf Medearis says, "I want to write the kind of books I always longed to find in the library when I was a child. I love introducing children all over the world to African American history and culture." Ms. Medearis has written over 60 books for children and adults. She lives in Austin, Texas.

About the illustrator John Kanzler admits, "I have never ridden a horse in my life," but he enjoyed the challenge of portraying the legendary cowboy Pecos Bill. He tried to create a different look for the modern and the tall/tale characters in the play.

Resources for

Meeting Individual Needs

LEVELED BOOKS

EASY
Pages 375A, 375D

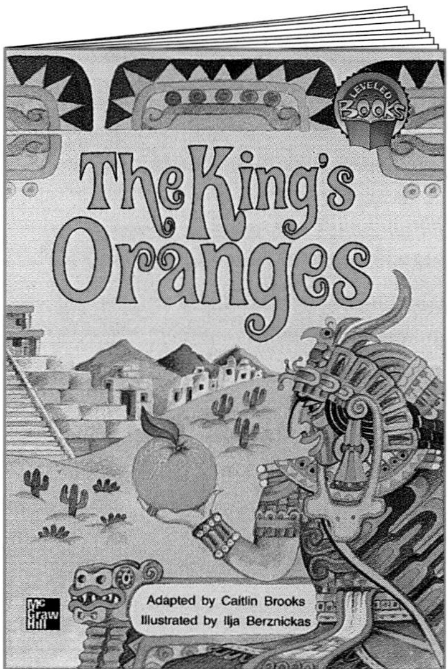

INDEPENDENT
Pages 375B, 375D

Take-Home version available

CHALLENGE
Pages 375C, 375D

LEVELED PRACTICE

Reteach, 96–102
blackline masters with reteaching opportunities for each assessed skill

Practice, 96–102
workbook with Take-Home Stories and practice opportunities for each assessed skill and story comprehension

Extend, 96–102
blackline masters that offer challenge activities for each assessed skill

ADDITIONAL RESOURCES

- **Language Support Book,** pp. 105–112
- **Take-Home Story, Practice** p. 97a
- **Alternate Teaching Strategies,** pp. T60–T66
- **Selected Quizzes Prepared by** Accelerated Reader

McGraw-Hill School TECHNOLOGY

Phonics CD-ROM provides extra phonics support.

interNET CONNECTION Research & Inquiry ideas. Visit ***www.mhschool.com/reading.***

Available on CD-ROM

Suggested Lesson Planner

READING AND LANGUAGE ARTS	DAY 1 Focus on Reading and Skills	 DAY 2 Read the Literature
Comprehension Vocabulary Phonics/Decoding Study Skills Listening, Speaking, Viewing, Representing	 **Read Aloud and Motivate,** 350E "Paul Bunyan, the Mightiest Logger of Them All" **Develop Visual Literacy,** 350/351 **Review Story Elements,** 352A–352B **Teaching Chart 79** **Reteach, Practice, Extend,** 96	**Build Background,** 352C Develop Oral Language **Vocabulary,** 352D ***combine*** ***located*** ***stumbled*** ***invented*** ***prairie*** ***wilderness*** **Teaching Chart 80** **Word Building Manipulative Cards** **Reteach, Practice, Extend,** 97  **Read the Selection,** 352–371 Guided Instruction Story Elements Make Inferences **Minilessons,** 359, 361, 363, 369 **Cultural Perspectives,** 358
 Curriculum Connections	 **Fine Arts,** 350/351	 **Drama,** 352C
Writing	 **Writing Prompt:** A little child just asked you how the moon got up in the sky. Invent a story that tells why a person or animal put it up there.	 **Writing Prompt:** A little boy wants to know why ocean water is salty. Invent a story to explain it. Write the story as if it is happening now.  **Journal Writing,** 371 Quick-Write
Grammar	**Introduce the Concept: Using Verb Tenses,** 375M Daily Language Activity 1. He chase the horse yesterday. chased 2. Cookie stirred the beans now. stirs 3. Ma counts the children last night. counted **Grammar Practice Book,** 83	**Teach the Concept: Using Verb Tenses,** 375M Daily Language Activity 1. Bill and Carl talked tomorrow. will talk 2. He watch the horses last week. watched 3. Cookie cleaned the dishes later. will clean **Grammar Practice Book,** 84
Spelling	**Introduce: Adding *-ed* and *-ing*,** 375O **Spelling Practice Book,** 83–84	**Explore the Pattern: Adding *-ed* and *-ing*,** 375O **Spelling Practice Book,** 85

Meeting Individual Needs

☑ = **Skill Assessed in Unit Test**

DAY 3 Read the Literature

Reread for Fluency, 370

Story Questions, 372
Reteach, Practice, Extend, 98
Story Activities, 373

Study Skill, 374
☑ Graphic Aids
Teaching Charts 81
Reteach, Practice, Extend, 99

Test Power, 375
TAAS Preparation and Practice Book, 46–47

Read the Leveled Books,
Guided Reading
/ou/ and /oi/
☑ Story Elements
☑ Instructional Vocabulary

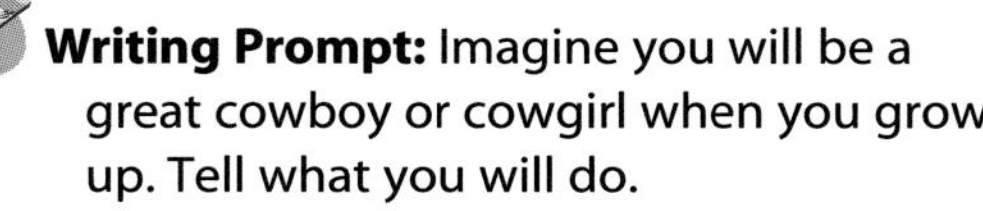
CD-ROM

Social Studies, 364

Writing Prompt: Imagine you will be a great cowboy or cowgirl when you grow up. Tell what you will do.

Writing Process: Persuasive Writing, 375K
Prewrite, Draft

Review and Practice: Using Verb Tenses, 375N
Daily Language Activity
1. Sue married Bill tomorrow. will marry
2. The rattlesnake helped Bill now. helps
3. The coyotes miss Bill last week. missed

Grammar Practice Book, 85

Practice and Extend: Adding *-ed* and *-ing*, 375P
Spelling Practice Book, 86

DAY 4 Build Skills

Read the Leveled Books and Self-Selected Books

☑ **Review Story Elements,** 375E–375F
Teaching Chart 82
Reteach, Practice, Extend, 100
Language Support, 110

☑ **Review Make Inferences,** 375G–375H
Teaching Chart 83
Reteach, Practice, Extend, 101
Language Support, 111

Math, 366

Writing Prompt: Write a conversation between two people who are imagining how mountains were formed.

Writing Process: Persuasive Writing, 375K
Revise

Meeting Individual Needs for Writing, 375L

Review and Practice: Using Verb Tenses, 375N
Daily Language Activity
1. Sue dances with Bill last night. danced
2. Sue sewed her dress now. sews
3. Cookie slice the pizza later. will slice

Grammar Practice Book, 86

Proofread and Write: Adding *-ed* and *-ing*, 375P
Spelling Practice Book, 87

DAY 5 Build Skills

Read Self-Selected Books

☑ **Review Multiple-Meaning Words,** 375I–375J
Teaching Chart 84
Reteach, Practice, Extend, 102
Language Support, 112

Listening, Speaking, Viewing, Representing, 375L
Draw Reviews
Character Interviews

Minilessons, 359, 361, 369

Phonics Review,
/ou/ and /oi/, 361
Phonics/Phonemic Awareness Practice Book, 61–64

CD-ROM

Music, 368

Writing Prompt: Invent a tall tale that explains why e-mail goes from here to there in seconds. Write it.

Writing Process: Persuasive Writing, 375K
Edit/Proofread, Publish

Assess and Reteach: Using Verb Tenses, 375N
Daily Language Activity
1. Bill play the guitar last year. played
2. Pa just join the wagon train. joined
3. Carl swim in the river later. will swim

Grammar Practice Book, 87–88

Assess and Reteach: Adding *-ed* and *-ing*, 375P
Spelling Practice Book, 88

Language Arts

Read Aloud and Motivate

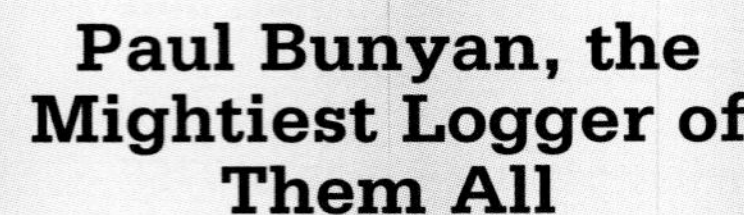

Paul Bunyan, the Mightiest Logger of Them All

retold by
Mary Pope Osborne

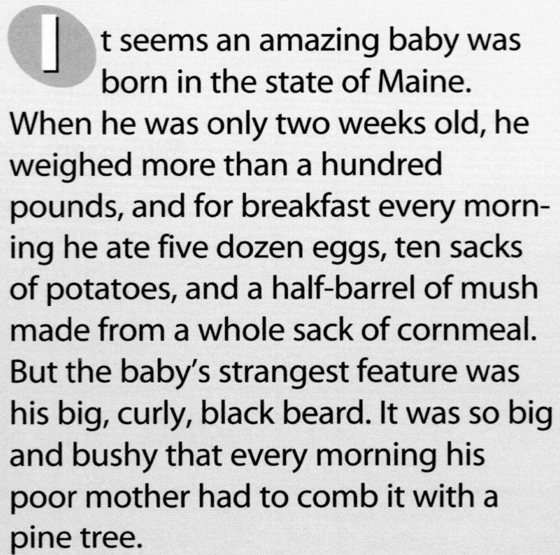

It seems an amazing baby was born in the state of Maine. When he was only two weeks old, he weighed more than a hundred pounds, and for breakfast every morning he ate five dozen eggs, ten sacks of potatoes, and a half-barrel of mush made from a whole sack of cornmeal. But the baby's strangest feature was his big, curly, black beard. It was so big and bushy that every morning his poor mother had to comb it with a pine tree.

Except for that black beard, the big baby wasn't much trouble to anybody until he was about nine months old. That was when he first started to crawl, and since he weighed over five hundred pounds, he caused an earthquake that shook the whole town.

The baby's parents tried putting him in a giant floating cradle off the coast of Maine, but every time he rolled over, huge waves drowned all the villages along the coast.

So his parents hauled the giant toddler to a cave in the Maine woods far away from civilization and said good-bye.

Continued on pages T2–T5

Oral Comprehension

LISTENING AND SPEAKING Read aloud this American tall tale about a giant woodsman. Ask students to weigh which events in the story could take place and which events would be impossible. When you have finished, ask, "Are there any parts of this story that could possibly take place?" Then ask, "Why might entertaining stories have been in such demand in the old pioneering days?

Activity Have students pretend that they are giants. Ask them to think about how a giant would walk down the street or do simple tasks with ordinary-sized objects. Invite each student to pantomime a Paul Bunyan activity.
▶ **Kinesthetic**

Develop Visual Literacy

Works of Art

Anthology pages 350-351

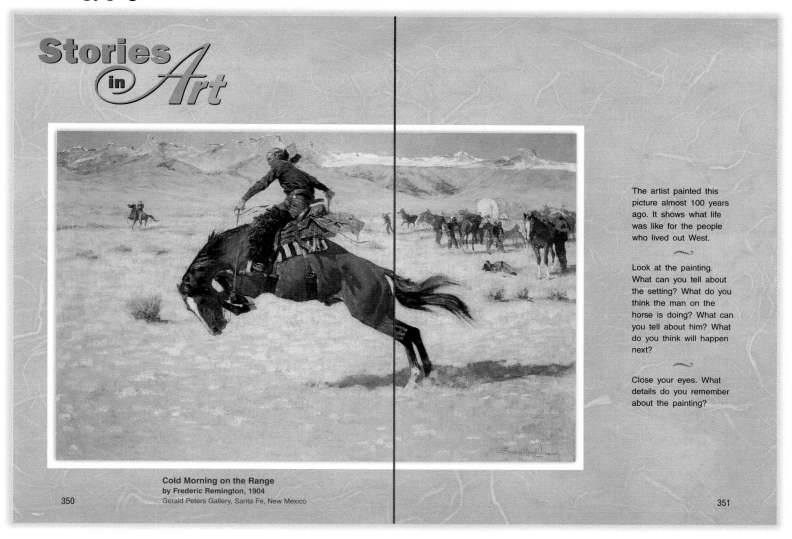

Stories in Art

The artist painted this picture almost 100 years ago. It shows what life was like for the people who lived out West.

Look at the painting. What can you tell about the setting? What do you think the man on the horse is doing? What can you tell about him? What do you think will happen next?

Close your eyes. What details do you remember about the painting?

Cold Morning on the Range
by Frederic Remington, 1904
Gerald Peters Gallery, Santa Fe, New Mexico

350

351

Objective: Analyze Character and Setting

VIEWING During the 1890s, a favorite subject of Frederic Remington's frontier paintings was the bucking horse. The animal testing the man's strength symbolized the struggle to tame the frontier wilderness. Ask students to comment on the setting in this painting. How does the artist convey a sense of space? Do they think the man or the horse will win the struggle? Read the page with students, encouraging individual interpretations of the painting.

Ask students to support any inferences they make about character and setting. For example:

- The main image of the man and the horse suggests the taming of the wilderness. The cowboy looks like he will bring the horse under his control.
- The horse and rider against the backdrop of huge mountains and empty space says something about people and nature. The human is seen as tiny in a vast land.

REPRESENTING Have students paint or draw a scene that shows people responding to a setting. Remind students that considering time, place, and climate will help them paint a convincing setting.

Students will analyze character, setting, and plot.

Review Story Elements

TEACHING TIP

MANAGEMENT If students will be looking for tall tales and other examples of character, setting, and plot in your classroom library, you may want to create a checkout system to keep track of the books. Write the titles and authors' names on individual index cards and keep them in an "IN" folder. When students take books out, have them move the cards into an "OUT" folder until the book is returned.

PREPARE

Discuss Familiar Characters, Settings, and Plots

Have students discuss a movie they have seen or a book they have read. Ask: Who were the main characters? Where did the story take place? What were the main events? Do you think that where the story took place affected the characters and what happened to them? How?

TEACH

Define Character, Setting and Plot

State that there are three main ingredients in every story: the characters (who is in the story), the plot (what happens in the story), and the setting (where the story takes place). Explain that all of these elements have an effect on each other.

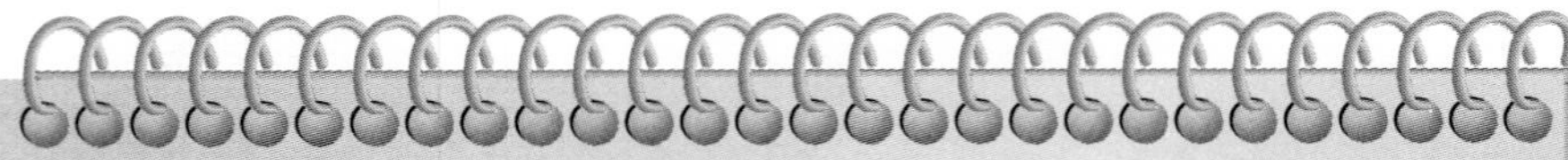

One Day

It was a hot, steamy summer day. A boy sat under a drooping tree in his backyard. "It must be at least 100 degrees," the boy thought, "I'm so sweaty and grumpy." Suddenly a large pink and purple bird flew down and sat right in front of the boy. "Hey there!" said the bird. "Birds can't talk," replied the boy in a grouchy voice. "I'm a magical bird," the bird tried again. "I grant wishes!" "Sure you do," said the boy, "Now GO AWAY!" The bird shrugged his shoulders and flew down the street, where he gave some kids air conditioning in their backyard.

Teaching Chart 79

Read the Passage and Model the Skill

Display **Teaching Chart 79**. Tell students to pay attention to clues about setting, characters, and plot.

MODEL The boy is hot, sweaty, and grumpy. I think the way he feels will affect the plot. These are clues that he is in a bad mood.

PRACTICE

Analyze Character, Setting, and Plot

Have students underline clues that show how the characters feel about the setting and the plot events. Then have students write a paragraph that explains what the setting of the scene is, how that setting affects the character of the boy, and how the boy's character affects the outcome of the plot. ▶ **Logical/Linguistic**

ASSESS/CLOSE

Rewrite "One Day"

Have students change an element of "One Day" and rewrite the scene with that change. For instance, they might change the setting to a lush, tropical forest. How would this change affect the character of the boy? (He probably wouldn't be so unhappy.) How might it change the outcome of the plot? (The boy would be more friendly to the talking bird, and they might become friends.)

SELECTION Connection

Students will analyze character, setting, and plot when they read *Pecos Bill: A Tall Tale Play* and the Leveled Books.

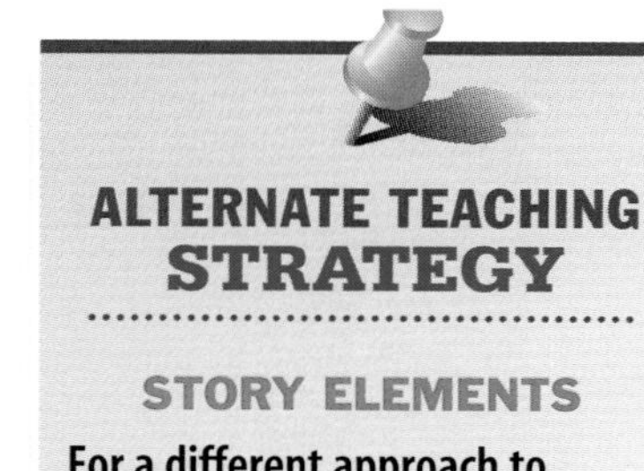

ALTERNATE TEACHING STRATEGY

STORY ELEMENTS

For a different approach to teaching this skill, see page T64.

Meeting Individual Needs for Comprehension

EASY

Name__________ Date______ **Reteach 96**

Story Elements

Characters are the people or the animals that are part of a story. The **setting** is when and where the story takes place. The **plot** tells about the events in a story.

Toshana, Tim, and their mom went into the city to see a movie called "Cooking Cowboys." It was about a group of cowboys who liked to cook together. At the end of the movie, the Cooking Cowboys won a cooking contest.

When they came out of the movie, Toshana said, "We should be like the cooking cowboys, too!"

"Yeah! Let's go buy some food and cook it, just like they did," said Tim.

Their mother said, "Cooking is a big job. Are you sure you want to do it?"

"We're sure," they both said. "We can do it!"

Circle the correct answer to the questions below.

1. Where does this story take place?
   a. on a boat (b.) in a city c. on a farm
2. Who are the main characters in the story?
   (a.) Toshana, Tim, and their mother b. Toshana, Tim, and their father c. Toshana and Tim
3. What movie did they see?
   a. "Cowboys" b. "Cowboys Who Care" (c.) "Cooking Cowboys"
4. What do Tim and Toshana decide to do at the end of the story?
   (a.) cook b. see another movie c. go to a museum

4 Book 3.1/Unit 3 **Pecos Bill: A Tall Tale Play** **At Home:** Have students write two sentences about what might happen next in the story. 96

Reteach, 96

ON-LEVEL

Name__________ Date______ **Practice 96**

Story Elements

Understanding the main **characters** and the **setting** can help you understand what happens in a story.

Read the story below. Then answer the questions.

Today in class, everyone was supposed to write a story. Jamar couldn't think of anything to write about, so he asked his friends for some ideas.

Erica said, "Write about horses."

Pedro said, "Write about a ship."

Bill suggested, "Write about a doctor."

He raised his hand. "Mr. Diaz, what should I do?" he said. "I'll never think of a story. I asked all my friends, but I don't want to write about the things they suggested."

Mr. Diaz said, "Usually, it's a good idea to write about things you like."

Jamar thought about it. "I like baseball. I know! I'll write a story about a baseball player who becomes an all-star!"

1. Where does the story take place? The story takes place in class.
2. Who is the main character? Jamar is the main character.
3. What is Jamar's problem? He can't think of anything to write about.
4. What does Jamar decide to do at the end of the story?
   He decides to write about something he likes—baseball.

4 Book 3.1/Unit 3 **Pecos Bill: A Tall Tale Play** **At Home:** Have students write a few sentences explaining how Jamar tries to solve his problem. 96

Practice, 96

CHALLENGE

Name__________ Date______ **Extend 96**

Story Elements

Complete the chart with information from your favorite fairy tale.

Title __________

Author __________

Setting __________

Main Characters __________

How did it begin? __________

What happened in the middle? __________

Answers will vary.

How did it end? __________

Book 3.1/Unit 3 **Pecos Bill** **At Home:** Have students illustrate a cover for the story they described. 96

Extend, 96

Build Background

Anthology and Leveled Books

Drama

Evaluate Prior Knowledge

CONCEPT: PLAYS These stories are all written as plays. Ask: How is a play written differently from a story? How do you know who is speaking when you read a play?

COMPARE FORMATS Help students make a Venn diagram of the differences and similarities between reading plays and novels.

▶ **Logical/Visual**

PLAY		NOVEL
Different	Alike	Different
told through dialogue and actors; has directions for acting out story; often separated into scenes and acts	has beginning middle and end; has character, plot, and setting	told through description and dialogue; tells reader the story; separated into chapters

Graphic Organizer 14

WRITE A PLAY ONE WRITING Pass out copies of well-known folk tales. Have students choose a folk tale and write a short scene from the story in play format.

Develop Oral Language

CREATE A SKIT ESL Display illustrations for stories that are familiar to students. Encourage students to tell what is happening in the illustrations and who the characters are. Ask: What might the characters in these illustrations say if they could speak? Record students' suggested dialogue on the board in play format. Explain any difficult words or concepts.

Have students work with partners or in small groups and pick a story and characters. Then have them act out an illustration or a scene from the story. Allow them to invent their own dialogue and to use props if possible. Have students share their skits with the rest of the class.

TEACHING TIP

INSTRUCTIONAL Tell students that stage directions (information in parentheses), help the action of a play. It is more interesting to watch characters do something than to listen to them talk about doing things.

LANGUAGE SUPPORT

See **Language Support Book, pages 105–108,** for teaching suggestions for Build Background and Vocabulary.

Vocabulary

Key Words

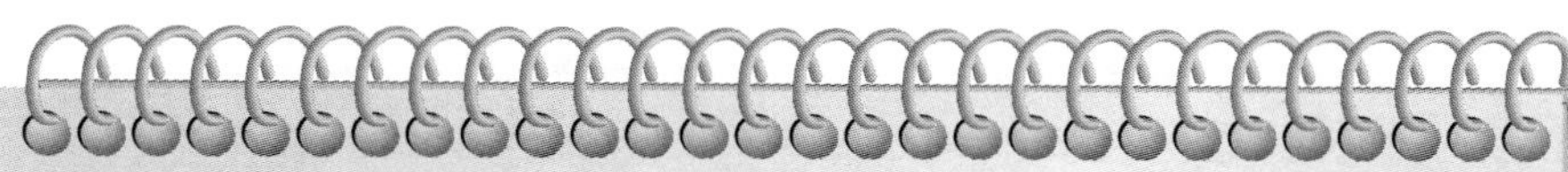

Pecos Bill

1. Pecos Bill's family moved to the wide-open, grassy prairie. 2. On the way, Bill slipped off his family's wagon, stumbled a bit, and almost fell down. 3. He was left alone in the wilderness, far from any other people. 4. To keep busy, Bill invented, or thought up, new ideas to help the world. 5. After a hard day's work inventing, Bill liked to combine ice cream and pickles for dinner, but his brother thought that was not a good mix. 6. If you are looking for the home of Pecos Bill, it is located in the great state of Texas.

Teaching Chart 80

Definitions

prairie (p. 366) flat or rolling land covered with grass and few or no trees

stumbled (p. 359) tripped or walked in a clumsy way

wilderness (p. 360) a place in nature where no people live

invented (p. 366) made or thought of for the first time; created

combine (p. 371) to join together; mix

located (p. 355) put or settled in a particular place

Vocabulary in Context

IDENTIFY VOCABULARY WORDS
Display **Teaching Chart 80** and read the passage with students. Have volunteers circle each vocabulary word and underline other words that are clues to its meaning.

DISCUSS MEANINGS Ask questions like these to help clarify word meanings:

- Would you find mountains on the prairie?
- If you stumbled, were you walking or sitting?
- Would you find a wilderness area in a city?
- Was the first airplane invented by the Wright Brothers, or did they grow it?
- Do you combine the ingredients when you make a cake?
- Will an address tell you where a place is located?

Practice

OPPOSITES Have partners pick three Vocabulary Cards each. Each says a sentence that uses the word's antonym. The partner guesses the word. ▶ Logical/Linguistic

Word Building Manipulative Cards

SYNONYMS Have students write a synonym for each vocabulary word. Partners exchange papers and guess each word. Have students refer to the Glossary as needed.
WRITING
▶ Linguistic/Interpersonal

SPELLING/VOCABULARY CONNECTIONS

See Spelling Challenge Words, page 375O–375P.

ON-LEVEL

Name________ Date________ **Practice 97**

Vocabulary

Write the vocabulary word that best fits in each of the sentences below.

combine invented located prairie stumbled wilderness

1. Let's combine your hard work with my good ideas. By joining together, we can do a much better job.
2. The scientist was well-known for thinking of useful new things. He invented egg timers and staplers, and he even made the first nonstick pan!
3. I live on Fire Street between the courthouse and the library. Where is your house located?
4. I was camping in the forest. Crickets were singing, and frogs were croaking. It was so lovely being out there in the wilderness.
5. The flat, grassy fields seemed like they would never end, and I hadn't seen a tree for miles. "This has to be the biggest prairie in the United States," I thought to myself.
6. My brother stepped on his shoelace, stumbled, and then cried out as he fell down.

97 **At Home:** Have students think of other words that mean almost the same thing as the vocabulary words. Then have them use these words as clues for

Book 3.1/Unit 3 **Pecos Bill: A Tall Tale Play** 6

Take-Home Story 97a
Reteach 97
Practice 97 • Extend 97

Guided Instruction

Preview and Predict

Have students read the title and take a **picture walk**, looking for clues about the characters.

- Will the selection be serious or humorous? How do the pictures help you decide?
- What will this selection be about?
- Is this a story or a play? How can you tell? (Each character's name precedes the dialogue. Stage directions are given.) ***Genre***

Have students record their predictions about the characters, setting, and plot.

PREDICTIONS	WHAT HAPPENED
Most of the characters will not act like real people.	
The setting of the story will change.	

Set Purposes

What do students want to find out by reading the story? For example:

- Who is Pecos Bill?
- What happens to the baby in the story?

Meet Angela Shelf Medearis

"As a child I loved to pretend I was the heroine in fairy tales," says Angela Shelf Medearis. "I've always loved to read but I can't recall ever reading any books by or about African Americans when I was in elementary school."

When Medearis grew up she changed all that. She became a children's book author and has made a difference with her writing. Funny and award-winning books like *Zebra Riding Cowboy*, *Dancing with the Indians*, and *Poppa's New Pants* have helped make Medearis one of Texas's most popular children's authors.

"I really, really like to make kids laugh," she says. "It's one of the happiest sounds in the world."

Meet John Kanzler

John Kanzler lives in Connecticut with his wife Diane, also an artist, in a small house surrounded by woods. Animals and insects are his favorite things to draw, and he can often see deer, turkey, and coyotes, running or napping in his yard. He says, "Although I have never ridden a horse in my life, I wanted painting Pecos Bill to feel like the closest thing to going out West and wrangling mustangs myself!"

352

Meeting Individual Needs • Grouping Suggestions for Strategic Reading

EASY

Read Together Read the story with students or have them use the **Listening Library Audiocassette**. Have students use the story props when they talk about the story elements. Guided Instruction and Prevention/Intervention prompts offer additional help with decoding, vocabulary, and comprehension.

ON-LEVEL

Guided Reading Preview the story words listed on page 353. Have students read the story first on their own, or listen to the **Listening Library Audiocassette**. Choose from the Guided Instruction questions as you read the story with students. Have them use the story props as they discuss story elements.

CHALLENGE

Read Independently Remind students that paying attention to setting and its effect on characters can help them make inferences about the characters and understand the plot. Have students use their story props as they think about and discuss connections between story elements.

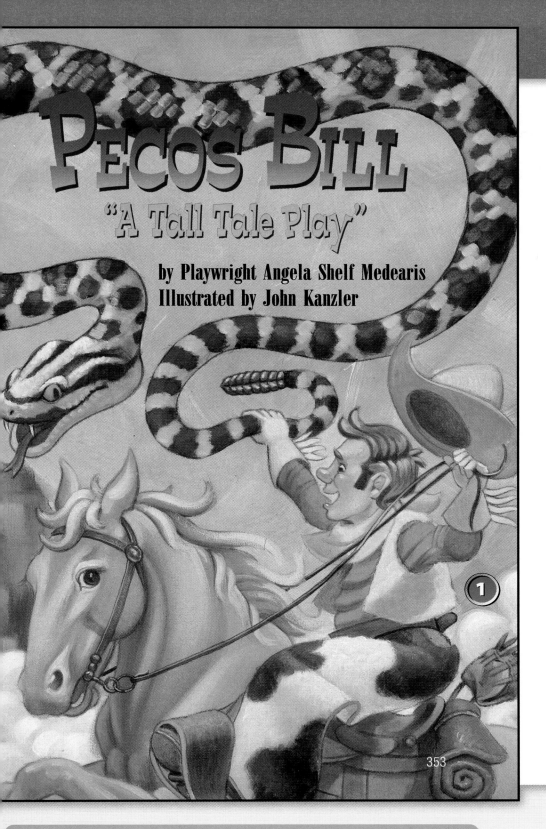

Pecos Bill
"A Tall Tale Play"

by Playwright Angela Shelf Medearis
Illustrated by John Kanzler

1

353

Guided Instruction

Story Elements

Make Inferences

Strategic Reading Paying attention to plot events and setting, and how a character responds to these elements, will help you understand the story and "know" the character. Before we begin reading, let's construct our cowboy hats to use when discussing the characters, setting, and plot of the play.

1 **SETTING** What do you think the setting of this story will be? What makes you think so?

MODEL In the pictures on pages 352 and 353 I see bulls or steer, rocky mountains in the background, and a cowboy-type person on a horse swinging a snake lasso. All these things make me think that this story will take place somewhere in the West.

LANGUAGE SUPPORT

A blackline master of the cowboy hat story prop is available in the **Language Support Book.**

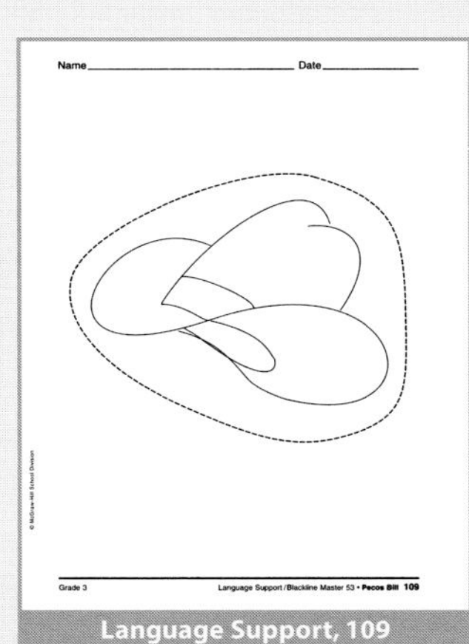

Language Support, 109

Story Words

The words below may be unfamiliar. Have students check their meanings and pronunciations in the Glossary beginning on page 388.

- tall tale, p. 354
- mustang, p. 365
- bronco-busting, p. 366
- lasso, p. 366
- longhorns, p. 366

Guided Instruction

2 **PLOT** What can you tell about the plot of the story based on the fact that there are two lists of characters? (There will be a story told within the play.) What words are clues that a story is going to be told? (*narrative, narrator*, and *tall tale*)

3 **CHARACTER** Why do you think some characters have names and some do not? (Some are more important than others.)

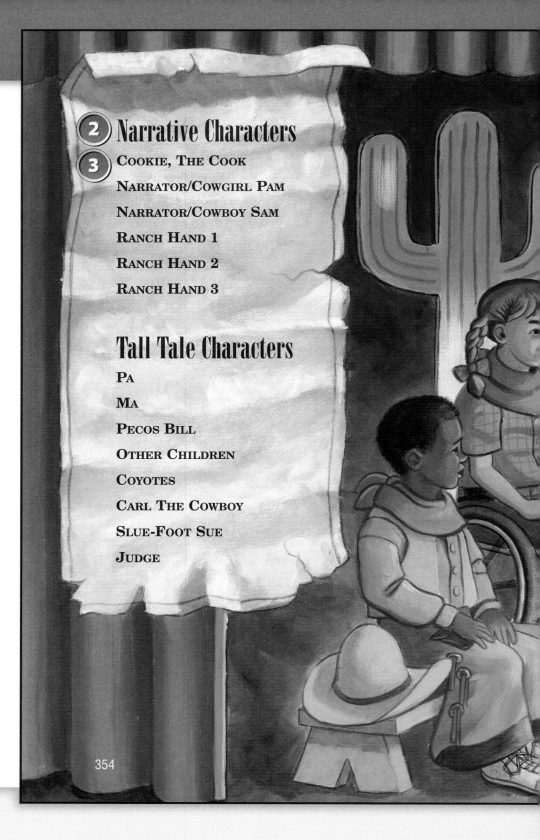

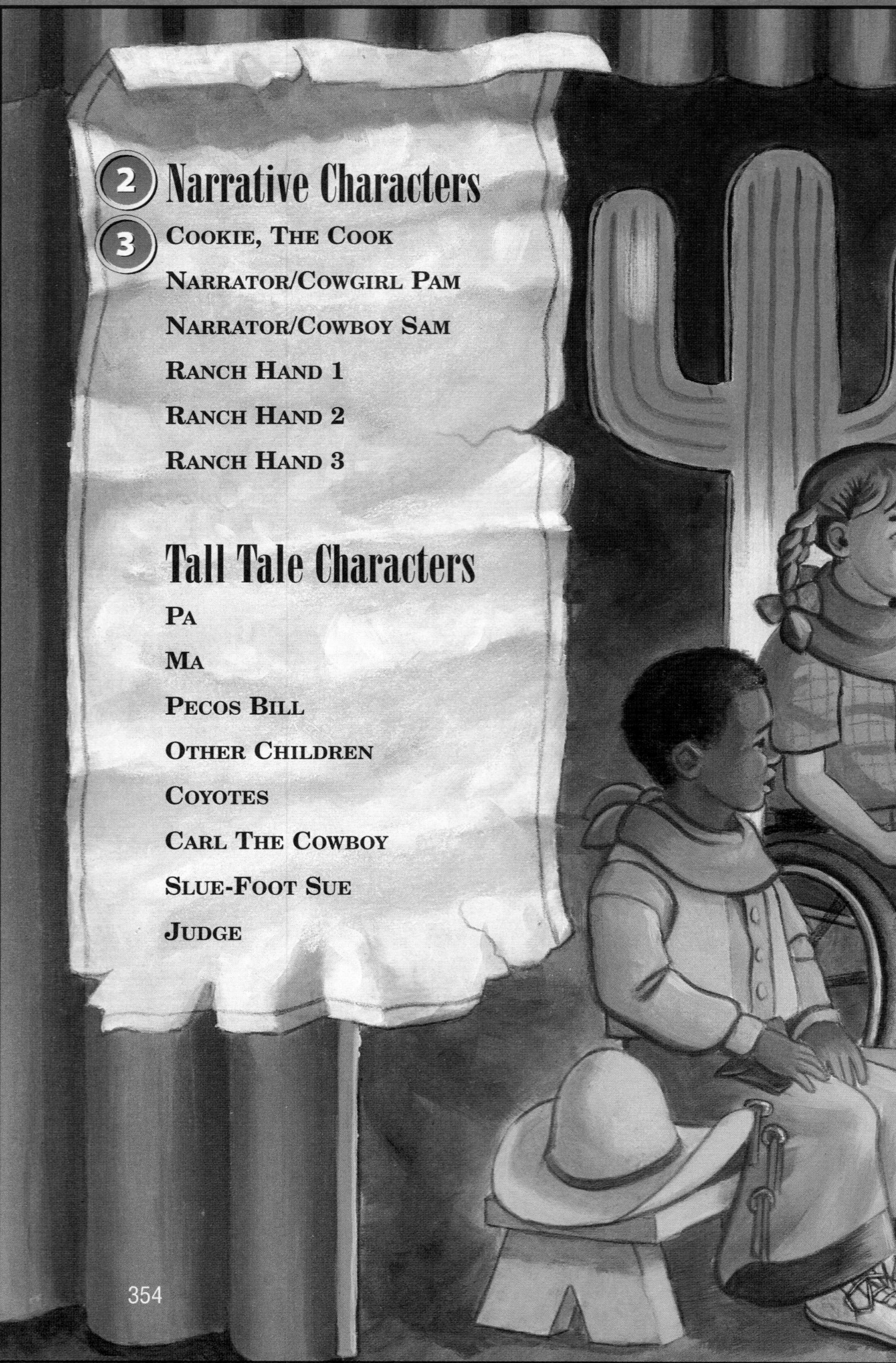

Visual Literacy

VIEWING AND REPRESENTING

Have students look at the illustrations on pages 354–355. Ask them if these look like real cowboys, cowgirls, and ranch hands. What can the students see that lets them know they are not? (fake mustache; they are just children)

Which set of characters do they think is drawn on these pages? (narrative) Why do they think that? (because there are no coyotes and there would need to be more characters for them to be the tall tale characters)

PRODUCTION NOTE: In this play the campfire and the benches should be placed stage left. The Narrative Characters will stay in this area during the whole play. Cowboy Sam and Cowgirl Pam will narrate the story. The action of the Tall Tale Characters will take place center stage and stage right.
SETTING: A cowboy camp located somewhere in the Southwest. Some benches are pulled up around a campfire. 4
COOKIE *(Enters while beating on a pan with a spoon):* Come and get it!
COWBOY SAM: What a day! I'm so hungry I could eat my boots.
RANCH HAND 1: What's for dinner, Cookie?
COOKIE: Beans.
355

Guided Instruction

4 **MAKE INFERENCES** What do you know about the setting of the play in this story now? Does the Production Note tell you something about the setting, and how it might change? Explain.

MODEL I can see by the picture and the Setting explanation that the play takes place around a campfire at a cowboy camp in the Southwest. But the Production Note says that the action of the tall tale will happen in a different spot, so I think the setting will change for the tall tale story.

TEACHING TIP

MANAGEMENT For ease in reading *Pecos Bill: A Tall Tale Play* aloud with the students, assign parts for each page. In lieu of having students act out the stage directions, which might get raucous, have one student read the stage directions.

LANGUAGE SUPPORT

ESL Point out the playwriting conventions on page 355 and discuss each one with students.

- A production note is a general statement about how the play will be performed.
- The setting tells where the play takes place.
- When a character speaks, his or her name is printed in dark capital letters followed by a colon.
- The words in parentheses after a character's name tell how he or she should act.

Guided Instruction

(5) **CHARACTER, SETTING, PLOT** Why do you think the characters are tired of eating beans? (because they've been eating them for 67 days) Why have they been eating them for so long? (They are working out on the range, far from a grocery store with a selection of foods.) What happens because they are so tired of beans? (They order pizza.) What is going to happen while they wait for the pizzas? (Cowboy Sam and Cowgirl Pam will tell the story of Pecos Bill.)

(6) Can you summarize briefly, and in your own words, what has happened on page 356? (The characters are tired of eating beans, so they order pizza, and while they wait they will tell the story of Pecos Bill and Slue-Foot Sue.) ***Summarize***

(P/i) **COMPOUND WORDS** Reread page 356. Which words are compound words, not including proper names? (*three-bean*, *anything*, *ten-gallon*, and *cowboys*)

RANCH HAND 2: Did you fix a salad?
COOKIE: I sure did. It's three-bean salad.
RANCH HAND 3: What's for dessert?
COOKIE: Bean pie.
COWGIRL PAM: Cookie, we're tired of eating beans!
RANCH HAND 1: We've had beans for sixty-seven days!
EVERYONE: All you ever cook is beans, beans, beans!
COWGIRL PAM: Don't you know how to cook anything else?
COOKIE: Nope! I only cook what I like to eat and I like beans.
COWBOY SAM: Well, I'm going to order some pizzas.
RANCH HANDS *(together)*: Yeah! Pizza!
COOKIE: Okay! Okay! If you don't want to eat these beans tonight, that's fine. I will just serve them for breakfast in the morning.
(Everyone groans. Cowboy Sam takes a cell phone out from under his cowboy hat and dials some numbers.)
COWGIRL PAM: So, that's why cowboys wear those ten-gallon hats!
COWBOY SAM *(into phone)*: Hello, four large cheese pizzas, please. Oh, you need our address? We're at 555 Middle of Nowhere Road. Okay, see you in thirty minutes.
RANCH HAND 1: Cowgirl Pam, will you tell us a story while we're waiting for our pizzas?
(5) **RANCH HAND 2:** I want to hear a story about Pecos Bill.
(6) **RANCH HAND 3:** I want to hear a story about Slue-Foot Sue.

356

PREVENTION/INTERVENTION

COMPOUND WORDS Remind students that all compound words are made up of two smaller words, some with a hyphen between them. Knowing the meaning of the smaller words can often help in understanding the meaning of a compound word.

- Write the words *three-bean*, *anything*, *ten-gallon*, and *cowboy* on the chalkboard.
- Ask students the definition of each base word, and write their responses beneath each one.
- Have students put the base word meanings together to arrive at a definition for the compound words.

Cowgirl Pam: I'll be glad to tell you all about Pecos Bill and Slue-Foot Sue. Will you help me, Cowboy Sam?

Cowboy Sam: Of course. Listen up, cowpokes! The legend of Pecos Bill and Slue-Foot started right here in the great state of Texas. Now, Bill's Pa couldn't stand to live around too many people. 

Cowgirl Pam: It's a good thing that Texas is a big state. Bill's Pa didn't have to move very far when he wanted to be alone. 

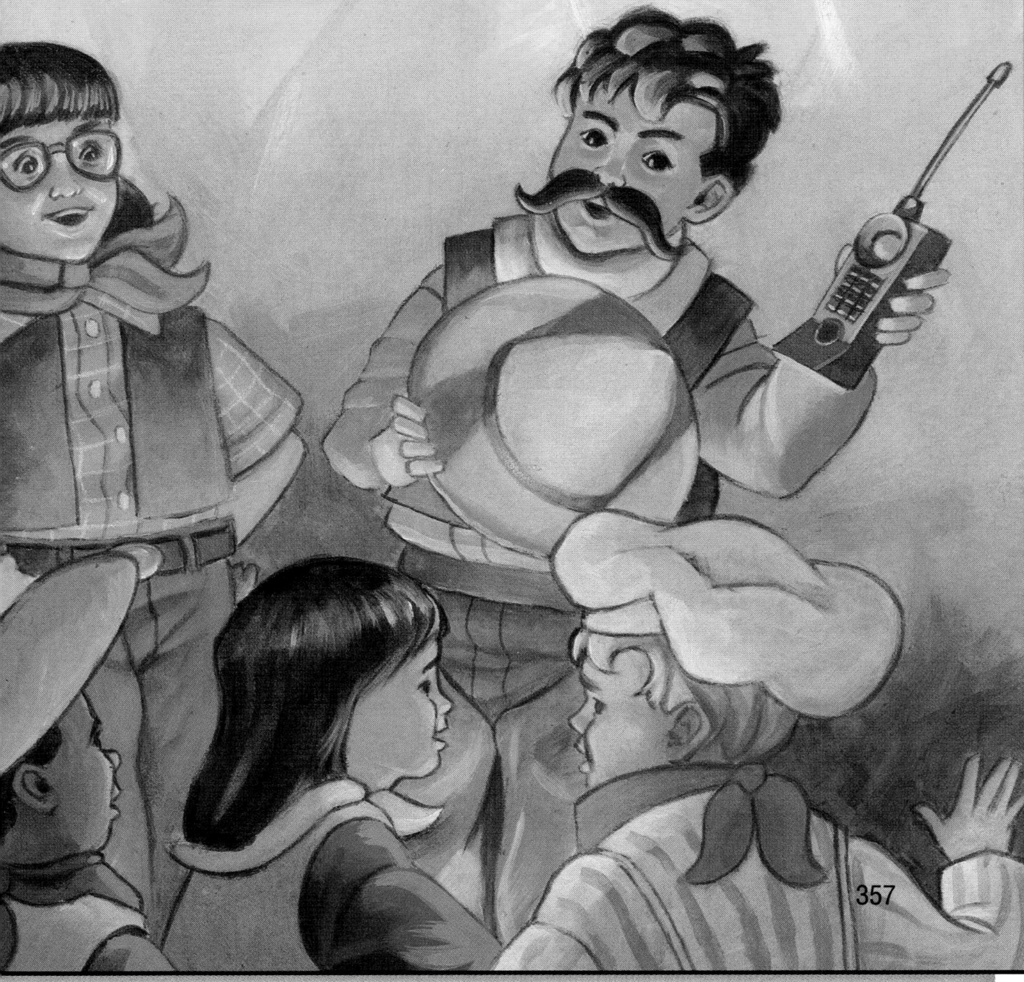

357

Guided Instruction

7 **SETTING** What is the same about the setting of the play and the setting of the tall tale? (Both are set in Texas.)

8 **PLOT** How do the stage directions—the words in parentheses—help you to understand the plot of the play? Hold up your cowboy hat as you discuss this. *Story Prop*

MODEL When I read the stage directions on page 356, I know that Cowboy Sam has a cell phone under his cowboy hat. If the stage directions didn't tell me this, I would not understand why Cowgirl Pam says, "So that's why cowboys wear those ten-gallon hats!" I would also not understand who Cowboy Sam was talking to when he ordered the pizzas. I'll read the play without the stage directions and see if it makes sense.

LANGUAGE SUPPORT

ESL Ask students to recap what has happened so far and what is about to happen. (The cowboys are unhappy because they're having beans for dinner again. Cowboy Sam uses a cell phone to order pizzas. Cowgirl Pam is about to tell a story about Slue-Foot Sue and Pecos Bill while they wait.)

Ask students to guess what a *legend* is using context clues. Explain that it is not a true story, but one that people have told over and over again through the years.

Guided Instruction

9 **MAKE INFERENCES** How do you explain the images drawn on this page? Do the cloudlike frames give you a clue as to what is happening with these illustrations?

MODEL The cloudlike frames remind me of thought bubbles, like I've seen in cartoons and comics. Maybe the pictures in the cloudlike frames are the way the people listening to the tall tale imagine the action of the tall tale looks.

TEACHING TIP

INSTRUCTIONAL Discuss with students how reading a play is different from watching a play be performed. Explain that the setting can change in a play. A reader can tell that the setting has changed by paying close attention to the stage directions and to the words and actions of the characters.

PA *(runs on stage)*: Ma, we've got new neighbors! It's time to move!

MA *(entering stage followed by some children)*: Where do they live, Pa?

PA: They live over the mountains and through the woods. They're only 150 miles away!

MA: 150 miles! Why, they're almost right in our backyard!

PA: Come on, Ma! Pack up all of the kids! *(exiting with Ma and the children)* Let's go west!

CULTURAL PERSPECTIVES

NEW HOMES Tell students that people all over the world move to new places.

RESEARCH AND INQUIRY Have students research groups of immigrants.

- Have students draw a suitcase. On the suitcase, have them write the location the immigrants moved from, the place they moved to, and the year.

▶ **Spatial/Intrapersonal**

Cowgirl Pam: So, Pa, Ma, Bill, and his fourteen brothers and sisters moved west. They were crossing the Pecos River when their wagon wheel hit a rock. Poor little Bill flew out of the wagon. He hit the ground and stumbled around like a tumbleweed in a Texas tornado.

(Pecos Bill stumbles across stage. He sits down in the center of the stage. He looks around, rubbing his head and looking puzzled.)

Cowboy Sam: Pa and Ma didn't hear a thing.

Ranch Hand 1: Didn't Ma and Pa notice that Pecos Bill was missing?

Cowgirl Pam: Well, Ma tried to count her children every day. But they kept moving around. Sometimes she even counted some of them twice.

359

Guided Instruction

10 **CHARACTER** What kind of a character is Pa? Do you think he is adventurous? What in the story helps you decide? (He moves his whole family without knowing exactly where they are going.) How would you describe the character of Ma? (absent-minded) What makes you think that? (She counts her children every day.)

11 **PLOT** What major event happens on page 359? (Baby Bill falls off the wagon.) How do you think this will affect Bill's life?

LANGUAGE SUPPORT

ESL Demonstrate the meaning of *tumbleweed* for students needing additional instruction. Write *tumbleweed* on the chalkboard.

Point out that *tumbleweed* is a compound word. Ask a volunteer to explain that a compound word is a word made up of two base words, and then have another volunteer circle the two words that make up *tumbleweed*. Brainstorm with students the meanings of each of these words. Then invite them to pantomime *tumble* and draw a weed on the chalkboard. Have students give a definition for the compound word *tumbleweed*. If necessary, bring in photos of tumbleweed.

Minilesson

REVIEW/MAINTAIN

Main Idea

Call on volunteers to tell the main idea of the story—what it is mainly about. Remind students that they should focus on the main events of the story, not every detail.

Activity Challenge students to write one sentence that explains the main idea of the story, as a whole. (Listening to a tall tale is a good way to pass the time when you are hungry and waiting for food.) If this proves too difficult, they can write about the main idea of the narrative play separately from the tall tale.

Guided Instruction

12 **CHARACTER** Hold up your cowboy hats. What can you tell about the character of Ranch Hand 3? Would you say that Ranch Hand 3 is absorbed by the tall tale, or not? Explain. (Ranch Hand 3 is crying about food while the other ranch hands are crying about Pecos Bill.) ***Story Prop***

13 **PLOT** What events are happening in the story of Pecos Bill that tell you this story is a tall tale? (Baby Bill falls out of a wagon and nobody notices; coyotes "understand" baby talk; coyotes take Bill to their den and feed him.)

MA *(counting children)*: One, two, five, eight, nine...or was that six?

COWBOY SAM: Poor little Bill was left out in the middle of nowhere all by himself.

RANCH HAND 1 *(crying)*: Poor little Bill!

RANCH HAND 2 *(crying)*: All alone in the Texas wilderness!

RANCH HAND 3 *(crying)*: When are those pizzas coming? *(everyone looks at Ranch Hand 3)*

12 **RANCH HAND 3:** Well, I'm hungry! Go on with the story, Cowboy Sam.

COWBOY SAM: There was a pack of friendly coyotes nearby. They were eating dinner. The coyotes looked at Bill. Bill looked at the coyotes. Pretty soon they came over to see what kind of animal Bill was.

(A mother coyote and her coyote children—about four to six children—run over to Bill.)

COYOTES *(together)*: AHOOOOO!

PECOS BILL: Goo-goo.

13 **COWBOY SAM:** Now, it turns out that goo-goo means "I'm lost, hungry, and feeling very alone, please help me right now!" in coyote language.

COWGIRL PAM: The kind mother coyote took Bill to her den. Then she gave him a nice, juicy piece of meat.

(Bill sniffs the meat and gobbles it down.)

COYOTES: AHOOOOO!

PECOS BILL: Goo-goo.

360

Cross Curricular: Science

DESERT LIFE Ask students who have been to the desert to describe the plants and animals they saw there.

RESEARCH AND INQUIRY

- Have students choose a favorite desert plant or animal to research and draw.
- Ask students to write captions under their drawings about their plant or animal. ▶ **Linguistic/Spatial**

Students can learn more about the desert by visiting ***www.mhschool.com/reading.***

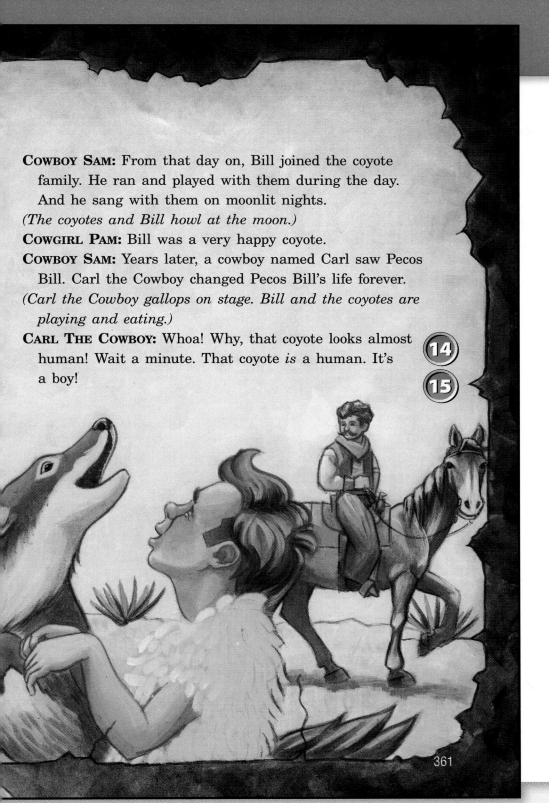

Cowboy Sam: From that day on, Bill joined the coyote family. He ran and played with them during the day. And he sang with them on moonlit nights.

(The coyotes and Bill howl at the moon.)

Cowgirl Pam: Bill was a very happy coyote.

Cowboy Sam: Years later, a cowboy named Carl saw Pecos Bill. Carl the Cowboy changed Pecos Bill's life forever.

(Carl the Cowboy gallops on stage. Bill and the coyotes are playing and eating.)

Carl the Cowboy: Whoa! Why, that coyote looks almost human! Wait a minute. That coyote *is* a human. It's a boy! 14 15

361

Guided Instruction

14 By the end of page 361, has a lot of time passed? How can you tell? (Bill looks older now.) What phrase on this page is a clue that time has passed? (*years later*) ***Sequence of Events***

15 Are the narrative characters different from or similar to the tall tale characters? (both) How? (They are different because the narrative characters are mostly just like real people, and the tall tale characters don't seem real. They are similar because they both do funny and unexpected things, like Ranch Hand 3 crying over pizza and Pecos Bill going to live with coyotes.) ***Compare and Contrast***

PHONICS KIT
HANDS-ON ACTIVITIES AND PRACTICE

Minilesson

REVIEW/MAINTAIN

/ou/ and /oi/

Write the word *counting* on the chalkboard. Have a volunteer underline the spelling of the /ou/ sound.

- Have students find other words on pages 360 and 361 with the /ou/ sound. (*cowgirl, cowboy, howl*)
- Repeat the procedure for the /oi/ sound with the words *joined* and *cowboy*.

Activity Have students brainstorm /ou/ and /oi/ words. Invite them to write a short dialogue between a cowboy and a cowgirl using the words from their list.

Phonics CD-ROM Have students use the interactive phonics activities on the CD-ROM for more reinforcement.

Guided Instruction

16 CHARACTER, SETTING, PLOT Would the tall tale be different if the setting was not the Texas wilderness and desert land? What plot events could not have happened if this were so? (Baby Bill might not have fallen out of the wagon; there would be no coyotes to take care of him.) Would the characters be the same? Explain. (If the setting was not the same, and that made the plot different, the characters would probably be different, too. Carl the Cowboy wouldn't be a cowboy, for instance.)

P/I INFLECTIONAL ENDINGS Can you find the words on page 362 that are in the comparative form? *(faster, higher, louder)*

Fluency

READ DIALOGUE

Have small groups choose roles and read the text you have covered so far. Help students prepare for their roles by discussing character. Ask students to describe the character they will read. Have them tell you what they infer about each character's personality, voice, mannerisms. Ask: Will this character speak very slowly? Is this character excited? Grumpy? Encourage students to read with appropriate vocal and facial expression.

(Carl the Cowboy grabs Bill by the leg. Bill tries to run away. The coyotes run offstage.)

CARL THE COWBOY: I'm Carl the Cowboy. What's your name?

PECOS BILL: AHOOOO! AHOOO! AH, AH, AH, BILLLLLLLLL!

CARL THE COWBOY: Did you say your name is Bill?

PECOS BILL: I, I—*(coughs loudly)* Yes! Yes! My name is Bill!

CARL THE COWBOY: Why in the world are you crawling around in the dirt like a coyote?

PECOS BILL: Because I am a coyote.

CARL THE COWBOY: Son, you are not a coyote.

PECOS BILL: Yes, I am. I can run faster than a lizard. I can jump higher than a jack rabbit. And I can howl louder than the wind.

CARL THE COWBOY: I can do all that stuff, too. Son, you need a good, hot bath. Come along with me. I'm going to teach you how to be a cowboy.

COWGIRL PAM: For three long days, Carl the Cowboy taught Pecos Bill how to think, walk, talk, and ride like a cowboy. He gave him a book called *How to Be a Cowboy in Ten Easy Lessons*.

(Carl shows him how cowboys walk. They skip around on the stage. He mimes how to ride a horse.)

CARL THE COWBOY: Well, I've taught you everything I know. I've got to go now. I'm on my way to see my Pa and help him with his ranch.

PECOS BILL: My Pa was named Pa, too.

CARL THE COWBOY: Was your Ma named Ma?

PECOS BILL: Yes!

362

P/I PREVENTION/INTERVENTION

INFLECTIONAL ENDINGS Review with children the inflectional ending *-er*. Tell them *-er* is a suffix that means "more." It shows that an adjective or an adverb is in its comparative form.

Have volunteers write the comparatives from page 362 on the chalkboard. *(faster, higher, louder)* Then ask students what the base word in each comparative is. Write their responses on the chalkboard. Use sentences to illustrate that the comparative form compares two things.

Carl the Cowboy: Do you have fourteen brothers and sisters?
Pecos Bill: I sure do!
Carl the Cowboy *(rapidly)*: Do you have a red-haired, freckled-faced brother named Clyde?
Pecos Bill *(sadly)*: No. No, I don't have a red-haired, freckled-faced brother named Clyde. 
Carl the Cowboy *(happily):* Neither do I! But I do have a brother named Bill. He fell out of a wagon while we were crossing the Pecos River. We always called him Pecos Bill. 

363

Guided Instruction

17 How do people look when they have found something or someone they have lost? How would it feel to find a long-lost brother or sister? Show me how it would feel. ***Pantomime***

18 What is the problem Carl the Cowboy faces on this page? (how to figure out if he and Bill are brothers) How does he solve his problem? (He asks if Bill's family was like his in this way or that, and Bill always answers "yes." Carl tests Bill when he asks about the brother named Clyde, because if Bill answers "yes" it means Bill is not telling the truth. So when Bill says "no," it's proof that they are brothers.) ***Problem and Solution***

Guided Instruction

19 PLOT What do you think is happening on this page? Can you tell just from looking at the illustration? (As Carl the Cowboy rides off with Pecos Bill toward a new life, Pecos Bill and the coyotes howl "good-bye" to each other.)

SELF-MONITORING

STRATEGY

REREAD Rereading what you have already read can help you remember the details of a story.

MODEL I can't remember all the details I have read so far. There are a lot of characters and two different stories to keep track of. I think I'll quickly glance at the pages I have read. I will go back to the first page and quickly review the characters in the narrative and the characters in the tall tale. Then I will look at the other pages. I probably won't need to go back and read every word because I have already read them. I just need to give my memory a little tap.

Activity

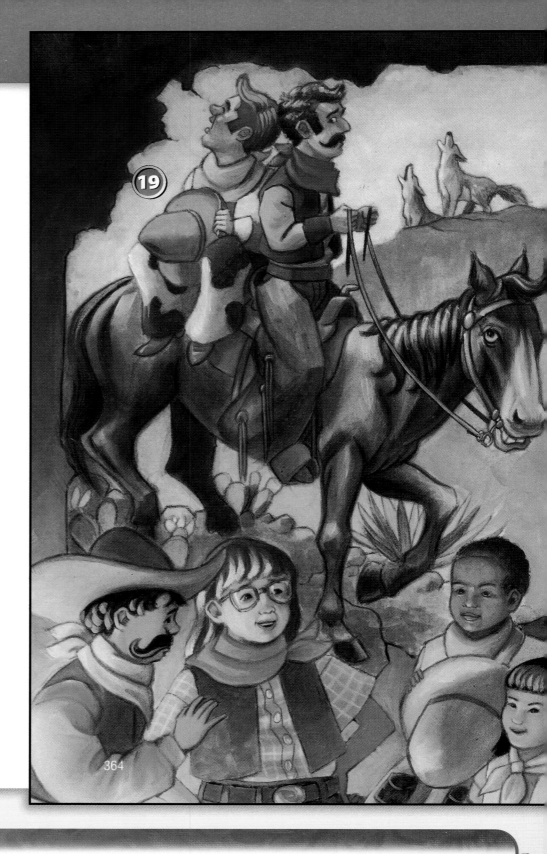

Cross Curricular: Social Studies

WILD WEST Discuss with students how difficult pioneer life must have been.

RESEARCH AND INQUIRY Have students research facts about pioneer life in the Southwest.

- Have students draw a scene of frontier life with a caption that explains the scene. ▶ **Linguistic/Interpersonal**

In the Old West, it was too dangerous to travel alone, so several families joined together to form wagon trains.

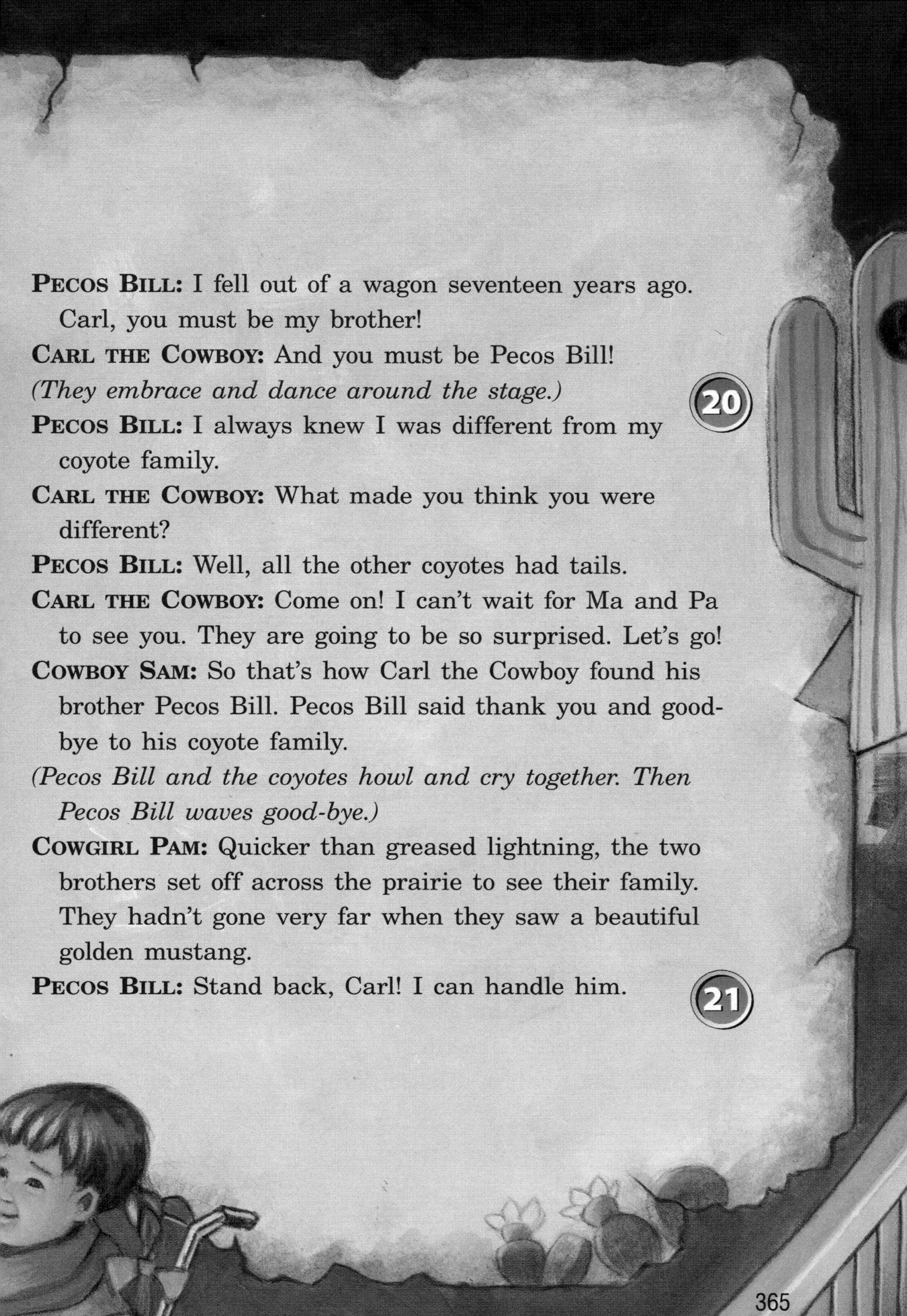

PECOS BILL: I fell out of a wagon seventeen years ago. Carl, you must be my brother!
CARL THE COWBOY: And you must be Pecos Bill!
(They embrace and dance around the stage.)
20
PECOS BILL: I always knew I was different from my coyote family.
CARL THE COWBOY: What made you think you were different?
PECOS BILL: Well, all the other coyotes had tails.
CARL THE COWBOY: Come on! I can't wait for Ma and Pa to see you. They are going to be so surprised. Let's go!
COWBOY SAM: So that's how Carl the Cowboy found his brother Pecos Bill. Pecos Bill said thank you and good-bye to his coyote family.
(Pecos Bill and the coyotes howl and cry together. Then Pecos Bill waves good-bye.)
COWGIRL PAM: Quicker than greased lightning, the two brothers set off across the prairie to see their family. They hadn't gone very far when they saw a beautiful golden mustang.
PECOS BILL: Stand back, Carl! I can handle him.
21
365

Guided Instruction

20 **CHARACTER** Put on your cowboy hat as you answer. How do you think Carl the Cowboy and Pecos Bill feel about discovering they are brothers? (They are very happy.) How can you tell? (The stage direction says they hug each other and dance around, and that seems like the kind of thing you do when you're happy.) ***Story Prop***

21 You know quite a bit about Pecos Bill and the unexpected, and somewhat unpredictable, kind of life he lives. What event happens on this page that distracts him from his journey, and fits in with his lifestyle? (He and Carl don't get far before they find a golden mustang that Bill says he can handle.) How likely is it that there will be other events that get in the way of Pecos Bill and Carl the Cowboy getting home right away? ***Make Predictions***

P/I **IDIOMS** Read what Cowgirl Pam says on page 365. Do you know what the phrase *quicker than greased lightning* means?

P/I PREVENTION/INTERVENTION

IDIOMS Tell students that the phrase *quicker than greased lightning* is an *idiom*—an expression whose meaning cannot be understood from the meanings of the separate words in it.

Ask students what something is like when it is *greased*, such as the gears on a bike. (slippery, fast) Then ask them to describe *lightning*. (quick flash of light) Finally, ask them if they can tell what *quicker than greased lightning* means. (even faster than something that is very fast)

Guided Instruction

22 **MAKE INFERENCES** What kind of person do you think Pecos Bill is? (adventurous, fearless, maybe a little crazy) What makes you think this? (He jumps on the back of a wild horse without even thinking about it; he grabs a rattlesnake without fear; his brother seems amazed by him.)

23 **CHARACTER, PLOT** How is the plot affected by Pecos Bill's character? What happens because he is adventurous, fearless, and a little crazy? (The Grand Canyon is created, and bronco-busting and the lasso are invented.)

COWBOY SAM: Pecos Bill ran as fast as a jack rabbit. He chased that horse across several states. Finally he got close enough to grab the mustang by its mane. Pecos Bill swung himself on the horse's back. The horse stopped so quick it plowed up miles and miles of earth. Pecos Bill and the mustang found themselves at the bottom of a deep canyon. Some folks call it the Grand Canyon.

CARL THE COWBOY: Well, if that don't beat all. I think you just invented something new. I've never seen anybody tame a wild horse like that.

PECOS BILL: Let's call it bronco-busting! We can teach it to all the cowboys.

CARL THE COWBOY: That's a great idea. I can't wait for Pa and Ma to see you riding on that wildcat.

PECOS BILL: I'm going to name this horse Widow Maker. Yee-haw!

COWGIRL PAM: Well, Pecos Bill and Carl the Cowboy hadn't gone very far when a big old rattlesnake appeared. Pecos Bill jumped off his horse, grabbed the snake, and held it tight. Next he whirled it around and around his head. That snake got so dizzy it forgot how
22 to bite. Then Pecos Bill used the rattler to rope all the longhorns he saw on the prairie.

CARL THE COWBOY: Well, if that don't beat all. I think you just invented something else! I've never seen anybody round up longhorns like that.

PECOS BILL: Let's call it a lasso! We can teach it to all
23 the cowboys.

366

Cross Curricular: Math

MEASURE THE GRAND CANYON Have students research numerical facts about the Grand Canyon, such as width, depth, and how many miles of trails it contains.

Have students chart their findings in a two-column chart. They may also want to research other measurements to compare with their findings, such as the length of their city or town in miles, or the depth of a local body of water.

▶ **Spatial/Mathematical**

The Grand Canyon	
depth	1 mile
width	18 miles
miles of trails	400 miles

Ranch Hand 1: So that's how a lasso was invented.
Ranch Hand 2: And bronco-busting!
Ranch Hand 3: Where is that pizza? *(Everyone looks at Ranch Hand 3.)* Well, I'm hungry! Go on with the story, Cowboy Sam.
Cowboy Sam: Guess what else Pecos Bill invented.
Cookie: The lima bean?
Cowboy Sam: No! He invented the guitar and cowboy songs. 24
Ranch Hand 1: How did he do that? 25

Guided Instruction

24 What is similar about the characters of Cookie and Ranch Hand 3? (They both seem to have only one thing on their minds: beans or pizza.) Why do you think the author created them this way? What do they bring to the narrative portions of the story which might otherwise not be there? (They are funny. Without them the tall tale would have all the funny characters.) ***Author's Purpose***

25 Can you summarize the events on page 366 in your own words? Remember to keep your summaries brief, focus on main events rather than details, and keep events in order. (Pecos Bill creates and invents familiar things in strange and unusual ways.) ***Summarize***

P/I **CONTEXT CLUES** Find the word *tame* on page 366. Do you know what *tame* means? (to bring under control) Can you tell by reading the rest of the sentence?

P/I PREVENTION/INTERVENTION

CONTEXT CLUES Remind students that they can come to understand the meaning of an unfamiliar word by looking at the words nearby.

Have students read Carl the Cowboy's first speech on page 366 to figure out the meaning of *tame* by using context clues. Ask them what context clues they found. (a wild horse) Help students see that in this selection *tame* means *to bring under control.*

Guided Instruction

26 **MAKE INFERENCES** Based on what you know about the names of the other tall tale characters, who do you think the person on the fish is in the illustration on page 368? What makes you think so? (Since this person is a female, and there is only one other female besides Bill's mother in the tall tale, it must be Slue-Foot Sue.)

27 Carl the Cowboy and Pecos Bill still have not reached home. How many of you correctly predicted that they would have several adventures before reaching home? *Confirm Predictions*

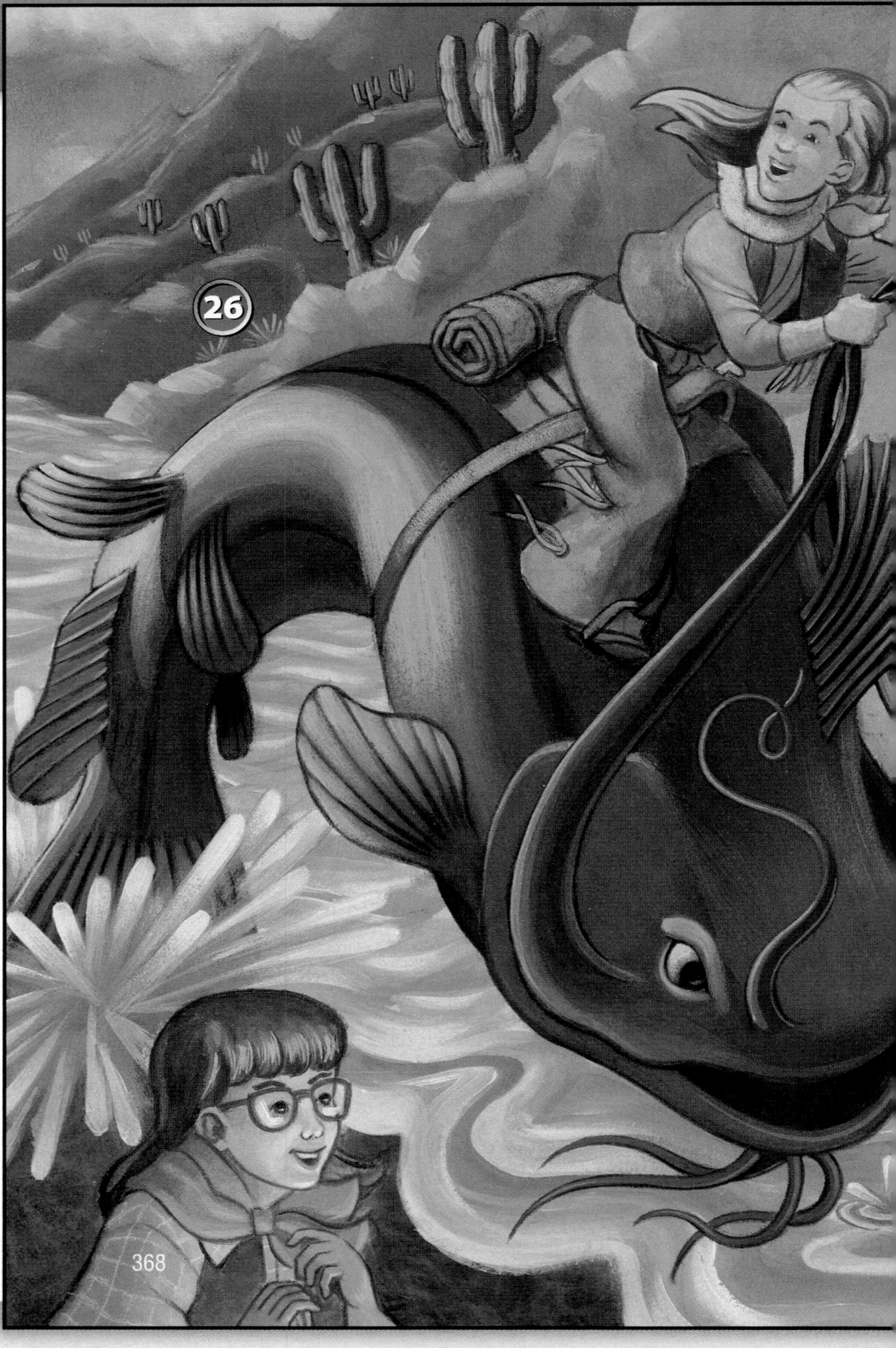

Activity

Cross Curricular: Music

COWBOY SONGS Share recordings of cowboy songs with students. Have them listen closely to the words and themes of the songs. Discuss how the life of a cowgirl or cowboy is reflected in the songs.

- Invite small groups to make up their own cowboy song. Suggest that they make up a song about Pecos Bill or another character in the story, using details they have learned about that character.
- Students can use a traditional cowboy melody for the tune of their song.

▶ **Musical/Interpersonal**

Cowgirl Pam: The moon was as large and round as a ripe peach. Carl the Cowboy and Pecos Bill stopped to rest for the night. Pecos Bill picked out a tree, tore it down with his bare hands, and twisted it into a guitar. He pulled some of the hair out of his head to use for guitar strings. Then he started to sing a song. 

Pecos Bill: This is a song the coyotes taught me, Carl. Just listen and sing along with me.

(Pecos Bill and Carl the Cowboy sing Home on the Range. *Everyone sings along.)*

Ranch Hand 1: What a beautiful song.

Ranch Hand 2: Now we know how the first guitar was made.

Ranch Hand 3: The pizza is here! Yes!

(Everyone gets a slice of pizza.)

Ranch Hand 2: Go on with the story, Cowgirl Pam.

Cowgirl Pam: Do you know how Pecos Bill met his wife, Slue-Foot Sue?

Ranch Hand 1: Tell us!

Cowboy Sam: One day, Pecos Bill and Carl the Cowboy decided to go for a swim in the Rio Grande River. While they were swimming, Pecos Bill saw something strange coming towards them.

Slue-Foot Sue: Out of my way you two! Yee-haw!

Pecos Bill: What was that? It looked like a catfish, but it's as big as a whale! And who is that riding that fish like a bronco?

Carl the Cowboy: That's Slue-Foot Sue!

Slue-Foot Sue: Howdy, Carl! Howdy, stranger! 

Carl: Howdy, Slue-Foot Sue. Sue, this is my brother, Pecos Bill.

369

Guided Instruction

28 **CHARACTER** What kind of person do you think Slue-Foot Sue is? (a friendly person; a daring person) What clues in the story help you know this? (She says "Howdy!" and she rides a huge catfish as if it's a horse.)

Minilesson

REVIEW/MAINTAIN

Context Clues

Remind students that other words in the story can provide clues to an unfamiliar word's meaning.

- Ask students to find clues to the meaning of *ripe* in Cowboy Pam's speech at the top of page 369. (*large, peach*)
- Ask students to give a definition for the word *ripe*.

Activity Have students write context sentences for the word *ripe*. Have them circle the context clues in their sentence.

Guided Instruction

29 What causes Pecos Bill to start howling like a coyote again? (He falls in love with Slue-Foot Sue.) ***Cause and Effect***

30 **CHARACTER, PLOT** Hold up your cowboy hat as you discuss this question. In tall tales, the characters are larger than life. The things they do are things that no real person could do. What are some things that Pecos Bill does that no real person could do? (He chased a mustang across several states. He made a lasso out of a rattlesnake. He tore down a tree with his bare hands.)

RETELL THE STORY Have volunteers retell the story in their own words. Then have them write one or two sentences that summarize the story. ***Summarize***

Student Self-Assessment

- How did using the strategy of Analyzing Character, Setting, and Plot help me to understand the story?
- Did using the story props help me to focus on the connections between story elements?

TRANSFERRING THE STRATEGY

- When might I use this strategy again? In what other reading could story props help me?

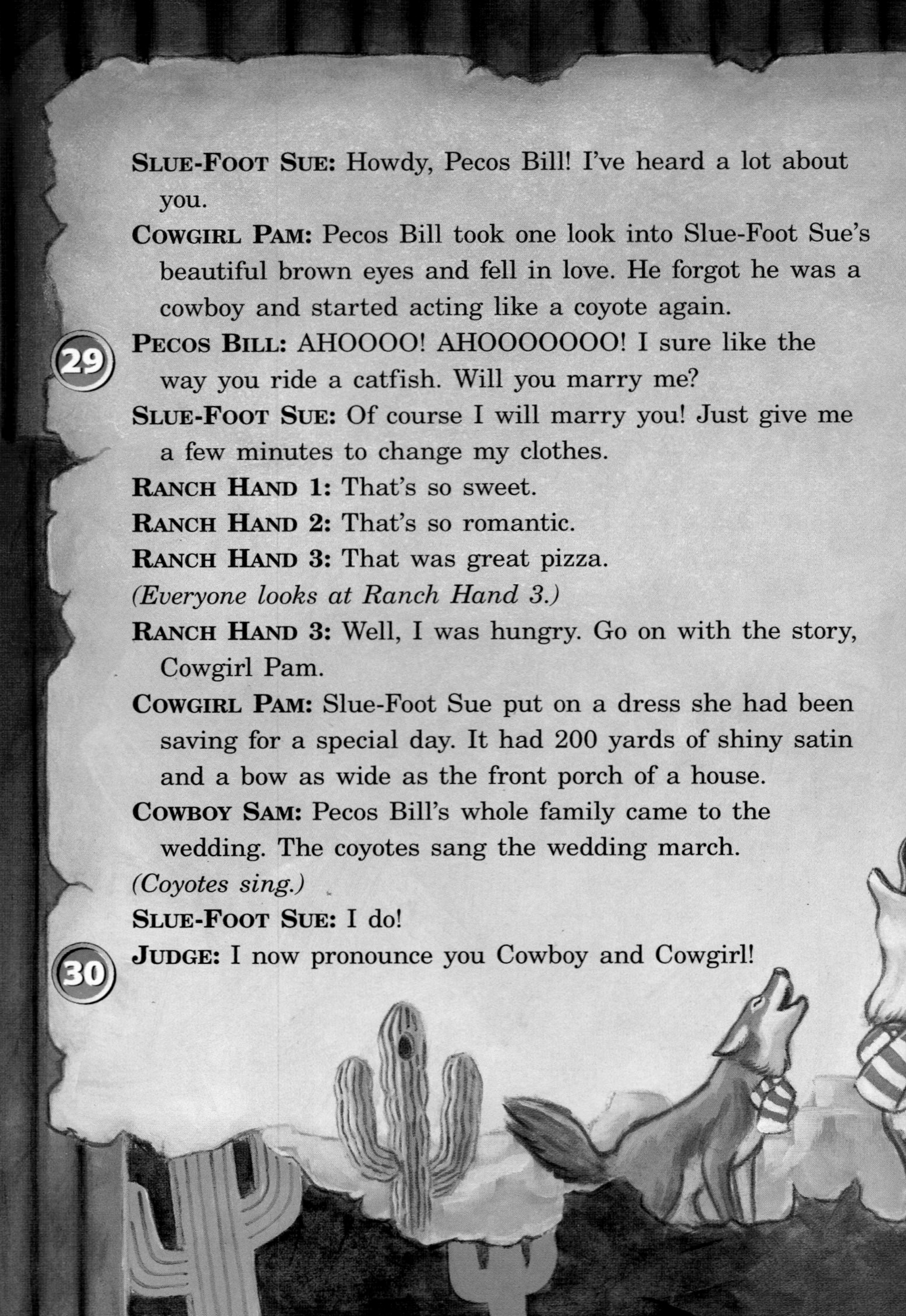

SLUE-FOOT SUE: Howdy, Pecos Bill! I've heard a lot about you.

COWGIRL PAM: Pecos Bill took one look into Slue-Foot Sue's beautiful brown eyes and fell in love. He forgot he was a cowboy and started acting like a coyote again.

29 **PECOS BILL:** AHOOOO! AHOOOOOOO! I sure like the way you ride a catfish. Will you marry me?

SLUE-FOOT SUE: Of course I will marry you! Just give me a few minutes to change my clothes.

RANCH HAND 1: That's so sweet.

RANCH HAND 2: That's so romantic.

RANCH HAND 3: That was great pizza.

(Everyone looks at Ranch Hand 3.)

RANCH HAND 3: Well, I was hungry. Go on with the story, Cowgirl Pam.

COWGIRL PAM: Slue-Foot Sue put on a dress she had been saving for a special day. It had 200 yards of shiny satin and a bow as wide as the front porch of a house.

COWBOY SAM: Pecos Bill's whole family came to the wedding. The coyotes sang the wedding march.

(Coyotes sing.)

SLUE-FOOT SUE: I do!

30 **JUDGE:** I now pronounce you Cowboy and Cowgirl!

370

REREADING FOR *Fluency*

GROUP Have students form two groups. Invite one group to read the narrative while the other group reads the tall tale. After reading, groups can exchange parts.

READING RATE You may want to evaluate a student's reading rate. Have the student read aloud from *Pecos Bill: A Tall Tale* for one minute. Ask the student to place a self-stick note after the last word read. Then count the number of words he or she has read. Alternatively, you could assess small groups or the whole class together by having students count words and record their own scores.

A Running Record form provided in **Diagnostic/Placement Evaluation** will help you evaluate reading rate(s).

Pecos Bill: AHOOOOOOO!
Slue-Foot Sue: He sure has a pretty way with words.
Cowgirl Pam: And they lived happily ever after.
Ranch Hand 1: That was a great tall tale.
Ranch Hand 2: That was fun.
Ranch Hand 3: That was great pizza.
Cookie: It sure was. I think I'll make pizza from now on. I know! I'll combine beans with pizza!
(Everyone looks at Cookie. They all get up and leave.)
Cookie *(follows after them)*: How does Lima Bean Pizza sound for breakfast?

The End

Literary Response

QUICK-WRITE Invite students to record their thoughts about the story. These questions may help them get started:

- Did you always know what was going to happen next in this play? Did you enjoy being surprised by events?
- How did you like the play having two sets of characters? Was it confusing?
- Would you like to read other tall tales? Why or why not?

ORAL RESPONSE Have students share their journal writings and discuss what part of the play they enjoyed most.

Guided Instruction

Return to Predictions and Purposes

Review with students their story predictions. Were their predictions correct? Did they find out what they wanted to know?

PREDICTIONS	WHAT HAPPENED
Most of the characters will not act like real people.	Pecos Bill and the other tall tale characters did things that real people can't do, such as creating the Grand Canyon, inventing cowboy songs, and riding catfish.
The setting of the story will change.	When the story switched to the tall tale, the setting changed from a cowboy camp to the Texas countryside.

STORY ELEMENTS

HOW TO ASSESS

- Ask students to draw conclusions about the main characters from their actions.
- Ask how the setting affected them.
- Have them discuss the plot events that revealed the most about the characters.

FOLLOW UP

If students have trouble analyzing character, setting, and plot, help them brainstorm words to describe the characters and ask them to point out moments in the story that support their descriptions.

Story Questions

Have students discuss or write answers to the questions on page 372.

Answers:

1. Cowgirl Pam and Cowboy Sam *Literal/Story Elements*
2. "Home on the Range" *Literal/Details*
3. Possible answer: Pecos Bill was brave because he tried lots of new things. *Inferential/Character*
4. It is mainly about a cowboy who does things no real person could do. *Critical/Summarize*
5. Possible answer: Cowgirl Pam might tell Phoebe a tall tale, and Phoebe might take some of the words that Pam used and make up her own story. *Critical/Reading Across Texts*

Write a Play Review For a full lesson related to persuasive writing, see pages 375K–375L.

Story Questions & Activities

1. Who is telling the story of Pecos Bill?
2. What did Pecos Bill learn from the coyotes?
3. Do you think Pecos Bill was brave? Explain.
4. What is this story mostly about?
5. Pretend that Cowgirl Pam meets Phoebe. What might they talk about? What kinds of stories might they tell each other?

Write a Play Review

Your class is about to put on a performance of "Pecos Bill." Write a review that will convince people to come and see the play. Describe your favorite part of the play.

Meeting Individual Needs

EASY

Name________________ Date__________ **Reteach 97**

Vocabulary

Fill in the sentences with the words below.

combine invented located prairie stumbled wilderness

1. First you ___combine___ sugar and butter.
2. I was lost deep in the ___wilderness___.
3. We lived on a grassy ___prairie___.
4. Who ___invented___ the first car?
5. I was so tired that I ___stumbled___ and almost fell down!
6. I finally ___located___ my lost sweater.

/6

Story Comprehension **Reteach 98**

Answer the following questions.

1. What happened after Bill fell out of the wagon? Some coyotes found him and raised him.
2. What noisy thing did Bill and the coyotes do at night? They all sang.
3. What did Carl the Cowboy teach Bill? Carl taught Bill how to be a cowboy.
4. Name one thing that Bill invented. Possible answers: the lasso, the guitar

97–98 **At Home:** Have students think of a synonym for each vocabulary word. Book 3.1/Unit 3 **Pecos Bill: A Tall Tale Play** /4

McGraw-Hill School Division

Reteach, 98

ON-LEVEL

Name________________ Date__________ **Practice 98**

Story Comprehension

In "Pecos Bill," Cowboy Sam and Cowgirl Pam tell a story to Cookie and the ranch hands. "Pecos Bill" is a story within a story. Fill in the chart for each story.

	Main Story	Story Within a Story
Setting	cowboy camp in Texas	Texas
Characters	Cowboy Sam, Cowgirl Pam, Cookie, and the ranch hands	Pa, Ma, Pecos Bill, the other children, coyotes, Carl the Cowboy, Slue-Foot Sue, and the Judge
Beginning	They order pizza. Sam and Pam start telling a story.	Bill's family decides to go west.
Middle	The pizza comes.	Baby Bill falls out of the wagon. Coyotes raise him. Years later, Carl the Cowboy finds Bill and teaches him how to be a cowboy. Bill invents different things.
End	Everyone goes to sleep.	Bill meets and marries Slue-Foot Sue.

98 **At Home:** Ask students to circle the part of the chart that represents the plot. Book 3.1/Unit 3 **Pecos Bill: A Tall Tale Play** /10

McGraw-Hill School Division

Practice, 98

CHALLENGE

Name________________ Date__________ **Extend 97**

Vocabulary

combine invented located prairie stumbled wilderness

Write a paragraph on another piece of paper telling about an adventure, using as many vocabulary words from the box as you can. Then erase those vocabulary words or cover them with tape. Exchange paragraphs with a partner and fill in the blanks.

Extend 98

Story Comprehension

Work with a partner to make up your own tall tales. Think of situations that might be difficult to get out of. Write one of these below. Take turns giving a tall tale response. Make your tales as tall as can be! When you are finished, choose your favorite tall tale and tell it to the rest of the class.

Answers will vary.

97–98 **At Home:** Have students give a tall tale response to a question about why they were late for an imaginary appointment. Book 3.1/Unit 3 **Pecos Bill**

McGraw-Hill School Division

Extend, 98

Make a Fact Card

Pecos Bill met Slue-Foot Sue on the Rio Grande. Make a fact card about the Rio Grande. How many miles is it? What states does it flow through? What kind of boats travel the Rio Grande?

Illustrate an Invention

Pecos Bill claims to be the inventor of many things. Can you think of something to invent? How about a new idea for a lunch box? An umbrella? Make an illustration of your invention. Write a caption that tells what your invention does.

Find Out More

What do you know about modern cowboys? Where do they live? What is a typical day like for a cowboy? Find a library book about cowboys and compare Pecos Bill's life with the way cowboys live today.

373

Story Activities

Make a Fact Card

Materials: blank index cards, felt-tipped markers, reference books

PARTNERS Have partners come up with questions they would like to answer about the Rio Grande, and decide who will research which questions for their fact cards. Provide reference materials about the Rio Grande. Make a Wall of Facts where students can display their fact cards.

Illustrate an Invention

Materials: paper, felt-tipped markers

ONE Brainstorm with students ideas for inventions. Have them illustrate their inventions, and write a caption underneath it that explains just what the invention does.

Find Out More

GROUP **RESEARCH AND INQUIRY** Divide students into groups to find out where and how modern cowboys live, and how their lives compare to the life of Pecos Bill. Then have groups report their findings. Suggest that students consult an encyclopedia, books on cowboys, or the Internet.

interNET CONNECTION For more information on the topic, have students go to ***www.mhschool.com/reading.***

FORMAL ASSESSMENT

After page 373, see the Selection Assessment.

Study Skills

GRAPHIC AIDS

Students will:

- identify locations on a map.
- explore maps for information.

PREPARE Preview the map with students, pointing out the compass rose.

TEACH Review with students how to read a map. Discuss the kinds of information found on a map, such as routes, location of bodies of water, places of interest, and distances between locations. Display **Teaching Chart 81**.

PRACTICE Have students answer questions **1–5**. Review the answers with them.
1. Austin **2.** San Antonio **3.** Northwest
4. Houston **5.** Answers will vary.

ASSESS/CLOSE Have students use the map to plan a trip they would take. They should write what sights they plan on seeing and the direction they would be traveling.

STUDY SKILLS

Use a Map

A **map** is a drawing that shows information about a place. You might use a map if you were going to visit a new place.

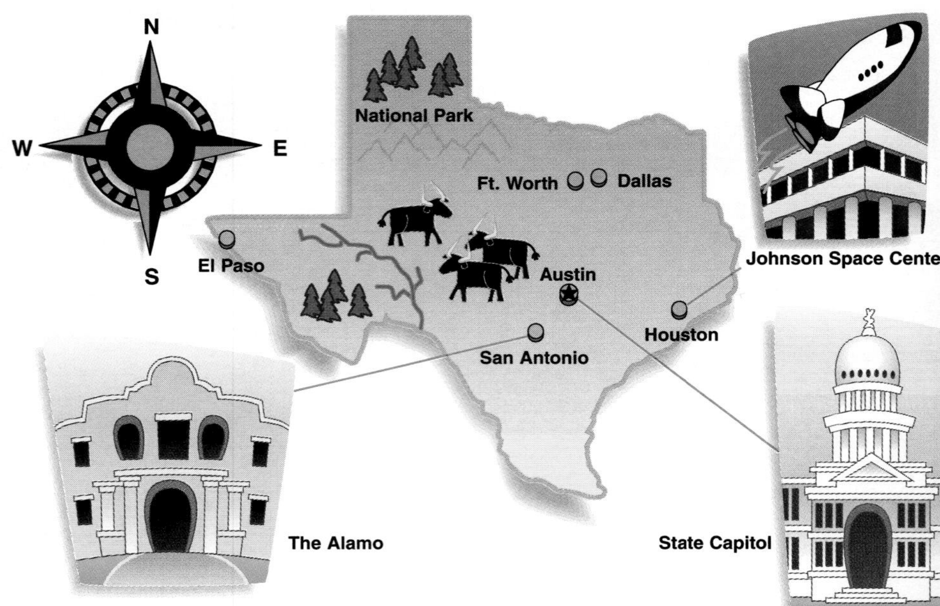

Use the map of Texas to answer these questions.

1. What is the state capital of Texas?
2. In which city is the Alamo located?
3. If you went from Houston to El Paso, which direction would you travel?
4. If you wanted to visit the Johnson Space Center, which city would you go to?
5. Which places would you like to visit in Texas? Give reasons for your answers.

Meeting Individual Needs

EASY

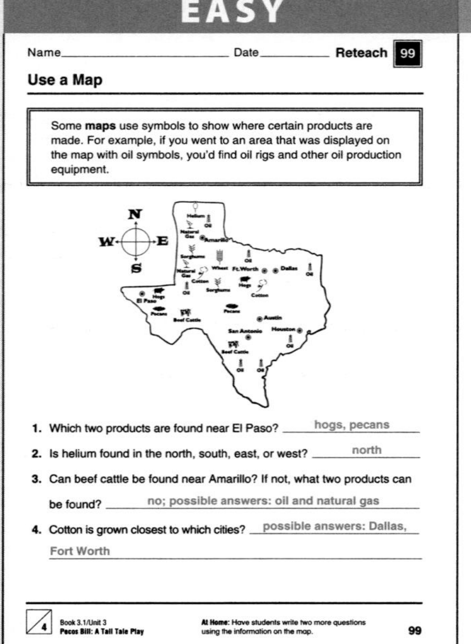

Name______________ Date________ **Reteach 99**

Use a Map

Some **maps** use symbols to show where certain products are made. For example, if you went to an area that was displayed on the map with oil symbols, you'd find oil rigs and other oil production equipment.

1. Which two products are found near El Paso? hogs, pecans
2. Is helium found in the north, south, east, or west? north
3. Can beef cattle be found near Amarillo? If not, what two products can be found? no; possible answers: oil and natural gas
4. Cotton is grown closest to which cities? possible answers: Dallas, Fort Worth

4 Book 3.1/Unit 3
Pecos Bill: A Tall Tale Play
At Home: Have students write two more questions using the information on the map. 99

Reteach, 99

ON-LEVEL

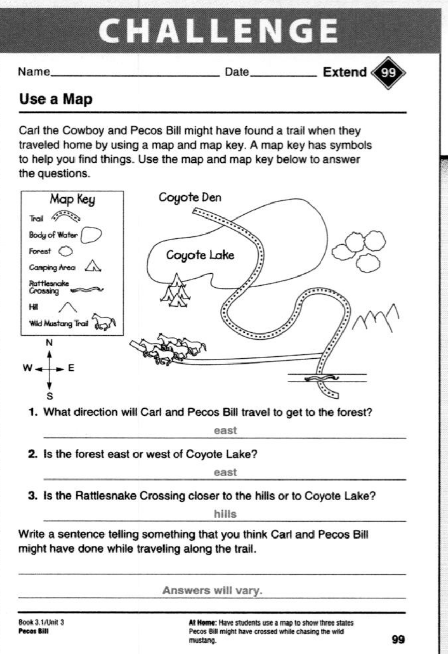

Name______________ Date________ **Practice 99**

Use a Map

Use the map to answer the questions.

1. Some farmers asked Paul and Babe to clear land for farming. In one day, with a few swings of his huge ax, Paul removed every tree in two states. In which two states did he do this? North Dakota, South Dakota
2. Paul Bunyan took a shovel and dug out Puget Sound on the West Coast. In which state did this take place? Washington
3. Babe needed new shoes. Paul needed a lot of iron to make four shoes Babe's size. Paul had to dig out three huge brand new iron mines. In which Midwestern state did he do this? Minnesota
4. When Babe was thirsty, Paul decided to dig out Lake Michigan so he could have a water bowl his own size. Between which two states is Lake Michigan? Wisconsin and Michigan

4 Book 3.1/Unit 3
Pecos Bill: A Tall Tale Play
At Home: Ask students to name the states on the map not mentioned in the questions above. 99

Practice, 99

CHALLENGE

Name______________ Date________ **Extend 99**

Use a Map

Carl the Cowboy and Pecos Bill might have found a trail when they traveled home by using a map and map key. A map key has symbols to help you find things. Use the map and map key below to answer the questions.

Map Key: Trail; Body of Water; Forest; Camping Area; Rattlesnake Crossing; Hill; Wild Mustang Trail

Coyote Den

Coyote Lake

N W E S

1. What direction will Carl and Pecos Bill travel to get to the forest? east
2. Is the forest east or west of Coyote Lake? east
3. Is the Rattlesnake Crossing closer to the hills or to Coyote Lake? hills

Write a sentence telling something that you think Carl and Pecos Bill might have done while traveling along the trail.

Answers will vary.

Book 3.1/Unit 3
Pecos Bill
At Home: Have students use a map to show three states Pecos Bill might have crossed while chasing the wild mustang. 99

Extend, 99

TEST POWER

Test Tip
Look for clues around the underlined word to figure out what it means.

DIRECTIONS:
Read the story. Then read each question about the story.

SAMPLE

All About the World

There was a little girl who loved to skip and sing. One day another child told the girl that she should not skip and sing at the same time. "If you sing and skip at the same time, you might miss the edge of the world and fall off!" he said.

The girl had never heard that the world had an edge nor that you could fall off. For the rest of the day she was careful not to sing and skip at the same time.

That night, she asked her mother if she could fall off the world if she skipped and sang at the same time.

Her mother smiled and said, "No, no, dear, the world is a sphere. It is round like a big ball and has no edges. Skip and sing as much as you like!"

1 When the child told the girl that the world had edges, she felt—

- ○ happy
- ● worried
- ○ excited
- ○ pleased

2 In this story, the word sphere means—

- ● shaped like a ball
- ○ shaped like a square
- ○ bouncy
- ○ blue and green

375

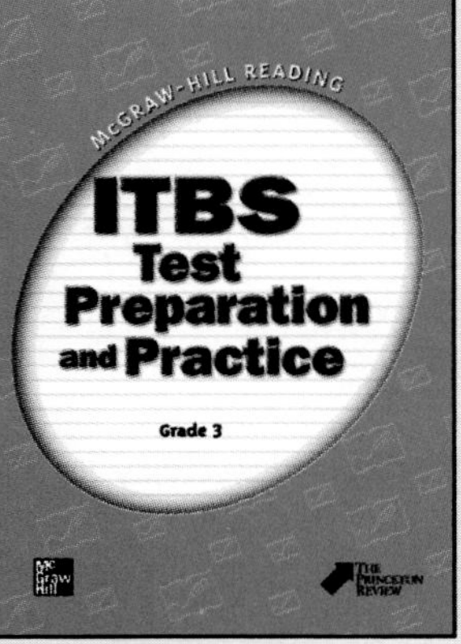

ITBS/TEST PREPARATION

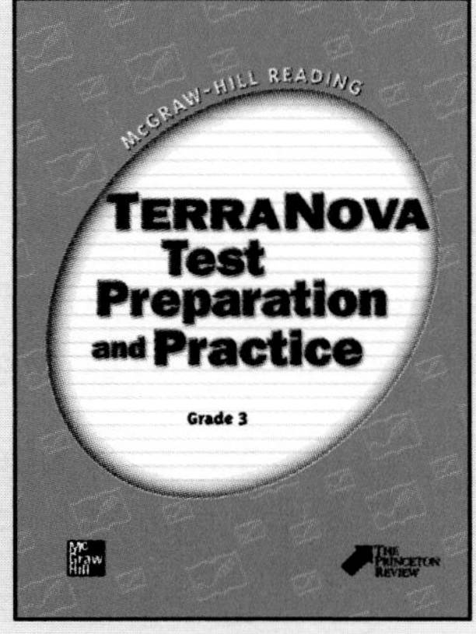

TERRANOVA/TEST PREPARATION

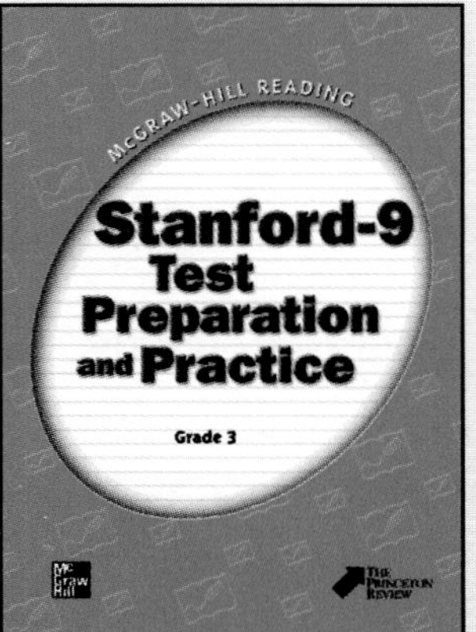

SAT 9/TEST PREPARATION

Test Power

THE PRINCETON REVIEW

Read the Page

As students read the story, remind them to note when events take place. Have students summarize the story in their own words.

Discuss the Questions

QUESTION 1: This question requires students to understand the feelings of a character. Ask: What did the girl do after the child told her that the world had edges? Instruct students to refer back to the point in the story *when* this occurred. Remind students that the girl's feelings change during the story. Use process of elimination.

QUESTION 2: This question asks students to define a word in context. Standardized tests provide a synonym (word or group of words) within the two sentences surrounding the word. Have students look for context clues within the surrounding sentences.

Leveled Books

EASY

Little Fox and Big Coyote

/ou/ and /oi/

☑ Story Elements

☑ Instructional Vocabulary: *combine, invented, located, prairie, stumbled, wilderness*

Answers to Story Questions

1. The main characters are Big Coyote and Little Fox.
2. They were afraid of the animals and didn't want them at the party.
3. Big Coyote is not as smart as Little Fox.
4. The story is about Little Fox, who keeps tricking Big Coyote so the coyote will not eat him up. The last trick that Little Fox plays outwits Big Coyote forever.
5. Answers will vary.

Story Questions and Writing Activity

1. Who are the main characters?
2. Why did the people at the party chase Little Fox and Big Coyote away?
3. Why do you think Big Coyote keeps falling for Little Fox's tricks?
4. What is the story mostly about?
5. Do you think if Little Fox and Pecos Bill met, they would become friends? Why or why not?

What's He Thinking?

Draw a line down the middle of a piece of paper. On one side, draw a picture of Big Coyote holding up the cliff. On the other side, show what you think Little Fox did after he escaped. Write two or three sentences telling what each animal is doing and thinking.

from *Little Fox and Big Coyote*

Guided Reading

PREVIEW AND PREDICT Conduct a **picture walk** up to page 14. Have students discuss the illustrations and make predictions about the story. They should record their predictions on a chart.

SET PURPOSES Have students write down questions that they would like to have answered by reading the story. For example, they might want to know how such a little fox could escape a hungry coyote.

READ THE BOOK After students have read the story independently, use the questions below to guide students' reading.

Pages 2–3: Where does this play take place? (the countryside) How would you describe Big Coyote's character? (He is lazy.) What makes you say so? (He doesn't chase Little Fox, he just tells him not to bother running away.) ***Character/Setting***

Pages 4–5: What words on these pages have the /ou/ and the /oi/ sounds? (*pointing, ground, join, count, down, annoying, growling*) How are these sounds spelled? (*ou, ow, oi, oy*) ***Phonics and Decoding***

Page 7: You have learned that *stumbled* means tripped or walked in a clumsy way. What do you think it means to have stumbled upon something? Does it mean that Big Coyote actually tripped over Little Fox? (No, it means that he discovered him.) ***Vocabulary***

Page 9: What do you think is the reason for the party being introduced into the plot of the play? (It will provide Little Fox with another way to escape Big Coyote.) ***Character/Setting/Plot***

RETURN TO PREDICTIONS AND PURPOSES Review students' predictions and reasons for reading.

LITERARY RESPONSE Discuss these questions:

- What other adjectives could be used to describe Little Fox besides little? Why?
- How else, besides lazy, would you describe Big Coyote?

Also see the story questions and activity in *Little Fox and Big Coyote*.

See the Phonics CD-ROM for practice using the /ou/ and /oi/ sounds.

Leveled Books

INDEPENDENT

The King's Oranges

- ☑ **Story Elements**
- ☑ **Instructional Vocabulary:** *combine, invented, located, prairie, stumbled, wilderness*

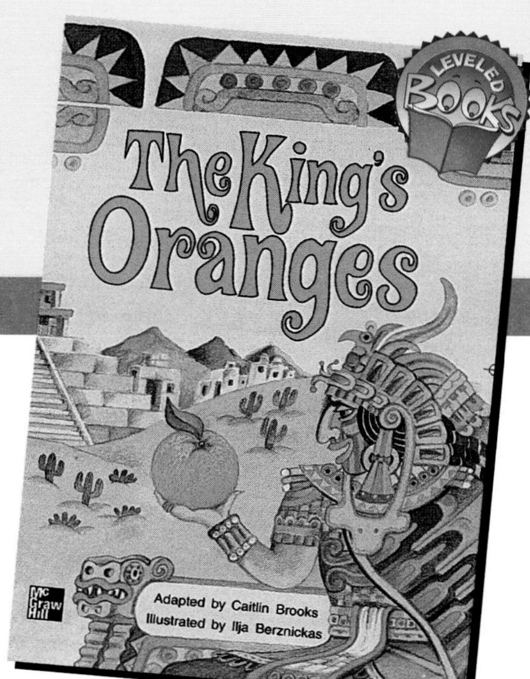

Guided Reading

PREVIEW AND PREDICT Have students read the title and take a **picture walk** through the illustrations to page 9. Have students record their predictions about the story in a journal.

SET PURPOSES Have students discuss and record what they want to find out when they read *The King's Oranges*.

READ THE BOOK Have students read the story independently. After they have read the story, return to the text to apply strategies.

Pages 2–3: What can you tell about Fernando's feeling about wealth and riches? (He thinks more about the beauty of his oranges than the money they might bring him.) ***Character***

Page 5: What does Isabel mean when she says she will combine nuts and raisins? (She will mix them together.) What other word or words could you use instead of *is located* on this page? (Possible answers: *is to be found; sits*) What words in the last sentence tell you what a prairie looks like? *(huge flat area)* ***Vocabulary***

Page 12: Why do you think it is important that the king gives Fernando a bag of gold for the orange? Who will be happy? Who will be upset? (The townspeople and Isabel will be happy, but Esteban will be upset. It might lead Esteban to take some action in the play.) ***Character/Plot***

Page 15: Does running away seem like something Esteban would normally do? (no) What do you think he is feeling? (scared of the king) ***Character/Make Inferences***

RETURN TO PREDICTIONS AND PURPOSES Review students' predictions and reasons for reading the story.

LITERARY RESPONSE Discuss these questions:

- What is the message of this play?
- How does having a good attitude and taking pride in your work lead to better results? Explain.
- If you met Esteban, what advice would you give him? Explain your answer.

Also see the story questions and activity in *The King's Oranges*.

Answers to Story Questions

1. Fernando and Isabel grew oranges.
2. The king thought Fernando was a good person who deserved a reward for bringing the fruit.
3. Esteban learned that being kind and taking pride in your work will earn a person rewards.
4. The story is about a kind man who grew some beautiful oranges and gave them to the king and a mean man who was jealous.
5. Answers will vary.

Story Questions and Writing Activity

1. What kind of fruit did Fernando and Isabel grow?
2. Why did the king reward Fernando?
3. What lesson do you think Esteban learned?
4. What is the story mostly about?
5. If Pecos Bill grew oranges, what do you think they might be like?

How Long Does It Take?

Look up "oranges" in the encyclopedia. Find out how long it takes for oranges to grow on a fully developed tree. Make a calendar and fill in dates to show the different stages of growing oranges.

from *The King's Oranges*

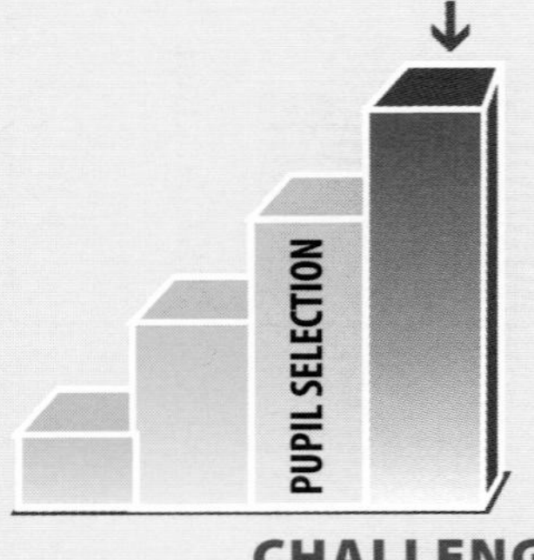

CHALLENGE

Answers to Story Questions

1. Sam
2. Barbara probably felt anxious at first, then happy.
3. They are a close family who love each other and who try to help each other in any way possible.
4. The story is about how Barbara feels about the new baby in her family.
5. Answers will vary.

Story Questions and Writing Activity

1. What name did Barbara decide to call her baby brother?
2. How do you think Barbara felt about getting a new baby in the house?
3. What can you tell about this family from the characters and the story?
4. What is the story mostly about?
5. Imagine if Pecos Bill got to meet Barbara's little brother. What are some things Pecos Bill could teach him?

How Many Days?

Draw a calendar and make a time line for this story. Begin with the day Barbara hit the home run. How many days do you think passed before the baby arrived? How many more days passed before Act III took place?

from *Barbara Becomes a Big Sister*

Leveled Books

CHALLENGE

Barbara Becomes a Big Sister
LEVELED BOOKS
Written by Dan Piparo and Patsy Jensen
Illustrated by Patty Fleckenstein

Barbara Becomes a Big Sister

- ☑ **Story Elements**
- ☑ **Instructional Vocabulary:** ***combine, invented, located, prairie, stumbled, wilderness***

Guided Reading

PREVIEW AND PREDICT Conduct a **picture walk** up to page 12. Then have students discuss the illustrations, and any predictions they make about the story. Have them record their predictions in a chart.

SET PURPOSES Have students write down their reasons for reading the story, and any questions they want answered by reading.

READ THE BOOK Have students first read the story independently and monitor their reading behaviors. Then return to the story for teaching opportunities.

Page 7: Can you tell me what Barbara's Grandpa might say to describe life on the prairie? Possible answer: There weren't many trees to climb, but there was lots of rolling land to run across.) ***Vocabulary***

Pages 8–9: How does the setting of the waiting room show you something about Barbara? (Because she can't go to her mother in her hospital room, we see that Barbara is very impatient for the arrival of her baby sister or brother.) How is this affecting the plot? (To pass the time, she is talking to her grandparents and learning how to be a good older sister.) ***Character/Setting/Plot***

Pages 14–16: Do you think Barbara enjoys being an older sister? (yes) How can you tell? (She is laughing and enjoying the things her baby brother is doing; she shares her special doll with Sam.) Do you think that Barbara has learned something about families that she didn't know before? Explain. ***Character/Make Inferences***

RETURN TO PREDICTIONS AND PURPOSES Have students revisit their predictions and purposes. Which predictions were accurate? Which were not?

LITERARY RESPONSE Discuss these questions:

- If you were Barbara's older brother or sister in this play, what would you do? What advice would you give to Barbara?
- Does each member of your family always play the same role? Or do the roles sometimes change?

Also see the story questions and activity in *Barbara Becomes a Big Sister.*

Activities

Anthology and Leveled Books

Connecting Texts

PLAY CHARTS
Write the play titles on a chart. Discuss with students that not all plays are structured exactly the same way. Remind them of the characteristics of a play, and ask them to think of which characteristics were present in the play they read. Call on volunteers from each reading level and write their suggestions on the chart.

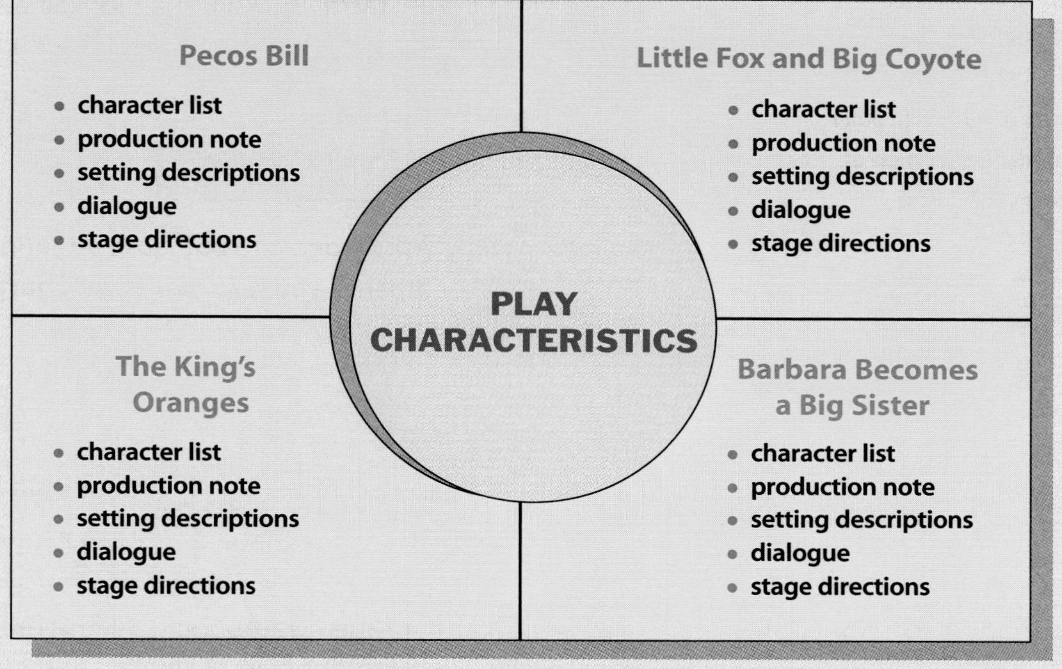

Viewing/Representing

GROUP PRESENTATIONS Divide the class into groups, one for each of the four books read in the lesson. (For *Pecos Bill,* combine students of different reading levels.) Have each group create story charts with columns labeled Character, Plot, and Setting. Allow students to use the chalkboard to present their frameworks to the class.

AUDIENCE RESPONSE
Ask students to pay attention to each group's presentation. Allow time for questions after each presentation.

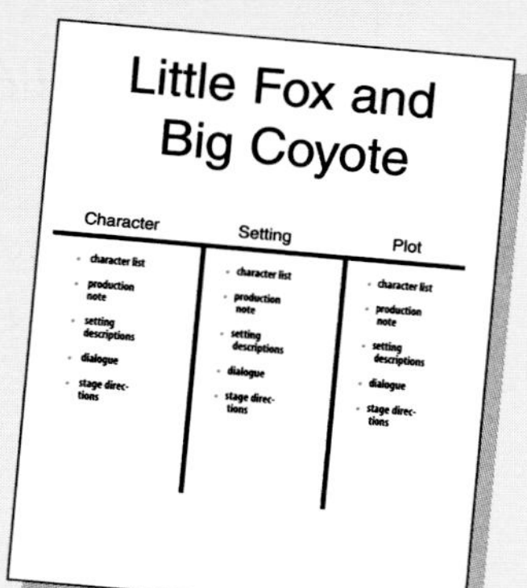

Research and Inquiry

PLAY ADAPTATIONS *Pecos Bill, Little Fox and Big Coyote*, and *The King's Oranges* are all play adaptations of previously written or told stories. Have students use literature books, books about legends, tall tales, fables, and the Internet to research the original stories that these plays came from. Have them:

- make a Venn diagram that lists how the play is different from, and similar to, the original story.
- illustrate one scene that is unique to either the play or the story.
- present their findings and illustrations to the class.

interNET CONNECTION Have students log on to ***www.mhschool.com/reading*** to find out more about plays.

Students will make inferences about and analyze character, setting, and plot.

TEACHING TIP

INSTRUCTIONAL Explain that many North American tall tales were created to explain how the United States came to be the way it is. Talk about other tall tales students may know of, such as stories about Paul Bunyan.

Review Story Elements

PREPARE

Discuss Character, Setting, and Plot

Remind students that paying attention to the connections between character, setting, and plot will help them to make inferences about characters and will add to their understanding and enjoyment of the story.

TEACH

Read "Pecos Bill and the Cloud" and Model the Skill

Ask students to pay close attention to how story elements affect each other as you read **Teaching Chart 82** with them.

Pecos Bill and the Cloud

The summer was so hot, everything was drooping. The cows were drooping, the grass was drooping, and even Slue-Foot Sue was drooping. All this drooping was making Pecos Bill mighty sad. He looked at the sky, but it was blue and clear of clouds. So Pecos Bill rode across the whole country until he found a big, fat cloud. "Yee haw!" he shouted. He roped that cloud, brought it back to the prairie, and squeezed it with his lasso until it split open and enough water poured out to last the rest of the summer.

Teaching Chart 82

Discuss how the setting of this passage affects the characters and plot.

MODEL The setting is a very hot summer, when everything is drooping. This makes Bill sad. I think he lassos a cloud to make rain so everything won't droop. Then he won't be sad.

PRACTICE

Analyze Character, Setting, and Plot

Have students underline clues that describe the setting of the passage on **Teaching Chart 82**. Then have them double underline those places where the setting is affecting the character, and circle the plot events that happen because of how the character is affected by the setting.
▶ **Logical/Linguistic**

ASSESS/CLOSE

Write a Story with a New Setting for Pecos Bill

Have students brainstorm a list of other settings for a Pecos Bill story, such as in a snowstorm, at the ocean, at a market, and so on. Ask them what might happen in these settings and how it might affect Pecos Bill and the events in the story. Invite students to work in groups and write a new story about Pecos Bill.

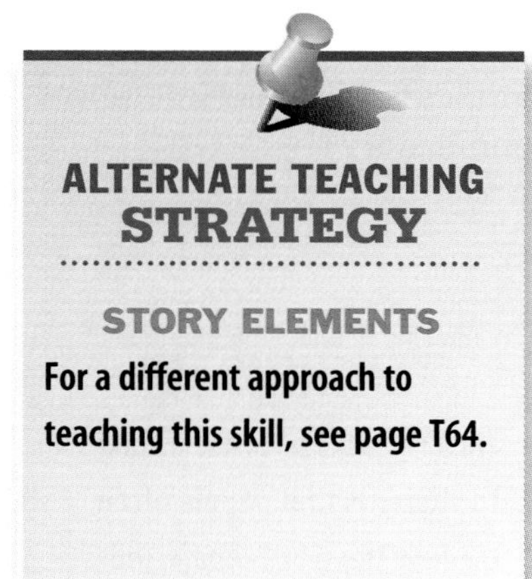

ALTERNATE TEACHING STRATEGY

STORY ELEMENTS

For a different approach to teaching this skill, see page T64.

SELF-SELECTED Reading

Students may choose from the following titles.

ANTHOLOGY

- *Pecos Bill*

LEVELED BOOKS

- *Little Fox and Big Coyote*
- *The King's Oranges*
- *Barbara Becomes a Big Sister*

Bibliography, pages T76–T77

Meeting Individual Needs for Comprehension

EASY

Name________ Date______ **Reteach 100**

Story Elements

Characters are *who* the story is about. **Setting** is *where* the story takes place. **Plot** is *what* the story is about.

Answer the questions.

1. **Character:** Who are the three main characters of the tall tale in "Pecos Bill"? Pecos Bill, Carl the Cowboy, and Slue-foot Sue
2. **Setting:** Where does the story of Pecos Bill take place? The story takes place in Texas.
3. **Setting:** Where does Bill fall out of his parents' wagon? at the Pecos River
4. **Plot:** Who finds baby Bill by the river and teaches him how to sing? the coyotes
5. **Plot:** Who finds Bill many years later and teaches him how to be a cowboy? Carl the Cowboy

At Home: Have students write sentences about how Bill invented bronco-busting, the guitar, cowboy songs, or the lasso.

100 Book 3.1/Unit 3 **Pecos Bill: A Tall Tale Play** 5

Reteach, 100

ON-LEVEL

Name________ Date______ **Practice 100**

Story Elements

Understanding what the **characters** in a story do as well as where they do it helps us to understand what the story is about.

Answer the following questions.

1. Where are Cookie, Cowgirl Pam, Cowboy Sam, and the cowhands? They are sitting around a fire in a cowboy camp in the Southwest.
2. Why do Sam and Pam have time to tell the story of Pecos Bill? They have time because they are waiting for pizza to be delivered.
3. Why was Bill's family always moving? The family was always moving because Bill's father didn't like living near other people.
4. How did Pecos Bill get his name? He fell off of his parents' wagon while they were crossing the Pecos River.
5. How did Bill invent the lasso? He grabbed a rattlesnake and used it to rope a steer.
6. How did Pecos Bill first meet Slue-Foot Sue? He saw her riding a catfish, and Cowboy Carl introduced him to her.

At Home: Have students organize their answers in a three-column chart. Have them label the columns as follows: Character, Setting, Plot.

100 Book 3.1/Unit 3 **Pecos Bill: A Tall Tale Play** 6

Practice, 100

CHALLENGE

Name________ Date______ **Extend 100**

Story Elements

Work with a group to present a "Pecos Bill" puppet show for your class. Decide which scene you will show. Fill out the chart.

Characters: ________

Setting: ________

What happens: ________

Follow the directions below to make stick puppets of the characters. Practice moving your puppet as you read its part out loud. Cover the front of a table with a piece of cloth or cardboard to create a theater for your puppet show. Crouch behind the table with your puppets, and let the show go on!

How to Make Stick Puppets
Draw your character on poster board with crayons or markers. Cut out your character and paste it to a craft stick. Hold the stick at the end. Raise it, lower it, and wave it from side to side as the puppet speaks.

At Home: Have students write a sentence telling which event in the plot of "Pecos Bill" was the funniest or most exciting.

100 Book 3.1/Unit 3 **Pecos Bill**

Extend, 100

LANGUAGE SUPPORT

Name________ Date______

A Round Story

Setting
Character
Problem
Solution

110 **Pecos Bill** • Language Support / Blackline Master 54 Grade 3

Language Support, 110

Students will make inferences about story characters.

TEACHING TIP

INSTRUCTIONAL Explain to students that people often confuse the words *imply* and *infer* (make an inference), because they are very closely related. Someone who hints at something is *implying*. The frown on your face *implied* that something was wrong. Someone who reaches a conclusion by examining things is *inferring*. I *inferred* (made an inference) from your smile that you won the game.

Review Make Inferences

PREPARE

Discuss the Use of Inferences Remind students that looking for clues to get more information about the characters will help them to better understand and enjoy the story. These clues are in the characters' actions, thoughts, and words.

TEACH

Read "The Party" and Model the Skill Ask students to pay attention to clues about the character as you read the passage on **Teaching Chart 83** with them.

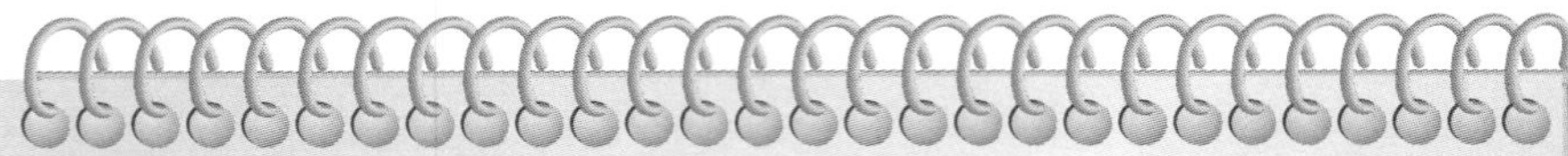

The Party

Slue-Foot Sue and Pecos Bill were going to a Texas-sized party. Sue asked the hostess what she could bring, and had made up a whole truckload of her famous five-alarm chili, enough to scorch the tastebuds of every person in Texas. She picked a bunch of red roses from her garden for the hostess, too, to thank her for the party. But when Sue looked up and saw where the sun was in the sky, she frowned. It was past three o'clock already! They were going to be late. "Pecos Bill, you get a move on!" Sue shouted. "There's a heap of hungry people waiting for that chili, and I don't want to disappoint them!"

Teaching Chart 83

Invite a volunteer to underline some clues that might help readers make inferences about what kind of person Slue-Foot Sue is.

MODEL I think Slue-Foot Sue is a responsible person. She made sure that she had enough chili for everyone at the party and knew that it was important to be on time.

PRACTICE

Make Inferences about a Character

PARTNERS

Have partners work on a Clue/Inference chart like the one below. Help them get started. ▶ **Spatial/Linguistic**

CLUE	INFERENCE
Sue makes chili for the party, and brings roses for the hostess.	She is a considerate person.
She frowns when she sees what time it is and tells Bill to get a move on.	She is a responsible person.

ASSESS/CLOSE

Write About Characters and Make Inferences

On one side of an index card, have students write down a specific quality or attitude of a character, for example: *This character loves the ocean. This character is angry at a neighbor. This character is timid.*

Instruct students to write sentences on the other side of their cards that give clues about the characters which would help a partner to make inferences. Have partners trade cards and try to make the correct inferences based on the sentences. Partners can check their inferences against the written statements on the index cards.

ALTERNATE TEACHING STRATEGY

MAKE INFERENCES

For a different approach to teaching this skill, see page T66.

LOOKING AHEAD

Students will apply this skill as they read the next selection, *A Very Cool Place to Visit.*

Meeting Individual Needs for Comprehension

EASY

Name_______________ Date_______ **Reteach 101**

Make Inferences

You can make an **inference,** or a good guess, about how characters feel by noticing what they say and do.

Read each passage. Then choose the correct inference. Circle the correct answer.

1. Paul laughed and jumped up and down. "Is it eight o'clock yet?" he asked. His mother smiled and replied, "As I said before, the party will start in an hour."
   - a. Paul felt sad about his mother.
   - b. Paul felt scared about the party.
   - (c.) Paul felt excited about the party.
2. When Dad asked Greg about losing Rashida's book, Greg frowned and hung his head.
   - (a.) Greg felt sorry.
   - b. Greg felt happy.
   - c. Greg felt tired.
3. Tad yawned. He'd had a long day and couldn't keep his eyes open anymore. He lay back against the pillows.
   - a. Tad felt awake.
   - (b.) Tad felt sleepy.
   - c. Tad felt happy.
4. The kitten ran back and forth across the room. Then she chewed on an old sock. After that, she played with a toy mouse.
   - (a.) The kitten was playing.
   - b. The kitten was tired.
   - c. The kitten was sick.

4 Book 3.1/Unit 3 **Pecos Bill: A Tall Tale Play** — **At Home:** Have students write a paragraph with a clear inference in it. Have them write the inference. 101

Reteach, 101

ON-LEVEL

Name_______________ Date_______ **Practice 101**

Make Inferences

Sometimes a character in a story doesn't say exactly how he or she feels about something. Readers must then **infer** how the character feels by thinking about what the character says or does, or how he or she acts.

Read the sentences below. Then, in the right column, write down how the character feels.

What Character Says or Does	How Character Feels
1. "No, I am not mad!" Michael yelled, angrily waving his fists in the air.	Michael feels angry.
2. "Kate!" Samantha shouted. "I can't believe you're finally here!" She hugged her friend tightly.	Samantha feels happy to see her friend.
3. Vera said, "We should try to stay calm." Her knees were shaking and her teeth were chattering.	Vera feels scared.
4. Shane had to make lunch for himself. Then he had to clean his room. After that, he had to finish his homework. He sat down at the table with a loud groan and closed his eyes.	Shane isn't happy about having so much to do.

4 Book 3.1/Unit 3 **Pecos Bill: A Tall Tale Play** — **At Home:** Ask students to explain an instance in their own lives when they had to make an inference. 101

Practice, 101

CHALLENGE

Name_______________ Date_______ **Extend 101**

Make Inferences

Play "Pass the Story" with a partner. Begin writing a story about anything you choose on the lines below.

Exchange pages with your partner. Finish the story you receive on the lines below. Use clues from the story and what you already know to make inferences about how it should end.

Exchange pages again. Read what your partner wrote. Did he or she end the story the way you would have?

Book 3.1/Unit 3 **Pecos Bill** — **At Home:** Read the first paragraph from a news story and have students write an ending to it. 101

Extend, 101

LANGUAGE SUPPORT

Name_______________ Date_______

Who and What?

If this	Then this	Because

If this:

Then this: He invented bronco busting.

Because: That is how cowboy's tame broncos.

If this:

Then this:

Because:

If this:

Then this:

Because:

Grade 3 — Language Support/Blackline Master 55 • **Pecos Bill** 111

Language Support, 111

TESTED OBJECTIVES

Students will:

- identify words with multiple meanings.
- define homographs.
- use context to determine which meaning of a homograph is being used.

MATERIALS

- **Teaching Chart 84**
- dictionary

TEACHING TIP

INSTRUCTIONAL Share information about homographs:

- The prefix *homo* means "the same." The word *graph* means "write or written."
- Together they mean "words that are spelled the same."
- *Homographs* have separate entries in the dictionary.
- Share examples such as *bear* ("to carry" or "a large, heavy animal").

Review Multiple-Meaning Words

PREPARE

Discuss Multiple-Meaning Words and Define Homographs

Remind students that many words share the same spelling but have different meanings. Sometimes the words may be close in meaning. At other times the words may mean something totally different. Those words are known as *homographs*. Besides having a different meaning, homographs may be pronounced differently.

TEACH

Read "Home on the Range" and Model the Skill

Have students read the passage on **Teaching Chart 84**. Suggest they look for multiple-meaning words.

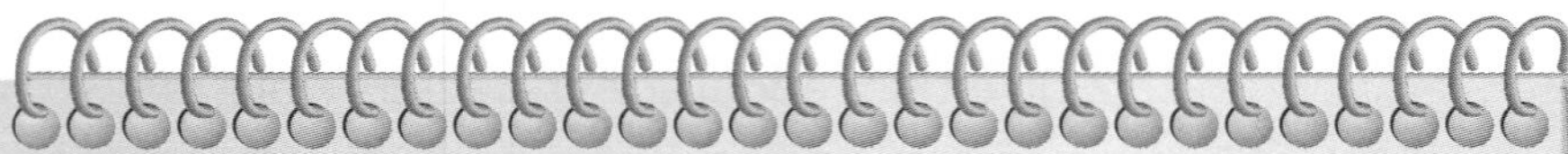

Home on the Range

While riding his pony across the range, Cookie had to steer around herds of steer. When he was a yard from his house he stopped to wind his watch. At home, Cookie turned on the range and started cooking up a pot of beans. Suddenly, there was a rap at the door. Three chaps came in. These boys were singing a rap song about how the desert wind chaps their lips. When their song was finished they took a bow, and Cookie gave them a can of beans with a bow on it as a gift, and said goodbye.

Teaching Chart 84

Explain that with homographs, it is important to pay attention to how the word is used in order to understand its meaning.

MODEL When a word has more than one meaning, I look at how the word is being used to make sure I understand the right meaning. In the first sentence, I know that *range* means "a place" because Cookie is riding across it.

Have students define *range* in the third sentence of the passage and tell how they know the meaning.

PRACTICE

Identify Homographs and Use Clues to Meaning

Invite volunteers to underline homographs in the passage and then circle the clues that help give the meanings of the words. Have groups discuss what each homograph means and write a short definition. They can use a dictionary to help them. ▶ **Logical/Linguistic**

ASSESS/CLOSE

Identify and Use Homographs

Invite students to brainstorm a list of homographs and write sentences that illustrate the words' meanings. Encourage them to use a dictionary to check to see if the words are true homographs.

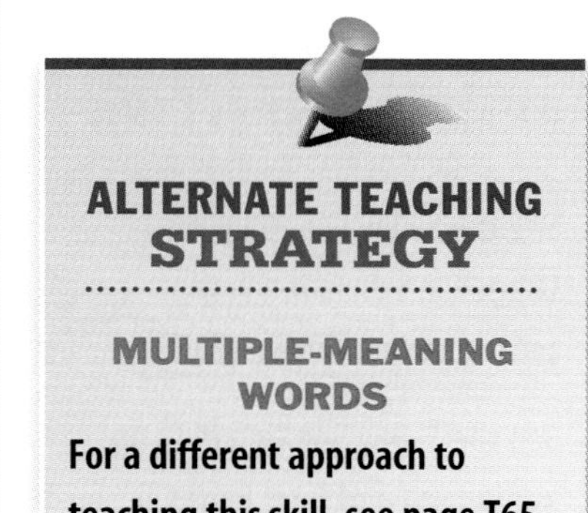

ALTERNATE TEACHING STRATEGY

MULTIPLE-MEANING WORDS

For a different approach to teaching this skill, see page T65.

Meeting Individual Needs for Vocabulary

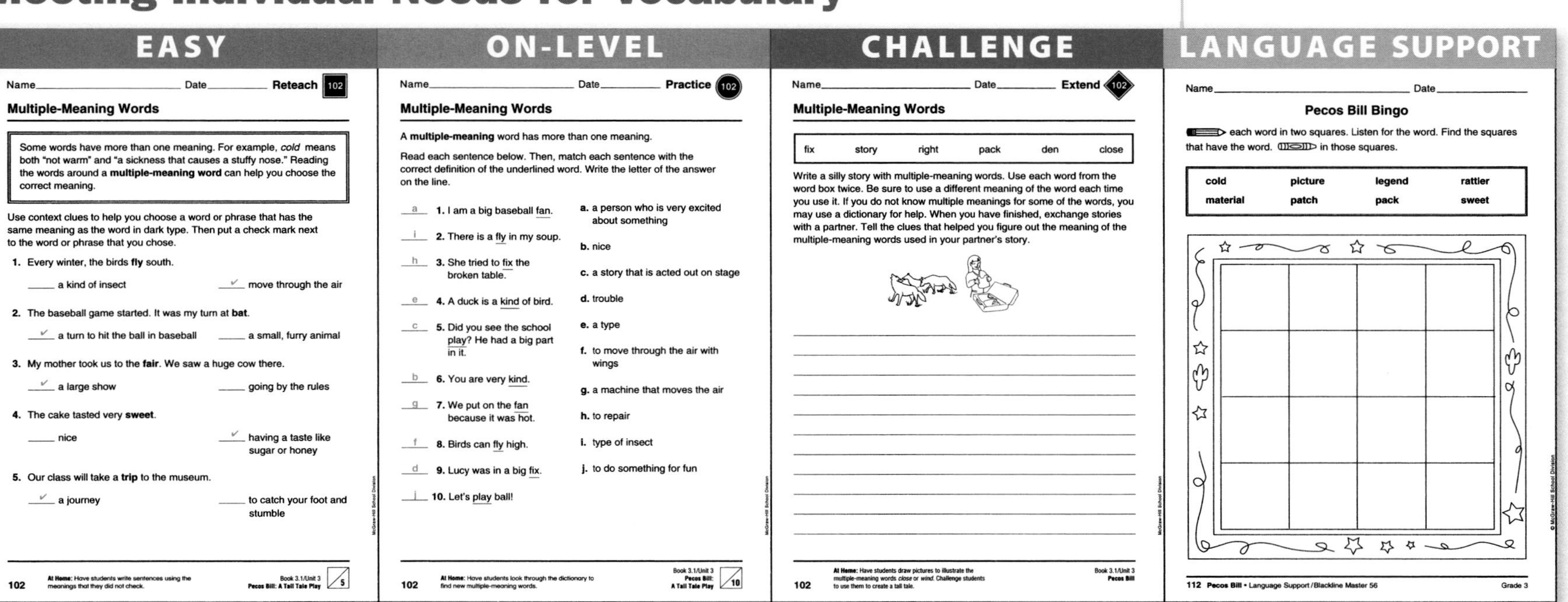

EASY

Name________________ Date________ **Reteach** 102

Multiple-Meaning Words

Some words have more than one meaning. For example, *cold* means both "not warm" and "a sickness that causes a stuffy nose." Reading the words around a **multiple-meaning word** can help you choose the correct meaning.

Use context clues to help you choose a word or phrase that has the same meaning as the word in dark type. Then put a check mark next to the word or phrase that you chose.

1. Every winter, the birds **fly** south.
   ____ a kind of insect ✓ move through the air
2. The baseball game started. It was my turn at **bat**.
   ✓ a turn to hit the ball in baseball ____ a small, furry animal
3. My mother took us to the **fair**. We saw a huge cow there.
   ✓ a large show ____ going by the rules
4. The cake tasted very **sweet**.
   ____ nice ✓ having a taste like sugar or honey
5. Our class will take a **trip** to the museum.
   ✓ a journey ____ to catch your foot and stumble

102 **At Home:** Have students write sentences using the meanings that they did not check. Book 3.1/Unit 3 **Pecos Bill: A Tall Tale Play** 5

McGraw-Hill School Division

Reteach, 102

ON-LEVEL

Name________________ Date________ **Practice** 102

Multiple-Meaning Words

A **multiple-meaning** word has more than one meaning.

Read each sentence below. Then, match each sentence with the correct definition of the underlined word. Write the letter of the answer on the line.

a	1. I am a big baseball fan.	a. a person who is very excited about something
i	2. There is a fly in my soup.	b. nice
h	3. She tried to fix the broken table.	c. a story that is acted out on stage
e	4. A duck is a kind of bird.	d. trouble
c	5. Did you see the school play? He had a big part in it.	e. a type
b	6. You are very kind.	f. to move through the air with wings
g	7. We put on the fan because it was hot.	g. a machine that moves the air
f	8. Birds can fly high.	h. to repair
d	9. Lucy was in a big fix.	i. type of insect
j	10. Let's play ball!	j. to do something for fun

102 **At Home:** Have students look through the dictionary to find new multiple-meaning words. Book 3.1/Unit 3 **Pecos Bill: A Tall Tale Play** 10

McGraw-Hill School Division

Practice, 102

CHALLENGE

Name________________ Date________ **Extend** 102

Multiple-Meaning Words

fix story right pack den close

Write a silly story with multiple-meaning words. Use each word from the word box twice. Be sure to use a different meaning of the word each time you use it. If you do not know multiple meanings for some of the words, you may use a dictionary for help. When you have finished, exchange stories with a partner. Tell the clues that helped you figure out the meaning of the multiple-meaning words used in your partner's story.

102 **At Home:** Have students draw pictures to illustrate the multiple-meaning words *close* or *wind*. Challenge students to use them to create a tall tale. Book 3.1/Unit 3 **Pecos Bill**

McGraw-Hill School Division

Extend, 102

LANGUAGE SUPPORT

Name________________ Date________

Pecos Bill Bingo

each word in two squares. Listen for the word. Find the squares that have the word. in those squares.

cold	picture	legend	rattler
material	patch	pack	sweet

112 **Pecos Bill** • Language Support/Blackline Master 56 Grade 3

Language Support, 112

GRAMMAR/SPELLING CONNECTIONS

See the 5-Day Grammar and Usage Plan on using verb tenses, pages 375M–375N.

See the 5-Day Spelling Plan on adding *-ed* and *-ing*, pages 375O–375P.

TECHNOLOGY TIP

When you are ready to publish your review, try experimenting with different type fonts for your title. Use a large font size and a style that suits your subject.

Persuasive Writing

Prewrite

WRITE A PLAY REVIEW Present this writing assignment: Your class is putting on a performance of *Pecos Bill*. Write a review that will convince people to come and see the play. Describe your favorite part of the play.

TALK ABOUT REVIEWS Explain that people write reviews to share their opinions and to try to get other people to see things their way. Point out their goal is to get others to agree with their opinions, so they should use persuasive language and support their opinions with facts.

Strategy: Make an Outline Have students create an outline for their reviews to help them organize their ideas. Tell them each opinion they express should be supported by examples from the play. Use the following as an example:

Topic: Review of *Pecos Bill*

I The play is funny.

A. cell phone under hat

B. too many kids to count

C. lasso from a snake

II The play is informative.

A. Cowhands eat lots of beans.

B. The Grand Canyon is big.

Draft

USE THE OUTLINE Ask students to write their reviews by using their outlines as guides. Remind them to use persuasive language, to elaborate when necessary to make themselves clear, and to organize facts.

Revise

TALK TO A PARTNER Have partners trade drafts. Remind them that sometimes other people can have ideas that they might not have thought about. Encourage them to listen to their partner's suggestions without getting upset, and to ask questions of their partner if there is something they don't understand.

Edit/Proofread

CHECK FOR ERRORS Students should reread their reviews to check their spelling, grammar, and punctuation.

Publish

POST REVIEWS Have students thumbtack their reviews on a classroom bulletin board where everyone can read them.

GREAT NEW COWBOY PLAY!

I loved the third grade class's performance of *Pecos Bill*. If you like cowboys and cowgirls as much as I do, and if you like to laugh, this is the play for you.

In the play, three ranch hands are sitting around a campfire with a cowboy and a cowgirl and their cook. These ranch hands are the funniest ranch hands I have ever seen! They all wore giant cowboy hats that were way too big for them. This added to the laughs a lot. The cowboy and the cowgirl told the ranch hands a tall tale about a cowboy named Pecos Bill. This tall tale was amazing!

I thought the whole play was written very well. The scenery was very colorful. I hope someone writes more about the adventures of Pecos Bill.

Presentation Ideas

DRAW REVIEWS Have students draw from one to five cowboy hats to use as a rating system in their reviews.
▶ **Representing/Viewing**

HAVE AN INTERVIEW SHOW "Hosts" can ask questions of "actors" from *Pecos Bill*. Have students prepare questions that are relevant to their reviews.
▶ **Speaking/Listening**

Consider students' creative efforts, possibly adding a plus (+) for originality, wit, and imagination.

Scoring Rubric

Excellent	Good	Fair	Unsatisfactory
4: The writer • states a clear opinion. • vividly describes examples from the play. • uses sophisticated ideas and language to sway his or her audience.	**3:** The writer • states a clear opinion. • attempts to use examples that will convince the reader. • has a good sense of audience.	**2:** The writer • attempts to state an opinion. • may not use specific examples to develop the argument. • presents vague or poorly-organized ideas.	**1:** The writer • may not express an opinion. • may present too few examples or irrevelant materials. • may present disconnected or disorganized ideas.

0: The writer leaves the page blank or fails to respond to the writing task. The student does not address the topic or simply paraphrases the prompt. The response is illegible or incoherent.

Meeting Individual Needs for Writing

EASY

Sketch Scenery Have students draw sketches for scenery that might be used in a play about a cowboy or cowgirl. Ask them to label their scenery and write a few sentences telling why this type of scenery is appropriate for their play.

ON-LEVEL

Comic Characters Ask students to think about characters in comedies they have seen on stage or screen. Have them write descriptions explaining why they thought these characters were funny, what they wore, and what they did.

CHALLENGE

Write a Tall Tale Invite students to write a tall-tale play about one of the characters in the play *Pecos Bill*. For example, they might write a play about a cook named Cookie who cooks so many beans that they fill up the Grand Canyon.

COMMUNICATION TIPS

REPRESENTING If you have students present their reviews orally, have them hold up the hats at the end. Encourage students to make each cowboy hat slightly different.

SPEAKING Interviewers should write a list of questions before they begin the interview. That way they can speak confidently.

LANGUAGE SUPPORT

ESL Students from other countries may enjoy performing a familiar play or story in their native language. Encourage them to use expression in their face, body, and voice so that viewers can try to understand what is happening. After the performance, the audience can ask the actors questions about the play and brainstorm ideas for a review.

PORTFOLIO Invite students to include their play reviews or another writing project in their portfolios.

5 Day Grammar and Usage Plan

LANGUAGE SUPPORT

ESL **Write *yesterday, today,* and *tomorrow* on the chalkboard. Then make up sentences using past, present, and future tense verbs. After each, ask a student to come to the board and point to the word that could be used with the sentence. For example if you say, *I will go to the library,* the student points to *tomorrow.* Vary the verbs in your sentences.**

DAILY LANGUAGE ACTIVITIES

Write the Daily Language Activities on the chalkboard each day or use **Transparency 14**. Have students orally correct the verb tenses to match the time clues.

Day 1

1. He chase the horse yesterday. chased
2. Cookie stirred the beans now. stirs
3. Ma counts the children last night. counted

Day 2

1. Bill and Carl talked tomorrow. will talk
2. He watch the horses last week. watched
3. Cookie cleaned the dishes next week. will clean

Day 3

1. Sue married Bill tomorrow. will marry
2. The rattlesnake helped Bill now. helps
3. The coyotes miss Bill last week. missed

Day 4

1. Sue dances with Bill last night. danced
2. Sue sewed her dress now. sews
3. Cookie slice the pizza later. will slice

Day 5

1. Bill play the guitar last year. played
2. Pa just join the wagon train. joined
3. Carl swim in the river later. will swim

Daily Language Transparency 14

DAY 1 Introduce the Concept

Oral Warm-Up Read aloud: The cowboy ropes longhorns. Ask students whether the sentence tells what is happening now or what happened in the past. Ask them to explain their answer.

Introduce Verb Tenses. Present the following:

Verb Tenses

- A **present-tense** verb tells what happens now.
- A **past-tense** verb tells about an action that already happened.

Present the Daily Language Activity and have students correct orally. Prompt students to identify clues to the tense (such as *just, last night, tomorrow*). Have each student write another sentence using one of the clue words.

Assign the daily Writing Prompt on page 350C.

Name________ Date________ Grammar 83

Using Verb Tenses

- A **present-tense verb** tells what happens now.
  Cookie cooks beans every day.
- A **past-tense verb** tells about an action that already happened.
  Pecos Bill jumped on the mustang.

Circle the verb in each sentence. Decide whether it is in the present tense or the past tense. Write **present** or **past** on the line.

1. Cowboy Sam orders pizza for dinner. present
2. Cowgirl Pam and Cowboy Sam tell a story. present
3. The legend of Pecos Bill started in Texas. past
4. Pecos Bill's family moved west. past
5. Bill dropped out of the wagon. past
6. Ranch Hand #3 wonders about the pizza. present
7. Pecos Bill joined a family of coyotes. past
8. Years later, Bill learned human ways from his brother. past
9. The pizza finally arrives. present
10. Pecos Bill married Slue-Foot Sue. past

10 Book 3.1/Unit 3 Pecos Bill

Extension: Have students work in small groups. Ask them to write short skits (five lines at most) using the same characters as those in *Pecos Bill.* They can write in either the present tense or the past tense. Later, they can act out their skits. 83

GRAMMAR PRACTICE BOOK, PAGE 83

DAY 2 Teach the Concept

Review Verb Tenses Ask students when the past tense is used and how most past-tense verbs end. *(-ed)* Ask how they know something is taking place in the present.

Introduce Future Tense Explain that some verbs tell about something that will happen in the future. Present the following:

Future Tense

- A verb in the **future tense** tells about an action that is going to happen.
- To write about the future, use the special verb *will*.

Present the Daily Language Activity. Then have students write three sentences using the future tense.

Assign the daily Writing Prompt on page 350C.

Name________ Date________ Grammar 84

Future Tense

- A verb in the **future tense** tells about an action that is going to happen.
- To write about the future, use the special verb *will.*
  Cookie will cook lima bean pizza.

Find the future tense verb in each sentence. Underline your answer.

1. Pecos Bill will become a legendary cowboy.
2. He will meet his brother, Carl the Cowboy.
3. Carl will teach him in three days.
4. Bill will surprise Carl with his abilities.
5. He will chase Widow Maker across several states.
6. Pecos Bill will invent the lasso.
7. He will make the world's first guitar.
8. In the Rio Grande, he will find his future wife, Slue-Foot Sue.
9. The coyotes will attend the wedding, too.
10. All of them will live happily ever after.

84 **Extension:** Have each student write about what they think they will be in the future. They can start with "I think that I..." Encourage them to be fanciful if they wish. If time allows, they can illustrate their statements.

Book 3.1/Unit 3 Pecos Bill 10

GRAMMAR PRACTICE BOOK, PAGE 84

Using Verb Tenses

DAY 3 Review and Practice

Learn from the Literature Review verb tenses. Read Slue-Foot Sue's sentence on page 370 of *Pecos Bill.*

Of course I will marry you!

Ask students to identify the tense of the verb. (future) Ask what word tells them the tense is future. (will) Have them explain how the spelling of the verb would change in the past tense.

Correct Verb Tenses Present the Daily Language Activity and have children correct the sentences orally.

Have students make a 3-column chart and write definitions of the three tenses. Have students find past, present, and future verbs in the play.

Assign the daily Writing Prompt on page 350D.

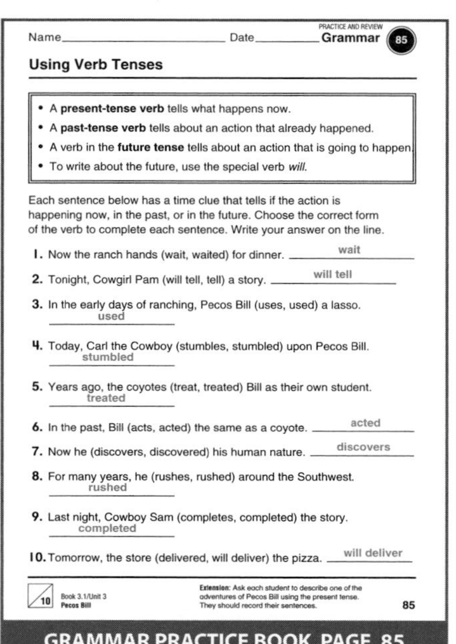

PRACTICE AND REVIEW

Name________________ Date________ **Grammar** 85

Using Verb Tenses

- A **present-tense verb** tells what happens now.
- A **past-tense verb** tells about an action that already happened.
- A verb in the **future tense** tells about an action that is going to happen.
- To write about the future, use the special verb *will.*

Each sentence below has a time clue that tells if the action is happening now, in the past, or in the future. Choose the correct form of the verb to complete each sentence. Write your answer on the line.

1. Now the ranch hands (wait, waited) for dinner. wait
2. Tonight, Cowgirl Pam (will tell, tell) a story. will tell
3. In the early days of ranching, Pecos Bill (uses, used) a lasso. used
4. Today, Carl the Cowboy (stumbles, stumbled) upon Pecos Bill. stumbled
5. Years ago, the coyotes (treat, treated) Bill as their own student. treated
6. In the past, Bill (acts, acted) the same as a coyote. acted
7. Now he (discovers, discovered) his human nature. discovers
8. For many years, he (rushes, rushed) around the Southwest. rushed
9. Last night, Cowboy Sam (completes, completed) the story. completed
10. Tomorrow, the store (delivered, will deliver) the pizza. will deliver

/10 Book 3.1/Unit 3 **Pecos Bill**

Extension: Ask each student to describe one of the adventures of Pecos Bill using the present tense. They should record their sentences.

85

GRAMMAR PRACTICE BOOK, PAGE 85

DAY 4 Review and Practice

Review Verb Tenses Write all the verbs from the Daily Language Activities for Days 1 through 3 on the chalkboard in the present tense. Ask students to change the verbs to their past-tense and future-tense forms, and use them in sentences. Then present the Daily Language Activity for Day 4.

Mechanics and Usage Before students begin the daily Writing Prompt on page 350D, review the following:

Quotation Marks and Commas

- Use quotation marks at the beginning and end of a person's exact words.
- Use a comma after the name of a person being spoken to.

Assign the daily Writing Prompt on page 350D.

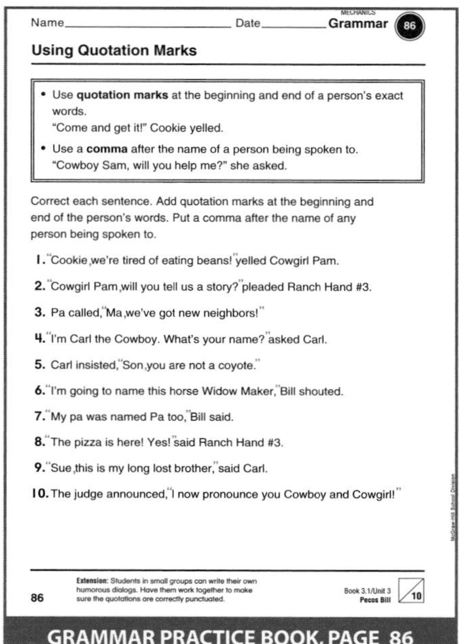

MECHANICS

Name________________ Date________ **Grammar** 86

Using Quotation Marks

- Use **quotation marks** at the beginning and end of a person's exact words.
  "Come and get it!" Cookie yelled.
- Use a **comma** after the name of a person being spoken to.
  "Cowboy Sam, will you help me?" she asked.

Correct each sentence. Add quotation marks at the beginning and end of the person's words. Put a comma after the name of any person being spoken to.

1. "Cookie, we're tired of eating beans!" yelled Cowgirl Pam.
2. "Cowgirl Pam, will you tell us a story?" pleaded Ranch Hand #3.
3. Pa called, "Ma, we've got new neighbors!"
4. "I'm Carl the Cowboy. What's your name?" asked Carl.
5. Carl insisted, "Son, you are not a coyote."
6. "I'm going to name this horse Widow Maker," Bill shouted.
7. "My pa was named Pa too," Bill said.
8. "The pizza is here! Yes!" said Ranch Hand #3.
9. "Sue, this is my long lost brother," said Carl.
10. The judge announced, "I now pronounce you Cowboy and Cowgirl!"

86

Extension: Students in small groups can write their own humorous dialogs. Have them work together to make sure the quotations are correctly punctuated.

Book 3.1/Unit 3 **Pecos Bill** /10

GRAMMAR PRACTICE BOOK, PAGE 86

DAY 5 Assess and Reteach

Assess Use the Daily Language Activity and page 87 of the **Grammar Practice Book** for assessment.

Reteach Have students write each rule about verb tenses from the lesson on an index card. Have them write an example sentence of each rule on the card using the same regular verb. For each verb in Daily Language Activity sentences, have students write the verb tense and its other tenses on the appropriate index card.

Have students create a word wall with lists of verbs in the three tenses.

Use page 88 of the **Grammar Practice Book** for additional reteaching.

Assign the daily Writing Prompt on page 350D.

TEST

Name________________ Date________ **Grammar** 87

Using Verb Tenses

A. Choose the correct form for each of the following verbs to go with the time clue in the sentence. Mark your answer.

1. Tomorrow, Sam ____ home.
   ⓐ walks ⓑ walk ● will walk ⓓ walked
2. You ____ right now.
   ⓐ steers ● will steer ⓒ steered ⓓ steer
3. They _____ last night.
   ● listened ⓑ listen ⓒ will listen ⓓ listens
4. In those days, he _____ behind.
   ⓐ lag ⓑ lags ● lagged ⓓ will lag

B. Decide if the verb in each sentence should be past tense, present tense, or future tense. Find the verb that correctly completes the sentence. Mark your answer.

5. Long ago, Pecos Bill _____ with the other young coyotes.
   ● played ⓑ plays ⓒ will play ⓓ plaied
6. One day perhaps he _____ to the Southwest.
   ⓐ return ● will return ⓒ returns ⓓ returned
7. In those days wild horses still _____ the Texas countryside.
   ⓐ roam ● roamed ⓒ roams ⓓ will roam
8. Tall tales ____ popular today.
   ⓐ remained ⓑ remains ⓒ will remain ● remain

/8 Book 3.1/Unit 3 **Pecos Bill**

87

GRAMMAR PRACTICE BOOK, PAGE 87

GRAMMAR PRACTICE BOOK, PAGE 88

5 Day Spelling Plan

LANGUAGE SUPPORT

To help with the different pronunciations of the *-ied* ending, ask why the long *e* sound is heard in *buried* but the long *i* sound in *fried*. (because the base words are *bury* and *fry*)

DICTATION SENTENCES

Spelling Words

1. The thief spied on her neighbor.
2. The hawk was moving through the sky.
3. The bank was robbed by a thief.
4. She likes saving money in a bank.
5. She blamed her friend for kicking the doll.
6. The race is beginning soon.
7. He had fried eggs for breakfast.
8. The ground was shaking.
9. The farmer supplied the eggs for breakfast.
10. The coins were buried in the ground.
11. The birds were escaping from the zoo.
12. She hurried so she would not be late.
13. He stirred the soup.
14. The farmer was splitting wood.
15. She divided the bread into three pieces.

Challenge Words

16. When you combine things, you put them together.
17. Who invented the car?
18. Where is the park located?
19. The herd walked through the prairie.
20. The town was a wilderness in the past.

DAY 1 Pretest

Assess Prior Knowledge Use the Dictation Sentences at left and **Spelling Practice Book page 83** for the pretest. Allow students to correct their own papers. If students have trouble, have partners give each other a midweek test on Day 3. Students who require a modified list may be tested on the first eight words.

Spelling Words		Challenge Words
1. spied	9. supplied	16. **combine**
2. moving	10. buried	17. **invented**
3. robbed	11. escaping	18. **located**
4. **saving**	12. hurried	19. **prairie**
5. blamed	13. stirred	20. **wilderness**
6. beginning	14. splitting	
7. fried	15. divided	
8. shaking		

*Note: Words in **dark type** are from the story.*

Word Study On page 84 of the **Spelling Practice Book** are word study steps and an at-home activity.

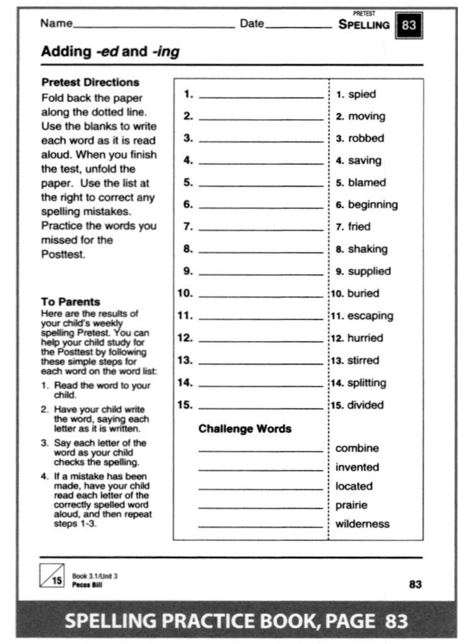

Name__________ Date______ PRETEST SPELLING 83

Adding *-ed* and *-ing*

Pretest Directions
Fold back the paper along the dotted line. Use the blanks to write each word as it is read aloud. When you finish the test, unfold the paper. Use the list at the right to correct any spelling mistakes. Practice the words you missed for the Posttest.

To Parents
Here are the results of your child's weekly spelling Pretest. You can help your child study for the Posttest by following these simple steps for each word on the word list:
1. Read the word to your child.
2. Have your child write the word, saying each letter as it is written.
3. Say each letter of the word as your child checks the spelling.
4. If a mistake has been made, have your child read each letter of the correctly spelled word aloud, and then repeat steps 1-3.

1. ____ 1. spied
2. ____ 2. moving
3. ____ 3. robbed
4. ____ 4. saving
5. ____ 5. blamed
6. ____ 6. beginning
7. ____ 7. fried
8. ____ 8. shaking
9. ____ 9. supplied
10. ____ 10. buried
11. ____ 11. escaping
12. ____ 12. hurried
13. ____ 13. stirred
14. ____ 14. splitting
15. ____ 15. divided

Challenge Words
____ combine
____ invented
____ located
____ prairie
____ wilderness

15 Book 3.1/Unit 3 Pecos Bill 83

SPELLING PRACTICE BOOK, PAGE 83

WORD STUDY STEPS AND ACTIVITY, PAGE 84

DAY 2 Explore the Pattern

Sort and Spell Words Explain that the endings *-ed* and *-ing* can be added to verbs, and that sometimes the spelling of the base word changes when endings are added. A final consonant may be doubled, a final *e* dropped, or a final *y* changed to *i*. Have students say each Spelling Word and sort the Spelling Words according to their spelling change.

Doubled consonant	Dropped *e*	*y* to *i*
robbed	moving	spied
beginning	saving	fried
stirred	blamed	supplied
splitting	shaking	buried
	escaping	hurried
	divided	

Word Wall Have students find other words ending in *-ed* or *-ing* and add them to a classroom word wall, noting any spelling changes.

Name__________ Date______ EXPLORE THE PATTERN SPELLING 85

Adding *-ed* and *-ing*

spied	saving	fried	buried	stirred
moving	blamed	shaking	escaping	splitting
robbed	beginning	supplied	hurried	divided

Pattern Power
Write the spelling words that show what you do before adding *-ed* or *-ing*.

double final consonant	drop e	change y to i
1. robbed	5. moving	11. spied
2. beginning	6. saving	12. fried
3. stirred	7. blamed	13. supplied
4. splitting	8. shaking	14. buried
	9. escaping	15. hurried
	10. divided	

Order, Please!
Write each group of spelling words in alphabetical order.

spied, saving, shaking, stirred

16. saving 17. shaking
18. spied 19. stirred

blamed, divided, escaping, beginning, buried

20. beginning 21. blamed
22. buried 23. divided
24. escaping

24 Book 3.1/Unit 3 Pecos Bill 85

SPELLING PRACTICE BOOK, PAGE 85

Adding -*ed* and -*ing*

DAY 3 Practice and Extend

Word Meaning: Base Words Remind students that the Spelling Words end with -*ed* or -*ing*. Review the rules for changing the spelling of the base words. Then ask students to list the base words. *(spy, move, rob, save, blame, begin, fry, shake, supply, bury, escape, hurry, stir, split, divide)*

Glossary Have students:

- identify which Challenge Words have endings. *(invented, located)*
- look up words in the Glossary and find what form of each word is listed. (the base word)
- find where the -*ed* form of each word appears in the entry. (at the end)
- write each Challenge Word and any forms that appear at the end of its Glossary entry.

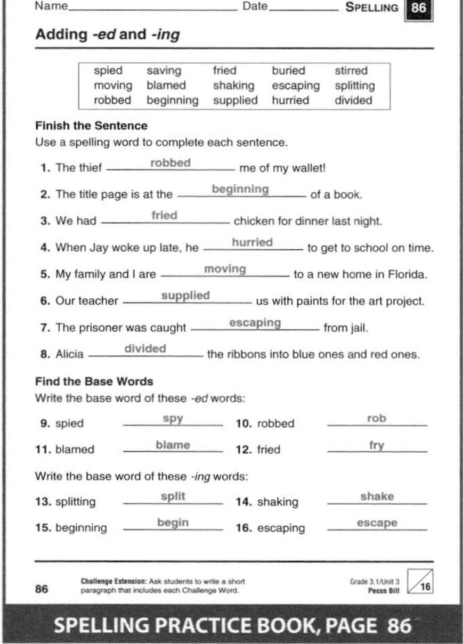

Name______________ Date__________ PRACTICE AND EXTEND SPELLING 86

Adding -*ed* and -*ing*

spied	saving	fried	buried	stirred
moving	blamed	shaking	escaping	splitting
robbed	beginning	supplied	hurried	divided

Finish the Sentence

Use a spelling word to complete each sentence.

1. The thief ___robbed___ me of my wallet!
2. The title page is at the ___beginning___ of a book.
3. We had ___fried___ chicken for dinner last night.
4. When Jay woke up late, he ___hurried___ to get to school on time.
5. My family and I are ___moving___ to a new home in Florida.
6. Our teacher ___supplied___ us with paints for the art project.
7. The prisoner was caught ___escaping___ from jail.
8. Alicia ___divided___ the ribbons into blue ones and red ones.

Find the Base Words

Write the base word of these -*ed* words:

9. spied ___spy___ 10. robbed ___rob___

11. blamed ___blame___ 12. fried ___fry___

Write the base word of these -*ing* words:

13. splitting ___split___ 14. shaking ___shake___

15. beginning ___begin___ 16. escaping ___escape___

86 **Challenge Extension:** Ask students to write a short paragraph that includes each Challenge Word. Grade 3.1/Unit 3 **Pecos Bill** 16

SPELLING PRACTICE BOOK, PAGE 86

DAY 4 Proofread and Write

Proofread Sentences Write these sentences on the chalkboard, including the misspelled words. Ask students to proofread, circling incorrect spellings and writing the correct spellings. There are two spelling errors in each sentence.

He spyied a man escapeing from the room. (spied, escaping)

She supplyed the fryed chicken for supper. (supplied, fried)

He dividded the wood by spliting it. (divided, splitting)

Have students create additional sentences with errors for partners to correct.

Have students use as many Spelling Words as possible in the daily Writing Prompt on page 350D. Remind students to proofread their writing for errors in spelling, punctuation, and grammar.

Name______________ Date__________ PROOFREAD AND WRITE SPELLING 87

Adding -*ed* and -*ing*

Proofreading Paragraph

There are six spelling mistakes in this paragraph. Circle the misspelled words. Write the words correctly on the lines below.

Two men robed a bank. They berryed all but one of the sacks of money. They devided the rest of the money equally between the two of them.

When the two men reached the next town, they stopped. "I smell fryed chicken," said Luke. "Let's eat!" So the hungry men hurried into a small coffee shop and ordered everything on the menu. But when the time came to pay the bill, neither of the robbers wanted to pay.

"Come on, Luke, pay up!" said Bart. "What are you sayving it for?"

"Why should I pay?" asked Luke.

While the two men were busy arguing, the sheriff and his deputies walked in. Each blammed the other for their bad luck.

1. ___robbed___ 2. ___buried___ 3. ___divided___

4. ___fried___ 5. ___saving___ 6. ___blamed___

Writing Activity

Write a short story that takes place in the Old West. How does the story begin? What do the characters do? How does the story end? Use six spelling words.

12 Book 3.1/Unit 3 **Pecos Bill** 87

SPELLING PRACTICE BOOK, PAGE 87

DAY 5 Assess and Reteach

Assess Students' Knowledge Use page 88 of the **Spelling Practice Book** or the Dictation Sentences on page 375O for the posttest.

Personal Word List Have students create a section of their journals called "*y* to *i*." In that section have them make columns with words such as *spy, spied, try, tried, supply, supplied*, and similar words that they encounter in other stories and texts. Students should refer to their lists during future writing activities.

Name______________ Date__________ POSTTEST SPELLING 88

Adding -*ed* and -*ing*

Look at the words in each set. One word in each set is spelled correctly. Use a pencil to color in the circle in front of that word. Before you begin, look at the sample sets of words. Sample A has been done for you. Do Sample B by yourself. When you are sure you know what to do, you may go on with the rest of the page.

Sample A
- (A) tried
- (B) tryed
- (C) treid
- (D) tride

Sample B
- (E) caried
- (F) carryed
- (G) caryed
- (H) carried

1. (A) devided (B) divided (C) divyded (D) deivided
2. (E) fried (F) fryed (G) freid (H) fride
3. (A) ciplied (B) suplied (C) supplied (D) sepplied
4. (E) movin (F) mooving (G) movving (H) moving
5. (A) begining (B) beginning (C) beggining (D) begineng
6. (E) rabbed (F) robbed (G) rawbed (H) raubed
7. (A) stird (B) stirred (C) stired (D) sturred
8. (E) eskaping (F) escayping (G) eschaping (H) escaping
9. (A) hurryed (B) hurried (C) herried (D) huried
10. (E) blaymed (F) blaimed (G) blamed (H) blamde
11. (A) spyed (B) spied (C) spide (D) spyde
12. (E) shaking (F) shaching (G) shakin (H) schaking
13. (A) buryed (B) berryed (C) barried (D) buried
14. (E) splittin (F) soppliting (G) splitting (H) splytting
15. (A) saiving (B) savving (C) saving (D) sayving

McGraw-Hill School Division

88 Grade 3.1/Unit 3 **Pecos Bill** 15

SPELLING PRACTICE BOOK, PAGE 88

Lesson Overview

A Very Cool Place to Visit

Selection Summary Students will read about a hotel in Sweden that has to be rebuilt every winter because it melts in the spring. It is made of ice and snow!

TIME
FOR KIDS
SPECIAL REPORT
A VERY COOL PLACE TO VISIT
A hotel in Sweden is made of ice and snow.

Listening Library Audiocassette

INSTRUCTIONAL
Pages 378–385

Resources for

Meeting Individual Needs

REVIEW LEVELED BOOKS

EASY
Pages 385A, 385D

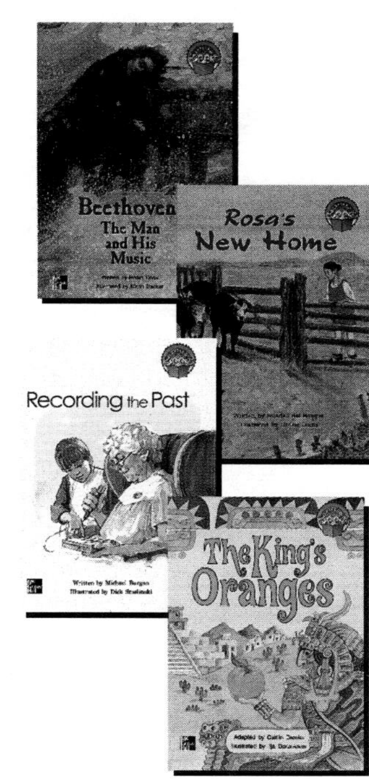

INDEPENDENT
Pages 385B, 385D

CHALLENGE
Pages 385C, 385D

Take-Home versions available

LEVELED PRACTICE

Reteach, 103–109
blackline masters with reteaching opportunities for each assessed skill

Practice, 103–109
workbook with Take-Home Stories and practice opportunities for each assessed skill and story comprehension

Extend, 103–109
blackline masters that offer challenge activities for each assessed skill

ADDITIONAL RESOURCES

- **Language Support Book** 133–120
- **Take-Home Story, Practice** p. 104a
- **Alternate Teaching Strategies** T60–T66
- **Selected Quizzes Prepared by** Accelerated Reader

McGraw-Hill School TECHNOLOGY

Phonics CD-ROM provides extra phonics support.

interNET CONNECTION Research & Inquiry ideas. Visit ***www.mhschool.com/reading.***

Suggested Lesson Planner

Available on CD-ROM

READING AND LANGUAGE ARTS	DAY 1 Focus on Reading and Skills	DAY 2 Read the Literature
Comprehension Vocabulary Phonics/Decoding Study Skills Listening, Speaking, Viewing, Representing	 **Read Aloud and Motivate,** 376E "Ice Cycle" **Develop Visual Literacy,** 376/377 ☑ **Review Main Idea,** 378A–378B **Teaching Chart 85** **Reteach, Practice, Extend,** 103	**Build Background,** 378C Develop Oral Language **Vocabulary,** 378D ***beauty*** ***creeps*** ***furniture*** ***palace*** ***pure*** ***visitors*** **Teaching Chart 86** **Word Building Manipulative Cards** **Reteach, Practice, Extend,** 104  **Read the Selection,** 378–381 Guided Instruction ☑ Main Idea ☑ Make Inferences
Curriculum Connections	 Fine Arts, 376/377	 Social Studies, 378C
Writing	 **Writing Prompt:** Would you like to sleep on an ice bed? Why or why not? Explain in a paragraph.	 **Writing Prompt:** Why do you think people like to come to the Ice Hotel? Tell why in a short essay.  **Journal Writing,** 381 Quick-Write
Grammar	**Introduce the Concept: Sentence Combining with Verbs,** 385M Daily Language Activity 1. The ice melts. The ice freezes. The ice melts and freezes. 2. The snow falls. The snow drifts quietly. The snow falls and drifts quietly. 3. The wind howls. The wind blows. The wind howls and blows. **Grammar Practice Book,** 89	**Teach the Concept: Sentence Combining with Verbs,** 385M Daily Language Activity 1. People visit. People leave the hotel. 2. Cold air creeps into the rooms. Cold air sneaks into the rooms. 3. A reindeer meets the visitors. A reindeer greets the visitors. **Grammar Practice Book,** 90
Spelling	**Pretest: Words from Science,** 385O **Spelling Practice Book,** 89–90	**Explore the Patterns: Words from Science,** 385O **Spelling Practice Book,** 91

Meeting Individual Needs

☑ = **Skill Assessed in Unit Test**

DAY 3 Read the Literature

Reread for Fluency, 380

Story Questions, 382
- **Reteach, Practice, Extend,** 105

Story Activities, 383

Study Skill, 384
- ☑ Graphic Aids
- **Teaching Chart 87**
- **Reteach, Practice, Extend,** 106

Test Power, 385

Read the Leveled Books
- Guided Reading
- ☑ Phonics Review
- ☑ Comprehension Review

Phonics Review

 CD-ROM

Science, 383

Writing Prompt: What do people make out of snow and ice? List three things and describe one of them.

Writing Process: Persuasive Writing, 385K
- Prewrite, Draft

Review and Practice: Sentence Combining with Verbs, 385N

Daily Language Activity
1. People exercise. People do push-ups.
2. Workers help. Workers give advice.
3. Children skate. Children slide on the ice.

Grammar Practice Book, 91

Practice and Extend: Words from Science, 385P
- **Spelling Practice Book,** 92

DAY 4 Build and Review Skills

Read the Leveled Books and Self-Selected Books

☑ **Review Summarize,** 385E–385F
- **Teaching Chart 88**
- **Reteach, Practice, Extend,** 107
- **Language Support,** 118

☑ **Review Multiple-Meaning Words,** 385G–385H
- **Teaching Chart 89**
- **Reteach, Practice, Extend,** 108
- **Language Support,** 119

Writing Prompt: If you could visit a hotel anywhere in the world, where would you go?

Writing Process: Persuasive Writing, 385K
- Revise

Meeting Individual Needs for Writing, 385L

Review and Practice: Sentence Combining with Verbs, 385N

Daily Language Activity
1. Visitors sleep. Visitors stay warm.
2. Stars twinkle. Stars glow in the sky.
3. The beds are made of ice. The beds are covered with reindeer skins.

Grammar Practice Book, 92

Proofread and Write: Words from Science, 385P
- **Spelling Practice Book,** 93

DAY 5 Build and Review Skills

Read Self-Selected Books

☑ **Review Context Clues,** 385I–385J
- **Teaching Chart 90**
- **Reteach, Practice, Extend,** 109
- **Language Support,** 120

Listening, Speaking, Viewing, Representing, 385L
- Design Ice Sculptures
- Persuasive Speaking

Writing Prompt: Write a paragraph telling how it feels to be in the ice hotel when it is melting.

Writing Process: Persuasive Writing, 385K
- Edit/Proofread, Publish

Assess and Reteach: Sentence Combining with Verbs, 385N

Daily Language Activity
1. The ice melts. The ice forms a pond.
2. Tom fell on the ice. Tom broke his wrist.
3. The fire crackles. The fire pops.

Grammar Practice Book, 93–94

Assess and Reteach: Words from Science, 385P
- **Spelling Practice Book,** 94

Language Arts

Read Aloud and Motivate

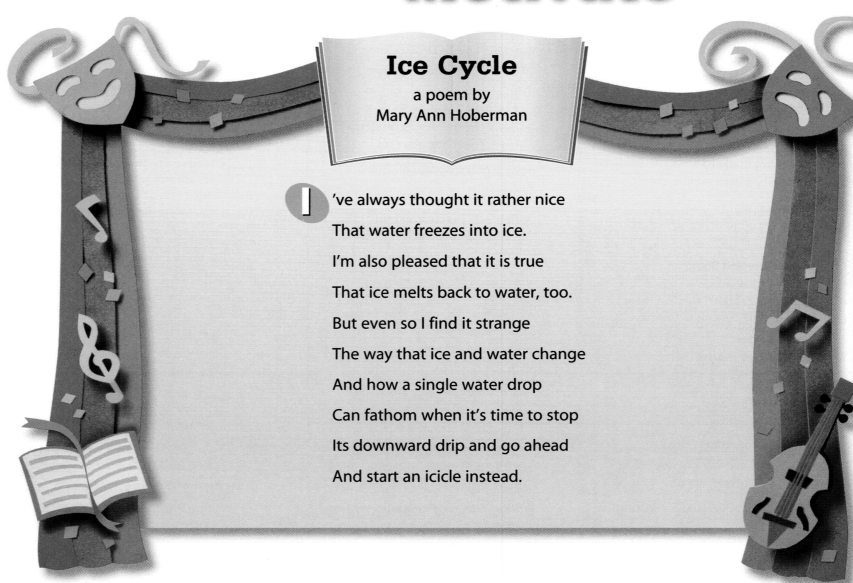

Ice Cycle

a poem by
Mary Ann Hoberman

I've always thought it rather nice
That water freezes into ice.
I'm also pleased that it is true
That ice melts back to water, too.
But even so I find it strange
The way that ice and water change
And how a single water drop
Can fathom when it's time to stop
Its downward drip and go ahead
And start an icicle instead.

Oral Comprehension

LISTENING AND SPEAKING Motivate students to think about rhythm and rhyme by reading aloud this poem about icicles. Ask students to pay attention to the rhythm of the words as you read and to listen for the rhyming words. When you have finished reading the poem, ask, "Which words rhymed in this poem?" Then ask, "Did the rhythm of the words help you enjoy the poem more than if it were written as prose? Why or why not?" Encourage students to listen for the rhythm in other poems they read.

Activity Have students create snowscape paintings with watercolor paints. For extra effect, encourage students to use silver glitter to highlight their paintings.

▶ **Visual/Kinesthetic**

Develop Visual Literacy

Works of Art

Anthology pages 376-377

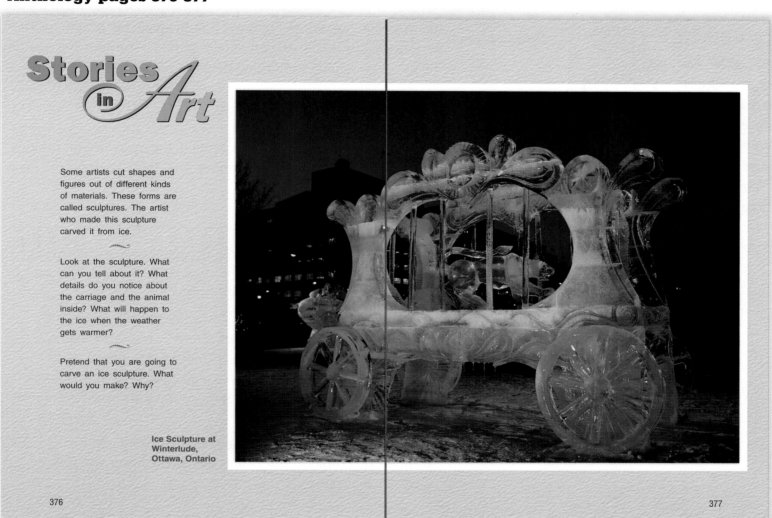

Stories in Art

Some artists cut shapes and figures out of different kinds of materials. These forms are called sculptures. The artist who made this sculpture carved it from ice.

Look at the sculpture. What can you tell about it? What details do you notice about the carriage and the animal inside? What will happen to the ice when the weather gets warmer?

Pretend that you are going to carve an ice sculpture. What would you make? Why?

Ice Sculpture at Winterlude, Ottawa, Ontario

376

377

Objective: Identify Main Idea

VIEWING This ice sculpture depicts a traveling circus wagon. Inside the cage on wheels is a fierce tiger. Ask students if they have ever seen a work of art carved in ice. Do they think the artist was successful in shaping the elegant wagon and the snarling wild cat within? Is this work of art a lasting one? Why or why not? Read the page with students, encouraging individual interpretations of the sculpture.

Have students comment on the impression the piece creates and its details.

For example:

- The carriage is meticulously rendered and has a fairy-tale quality.
- In contrast, the animal inside seems ready to spring.

REPRESENTING Students might make their own sculptures from clay or achieve a sense of three-dimensional design by gluing objects to construction paper to form a design.

Students will distinguish between main idea and supporting details.

TEACHING TIP

MANAGEMENT Glue a red and green one-inch cube together. When working independently on a project, a student turns the block to show his/her need for help—green means "Keep moving!" and red means "Stop to help me!"

Review Main Idea

PREPARE

Recognizing Main Ideas in Everyday Life

Ask students to recall times when their mother has told them to go to the store and buy bread. Point out that the main idea of her instruction was to buy bread. Any other information—the kind, the quantity, the price—would be supporting details.

TEACH

Define Main Idea and Supporting Details

Remind students that in pieces of writing, the main idea, or topic, is what the essay, book, or story is about. The details support the main idea, or topic.

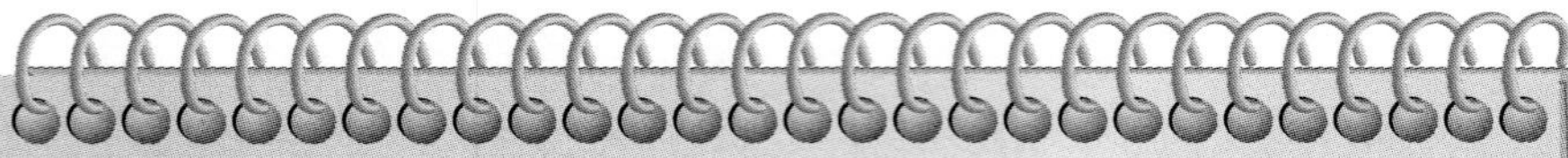

The Snow Igloo

The snow igloo gives a surprising amount of protection in one of the coldest places on earth. Snow is a good insulator. This means that once the inside of an igloo is warmed up, it remains warm. When two or three Inuits go inside their snow house and light their oil lamps, they can take off their furs and bask in the heat.

To keep cold air from coming in the front door, the Inuit build a long entrance tunnel that traps the cold air and prevents it from coming into the living space.

Teaching Chart 85

Read the Passage Aloud and Model the Skill

Display **Teaching Chart 85**. Have students pay attention to the main idea and supporting details as the passage is read.

MODEL The first sentence in the passage states that snow igloos can protect people from the cold. I think the writer has written the passage to tell how this works. All the other facts in the passage explain how a snow igloo keeps people warm. These must be the supporting details.

PRACTICE

Identify Main Idea and Supporting Details

Have students circle the main idea and underline the supporting details. Then have students record the main idea and the supporting details of the **Teaching Chart** passage in a Main Idea and Supporting Details chart.
▶ **Linguistic/Logical**

MAIN IDEA	SUPPORTING DETAILS
Snow igloos protect against the cold.	1. Snow is a good insulator.
	2. Long entrance tunnels prevent the cold from entering the living space.

ASSESS/CLOSE

Write Another Main Idea and Supporting Details Chart

Have students think of other kinds of homes. Have them describe the important aspect about each type of place by writing a main idea and supporting details.

SELECTION Connection

Students will compare and contrast when they read *A Very Cool Place to Visit* and the Leveled Books.

ALTERNATE TEACHING STRATEGY

MAIN IDEA

For a different approach to teaching this skill, see page T60.

Meeting Individual Needs for Comprehension

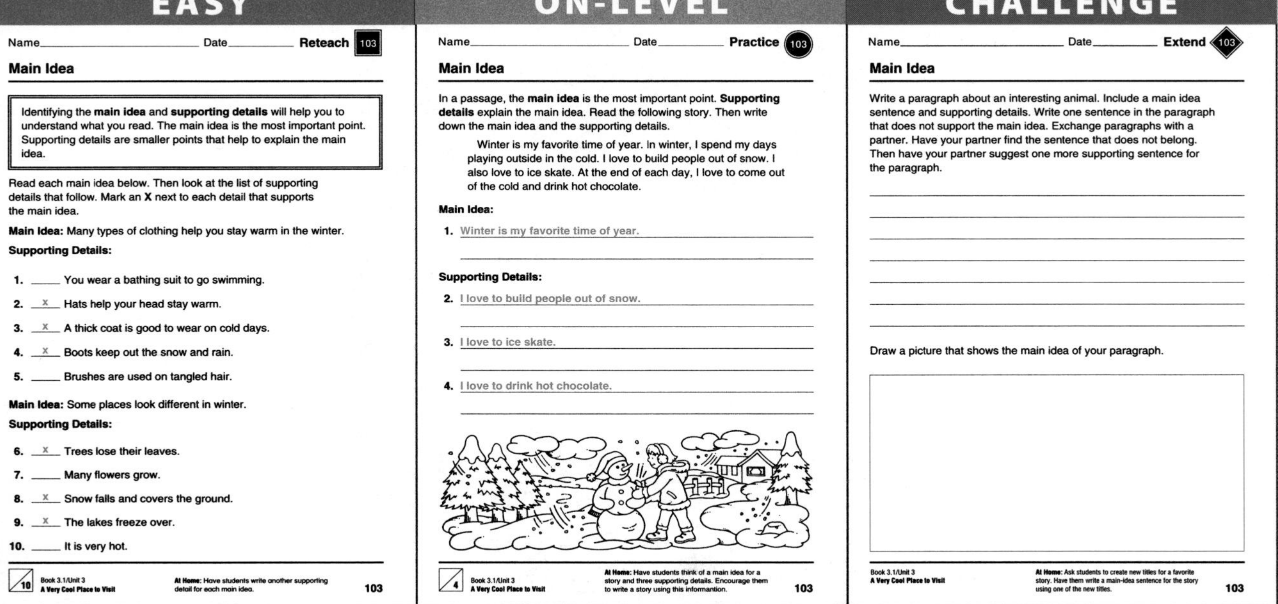

EASY

Name________ Date______ Reteach 103

Main Idea

Identifying the **main idea** and **supporting details** will help you to understand what you read. The main idea is the most important point. Supporting details are smaller points that help to explain the main idea.

Read each main idea below. Then look at the list of supporting details that follow. Mark an **X** next to each detail that supports the main idea.

Main Idea: Many types of clothing help you stay warm in the winter.
Supporting Details:

1. ____ You wear a bathing suit to go swimming.
2. _x_ Hats help your head stay warm.
3. _x_ A thick coat is good to wear on cold days.
4. _x_ Boots keep out the snow and rain.
5. ____ Brushes are used on tangled hair.

Main Idea: Some places look different in winter.
Supporting Details:

6. _x_ Trees lose their leaves.
7. ____ Many flowers grow.
8. _x_ Snow falls and covers the ground.
9. _x_ The lakes freeze over.
10. ____ It is very hot.

10 Book 3.1/Unit 3 **A Very Cool Place to Visit** **At Home:** Have students write another supporting detail for each main idea. 103

ON-LEVEL

Name________ Date______ Practice 103

Main Idea

In a passage, the **main idea** is the most important point. **Supporting details** explain the main idea. Read the following story. Then write down the main idea and the supporting details.

Winter is my favorite time of year. In winter, I spend my days playing outside in the cold. I love to build people out of snow. I also love to ice skate. At the end of each day, I love to come out of the cold and drink hot chocolate.

Main Idea:
1. Winter is my favorite time of year.

Supporting Details:
2. I love to build people out of snow.
3. I love to ice skate.
4. I love to drink hot chocolate.

4 Book 3.1/Unit 3 **A Very Cool Place to Visit** **At Home:** Have students think of a main idea for a story and three supporting details. Encourage them to write a story using this informantion. 103

CHALLENGE

Name________ Date______ Extend 103

Main Idea

Write a paragraph about an interesting animal. Include a main idea sentence and supporting details. Write one sentence in the paragraph that does not support the main idea. Exchange paragraphs with a partner. Have your partner find the sentence that does not belong. Then have your partner suggest one more supporting sentence for the paragraph.

Draw a picture that shows the main idea of your paragraph.

Book 3.1/Unit 3 **A Very Cool Place to Visit** **At Home:** Ask students to create new titles for a favorite story. Have them write a main-idea sentence for the story using one of the new titles. 103

Reteach, 103 **Practice, 103** **Extend, 103**

Build Background

Social Studies

Evaluate Prior Knowledge

CONCEPT: LIVING IN A COLD CLIMATE This selection shows that people who live in cold climates have special experiences. Have students discuss how life in a cold climate is different from life in a warm one.

COMPARE CLIMATES Have students list ways in which living in a cold climate is the same as or different from living in a warm climate. Create a Venn diagram.

▶ Logical/Visual

COLD CLIMATE		WARM CLIMATE
Different	Alike	Different
well-built house heating system warm clothing snow and ice skating and skiing	schools work friends	house with open areas air conditioning light-weight clothing swimming and beaches

Graphic Organizer 14

MENU FOR KEEPING WARM Have

students work in pairs to plan menus for a cold day. Ask them if they would send their parents off to work with hot cereal and hot chocolate or cold cereal and cold milk.

Develop Oral Language

LOOKING AT LIFE IN A COLD CLIMATE

ESL Bring in photographs of scenes from really cold climates. Have students brainstorm a list of things they might see or experience in this environment.

Write the list on the chalkboard. Discuss the meaning of each word and ask students to use it in a sentence.

Have students work with partners to present a skit about getting to school in a place with a frigid climate. Encourage them to use some of the words listed on the chalkboard.

TEACHING TIP

INSTRUCTIONAL Have students discuss books or movies about life in a very cold place. Guide them to recall how the cold affected people's daily lives—their clothes, their food, their recreations.

LANGUAGE SUPPORT

See Language Support Book, pages 113–116, for teaching suggestions for Build Background and Vocabulary.

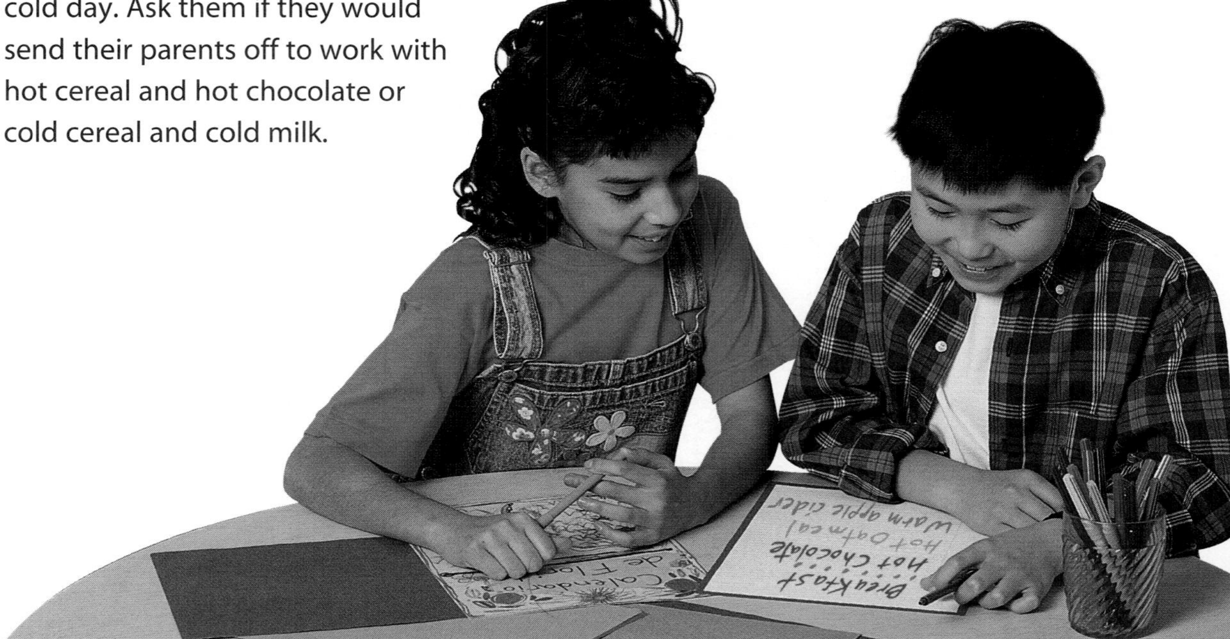

Vocabulary

Key Words

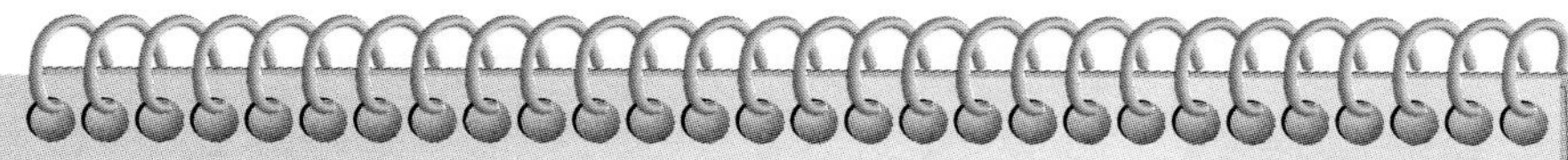

A Special Place to Stay

1. The great building sparkled like a palace made of crystal. **2.** It was made of pure ice that was not mixed with any other material. **3.** The travelers' guide told them that they could spend the night there as visitors. **4.** The travelers were delighted by the building's shining beauty. **5.** "I hope the chairs and other furniture aren't made out of ice," one said. **6.** "I hope it shuts out this sneaky chill that creeps down my collar and up my sleeves," said the other.

Teaching Chart 86

Definitions

palace (p. 380) the home of a ruler; a large, expensive house

pure (p. 379) not mixed with anything

visitors (p. 381) people staying in a different place for a while

beauty (p. 379) a pleasing quality

furniture (p. 379) large, useful household articles

creeps (p. 379) moves slowly and sneakily

SPELLING/VOCABULARY CONNECTIONS

See Spelling Challenge Words, pages 385O–385P.

Vocabulary in Context

IDENTIFY VOCABULARY WORDS Display **Teaching Chart 86** and read the passage with students. Have volunteers circle each vocabulary word and underline other words that are clues to its meaning.

DISCUSS MEANINGS Ask questions like these to help clarify word meanings:

- Would a king or a school teacher live in a palace?
- Is water mixed with mud pure?
- Do visitors come for good or just for a while?
- If you love the way something looks, do you enjoy its beauty?
- Which is furniture, a chair or a car?
- When a cat creeps, does it move quickly or slowly?

Practice

MOVING PICTURES Have students work in small groups. Have each group pick a Vocabulary Card. Then have each member draw a different picture illustrating the word. Each group can make a mobile with their pictures by tying them onto wire coat hangers.
▶ **Linguistic/Spatial**

Word Building Manipulative Cards

WRITE A STORY Have pairs of students write a brief story about a visit to a family on another planet, using all the vocabulary words. Have students refer to their Glossary as needed.
PARTNERS WRITING
▶**Linguistic**

ON-LEVEL

Name______ Date______ Practice 104

Vocabulary

Write the vocabulary word that fits in each of the sentences below.

beauty creeps furniture palace pure visitors

1. The cat __creeps__ quietly toward the old sock. Does the cat think the sock is a mouse?
2. Everyone was surprised when the king and queen sold the royal __palace__. A week after that, they moved into a two-bedroom apartment.
3. My next-door neighbor had many friends. She always welcomed __visitors__ into her home.
4. Mary bought the brown table. She thought it would look good with her other __furniture__.
5. This water is very clean and __pure__. It comes from a spring in the mountains.
6. The ugly duckling did not know that one day it would be a bird of great __beauty__.

104 At Home: Have students write a story about a visit to an abandoned castle using the vocabulary words. Book 3.1/Unit 3 A Very Cool Place to Visit 6

Take-Home Story 104a
Reteach 104
Practice 104 • Extend 104

Guided Instruction

Preview and Predict

Have students preview the article by skimming it, looking at the pictures, and reading the captions.

- What is this article mainly about?
- Where do the events it describes take place?
- Is it nonfiction or a fantasy? How can you tell? (Nonfiction; it is illustrated by photographs.) ***Genre***

Have students record their predictions about the selection.

Set Purposes

What do students want to find out by reading the selection? For example:

- Why would anyone want to stay in a hotel made of ice?
- What experiment can you do with an ice cube?

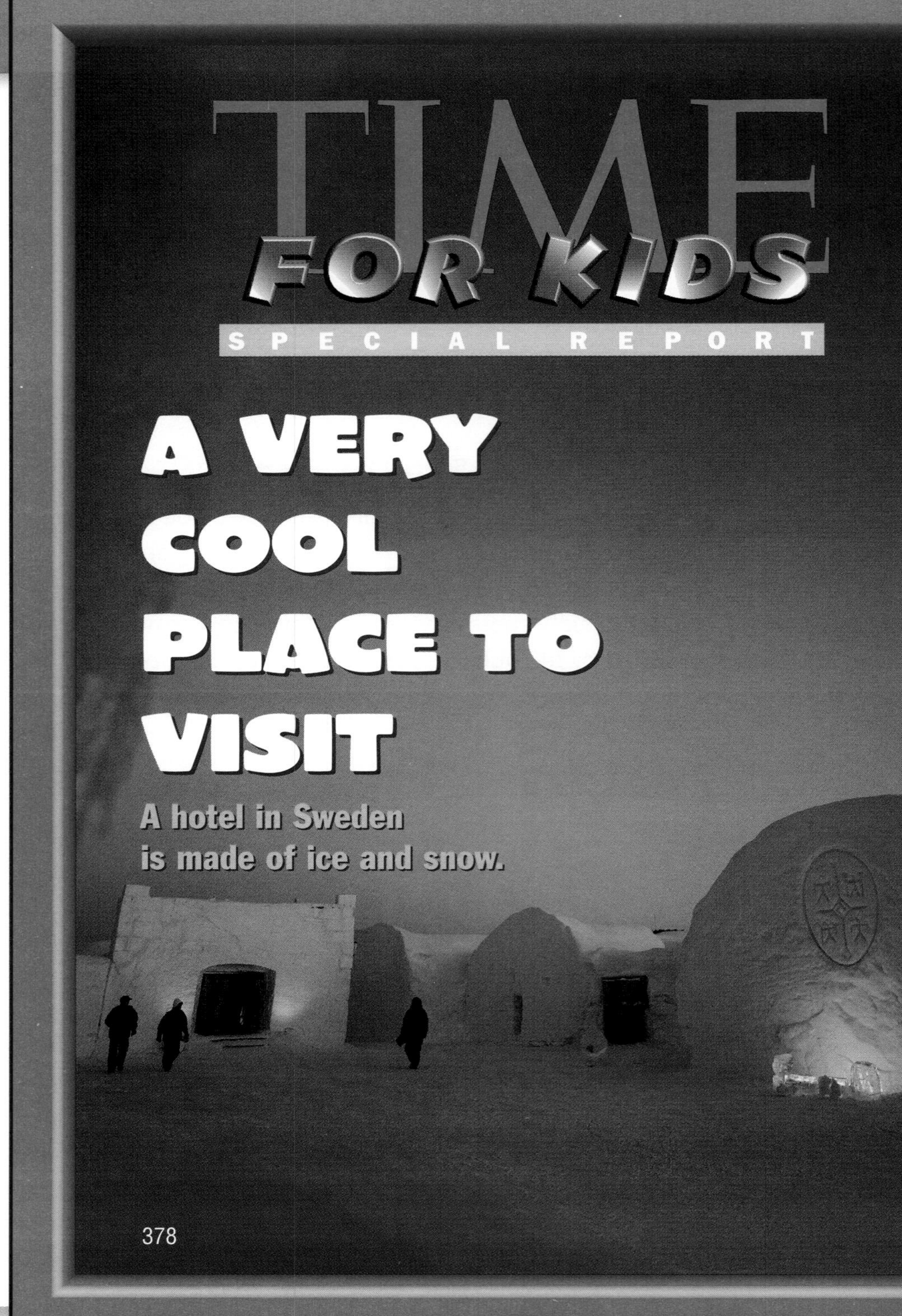

TIME FOR KIDS
SPECIAL REPORT
A VERY COOL PLACE TO VISIT
A hotel in Sweden is made of ice and snow.
378

Meeting Individual Needs • Grouping Suggestions for Strategic Reading

EASY	ON-LEVEL	CHALLENGE
Read Together Read the article with students or have them use the **Listening Library Audiocassette.** Have students use the Main Ideas and Supporting Details chart to organize the information in the story. Guided Instruction and Intervention prompts offer additional help with decoding, vocabulary, and comprehension.	**Guided Reading** Display the story words listed on page 379. Choose from the Guided Instruction questions as you read the article with students or after they have played the **Listening Library Audiocassette.** Have them use the Main Idea and Supporting Details chart to record meaningful information during reading.	**Read Independently** Remind students that being able to identify main ideas and supporting details will help them understand the information given in the article. Have students set up a Main Idea and Supporting Details chart as on page 379. After reading they can use their charts to summarize facts about *A Very Cool Place to Visit*.

TIME FOR KIDS

Chill Out!

Sometimes on a winter night, the cold creeps in. It creeps under wool blankets. It creeps into the warmest pajamas. It creeps inside the heaviest socks. *Brrr!* It finds a set of toes to nip.

At one hotel in Sweden, the cold doesn't have to sneak in. Guests *know* it will nip at their toes, fingers, and noses. Welcome to the Ice Hotel! The building and some of the furniture are made of ice and snow.

Why would anyone spend money to stay in a hotel like this? Kerstin Nilsson, who works there, says people love the beauty of the place. "It is pure winter—white and fresh snow." And she says there are "beautiful northern lights in the sky." It is also very quiet.

Guests sleep on beds made of ice and covered with reindeer skins.

A reindeer greets visitors as they arrive at the hotel.

379

Guided Instruction

- Main Idea
- Make Inferences

Strategic Reading Looking for the main idea and supporting details can help you understand an article better. As we read, we will make a Main Idea and Supporting Details chart.

1 MAIN IDEA What is the main idea of this article and how can you tell? (The main idea is that a hotel made of ice exists in Sweden. I know this because all the other information explains this statement.)

2 MAKE INFERENCES How can the guests be sure that Sweden's Ice Hotel won't melt? (The temperature in that part of Sweden must stay below freezing all winter. No one would ask guests to stay there if the ice were likely to melt.)

Story Words

The words below may be unfamiliar. Have students check the meanings and pronunciations of each word in the Glossary on page 388.

- Kerstin Nilsson, p. 379
- northern lights, p. 379
- Sweden, p. 379
- Johan Woutilainen, p. 380

LANGUAGE SUPPORT

This chart is available as a blackline master in the **Language Support Book.**

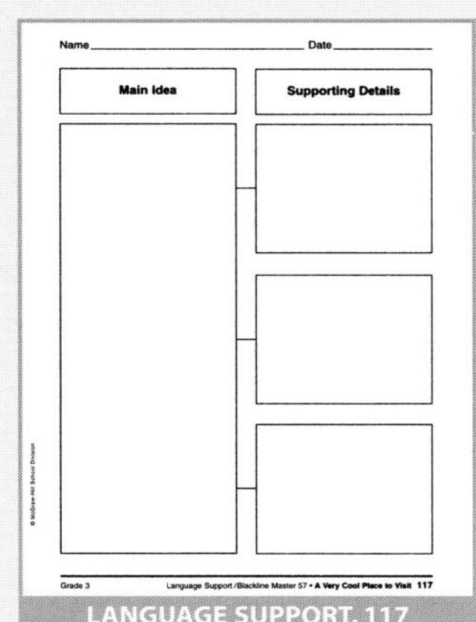

Name ____________ Date ________

Main Idea	Supporting Details

LANGUAGE SUPPORT, 117

Guided Instruction

3 MAKE INFERENCES Why should guests at the Ice Hotel do push-ups before they go to bed? (The hotel is not heated; exercise makes you warm.)

4 MAIN IDEA Let's use the Main Idea and Supporting Details chart to organize information about the Ice Hotel.

MAIN IDEA	SUPPORTING DETAILS
People visit the Ice Hotel to experience Sweden in the winter.	The white, fresh snow around the hotel is beautiful.
	The hotel is located so far north that guests can see the northern lights.
	Guests of the hotel pride themselves on having experienced something unusual.

ORGANIZE INFORMATION Ask volunteers to use their Main Idea and Supporting Details charts to organize the rest of the information in this article. Then have them write an outline of the article. *Summarize*

KAREN SU/CORBIS

This isn't an ice hotel. It's an ice palace! It was built for a winter carnival in Harbin, China.

Each guest gets an extra-warm snowsuit and a sleeping bag for the night. Guests need all the warm things they can get. The hotel's 100 beds are made from ice blocks covered with reindeer skins.

You have to warm yourself up before you get into bed. "Do some push-ups at bedtime," says Johan Woutilainen, a hotel worker. Once inside their sleeping bags, guests stay warm through the night. **3**

FIND OUT MORE
Visit our website:
www.mhschool.com/reading

interNET CONNECTION

380

REREADING FOR *Fluency*

PARTNERS Have partners take turns reading the different sections of *Nice Ice Experiment.*

READING RATE You may want to evaluate a student's reading rate. Have the student read aloud from *A Cool Place to Visit* for one minute. Ask the student to place a self-stick note after the last word read. Then count the number of words he or she has read.

Alternatively, you could assess small groups or the whole class together by having students count words and record their own scores.

A Running Record form provided in **Diagnostic/Placement Evaluation** will help you evaluate reading rate(s).

When visitors leave in the morning, they get a special card. It proves they have conquered the cold by staying at the hotel.

Each spring, when the weather warms up, the hotel melts. When winter comes, a new hotel is built from fresh ice and snow. Once again, the Ice Hotel is ready to welcome people into the cold.

NICE ICE EXPERIMENT

Here is a cold experiment you can do even in the middle of summer!

What You Need

- table salt
- an ice cube
- a piece of string

What You Do

1. Place one end of the string on the ice cube.
2. Sprinkle some salt over the string and the cube.
3. Wait a few seconds. Gently lift the string. The cube will come up with it.

Why It Works

Salt warms the ice and makes it melt. When the salt melts away, the ice freezes again.

ILLUSTRATION FOR TIME FOR KIDS BY BOB STAAKE

Based on an article in *TIME FOR KIDS.*

Guided Instruction

Return to Predictions and Purposes

Review with students the predictions they made earlier. Were their predictions correct? Did they find out what they wanted to know?

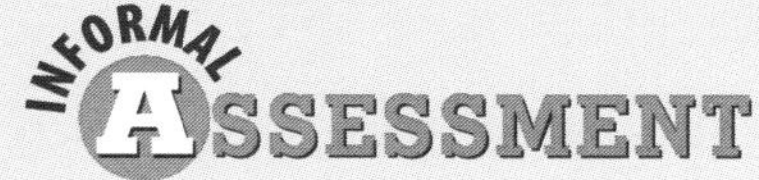

MAIN IDEAS

HOW TO ASSESS
Ask students to identify three supporting details to the main idea of this article—people visit the Ice Hotel to experience Sweden in the winter.

Students should be able to explain how the details support the main idea.

FOLLOW UP If students have trouble identifying three supporting details, have them review their Main Idea and Supporting Details charts.

LITERARY RESPONSE

QUICK-WRITE Invite students to record their thoughts about the selection. This questions may help them get started.

JOURNAL

- Would you accept an invitation to stay at the Ice Hotel?

ORAL RESPONSE Have students share their journal writings and discuss what part of the article they enjoyed most.

RESEARCH AND INQUIRY
Ice sculptures are featured at winter carnivals in many cities around the world. Have students look on the Internet to find and list five such cities.

For more information or activities on this topic go to ***www.mhschool.com/reading***.

Story Questions

Have students discuss or write answers to the questions on page 382.

Answers:

1. They wear snowsuits and use sleeping bags. *Literal/Details*
2. Besides exercising, they might drink something hot. *Inferential/Cause and Effect*
3. To prove that they slept there; only guests of the Ice Hotel can get the cards *Inferential/Make Inferences*
4. An Ice Hotel can be a fun place to visit. *Critical/Summarize*
5. Different: The Ice Hotel is made of ice; Fernando's house was made of adobe. Alike: Both are made of natural materials. *Critical/Reading Across Texts*

Write a Letter For a full lesson on Persuasive Writing see pages 385K–385L.

Story Questions & Activities

1. How do people stay warm when they sleep on beds made of ice?
2. How do you think people might warm up before going to bed?
3. Why do you think visitors get a special card when they leave in the morning? Explain.
4. What is the main idea of this selection?
5. How is the Ice Hotel different from Fernando's house in "The Little Painter of Sabana Grande"? How is it the same?

Write a Letter

Write a letter to your family to persuade them to visit the Ice Hotel for a family vacation. Give reasons why it would be a fun place to visit.

Meeting Individual Needs

EASY

Name________ Date______ **Reteach 104**

Vocabulary

Write the correct words from the list in the sentences.

beauty creeps furniture palace pure visitors

He opens the door and ___creeps___ into the ___palace___. He never imagined that a place could look so wonderful—its ___beauty___ surprises him. All of the ___furniture___ is special; each chair, table, and desk is like a work of art. "Why aren't there any other ___visitors___?" He gets a glass, and pours himself some fresh, ___pure___ water. 6

Story Comprehension **Reteach 105**

Think about what you learned in "A Very Cool Place to Visit." Then complete the summary below.

At the Ice Hotel, th ___building___ and some of the furniture are made of ice and snow. People stay at the hotel because they love the ___beauty___ and quiet there.

Visitors are given extra-warm snowsuits and sleeping bags. They are told to do some ___push-ups___ to warm themselves before going to bed.

When visitors leave the hotel, they get a special ___card___ that says they have stayed there.

104-105 **At Home:** Have students write sentences explaining why they would or would not like to stay at the Ice Hotel. Book 3.1/Unit 3 **A Very Cool Place to Visit** 4

Reteach, 105

ON-LEVEL

Name________ Date______ **Practice 105**

Story Comprehension

Answer the following questions about "A Very Cool Place to Visit."

1. What parts of the hotel are made out of ice and snow? The building and some of the furniture are made out of ice and snow.
2. Why do people want to stay at the hotel? People want to stay there because it's beautiful and quiet.
3. Name two ways that guests stay warm at the Ice Hotel. Answers may vary. Guests use extra-warm clothes and sleeping bags; they exercise before going to bed; they cover their beds with skins.
4. What greets visitors as they arrive at the hotel? A reindeer greets guests.
5. What happens each spring? The hotel melts.

105 **At Home:** Have students imagine that they are visiting the Ice Hotel for a night, and have them write about their experiences. Book 3.1/Unit 3 **A Very Cool Place to Visit** 5

Practice, 105

CHALLENGE

Name________ Date______ **Extend 104**

Vocabulary

beauty creeps furniture palace pure visitors

Write a paragraph about going to visit a castle. Use as many words from the box as you can to describe the people and the things that you see there.

Extend 105

Story Comprehension

Imagine that you are responsible for selling trips to the Ice Hotel. Work in a group to write advertisements and make posters for the Ice Hotel. Include information in your advertisements and posters that will make people want to visit. Write a slogan, or clever saying, about the Ice Hotel that you can use in your ads.

104–105 **At Home:** Have students write a sentence that might describe people who visit the Ice Hotel. Book 3.1/Unit 3 **A Very Cool Place to Visit**

Extend, 105

Design a Sugar Hotel

Make a plan to construct a hotel out of sugar cubes. Then use sugar cubes and glue to build the palace. Compare your plan to the finished hotel. Did you make any changes? Display your plan and the hotel in your classroom.

Make a Poster

At what temperature does water freeze and turn into ice? Make a poster showing water turning into ice. Include a thermometer in your drawing showing the temperature at which water freezes. Write some fun facts about ice on your poster.

Find Out More

At the Ice Hotel, guests are greeted by a reindeer. Find out more about reindeer. What kinds of things do they eat? Where do they live? Make a reindeer fact card and illustrate it.

Story Activities

Design a Sugar Hotel

Materials: sugar cubes and glue

GROUP Ask students to decide in advance how many stories the hotel will be, the size of its rooms, and the position and number of doors and windows.

Make a Poster

Materials: drawing materials, poster board

PARTNERS Remind students to research interesting information about ice. They may also want to illustrate their poster with snowflakes or with pictures of ice palaces and ice sculptures.

Find Out More

RESEARCH AND INQUIRY Before students begin to make their fact cards, ask them to make a list of questions to guide their research. Have them use encyclopedias, nature magazines, books about Sweden, and the Internet.

interNET CONNECTION Go to ***www.mhschool.com/reading*** for more information or activities on the topic.

After page 383, see Selection and Unit Assessment.

Study Skills

GRAPHIC AIDS

Students will use a climate map.

PREPARE Look over the maps with students. Display **Teaching Chart 87.**

TEACH Point out the labels on these maps. Have students identify them as maps that show average temperatures in Sweden for January and July.

PRACTICE Have students answer questions 1–5. Point out "61°F" stands for "61 degrees Fahrenheit." Review the answers with them.
1. average temperature and precipitation
2. July **3.** Temperatures in Sweden may be lowest in January and highest in July.
4. Särna, Lulea, Kiruna **5.** Lulea, Stockholm, Malmö

ASSESS/CLOSE Ask students to use the climate maps to plan a trip to Sweden. Have them tell which month they will go to Sweden and what the weather will be like.

Use a Map

Maps are used to locate places such as countries or cities. They can also show geographical features such as elevation or climate.

CLIMATE OF SWEDEN

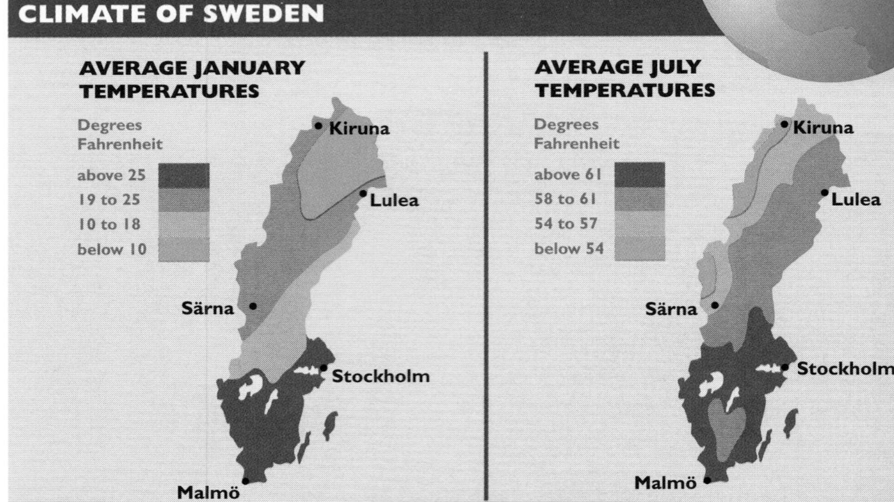

Use the climate map to answer these questions.

1. What kind of information does a climate map give you?
2. If you wanted to visit Stockholm when the temperature was above 61°F, what month would you go?
3. Why do you think the map gives the temperatures for January and July?
4. Which cities have an average January temperature below 25°F?
5. Which cities have an average July temperature above 57°F?

Meeting Individual Needs

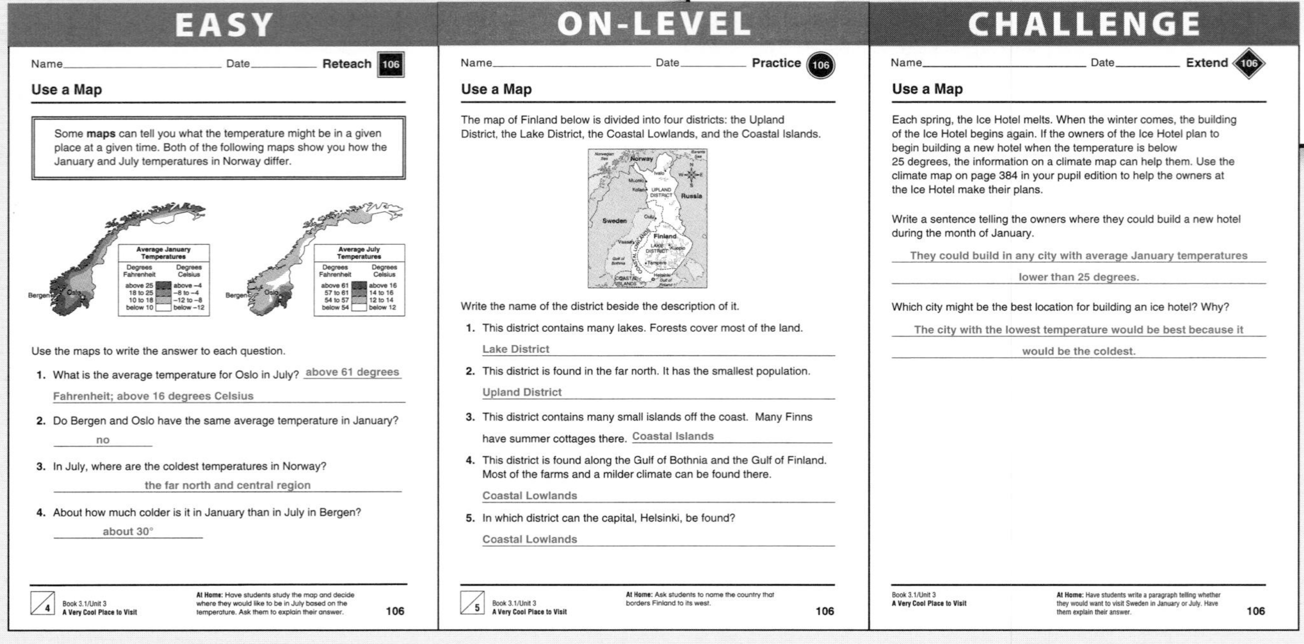

EASY

Name________ Date______ Reteach 106

Use a Map

Some **maps** can tell you what the temperature might be in a given place at a given time. Both of the following maps show you how the January and July temperatures in Norway differ.

Use the maps to write the answer to each question.

1. What is the average temperature for Oslo in July? above 61 degrees Fahrenheit; above 16 degrees Celsius
2. Do Bergen and Oslo have the same average temperature in January? no
3. In July, where are the coldest temperatures in Norway? the far north and central region
4. About how much colder is it in January than in July in Bergen? about 30°

Book 3.1/Unit 3 A Very Cool Place to Visit
At Home: Have students study the map and decide where they would like to be in July based on the temperature. Ask them to explain their answer. 106

ON-LEVEL

Name________ Date______ Practice 106

Use a Map

The map of Finland below is divided into four districts: the Upland District, the Lake District, the Coastal Lowlands, and the Coastal Islands.

Write the name of the district beside the description of it.

1. This district contains many lakes. Forests cover most of the land. Lake District
2. This district is found in the far north. It has the smallest population. Upland District
3. This district contains many small islands off the coast. Many Finns have summer cottages there. Coastal Islands
4. This district is found along the Gulf of Bothnia and the Gulf of Finland. Most of the farms and a milder climate can be found there. Coastal Lowlands
5. In which district can the capital, Helsinki, be found? Coastal Lowlands

Book 3.1/Unit 3 A Very Cool Place to Visit
At Home: Ask students to name the country that borders Finland to its west. 106

CHALLENGE

Name________ Date______ Extend 106

Use a Map

Each spring, the Ice Hotel melts. When the winter comes, the building of the Ice Hotel begins again. If the owners of the Ice Hotel plan to begin building a new hotel when the temperature is below 25 degrees, the information on a climate map can help them. Use the climate map on page 384 in your pupil edition to help the owners at the Ice Hotel make their plans.

Write a sentence telling the owners where they could build a new hotel during the month of January.

They could build in any city with average January temperatures lower than 25 degrees.

Which city might be the best location for building an ice hotel? Why?

The city with the lowest temperature would be best because it would be the coldest.

Book 3.1/Unit 3 A Very Cool Place to Visit
At Home: Have students write a paragraph telling whether they would want to visit Sweden in January or July. Have them explain their answer. 106

Reteach, 106 Practice, 106 Extend, 106

TEST POWER

Test Tip
If you do not understand a question, read it and the answer choices again.

DIRECTIONS:
Read the story. Then read each question about the story.

SAMPLE

An Instrument for Vincent

Vincent had always liked the guitar and he wanted to learn how to play one. His mother was excited that he wanted to learn how to play a musical instrument. She enrolled Vincent in guitar lessons the next day.

A guitar, Vincent learned, has six strings. The strings go from one end of the instrument to the other. The long part of the guitar is called the neck. Vincent could press the strings on the neck to make different sounds. Vincent learned many ways to use his fingers to make different notes.

Vincent practiced a little every day. Soon he was able to play a short song for his mother.

1 This story is mostly about—

- ● learning to play the guitar
- ○ deciding what instrument to play
- ○ how to play the piano
- ○ Vincent's mother taking lessons

2 In this story, enrolled means—

- ● signed up
- ○ gave
- ○ sang
- ○ walked around

385

Test Power

THE PRINCETON REVIEW

Read the Page

Tell students to note the underlined words as they read the story.

Discuss the Questions

QUESTION 1: This question asks students to determine the best summary of the whole story. Have students work through all of the answer choices. As they look at each answer choice, have them be ready to discuss *why* a choice is incorrect even if it is a fact that is stated in the story.

QUESTION 2: This question asks students to define a word in context. Ask students to find the clue that will help them answer this question: What might Vincent do if he wants to learn how to play the guitar? Use process of elimination. Remind students that this is not a test of vocabulary words, but rather a test of their use in context.

ITBS/TEST PREPARATION

TERRANOVA/TEST PREPARATION

SAT 9/TEST PREPARATION

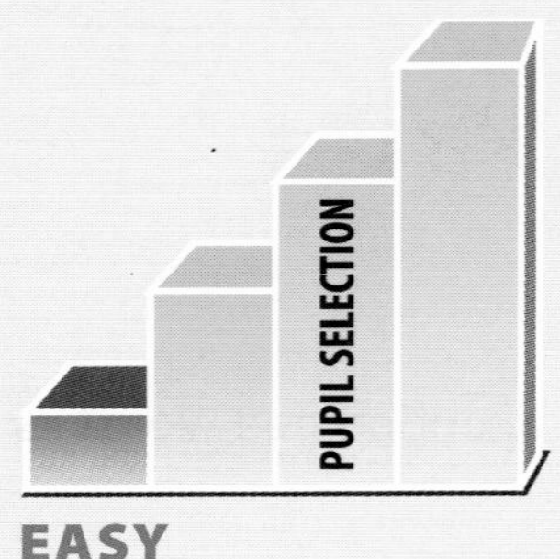

EASY

Self-Selected Reading
Leveled Books

EASY

UNIT SKILLS REVIEW

Phonics

Comprehension

Help students self-select an Easy Book to read and apply phonics and comprehension skills.

Guided Reading

PREVIEW AND PREDICT Discuss the illustrations in the beginning of the book. As you take the **picture walk**, have students predict what the story will be about. List their ideas.

SET PURPOSES Have students write why they want to read the book. Have them share their purposes.

READ THE BOOK Use items like the following to guide students' reading or to discuss after they have read the story independently:

- Reread the story and look for words with consonant clusters, double consonants and the sounds /ou/ and /oi/. Make a list of the words that you find. *Phonics and Decoding*
- How do you think the characters' personalities affected the plot? *Make Inferences*
- Where does the story take place? *Setting*
- Summarize the story by stating its main idea and supporting details. *Main Idea*
- Why might the author have written this story? *Author's Purpose*

RETURN TO PREDICTIONS AND PURPOSES Discuss students' predictions. Ask which were close to the book's contents and why. Have students review their purposes for reading. Did they find out what they wanted to know?

LITERARY RESPONSE Have students discuss questions like the following:

- What problem did the characters in the story face?
- How would you have solved the problem?
- Which movie, television show, or cartoon does this story resemble?

See the Phonics **CD-ROM** for practice using words with consonant clusters, double consonants, /ou/ and /oi/.

Phonics

- consonant clusters
- double consonants
- /ou/ and /oi/

Comprehension

- main idea
- story elements
- make inferences

Answers will vary. Have students cite examples from the story to support their answers.

EASY

Story Questions for Selected Reading

1. How do the characters in this story show their creativity or ingenuity?
2. What is the main idea of this story?
3. Could all the events in this story have really happened?
4. In what ways is their work or art important to the characters in this story?
5. How else might this story have ended?

Make a Poster

Make an illustrated poster that tells what the book is about.

Self-Selected Reading
Leveled Books

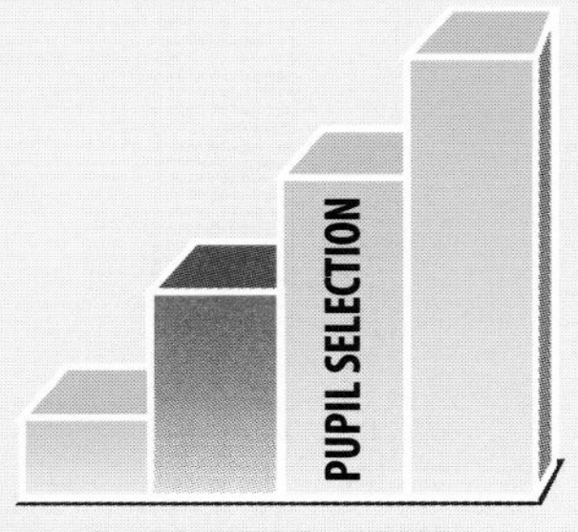

INDEPENDENT

INDEPENDENT

UNIT SKILLS REVIEW

Help students self-select an Independent Book to read and apply comprehension skills.

Guided Reading

PREVIEW AND PREDICT Discuss the illustrations in the beginning of the book. As you take the **picture walk**, have students predict what the story will be about. If the book has chapter headings, ask students to use the headings to predict the kind of information in the book or under each heading. List their ideas.

SET PURPOSES Have students write about why they want to read the book. Have them share their purposes.

READ THE BOOK Use items like the following to guide students' reading or to discuss after they have read the story independently:

- What do you think is the main idea of this story? *Cause and Effect*
- What is one lesson that this story teaches? *Author's Purpose*
- How would you describe the main character of this story? *Character*
- How do you think the main character felt at the beginning of the story? Why? *Make Inferences*
- Write a list of the story's most important events in the order in which they occurred. *Plot*

RETURN TO PREDICTIONS AND PURPOSES Have students review their predictions. Students can talk about whether their purposes were met, and if they have any questions that the story left unanswered.

LITERARY RESPONSE The following questions will help focus students' responses:

- Which character was most unlike the main character? How did these differences affect the plot?
- Which events in the story reminded you of experiences that you have had? Did reading the story change the way you feel about those experiences?
- How did the characters change during the story?

☑ Comprehension

- main idea
- story elements
- make inferences

Answers will vary. Have students cite examples from the story to support their answers.

INDEPENDENT

Story Questions for Selected Reading

1. What is the setting of story?
2. Was the story about events that actually happened?
3. What other stories have you read that express similar ideas?
4. What changes would you like to make in the story?
5. Did the story have a sad or happy ending?

Draw a Picture

Draw a picture of one of the scenes in this story.

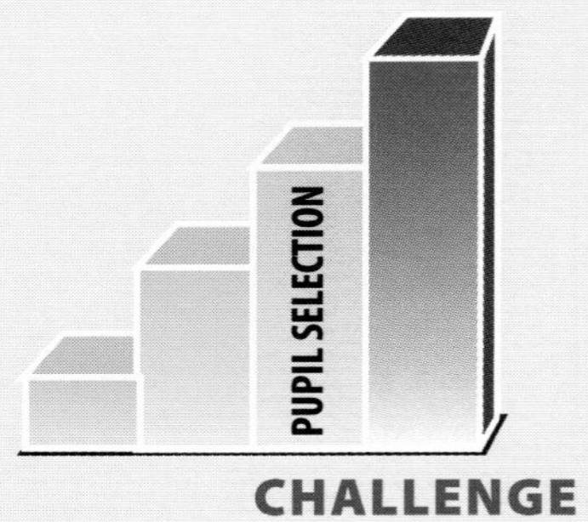

☑ Comprehension

- main idea
- story elements
- make inferences

Answers will vary. Have students cite examples from the story to support their answers.

CHALLENGE

Story Questions for Selected Reading

1. How do family or cultural traditions affect the events in this story?
2. How do the characters in the story change?
3. Does learning about the past help the characters in the story?
4. How was art or a special ability important to the story?
5. What caused the events in this story to happen?

Draw a Setting

Draw a picture showing the setting of the story.

Self-Selected Reading Leveled Books

CHALLENGE

UNIT SKILLS REVIEW

☑ Comprehension

Help students self-select a Challenge Book to read and apply comprehension skills.

Guided Reading

PREVIEW AND PREDICT Discuss the illustrations in the beginning of the book. As you take the **picture walk**, have students predict what the story will be about. If the book has chapter headings, ask students to use them to predict the kind of information in the book or under each heading. List their ideas.

SET PURPOSES Have students write about or draw why they want to read the book. Have them share their purposes.

READ THE BOOK Use items like the following to guide students' reading or to discuss after they have read the story independently:

- What do you think the characters in the story are going to do next? *Make Predictions*
- State the main idea of the story and list the details that support it. *Main Idea*
- Which event came last in the story? *Plot*
- Why do you think the author wrote this book? *Author's Purpose*
- How do you think that learning about the past makes the characters feel about one another? *Make Inferences*

RETURN TO PREDICTIONS AND PURPOSES Discuss students' predictions. Ask which were close to the story and why. If the book had chapter headings were the headings useful? How? Have students review their purposes for reading. Did they find out what they wanted to know?

LITERARY RESPONSE Have students discuss questions like the following:

- Did the story make you want to find out more about your family's past? Why or why not?
- How did the setting affect the characters in the story?
- If you were to meet one of the characters from the story, what would you talk about?

Connecting Texts

CLASS DISCUSSION
Divide the class into groups representing the books in the unit. Have the groups choose a theme to link the different books together in a chart. For example, write these five story titles on a chart with the heading *The Past Comes Alive: Recording the Past, All That Jazz, Aborigines of the Australian Outback, Rosa's New Home, An Ancient Art.* Have students chart the ways in which the characters learn to appreciate the past.

The Past Comes Alive

Recording the Past	All That Jazz	Aborigines of the Australian Outback	Rosa's New Home	An Ancient Art
• the grand-mother's stories	• phonograph records	• practicing ancient customs	• moving to a family home	• learning a traditional art from a family member

Viewing/Representing

GROUP PRESENTATIONS Divide the class into groups representing the five stories in the unit. Each group will be made up of students who have read the same story. Have students create a collage showing the elements of the story that come from the past and elements that come from the present. They might combine photographs, pieces of cloth, drawings, fragments of calligraphy, musical notes, and so on.

AUDIENCE RESPONSE Ask students to look carefully at the collages made by each group. See if students can determine what aspects of past and present are represented by the collages. Allow time for questions after each presentation.

Research and Inquiry

INVESTIGATE Have students further investigate one of the topics featured in the books. Invite students to:

- Make a list of the questions they have about the topic.
- Use reference books, encyclopedias, magazines, newspapers, and interviews with older family members to learn more about the topic.
- Create a report that summarizes their findings.

*inter***NET** **CONNECTION** Have students log on to ***www.mhschool.com/reading*** for links to sites about family traditions.

Students can write and draw what they learned in their journals.

TESTED OBJECTIVES

Students will summarize an article.

TEACHING TIP

INSTRUCTIONAL Ask students to summarize what they learned in their social studies lesson. Encourage them to find the main ideas of the lesson. Then have them restate those ideas in their own words. Help them make an outline of this summary.

Review Summarize

PREPARE

Discuss How to Summarize

Remind students that one way to summarize a piece of writing is to identify the main topic and the most important points, and state it in their own words.

TEACH

Read "Ice Is Nice for Visitors in Sweden" and Model the Skill

Ask students to look for the important information as you read **Teaching Chart 88** with them.

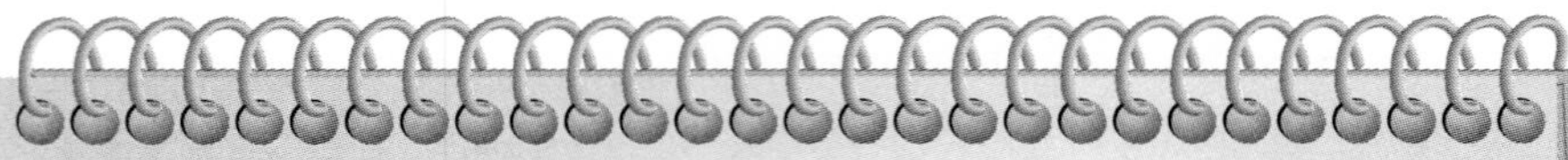

Ice Is Nice for Visitors in Sweden

In Sweden, visitors can top off a day of skating and skiing by checking into the famous Ice Hotel. The hotel and all the beds are carved from ice. Of course, even visitors have to keep warm. So the staff provides snowsuits and extra-warm sleeping bags for them to snuggle in. The staff also encourages guests to do warming exercises before going to bed.

Ice Hotel guests cannot only enjoy the pure snow and spectacular northern lights of the Swedish winter, they can brag of having slept in it.

Teaching Chart 88

MODEL This passage tells about Sweden's Ice Hotel, and how much guests enjoy it. One important point in the article is that the hotel is made from ice. I would make sure to include this information in my summary.

PRACTICE

Identify Important Information to Summarize

Have students circle the topic and underline the important points on the chart. Then have them write a brief summary.
▶ **Linguistic/Logical**

ASSESS/CLOSE

Summarize an Article

Have students choose another article or story they have read recently to summarize. For example, they might choose a story or article from Unit 2.

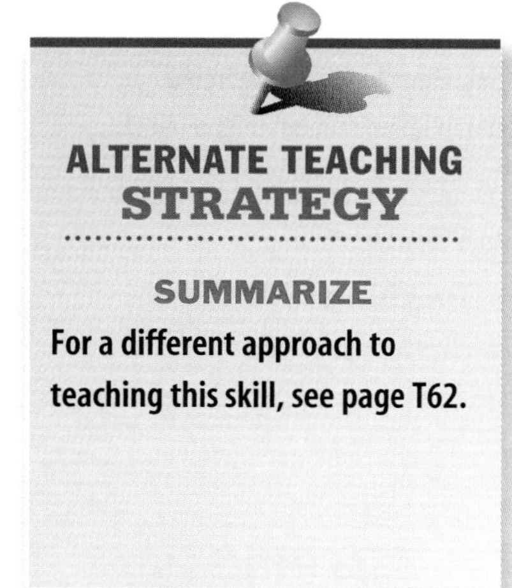

ALTERNATE TEACHING
STRATEGY
SUMMARIZE
For a different approach to teaching this skill, see page T62.

SELF-SELECTED Reading

Students may choose from the following titles.

ANTHOLOGY

- *A Very Cool Place to Visit*

LEVELED BOOKS

All titles for the unit.

Bibliography, pages T76–T77

Meeting Individual Needs for Comprehension

EASY

Name__________ Date______ **Reteach 107**

Summarize

A **summary** tells the important ideas of a selection.

Read the paragraphs about "A Very Cool Place to Visit." Then circle the sentence that best summarizes the paragraphs.

1. At one place in Sweden, the cold comes right in the door. Guests know it will nip at their entire bodies. The place is the Ice Hotel. Here, most of the furniture is made of snow and ice.
   - (a.) It is cold at the Ice Hotel.
   - b. Sometimes your toes, fingers, and nose can get cold.
   - c. Some of the furniture at the Ice Hotel is made out of ice.
2. Why would a person pay money to stay in a place like this? One worker at the hotel says people love the way the hotel looks.
   - a. There are lovely lights in the sky at night.
   - b. The Ice Hotel is in France.
   - (c.) People stay in the Ice Hotel because they love the look of the hotel.
3. When people check out of the hotel in the morning, they get a special card. The note proves that they beat the cold and slept in the hotel.
   - a. Visitors leave the hotel in the morning.
   - b. Some visitors think the hotel is too cold.
   - (c.) When visitors leave, they get a card.
4. Each spring, the weather gets warmer and the hotel melts. When winter comes, a new building is made from fresh ice and snow. And all over again, the Ice Hotel opens its chilly doors to fun-loving guests.
   - (a.) Every year, the hotel melts and a new hotel has to be built.
   - b. The hotel melts each spring.
   - c. People build a new hotel each winter.

107 **At Home:** Have students write a paragraph that summarizes the four paragraphs above. Book 3.1/Unit 3 **A Very Cool Place to Visit** 4

Reteach, 107

ON-LEVEL

Name__________ Date______ **Practice 107**

Summarize

A **summary** tells the main ideas of a story.

Read the paragraphs about "A Very Cool Place to Visit." Then summarize each paragraph in one sentence.

1. At one place in Sweden, the cold is everywhere. Guests feel it in their toes, fingers, and noses. Welcome to the Ice Hotel, where the building and even some of the furniture are made of snow and ice.
   It is very cold at the Ice Hotel.
2. Why would people want to stay in a hotel that was cold and frozen? A worker at the hotel, says people love the hotel for its beauty. "The white fresh snow is pure winter." She also says that people want to see the northern lights.
   People stay at the hotel because it is beautiful.
3. Before you get into bed, you have to warm yourself up. Doing some push-ups at bedtime will help you feel warm even before you get into bed!
   Guests exercise to warm themselves up before bed.
4. In the springtime, when the weather gets warmer, the hotel melts. When winter returns, a new building is built from fresh snow and ice. And once again, the Ice Hotel welcomes everyone into its cold and wintry world.
   Every year, the hotel melts and a new hotel is built.

107 **At Home:** Have students summarize "A Very Cool Place to Visit." Book 3.1/Unit 3 **A Very Cool Place to Visit** 4

Practice, 107

CHALLENGE

Name__________ Date______ **Extend 107**

Summarize

Review "A Very Cool Place to Visit." Write a short summary of the article in the space below. Then use the summary to write a television commercial that you might make telling people what a great place the Ice Hotel is to visit on vacation. Present your commercial to your classmates.

"A Very Cool Place to Visit" tells about __________

107 **At Home:** Have students write a paragraph summarizing a visit they have made or would like to make to a special place. Book 3.1/Unit 3 **A Very Cool Place to Visit**

Extend, 107

LANGUAGE SUPPORT

Name__________ Date______

A Postcard from the Ice Hotel

funiture	blankets	melts	winter
future	bulbs	mess	water

Dear Friends,

I am at the Ice Hotel.
It has f_urnitur_e made from ice.
The beds are made form ice, too.
If you stay in a sleeping bag with lots of bl_anket_s, you will stay warm.
Every summer the hotel m_elt_s when it gets warm.
So, you must stay here in the w_inte_r season.

118 **A Very Cool Place to Visit** • Language Support / Blackline Master 58 Grade 3

Language Support, 118

Students will identify multiple-meaning words.

MATERIALS

- **Teaching Chart 89**
- **dictionary**

TEACHING TIP

INSTRUCTIONAL

Students have learned that homographs have separate dictionary entries. Other words with multiple meanings may have only one entry, but several numbered definitions. Compare *date* and *dash.*

Review Multiple-Meaning Words

PREPARE

Examine a Multiple-Meaning Word

Write *date* on the chalkboard. Ask volunteers if they know two meanings for this word. (a kind of fruit or a day of the month or year) Explain that this is a multiple-meaning word.

TEACH

Read "First Day on the Slopes" and Model the Skill

Ask students to look for multiple-meaning words as you read the passage on **Teaching Chart 89** with students. Remind students that multiple-meaning words may sometimes have two different pronunciations.

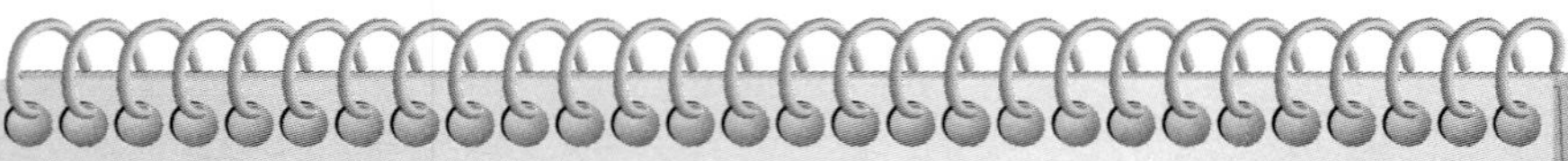

First Day on the Slopes

On Ronnie's first day at the ski resort, he started to trail behind the ski instructor. She told him to ski between a row of flags, but he insisted on going down a steep, unmarked trail.

The trail passed trees with low branches. Skiers had to be careful or they would bump into them. Ronnie forgot to duck. He had a big bump on his forehead. Ronnie wished he had followed the instructor's lead. His legs felt stiff and as heavy as lead. He took off his skis and walked like a duck down the trail.

Teaching Chart 89

Ask volunteers to circle sets of multiple-meaning words. Then model the skill beginning with the word *trail.*

MODEL I see that *trail* is used to refer to both following someone and a path. This must be a multiple-meaning word. It is used first as a verb then as a noun.

PRACTICE

Create a Multiple-Meaning Chart Help students create a Multiple-Meaning chart using the words from **Teaching Chart 89.** ▶ **Visual/Logical**

WORDS	MEANINGS
trail	1. to follow 2. a path
lead	1. example 2. a heavy metal
bump	1. knock out of place 2. swelling on skin
duck	1. lower head 2. swimming bird

ASSESS/CLOSE

Chart the Different Meanings Have students make a Multiple-Meaning chart to show the different meanings of the words below. Encourage students to use a dictionary to define the words.

wind **fine** **rock** **stick**

ALTERNATE TEACHING STRATEGY

MULTIPLE-MEANING WORDS

For a different approach to teaching this skill, see page T65.

Meeting Individual Needs for Vocabulary

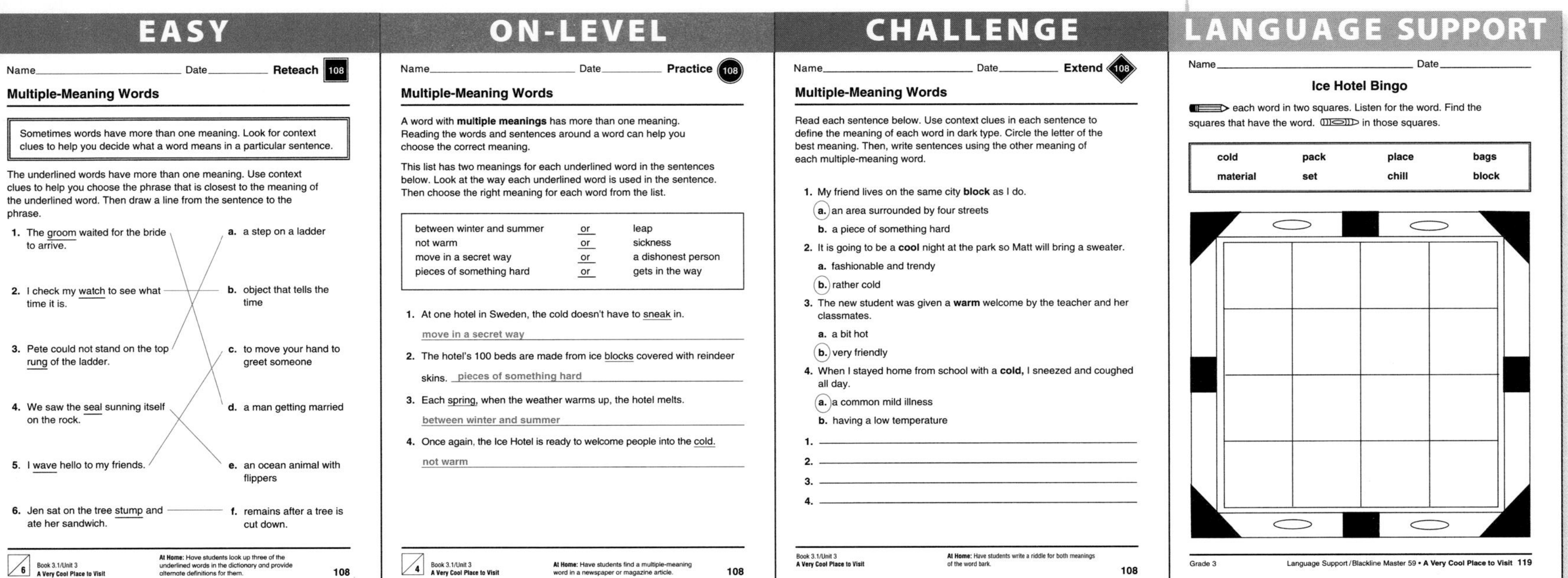

EASY

Name______ Date______ Reteach 108

Multiple-Meaning Words

Sometimes words have more than one meaning. Look for context clues to help you decide what a word means in a particular sentence.

The underlined words have more than one meaning. Use context clues to help you choose the phrase that is closest to the meaning of the underlined word. Then draw a line from the sentence to the phrase.

1. The groom waited for the bride to arrive. — a. a step on a ladder
2. I check my watch to see what time it is. — b. object that tells the time
3. Pete could not stand on the top rung of the ladder. — c. to move your hand to greet someone
4. We saw the seal sunning itself on the rock. — d. a man getting married
5. I wave hello to my friends. — e. an ocean animal with flippers
6. Jen sat on the tree stump and ate her sandwich. — f. remains after a tree is cut down.

6 Book 3.1/Unit 3 A Very Cool Place to Visit — At Home: Have students look up three of the underlined words in the dictionary and provide alternate definitions for them. 108

ON-LEVEL

Name______ Date______ Practice 108

Multiple-Meaning Words

A word with **multiple meanings** has more than one meaning. Reading the words and sentences around a word can help you choose the correct meaning.

This list has two meanings for each underlined word in the sentences below. Look at the way each underlined word is used in the sentence. Then choose the right meaning for each word from the list.

between winter and summer	or	leap
not warm	or	sickness
move in a secret way	or	a dishonest person
pieces of something hard	or	gets in the way

1. At one hotel in Sweden, the cold doesn't have to sneak in. move in a secret way
2. The hotel's 100 beds are made from ice blocks covered with reindeer skins. pieces of something hard
3. Each spring, when the weather warms up, the hotel melts. between winter and summer
4. Once again, the Ice Hotel is ready to welcome people into the cold. not warm

4 Book 3.1/Unit 3 A Very Cool Place to Visit — At Home: Have students find a multiple-meaning word in a newspaper or magazine article. 108

CHALLENGE

Name______ Date______ Extend 108

Multiple-Meaning Words

Read each sentence below. Use context clues in each sentence to define the meaning of each word in dark type. Circle the letter of the best meaning. Then, write sentences using the other meaning of each multiple-meaning word.

1. My friend lives on the same city **block** as I do.
   a. an area surrounded by four streets
   b. a piece of something hard
2. It is going to be a **cool** night at the park so Matt will bring a sweater.
   a. fashionable and trendy
   b. rather cold
3. The new student was given a **warm** welcome by the teacher and her classmates.
   a. a bit hot
   b. very friendly
4. When I stayed home from school with a **cold,** I sneezed and coughed all day.
   a. a common mild illness
   b. having a low temperature

1. ______
2. ______
3. ______
4. ______

Book 3.1/Unit 3 A Very Cool Place to Visit — At Home: Have students write a riddle for both meanings of the word bark. 108

LANGUAGE SUPPORT

Name______ Date______

Ice Hotel Bingo

each word in two squares. Listen for the word. Find the squares that have the word. in those squares.

cold	pack	place	bags
material	set	chill	block

Grade 3 Language Support/Blackline Master 59 • A Very Cool Place to Visit 119

Reteach, 108 Practice, 108 Extend, 108 Language Support, 119

Review Context Clues

TESTED OBJECTIVES

Students will:

- recognize that different content areas have specialized vocabularies.
- try to figure out word meaning from context clues.

MATERIALS

- **Teaching Chart 90**

TEACHING TIP

MANAGEMENT Encourage students to talk about their favorite hobby or sport. Point out that they use many words that are special to that activity. Tell them that most content areas have such words.

PREPARE

Discuss Specialized Vocabularies Explain that specialized vocabulary is often used by people who come from the same region, do the same kind of work, or engage in other organized activities.

TEACH

Read the Passage and Model the Skill Ask students to note the words for cold-weather equipment that they do not understand as you read the passage on **Teaching Chart 90**.

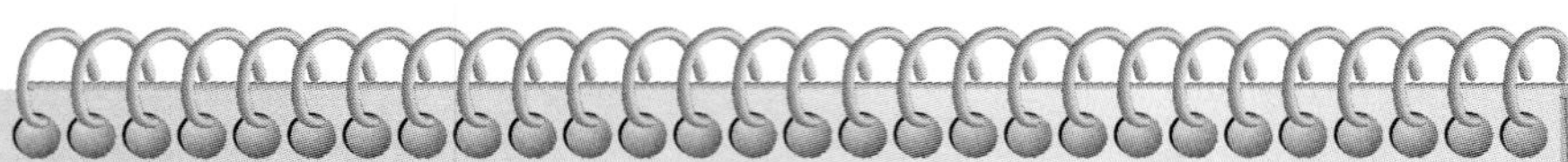

Cold Weather Equipment

Guests of the Ice Hotel wear snowsuits and sleep in sleeping bags in order to stay warm in the winter night. The Inuits wear anoraks and mukluks in the bitter Arctic cold. Anoraks, made of caribou skin, keep the upper body warm and allow freedom of movement for activities. Mukluks keep the feet warm. Their sealskin soles cannot be cut easily by sharp pieces of ice.

Teaching Chart 90

MODEL I don't recognize the word *anorak*. But I may be able to figure out what it means if I look at the words around it. I see that it is something that covers the upper body. It may be a jacket.

PRACTICE

Use Context Clues

Have volunteers circle words that name cold-weather equipment and underline clues that point to their meaning. ▶ **Kinesthetic/Linguistic**

ASSESS/CLOSE

Write Context Sentences for Specialized Words

Encourage students to choose a favorite sport or hobby. Have them write a list of words special to the activity. Ask them to write sentences that explain the meaning of three of the special words. Then have them exchange sentences with a classmate, and see if the classmate can understand the words' meanings.

ALTERNATE TEACHING STRATEGY

CONTEXT CLUES

For a different approach to teaching this skill, see page T63.

Meeting Individual Needs for Vocabulary

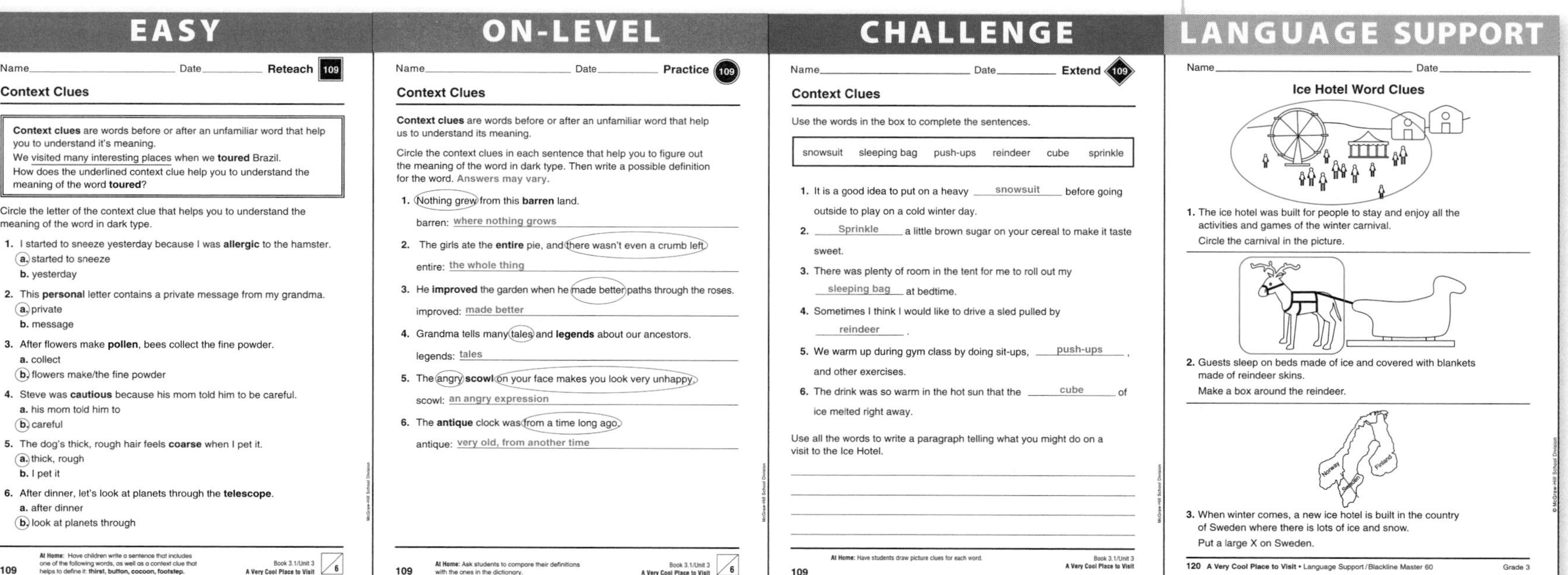

EASY

Name__________ Date__________ Reteach 109

Context Clues

Context clues are words before or after an unfamiliar word that help you to understand it's meaning.
We visited many interesting places when we **toured** Brazil.
How does the underlined context clue help you to understand the meaning of the word **toured**?

Circle the letter of the context clue that helps you to understand the meaning of the word in dark type.

1. I started to sneeze yesterday because I was **allergic** to the hamster.
   a. started to sneeze
   b. yesterday
2. This **personal** letter contains a private message from my grandma.
   a. private
   b. message
3. After flowers make **pollen**, bees collect the fine powder.
   a. collect
   b. flowers make/the fine powder
4. Steve was **cautious** because his mom told him to be careful.
   a. his mom told him to
   b. careful
5. The dog's thick, rough hair feels **coarse** when I pet it.
   a. thick, rough
   b. I pet it
6. After dinner, let's look at planets through the **telescope**.
   a. after dinner
   b. look at planets through

At Home: Have children write a sentence that includes one of the following words, as well as a context clue that helps to define it: **thirst, button, cocoon, footstep.**

109 Book 3.1/Unit 3 A Very Cool Place to Visit 6

ON-LEVEL

Name__________ Date__________ Practice 109

Context Clues

Context clues are words before or after an unfamiliar word that help us to understand its meaning.

Circle the context clues in each sentence that help you to figure out the meaning of the word in dark type. Then write a possible definition for the word. Answers may vary.

1. Nothing grew from this **barren** land.
   barren: where nothing grows
2. The girls ate the **entire** pie, and there wasn't even a crumb left.
   entire: the whole thing
3. He **improved** the garden when he made better paths through the roses.
   improved: made better
4. Grandma tells many tales and **legends** about our ancestors.
   legends: tales
5. The angry **scowl** on your face makes you look very unhappy.
   scowl: an angry expression
6. The **antique** clock was from a time long ago.
   antique: very old, from another time

At Home: Ask students to compare their definitions with the ones in the dictionary.

109 Book 3.1/Unit 3 A Very Cool Place to Visit 6

CHALLENGE

Name__________ Date__________ Extend 109

Context Clues

Use the words in the box to complete the sentences.

snowsuit	sleeping bag	push-ups	reindeer	cube	sprinkle

1. It is a good idea to put on a heavy snowsuit before going outside to play on a cold winter day.
2. Sprinkle a little brown sugar on your cereal to make it taste sweet.
3. There was plenty of room in the tent for me to roll out my sleeping bag at bedtime.
4. Sometimes I think I would like to drive a sled pulled by reindeer.
5. We warm up during gym class by doing sit-ups, push-ups, and other exercises.
6. The drink was so warm in the hot sun that the cube of ice melted right away.

Use all the words to write a paragraph telling what you might do on a visit to the Ice Hotel.

At Home: Have students draw picture clues for each word.

109 Book 3.1/Unit 3 A Very Cool Place to Visit

LANGUAGE SUPPORT

Name__________ Date__________

Ice Hotel Word Clues

1. The ice hotel was built for people to stay and enjoy all the activities and games of the winter carnival.
   Circle the carnival in the picture.
2. Guests sleep on beds made of ice and covered with blankets made of reindeer skins.
   Make a box around the reindeer.
3. When winter comes, a new ice hotel is built in the country of Sweden where there is lots of ice and snow.
   Put a large X on Sweden.

120 A Very Cool Place to Visit • Language Support/Blackline Master 60 Grade 3

Reteach, 109

Practice, 109

Extend, 109

Language Support, 120

GRAMMAR/SPELLING CONNECTIONS

See the 5-Day Grammar and Usage Plan on Sentence Combining with Verbs, pages 385M–385N.

See the 5-Day Spelling Plan on pages 385O–385P.

TECHNOLOGY TIP

Many word processing programs allow you to set margins so that the first line of a paragraph indents automatically. Help students to use this feature.

Persuasive Writing

Prewrite

WRITE A LETTER Present this writing assignment: Write a letter to your family to persuade them to visit the Ice Hotel for a family vacation. Give three good reasons why it would be a fun place to visit.

DISCUSS THE TOPIC Have students discuss the article *A Very Cool Place to Visit*. Have them use their own words to tell why staying in such a place would be fun. Ask them what a visit to the Ice Hotel has in common with a camping trip.

Strategy: Make a Chart Have students make a chart outlining their own reasons for wanting to visit the Ice Hotel. Encourage them to explore imaginative and original ideas for what they would do in a place like that.

Draft

FREE WRITE Guide students to use their creativity as a basis for drafting. Invite them to enhance their reasons by describing activities that will make their vacation proposal attractive to their own families.

Revise

SELF-QUESTIONING Have students ask themselves the following questions:

- Have I described the Ice Hotel vividly?
- Have I listed at least three reasons to visit that will appeal to my family?

Have students trade letters with a peer and ask for suggestions.

Edit/Proofread

CHECK FOR ERRORS Students should check spelling, grammar, and punctuation.

Publish

DELIVER THE LETTERS Have students give the letters to their families. Have them report their families' reactions.

September 14, 20–

Dear Dad, Mom, and Molly,

I read about a really cool place to visit. It is the Ice Hotel in Sweden. It is made of ice! The ice melts in summer so you have to go in winter.

Mom and Dad, I know you like to camp out. Sleeping in beds of ice would be like camping in the snow! Molly, you love animals. At the Ice Hotel, they have a reindeer in the lobby! We all like to watch sunsets. In Sweden, it's very dark during the winter. But the night sky is lit up by the northern lights.

I would like to go to the Ice Hotel. How about you?

Love,

Mattie

Presentation Ideas

DESIGN ICE SCULPTURES Have students sculpt or draw designs for their own ice palace or ice sculpture garden.
▶ **Viewing/Representing**

PERSUASIVE SPEAKING Have students prepare and perform commercials for the Ice Hotel. Videotape or make audiocassettes of the commercials, if possible.
▶ **Speaking/Listening**

Consider students' creative efforts, possibly adding a plus (+) for originality, wit, and imagination.

Scoring Rubric

Excellent	Good	Fair	Unsatisfactory
4: The writer • makes an imaginative proposal. • uses descriptive and original ideas to make the proposal attractive. • gives three reasons to visit the hotel designed to appeal to the family.	**3:** The writer • presents a well-thought-out proposal. • keeps to the letter form and organizes ideas well. • attempts to explore reasons that make the proposal attractive to his/her family.	**2:** The writer • attempts to promote a family trip. • may show some gaps in letter form. • may have trouble organizing or clearly stating reasons. • may not clearly relate the idea for the trip to family preferences.	**1:** The writer • may not grasp the task to propose a family visit. • may not use letter form or organize text. • may present vague or disconnected descriptions without an intent to persuade.

0: The writer leaves the page blank or fails to respond to the writing task. The student does not address the topic or simply paraphrases the prompt. The response is illegible or incoherent.

Meeting Individual Needs for Writing

EASY

Winter Skies Have students make posters illustrating winter skies and the northern lights. Have them show and label at least one constellation. They can use black paper with bright-colored chalk.

ON-LEVEL

Cool Recreation Have students write a story about a favorite winter activity. Ask them to explore vocabulary that will bring the activity to life and make others want to try it.

CHALLENGE

Hot Spots Have students research and write about a place in another country where people might go to warm up after a visit to the Ice Hotel. They should choose a place that is sunny and hot and unique in a different way. They can illustrate their report with photographs or drawings.

COMMUNICATION TIPS

REPRESENTING If students need models, show them photos of ice sculptures from Quebec City, Canada, and Harbin, China.

SPEAKING Pairs of students can take turns rehearsing their commercials and giving each other feedback.

LANGUAGE SUPPORT

ESL Ask ESL students to share the first drafts of their letters with an English-fluent student. Suggest that they work together to make sure each idea is expressed as simply and clearly as possible.

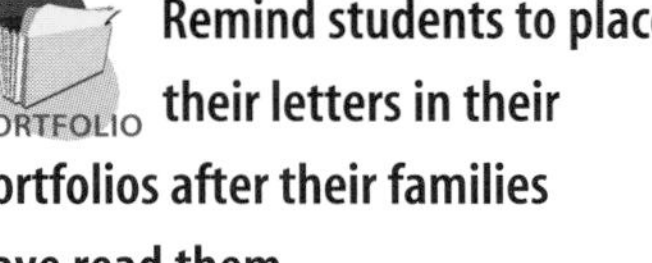

Remind students to place their letters in their portfolios after their families have read them.

5 Day Grammar and Usage Plan

LANGUAGE SUPPORT

Write on the chalkboard: *I run. I climb.* Model how to combine the sentences, and ask students to combine their own sentences.

DAILY LANGUAGE ACTIVITIES

Write each day's activities on the board, or use **Transparency 15.** Students combine sentences orally. Answers given for Day 1; remaining answers follow same pattern.

Day 1

1. The ice melts. The ice freezes. The ice melts and freezes.
2. The snow falls. The snow drifts quietly. The snow falls and drifts quietly.
3. The wind howls. The wind blows. The wind blows and howls.

Day 2

1. People visit. People leave the hotel.
2. Cold air creeps into the rooms. Cold air sneaks into the rooms.
3. A reindeer meets the visitors. A reindeer greets the visitors.

Day 3

1. People exercise. People do push-ups.
2. Workers help. Workers give advice.
3. Children skate. Children slide on the ice.

Day 4

1. Visitors sleep. Visitors stay warm.
2. Stars twinkle. Stars glow in the sky.
3. The beds are made of ice. The beds are covered with reindeer skins.

Day 5

1. The ice melts. The ice forms a pond.
2. Tom fell on the ice. Tom broke his wrist.
3. The fire crackles. The fire pops.

Daily Language Transparency 15

DAY 1 Introduce the Concept

Oral Warm-Up Read these sentences aloud: *The girl skipped. The girl hopped.* Ask students which words are the same in both sentences, and how the sentences might be combined.

Introduce Sentence Combining with Verbs Remind students that two sentences with words in common can often be combined into one. Present:

> **Sentence Combining with Verbs**
>
> Two sentences can be combined by joining the predicates with *and*.

Present the Daily Language Activity and have students combine each pair of sentences. Then have students complete these sentences with verbs: I _______. I _______. Have them combine the sentences using *and*. Example: *I run and jump.*

Assign the daily Writing Prompt on page 376C.

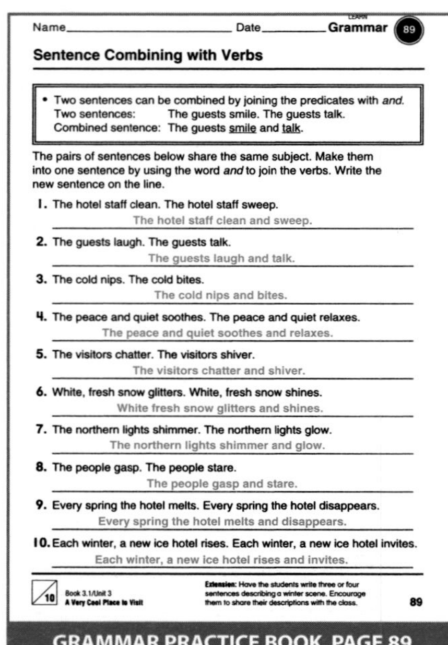

Name__________ Date________ LEARN Grammar 89

Sentence Combining with Verbs

- Two sentences can be combined by joining the predicates with *and*.
  Two sentences: The guests smile. The guests talk.
  Combined sentence: The guests smile and talk.

The pairs of sentences below share the same subject. Make them into one sentence by using the word *and* to join the verbs. Write the new sentence on the line.

1. The hotel staff clean. The hotel staff sweep.
   The hotel staff clean and sweep.
2. The guests laugh. The guests talk.
   The guests laugh and talk.
3. The cold nips. The cold bites.
   The cold nips and bites.
4. The peace and quiet soothes. The peace and quiet relaxes.
   The peace and quiet soothes and relaxes.
5. The visitors chatter. The visitors shiver.
   The visitors chatter and shiver.
6. White, fresh snow glitters. White, fresh snow shines.
   White fresh snow glitters and shines.
7. The northern lights shimmer. The northern lights glow.
   The northern lights shimmer and glow.
8. The people gasp. The people stare.
   The people gasp and stare.
9. Every spring the hotel melts. Every spring the hotel disappears.
   Every spring the hotel melts and disappears.
10. Each winter, a new ice hotel rises. Each winter, a new ice hotel invites.
    Each winter, a new ice hotel rises and invites.

10 Book 3.1/Unit 3 A Very Cool Place to Visit

Extension: Have the students write three or four sentences describing a winter scene. Encourage them to share their descriptions with the class. 89

GRAMMAR PRACTICE BOOK, PAGE 89

DAY 2 Teach the Concept

Review Sentence Combining with Verbs Ask students how two sentences with the same subject can be combined, and what word is used to join them. Review the rule from Day 1. Then have students combine the following sentences: *The dog barked loudly. The dog leaped at the cat.* (The dog barked loudly and leaped at the cat.)

Present the Daily Language Activity. Then have students make up additional sentences about the dog using the model given.

Assign the daily Writing Prompt on page 376C.

Name__________ Date________ LEARN AND PRACTICE Grammar 90

Sentence Combining with Verbs

- Two sentences can be combined by joining the predicates with *and*.
  Two sentences: Guests wear snowsuits. Guests use sleeping bags.
  Combined sentence: Guests wear snowsuits and use sleeping bags.

Underline the predicate in each pair of sentences. Then combine the two sentences and write your one sentence on the line.

1. Guests visit Sweden. Guests stay at the Ice Hotel.
   Guests visit Sweden and stay at the Ice Hotel.
2. Johan helps the guests. Johan advises them.
   Johan helps the guests and advises them.
3. People love the beauty. People enjoy the quiet.
   People love the beauty and enjoy the quiet.
4. The northern lights astonish them. The northern lights delight them.
   The northern lights astonish and delight them.
5. Kerstin works at the hotel. Kerstin waits on the guests.
   Kerstin works at the hotel and waits on the guests.
6. Guests need snowsuits. Guests sleep on ice beds.
   Guests need snowsuits and sleep on ice beds.
7. Visitors conquer the cold. Visitors receive a special card.
   Visitors conquer the cold and receive a special card.
8. The ice melts from the salt. The ice freezes around the string.
   The ice melts from the salt and freezes around the string.

90 **Extension:** Have students work with partners. Each student writes pairs of sentences that have the same subject. The partners then join each other's sentences using *and*.

Book 3.1/Unit 3 A Very Cool Place to Visit 8

GRAMMAR PRACTICE BOOK, PAGE 90

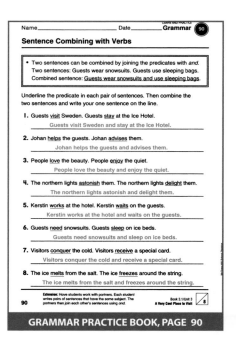

Sentence Combining with Verbs

DAY 3 Review and Practice

Learn from the Literature Review combining sentences with verbs. Read the next-to-last sentence in the box on page 381 of *A Very Cool Place to Visit.*

Salt warms the ice and makes it melt.

Ask students to identify the predicates and the word that joins them together.

Combine Sentences Present the Daily Language Activity. Then, have students brainstorm about things people can do in the snow. Ask students to write pairs of sentences with the same subject about the topic. For example, *Sam packs the snow. Sam builds a fort. Sarah pulls her sleigh up the hill. Sarah glides swiftly down.* Then have students exchange papers with a partner, who combines the sentences. Invite volunteers to share their combined sentences aloud.

Assign the daily Writing Prompt on page 376D.

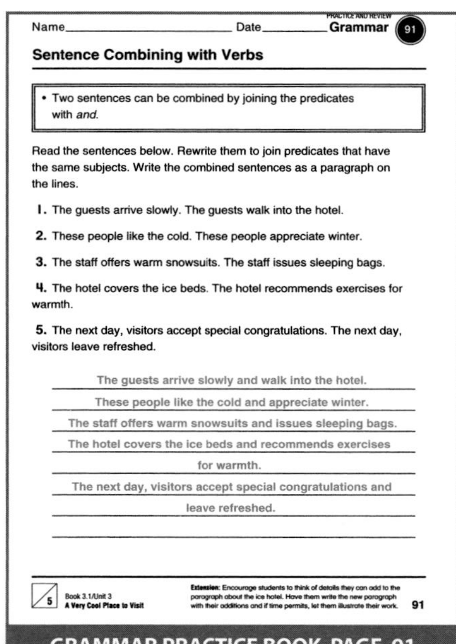

Name________ Date________ PRACTICE AND REVIEW Grammar 91

Sentence Combining with Verbs

- Two sentences can be combined by joining the predicates with *and.*

Read the sentences below. Rewrite them to join predicates that have the same subjects. Write the combined sentences as a paragraph on the lines.

1. The guests arrive slowly. The guests walk into the hotel.
2. These people like the cold. These people appreciate winter.
3. The staff offers warm snowsuits. The staff issues sleeping bags.
4. The hotel covers the ice beds. The hotel recommends exercises for warmth.
5. The next day, visitors accept special congratulations. The next day, visitors leave refreshed.

The guests arrive slowly and walk into the hotel. These people like the cold and appreciate winter. The staff offers warm snowsuits and issues sleeping bags. The hotel covers the ice beds and recommends exercises for warmth. The next day, visitors accept special congratulations and leave refreshed.

5 Book 3.1/Unit 3 A Very Cool Place to Visit

Extension: Encourage students to think of details they can add to the paragraph about the ice hotel. Have them write the new paragraph with their additions and if time permits, let them illustrate their work. 91

GRAMMAR PRACTICE BOOK, PAGE 91

DAY 4 Review and Practice

Review Sentence Combining with Verbs Ask students to list the verbs from the Daily Language Activity for Day 3, and then use them in new sentences with compound predicates. Introduce the Daily Language Activity for Day 4.

Mechanics and Usage Before students begin the daily Writing Prompt on page 376D, review the following:

Sentence Punctuation

- Every sentence begins with a capital letter.
- Statements and commands end with a period.
- A question ends with a question mark.
- An exclamation ends with an exclamation point.

Assign the daily Writing Prompt on page 376D.

Name________ Date________ MECHANICS Grammar 92

Correcting Sentences

- Every sentence beings with a capital letter.
- A statement ends with a period.
- A question ends with a question mark.
- A command ends with a period.
- An exclamation ends with an exclamation point.

Correct each sentence. Write the capital letter over the small letter. Add the end mark.

1. T the hotel is made of ice and snow.
2. T the hotel is a very cold place.
3. C can you imagine sleeping on ice?
4. C can you imagine how strange that is?
5. H how chilly it is!
6. H how quiet it is!
7. P place one end of the string on the ice cube.
8. S sprinkle salt on the ice cube and string.

Combine the predicates of two pairs of sentences above. Write them on the lines.

9. ________
10. ________

92 **Extension:** Have students in pairs try the "nice ice experiment." Ask them to write one of each kind of sentence—statement, question, command, and exclamation—about the experiment.

Book 3.1/Unit 3 A Very Cool Place to Visit 10

GRAMMAR PRACTICE BOOK, PAGE 92

DAY 5 Assess and Reteach

Assess Use the Daily Language Activity and page 93 of the **Grammar Practice Book** for assessment.

Reteach Review the rule from Day 1 on combining sentences with verbs. Then, have students work in pairs. Each pair should choose an animal and write two sentences describing its behavior. Then, have them combine the predicates to form a new sentence. Ask partners to share their sentences aloud. Example: *Black bears live in caves. Black bears eat insects and berries.* (Black bears live in caves and eat insects and berries.)

Use page 94 of the **Grammar Practice Book** for additional reteaching.

Assign the daily Writing Prompt on page 376D.

Name________ Date________ TEST Grammar 93

Sentence Combining with Verbs

Each pair of sentences below shares a subject. On the line, write the predicate of the first sentence. Then write the word *and* followed by the predicate of the second sentence.

1. The guests danced. The guests sang. danced and sang
2. The night sky sparkled. The night sky shone brightly. sparkled and shone
3. The staff announced dinner. The staff served the guests. announced and served
4. The cold air stung our faces. The cold air frosted our breath. stung and frosted

Join the sentence pairs below into single sentences. Write your answers.

5. A reindeer stands in front. A reindeer greets hotel visitors. A reindeer stands in front and greets hotel visitors.
6. Snow suits prevent chills. Snow suits allow guests to sleep. Snow suits prevent chills and allow guests to sleep.
7. Guests sleep soundly in their sleeping bags. Guests rise early. Guests sleep soundly in their sleeping bags and rise early.
8. The hotel boasts 100 ice beds. The hotel attracts many visitors. The hotel boasts 100 ice beds and attracts many visitors.
9. Winter pleases the guests. Winter makes the ice hotel possible. Winter pleases the guests and makes the ice hotel possible.
10. Warm weather ruins the ice hotel. Warm weather ends the season. Warm weather ruins the ice hotel and ends the season.

10 Book 3.1/Unit 3 A Very Cool Place to Visit 93

GRAMMAR PRACTICE BOOK, PAGE 93

GRAMMAR PRACTICE BOOK, PAGE 94

5 Day Spelling Plan

LANGUAGE SUPPORT

To help students find the number of syllables in a word, have them tap out the number of vowel sounds. Distinguish between vowels, which may be silent, and vowel sounds.

DICTATION SENTENCES

Spelling Words

1. The ice was very hard.
2. The rock was heavy and solid.
3. Hot toast can melt cold butter.
4. Northern weather can be very cold.
5. The heat from the flame made us hot.
6. Water freezes on this lake.
7. It does not matter if we finish.
8. The field had a cover of frost.
9. Every snowflake is white.
10. The creek could thaw if the weather is hot.
11. Arctic rivers are hard as rocks.
12. The woods are dense with trees.
13. It was more than one degree too hot.
14. The breeze made a chill in the room.
15. They live in a small igloo.

Challenge Words

16. A flower is a thing of beauty.
17. A chair is a piece of furniture.
18. The giant house is like a palace.
19. The water from the creek is pure.
20. Many visitors go to the park.

DAY 1 Pretest

Assess Prior Knowledge Use the Dictation Sentences at left and **Spelling Practice Book** page 89 for the pretest. Allow students to correct their own papers. If students have trouble, have partners give each other a midweek test on Day 3. Students who require a modified list may be tested on the first eight words.

Spelling Words		Challenge Words
1. ice	9. snowflake	16. beauty
2. solid	10. thaw	17. furniture
3. **melt**	11. arctic	18. palace
4. **northern**	12. dense	19. pure
5. heat	13. degree	20. visitors
6. **freezes**	14. chill	
7. matter	15. igloo	
8. frost		

*Note: Words in **dark type** are from the story.*

Word Study On page 90 of the **Spelling Practice Book** are word study steps and an at-home activity.

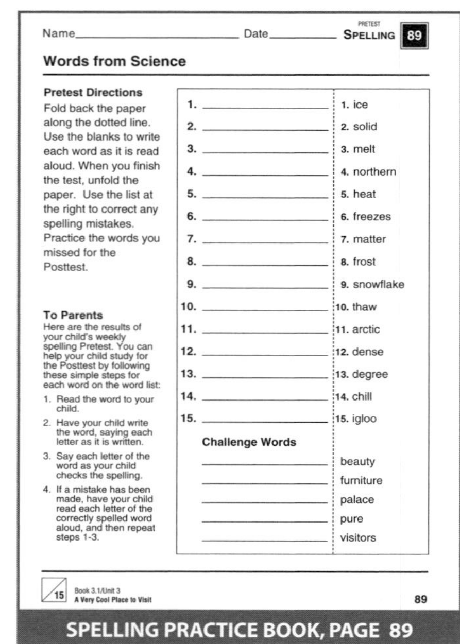

Name________ Date______ PRETEST SPELLING 89

Words from Science

Pretest Directions
Fold back the paper along the dotted line. Use the blanks to write each word as it is read aloud. When you finish the test, unfold the paper. Use the list at the right to correct any spelling mistakes. Practice the words you missed for the Posttest.

To Parents
Here are the results of your child's weekly spelling Pretest. You can help your child study for the Posttest by following these simple steps for each word on the word list:
1. Read the word to your child.
2. Have your child write the word, saying each letter as it is written.
3. Say each letter of the word as your child checks the spelling.
4. If a mistake has been made, have your child read each letter of the correctly spelled word aloud, and then repeat steps 1-3.

1. ____ 1. ice
2. ____ 2. solid
3. ____ 3. melt
4. ____ 4. northern
5. ____ 5. heat
6. ____ 6. freezes
7. ____ 7. matter
8. ____ 8. frost
9. ____ 9. snowflake
10. ____ 10. thaw
11. ____ 11. arctic
12. ____ 12. dense
13. ____ 13. degree
14. ____ 14. chill
15. ____ 15. igloo

Challenge Words
____ beauty
____ furniture
____ palace
____ pure
____ visitors

15 Book 3.1/Unit 3 A Very Cool Place to Visit 89

SPELLING PRACTICE BOOK, PAGE 89

WORD STUDY STEPS AND ACTIVITY, PAGE 90

DAY 2 Explore the Pattern

Sort and Spell Words Say the phrase *ice freezes*. Ask students to listen for the number of vowel sounds in each word. Tell them that *ice* has one syllable, while *freezes* has two.

Ask students to read aloud the 15 Spelling Words and sort them according to the number of syllables.

Words with one syllable	Words with two syllables
ice	solid
melt	northern
heat	freezes
frost	matter
thaw	snowflake
dense	arctic
chill	degree
	igloo

Word Wall Have students look for other one- and two-syllable words from social studies and add them to a classroom word wall.

Name________ Date______ EXPLORE THE PATTERN SPELLING 91

Words from Science

ice	northern	matter	thaw	degree
solid	heat	frost	arctic	chill
melt	freezes	snowflake	dense	igloo

Pattern Power
Write the spelling words that have one syllable.
1. ice 2. melt 3. heat
4. frost 5. thaw 6. dense
7. chill

Write the spelling words that have two syllables.
8. solid 9. northern 10. freezes
11. matter 12. snowflake 13. arctic
14. degree 15. igloo

Rhyme Time
Write a spelling word that rhymes with each of these words.
16. fatter matter 17. claw thaw
18. sense dense 19. lost frost
20. seat heat 21. sneezes freezes

Word Scramble
Unscramble each spelling word.
22. nowesfakl s n o w f l a k e
23. ologi i g l o o
24. edgere d e g r e e
25. iec i c e

25 Book 3.1/Unit 3 A Very Cool Place to Visit 91

SPELLING PRACTICE BOOK, PAGE 91

Words from Science

DAY 3 Practice and Extend

Word Meaning: Analogies Explain to students that analogies are words that are grouped together to show a relationship—*dog* is to *bark* as *cat* is to *meow*. The relationship is sounds made by pets. Have students complete these analogies by filling in the blanks with words from the list.

Solid is to ___ as *liquid* is to *water*. (ice)

Wood is to *house* as *ice* is to ___. (igloo)

Cold is to ___ as ___ is to *southern*. (northern, heat)

Raindrop is to rain as ___ is to snow. (snowflake)

Glossary Ask students to look up Challenge Words in the glossary and divide them into syllables. Have them note which word has only one syllable.

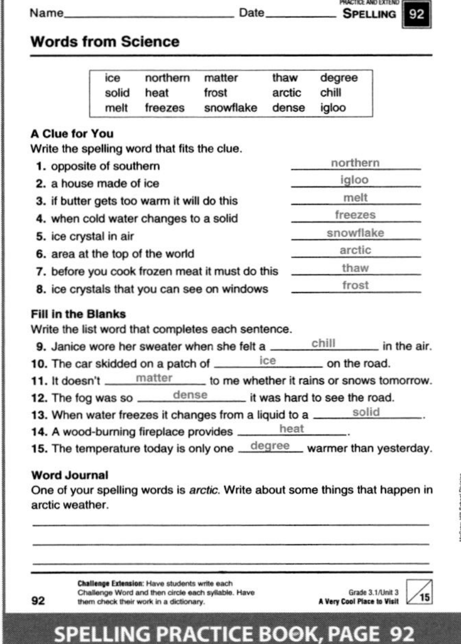

Name________________ Date__________ PRACTICE AND EXTEND **SPELLING 92**

Words from Science

ice	northern	matter	thaw	degree
solid	heat	frost	arctic	chill
melt	freezes	snowflake	dense	igloo

A Clue for You

Write the spelling word that fits the clue.

1. opposite of southern ___northern___
2. a house made of ice ___igloo___
3. if butter gets too warm it will do this ___melt___
4. when cold water changes to a solid ___freezes___
5. ice crystal in air ___snowflake___
6. area at the top of the world ___arctic___
7. before you cook frozen meat it must do this ___thaw___
8. ice crystals that you can see on windows ___frost___

Fill in the Blanks

Write the list word that completes each sentence.

9. Janice wore her sweater when she felt a ___chill___ in the air.
10. The car skidded on a patch of ___ice___ on the road.
11. It doesn't ___matter___ to me whether it rains or snows tomorrow.
12. The fog was so ___dense___ it was hard to see the road.
13. When water freezes it changes from a liquid to a ___solid___.
14. A wood-burning fireplace provides ___heat___.
15. The temperature today is only one ___degree___ warmer than yesterday.

Word Journal

One of your spelling words is *arctic*. Write about some things that happen in arctic weather.

92 **Challenge Extension:** Have students write each Challenge Word and then circle each syllable. Have them check their work in a dictionary. Grade 3.1/Unit 3 **A Very Cool Place to Visit** 15

SPELLING PRACTICE BOOK, PAGE 92

DAY 4 Proofread and Write

Proofread Sentences Write these sentences on the chalkboard, including the misspelled words. Ask students to proofread, circling incorrect spellings and writing the correct spellings. There are two spelling errors in each sentence.

He felt a chil inside the iglue. (chill, igloo)

Ice does not often thauw in the artic. (thaw, arctic)

The northern ice is solit and dence. (solid, dense)

Have students create additional sentences with errors for partners to correct.

WRITING Have students use as many Spelling Words as possible in the daily Writing Prompt on page 376D. Remind students to proofread their writing for errors in spelling, punctuation, and grammar.

Name________________ Date__________ PROOFREAD AND WRITE **SPELLING 93**

Words from Science

Proofreading Paragraph

There are six spelling mistakes in this weather report. Circle the misspelled words. Write the words correctly on the lines below.

In the northarn states, the weather will be quite cold tomorrow. The temperature may even reach one digre below zero. Now that's artic weather! This chill will last for several days. Anyone care to build an iglo?

Now, there's another mattir to report. Our friends down south, of course, have a different weather problem. They are complaining about the hete!

1. ___northern___ 2. ___degree___ 3. ___arctic___
4. ___igloo___ 5. ___matter___ 6. ___heat___

Writing Activity

What questions would you like to ask someone who lives in a very cold climate? Write your interview questions, using at least six spelling words.

12 Book 3.1/Unit 3 **A Very Cool Place to Visit** 93

SPELLING PRACTICE BOOK, PAGE 93

DAY 5 Assess

Assess Students' Knowledge Use page 94 of the **Spelling Practice Book** or the Dictation Sentences on page 385O for the posttest.

Personal Word List If students have trouble with any words in the lesson, have them add the words to their personal list of troublesome words in their journal. They may want to create a category for words from science.

Students should refer to their lists during future writing activities.

Name________________ Date__________ POSTTEST **SPELLING 94**

Words from Science

Look at the words in each set. One word in each set is spelled correctly. Use a pencil to color in the circle in front of that word. Before you begin, look at the sample sets of words. Sample A has been done for you. Do Sample B by yourself. When you are sure you know what to do, you may go on with the rest of the page.

Sample A
(A) spil
● (B) spill
(C) spile
(D) spille

Sample B
(E) sothern
(F) suthern
● (G) southern
(H) southurn

1. (A) taw (B) thawe ● (C) thaw (D) thow
2. (E) chil ● (F) chill (G) chille (H) chell
3. ● (A) heat (B) heet (C) hete (D) heyt
4. (E) eyce (F) ise ● (G) ice (H) iece
5. ● (A) snowflake (B) snoflake (C) snowflace (D) snowfake
6. ● (E) solid (F) solled (G) sullid (H) solide
7. (A) mellt (B) melet (C) mellet ● (D) melt
8. (E) frawst (F) frast (G) forst ● (H) frost
9. (A) dence (B) dens ● (C) dense (D) deanse
10. (E) iglu ● (F) igloo (G) iglue (H) ickloo
11. ● (A) northern (B) nothern (C) northurn (D) norturn
12. ● (E) arctic (F) artic (G) arktic (H) artick
13. (A) freeses (B) freecez (C) freazes ● (D) freezes
14. (E) dagree ● (F) degree (G) digree (H) diggrea
15. (A) maturr ● (B) matter (C) mattar (D) matture

94 Grade 3.1/Unit 3 **A Very Cool Place to Visit** 15

SPELLING PRACTICE BOOK, PAGE 94

UNIT 3

Unit Closer

Wrap Up the Theme

Be Creative!

We can all express ourselves in creative, wonderful ways.

REVIEW THE THEME Remind students that all of the selections in this unit relate to the theme, Be Creative! Were students surprised at any of the ways the characters found to express themselves? Ask students to name other stories or movies they know that also fit the theme, Be Creative!

READ THE POEM Read aloud to students "My Pencil" by Shirley R. Williams. As they listen, ask students to think about how she feels about her pencil. After reading, discuss how the poem connects to the theme, Be Creative! What is surprising or fun about the way the pencil is used in the poem?

Reread the poem, having students echo the last word in each line. Encourage students to listen for the rhymes.

LISTENING LIBRARY AUDIOCASSETTE

GROUP **MAKE CONNECTIONS** Have students work in small groups to brainstorm a list of ways that the stories, poems, and the *Time for Kids* magazine article relate to the theme, Be Creative!

Groups can then compare their lists as they share them with the class.

LOOKING AT GENRE

Have students review *The Patchwork Quilt* and *Pecos Bill: A Tall Tale Play.* What makes *The Patchwork Quilt* realistic fiction? What makes *Pecos Bill* a tall tale?

Help students list the key characteristics of each literary form or genre. Can they name other tall tales and fiction stories that have these same characteristics?

REALISTIC FICTION *The Patchwork Quilt*	TALL TALE *Pecos Bill*
• Characters seem real. • Settings look and sound real. • Characters' problems and actions could happen in real life.	• Characters and actions seem larger than life. • Heroes perform impossible deeds. • A tall tale has boastful humor.

My Pencil

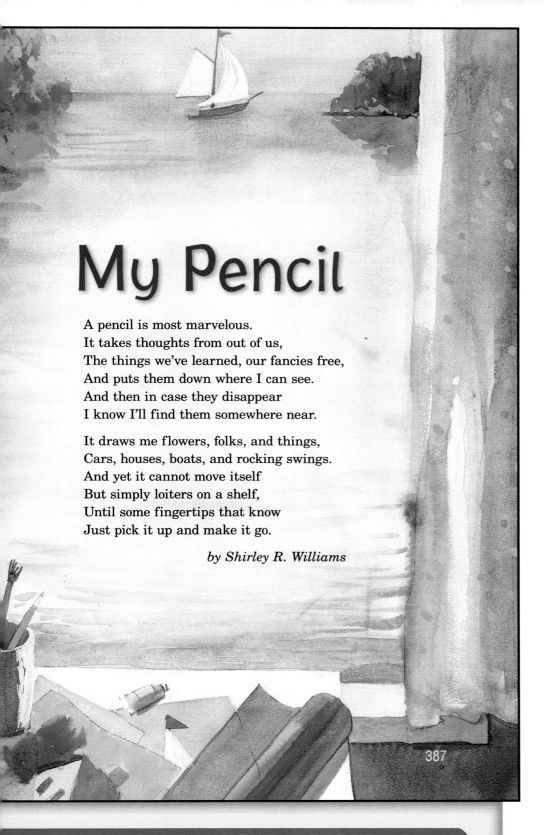

A pencil is most marvelous.
It takes thoughts from out of us,
The things we've learned, our fancies free,
And puts them down where I can see.
And then in case they disappear
I know I'll find them somewhere near.

It draws me flowers, folks, and things,
Cars, houses, boats, and rocking swings.
And yet it cannot move itself
But simply loiters on a shelf,
Until some fingertips that know
Just pick it up and make it go.

by Shirley R. Williams

387

LEARNING ABOUT POETRY

iterary Devices: Rhyme Pattern oint out the *aabbcc* rhyme pattern nroughout the poem by having stu-ents name the rhyming words. Then ave them clap as they read aloud the rst stanza to feel the driving rhythm hat the simple rhyme scheme pro-ides. Ask students how they feel bout this rhyme pattern. Does it nake the poem fun to read aloud? oint out that playing with rhythm adds an element of interest to the poem and holds the reader's attention.

Poetry Activity Ask students to respond to the poem by drawing. First, have them create pictures of some things the poet says her pencil draws. Then have students create pictures that express their own thoughts and feelings.

Research and Inquiry

GROUP **Complete the Theme Project** Have students work in teams to complete their group project. Remind students that the information they have gathered about the historical event, landmark, or product can be presented in any creative way. Encourage them to share the tasks of making visual aids or scenery or writing the scripts so that each member of the team can contribute to the project.

Make a Classroom Presentation Have teams take turns presenting their projects. Be sure to include time for questions from the audience.

Draw Conclusions Have students draw conclusions about what they learned from researching and preparing their projects. Discuss any experiences they had using the Internet for research. Was the resource chart they made helpful? What conclusions have students drawn about their topic? Was their presentation effective? Finally, ask students if doing the research changed their opinion about their community in any way. What conclusions can they draw from this?

Ask More Questions What additional questions do students now have about the community? What else would students like to find out? Do students have questions about other communities and how they might compare with their own? You might encourage the teams to continue their research and prepare another presentation.

UNIT 3

Writing Process

Persuasive Writing

CONNECT TO LITERATURE In *The Little Painter of Sabana Grande,* GROUP Fernando convinces his neighbors to let him paint their houses. Engage the class in a discussion of how and why they think Fernando was able to persuade them. Have students make a list of their classmates' responses.

Our neighborhood has too many stray animals. They're hungry, so they sometimes dig up people's gardens or get into the trash. I think we should start a pet adoption center.

Volunteers could take care of the animals. I think this plan would help animals by giving them good homes. It would also help people, by keeping strays out of their gardens and by giving them pets to love and care for.

Prewrite

PURPOSE AND AUDIENCE Tell students that they will write speeches whose purpose will be to persuade their neighbors and friends to work on a community project. Students can pretend that the speeches are for a town meeting. Encourage students to keep their purpose and audience in mind as they write.

STRATEGY: BRAINSTORM Have students brainstorm ideas to improve their neighborhood or school. Then have them vote on three of the best ideas. Invite students to select one of the ideas for their writing project.

Use **Writing Process Transparency 3A** as a model.

FEATURES OF PERSUASIVE WRITING

- clearly states a position on a specific topic
- offers convincing reasons and facts to persuade an audience
- makes clear connections among the ideas presented
- draws a concrete, practical conclusion

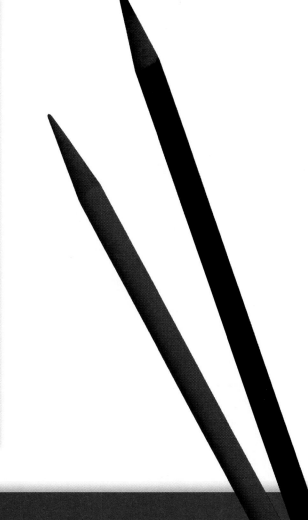

PREWRITE **TRANSPARENCY**

Making a Student Recycling Center

POSITION STATEMENT:

We need a recycling center at school.

1. helps the environment
2. makes students aware of recycling
3. sets example for younger students

McGraw-Hill School Division

Book 3.1/Unit 3: Persuasive Writing / Prewriting 3A

TEACHING TIP

ORGANIZATION Have students focus on organizing facts and reasons in the planning stage. Remind them to think about the pros and cons of their positions and to include answers to potential arguments. Give concrete examples of how to support personal opinion with detailed information.

Draft

STRATEGY: DEVELOP A MAIN IDEA Instruct students to begin with a strong opening sentence declaring their position on a specific issue. From there, encourage them to freely write their opinions without self-editing. Urge them to consult their prewriting organizers, and to include their supporting facts in their speech. Remind them that good persuasive writing concludes with a well-stated practical plan.

Use **Writing Process Transparency 3B** to model a first draft.

LANGUAGE CONTROL Give students copies of an age-appropriate opinion article. Have them identify and circle words that they feel best express and support the author's opinion. They can write a comment sheet telling why they chose each word, and save it in their portfolio.

LANGUAGE SUPPORT

Conference individually, or in small groups, with students who need help with their main idea. Ask them to name issues they feel strongly about in their own lives at home or in school. Help them to identify a position, and to list persuasive words and pertinent facts under a topic sentence.

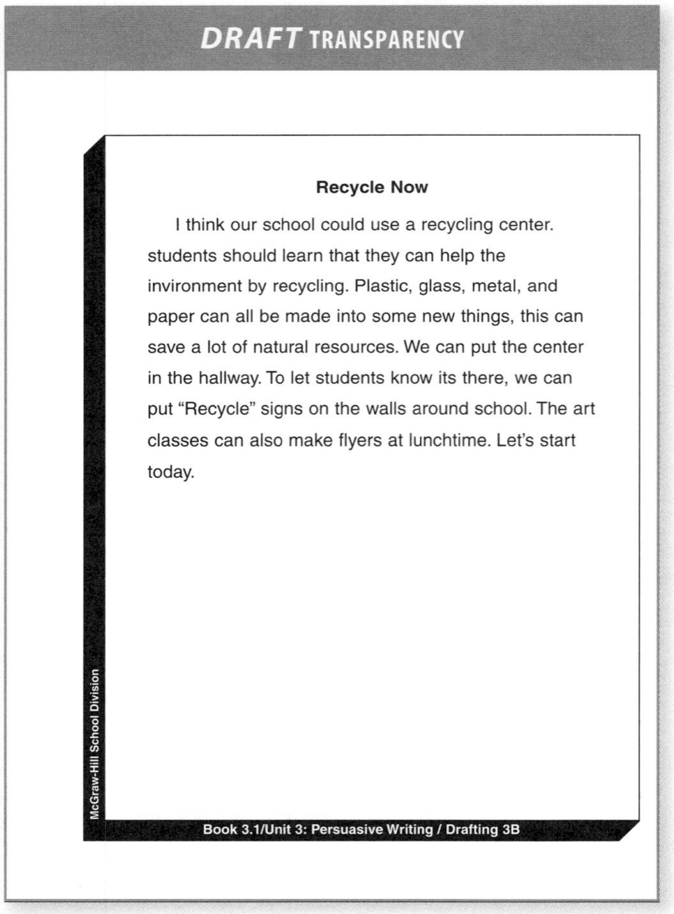

***DRAFT* TRANSPARENCY**

Recycle Now

I think our school could use a recycling center. students should learn that they can help the invironment by recycling. Plastic, glass, metal, and paper can all be made into some new things, this can save a lot of natural resources. We can put the center in the hallway. To let students know its there, we can put "Recycle" signs on the walls around school. The art classes can also make flyers at lunchtime. Let's start today.

McGraw-Hill School Division

Book 3.1/Unit 3: Persuasive Writing / Drafting 3B

Revise

Place students in topic-based pairs, pro and con. Have them write comment sheets telling what they find convincing about each other's speeches. Explain to students that the comments should be constructive and help their partner think of ways to improve his or her argument.

Use **Writing Process Transparency 3C** for classroom discussion on the revision process. Ask students to comment on how revisions may have improved this writing example.

STRATEGY: ELABORATION Have students examine their work for changes and additions that will strengthen their arguments. Ask them to consider how an audience would react to their writing. Use the following questions to help the revision process:

- Do my written words completely express my opinion?
- Have I offered a strong plan of action?
- Would an audience agree with me, and if so, why?

TEACHING TIP

TEACHER CONFERENCE

Reinforce the importance of balancing a strong opinion with solid facts and details. Ask students to consider these questions while revising:

- **Did you begin with a strong opening statement? What are the most important words?**
- **How have you backed up your opinions with facts and examples?**
- **Is your speech presented in a logical order?**

***REVISE* TRANSPARENCY**

Recycle Now !

~~I think~~ our school ~~could use~~ needs a recycling center. students should learn that they can help the inviornment by recycling. Recycled Plastic, glass, metal, and paper can all be made into some new things, this can save a lot of natural resources. We can put the center in the hallway next to the gym. To let students know its there, we can put "Recycle" signs on the walls around school. The art classes can also make flyers to give out at lunchtime. Let's start today. !

McGraw-Hill School Division

Book 3.1/Unit 3: Persuasive Writing / Revising 3C

Persuasive Writing

Edit/Proofread

After students finish revising their texts, have them proofread for final corrections and additions.

GRAMMAR/SPELLING CONNECTIONS

See the 5-Day Grammar and Usage Plans on verbs, pages 289M–289N, 317M–317N, 349M–349N, 375M–375N, and 385M–385N.

See the 5-Day Spelling Plans, pages 289O–289P, 317O–317P, 349O–349P, 375O–375P, and 385O–385P.

GRAMMAR, MECHANICS, USAGE

- Begin abbreviations with a capital letter and end with a period.
- Use a comma between the names of a city and a state.
- Add an apostrophe and an *s* to make a singular noun possessive.

Publish

MAKE A DISPLAY Display students' speeches on a hall bulletin board. Staple a large envelope to the board, with a sign asking for pro and con response votes to the opinions posted.

Use **Writing Process Transparency 3D** as a proofreading model and **Writing Process Transparency 3E** to discuss presentation ideas.

***PROOFREAD* TRANSPARENCY**

Recycle Now !

~~I think~~ our school ~~could use~~ needs a recycling center. students should learn that they can help the invironment by recycling. Recycled Plastic, glass, metal, and paper can all be made into some new things, this can save a lot of natural resources. We can put the center in the hallway next to the gym. To let students know its there, we can put "Recycle" signs on the walls around school. The art classes can also make flyers to give out at lunchtime. Let's start today. !

McGraw-Hill School Division

Book 3.1/Unit 3: Persuasive Writing / Proofreading 3D

***PUBLISH* TRANSPARENCY**

Recycle Now!

Our school needs a recycling center. Students should learn that they can help the environment by recycling. Recycled plastic, glass, metal, and paper can all be made into some new things. This can save a lot of natural resources. We can put the center in the hallway next to the gym. To let students know it's there, we can put "Recycle" signs on the walls around school. The art classes can also make flyers to give out at lunchtime. Let's start today!

McGraw-Hill School Division

Book 3.1/Unit 3: Persuasive Writing / Publishing 3E

Presentation Ideas

STAGE A DEBATE Organize student teams to debate the pros and cons of their chosen writing topics. Invite other classes to attend, and ask them to vote on each idea debated. ▶ **Representing/Speaking**

MAKE AN AUDIOTAPE Tape the finished debate speeches, and invite students to listen to it. If you have a school newspaper, ask the editors to publish some of the speeches. ▶ **Listening/Speaking**

Assessment

SCORING RUBRIC When using the rubric, please consider students' creative efforts, possibly adding a plus (+) for originality, wit, and imagination.

SELF-ASSESSMENT Present the Features of Persuasive Writing on page 387B in question form. Have students use these questions to self-assess their speeches.

COMMUNICATION TIPS

REPRESENTING Have students design posters advertising the debate.

SPEAKING Give students a chance to rehearse their speeches before the debate. Have students work with a partner and take turns reading their speeches to each other.

Scoring Rubric: 6-Trait Writing

4 Excellent	3 Good	2 Fair	1 Unsatisfactory
Ideas & Content • crafts an unusually convincing argument with extensive supporting details and ideas.	Ideas & Content • crafts a solid, well-thought-out argument, with a set of details that show knowledge of the topic; may make some new connections in the topic.	Ideas & Content • has some control of argument, but may not offer clear or thorough details; may not hold the reader's attention.	Ideas & Content • does not successfully argue a position; it is hard to tell what the writer thinks or feels.
Organization • carefully-planned persuasive strategy moves the reader logically and evenly through the text; ideas and details strengthen the argument.	Organization • presents a capable, easy-to-follow strategy; reader can understand the argument from beginning to end; details fit and build on each other.	Organization • tries to structure an argument, but has trouble ordering facts and ideas; may lose control of topic after stating the main idea.	Organization • extreme lack of organization makes the text difficult to follow; ideas and details are not connected.
Voice • conveys a strong personal message, with potential to influence the reader's opinion; deep involvement with the topic.	Voice • shows who is behind the words; personal style matches purpose and reaches out to convince the reader.	Voice • communicates the main argument, with some hint of who is behind the words; writer may seem uninvolved with the topic and the audience.	Voice • is not involved in the topic; lacks interaction with reader.
Word Choice • makes thoughtful, imaginative use of specific language.	Word Choice • uses a variety of accurate, specific words to communicate opinions and details; may experiment with new words.	Word Choice • gets the message across, but experiments with few new words; may not use specific or colorful words.	Word Choice • does not use words that express an opinion; some words may detract from the meaning of the text; words do not fit, or are overused.
Sentence Fluency • crafts varied, effective sentences that flow with a natural rhythm; sentences have a variety of beginnings, lengths, and patterns.	Sentence Fluency • crafts careful sentences that make sense and are easy to read and understand; sentence lengths and patterns vary, and fit together well.	Sentence Fluency • sentences are understandable, but may be choppy, rambling, or awkward; some writing may be difficult to follow.	Sentence Fluency • uses choppy, rambling, or confusing sentences; does not understand how words and sentences fit together; writing is hard to read aloud.
Conventions • shows strong skills in most writing conventions; proper use of the rules of English enhances clarity, personal style, and cohesion; editing is largely unnecessary.	Conventions • uses a variety of conventions correctly; some editing may be needed. Errors are few.	Conventions • makes frequent mistakes which may interfere with a smooth reading; extensive need for editing.	Conventions • has repeated errors in spelling, word choice, punctuation and usage; sentence structures may be confused.

This piece is either blank, or fails to respond to the writing task. The topic is not addressed, or the student simply paraphrases the prompt. The response may be illegible or incoherent.

UNIT 3

Unit Assessment

VOCABULARY

GROUP Divide the class into groups. Assign a selection to each team. Have each group make up and tell a story using as many words from the selection as they can. As soon as they hear a vocabulary word, the other groups must raise their hands. Have volunteers from each group define each word.

Unit Review

Moses Goes to a Concert

concert	ill	musician
conductor	instrument	orchestra

The Little Painter of Sabana Grande

blossom	faded	miserable
dawn	imaginary	shallow

The Patchwork Quilt

anxious	costume	gazed
attic	examined	pattern

Pecos Bill

combine	located	stumbled
invented	prairie	wilderness

A Very Cool Place to Visit

beauty	furniture	pure
creeps	palace	visitors

Name__________ Date______ **Practice 110**

Unit 3 Vocabulary Review

A. Supply the correct word from the box.

orchestra	concert	imaginary	conductor	musician

Helen pretended she was the __conductor__ of an __orchestra__. She could hear the __imaginary__ music in her head. When she waved her arms, each __musician__ played faster. The pretend audience clapped wildly. At the end of the __concert__, they threw her flowers.

B. Read each word in Column 1. Then find a word in Column 2 that means the opposite. Write the letter of the word on the line.

1. shallow __c__	**a.** bright
2. ill __e__	**b.** cellar
3. miserable __f__	**c.** deep
4. faded __a__	**d.** lost
5. attic __b__	**e.** well
6. stumbled __g__	**f.** happy
7. located __d__	**g.** leaped

PRACTICE BOOK, 110–111

GRAMMAR

PARTNERS To review the grammar lesson skills, have students work together to write a short essay about a trip to a zoo. Explain that all verbs must be in the past tense. Then have them rewrite it, changing all the past-tense verbs to present tense.

Unit Review

Moses Goes to a Concert
Action Verbs

The Little Painter of Sabana Grande
Present-Tense Verbs

The Patchwork Quilt
Past-Tense Verbs

Pecos Bill
Using Verb Tenses

A Very Cool Place to Visit
Sentence Combining with Verbs

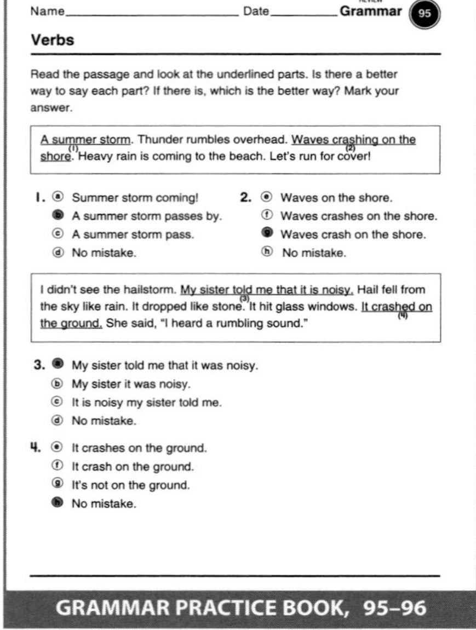

Name__________ Date______ REVIEW **Grammar 95**

Verbs

Read the passage and look at the underlined parts. Is there a better way to say each part? If there is, which is the better way? Mark your answer.

A summer storm.(1) Thunder rumbles overhead. Waves crashing on the shore.(2) Heavy rain is coming to the beach. Let's run for cover!

1.
- ⓐ Summer storm coming!
- ● A summer storm passes by.
- ⓒ A summer storm pass.
- ⓓ No mistake.

2.
- ⓔ Waves on the shore.
- ⓕ Waves crashes on the shore.
- ● Waves crash on the shore.
- ⓗ No mistake.

I didn't see the hailstorm. My sister told me that it is noisy.(3) Hail fell from the sky like rain. It dropped like stone. It hit glass windows. It crashed on the ground.(4) She said, "I heard a rumbling sound."

3.
- ● My sister told me that it was noisy.
- ⓑ My sister it was noisy.
- ⓒ It is noisy my sister told me.
- ⓓ No mistake.

4.
- ⓔ It crashes on the ground.
- ⓕ It crash on the ground.
- ⓖ It's not on the ground.
- ● No mistake.

GRAMMAR PRACTICE BOOK, 95–96

SPELLING

GROUP Divide the class into teams. Write the review words on cards and give a card to each student. Have students draw pictures representing each word. Then have the teams take turns showing their pictures to the other teams. The team that guesses and spells the word correctly gets a point. The team with the most points wins.

Unit Review

Consonant Clusters
paint
thank
friend
thump
belong

Adding *-ed* and *-ing*
spied
moving
robbed
shaking
hurried

Double Consonants
ladder
ribbon
silly
butter
supper

Science Words
melt
northern
heat
freezes
snowflake

/ou/ and /oi/
power
enjoy
cloudy
noisy
shout

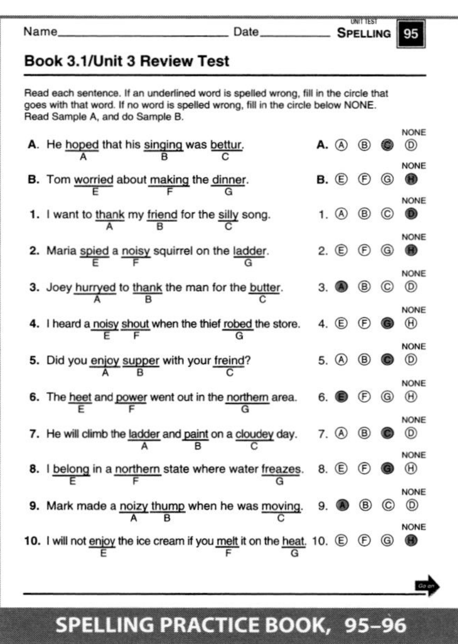

Name________________ Date__________ UNIT TEST SPELLING 95

Book 3.1/Unit 3 Review Test

Read each sentence. If an underlined word is spelled wrong, fill in the circle that goes with that word. If no word is spelled wrong, fill in the circle below NONE. Read Sample A, and do Sample B.

A. He hoped (A) that his singing (B) was bettur (C). — A. Ⓐ Ⓑ ● NONE Ⓓ
B. Tom worried (E) about making (F) the dinner (G). — B. Ⓔ Ⓕ Ⓖ NONE ●
1. I want to thank (A) my friend (B) for the silly (C) song. — 1. Ⓐ Ⓑ Ⓒ NONE ●
2. Maria spied (E) a noisy (F) squirrel on the ladder (G). — 2. Ⓔ Ⓕ Ⓖ NONE ●
3. Joey hurryed (A) to thank (B) the man for the butter (C). — 3. ● Ⓑ Ⓒ NONE Ⓓ
4. I heard a noisy (E) shout (F) when the thief robed (G) the store. — 4. Ⓔ Ⓕ ● NONE Ⓗ
5. Did you enjoy (A) supper (B) with your freind (C)? — 5. Ⓐ Ⓑ ● NONE Ⓓ
6. The heet (E) and power (F) went out in the northern (G) area. — 6. ● Ⓕ Ⓖ NONE Ⓗ
7. He will climb the ladder (A) and paint (B) on a cloudey (C) day. — 7. Ⓐ Ⓑ ● NONE Ⓓ
8. I belong (E) in a northern (F) state where water freazes (G). — 8. Ⓔ Ⓕ ● NONE Ⓗ
9. Mark made a noizy (A) thump (B) when he was moving (C). — 9. ● Ⓑ Ⓒ NONE Ⓓ
10. I will not enjoy (E) the ice cream if you melt (F) it on the heat (G). — 10. Ⓔ Ⓕ Ⓖ NONE ●

Go on

SPELLING PRACTICE BOOK, 95–96

SKILLS & STRATEGIES

Comprehension
- ☑ Main Idea
- ☑ Summarize
- ☑ Story Elements
- ☑ Make Inferences

Vocabulary Strategy
- ☑ Context Clues
- ☑ Multiple-Meaning Words

Study Skills
- ☑ Graphic Aids

Writing
- ☑ Persuasive Writing

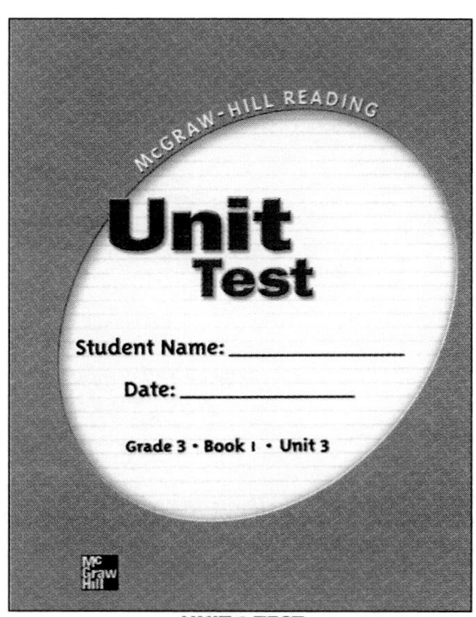

McGRAW-HILL READING
Unit Test
Student Name: ____________
Date: ____________
Grade 3 • Book 1 • Unit 3
McGraw Hill

UNIT 3 TEST

Assessment Follow-Up

Use the results of the informal and formal assessment opportunities in the unit to help you make decisions about future instruction.

SKILLS AND STRATEGIES	Reteaching Blackline Masters	Alternate Teaching Strategies
Comprehension		
Main Idea	75, 79, 94, 103	T60
Summarize	80, 87, 107	T62
Story Elements	82, 86, 96, 100	T64
Make Inferences	89, 93, 101	T66
Vocabulary Strategy		
Context Clues	81, 88, 109	T63
Multiple-Meaning Words	95, 102, 108	T65
Study Skills		
Graphic Aids	78, 85, 92, 99, 106	T61

	Alternate Writing Project–Easy	Unit Writing Process Lesson
Writing		
Persuasive Writing	289L, 317L, 349L, 375L, 385L	387A–387F

CD-ROM provides extra phonics support.

Research & Inquiry ideas. Visit ***www.mhschool.com/reading.***

Glossary

Introduce students to the Glossary by reading through the introduction and looking over the pages with them. Encourage the class to talk about what they see.

Words in a glossary, like words in a dictionary, are listed in **alphabetical order.** Point out the **guide words** at the top of each page that tell the first and last words appearing on that page.

Point out examples of **entries** and **main entries.** Read through a simple entry with the class, identifying each part. Have students note the order in which information is given: entry words(s), definition(s), example sentence, syllable division, pronunciation respelling, part of speech, plural/verb/adjective forms.

Note that if more than one definition is given for a word, the definitions are numbered. Note also the format used for a word that is more than one part of speech.

Review the parts of speech by identifying each in a sentence:

inter.	*adj.*	*n.*	*conj.*	*adj.*	*n.*
Wow!	**A**	**dictionary**	**and**	**a**	**glossary**
v.	*adv.*	*pron.*	*prep.*	*n.*	
tell	**almost**	**everything**	**about**	**words!**	

Explain the use of the **pronunciation key** (either the **short key,** at the bottom of every other page, or the **long key,** at the beginning of the glossary). Demonstrate the difference between **primary** stress and **secondary** stress by pronouncing a word with both.

Point out an example of the small triangle signaling a homophone. **Homophones** are words with different spellings and meanings but with the same pronunciation. Explain that a pair of words with the superscripts **1** and **2** are **homographs**—words that have the same spelling, but different origins and meanings, and in some cases, different pronunciations.

The **Word History** feature tells what language a word comes from and what changes have occurred in its spelling and/or meaning. Many everyday words have interesting and surprising stories behind them. Note that word histories can help us remember the meanings of difficult words.

Allow time for students to further explore the Glossary and make their own discoveries.

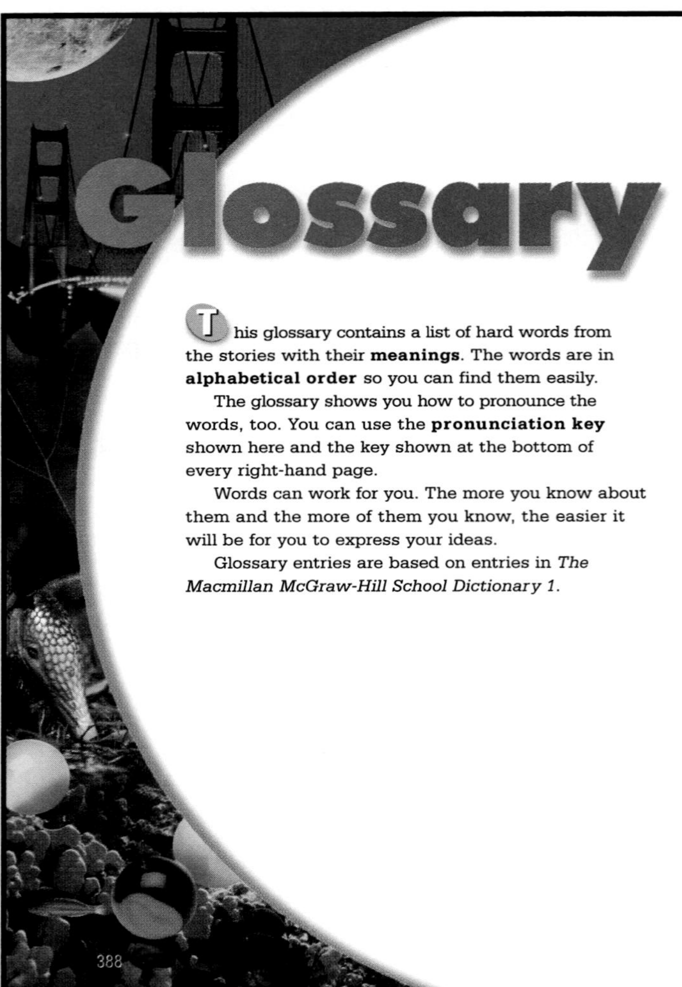

This glossary contains a list of hard words from the stories with their **meanings**. The words are in **alphabetical order** so you can find them easily.

The glossary shows you how to pronounce the words, too. You can use the **pronunciation key** shown here and the key shown at the bottom of every right-hand page.

Words can work for you. The more you know about them and the more of them you know, the easier it will be for you to express your ideas.

Glossary entries are based on entries in *The Macmillan McGraw-Hill School Dictionary 1.*

Guide Words

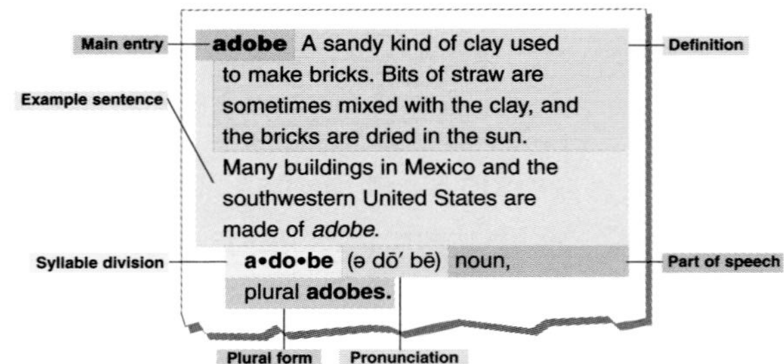

Sample Entry

Main entry — Definition — Example sentence — Syllable division — Part of speech — Plural form — Pronunciation

adobe A sandy kind of clay used to make bricks. Bits of straw are sometimes mixed with the clay, and the bricks are dried in the sun. Many buildings in Mexico and the southwestern United States are made of *adobe.*
a•do•be (ə dō′ bē) noun, plural **adobes.**

a	at, bad	**d**	dear, soda, bad
ā	ape, pain, day, break	**f**	five, defend, leaf, off, cough, elephant.
ä	father, car, heart	**g**	game, ago, fog, egg
âr	care, pair, bear, their, where	**h**	hat, ahead
e	end, pet, said, heaven, friend	**hw**	white, whether, which
ē	equal, me, feet, team, piece, key	**j**	joke, enjoy, gem, page, edge
i	it, big, English, hymn	**k**	kite, bakery, seek, tack, cat
ī	ice, fine, lie, my	**l**	lid, sailor, feel, ball, allow
îr	ear, deer, here, pierce	**m**	man, family, dream
o	odd, hot, watch	**n**	not, final, pan, knife
ō	old, oat, toe, low	**ng**	long, singer, pink
ô	coffee, all, taught, law, fought	**p**	pail, repair, soap, happy
ôr	order, fork, horse, story, pour	**r**	ride, parent, wear, more, marry
oi	oil, toy	**s**	sit, aside, pets, cent, pass
ou	out, now	**sh**	shoe, washer, fish, mission, nation
u	up, mud, love, double	**t**	tag, pretend, fat, button, dressed
ū	use, mule, cue, feud, few	**th**	thin, panther, both,
ü	rule, true, food	**<u>th</u>**	this, mother, smooth
ů	put, wood, should	**v**	very, favor, wave
ûr	burn, hurry, term, bird, word, courage	**w**	wet, weather, reward
ə	about, taken, pencil, lemon, circus	**y**	yes, onion
b	bat, above, job	**z**	zoo, lazy, jazz, rose, dogs, houses
ch	chin, such, match	**zh**	vision, treasure, seizure

adobe A sandy kind of clay used to make bricks. Bits of straw are sometimes mixed with the clay, and the bricks are dried in the sun. Many buildings in Mexico and the southwestern United States are made of *adobe.*
a•do•be (ə dō′ bē) *noun, plural* **adobes.**

Word History
The word **adobe** comes from the Spanish word of the same spelling, meaning "sun-dried brick." But the Spanish got this word from an even earlier Arabic word, *at-tob,* meaning "the brick."

anxious 1. Wanting very much; eager. I was *anxious* to make friends at my new school. **2.** Nervous, worried or fearful about what may happen. My cousin was *anxious* about driving on the slippery roads.
anx•ious (angk′ shəs *or* ang′ shəs) *adjective.*

appendix A short, hollow pouch that is attached to the large intestine.
ap•pen•dix (ə pen′ diks) *noun, plural* **appendixes.**

applaud To show approval or enjoyment of something by clapping the hands. The children *applauded* the clown's funny tricks.
ap•plaud (ə plôd′) *verb,* **applauded, applauding.**

arachnid Any of a large group of small animals without a backbone. The body of an arachnid is divided into two parts. Arachnids have four pairs of legs and no antennae or wings. Spiders, scorpions, mites, and ticks are *arachnids.*
ar•ach•nid (ə rak′ nid) *noun, plural* **arachnids.**

area A particular space, region, or section. We moved from the city to a rural *area.*
ar•e•a (âr′ ē ə) *noun, plural* **areas.**

astonish To surprise very much; amaze. The news that I had won the contest *astonished* me.
▲ **Synonym:** astound
as•ton•ish (ə ston′ ish) *verb,* **astonished, astonishing.**

Language Note
A **synonym** is a word that can be used for another word. A synonym for *astonish* is *surprise.*

attic The space just below the roof of a house. We use our *attic* to store trunks of old clothes.
at•tic (at′ ik) noun, plural **attics.**

autograph To write one's name in one's own handwriting. Will you *autograph* a copy of your book for me? *Verb.* —A person's signature written in that person's own handwriting. *Noun.*
au•to•graph (ô′ tə graf′) *verb,* **autographed, autographing;** *noun, plural* **autographs.**

Word History
The word **autograph** comes from the Greek words *autos,* meaning "self," and *graphein,* meaning "to write."

banner A flag or other piece of cloth that has a design and sometimes writing on it. The fans at the baseball game held up a *banner.*
ban•ner (ban′ ər) *noun, plural* **banners.**

beauty A quality that makes a person or a thing pleasing to look at, hear, or think about. The garden is a place of *beauty.*
beau•ty (bū′ tē) *noun, plural* **beauties.**

bewilder To confuse or puzzle; mix up. The student was *bewildered* by the math problem.
be•wil•der (bi wil′ dər) *verb,* **bewildered, bewildering.**

black widow A black spider. The female black widow is poisonous and has a red mark on her body. The female black widow is larger than the male.
black wi•dow (blak wid′ ō) *noun, plural* **black widows.**

blossom The flower of a plant or tree, especially one that produces fruit. We gathered *blossoms* from the apple trees. *Noun.*—To have flowers or blossoms; bloom. The peach trees *blossom* in the spring. *Verb.*
blos•som (blos′ əm) *noun, plural* **blossoms;** *verb,* **blossomed, blossoming.**

at; āpe; fär; câre; end; mē; it; īce; pîerce; hot; ōld; sông; fôrk; oil; out; up; ūse; rüle; pu̇ll; tûrn; chin; sing; shop; thin; <u>th</u>is; **hw** in white; **zh** in treasure. The symbol **ə** stands for the unstressed vowel sound in about, taken, pencil, lemon, and circus.

bronco busting The act of taming and training wild horses. The cowboys spent part of each day *bronco busting.*
bron•co bust•ing (brong′ kō bust′ ing) *noun.*

buffalo 1. A large North American animal that has a big shaggy head with short horns and a hump on its back; bison. **2.** Any of various oxen of Europe, Asia, and Africa.
buf•fa•lo (buf′ ə lō′) *noun, plural* **buffaloes** *or* **buffalos** *or* **buffalo.**

canyon A deep valley with very high, steep sides. A *canyon* often has a stream running through it.
can•yon (kan′ yən) *noun, plural* **canyons.**

capture To catch and hold a person, animal, or thing. The explorers *captured* the tiger in a large net. ▲**Synonyms:** take, seize
cap•ture (kap′ chər) *verb* **captured, capturing.**

ceiling The inside overhead surface of a room. The tall guest reached up and almost touched the *ceiling.*
ceil•ing (sē′ ling) *noun, plural* **ceilings.**

celebrate To observe or honor a special day or event with ceremonies and other activities. We *celebrated* Grandma's birthday with a big party.
cel•e•brate (sel′ ə brāt′) *verb,* **celebrated, celebrating.**

cent A coin of the United States and Canada. One hundred *cents* is equal to one dollar. ▲Other words that sound like this are **scent** and **sent.**
▲**Synonym:** penny
cent (sent) *noun, plural,* **cents.**

Language Note
A **homonym** is a word that sounds like another word but has a different meaning. A homonym for *cent* is *sent.*

combine To cause to mix together; blend. We *combined* eggs, flour, and milk to make the batter for the pancakes.
▲**Synonyms:** blend, mix
com•bine (kəm bīn′) *verb,* **combined, combining.**

concert A performance, usually a musical performance by a number of musicians. We went to a *concert* in the park.
▲**Synonyms:** show, recital, symphony
con•cert (kon′ sərt) *noun, plural* **concerts.**

conductor 1. A person who leads a group of musicians. Our music teacher is also the *conductor* of the school orchestra. **2.** A person on a train or bus who collects fares and assists passengers. The *conductor* walked down the aisle and called out the name of the next stop.
con•duc•tor (kən duk′ tər) *noun, plural* **conductors.**

consonant A letter of the alphabet that is not a vowel. *Consonants* include the letters *b, d, f, g, m, p, t,* and others.
con•so•nant (kon′ sə nənt) *noun, plural* **consonants.**

continue 1. To go on or do after stopping. We will *continue* the meeting after lunch. **2.** To keep on happening, being, or doing; go on without stopping. The rain had *continued* for two days.
con•tin•ue (kən tin′ ū) *verb,* **continued, continuing.**

cork The light, thick outer bark of a kind of oak tree. *Cork* is used for such things as bottle stoppers, insulation, and floats for rafts.
cork (kôrk) *noun, plural* **corks.**

correct Not having any mistakes; accurate. This is the *correct* answer to the arithmetic problem. *Adjective.* —To mark the mistakes in; change to make right. The teacher *corrected* our spelling tests. *Verb.*
cor•rect (kə rekt′) *adjective; verb,* **corrected, correcting.**

costume Clothes worn in order to look like someone or something else. I wore a cowboy *costume* to the Halloween party.
cos•tume (kos′ tüm *or* kos′ tūm) *noun, plural* **costumes.**

at; **ā**pe; f**ä**r; c**â**re; **e**nd; m**ē**; **i**t; **ī**ce; p**î**erce; h**o**t; **ō**ld; s**ô**ng; f**ô**rk; **oi**l; **ou**t; **u**p; **ū**se; r**ü**le; p**ů**ll; t**û**rn; **ch**in; si**ng**; **sh**op; **th**in; **th**is; **hw** in **wh**ite; **zh** in trea**s**ure. The symbol **ə** stands for the unstressed vowel sound in **a**bout, tak**e**n, penc**i**l, lem**o**n, and circ**u**s.

creep To move slowly along the ground or over a surface. The wind *creeps* in through the window.
creep (krēp) *verb,* **crept, creeping.**

crooked Not straight; bent or curving. The path through the woods was very *crooked.*
▲**Synonyms:** bent, winding
crook•ed (krůk′ id) *adjective.*

crop Plants that are grown to be used as a food or to be sold for profit. Wheat and corn are two *crops* grown in the Midwest.
crop (krop) *noun, plural* **crops.**

crumble 1. To break into small pieces. The muffin *crumbled* when I tried to butter it. **2.** To fall apart or be destroyed. The old house is slowly *cumbling.*
crum•ble (krum′ bəl) *verb,* **crumbled, crumbling.**

daddy-longlegs A kind of bug that looks like a spider. A daddy-longlegs has a small, round body and eight very long, thin legs.
dad•dy long•legs (dad′ē lông′ legz′) *noun, plural* **daddy-longlegs.**

darkness A partial or total absence of light; the result of a light going out. The sun dipped behind the hilltops and *darkness* fell.
dark•ness (därk′ nis) *noun.*

dawn The first light that appears in the morning. We left our house before *dawn.*
▲**Synonym:** daybreak
dawn (dôn) *noun, plural* **dawns.**

deaf Not able to hear, or not able to hear well. The *deaf* children were using sign language to speak to one another
deaf (def) *adjective,* **deafer, deafest.**

decimal 1. A period put before a decimal fraction. The periods in .5, .30, and .052 are *decimals.* **2.** A fraction with a denominator of 10, or a multiple of 10 such as 100 or 1,000. The *decimal* .5 is another way of writing $\frac{5}{10}$.
dec•i•mal (des′ ə məl) *noun, plural* **decimals.**

den A place where wild animals rest or sleep. The bear uses a cave as a *den* during its long winter sleep.
den (den) *noun, plural* **dens.**

disaster An event that causes much suffering or loss. The flood was a *disaster.*
▲**Synonyms:** tragedy, trouble
dis•as•ter (di zas′ tər) *noun, plural* **disasters.**

Word History
The word **disaster** comes from the Latin *dis,* meaning "away," and *astrum,* meaning "star."

dragonfly An insect that has a long, thin body and two pairs of wings. *Dragonflies* eat mosquitoes and live near fresh water.
drag•on•fly (drag′ ən flī′) *noun, plural* **dragonflies.**

eager Wanting very much to do something. A person who is *eager* is full of interest and enthusiasm.
▲**Synonym:** excited
ea•ger (ē′ gər) *adjective.*

earthquake A shaking or trembling of the ground. Earthquakes are caused by rock, lava, or hot gases moving deep inside the earth. Some *earthquakes* are so powerful that they cause the ground to split.
earth•quake (ûrth′ kwāk′) *noun, plural* **earthquakes.**

echo The repeating of a sound. Echoes are caused when sound waves bounce off a surface. We shouted "hello" and soon heard the *echo* of our voices.
ech•o (ek′ ō) *noun, plural* **echoes.**

embarrass To make someone feel shy, uncomfortable, or ashamed. My foolish mistake *embarrassed* me.
em•bar•rass (em bar′ əs) *verb,* **embarrassed, embarrassing.**

enormous Much greater than the usual size or amount; very large. The flood caused an *enormous* amount of damage.
▲**Synonyms:** large, gigantic
e•nor•mous (i nôr′ məs) *adjective.*

at; **ā**pe; f**ä**r; c**â**re; **e**nd; m**ē**; **i**t; **ī**ce; p**î**erce; h**o**t; **ō**ld; s**ô**ng; f**ô**rk; **oi**l; **ou**t; **u**p; **ū**se; r**ü**le; p**ů**ll; t**û**rn; **ch**in; si**ng**; **sh**op; **th**in; **th**is; **hw** in **wh**ite; **zh** in trea**s**ure. The symbol **ə** stands for the unstressed vowel sound in **a**bout, tak**e**n, penc**i**l, lem**o**n, and circ**u**s.

eon A very long period of time. That deposit of coal was formed *eons* ago.
e•on (ē′ ən *or* ē′ on) *noun, plural* **eons.**

Espino, Fernando
(es pē′ nō, fûr nän′ dō)

examine 1. To look at closely and carefully; check. We *examined* the baseball bat to be sure it wasn't cracked. **2.** To question in a careful way or test, usually to discover what a person knows. The lawyer *examined* the witness during the trial.
▲**Synonyms:** inspect, study
ex•am•ine (eg zam′ in) *verb,* **examined, examining.**

excitement The condition of being excited. We could hardly sleep because of our *excitement* about starting the trip tomorrow.
ex•cite•ment (ek sīt′ mənt) *noun.*

fade 1. To lose freshness; wither. The flowers *faded* after three days. **2.** To lose or cause to lose color or brightness. Blue jeans may *fade* when they are washed.
fade (fād) *verb,* **faded, fading.**

fan A person who is very interested in or enthusiastic about something. The *fans* ran up to the movie star.
▲**Synonym:** admirer
fan (fan) *noun, plural* **fans.**

feelers A part of an animal's body that is used for touching things. Many insects have *feelers* on their heads.
feel•er (fē′ lər) *noun, plural* **feelers.**

flex To bend. If your arm is tired, *flex* it to keep it loose.
flex (fleks) *verb,* **flexed, flexing.**

flow To move along steadily in a stream. Water *flows* through these pipes.
flow (flō) *verb,* **flowed, flowing.**

furniture Tables, chairs, beds, and other movable articles used in a home or office. Our living room is full of *furniture.*
fur•ni•ture (fûr′ ni chər) *noun.*

gaze To look at something a long time. We all *gazed* at the beautiful sunset. *Verb.*—A long steady look. Our *gaze* rested on the bear and its two playful cubs. *Noun.*
gaze (gāz) *verb,* **gazed, gazing;** *noun, plural* **gazes.**

Genghis Khan
(geng′ gis kän′)

gift 1. Something given; a present. This basketball was a *gift* from my parents. **2.** Talent; ability. That student has a *gift* for dancing.
gift (gift) *noun, plural* **gifts.**

grain 1. A tiny, hard piece of something. *Grains* of sand fell from the beach towel. **2.** The seed of wheat, corn, rice, oats, and other cereal plants. Breakfast cereal is made from *grains.*
grain (grān) *noun, plural* **grains.**

groan To make a deep, sad sound. I *groaned* when the doctors touched my injured ankle.
▲**Synonym:** moan ▲ Another word that sounds like this is **grown.**
groan (grōn) *verb,* **groaned, groaning.**

guard A person who is assigned to watch over things. The museum *guard* collected our tickets at the door. *Noun.*—To keep safe from harm or danger; protect. The dog *guarded* the house. *Verb.*
guard (gärd) *noun, plural* **guards;** *verb,* **guarded, guarding.**

halfway To or at half the distance; midway. We climbed *halfway* up the mountain.
half•way (haf′ wā′) *adverb.*

handful 1. The amount the hand can hold at one time. Each child took a *handful* of peanuts. **2.** A small number. Only a *handful* of people showed up.
hand•ful (hand′ fool′) *noun, plural* **handfuls.**

at; āpe; fär; câre; end; mē; it; īce; pîerce; hot; ōld; sông; fôrk; oil; out; up; ūse; rüle; pu̇ll; tûrn; chin; sing; shop; thin; <u>th</u>is; hw in white; zh in treasure. The symbol ə stands for the unstressed vowel sound in about, taken, pencil, lemon, and circus.

hatch To come from an egg. We are waiting for these chicks to *hatch.*
hatch (hach) *verb,* **hatched, hatching.**

haunch A part of the body of a person or animal including the hip and upper thigh. The lion sat on its *haunches.*
haunch (hônch) *noun, plural* **haunches.**

heap A collection of things piled together. We left a *heap* of peanut shells on the kitchen table.
▲**Synonyms:** pile, load, mound
heap (hēp) *noun, plural* **heaps.**

herd A group of animals that live or travel together. A *herd* of cattle grazed in the pasture.
▲Another word that sounds like this is **heard.**
herd (hûrd) *noun, plural* **herds;** *verb,* **herded, herding.**

ill Not healthy or well; sick. Many children in our class were *ill.*
ill (il) *adjective.*

imaginary Existing only in the mind; unreal. Most people believe that elves are *imaginary.*
▲**Synonyms:** unreal, fictional
i•mag•i•nary (i maj′ə ner′ē) *adjective.*

include To have as part of the whole; contain. You don't have to buy batteries for that toy because they are already *included* in the box.
in•clude (in klüd′) *verb,* **included, including.**

instrument 1. A device for producing musical sounds. Our music teacher plays the guitar, flute, and several other *instruments.* **2.** A device used for doing a certain kind of work; tool. The dental hygienist used a sharp *instrument* to scrape my teeth.
in•stru•ment (in′strə mənt) *noun, plural* **instruments.**

invent 1. To make or think of for the first time; create. Do you know who *invented* the phonograph? **2.** To make up. I'm ashamed to say I *invented* an excuse for being late.
in•vent (in vent′) *verb,* **invented, inventing.**

Word History

The word **invent** comes from a Latin word meaning "to come upon" or "find." The word *invent* was originally used to describe the finding of an answer, the solution to a problem, or the means to do something.

jagged Having sharp points that stick out. Some eagles build nests on *jagged* cliffs.
jag•ged (jag′ id) *adjective.*

jingle To make or cause to make a tinkling or ringing sound. When the bell moved, it *jingled.*
jingle (jing′gəl) *verb,* **jingled, jingling.**

journey A long trip. The Pilgrims crossed the Atlantic on their *journey* to the New World.
jour•ney (jûr′ nē) *noun, plural* **journeys.**

kinship A relationship or close connection. There has always been a *kinship* between the two villages.
kin•ship (kin′ ship′) *noun, plural* **kinships.**

lasso A long rope with a loop. A *lasso* is used to catch animals. *Noun.*
—To catch with a lasso. The cowhands will *lasso* the steer. *Verb.*
las•so (la′sō *or* lasü′) *noun, plural* **lassos** *or* **lassoes;** *verb,* **lassoed, lassoing.**

lease To rent. The family *leased* a cabin for the summer. *Verb.*
—A written agreement for renting a house, apartment, or land. My parents signed a new *lease. Noun.*
lease (lēs) *verb,* **leased, leasing;** *noun, plural* **leases.**

at; āpe; fär; câre; end; mē; it; īce; pîerce; hot; ōld; sông; fôrk; oil; out; up; ūse; rüle; pu̇ll; tûrn; chin; sing; shop; thin; <u>th</u>is; hw in white; zh in treasure. The symbol ə stands for the unstressed vowel sound in about, taken, pencil, lemon, and circus.

legend A story passed down through the years that many people believe, but that is not entirely true. There are many *legends* about the knights of the Middle Ages.
leg•end (lej′ənd) *noun, plural* **legends.**

length The distance from one end to the other end. The *length* of a football field is 100 yards.
▲**Synonym:** measure
length (lengkth *or* length) *noun, plural* **lengths.**

liquid A form of matter that is not a solid or a gas. A liquid can flow easily. It can take on the shape of any container into which it is poured. Milk is a *liquid.*
liq•uid (lik′wid) *noun, plural* **liquids.**

Little League A baseball league for children under thirteen years of age. We play for the West Side *Little League* on Saturday.
Lit•tle League (lit′ əl lēg) *noun.*

locate 1. To put or settle in a particular place. The baker *located* the bakery in the shopping mall. **2.** To find the place or position of. He could not *locate* his glasses.
lo•cate (lō′kāt) *verb,* **located, locating.**

longhorn A breed of cattle with very long horns. *Longhorns* were once common in the southwestern United States.
long•horn (lông′ hôrn) *noun, plural* **longhorns.**

Mm

marvel To feel wonder and astonishment. We *marveled* at the acrobat's skill.
mar•vel (mär′vəl) *verb,* **marveled, marveling.**

McGwire, Mark
(məgwir′, märk)

mischievous Playful but naughty. That *mischievous* child hid my slippers again.
mis•chie•vous (mis′chə vəs) *adjective.*

miserable 1. Very unhappy; wretched. We all felt *miserable* about losing our dog. **2.** Causing discomfort or unhappiness. I had a *miserable* cold.
▲**Synonyms:** sad, horrible, unpleasant
mis•er•a•ble (miz′ ər ə bəl) *adjective.*

mob To crowd around in excitement or anger. Shoppers *mobbed* the store during the big sale. *Verb.* —A large number of people; crowd. A *mob* is sometimes made up of people who are so angry or upset about something that they break the law and cause damage. *Noun.*
mob (mob) *verb,* **mobbed, mobbing;** *noun, plural* **mobs.**

mock Not real; imitation. In history class we had a *mock* battle with cardboard shields. *Adjective.*—To make fun of in a mean way. Instead of helping, they laughed and *mocked* me when I fell off my bike. *Verb.*
mock (mok) *adjective; verb,* **mocked, mocking.**

musician A person who is skilled in playing a musical instrument, composing music, or singing. My brother studied piano for years and became a talented *musician.*
mu•si•cian (mū zish′ ən) *noun, plural* **musicians.**

mustang A wild horse that lives on the American plains; bronco. We watched the *mustangs* go down to the river for a cool drink of water.
mus•tang (mus′tang) *noun, plural* **mustangs.**

Nn

New World North and South America; the Western Hemisphere.
New World (nü wûrld)

Nilsson, Kerstin
(Nil′sən, Ker′stin)

northern lights Shining bands of light that can be seen in the night sky in the Northern Hemisphere. In the winter, you can see the *northern lights* in Alaska.
north•ern lights (nôr′th ərn līts) *noun.*

at; āpe; fär; câre; end; mē; it; īce; pîerce; hot; ōld; sông; fôrk; oil; out; up; ūse; rüle; pu̇ll; tûrn; chin; sing; shop; thin; this; hw in white; zh in treasure. The symbol ə stands for the unstressed vowel sound in about, taken, pencil, lemon, and circus.

Glossary

orchestra 1. A group of musicians playing together on various instruments. **2.** The area just in front of a stage in which the orchestra plays.
▲**Synonyms:** symphony, band
or•ches•tra (ôr′ kə strə) *noun, plural* **orchestras.**

Word History

The word **orchestra** comes from a Greek word meaning "dance area." In the theater of ancient Greece, one section of the stage was called the *orchestra.* It was there that a chorus of performers danced and sang during a performance.

palace A very large, grand building where a king, queen, or other ruler usually lives. In London, we got to visit Buckingham *Palace.*
pal•ace (pal′ is) *noun, plural* **palaces.**

Panama A country in Central America.
Pan•a•ma (pan′ ə mä′) *noun.*

pattern The way in which colors, shapes, or lines are arranged or repeated in some order. The wallpaper was printed with a pretty flower *pattern.*
▲**Synonym:** design
pat•tern (pat′ ərn) *noun, plural* **patterns.**

peak 1. A high mountain, or the pointed top of a high mountain. We could see the snowy *peaks* in the distance. **2.** A sharp or pointed end or top. If you stand on the *peak* of our roof, you can see the ocean.
▲**Synonyms:** mountain top, crest, summit
peak (pēk) *noun, plural* **peaks.**

pedestrian A person who travels on foot; walker. Sidewalks are for *pedestrians.*
ped•es•tri•an (pə des′trē ən) *noun, plural* **pedestrians.**

Word History

The word **pedestrian** comes to us from the Latin root *pedis,* meaning "on foot."

percussionist One who is skilled in playing percussion instruments, such as the drum, cymbal, xylophone, and piano. The *percussionist* in the orchestra played the bass drum and cymbals.
per•cus•sion•ist (pər kush′ ən ist) *noun, plural* **percussionists.**

petition A formal request that is made to a person in authority. All the people on our street signed a *petition* asking the city to put a stop sign on the corner. *Noun.*—To make a formal request to. The students in our school *petitioned* the principal to keep the library open on weekends. *Verb.*
pe•ti•tion (pə tish′ ən) *noun, plural* **petitions;** *verb,* **petitioned, petitioning.**

pitcher A baseball player who throws the ball to the batter. The *pitcher* stands near the middle of the diamond facing home place.
pitch•er (pich′ ər) *noun, plural* **pitchers.**

pitcher

prairie Flat or rolling land covered with grass. A *prairie* has few trees.
▲**Synonym:** plains
prai•rie (prâr′ ē) *noun, plural* **prairies.**

prey An animal that is hunted by another animal for food. Rabbits and birds are the *prey* of foxes.
prey (prā) *noun, plural* **prey.**

prong One of the pointed ends of an antler or of a fork or other tool. My grandmother's forks have only three *prongs.*
▲**Synonym:** point
prong (prông *or* prong) *noun, plural* **prongs.**

at; āpe; fär; câre; end; mē; it; īce; pîerce; hot; ōld; sông; fôrk; oil; out; up; ūse; rüle; pu̇ll; tûrn; chin; sing; shop; thin; this; hw in white; zh in treasure. The symbol ə stands for the unstressed vowel sound in about, taken, pencil, lemon, and circus.

pure **1.** Nothing but. We won that game with *pure* luck. **2.** Not mixed with anything else. This bracelet is made of *pure* silver.
▲**Synonyms:** true, actual
pure (pyůr) *adjective,* **purer, purest.**

respect High regard or consideration. We show *respect* for our teacher. *Noun.*—To have or show honor or consideration for. I *respect* your opinion. *Verb.*
▲**Synonyms:** admiration, esteem
re•spect (ri spekt′) *noun; verb,* **respected, respecting.**

ripe Fully grown and ready to be eaten. The tomatoes in the garden are *ripe* now.
ripe (rīp) *adjective,* **riper, ripest.**

royal Of or pertaining to a king or queen or their family. The *royal* family lives in the palace.
roy•al (roi′ əl) *adjective.*

rubble Rough, broken pieces of stone, rock, or other solid material. The rescue workers searched through the *rubble* of the collapsed building.
rub•ble (rub′ əl) *noun.*

ruin Harm or damage greatly. The earthquake *ruined* the town. *Verb.* —Destruction, damage, or collapse. The storekeeper faced financial *ruin. Noun.*
▲**Synonym:** destroy
ru•in (rü′ in) *verb,* **ruined, ruining;** *noun, plural* **ruins.**

Sabana Grande
(sə bän′ə grän′ dā)

scatter **1.** To spread or throw about in various places. The wind *scattered* the leaves all over the yard. **2.** To separate or cause to separate and go in different directions. The loud thunder *scattered* the cattle.
▲**Synonyms:** cast, fling, sprinkle
scat•ter (skat′ ər) *verb,* **scattered, scattering.**

scene **1.** The place where something happens. The police arrived on the *scene* just as the thieves were escaping. **2.** A part of an act in a play or movie.
▲Another word that sounds like this is **seen.**
scene (sēn) *noun, plural* **scenes.**

schedule The time at which something is supposed to happen. The train was running behind *schedule* because of the weather.
sched•ule (skej′ ül) *noun, plural* **schedules.**

score The points or a record of the points made in a game or on a test. The final *score* of the game was 5 to 4. *Noun.*—To make a point or points in a game or test. She *scored* 10 points for her basketball team. *Verb.*
score (skôr) *noun, plural* **scores;** *verb,* **scored, scoring.**

season **1.** Any special part of the year. There is almost no rain during the dry *season.* **2.** One of the four parts of the year: spring, summer, fall, or winter.
sea•son (sē′ zən) *noun, plural* **seasons.**

season

Word History
The word **season** comes from a French word that originally meant, "the season of spring," or "planting time."

section **1.** A part of an area or group. We visited the old *section* of the city. **2.** A part taken from a whole; portion. Please cut the apple into four *sections.*
▲**Synonym:** quarter
sec•tion (sek′ shən) *noun, plural* **sections.**

serious **1.** Dangerous. Sam risked *serious* injury when he drove so fast on that icy road. **2.** Not joking; sincere. Were you *serious* about taking piano lessons?
▲**Synonyms:** grave, critical
se•ri•ous (sîr′ ē əs) *adjective.*

at; āpe; fär; câre; end; mē; it; īce; pîerce; hot; ōld; sông; fôrk; oil; out; up; ūse; rüle; půll; tûrn; chin; sing; shop; thin; this; hw in white; zh in treasure. The symbol ə stands for the unstressed vowel sound in about, taken, pencil, lemon, and circus.

shallow Not deep. The water in the pond is *shallow.*
shallow (shal′ ō) *adjective,* **shallower, shallowest.**

shelter **1.** To find or take refuge. It is not safe to take *shelter* under a tree during an electrical storm. **2.** To give shelter to. The umbrella *sheltered* us from the rain. *Verb.* —Something that covers or protects. The hikers used a cave as *shelter* during the thunderstorm. *Noun.*
shel•ter (shel′ tər) *verb,* **sheltered, sheltering;** *noun, plural* **shelters.**

skill The power or ability to do something. Swimming is an important *skill* to know when you are out on a boat.
▲**Synonym:** talent
skill (skil) *noun, plural* **skills.**

sloth A slow-moving animal that lives in the forests of South America. *Sloths* use their long arms and legs and their curved claws to hang upside down from trees.
sloth (slôth *or* slōth) *noun, plural* **sloths.**

snipping The act or sound of cutting with scissors in short, quick strokes. *Snipping* coupons from the newspaper is a way to save money on groceries.
snip•ping (snip′ ing) *noun.*

soldier A person who is a member of an army. The *soldiers* marched in a parade.
sol•dier (sōl′ jər) *noun, plural* **soldiers.**

Sosa, Sammy
(sō′ sə, sam′ mē)

souvenir Something that is kept because it reminds one of a person, place, or event. I kept my ticket as a *souvenir* of my first play.
▲**Synonym:** keepsake, memento
sou•ve•nir (sü′ və nîr′ *or* sü′ və nîr′) *noun, plural* **souvenirs.**

steamship A large ship that is powered by steam.
steam•ship (stēm′ ship) *noun, plural* **steamships.**

stem The main part of a plant that supports the leaves and flowers. Water and food travel through the *stem* to all parts of the plant.
▲**Synonym:** stalk
stem (stem) *noun, plural* **stems.**

straighten **1.** To make or become straight. The picture on the wall slanted to the left, so I *straightened* it. **2.** To put into proper order. I asked you to *straighten* your room.
straight•en (strā′tən) *verb,* **straightened, straightening.**

struggle To make a great effort. The children *struggled* through the heavy snow.
strug•gle (strug′ əl) *verb,* **struggled, struggling.**

stumble To lose one's balance; trip. I *stumbled* over the rake.
stum•ble (stum′ bəl) *verb,* **stumbled, stumbling.**

surround To be on all sides of; form a circle around. A fence *surrounds* our yard.
▲**Synonym:** enclose
sur•round (sə round′) *verb,* **surrounded, surrounding.**

Sweden A country in northern Europe.
Swe•den (swē′ dən) *noun.*

Tt

tall tale A made-up or exaggerated story; a tale too fantastic to believe.
tall tale (tôl tāl) *noun, plural* **tall tales.**

Tanksi
(tawnk′ shē)

tarantula A hairy spider that is found in warm areas. The *tarantula* has a painful bite.
ta•ran•tu•la (tə ran′ chə lə) *noun, plural* **tarantulas.**

Tiblo
(tē′ blo)

toucan A bird that has a heavy body, a very large beak, and colorful feathers. *Toucans* are found in Central America.
tou•can (tü′ kan) *noun, plural* **toucans.**

at; āpe; fär; câre; end; mē; it; īce; pîerce; hot; ōld; sông; fôrk; oil; out; up; ūse; rüle; půll; tûrn; chin; sing; shop; thin; this; hw in white; zh in treasure. The symbol ə stands for the unstressed vowel sound in about, taken, pencil, lemon, and circus.

towering Very tall; lofty. *Towering* palm trees lined the beach.
tow•er•ing (tou′ ər ing) *adjective.*

trade To give one thing in return for something else. I'll *trade* you two of my cards for one of yours.
▲**Synonyms:** exchange, swap
trade (trād) *verb,* **traded, trading.**

triangle **1.** A musical instrument made of a metal bar bent in the shape of a triangle. A *triangle* sounds like a bell when it is hit. **2.** A figure or object with three sides and three angles.
tri•an•gle (trī′ang′əl) *noun, plural* **triangles.**

trim To cut away or remove parts to make something neat and orderly. Please *trim* the hedge evenly.
trim (trim) *verb,* **trimmed, trimming.**

unusual Not usual, common, or ordinary. It is very *unusual* for them not to want to go to a movie.
un•u•su•al (un ū′ zhü əl) *adjective.*

vibration Rapid movement back and forth or up and down. People many miles away could feel the *vibration* of the earthquake.
▲**Synonym:** shaking
vi•bra•tion (vi brā′ shən) *noun, plural* **vibrations.**

visitor A person who visits. I have to clean my room because we're having *visitors* this afternoon.
▲**Synonym:** guest
vis•i•tor (viz′ i tər) *noun, plural* **visitors.**

wilderness A natural place where no people live. In a *wilderness* there may be a dense forest and wild animals.
wil•der•ness (wil′ dər nis) *noun, plural* **wildernesses.**

within In or into the inner part or parts of. The troops camped *within* the walls of the fort.
with•in (wi<u>th</u> in′ *or* with in′) *preposition.*

Woutilainen, Johan
(woo ti lā′ nən, yō′ han)

woven Formed or made by lacing together thread, yarn, or strips of straw or other material. Gold thread had been *woven* into the blouse.
wo•ven (wō′ vən) *past particple of* **weave.**

wrap To cover by putting something around. Please help me *wrap* these presents.
wrap (rap) *verb,* **wrapped, wrapping.**

zinnia A garden plant that has rounded, brightly colored flowers.
zin•ni•a (zin′ ē ə) *noun, plural* **zinnias.**

at; **ā**pe; f**ä**r; c**â**re; **e**nd; m**ē**; **i**t; **ī**ce; p**î**erce; h**o**t; **ō**ld; s**ô**ng; f**ô**rk; **oi**l; **ou**t; **u**p; **ū**se; r**ü**le; p**u̇**ll; t**û**rn; **ch**in; si**ng**; **sh**op; **th**in; <u>th</u>is; **hw** in **wh**ite; **zh** in trea**s**ure. The symbol **ə** stands for the unstressed vowel sound in **a**bout, tak**e**n, penc**i**l, lem**o**n, and circ**u**s.

Glossary

Acknowledgments

Cover Illustration: Lori Lohstoeter

The publisher gratefully acknowledges permission to reprint the following copyrighted material:

"The Ants" from BEAST FEAST by Douglas Florian. Copyright © 1994 by Douglas Florian. Used by permission of Harcourt Brace & Company.

"Arachne the Spinner" from GREEK MYTHS retold by Geraldine McCaughrean. Text copyright © 1992 by Geraldine McCaughrean. Illustrations copyright © 1992 by Emma Chichester Clark. Used by permission of Margaret K. McElderry Books, Macmillan Publishing Company.

"Arkansas Traveler" from GONNA SING MY HEAD OFF! Used by permission of Alfred A. Knopf.

"At the Flick of a Switch" from EARTH LINES, POEMS FOR THE GREEN AGE by Pat Moon. Copyright © 1991 by Pat Moon. Used by permission of Greenwillow Books, a division of William Morrow & Company, Inc.

"Basket" from WORLDS I KNOW AND OTHER POEMS by Myra Cohn Livingston. Copyright © 1985 by Myra Cohn Livingston. Used by permission of Marian Reiner for the author.

"Frog and Locust" from A HEART FULL OF TURQUOISE by Joe Hayes. Copyright © 1988 by Joe Hayes. Used by permission of Mariposa Publishing.

"From the Bellybutton of the Moon/Del ombligo de la luna" from FROM THE BELLY-BUTTON OF THE MOON AND OTHER SUMMER POEMS by Francisco X. Alarcón. Poems copyright © 1998 by Francisco X. Alarcón. Illustrations copyright © 1998 by Maya Christina Gonzalez. Used by permission of Children's Book Press.

"A Garden" from ALWAYS WONDERING by Aileen Fisher. Text copyright © 1991 by Aileen Fisher. Illustrations copyright © 1991 by Joan Sandin. Used by permission of HarperCollins Publishers.

"The Hen and the Apple Tree" from FABLES by Arnold Lobel. Copyright © 1980 by Arnold Lobel. Used by permission of HarperCollins Publishers.

"The Hurricane" from SING TO THE SUN by Ashley Bryan. Copyright © 1992 by Ashley Bryan. Used by permission of HarperCollins.

"Ice Cycle" from ONCE UPON ICE AND OTHER FROZEN POEMS by Mary Ann Hoberman. Copyright © 1997 by Mary Ann Hoberman. Used by permission of Wordsong/Boyds Mills Press, Inc.

"If I Find a Penny" from THE BUTTERFLY JAR by Jeff Moss. Text copyright © 1988 by Jeff Moss. Illustrations copyright © 1988 by Chris Demarest. Used by permission of Bantam Doubleday Dell Publishing Group.

"In Daddy's Arms" from IN DADDY'S ARMS I AM TALL, AFRICAN AMERICANS CELEBRATING FATHERS by Folami Abiade. Text copyright © 1997 by Folami Abiade. Illustrations copyright © 1997 by Javaka Steptoe. Used by permission of Lee & Low Books, Inc.

ACKNOWLEDGMENTS

The publisher gratefully acknowledges permission to reprint the following copyrighted material:

"Abuelita's Lap" by Pat Mora from CONFETTI: POEMS FOR CHILDREN by Pat Mora. Text copyright © 1996 by Pat Mora. Reprinted by permission of Lee & Low Books Inc.

"Baseballs for Sale" from MAX MALONE MAKES A MILLION by Charlotte Herman. Text copyright © 1991 by Charlotte Herman. Illustrations copyright © 1991 by Catherine Bowman Smith. Reprinted by permission of Henry Holt and Company, Inc.

Entire text and art and cover of CITY GREEN by DyAnne DiSalvo-Ryan. Copyright © 1994 by DyAnne DiSalvo-Ryan. By permission of Morrow Junior Books, a division of William Morrow and Company, Inc.

"Closed, I am a mystery" by Myra Cohn Livingston from A PLACE TO DREAM. From My Head is Red and Other Riddle Rhymes by Myra Cohn Livingston. Copyright © 1990 by Myra Cohn Livingston (Published by Holliday House, NY) by presmission of Marian Reiner.

"Different Drum" by Joe Scruggs from ANTS by Joe Scuggs. (Produced by Gary Powell.) Copyright © 1994 by Educational Graphics Press, Inc.

"Dream Wolf" is from DREAM WOLF by Paul Goble. Copyright © 1990 by Paul Goble. Reprinted with the permission of Simon & Schuster Books For Young Readers.

"Fog" by Carl Sandburg from CHICAGO POEMS by Carl Sandburg. Copyright © 1916 by Holt Reinhart & Winston Inc.; renewed 1944 by Carl Sandburg. Reprinted by permission of Harcourt Brace Jovanovich, Inc.

Cover permission for THE GIRL WHO LOVED WILD HORSES by Paul Goble. Copyright © 1978 by Paul Goble. Reprinted by permission of Simon & Schuster Books for Young Readers.

"Grandfather's Journey" by Allen Say. Copyright © 1993 by Allen Say. Reprinted with the permission of Houghton Mifflin Company. All rights reserved.

"The Little Painter of Sabana Grande" by Patricia Maloney Markun, illustrated by Robert Casilla. Text copyright © 1993 by Patricia Maloney Markun. Illustrations copyright © 1993 by Robert Casilla. Published by Simon & Schuster Books for Young Readers. Reprinted by permission.

"Moses Goes to a Concert" by Issac Millman. Copyright © 1998 by Isaac Millman. Reprinted by permission of Frances Foster Books/Farrar, Straus and Giroux.

"My Pencil" by Shirley R. Williams from POETRY PLACE ANTHOLOGY by Instructor Publications, Inc. Text copyright © 1983 by Instructor Publications, Inc.

"Opt: An Illusionary Tale" from OPT: AN ILLUSIONARY TALE by Arline and Joseph Baum. Copyright © 1987 by Arline and Joseph Baum. Used by permission of Viking Penguin, a division of Penguin Putnam, Inc.

"The Patchwork Quilt" from THE PATCHWORK QUILT by Valerie Flournoy, illustrations by Jerry Pinkney. Text copyright © 1985 by Valerie Flournoy. Illustrations copyright © 1985 by Jerry Pinkney. Published by arrangment Dial Books for Young Readers, a division of Penguin Putnam, Inc.

"Phoebe and the Spelling Bee" by Barney Saltzberg. Text and illustrations © 1996 by Barney Saltzberg. Reprinted by permission of Hyperion Books for Children.

Cover permission for RABBIT MAKES A MONKEY OUT OF LION by Verna Aardema; pictures by Jerry Pinkney. Pictures copyright © 1989 by Jerry Pinkney. Reprinted with the permission of Dial Books for Young Readers, a division of Penguin Books USA, Inc.

"The Sun, the Wind and the Rain" from THE SUN, THE WIND AND THE RAIN by Lisa Westberg Peters. Text copyright © 1988 by Lisa Westberg Peters. Illustrations copyright © 1988 by Ted Rand. Reprinted by permission of Henry Holt and Co., Inc.

Cover permission for TURTLE IN JULY by Marilyn Singer; illustrated by Jerry Pinckney. Illustrations copyright © 1989 by Jerry Pinckney. Reprinted with the permission of Atheneum Books for Young Readers, an imprint of Simon & Schuster.

"Who Am I?" by Felice Holman. Copyright © Felice Holman from AT THE TOP OF MY VOICE AND OTHER POEMS. Published by Charles Scribner's Sons, 1970.

"My Pencil" by Shirley R. Williams in POETRY PLACE ANTHOLOGY, published by Scholastic Professional Books. Copyright © 1983 by Edgell Communications, Inc. Reprinted with premission of Scholastic Inc.

Illustration

Myron Grossman, 105; B.B. Sams, 108–123; Pat Rasch, 107; Andy Levine, 171; Pat Rasch, 224; Vilma Ortiz–Dillon, 231, 234, 236; Mike DiGiorgio, 232, 237, 242; Andy Levine, 243; Mike DiGiorgio, 288; John Kanzler, 352–371; Leonor Glynn, 374; Tom Foty, 10–11 Marni Backer, 138–139 Greg Couch, 140–141 Christopher Zacharow, 254–255 Steve Barbaria, 256–257 Peter M. Fiore, 386–387; Rodica Prato, 391, 396, 407; George Thompson, 399.

Photography

12–13: The Bridgeman Art Library International/Christopher Wood Gallery, London UK. 48–49: Jane Wooster Scott/Superstock. 78–79: Art Resource, Inc./Herscovici. 50: t.l. Courtesy of Hyperion Press/Barry E. Levine, Inc. 106–107: The Norman Rockwell Museum at Stockbridge. 128–129: The Bridgeman Art Library International/Wingfield Sporting Gallery, London, UK. 135: Duomo/William Sallaz. 142–143: The Image Works/Cameramann. 172–173: The Bridgeman Art Library International/Bonhams, London, UK. 204–205: Art Resource, Inc./K.S. Art. 226–227: Madison Press Books. 228: m.l. Courtesy of Diane Hoyt–Goldsmith/Lawrence Migdale. 228–229: DRK Photo/(c) Tom Bean 1990. 230: DRK Photo/(c) Larry Ulrich. 231: Animals Animals/(c) Bill Beatty. 233: DRK Photo/(c) Stephen J. Kraseman. 236: Photo Researchers, Inc./(c) Scott Camazine. 238: ENP Images/(c) Gerry Ellis. 239: Photo Researchers, Inc./(c) Jewel Craig. 244–245: The Bridgeman Art Library International/Kathryn Kooyahoema/Jerry Jacka Photography. 250: b. Photo Researchers, Inc.. m. Photo Researchers, Inc. 258–259: Superstock/Gil Mayers. 260: t.r. reprinted by permission of Farrar, Straus and Giroux Books for Young Readers/(c) Daniel Lee. 318–319: Photo by William C.L. Weintraub for the Georgia Quilt Project, Inc. . 350–351: Gerald Peters Gallery, Santa Fe, New Mexico. . 376–377: Superstock. 383: Peter Arnold, Inc./(c) Kim Heacox.

"Paul Bunyan, the Mightiest Logger of Them All" from AMERICAN TALL TALES by Mary Pope Osborne. Copyright © 1991 by Mary Pope Osborne. Used by permission of Alfred A. Knopf, Inc.

"Pincushion Cactus" from WHISPERS AND OTHER POEMS by Myra Cohn Livingston. Copyright © 1958, 1986 by Myra Cohn Livingston. Used by permission of Marian Reiner for the author.

"The Rabbit's Tale" from THE DRAGON'S TALE AND OTHER ANIMAL FABLES OF THE CHINESE ZODIAC by Demi. Copyright © 1996 by Demi. Used by permission of Henry Holt and Company, Inc.

"Seeing the Animals" from NATIVE AMERICAN ANIMAL STORIES by Joseph Bruchac. Copyright © 1992 by Joseph Bruchac. Used by permission of Fulcrum Publishing.

"The Song of the World's Last Whale" words and music by Pete Seeger. Copyright © 1970, 1994 by Stormking Music Inc.

"Spider on the Floor" from RAFFI'S TOP 10 SONGS TO READ. Words and music by Bill Russell. Text copyright © 1976 by Egos Anonymous (PRO). Illustrations copyright © 1993 by True Kelley. Used by permission of Crown Publishers, Inc., a Random House company.

"Take a Bite Out of Music" from TAKE A BITE OUT OF MUSIC, IT'S YUMMY by Mary Ann Hall. Copyright © 1986 by Mary Ann Hall's Music for Children.

"Take Me Out to the Ballgame" words by Jack Norworth, music by Albert von Tilzer from GONNA SING MY HEAD OFF! Used by permission of Alfred A. Knopf.

"Toad's Trick" from TO RIDE A BUTTERFLY by Verna Aardema. Text copyright © 1991 by Verna Aardema. Illustrations copyright © 1991 by Will Hillenbrand. Used by permission of Bantam Doubleday Dell Publishing Group, Inc.

"Using Your Head" from JATAKA TALES edited by Nancy DeRoin. Text copyright © 1975 by Nancy DeRoin. Drawings copyright © 1975 by Ellen Lanyon. Used by permission of Houghton Mifflin Company.

"Whale" from THE RAUCOUS AUK by Mary Ann Hoberman. Copyright © 1973 by Mary Ann Hoberman. Used by permission of The Viking Press.

"Why Bears Have Short Tails" from AND IT IS STILL THAT WAY by Byrd Baylor. Copyright © 1976 by Byrd Baylor. Used by permission of Trails West Press.

"The Wind and the Sun" told by Margaret Hughes from AESOP'S FABLES. Copyright © 1979 by Albany Books. Used by permission of Chartwell Books Inc., a division of Book Sales Inc.

"The Wolf and His Shadow" from THE BEST OF AESOP'S FABLES retold by Margaret Clark. Text copyright © 1990 by Margaret Clark. Illustrations copyright © 1990 by Charlotte Voake. Used by permission of Little, Brown and Company.

Notes

Backmatter Contents

Take a Bite of Music
Mary Ann Hall

Take a bite of music, it really is a treat.
Take a bite of music, serve it with a beat.
Take a bite of music, there are many ways to play.
Ev'rybody needs it every day.

The Crow and the Pitcher
a fable by Aesop

A crow perched on a tree branch to rest. He'd been flying for hours and was very thirsty. Looking down, he noticed a fat clay pitcher under the tree. He flew down to take a closer look.

"It has some water in it!" he shouted, amazed at his good luck.

The crow put his beak into the pitcher to take a drink. But he couldn't reach the water with his beak. He tried to stick his head in all the way, only to find that the opening was too small, and his head too big.

"Now what?" he muttered. He glared at the pitcher. "Here I am, dying of thirst, and over there is a pitcher of water. If the pitcher were full, then the water would come right up to the top and I could have all the water I wanted."

The crow looked around. Lots of small rocks lay in the grass. "Rocks and grass, rocks and . . . that's it! I have an idea! A terrific idea, if I say so myself."

The crow picked up a rock and dropped it into the pitcher. Then he took another rock and dropped it in. Then he took another, and another, and another, and dropped them one-at-a-time into the pitcher. Each made a satisfying little splash as it fell to the bottom. With each rock, the water rose a little higher up the sides of the pitcher. Finally the water reached to the top. The crow dipped his beak into the pitcher and took a long drink.

"That was the best water I've ever had," he said.

Moral: *Where there is a will, there is a way.*

Basket
Myra Cohn Livingston

Grandmother's basket
of ribbon and lace
is kept in a high-up closet place.

But when I go over
she'll take it out
and let me rummage all about

and find materials.
I can choose
whatever Grandmother doesn't use

when she knits an afghan
or sews a gown.
So whenever I see her take it down

I think of the things
my dolls could wear
of whatever my grandmother has to spare.

Paul Bunyan, the Mightiest Logger of Them All

retold by Mary Pope Osborne

It seems an amazing baby was born in the state of Maine. When he was only two weeks old, he weighed more than a hundred pounds, and for breakfast every morning he ate five dozen eggs, ten sacks of potatoes, and a half-barrel of mush made from a whole sack of cornmeal. But the baby's strangest feature was his big, curly black beard. It was so big and bushy that every morning his poor mother had to comb it with a pine tree.

Except for that black beard, the big baby wasn't much trouble to anybody until he was about nine months old. That was when he first started to crawl, and since he weighed over five hundred pounds, he caused an earthquake that shook the whole town.

The baby's parents tried putting him in a giant floating cradle off the coast of Maine, but every time he rolled over, huge waves drowned all the villages along the coast.

So his parents hauled the giant toddler to a cave in the Maine woods far away from civilization and said good-bye. His father gave him a fishing pole, a knife, some flint rocks, and an axe. "We'll think of you often, honey," his mother said, weeping. "But you can't come back—home—you're just too big."

That's the story of how Paul Bunyan came to take care of himself in the Maine woods. And even though he lived alone for the next twenty years, he got along quite well.

In those times, huge sections of America were filled with dark green forests. It would be nice if those trees could have stayed tall and thick forever. But the pioneers needed them to build houses, churches, ships, wagons, bridges, and barns. So one day Paul Bunyan took a good look at all those trees and decided to invent logging.

"Tim-ber!" he yelled, and he swung the bright steel axe his father had given him in a wide circle. There was a terrible crash, and when Paul looked around, he saw he'd felled ten white pines with a single swing.

After that Paul traveled plenty fast through the untamed North Woods. He cut pine, spruce, and red willow in Minnesota, Michigan, and Wisconsin. He cleared cottonwoods out of Kansas so farmers could plant wheat and oaks out of Iowa so farmers could plant corn.

When next heard of, Paul was headed to Arizona. He dragged his pickaxe behind him on that trip, not realizing he was leaving a big ditch in his tracks. Today that ditch is called the Grand Canyon.

When Paul got back from the West, he decided to start a logging camp. Word spread fast. Since all the woodsmen had heard of Paul Bunyan, thousands of them hurried to Paul's headquarters at Big Onion on the Big Onion River in Minnesota to be part of his crew.

"There's only two requirements," Paul announced to the men who'd gathered to apply for the job. "All my loggers have to be over ten feet tall and able to pop six buttons off their shirts with one breath."

Well, about a thousand of the lumberjacks met those requirements, and Paul hired them all. Then he built a gigantic logging camp with bunkhouses a mile long and bunks ten beds high. The camp's chow table was so long that it took a week to pass the salt and pepper from one end to the other. Paul dug a few ponds to provide drinking water for everyone. Today we call those ponds the Great Lakes.

Things went pretty well at the Big Onion Lumber Company until the Year of the Hard Winter. One day Shot Gunderson, the crew boss, complained to Paul, "Boss, it's so cold that the flames for all the lanterns are freezing. And, Boss, when I give orders to the woods crew, all my words freeze in the air and hang there stiff as icicles."

"Well, haul away your frozen words and store them somewhere next to the lantern flames," Paul advised. "They'll both thaw out in the spring."

Sure enough, they did. The only problem was that, come spring, the melting lantern flames started some mean little brush fires. And when Shot's frozen words thawed, old cries of "Timber!" and "Chow time!" started to echo throughout the woods, causing all sorts of confusion. But other than that, things ran pretty smoothly.

Well, there's stories and stories about Paul Bunyan. For many years, old loggers sat around potbellied stoves and told about the good old times with Paul. Those loggers are all gone now, but many of their stories still hang frozen in the cold forest air of the North Woods, waiting to be told. Come spring, when they start to thaw, some of them might just start telling themselves. It's been known to happen.

Ice Cycle

Mary Ann Hoberman

I've always thought it rather nice
That water freezes into ice.
I'm also pleased that it is true
That ice melts back to water, too.
But even so I find it strange
The way that ice and water change
And how a single water drop
Can fathom when it's time to stop
Its downward drip and go ahead
And start an icicle instead.

Moses Goes to a Concert • PRACTICE

Name__________ Date________ **Practice 75**

Main Idea

The **main idea** is the major point that an author wants readers to understand. **Supporting details** are small examples and reasons that explain the main idea.

For each main idea below, write some possible supporting details. Answers will vary.

Main Idea: Matt helps out around the house.

Supporting Details:

1. He makes his bed.
2. Matt helps his parents make dinner.
3. Matt and his sister feed the goldfish.

Main Idea: Ashley is a great baseball player.

Supporting Details:

4. Ashley hit three home runs in the last game.
5. She kept the other team from scoring any points.
6. The team voted Ashley captain.

At Home: Have students add one more supporting detail to each of the main ideas above.

Name__________ Date________ **Practice 76**

Vocabulary

Supply the correct answers. Answers may vary.

1. If you wanted to hear music at your party, why would you invite a **musician**? because he or she can play songs on an instrument
2. What would you hear at a **concert**? a musical performance
3. After learning how to play the drums, a person might join an **orchestra**. What is that? a group of people who play music together
4. What are some musical **instruments**? piano, drums, guitar, violin, saxophone
5. How does a **conductor** help members of a band to play music? by telling them when to start and how fast to play
6. Why would you stay home from school if you felt **ill**? to rest and get better

At Home: Have students write a story using all the vocabulary words.

A Special Touch

The *concert* was about to begin. But where was the *conductor*? Oh no! He was *ill*! How would the *orchestra* know what to do?

Each *musician* had a different idea. The violin player thought the orchestra should play without the conductor. The piano player thought she should be the conductor. The horn player thought the musicians should give a speech about each *instrument* they played. The drum player thought they should all go out to lunch.

Then the conductor's wife came in. "I have watched my husband practice. I can do his job," she said.

That night the orchestra gave one of its greatest concerts! Even the local newspapers agreed.

1. What is a person who plays music called? a musician
2. What are a violin, a piano, and a horn each called? an instrument
3. What is another name for a group of *musicians* playing together? an orchestra
4. Who was too ill to be in the concert? the conductor
5. How was the orchestra's problem solved? The conductor's wife conducted the concert.

At Home: Ask students how they would have solved the problem faced by the orchestra.

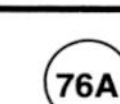

Name__________ Date________ **Practice 77**

Story Comprehension

Match each character from "Moses Goes to a Concert" with each statement in the right column. Write the letter on the line.

1. Moses c	a. feels vibrations with her feet.
2. Mr. Samuels d	b. plays on the marimba.
3. Ann b	c. has a new set of drums.
4. The percussionist a	d. takes his students to a concert.

Answer the following questions about "Moses Goes to a Concert."

5. Who do the children meet at the concert? The children meet Ms. Elwyn.
6. Why did Mr. Samuels give the children balloons before the concert? If they held the balloons, they could feel the vibrations of the music.
7. What is a percussionist? a musician who plays drums, a huge gong, a marimba, and other instruments that are struck
8. What does Moses tell his parents at the end of the story? "When you set your mind to it, you can become anything you want when you grow up." He says he wants to be a percussionist.

At Home: Have students write a sentence about how Moses feels at the end of the story.

Moses Goes to a Concert • PRACTICE

Name_____________________ Date__________ **Practice 78**

Use a Diagram

Some of the hand positions for letters in American Sign Language look like the written letters. Others use movements that appear to be drawing the letter in the air.

Study these letters. Explain how the fingers are positioned to look like the letter they represent. The first one is done for you.

1. C — **The thumb and other four fingers form a C shape.**
2. I — The pinky is held up alone like an I.
3. J — The pinky is moved down and up like a J.
4. L — The thumb and forefinger form an L.
5. V — The forefinger and middle finger form a V.
6. W — The forefinger, middle finger, and ring finger form a W.
7. Y — The thumb and pinky form a Y with the arm.
8. Z — The forefinger moves across, down, and across to make a Z.

At Home: Have students demonstrate the American Sign Language letters shown on this page.

Name_____________________ Date__________ **Practice 79**

Main Idea

To understand a passage better, separate the main idea from the details that support it. The **main idea** is the most important point. **Supporting details** are smaller points that explain the main idea.

Read the following sentences about "Moses Goes to a Concert." Write the main idea of the passage and then write the supporting details. Answers will vary.

Moses has a new set of drums. He likes to play with his new drums, but he can't hear the sound they make. Moses is deaf. He can, however, feel the vibration of his drums with his hands. To feel even more of the vibrations, Moses takes off his shoes. Now he can feel his new drums with his hands and his feet!

Main Idea:

1. Moses can play his drums, even though he is deaf.

Supporting Details:

2. Moses has a new set of drums.
3. Moses plays by feeling the vibrations of the drum through his hands.
4. Moses has also taken off his shoes, so he can feel the vibrations through his feet.

At Home: Have students read a paragraph from an article in a childrens' magazine or newspaper. Then ask them to write down the main idea and supporting details of the paragraph.

Name_____________________ Date__________ **Practice 80**

Summarize

When you **summarize**, you tell only the most important things that happened. Read each passage below. Then write a summary. Answers may vary.

1. Last summer, Crystal and her parents drove to Florida. On the way, their car broke down. They worried that they might not make it to Florida. However, they got their car fixed and drove there the next morning.

   Summary: Crystal and her parents had car trouble during their drive to Florida.

2. In Florida, they visited Crystal's grandma. Grandma loved to garden. She grew lemon trees, orange trees, and many different types of flowers. She gardened every day.

   Summary: In Florida, they visited Crystal's grandma, who loved to garden.

3. Crystal asked Grandma, "Can I work in the garden, too?" Grandma said yes. First, Crystal chose the kind of flowers she wanted. Crystal chose roses. Then, she planted seeds and watered them every day. Grandma said that Crystal's roses would bloom in the spring.

   Summary: Crystal planted roses in Grandma's garden.

4. After two weeks in Florida, it was time to go home. Crystal and her parents hugged Grandma. Crystal felt sad about leaving, but she knew that they would come back in the spring.

   Summary: After two weeks in Florida, Crystal and her parents headed home.

At Home: Have students write a one-paragraph summary of the story on this page.

Name_____________________ Date__________ **Practice 81**

Context Clues

When you find an unfamiliar word, read the words and sentences around it. They often can help you figure out the word's meaning.

Look at the underlined word in each example. Circle the words and phrases that help you tell what the word means. Then mark an **X** next to the meaning that fits the underlined word.

1. The musicians walked onto the stage. People clapped and waved. The concert was about to begin.

   ____ drums __X__ musical performance ____ game

2. The singer sang a very high note. She broke a window.

   ____ red ____ apple pie __X__ sound in music

3. She is a percussionist. She plays the piano, the drums, and many other instruments.

   __X__ type of musician ____ large van ____ baby duck

4. Mozart is a famous composer. He wrote many beautiful songs.

   ____ cab driver ____ dog food __X__ person who creates a musical work

5. He played a pretty melody on the piano. I asked, "What is the name of that song?"

   ____ green __X__ tune ____ bat

At Home: Have students look up each underlined word in a dictionary to check the meaning.

Name______________________ Date__________ **Reteach 75**

Main Idea

> The **main idea** is the most important point an author wants to make. **Supporting details** tell us more about the main idea.

Keep the main idea in mind as you read each list of supporting details. Put an **X** next to each detail that supports the main idea.

1. Main Idea: My dog is huge!

Supporting Details:

__x__ He is larger than I am.

_____ He never barks.

__x__ He weighs two hundred pounds.

2. Main Idea: I do a lot of things to keep my dog in good shape.

Supporting Details:

__x__ I take him on walks.

_____ I do my homework.

__x__ I play games with him.

3. Main Idea: My friend Margo has lots of pets.

Supporting Details:

__x__ She has a parrot.

__x__ She has some fish.

_____ She bought a dog bone.

4. Main Idea: Margo takes her pets everywhere.

Supporting Details:

__x__ She takes her cat to the library.

_____ She buys pet food at the pet shop.

__x__ She brings her parrot to the store.

At Home: Have students write one more supporting detail for each main idea.

Name______________________ Date__________ **Reteach 76**

Vocabulary

Supply the correct words from the list.

concert ill instruments conductor musicians orchestra

1. Some ___musicians___ can play both the tuba and the guitar.
2. The music show was the best ___concert___ I ever attended.
3. When people are ___ill___, they feel sick.
4. Pianos and drums are my favorite ___instruments___.
5. The ___conductor___ is the person who leads the orchestra.
6. There were six violins in the ___orchestra___.

6

Story Comprehension — Reteach 77

Circle the correct words for the sentences below.

1. Moses plays the
   a. piano b. flute **(c. drums)**
2. The name of Moses' teacher is
   a. Ms. Elwyn **(b. Mr. Samuels)** c. John
3. The teacher brought a surprise to give to the students. The surprise is
   a. lunch **(b. balloons)** c. a bus
4. When Moses grows up, he wants to be a
   (a. percussionist) b. teacher c. fireman

At Home: Have students write a sentence explaining how Ms. Elwyn became a percussionist.

Name______________________ Date__________ **Reteach 78**

Use a Diagram

> The words of our language are spelled out using letters. Words can be spelled out in other ways as well. Sign language is one example. You can also use **symbols** to represent letters.

A	=	□
B	=	○
C	=	+
D	=	△
E	=	#
F	=	$
G	=	%
H	=	×
I	=	☆
J	=	÷
K	=	¢
L	=	=
M	=	···

N	=	√
O	=	∅
P	=	‖
Q	=	≠
R	=	–
S	=	◇
T	=	⊗
U	=	♡
V	=	→
W	=	⊠
X	=	~
Y	=	!
Z	=	?

Use the diagram above to decode the words. When you have finished, read the secret question.

1. ⊠ × □ ⊗ ___what___
2. ☆ ◇ ___is___
3. ⊗ × # ___the___
4. ⊠ # □ ⊗ × # – ___weather___
5. ⊗ ∅ △ □ ! ___today___

Use the codes to spell your name. ___Answers will vary.___

At Home: Have students make up their own symbol for each letter of the alphabet. Ask them to write a sentence in their code.

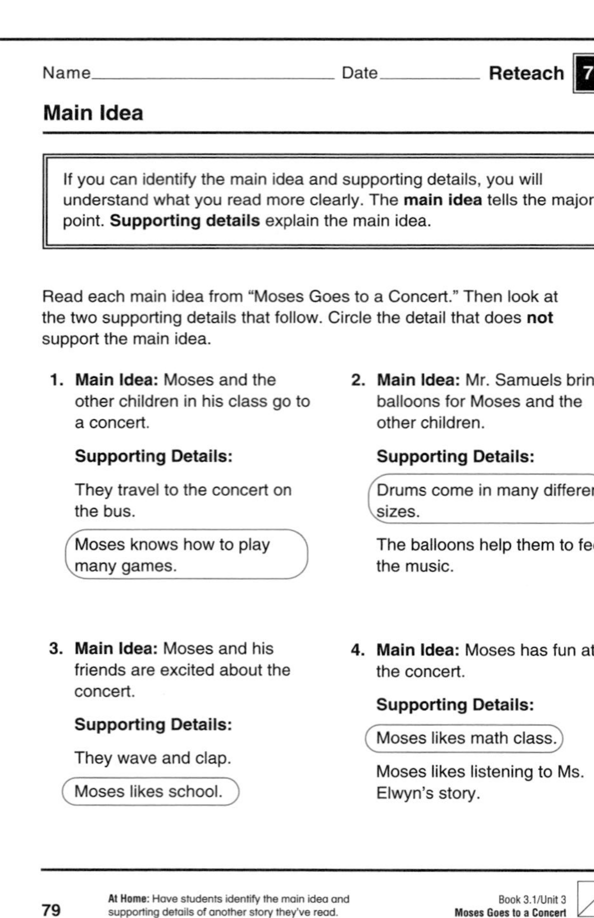

Name______________________ Date__________ **Reteach 79**

Main Idea

> If you can identify the main idea and supporting details, you will understand what you read more clearly. The **main idea** tells the major point. **Supporting details** explain the main idea.

Read each main idea from "Moses Goes to a Concert." Then look at the two supporting details that follow. Circle the detail that does **not** support the main idea.

1. Main Idea: Moses and the other children in his class go to a concert.

Supporting Details:

They travel to the concert on the bus.

(Moses knows how to play many games.)

2. Main Idea: Mr. Samuels brings balloons for Moses and the other children.

Supporting Details:

(Drums come in many different sizes.)

The balloons help them to feel the music.

3. Main Idea: Moses and his friends are excited about the concert.

Supporting Details:

They wave and clap.

(Moses likes school.)

4. Main Idea: Moses has fun at the concert.

Supporting Details:

(Moses likes math class.)

Moses likes listening to Ms. Elwyn's story.

At Home: Have students identify the main idea and supporting details of another story they've read.

Moses Goes to a Concert • RETEACH

Name____________________ Date__________ **Reteach 80**

Summarize

When you write a **summary**, you give only the most important events or information. You do not include small details when you summarize.

Read each paragraph. Underline the sentence that best summarizes the paragraph.

1. Sarah and her father both felt hungry. Their stomachs growled. They both wanted to eat cheese sandwiches for dinner that night.
   - Sarah's stomach growled.
   - Sarah's father felt hungry.
   - Sarah and her father both felt hungry.
2. Sarah and her father went to the store. They bought cheese and bread. They also bought six plums, a bunch of grapes, and a box of cookies.
   - Sarah and her father went to the store.
   - Sarah and her father bought cookies.
   - Sarah and her father saw a movie.
3. When they got home, it was almost time for dinner. Sarah and her father decided to make cheese sandwiches. Sarah and her father put the cheese on the bread. Then they put the bread in the oven.
   - Sarah and her father made dinner.
   - Sarah and her father put the cheese on the bread.
   - Sarah and her father ate plums.
4. Sarah and her father sat down to eat dinner. Sarah only ate one cheese sandwich, but her father ate four! For dessert, they ate the cookies, plums, and grapes.
   - Sarah and her father ate cookies, plums, and grapes for dessert.
   - Sarah and her father ate dinner.
   - Sarah's father ate four cheese sandwiches.

At Home: Have students use the four paragraphs as one story and summarize it.

Name____________________ Date__________ **Reteach 81**

Context Clues

Reading the words and sentences around an unfamiliar word can help you figure out what the word means. Then, you can use a dictionary or glossary to check your meaning or to find a more specific meaning.

Read each passage below. Use the words and phrases in dark type to help you decide what each underlined word means. Then write the meaning of the underlined word on the line.

1. There were **drummers, piano players, and many other musicians** in the orchestra. The children couldn't wait for the **concert** to begin.

   orchestra: a group of musicians playing on different instruments

2. When **Ms. Elwyn comes onto the stage**, people stand up and start to applaud. Some of the children in Moses's class do not **clap**, though. They wave instead.

   applaud: clap

3. I can play the **drums**. She can play the **piano**. Which instrument can you play?

   instrument: something that makes music

4. The musicians rehearsed for many days. They sounded **better each day**. After **practicing** for almost a month, they were ready for the concert.

   rehearsed: practiced

At Home: Have students write sentences using the underlined words above.

Name______________________ Date__________ **Extend 75**

Main Idea

Read the story. Use the information to write a main-idea statement.

what? where? who? when? why?

Matthew is too excited to sleep tonight. He is thinking about what will happen tomorrow when he wakes up. Early in the morning the whole family will drive to the airport to pick up Grandma and Grandpa. Aunt Lisa will arrive around lunchtime. After lunch everyone will go to the high school where Matthew will compete in his town's debating contest.

Mom comes in with a book and sits on Matthew's bed. They take turns reading pages from one of his favorite books. Matthew starts jumping on the bed. Mom tells him that she knows he is excited but he should just relax and listen. He asks for a drink of water. Mom brings him a glass of water and puts it on his dresser next to his bed. He reaches over and takes a sip of the water.

Mom tells Matthew that he can count sheep. Even after counting fifty sheep, he still can't sleep.

It is almost ten o'clock. Mom starts to hum a lullaby that she sang to Matthew when he was small. The music sounds soft and special to him. The melody is the last thing he remembers before falling asleep.

Now write your main-idea statement.

Matthew is too excited to sleep.

Write about a time you were so excited that you couldn't sleep.

Name______________________ Date__________ **Extend 76**

Vocabulary

concert	instrument	musician	conductor	orchestra	ill

You have been asked to take part in a special musical performance. Write the name of your instrument and draw its picture. Write to a family member or friend on another piece of paper. Use as many words from the box as you can to invite them to your performance.

Instrument ______________________

Extend 77

Story Comprehension

Work with a group to write a scene from "Moses Goes to a Concert." Choose actors. Have them use spoken words and sign language to play their parts. Present your scene to the class.

Name______________________ Date__________ **Extend 78**

Use a Diagram

Moses and the other children at his school communicate by using American Sign Language. In this language, a sign can stand for a letter of the alphabet, a whole word, or even an idea. The diagram below shows the hand signs for letters in American Sign Language. This alphabet is important because for some words, such as names, there are no signs.

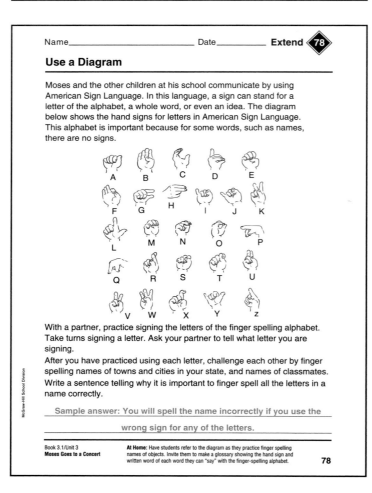

A B C D E
F G H I J K
L M N O P
Q R S T U
V W X Y Z

With a partner, practice signing the letters of the finger spelling alphabet. Take turns signing a letter. Ask your partner to tell what letter you are signing.

After you have practiced using each letter, challenge each other by finger spelling names of towns and cities in your state, and names of classmates. Write a sentence telling why it is important to finger spell all the letters in a name correctly.

Sample answer: You will spell the name incorrectly if you use the wrong sign for any of the letters.

Name______________________ Date__________ **Extend 79**

Main Idea

Write a main-idea sentence for "Moses Goes to a Concert."

Answers will vary. For example, "When you set your mind to it, you can be anything you want when you grow up."

Develop an idea for another story about Moses and his friends. Write a main idea sentence for this story.

Answers will vary.

Write three or four sentences giving supporting details for your story.

Name_______________ Date__________ **Extend 80**

Summarize

Read the paragraphs about the planet Earth.

The planet earth is the only planet in the solar system with large amounts of water on its surface and in its atmosphere. Earth is the third planet from the sun. The water in the oceans would boil away if the sun were much closer. If the earth were farther away from the sun, the water would turn to ice. The sun is just the right distance away.

Earth is larger than Mercury, Mars, Venus, and Pluto but smaller than all of the other planets. From space earth looks like a perfectly round ball, but it is really wider in the middle than at the top and bottom.

Earth is tilted a little to one side as it travels around the sun. As it goes around the sun, it spins like a big top. Each spin takes about twenty-four hours and is called a day.

A blanket of air circles the earth to keep the temperature from changing too much. This blanket of air is called the atmosphere. The people on the planet Earth live at the bottom of the atmosphere.

Write a paragraph summarizing the information about planet Earth. Be sure to include important information from each of the paragraphs.

Answers will vary.

At Home: Have students draw pictures to summarize the paragraphs about planet Earth.

Name_______________ Date__________ **Extend 81**

Context Clues

Use the words in the box to complete the story.

conductor	orchestra	marimba	kettledrum
snare drum	percussion	cymbal	triangle

Our class went to hear a concert performed by our town's **orchestra**. The musicians knew exactly when they were supposed to play. The **conductor** stood in front of them with his baton in his hand, and directed their playing. There were many different **percussion** instruments that were played by being hit or shaken. There were several kinds of drums, including a small double-headed drum called a **snare drum** because of the snares across its lower head. It made a sound like a rattle when it was played. I liked the drum that looked like a giant covered soup bowl. It is called a **kettledrum**.

There were other instruments, too. One of my favorites, the **marimba** looked a little like a piano keyboard, but you play it with sticks and not your fingers. The brass **cymbal** is shaped like a plate, but I can't imagine eating my dinner on it! To play it you strike it with a stick or even with another instrument just like it. I think the steel **triangle** has the funniest name of all. It makes me think of shapes we study in school.

At Home: Have students underline the context clues in the story that helped them fill in the correct word.

Moses Goes to a Concert • GRAMMAR

Name______________________ Date__________ LEARN **Grammar** 65

What Is an Action Verb?

- An **action verb** is a word that shows action.
  The students clap to the music.
  Moses beats a drum.

Each sentence has an action verb. Find the verb and write it on the line.

1. Mr. Samuels's class rides on a bus. ___rides___
2. Mr. Samuels carries his bag. ___carries___
3. He takes them to a concert. ___takes___
4. Moses sits in the front row. ___sits___
5. A young woman walks onstage. ___walks___
6. The percussionist bows. ___bows___
7. Some of the students wave. ___wave___
8. The conductor raises his baton. ___raises___
9. The percussionist hits the gong. ___hits___
10. The students thank Ms. Elwyn. ___thank___

Extension: Have students work together in pairs. Ask them to list verbs that show the actions of playing instruments. Once they have completed their lists, they can check the story to see if they can find additional musical action verbs.

Name______________________ Date__________ LEARN AND PRACTICE **Grammar** 66

Finding Action Verbs

- An **action verb** is a word that shows action. Some action verbs tell about actions that are hard to see.
  The students listen to the music.
  Moses likes the vibrations.

Circle the action verb in each sentence.

1. The teacher (waits) for the class.
2. The conductor (smiles) at the audience.
3. The students (watch) the conductor carefully.
4. They (enjoy) the concert!
5. Moses (feels) the vibrations in the balloon.
6. The students (learn) the music.
7. The drums (make) a lot of noise.
8. They (practice) their instruments.
9. They (helped) each other.
10. Moses (remembers) that field trip.

Extension: Have the students work in pairs and list four action verbs. Using their list, they should take turns writing sentences using the verbs.

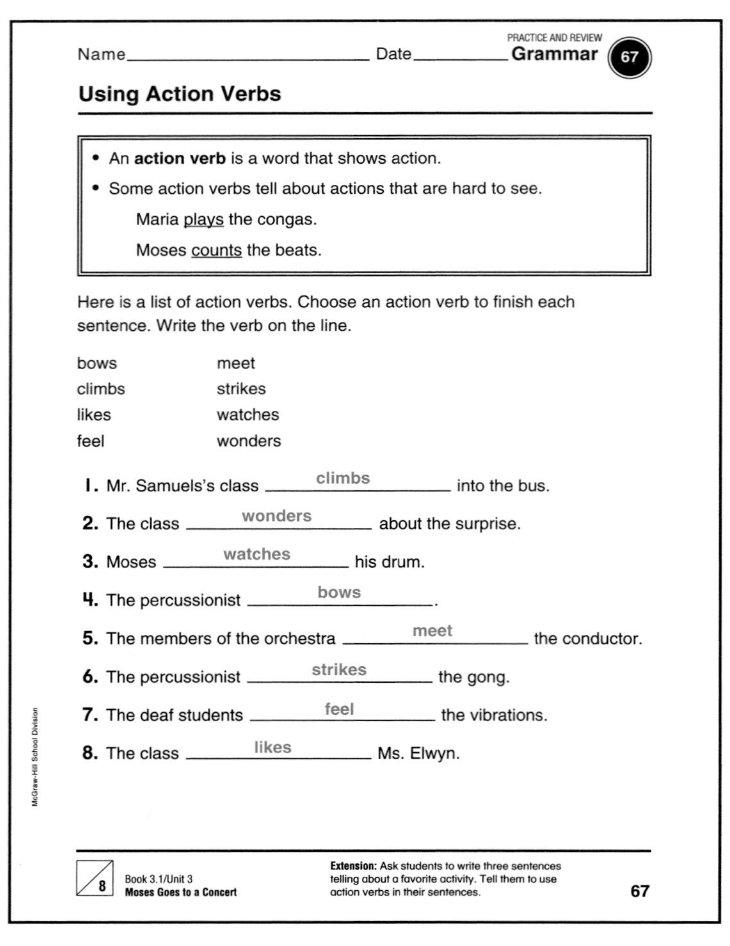

Name______________________ Date__________ PRACTICE AND REVIEW **Grammar** 67

Using Action Verbs

- An **action verb** is a word that shows action.
- Some action verbs tell about actions that are hard to see.
  Maria plays the congas.
  Moses counts the beats.

Here is a list of action verbs. Choose an action verb to finish each sentence. Write the verb on the line.

bows	meet
climbs	strikes
likes	watches
feel	wonders

1. Mr. Samuels's class ___climbs___ into the bus.
2. The class ___wonders___ about the surprise.
3. Moses ___watches___ his drum.
4. The percussionist ___bows___.
5. The members of the orchestra ___meet___ the conductor.
6. The percussionist ___strikes___ the gong.
7. The deaf students ___feel___ the vibrations.
8. The class ___likes___ Ms. Elwyn.

Extension: Ask students to write three sentences telling about a favorite activity. Tell them to use action verbs in their sentences.

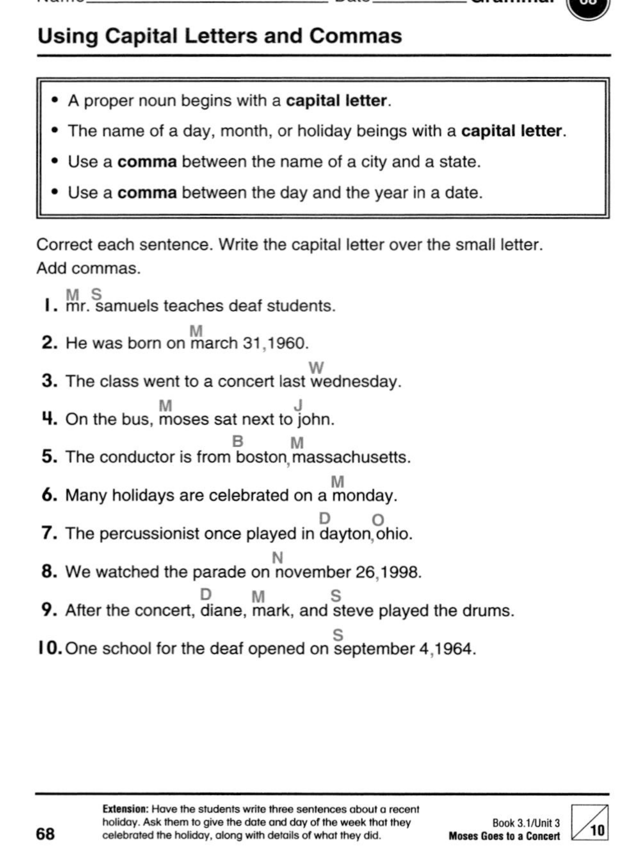

Name______________________ Date__________ MECHANICS **Grammar** 68

Using Capital Letters and Commas

- A proper noun begins with a **capital letter**.
- The name of a day, month, or holiday beings with a **capital letter**.
- Use a **comma** between the name of a city and a state.
- Use a **comma** between the day and the year in a date.

Correct each sentence. Write the capital letter over the small letter. Add commas.

1. M S
   mr. samuels teaches deaf students.
2. M
   He was born on march 31, 1960.
3. W
   The class went to a concert last wednesday.
4. M J
   On the bus, moses sat next to john.
5. B M
   The conductor is from boston, massachusetts.
6. M
   Many holidays are celebrated on a monday.
7. D O
   The percussionist once played in dayton, ohio.
8. N
   We watched the parade on november 26, 1998.
9. D M S
   After the concert, diane, mark, and steve played the drums.
10. S
    One school for the deaf opened on september 4, 1964.

Extension: Have the students write three sentences about a recent holiday. Ask them to give the date and day of the week that they celebrated the holiday, along with details of what they did.

Moses Goes to a Concert • GRAMMAR

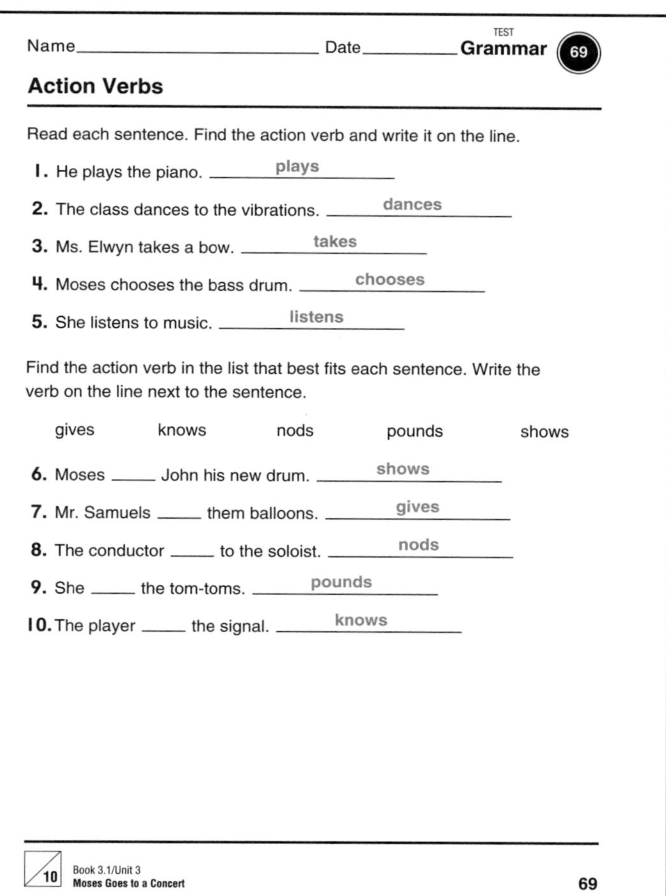

Name________________________ Date__________ TEST Grammar 69

Action Verbs

Read each sentence. Find the action verb and write it on the line.

1. He plays the piano. ___plays___
2. The class dances to the vibrations. ___dances___
3. Ms. Elwyn takes a bow. ___takes___
4. Moses chooses the bass drum. ___chooses___
5. She listens to music. ___listens___

Find the action verb in the list that best fits each sentence. Write the verb on the line next to the sentence.

gives knows nods pounds shows

6. Moses _____ John his new drum. ___shows___
7. Mr. Samuels _____ them balloons. ___gives___
8. The conductor _____ to the soloist. ___nods___
9. She _____ the tom-toms. ___pounds___
10. The player _____ the signal. ___knows___

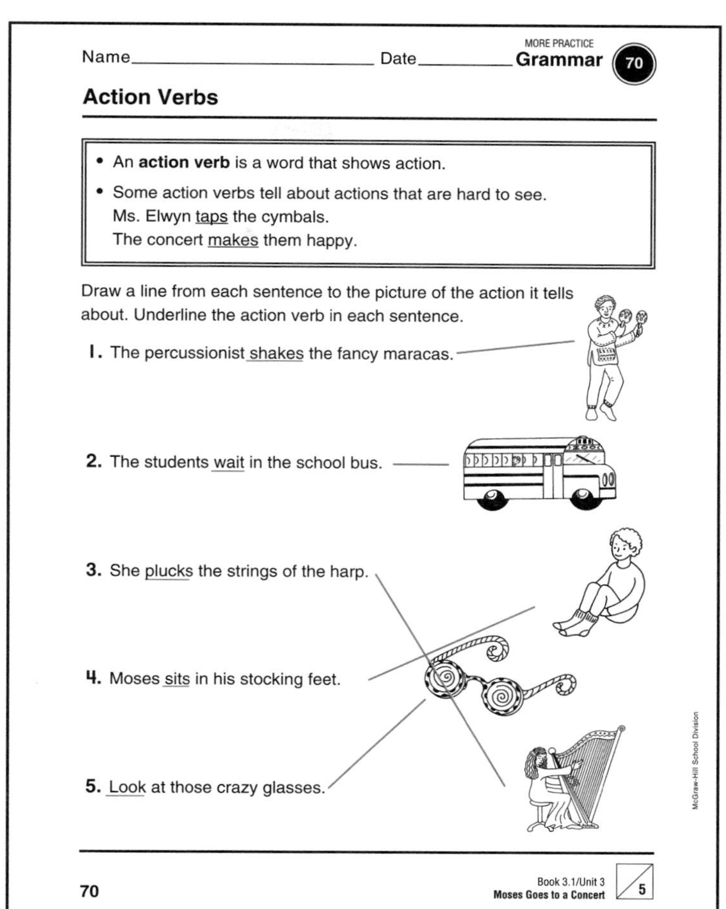

Name________________________ Date__________ MORE PRACTICE Grammar 70

Action Verbs

- An **action verb** is a word that shows action.
- Some action verbs tell about actions that are hard to see.
  Ms. Elwyn taps the cymbals.
  The concert makes them happy.

Draw a line from each sentence to the picture of the action it tells about. Underline the action verb in each sentence.

1. The percussionist shakes the fancy maracas.
2. The students wait in the school bus.
3. She plucks the strings of the harp.
4. Moses sits in his stocking feet.
5. Look at those crazy glasses.

Moses Goes to a Concert • SPELLING

Name________________ Date________ PRETEST SPELLING 65

Words with Consonant Clusters

Pretest Directions
Fold back the paper along the dotted line. Use the blanks to write each word as it is read aloud. When you finish the test, unfold the paper. Use the list at the right to correct any spelling mistakes. Practice the words you missed for the Posttest.

To Parents
Here are the results of your child's weekly spelling Pretest. You can help your child study for the Posttest by following these simple steps for each word on the word list:
1. Read the word to your child.
2. Have your child write the word, saying each letter as it is written.
3. Say each letter of the word as your child checks the spelling.
4. If a mistake has been made, have your child read each letter of the correctly spelled word aloud, and then repeat steps 1-3.

1. ________ 1. paint
2. ________ 2. young
3. ________ 3. stamp
4. ________ 4. thank
5. ________ 5. friend
6. ________ 6. ink
7. ________ 7. behind
8. ________ 8. faint
9. ________ 9. swing
10. ________ 10. thump
11. ________ 11. belong
12. ________ 12. student
13. ________ 13. husband
14. ________ 14. parent
15. ________ 15. trunk

Challenge Words
________ concert
________ conductor
________ instrument
________ musician
________ orchestra

Name________________ Date________ AT-HOME WORD STUDY SPELLING 66

Words with Consonant Clusters

Using the Word Study Steps
1. LOOK at the word.
2. SAY the word aloud.
3. STUDY the letters in the word.
4. WRITE the word.
5. CHECK the word.
   Did you spell the word right?
   If not, go back to step 1.

Spelling Tip
Use words that you know how to spell to help you spell new words.
thin + b**ank** = **thank**

X the Word
Put an X on the word that does not match the pattern in each row.

1.	thank	ink	trunk	~~truck~~
2.	stamp	thump	~~stop~~	bump
3.	~~below~~	swing	belong	young
4.	friend	husband	behind	~~hushed~~
5.	paint	~~study~~	student	parent

To Parents or Helpers:
Using the Word Study Steps above as your child comes across any new words will help him or her spell well.
Review the steps as you both go over this week's spelling words.
Go over the Spelling Tip with your child. Help him or her spell new words by using familiar words.
Help your child cross out the word that does not match the pattern in each row.

Name________________ Date________ EXPLORE THE PATTERN SPELLING 67

Words with Consonant Clusters

paint	thank	behind	thump	husband
young	friend	faint	belong	parent
stamp	ink	swing	student	trunk

Pattern Power
Write the spelling words for each of these clusters below.

nk
1. thank
2. ink
3. trunk

mp
4. stamp
5. thump

ng
6. young
7. swing
8. belong

nd
9. friend
10. behind
11. husband

nt
12. paint
13. faint
14. student
15. parent

Guide Words
Dictionary guide words help you find your way. Which spelling words will you find between each pair of words?

than/thunder 16. thank 17. thump
pail/part 18. paint 19. parent
face/front 20. faint 21. friend

Word Hunt
Write the spelling word in which you can find the smaller word.

22. *hum* thump 23. *end* friend
24. *win* swing 25. *rent* parent
26. *long* belong 27. *dent* student
28. *band* husband

Name________________ Date________ PRACTICE AND EXTEND SPELLING 68

Words with Consonant Clusters

paint	thank	behind	thump	husband
young	friend	faint	belong	parent
stamp	ink	swing	student	trunk

Opposites
An antonym is a word that has the opposite meaning of another word. Write the spelling word that is the antonym of each of the following words.

1. old young 2. enemy friend
3. ahead behind 4. wife husband

What's the Word?
Write a spelling word that correctly completes the sentence.

5. The student studies math in the third grade.
6. This parent spoke to the principal about her son.
7. I will paint a picture with watercolors.
8. A husband is married to his wife.
9. He keeps his spare tire in the trunk of his car.
10. Swing your arms left and right to the music.
11. Friend is the opposite of enemy.
12. The person sitting in back of you is behind you.

Make a Sentence
Use each word in a sentence.

13. thank ________
14. faint ________
15. thump ________
16. belong ________

Challenge Extension: Have students draw and label a picture to illustrate each Challenge Word.

Moses Goes to a Concert • SPELLING

Name____________________ Date__________ PROOFREAD AND WRITE **SPELLING 69**

Words with Consonant Clusters

Proofreading Paragraph

There are six spelling mistakes in this paragraph. Circle the misspelled words. Write the words correctly on the lines below.

"How do the artists draw their cartoons?" Lisa asked.

"Some people use black inck to outline their figures," Mr. Lopez said. "I know other artists who use paynt."

"Who writes the studnt pages in your newspaper?" the girl asked.

"The group is made up of reporters and yung volunteers," the editor answered. "A parrunt is also part of this team."

"Can a frind and I join this group?" she asked.

"Well, you'll both have to take a writing test," he said.

1. ink 2. paint 3. student
4. young 5. parent 6. friend

Writing Activity

What questions would you like to ask someone who works on a newspaper? Write your interview questions, using at least four spelling words.

____

____

____

____

____

____

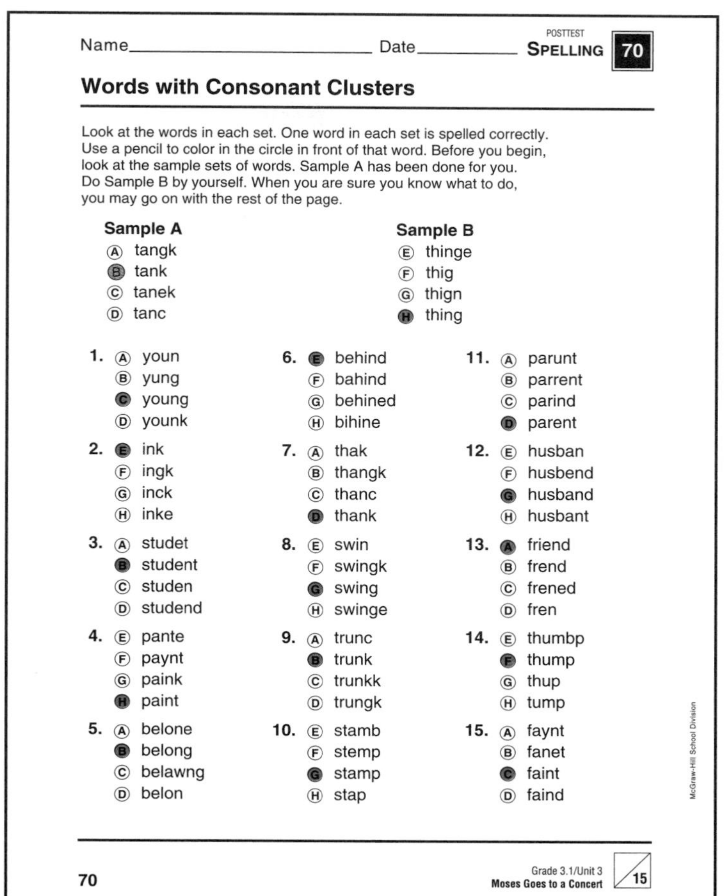

Name____________________ Date__________ POSTTEST **SPELLING 70**

Words with Consonant Clusters

Look at the words in each set. One word in each set is spelled correctly. Use a pencil to color in the circle in front of that word. Before you begin, look at the sample sets of words. Sample A has been done for you. Do Sample B by yourself. When you are sure you know what to do, you may go on with the rest of the page.

Sample A
- Ⓐ tangk
- ● tank
- Ⓒ tanek
- Ⓓ tanc

Sample B
- Ⓔ thinge
- Ⓕ thig
- Ⓖ thign
- ● thing

1. Ⓐ youn · Ⓑ yung · ● young · Ⓓ younk
2. ● ink · Ⓕ ingk · Ⓖ inck · Ⓗ inke
3. Ⓐ studet · ● student · Ⓒ studen · Ⓓ studend
4. Ⓔ pante · Ⓕ paynt · Ⓖ paink · ● paint
5. Ⓐ belone · ● belong · Ⓒ belawng · Ⓓ belon
6. ● behind · Ⓕ bahind · Ⓖ behined · Ⓗ bihine
7. Ⓐ thak · Ⓑ thangk · Ⓒ thanc · ● thank
8. Ⓔ swin · Ⓕ swingk · ● swing · Ⓗ swinge
9. Ⓐ trunc · ● trunk · Ⓒ trunkk · Ⓓ trungk
10. Ⓔ stamb · Ⓕ stemp · ● stamp · Ⓗ stap
11. Ⓐ parunt · Ⓑ parrent · Ⓒ parind · ● parent
12. Ⓔ husban · Ⓕ husbend · ● husband · Ⓗ husbant
13. ● friend · Ⓑ frend · Ⓒ frened · Ⓓ fren
14. Ⓔ thumbp · ● thump · Ⓖ thup · Ⓗ tump
15. Ⓐ faynt · Ⓑ fanet · ● faint · Ⓓ faind

Name_______________ Date_________ **Practice 82**

Story Elements

Understanding the **characters** and the **setting** of a story can help you determine the **plot** of the story.

Read the passage below. Then answer the questions. Answers will vary.

Ricardo's art teacher said, "For homework tonight, I would like each of you to paint someone who is special to you." Ricardo decided to paint his cat, Speedy.

That night, Ricardo took out some paint and paper. "Okay, Speedy," he said. "I'm going to paint you. Stand still!" Speedy ran over to Ricardo, jumped on his lap, jumped off his lap, ran into the kitchen, ran into Ricardo's room, pushed a pillow off the bed, and disappeared into the bathroom. "Speedy, stay still!" Ricardo shouted out. "I have to paint you!"

Suddenly the cat appeared again and began to run in circles around Ricardo. Ricardo sat down and thought about what to do next. Suddenly, Ricardo had an idea. "I know—I'll paint Speedy on the go!" he said.

When Ricardo brought his picture to school the next day, everyone liked it. "I'm lucky to have such a fast cat," he said.

1. Who are the main characters in this story? Ricardo and Speedy
2. Where does the story take place? in school and at Ricardo's house
3. What is Ricardo's problem? Speedy won't stand still.
4. How does Ricardo solve this problem? He decides to paint Speedy on the go.
5. What is the plot of this story? Ricardo is having a problem finishing his art homework.

At Home: Have students write a few sentences explaining why they would or would not like to have Speedy as a pet.

Name_______________ Date_________ **Practice 83**

Vocabulary

Supply the correct words from the list.

blossoms dawn faded imaginary miserable shallow

1. When a flower loses its color, it has faded.
2. A very unhappy person feels miserable.
3. If a pond or lake is not deep, we describe it as shallow.
4. Dawn is the time of day when the sun first rises.
5. A story that you make up in your mind is imaginary.
6. In spring, many fruit trees produce lovely flowers called blossoms.

At Home: Have students look up the vocabulary words in a dictionary and make vocabulary cards for each word to use as a study tool.

Carmen's Garden

One day a mouse named Carmen woke up at *dawn*. She liked to garden early in the morning.

Carmen's garden was behind her house near a stream that was *shallow*. Every day Carmen began by watering seeds she had planted. For weeks she watered and waited. But nothing happened! Waiting made Carmen *miserable*. After weeks of waiting, her hope for pretty flowers had *faded*.

Then one day, she spotted little green stems popping up. She couldn't believe it. "This must be *imaginary*!" she shouted. "The seeds are growing!"

Soon her garden was filled with the *blossoms* of hundreds of flowers.

1. What is the first moment of day called?
   dawn
2. When a stream is not deep, what is it?
   shallow
3. How does waiting make Carmen feel?
   miserable
4. Why does the garden seem *imaginary* to Carmen?
   She had to wait so long for the flowers, she couldn't believe it.
5. Why did Carmen have to wait so long?
   It takes time for flowers to grow.

At Home: Ask students to identify the main idea of the story. Then ask them to point out the supporting details.

Name_______________ Date_________ **Practice 84**

Story Comprehension

Think about the story of Fernando, the little painter. Then finish each sentence by writing the missing word on the blank line. Write that word on the crossword puzzle.

ACROSS

1. The smooth and white adobe houses reminded Fernando of paper.
4. Fernando lived in the village of Sabana Grande.
6. Everyone said kind words about Fernando's paintings.
8. The color yellow is made from dried grasses in the meadow.
9. Soon all the neighbors asked Fernando if he would paint their houses.
10. Above the door Fernando painted the words Casa Familia Espino.

DOWN

2. The color black is made from the charcoal of a burned tree stump.
3. Fernando's teacher taught him how the country people of Panama made their paints.
5. The color blue is made from berries that grow deep in the jungle.
7. The neighbors brought out chairs and watched Fernando paint.

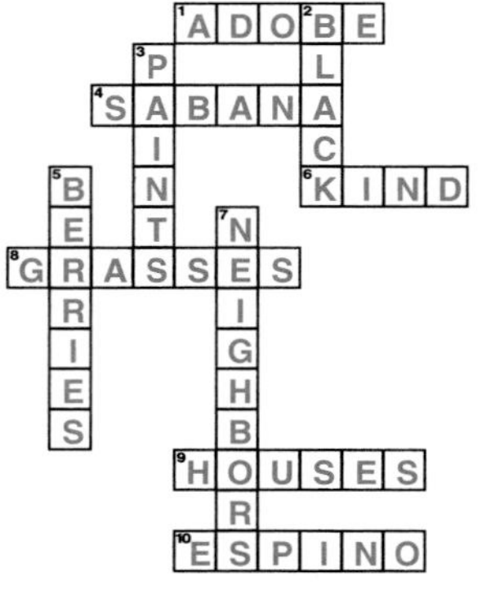

At Home: Have students think of two more clues and words to add to the puzzle.

Little Painter/S. Grande • PRACTICE

Name____________________ Date__________ **Practice 85**

Use a Map

Maps often show more than roads, towns, and the borders of countries. Lines drawn on a map can show many different kinds of information. Sometimes an area on a map is colored or shaded to give information about that area.

Look at this map of a playground. Follow the instructions below to add more information to this map.

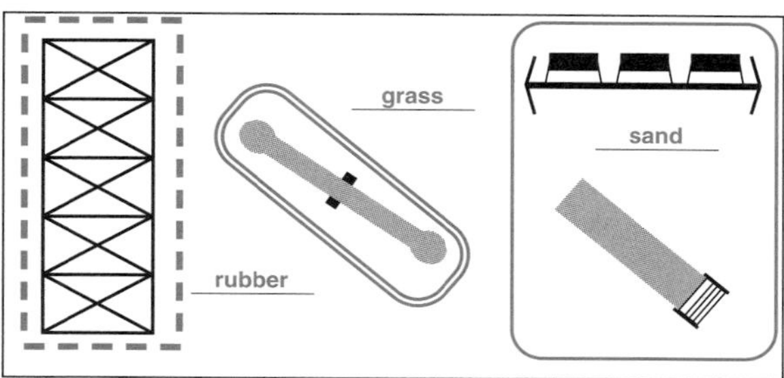

1. Draw a solid line around the swing sets and slides. This area has sand on the ground.
2. Write the word *sand* inside the area marked off by the solid line.
3. Draw a broken line around the gym bars. This area has rubber mats on the ground.
4. Write the word *rubber* next to this area.
5. Draw a double line around the seesaw. This area has grass on the ground.
6. Write the word *grass* next to this area.

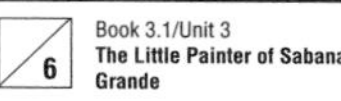

At Home: Ask students to make a map of the playground at their school or in their neighborhood.

Name____________________ Date__________ **Practice 86**

Story Elements

Choose a word from the list that describes Fernando, and write it on the line. Answers may vary.

happy bored busy tired sad talented

1. Fernando is busy.
2. Explain your word choice. Possible answer: In the story, Fernando is always doing something. He is busy making paint, searching for paper, and painting the outside of his house.
3. Where does the story take place? The story takes place in the village of Sabana Grande in Panama.
4. What is Fernando's problem in the story? He doesn't have paper to paint on.
5. How does Fernando solve his problem? Fernando solves his problem by painting his house.
6. What do people from the village ask Fernando to do at the end of the story? People ask Fernando to paint their houses, too.

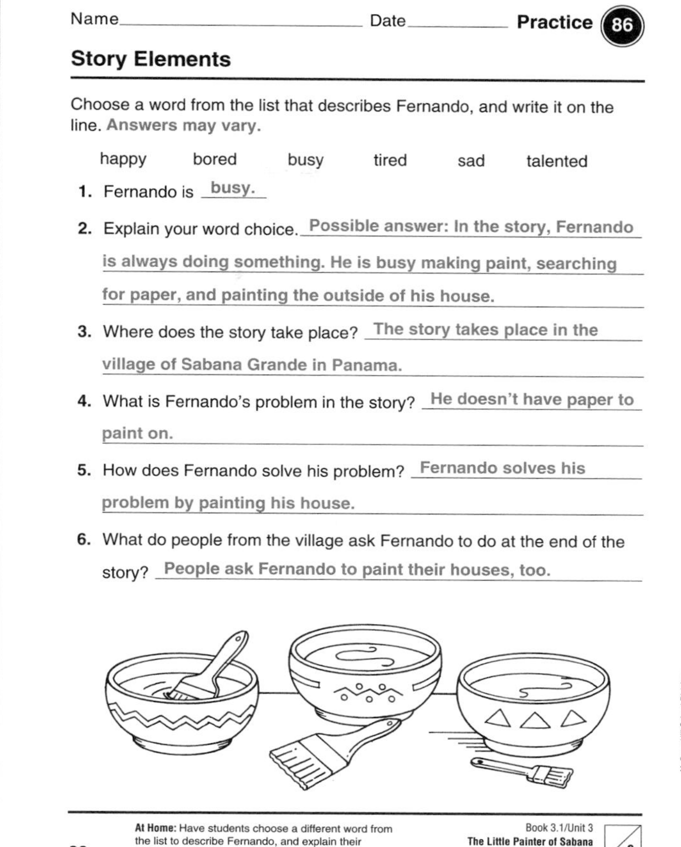

At Home: Have students choose a different word from the list to describe Fernando, and explain their choice.

Name____________________ Date__________ **Practice 87**

Summarize

Summarize each of the events in the story below. You may want to describe how Bonita feels as well as what she does. Answers may vary.

1. **Event 1:** Bonita and her class were writing short stories about their families. Bonita felt excited. She brought in some old family pictures to help give her ideas about her story.

   Bonita looked at family pictures before writing about her family.

2. **Event 2:** Bonita wrote about her grandfather. Then, Bonita painted a picture of him to go along with her story. Bonita was happy with the way her story was turning out.

   Bonita wrote a story about her grandfather.

3. **Event 3:** Just then, a gust of wind blew through an open window. Bonita's story flew right out the window. "Now my story is ruined!" Bonita said sadly.

   A gust of wind blew Bonita's story out the window.

4. **Event 4:** Bonita looked at her family photos. Her grandfather was smiling. Suddenly, Bonita began to smile. "I bet I can write another story about my grandfather," she said. "This one will be even better than the last!"

   Bonita looked at her grandfather's smiling picture and decided to write another, even better, story about him.

At Home: Have students watch a TV show and write a one-paragraph summary of it.

Name____________________ Date__________ **Practice 88**

Context Clues

When you are reading, you often discover new words. When you come across a puzzling word, look at the words and phrases near it and think about what is happening in the story. These **context clues** often can help you figure out what the word means.

Read each passage. Then use context clues to decide what the underlined word means. Circle the letter next to the correct meaning.

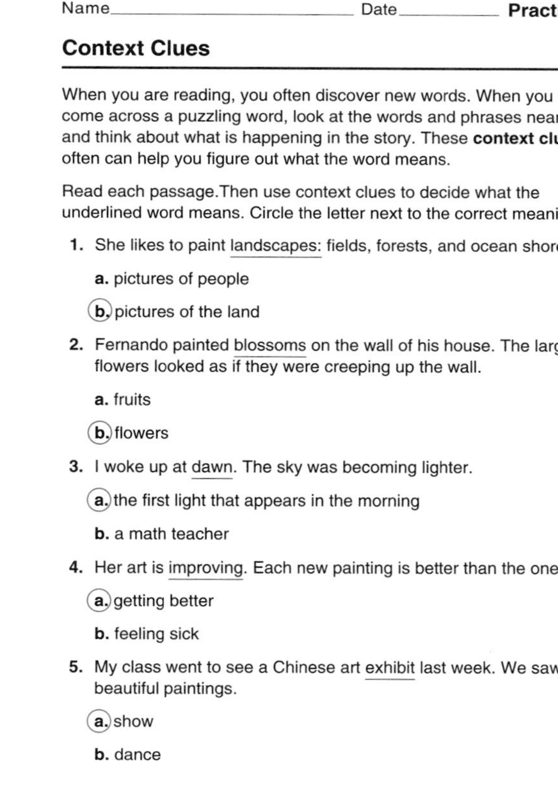

1. She likes to paint landscapes: fields, forests, and ocean shores.
   - **a.** pictures of people
   - **(b.)** pictures of the land
2. Fernando painted blossoms on the wall of his house. The large purple flowers looked as if they were creeping up the wall.
   - **a.** fruits
   - **(b.)** flowers
3. I woke up at dawn. The sky was becoming lighter.
   - **(a.)** the first light that appears in the morning
   - **b.** a math teacher
4. Her art is improving. Each new painting is better than the one before.
   - **(a.)** getting better
   - **b.** feeling sick
5. My class went to see a Chinese art exhibit last week. We saw many beautiful paintings.
   - **(a.)** show
   - **b.** dance

At Home: Have students write a short story using some of the words above.

Name____________________ Date__________ **Reteach 82**

Story Elements

> **Characters** are the people or animals in a story. The **setting** is where a story takes place. The **plot** is the events that take place in a story.

Read the passage below. Then circle the answer to each question.

Kelly and Sean were partners in art class. Today they were sharing paint. Kelly wanted to paint an orange car. Sean was going to paint an orange house.

Kelly and Sean started to have problems. "Please give me the orange paint," Sean said.

"I'm using it," Kelly said.

"But I want it. It's my favorite color!" Sean replied.

Kelly and Sean began to get angry with one another. Finally, Kelly had an idea. "Let's take turns with the orange paint," she said. Sean agreed and the partners finished their paintings.

1. Where is the setting of the story?
   a. Kelly's house (**b.**) art class **c.** music class
2. Who are the characters in the story?
   (**a.**) Kelly and Sean **b.** Kelly and the art teacher
   c. Kelly and her mother
3. Why did Kelly and Sean get angry with one another?
   a. They were best friends.
   b. They were tired.
   (**c.**) They both wanted the orange paint.
4. How did Kelly and Sean solve their problem?
   a. They went home.
   b. Kelly used colored pencils instead of paint.
   (**c.**) They shared the paint.

At Home: Have students explain in a few sentences whether or not they agree with the way Kelly and Sean solved their problem.

Name____________________ Date__________ **Reteach 83**

Vocabulary

Match each word below with its definition.

1. blossoms	a. when the sun first comes up
2. dawn	b. not deep
3. faded	c. very unhappy
4. imaginary	d. lost color
5. miserable	e. make-believe
6. shallow	f. flowers

6

Story Comprehension

Reteach 84

Write an answer to each question below.

1. When Fernando couldn't find any paper to paint on, what did he ask his parents if he could do? Fernando asked his parents if he could paint the outside of their house.
2. How did the people in Fernando's village react to his painting?
   They asked him to paint their houses, too.

At Home: Have students identify one problem and the solution to that problem in the story.

Name____________________ Date__________ **Reteach 85**

Use a Map

> **Maps** use lines, dots, and symbols to show what the land and cities look like. You can use maps to see how far one place is from another, and in what direction you would have to travel if you wanted to go from one place to another.

Study the map of Costa Rica below. Underline the correct answer to each question.

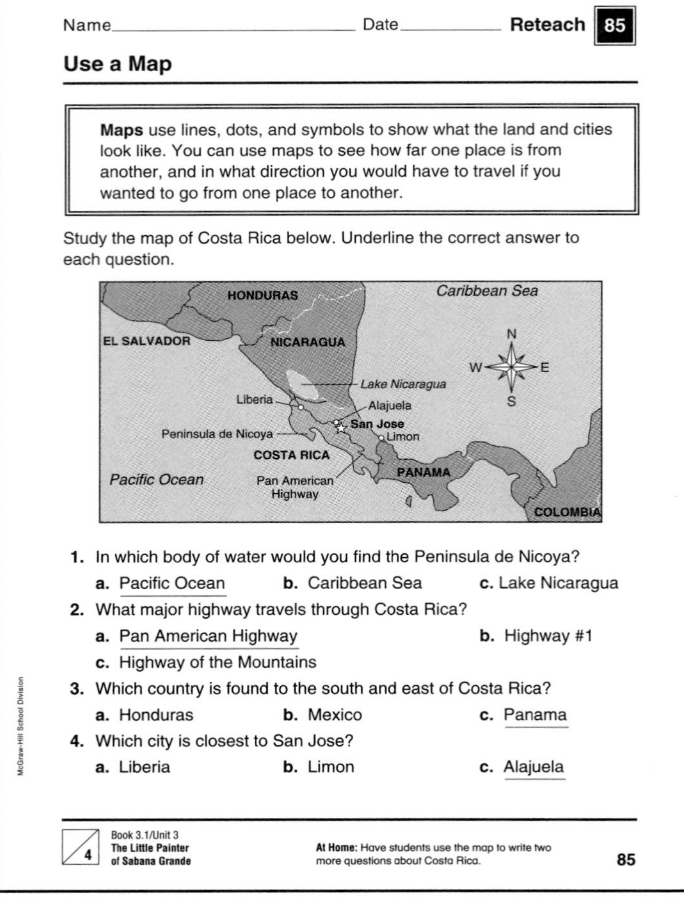

1. In which body of water would you find the Peninsula de Nicoya?
   a. Pacific Ocean **b.** Caribbean Sea **c.** Lake Nicaragua
2. What major highway travels through Costa Rica?
   a. Pan American Highway **b.** Highway #1
   c. Highway of the Mountains
3. Which country is found to the south and east of Costa Rica?
   a. Honduras **b.** Mexico **c.** Panama
4. Which city is closest to San Jose?
   a. Liberia **b.** Limon **c.** Alajuela

At Home: Have students use the map to write two more questions about Costa Rica.

Name____________________ Date__________ **Reteach 86**

Story Elements

> Every story has **characters** and a **plot**. Thinking about the characters and the plot will help you understand what is important in the story.

Write an answer to each question about "The Little Painter of Sabana Grande."

1. Who are the main characters in the story?
   Papa, Mama, Fernando, Señora Arias
2. What does Fernando decide to do on his vacation?
   He wishes to paint a picture.
3. What problem does Fernando face before he can start his project?
   He has no paper.
4. Who does Fernando ask for help in solving this problem?
   Papa and Mama
5. Who has to agree to his solution before he can carry out his project?
   Papa and Mama
6. How do Fernando's parents and the villagers react to his project?
   At first Papa and Mama say, "No." The neighbors are surprised to see the painting. But soon the villagers say kind words about Fernando's paintings.

At Home: Have students draw a picture of one of the characters in the story.

Name________________________ Date__________ **Reteach 87**

Summarize

Study the story and the summary.

Story	Summary
Jada and her mother worked together to build a shelf. They got a hammer, some nails, and some boards. Then they hammered the boards together and nailed the shelf onto the wall.	Jada and her mother built a shelf.

Now read the following stories. Circle the best summary for each one.

1. Carlos looked out the window. It was raining outside. Big drops of rain fell on the trees and houses. People held umbrellas and newspapers over their heads.
   - (a.) It was raining.
   - b. Carlos loved the rain.
   - c. People held umbrellas.
2. Carlos felt sad. He wanted to play baseball. He wanted to go to the park, but now he couldn't because it was raining.
   - a. Carlos liked baseball.
   - b. Carlos went to the park.
   - (c.) Carlos felt sad.
3. Carlos had an idea. He would paint a picture. He could still have fun, even though it was raining! Carlos decided that he would paint a picture of a baseball game.
   - a. Painting was fun.
   - (b.) Carlos decided to paint.
   - c. Carlos watched the rain.
4. Carlos got a paintbrush, a paint set, and a piece of paper. He painted a picture of himself hitting a home run. At the end of the day, Carlos was pleased with his work!
   - (a.) Carlos painted a picture.
   - b. Carlos played baseball.
   - c. Carlos got a paintbrush.

At Home: Have students illustrate one of the paragraphs.

Name________________________ Date__________ **Reteach 88**

Context Clues

When you see an unfamiliar word, you can often use the words around it to help you figure out the meaning. This is called using **context clues**.

Read the following passages. Think about the meaning of the underlined word as you read each passage. Then write **True** or **False** next to each statement below.

1. At first, the water was too deep for Fernando. But then he came to a shallow part of the water.

   Shallow means not deep. ___True___
2. I painted a portrait of my father in art class. My father said it looked just like him.

   A *portrait* is a young tree. ___False___
3. Fernando was very unhappy. His father hated to see him so miserable.

   Miserable means very unhappy. ___True___
4. There is a wooden frame around the painting.

   A *frame* is a pillow. ___False___
5. The sun rose at dawn and the rooster crowed.

   Dawn means sunset. ___False___
6. Fernando had nothing to paint on. He couldn't find even a scrap of paper.

   A *scrap* is a very small piece. ___True___

At Home: Have students illustrate some of the sentences above.

Name________________________ Date__________ Extend 82

Story Elements

Follow the directions to create a setting for a story of farm life.

1. Place a sheet of paper over a large piece of coarse fabric, such as burlap, muslin, denim, terry cloth, or corduroy.
2. Use colored chalk or charcoal pencil to draw a farm scene on the paper. Be sure to include some people or animals in your drawing.
3. Separate your drawing from the fabric.
4. Write a title on your picture, and sign your name.

Use the lines below to write names for the people and animals in your drawing.

Answers will vary. For example Mr. Jones, a farmer; Dr. Smith, a vet; Billy and Jeannie Jones, children of Mr. Jones; cows, chickens, goats, horses

Write a few sentences about the story's plot.

Share your picture with the rest of the class. Tell about the setting, characters, and plot.

At Home: Have students use their notes to write a farm story.

Name________________________ Date__________ Extend 83

Vocabulary

blossoms	dawn	faded
imaginary	miserable	shallow

Work with a partner to make up a newspaper story. Use the words in the box to answer these questions: Who is the story about? What happened? When did it happen? Where did it happen? Why did it happen? Write your story on another piece of paper.

Answers will vary.

Extend 84

Story Comprehension

Write a new ending for "The Little Painter of Sabana Grande." Try to imagine what might have happened if Fernando had plenty of paper to paint on.

Answers will vary.

At Home: Have students draw a picture of an adobe house painted by Fernando.

Name________________________ Date__________ Extend 85

Use a Map

Work with a group to create a "picture map" of Panama and the rest of Central America. Find a large map of Central America. Trace the outline of Central America on a sheet of paper. Then think of things you can draw on your map to show important products, land features, plants, and animals. Take turns drawing the things you think of. Look at the real map to make sure you draw your pictures in the right places.

To find things to add to your map, have each member of the group research one of the countries in Central America. Look in books about Central America to find out about important products and other things you can add to your map. Display your picture map in the classroom for everyone to see.

United States
Gulf of Mexico
Atlantic Ocean
Cuba
Mexico
Carribean Sea
Central America
Pacific Ocean
South America

Answers will vary.

At Home: Have students write a paragraph describing the different plants and animals pictured on their map.

Name________________________ Date__________ Extend 86

Story Elements

Imagine what it might be like to spend the day with Fernando, the main character in "The Little Painter of Sabana Grande." Write a paragraph telling about your imagined day.

Answers will vary.

Illustrate the setting of your imagined day with Fernando.

Share your paragraph and illustration with the rest of the class. Tell about the setting, characters, and plot.

At Home: Have students make up a simple plot for a story about something Fernando might do when he grows up.

Name____________________ Date__________ **Extend 87**

Summarize

Make a list of the things you do during a day at your school. Use the list to write a letter to a friend summarizing what your school day is like. Tell only the important points. Include sentences describing the setting and the people at your school.

Dear ____________________,

Answers will vary.

Your friend,

At Home: Have students summarize a favorite story. Tell them to keep their summary to a few sentences.

Name____________________ Date__________ **Extend 88**

Context Clues

Write a sentence telling the meaning of the word in dark type in each sentence.

Circle the words that helped you figure out the meaning.

1. There are only a few houses made of clay **adobe** in our small village.
   Answer: brick made of clay; students will circle the words *houses made of* and clay.
2. At dinner, we fill our warm, fried, flour **tortillas** with meat and cheese.
   Answer: a type of bread served with a filling; students will circle the words *fried, flour, meat,* and *cheese*

Work with a partner to play Word Detective. Have each person make a list of four words. Write a sentence using context clues for each of the words. Draw a picture or cartoon with clues to illustrate the meaning of each word. Exchange sentences and pictures. Try to guess all the meanings of the words on your partner's list.

At Home: Have students draw a picture illustrating the meaning of the words *adobe* and *tortillas*.

Name_______________ Date_______ LEARN Grammar 71

Present-Tense Verbs

- A verb in the **present tense** tells what happens now.
- A present-tense verb must **agree** with its subject.
- Add *–s* to most verbs if the subject is singular.
- Do not add *–s* to a present-tense verb when the subject is plural or *I* or *you*.

Each sentence below is followed by two forms of a verb. Choose the form of the verb that correctly agrees with the subject of the sentence. Circle your answer.

1. Fernando _____ in a tiny village. live **(lives)**
2. His parents _____ hard. **(work)** works
3. "I _____ paper for my paintings." **(need)** needs
4. "You _____ to paint our house?" **(want)** wants
5. His neighbors _____ what he is doing. **(wonder)** wonders
6. Fernando's plan _____ good. look **(looks)**
7. He _____ vines, trees, and animals. paint **(paints)**
8. Señora Alfaro _____ Fernando to paint her house also. ask **(asks)**

Extension: Have students write about the actions they do every afternoon when they get home from school.

Name_______________ Date_______ LEARN AND PRACTICE Grammar 72

Present-Tense Verbs

- A verb in the **present tense** tells what happens now.
- A present-tense verb must **agree** with its subject.
- Add *–es* to verbs that end in *s, ch, sh, x,* or *z* if the subject is singular.
- Change *y* to *i* and add *–es* to verbs that end with a consonant and *y*.
- Do not add *–es* to a present-tense verb when the subject is plural or *I* or *you*.

He fishes. The paint dries.
They fish. The dishes dry.

For each verb below, write the form that agrees with the subject given.

1. hurry — Fernando hurries.
2. catch — We catch.
3. brush — They brush.
4. fix — Señor Espino fixes.
5. carry — You carry.
6. bless — Señora Arias blesses.
7. wax — The painter waxes.
8. search — I search.

Extension: Have students write three or four sentences telling the story of the little painter in the present tense.

Name_______________ Date_______ PRACTICE AND REVIEW Grammar 73

Present-Tense Verbs

- A verb in the **present tense** tells what happens now.
- A present tense verb must **agree** with its subject.
- Add *–s* to most verbs if the subject is singular.
- Add *–es* to verbs that end in *s, ch, sh, x,* or *z* if the subject is singular.
- Change *y* to *i* and add *–es* to verbs that end with a consonant and *y*.
- Do not add *–s* or *–es* to a present-tense verb when the subject is plural or *I* or *you*.

Pick the correct singular or plural form of the verb in each sentence below. Underline your answer.

1. The Panama country people (<u>mix</u>, mixes) paint using natural dyes.
2. The water (flow, <u>flows</u>) fast in the brook.
3. Fernando (scratch, <u>scratches</u>) pictures in the dirt.
4. His parents (<u>wish</u>, wishes) he could find paper.
5. Fernando's mama (worry, <u>worries</u>) about his painting the house.
6. The neighbors (<u>gather</u>, gathers) to see him paint.
7. The painted vine (reach, <u>reaches</u>) almost to the roof.
8. "You (<u>paint</u>, paints) very well," his teacher tells him.
9. They (<u>confess</u>, confesses) that they like the result.
10. The villagers (<u>enjoy</u>, enjoys) Fernando's pictures.

Extension: Have students work in pairs to write sentences using singular verbs that end in *s, ch, sh, x, z,* and a consonant followed by *y*. The class may need to brainstorm together to come up with at least one verb for each type.

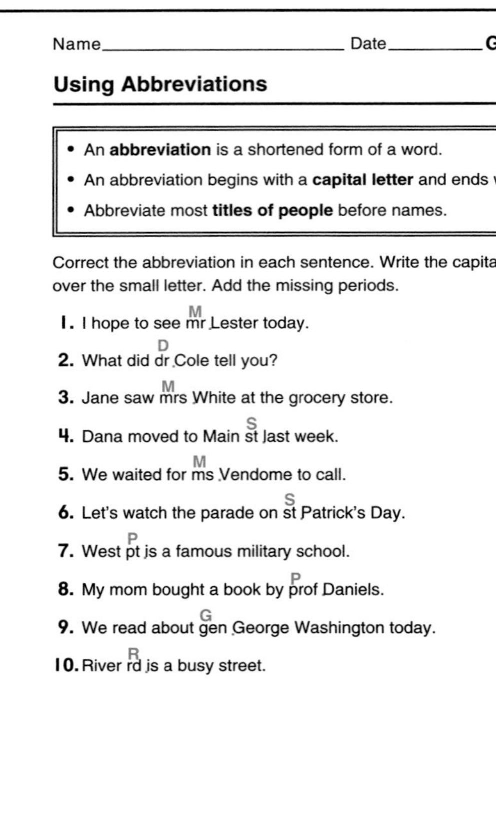

Name_______________ Date_______ MECHANICS Grammar 74

Using Abbreviations

- An **abbreviation** is a shortened form of a word.
- An abbreviation begins with a **capital letter** and ends with a **period.**
- Abbreviate most **titles of people** before names.

Correct the abbreviation in each sentence. Write the capital letter over the small letter. Add the missing periods.

1. I hope to see mr (M) Lester today.
2. What did dr (D) Cole tell you?
3. Jane saw mrs (M) White at the grocery store.
4. Dana moved to Main st (S) last week.
5. We waited for ms (M) Vendome to call.
6. Let's watch the parade on st (S) Patrick's Day.
7. West pt (P) is a famous military school.
8. My mom bought a book by prof (P) Daniels.
9. We read about gen (G) George Washington today.
10. River rd (R) is a busy street.

Extension: Have small groups of students create lists of capitalized abbreviations. Using the individual lists, create a class list for later review.

Little Painter/S. Grande • GRAMMAR

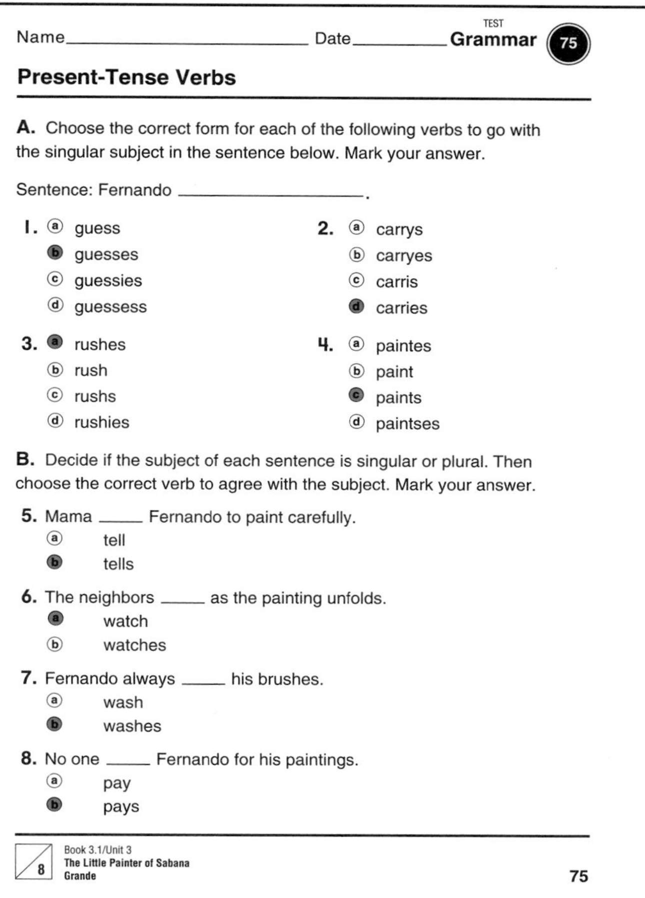

Name____________________ Date__________ TEST Grammar 75

Present-Tense Verbs

A. Choose the correct form for each of the following verbs to go with the singular subject in the sentence below. Mark your answer.

Sentence: Fernando ________________.

1. ⓐ guess
   ● guesses
   ⓒ guessies
   ⓓ guessess

2. ⓐ carrys
   ⓑ carryes
   ⓒ carris
   ● carries

3. ● rushes
   ⓑ rush
   ⓒ rushs
   ⓓ rushies

4. ⓐ paintes
   ⓑ paint
   ● paints
   ⓓ paintses

B. Decide if the subject of each sentence is singular or plural. Then choose the correct verb to agree with the subject. Mark your answer.

5. Mama _____ Fernando to paint carefully.
   ⓐ tell
   ● tells

6. The neighbors _____ as the painting unfolds.
   ● watch
   ⓑ watches

7. Fernando always _____ his brushes.
   ⓐ wash
   ● washes

8. No one _____ Fernando for his paintings.
   ⓐ pay
   ● pays

Name____________________ Date__________ MORE PRACTICE Grammar 76

Present-Tense Verbs

- A present tense verb must **agree** with its subject.
- Add *–s* or *–es* to verbs if the subject is singular.
- Change *y* to *i* and add *-es* to verbs that end with a consonant and *y*.
- Do not add *–s* or *–es* to a present-tense verb when the subject is plural or *I* or *you*.

  He fishes. The paint dries.
  I fish. We dry the dishes.

Work with a partner. One of you can read each sentence aloud while the other person writes down and corrects the verb in the sentence. The verbs are underlined.

1. Fernando's teacher tell him how to make paints. tells
2. It tax his patience to make them. taxes
3. He try to find paper. tries
4. Fernando's fingers itches to paint. itch
5. His parents sees his sadness. see
6. He wish to paint on the white adobe house. wishes
7. Mama and Papa finally agrees to let Fernando paint the house. agree
8. Fernando sketch a tiny plan. sketches
9. "I likes your plan," Papa says. like
10. The village buzz with excitement. buzzes

Now the partner who corrected the sentences can read them aloud.

Little Painter/S. Grande • SPELLING

Name________________________ Date__________ PRETEST SPELLING **71**

Words with Double Consonants

Pretest Directions
Fold back the paper along the dotted line. Use the blanks to write each word as it is read aloud. When you finish the test, unfold the paper. Use the list at the right to correct any spelling mistakes. Practice the words you missed for the Posttest.

1. ____________	1. small
2. ____________	2. ladder
3. ____________	3. little
4. ____________	4. happen
5. ____________	5. rubber
6. ____________	6. grass
7. ____________	7. ribbon
8. ____________	8. lesson
9. ____________	9. silly
10. ____________	10. butter
11. ____________	11. supper
12. ____________	12. middle
13. ____________	13. possible
14. ____________	14. hobby
15. ____________	15. unhappy
Challenge Words	
____________	blossoms
____________	dawn
____________	imaginary
____________	miserable
____________	shallow

To Parents
Here are the results of your child's weekly spelling Pretest. You can help your child study for the Posttest by following these simple steps for each word on the word list:

1. Read the word to your child.
2. Have your child write the word, saying each letter as it is written.
3. Say each letter of the word as your child checks the spelling.
4. If a mistake has been made, have your child read each letter of the correctly spelled word aloud, and then repeat steps 1-3.

Name________________________ Date__________ AT-HOME WORD STUDY SPELLING **72**

Words with Double Consonants

Using the Word Study Steps

1. LOOK at the word.
2. SAY the word aloud.
3. STUDY the letters in the word.
4. WRITE the word.
5. CHECK the word.
   Did you spell the word right?
   If not, go back to step 1.

Spelling Tip
If you hear a short vowel sound followed by one consonant sound, it is often a double consonant. See if the spelling looks right with a double consonant. Use your dictionary if you are not sure.

Find and Circle
Where are the spelling words?

m i d d l e t l a d d e r u l i t t l e
u n h a p p y v s u p p e r x s i l l y
q s m a l l u l e s s o n o r i b b o n
p o s s i b l e n g r a s s h h o b b y
a b u t t e r x r u b b e r h a p p e n

To Parents or Helpers:
Using the Word Study Steps above as your child comes across any new words will help him or her spell well. Review the steps as you both go over this week's spelling words.
Go over the Spelling Tip with your child. Point out how each spelling word follows this pattern. Help your child use the dictionary to look up words. Help your child find and circle the spelling words in the puzzle.

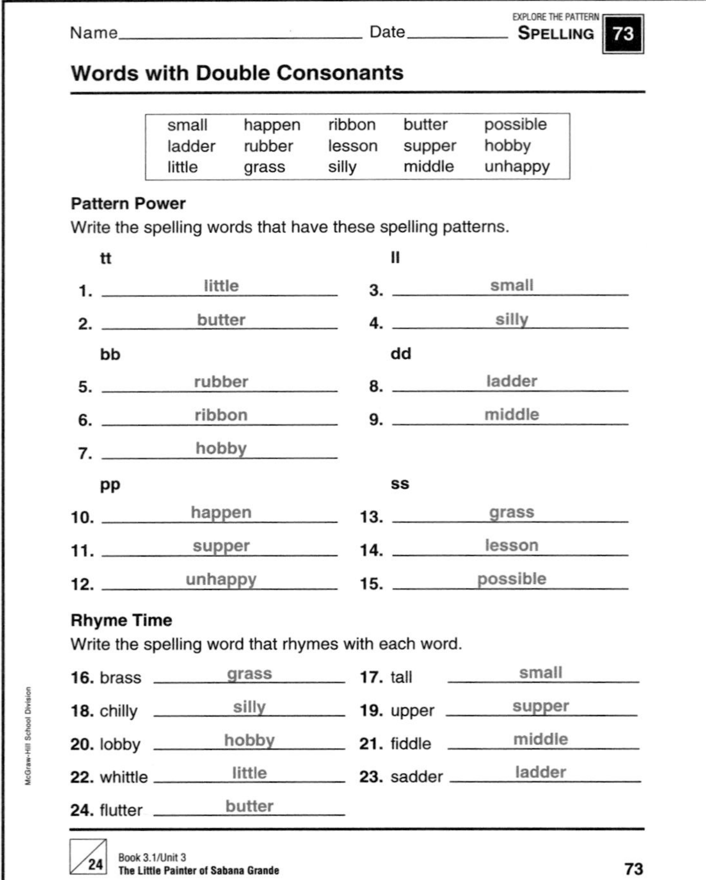

Name________________________ Date__________ EXPLORE THE PATTERN SPELLING **73**

Words with Double Consonants

small	happen	ribbon	butter	possible
ladder	rubber	lesson	supper	hobby
little	grass	silly	middle	unhappy

Pattern Power
Write the spelling words that have these spelling patterns.

tt
1. little
2. butter

ll
3. small
4. silly

bb
5. rubber
6. ribbon
7. hobby

dd
8. ladder
9. middle

pp
10. happen
11. supper
12. unhappy

ss
13. grass
14. lesson
15. possible

Rhyme Time
Write the spelling word that rhymes with each word.

16. brass grass
17. tall small
18. chilly silly
19. upper supper
20. lobby hobby
21. fiddle middle
22. whittle little
23. sadder ladder
24. flutter butter

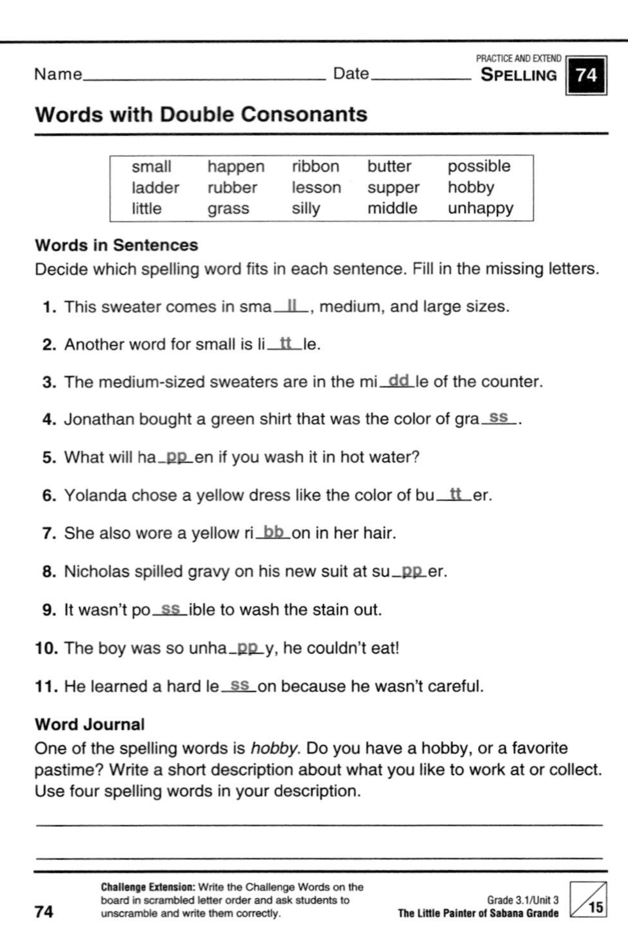

Name________________________ Date__________ PRACTICE AND EXTEND SPELLING **74**

Words with Double Consonants

small	happen	ribbon	butter	possible
ladder	rubber	lesson	supper	hobby
little	grass	silly	middle	unhappy

Words in Sentences
Decide which spelling word fits in each sentence. Fill in the missing letters.

1. This sweater comes in sma_ll_, medium, and large sizes.
2. Another word for small is li_tt_le.
3. The medium-sized sweaters are in the mi_dd_le of the counter.
4. Jonathan bought a green shirt that was the color of gra_ss_.
5. What will ha_pp_en if you wash it in hot water?
6. Yolanda chose a yellow dress like the color of bu_tt_er.
7. She also wore a yellow ri_bb_on in her hair.
8. Nicholas spilled gravy on his new suit at su_pp_er.
9. It wasn't po_ss_ible to wash the stain out.
10. The boy was so unha_pp_y, he couldn't eat!
11. He learned a hard le_ss_on because he wasn't careful.

Word Journal
One of the spelling words is *hobby*. Do you have a hobby, or a favorite pastime? Write a short description about what you like to work at or collect. Use four spelling words in your description.

____

____

Challenge Extension: Write the Challenge Words on the board in scrambled letter order and ask students to unscramble and write them correctly.

Name____________________ Date__________ PROOFREAD AND WRITE SPELLING **75**

Words with Double Consonants

Proofreading Paragraph

There are six spelling mistakes in this report. Circle the misspelled words. Write the words correctly on the lines below.

My Visit to America

I noticed many differences between American things and Japanese things. Some of them seem sily, but I'll include them anyway. The gras looks greener in Vermont than in Tokyo. However, the buter tastes sweeter in my home country. I eat supperr earlier at home.

At first, I felt unhapy in a new country. How strange everything was! Then my American friend showed me his baseball card collection. When I helped him with his hoby, I was no longer sad. I learned an important lesson from my trip. If you don't want to be homesick, keep busy.

1. silly 2. grass 3. butter
4. supper 5. unhappy 6. hobby

Writing Activity

Imagine that you are a visitor to a foreign country. For a school report, write about what you saw and did as a visitor. What things did you find the same or different? Write a short report below using six spelling words.

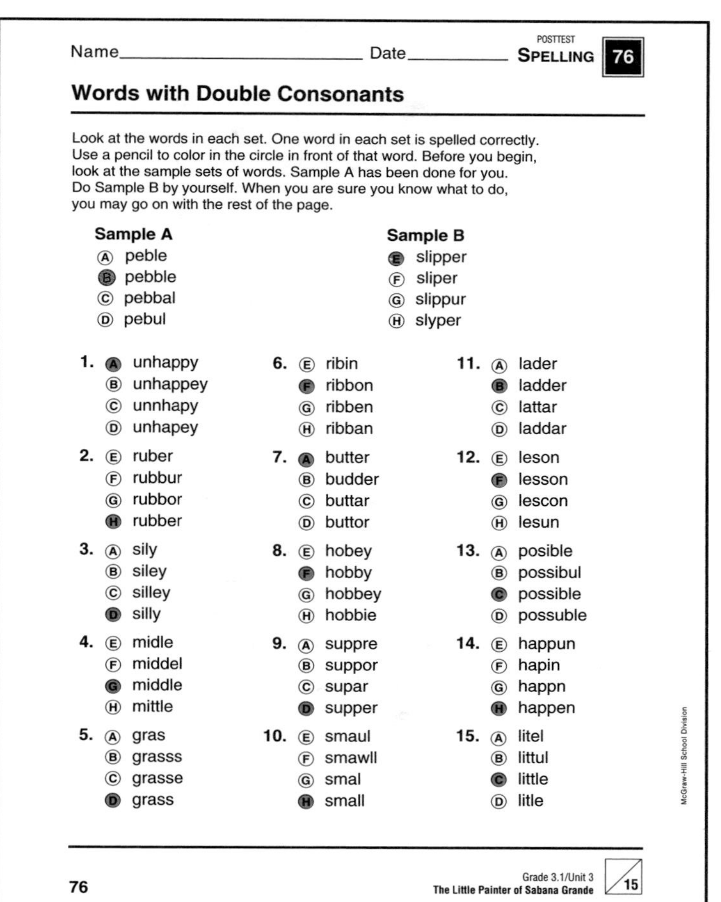

Name____________________ Date__________ POSTTEST SPELLING **76**

Words with Double Consonants

Look at the words in each set. One word in each set is spelled correctly. Use a pencil to color in the circle in front of that word. Before you begin, look at the sample sets of words. Sample A has been done for you. Do Sample B by yourself. When you are sure you know what to do, you may go on with the rest of the page.

Sample A
(A) peble
(B) pebble
(C) pebbal
(D) pebul

Sample B
(E) slipper
(F) sliper
(G) slippur
(H) slyper

1. **(A) unhappy** (B) unhappey (C) unnhapy (D) unhapey
2. (E) ruber (F) rubbur (G) rubbor **(H) rubber**
3. (A) sily (B) siley (C) silley **(D) silly**
4. (E) midle (F) middel **(G) middle** (H) mittle
5. (A) gras (B) grasss (C) grasse **(D) grass**
6. (E) ribin **(F) ribbon** (G) ribben (H) ribban
7. **(A) butter** (B) budder (C) buttar (D) buttor
8. (E) hobey **(F) hobby** (G) hobbey (H) hobbie
9. (A) suppre (B) suppor (C) supar **(D) supper**
10. (E) smaul (F) smawll (G) smal **(H) small**
11. (A) lader **(B) ladder** (C) lattar (D) laddar
12. (E) leson **(F) lesson** (G) lescon (H) lesun
13. (A) posible (B) possibul **(C) possible** (D) possuble
14. (E) happun (F) hapin (G) happn **(H) happen**
15. (A) litel (B) littul **(C) little** (D) litle

The Patchwork Quilt • PRACTICE

Name_______________ Date_______ **Practice 89**

Make Inferences

Sometimes you must **infer**, or figure out, what is happening in a story from clues that the author gives. Read each of the following passages. Then answer each question.

It was Roxanne's birthday, and she was hoping that someone would give her a book about airplanes. Her Aunt Jackie brought her a present in a box. It was just the right size for a book. Roxanne tore open the package. "I can't wait to find out what is!" she said.

1. How do you think Roxanne felt as she opened up the package? excited
2. Which clues helped you make your inference? Roxanne tore open the package. She couldn't wait to see what it was.

Roxanne opened the box and took out a pair of socks. She looked down at them for a minute and sighed very quietly. "Oh . . ." Then she smiled. "Thanks, Aunt Jackie. Just what I needed." Roxanne hugged her aunt.

3. How does Roxanne feel about her present? She feels disappointed.
4. Which clues helped you make your inference? After Roxanne opens her present, she says "Oh," and she sighs.
5. How does Roxanne feel about her Aunt Jackie? She likes her and doesn't want to hurt her feelings.
6. Which clues helped you make your inference? Roxanne pretends to like the present. When she sees the socks, she sighs very quietly so that Aunt Jackie won't hear. She smiles, and hugs her.

At Home: Have students write a sentence or two describing what they think will happen next.

Name_______________ Date_______ **Practice 90**

Vocabulary

gazed costume pattern attic examined anxious

Answer the following questions.

1. If you were *anxious* about something, would you be worried or calm? You would be worried.
2. Would you be more likely to find a *pattern* on flowery wallpaper or in a pile of mud? on flowery wallpaper
3. If you *gazed* at the sky, would you look at it for a long time or a short time? for a long time
4. When you are in an *attic* are you in the basement of a house or just under the roof? just under the roof

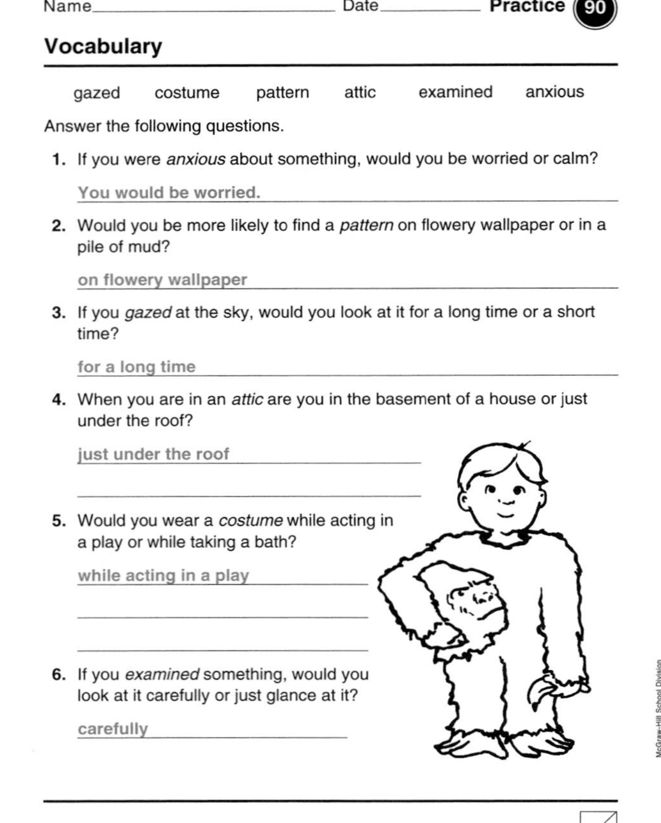

5. Would you wear a *costume* while acting in a play or while taking a bath? while acting in a play
6. If you *examined* something, would you look at it carefully or just glance at it? carefully

At Home: Have students use each of the vocabulary words in a sentence.

Guy's Holiday

Guy could not wait for Thanksgiving. He was *anxious* to show his Aunt Cora his Pilgrim *costume.*

When Aunt Cora arrived, she *gazed* at Guy. "My, Pilgrim, how you have grown!" she said.

After dinner, Aunt Cora and Mama told stories of their childhood. Mama went up to the *attic* and brought down a box filled with photos. Guy *examined* each photo.

In one, young Aunt Cora wore a dress with a *pattern* of leaves. It looked just like the dress she had on! "I guess some things never change!" Aunt Cora exclaimed.

After they finished looking at the photographs they ate dessert. This year they had four different kinds of pie.

1. What did Guy wear on Thanksgiving? a Pilgrim costume
2. How did Guy feel about showing his costume to his aunt? anxious
3. What did Guy's mother get from the *attic*? a box of photos
4. What was on Aunt Cora's dress? a pattern of leaves
5. Why did Aunt Cora say that some things never change? The dress she had on had leaves, like a childhood dress.

At Home: Have students list some of the things they do on Thanksgiving or on another special holiday.

Name_______________ Date_______ **Practice 91**

Story Comprehension

Look back over "The Patchwork Quilt." Then complete the chart below. Answers may vary.

1. Setting of story	Tanya's house
2. Main characters	Tanya, Grandma, Mama, Papa, Ted, and Jim
3. Beginning of story	Grandma tells Tanya about the patchwork quilt she wants to make. Tanya says that she will help her.
4. Middle of story	Grandma gathers patches for her quilt from the family's clothes. Mama decides to help. After Grandma gets sick, the whole family helps cut and prepare patches for the quilt.
5. End of story	Grandma feels better and sews the patches of the quilt together.

Now match each patch of clothing or fabric with the person it belonged to in the story.

b 6. gold dress — **a.** Grandma
a 7. piece of old quilt — **b.** Mama
e 8. red shirt — **c.** Tanya
c 9. African princess costume — **d.** Jim
d 10. blue corduroy pants — **e.** Ted

At Home: Have students write a sentence explaining why the patchwork quilt was important to Tanya and her family.

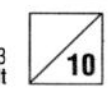

The Patchwork Quilt • PRACTICE

Name_______________________ Date__________ **Practice 92**

Use a Diagram

A **diagram** can help you see how to put something together. Use these diagrams and directions to create a square from a traditional quilt pattern.

This square is called an Indian Trail. It's also been called Forest Path or Winding Walk. As you can see, it looks like a path winding around and around.

Here are the two sizes of triangles that complete the diagram.

1. Start by drawing four sets of three small triangles. Draw them from each corner as shown at right. Then color them in. Use the dotted outlines as a guide.
2. Add four big triangles to the square as shown. Then color in.
3. Add four sets of three small triangles to the inside of the square as shown.
4. Color in those triangles to complete the quilt.

At Home: Ask students to make their own simple design for a quilt.

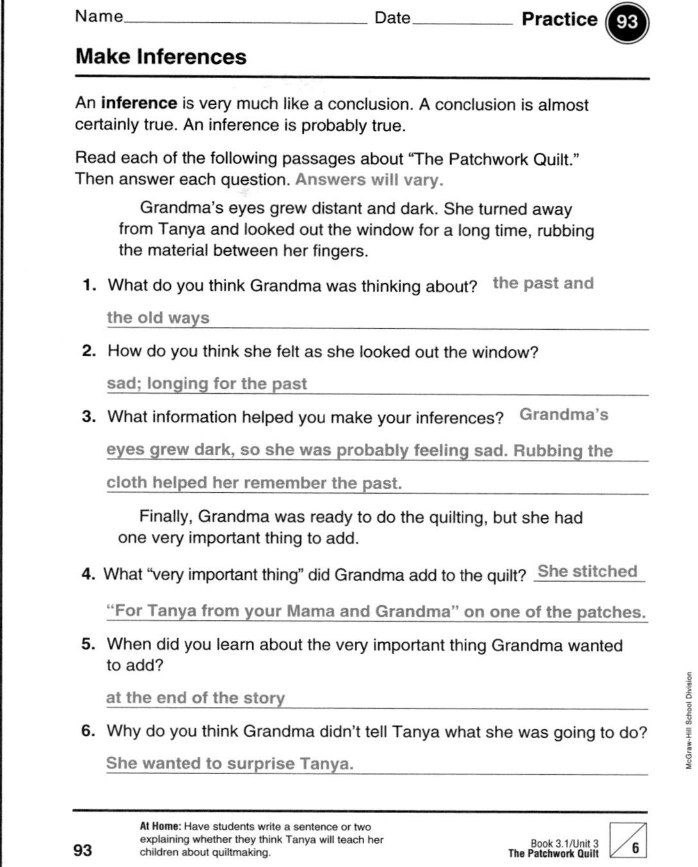

Name_______________________ Date__________ **Practice 93**

Make Inferences

An **inference** is very much like a conclusion. A conclusion is almost certainly true. An inference is probably true.

Read each of the following passages about "The Patchwork Quilt." Then answer each question. Answers will vary.

Grandma's eyes grew distant and dark. She turned away from Tanya and looked out the window for a long time, rubbing the material between her fingers.

1. What do you think Grandma was thinking about? the past and the old ways
2. How do you think she felt as she looked out the window? sad; longing for the past
3. What information helped you make your inferences? Grandma's eyes grew dark, so she was probably feeling sad. Rubbing the cloth helped her remember the past.

Finally, Grandma was ready to do the quilting, but she had one very important thing to add.

4. What "very important thing" did Grandma add to the quilt? She stitched "For Tanya from your Mama and Grandma" on one of the patches.
5. When did you learn about the very important thing Grandma wanted to add? at the end of the story
6. Why do you think Grandma didn't tell Tanya what she was going to do? She wanted to surprise Tanya.

At Home: Have students write a sentence or two explaining whether they think Tanya will teach her children about quiltmaking.

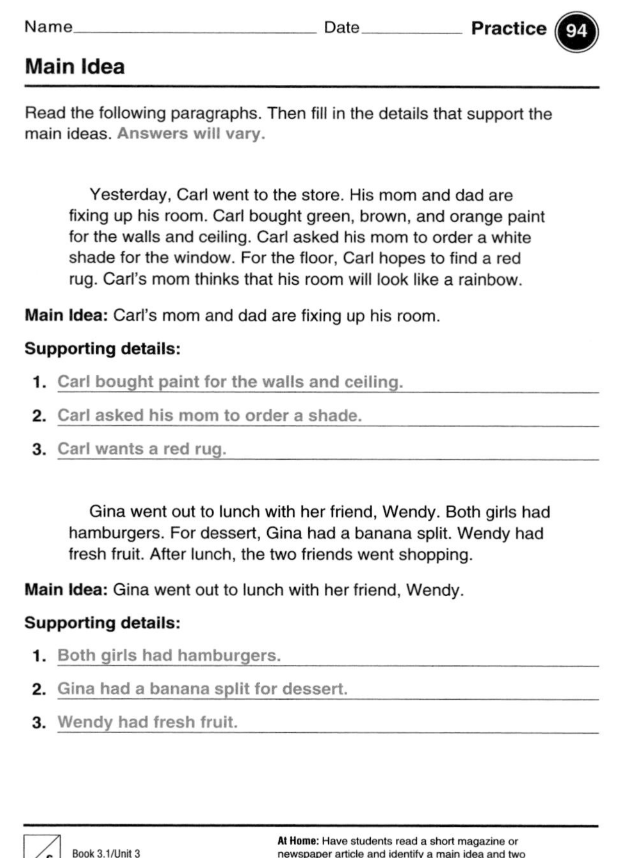

Name_______________________ Date__________ **Practice 94**

Main Idea

Read the following paragraphs. Then fill in the details that support the main ideas. Answers will vary.

Yesterday, Carl went to the store. His mom and dad are fixing up his room. Carl bought green, brown, and orange paint for the walls and ceiling. Carl asked his mom to order a white shade for the window. For the floor, Carl hopes to find a red rug. Carl's mom thinks that his room will look like a rainbow.

Main Idea: Carl's mom and dad are fixing up his room.

Supporting details:

1. Carl bought paint for the walls and ceiling.
2. Carl asked his mom to order a shade.
3. Carl wants a red rug.

Gina went out to lunch with her friend, Wendy. Both girls had hamburgers. For dessert, Gina had a banana split. Wendy had fresh fruit. After lunch, the two friends went shopping.

Main Idea: Gina went out to lunch with her friend, Wendy.

Supporting details:

1. Both girls had hamburgers.
2. Gina had a banana split for dessert.
3. Wendy had fresh fruit.

At Home: Have students read a short magazine or newspaper article and identify a main idea and two supporting details.

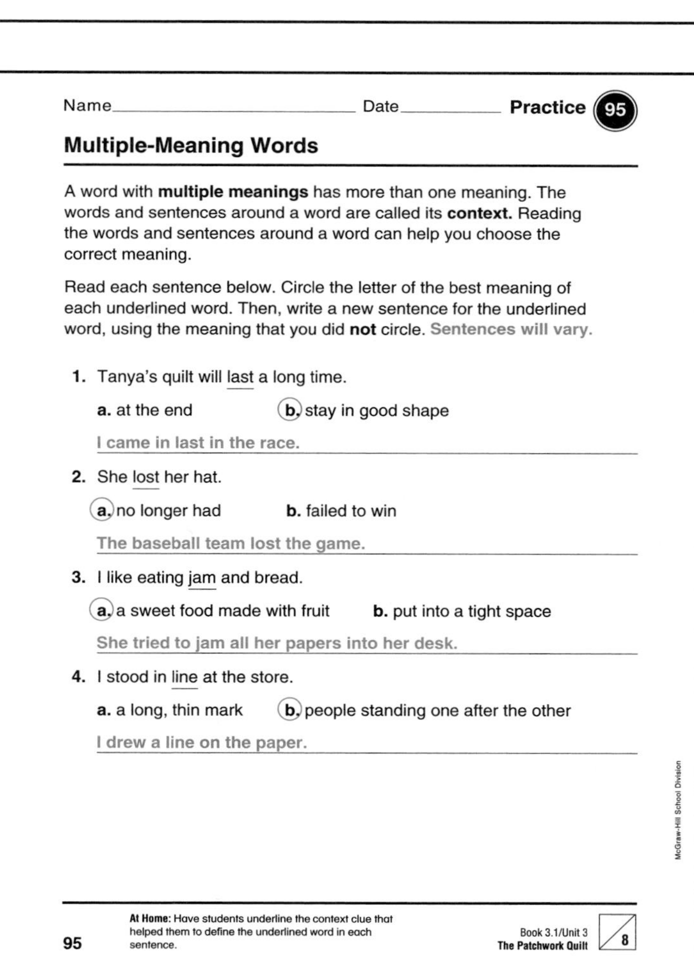

Name_______________________ Date__________ **Practice 95**

Multiple-Meaning Words

A word with **multiple meanings** has more than one meaning. The words and sentences around a word are called its **context.** Reading the words and sentences around a word can help you choose the correct meaning.

Read each sentence below. Circle the letter of the best meaning of each underlined word. Then, write a new sentence for the underlined word, using the meaning that you did **not** circle. Sentences will vary.

1. Tanya's quilt will last a long time.
   a. at the end **(b.)** stay in good shape
   I came in last in the race.
2. She lost her hat.
   (a.) no longer had **b.** failed to win
   The baseball team lost the game.
3. I like eating jam and bread.
   (a.) a sweet food made with fruit **b.** put into a tight space
   She tried to jam all her papers into her desk.
4. I stood in line at the store.
   a. a long, thin mark **(b.)** people standing one after the other
   I drew a line on the paper.

At Home: Have students underline the context clue that helped them to define the underlined word in each sentence.

The Patchwork Quilt • RETEACH

Name________________________ Date__________ **Reteach 89**

Make Inferences

> Authors do not always **tell** readers how characters feel. Sometimes they **show** readers how the character feels through his or her actions.

Read the following passages. Then circle the answer to each question and explain your answer.

The school play was about to start. Shara was playing the princess.

"I don't know if I can go on stage," Shara said. "There are so many people here. What if I forget what I'm supposed to say?" Her hands were shaking, and her stomach felt funny.

1. Based on this passage, how do you think Shara feels?

   (a.) afraid **b.** happy **c.** angry

2. Explain your answer. Shara says that she's not sure that she'll be able to go on stage. Her hands are shaking, and her stomach feels strange.

Once Shara walked on stage, her hands stopped shaking and her stomach felt better. Her voice was clear and strong. "What was I thinking? I'm great at this," she thought.

3. How does Shara feel now?

   a. sad (b.) happy **c.** disappointed

4. Explain your answer. Shara's hands stop shaking, her stomach feels better, and she speaks in a clear, strong voice. She says that she is "great."

At Home: Have students write a sentence or two explaining how they think Shara might feel after the performance.

Name________________________ Date__________ **Reteach 90**

Vocabulary

costume attic gaze pattern examined anxious

Choose the vocabulary word that matches each meaning. Then complete the puzzle.

Across

3. excited anxious
5. looked at examined
6. the space just below the roof of a house attic

Down

1. to look at something for a long time gaze
2. clothes worn to look like someone or something else costume
4. a design pattern

Story Comprehension **Reteach 91**

Put an **X** next to the sentences that describe "The Patchwork Quilt."

x Tanya agrees to help Grandma make the quilt.

x Grandma sews the last pieces of the quilt together.

x Everyone works on the quilt when Grandma gets sick.

____ Grandma sells the finished quilt.

x Grandma makes the quilt patches from old clothes.

At Home: Have students write a sentence explaining why the patchwork quilt is important to Tanya and her family.

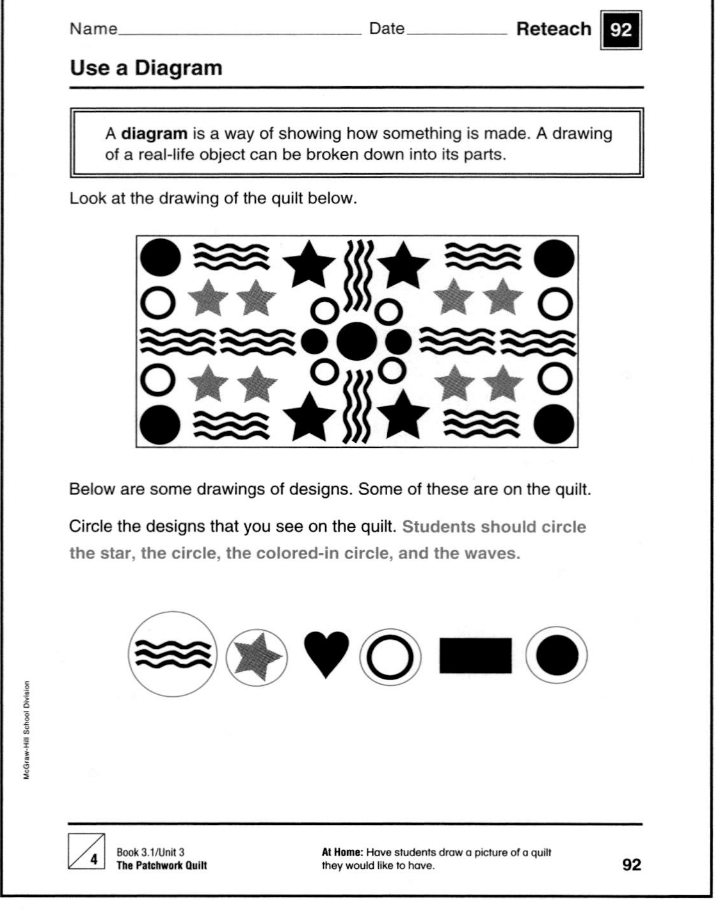

Name________________________ Date__________ **Reteach 92**

Use a Diagram

> A **diagram** is a way of showing how something is made. A drawing of a real-life object can be broken down into its parts.

Look at the drawing of the quilt below.

Below are some drawings of designs. Some of these are on the quilt.

Circle the designs that you see on the quilt. Students should circle the star, the circle, the colored-in circle, and the waves.

At Home: Have students draw a picture of a quilt they would like to have.

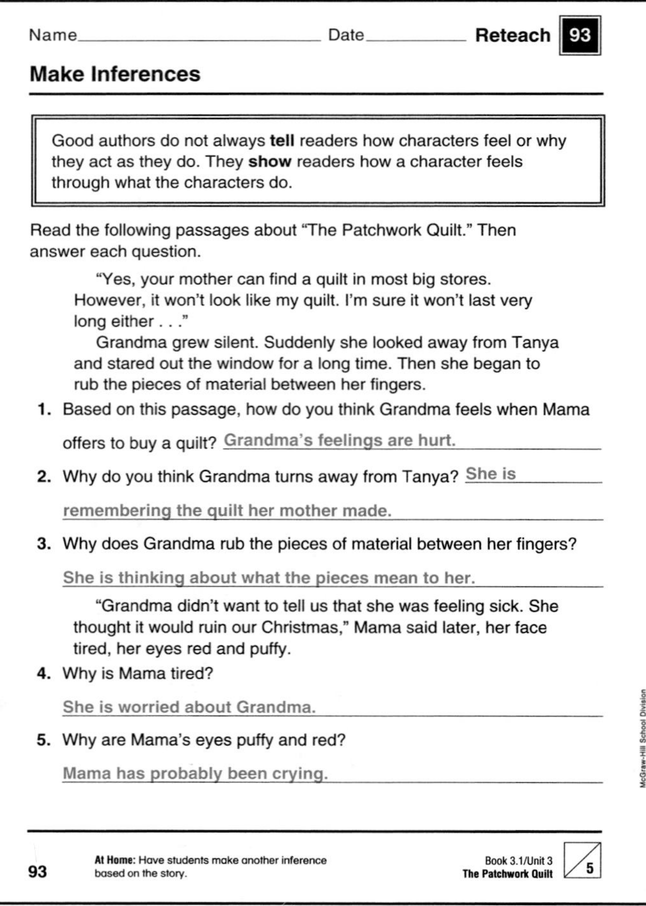

Name________________________ Date__________ **Reteach 93**

Make Inferences

> Good authors do not always **tell** readers how characters feel or why they act as they do. They **show** readers how a character feels through what the characters do.

Read the following passages about "The Patchwork Quilt." Then answer each question.

"Yes, your mother can find a quilt in most big stores. However, it won't look like my quilt. I'm sure it won't last very long either . . ."

Grandma grew silent. Suddenly she looked away from Tanya and stared out the window for a long time. Then she began to rub the pieces of material between her fingers.

1. Based on this passage, how do you think Grandma feels when Mama offers to buy a quilt? Grandma's feelings are hurt.
2. Why do you think Grandma turns away from Tanya? She is remembering the quilt her mother made.
3. Why does Grandma rub the pieces of material between her fingers? She is thinking about what the pieces mean to her.

"Grandma didn't want to tell us that she was feeling sick. She thought it would ruin our Christmas," Mama said later, her face tired, her eyes red and puffy.

4. Why is Mama tired? She is worried about Grandma.
5. Why are Mama's eyes puffy and red? Mama has probably been crying.

At Home: Have students make another inference based on the story.

Name________________________ Date__________ **Reteach 94**

Main Idea

> You can better understand what you read if you notice the **main idea** and **supporting details**. The main idea tells the most important point the author wants to make. The supporting details are smaller points that explain the main idea.

Read the story below. First write the main idea of the story. Then write the supporting details.

When it was time to make lunch, the whole family helped out. Dad cut the bread. I set the table. My sister, Betty, folded the napkins. Mom made sandwiches.

Our dog, Lenny, didn't help. He just waited for the leftovers.

Main Idea:

1. The whole family helped prepare lunch.

Supporting Details:

2. I set the table.
3. Betty folded the napkins.
4. Dad cut the bread.
5. Mom made sandwiches.

At Home: Encourage students to add two more supporting details to the story.

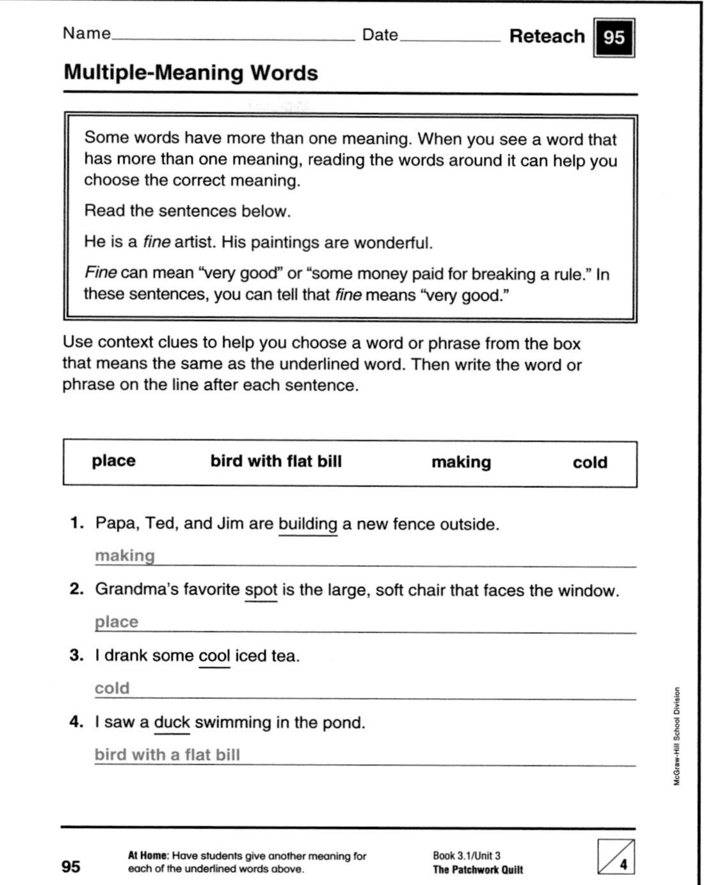

Name________________________ Date__________ **Reteach 95**

Multiple-Meaning Words

> Some words have more than one meaning. When you see a word that has more than one meaning, reading the words around it can help you choose the correct meaning.
>
> Read the sentences below.
>
> He is a *fine* artist. His paintings are wonderful.
>
> *Fine* can mean "very good" or "some money paid for breaking a rule." In these sentences, you can tell that *fine* means "very good."

Use context clues to help you choose a word or phrase from the box that means the same as the underlined word. Then write the word or phrase on the line after each sentence.

place	bird with flat bill	making	cold

1. Papa, Ted, and Jim are building a new fence outside.
   making
2. Grandma's favorite spot is the large, soft chair that faces the window.
   place
3. I drank some cool iced tea.
   cold
4. I saw a duck swimming in the pond.
   bird with a flat bill

At Home: Have students give another meaning for each of the underlined words above.

Name______________________ Date__________ **Extend 89**

Make Inferences

Read the story. Use story clues and what you already know to find out how Jenna feels about Anna's pet bird.

"This is my bird, Peppa," said Anna. "I'll let him out so you can hold him."

Jenna did not want Anna to let Peppa out. She said, "I can see that Peppa is a very beautiful bird. You don't have to let him out."

"Oh, but he is so sweet. You won't know how soft he feels if I don't let him out," said Anna.

Anna opened Peppa's cage and out he flew. First he landed on Anna's shoulder. She rubbed his neck and let him go. He flew in circles and then landed right on Jenna's arm.

Jenna didn't move. She let out a small scream.

"Jenna, he likes you!" cried Anna excitedly.

Jenna did not even answer her.

What clues in the text help you know how Jenna feels?

Answers will vary. For example, Jenna did not want Anna to open the cage.

What do you know about people and pets that will help you know how Jenna feels?

Answers will vary. For example, some people are afraid of birds.

What can you infer about how Jenna feels?

Answers will vary. For example, Jenna is afraid of birds and did not want Peppa near her.

At Home: Have students make an inference about how Anna was feeling.

Name______________________ Date__________ **Extend 90**

Vocabulary

anxious	attic	costume	examined	gazed	pattern

Make up a story with a partner. First make a list of the events that will happen in the story. Then use words in the box to tell how the characters feel or what they will do. Write your story on another piece of paper.

Answers will vary.

Extend 91

Story Comprehension

Work with a group to make a patchwork quilt "drawing" about your class that you "won't forget." Group members can include a drawing that tells something special about themselves. Write a sentence under each picture that tells what is important about it.

At Home: Have students write a paragraph about other ways besides quilting that families might use to record special memories.

Name______________________ Date__________ **Extend 92**

Use a Diagram

Make your own quilt pattern. Use colored pencils or markers and the graph paper below to make a design for a quilt. Exchange patterns with a partner. Try creating a paper quilt. Use colored construction paper, scissors, and glue to create a paper quilt by following your partner's design.

At Home: Have students make a pattern showing a design for a decorative screen or wall hanging.

Name______________________ Date__________ **Extend 93**

Make Inferences

Write a sentence or two about "The Patchwork Quilt" telling how you think Grandma feels about the past.

Answers will vary. For example, She longs for the past. She wants to remember the past and the old ways of doing things.

What clues in the story helped you infer this?

Answers will vary. For example, Grandma tells Tanya about the quilt her own mother made.

Work with a partner to write interview questions to ask Grandma about her past. Act out the interview.

At Home: Have students write a sentence telling why they think Tanya removed a few squares from Grandma's old quilt.

Name_______________ Date_______ **Extend 94**

Main Idea

Work with a group to read copies of a short newspaper article. Write a sentence stating the main idea of the article. List the supporting details from the article. List any details from the article that do not support the main idea. Answers will vary.

MAIN IDEA:

SUPPORTING DETAILS:

OTHER DETAILS:

Write a sentence telling why you think the article might have included details that do not support the main idea.

Answers may vary. For example, the author wanted to include an interesting fact.

At Home: Have students read a short magazine or newspaper article and identify the main idea and two supporting details.

Name_______________ Date_______ **Extend 95**

Multiple-Meaning Words

Read each joke. Then write a sentence below the joke using the word in dark type. Sentences will vary.

1. Why is the river rich? Because it has two **banks.**
2. What did the elephant take on vacation? His **trunk.**
3. Why is a tall building like a book of fairy tales? It has lots of **stories.**

Write your own joke using any of the following multiple-meaning words: **cold, fresh, soft,** and **worn.** Jokes will vary.

At Home: Have students draw a picture illustrating two meanings for the word bank.

Name__________ Date______ LEARN Grammar 77

Past-Tense Verbs

- A verb in the **past tense** tells about an action that already happened.
- Add *–ed* to most verbs to show past tense.
  Grandma waited for the scraps.

Find the past-tense verb in each sentence. Write it on the line.

1. Tanya wanted to go outside. wanted
2. She looked longingly out the window. looked
3. Grandma flexed her fingers. flexed
4. Tanya remembered some of the fabrics in the scraps. remembered
5. Mama complained about the mess. complained
6. "A year," shouted Tanya. shouted
7. One by one, Grandma added each person to the quilt. added
8. Tanya and her family romped in the snow. romped
9. Grandma grouped the scraps in a pattern of colors. grouped
10. Mama helped Grandma with the quilt. helped

Extension: Have students write present-tense verbs on scraps of paper, and shuffle the scraps for them to pick. Have each student spell the past-tense form of his or her verb and use it in a sentence.

Name__________ Date______ LEARN AND PRACTICE Grammar 78

Past-Tense Verbs

- If a verb ends with *e*, drop the *e* and add *–ed* to show past tense.
- If a verb ends with a consonant and *y*, change *y* to *i* and add *–ed.*
- If a verb ends with one vowel and one consonant, double the consonant and add *–ed.*
  pull, **pulled** carry, **carried**
  arrive, **arrived** clap, **clapped**

Change each underlined verb to past tense. Write the past-tense verb on the line.

1. All last year, Grandma trim scraps for the quilt. trimmed
2. That December, Mama cook for Christmas all day. cooked
3. At that time, Grandma join her in the kitchen. joined
4. Last night, she fold the quilt neatly. folded
5. A week ago, Mama and Papa permit them to see Grandma. permitted
6. Last night, Grandma smile at Ted, Jim, and Tanya. smiled
7. That spring, Tanya hurry home each day to work on the quilt. hurried
8. Last week, Tanya stop working on the quilt. stopped
9. Yesterday, she tiptoe into Grandma's room. tiptoed
10. Starting last month, Papa carry Grandma to her chair. carried

Extension: Have students work in pairs to list ten past-tense verbs that describe the actions of making a quilt. Develop a glossary page, giving their own definition for each verb. Encourage them to illustrate their glossary pages.

Name__________ Date______ PRACTICE AND REVIEW Grammar 79

Past-Tense Verbs

- A verb in the **past tense** tells about an action that already happened.
- Add *–ed* to most verbs to show past tense.
- If a verb ends in *e*, drop the *e* and add *–ed* to show past tense.
- If a verb ends with a consonant and *y*, change *y* to *i* and add *–ed.*
- If a verb ends with one vowel and one consonant, double the consonant and add *–ed.*

Choose the correct past-tense verb for each sentence. Circle your answer.

1.	Grandma ____ together the quilt all year.	pieces	(pieced)
2.	Tanya ____ her head.	(tilted)	tiltted
3.	Grandma never ____ old material.	(scrapped)	scraped
4.	Often that year, Mama ____ about Grandma.	worry	(worried)
5.	Yesterday, Jim ____ Grandma.	hugs	(hugged)
6.	All last winter, Mama ____ his pants again and again.	(patched)	patches
7.	In her flowing costume, Tanya ____.	danceded	(danced)
8.	"Look at the snow!" they ____.	cryed	(cried)
9.	Mama ____ the fabric between her fingers.	(rubbed)	rubs
10.	That first night, the quilt ____ each person of something different.	remind	(reminded)

Extension: Have students write brief paragraphs about a past holiday celebration in their families.

Name__________ Date______ MECHANICS Grammar 80

Using Commas

- Use commas to separate three or more words in a series.
  Mama shopped, cooked, and served dinner.

Correct the sentences by changing the verbs to past-tense. Add a comma after words in a series. Write the new sentence on the line.

1. Mama look at Grandma pick up Tanya's glass and went out.
   Mama looked at Grandma, picked up Tanya's glass, and went out.
2. Grandma turn away gaze out the window and rub the cloth.
   Grandma turned away, gazed out the window, and rubbed the cloth.
3. Grandma say, "I need more gold blue green and red material."
   Grandma said, "I needed more gold, blue, green, and red material."
4. Grandma and Mama hum talk and laugh as they work.
   Grandma and Mama hummed, talked, and laughed as they worked.
5. The two women cut place and sew the scraps.
   The two women cut, placed, and sewed the scraps.
6. The quilt include scraps from Ted Jim Tanya Mama and Papa.
   The quilt included scraps from Ted, Jim, Tanya, Mama, and Papa.
7. Tanya work all February March and April on the quilt.
   Tanya worked all February, March, and April on the quilt.
8. The finished quilt look big bright and colorful.
   The finished quilt looked big, bright, and colorful.

Extension: Hold a "scavenger hunt" for verbs, nouns, and adjectives in a series. The first student to find a series of each kind of word wins the hunt. The students can search in magazines, catalogs, and newspapers.

Name________________ Date__________ TEST Grammar 81

Past-Tense Verbs

Read each sentence. Find the past-tense verb and write it on the line.

1. Tanya hoped to go outside. hoped
2. She leaned against Grandma's chair. leaned
3. Grandma patted Tanya's head. patted
4. The students scurried outside to enjoy the snow. scurried

Spell the past-tense form of the action verb in each sentence. Write the answer on the line.

5. "A whole year!" Tanya (cry) last spring. cried
6. Beginning that day, Grandma (plan) her quilt. planned
7. Tanya (amaze) her family that year. amazed
8. All that spring, they (watch) her working on the quilt. watched
9. That day, Grandma (pin) some scraps together. pinned
10. Back then, nobody (imagine) the quilt's final size. imagined

Name________________ Date__________ MORE PRACTICE Grammar 82

Past Tense Verbs

- A verb in the **past tense** tells about an action that already happened.
- Add *–ed* to most verbs to show past tense.
- If a verb ends in *e*, drop the *e* and add *–ed* to show past tense.
- If a verb ends with a consonant and *y*, change *y* to *i* and add *–ed.*
- If a verb ends with one vowel and one consonant, double the consonant and add *–ed.*

Look at the picture and read the paragraph that tells what happened. Cross out each verb that is not spelled correctly to show a past action. Write the correct past tense verb above the crossed out verb.

Yesterday, we ~~bakeed~~ baked a cake together.
Mama ~~explainned~~ explained the directions.
Grandma ~~measure~~ measured the flour and sugar.
I ~~stired~~ stirred the batter.
I ~~trys~~ tried not to spill any!

Now write two or three sentences about how the cake was finished.

answers will vary

Name________________ Date________ PRETEST SPELLING **77**

Words with /ou/ and /oi/

Pretest Directions

Fold back the paper along the dotted line. Use the blanks to write each word as it is read aloud. When you finish the test, unfold the paper. Use the list at the right to correct any spelling mistakes. Practice the words you missed for the Posttest.

1. ________	1. found
2. ________	2. spoil
3. ________	3. power
4. ________	4. enjoy
5. ________	5. foil
6. ________	6. clown
7. ________	7. voyage
8. ________	8. cloudy
9. ________	9. noisy
10. ________	10. count
11. ________	11. poison
12. ________	12. loyal
13. ________	13. allow
14. ________	14. choice
15. ________	15. shout
Challenge Words	
________	anxious
________	attic
________	costume
________	examined
________	pattern

To Parents

Here are the results of your child's weekly spelling Pretest. You can help your child study for the Posttest by following these simple steps for each word on the word list:

1. Read the word to your child.
2. Have your child write the word, saying each letter as it is written.
3. Say each letter of the word as your child checks the spelling.
4. If a mistake has been made, have your child read each letter of the correctly spelled word aloud, and then repeat steps 1-3.

15

Name________________ Date________ AT-HOME WORD STUDY SPELLING **78**

Words with /ou/ and /oi/

Using the Word Study Steps

1. LOOK at the word.
2. SAY the word aloud.
3. STUDY the letters in the word.
4. WRITE the word.
5. CHECK the word.
   Did you spell the word right?
   If not, go back to step 1.

Spelling Tip

- The sound /oi/ in the middle of a word or syllable is usually spelled **oi**; at the end it is usually spelled **oy**.
- The sound /ou/ at the end of a word or syllable is usually spelled **ow**.

Circle the Rhyming Word

Circle the word in each row that rhymes with the word in dark type.

1.	**power**	poison	tower	pear
2.	**clown**	allow	cloudy	town
3.	**spoil**	foil	pail	spill
4.	**loyal**	noisy	enjoy	royal
5.	**shout**	out	shot	short
6.	**count**	coat	mount	moth
7.	**choice**	voice	voyage	enjoy
8.	**found**	bound	do	drew

To Parents or Helpers:

Using the Word Study Steps above as your child comes across any new words will help him or her spell well. Review the steps as you both go over this week's spelling words.

Go over each Spelling Tip with your child. Point out the spelling words that follow the pattern. Help your child complete the spelling activity.

8

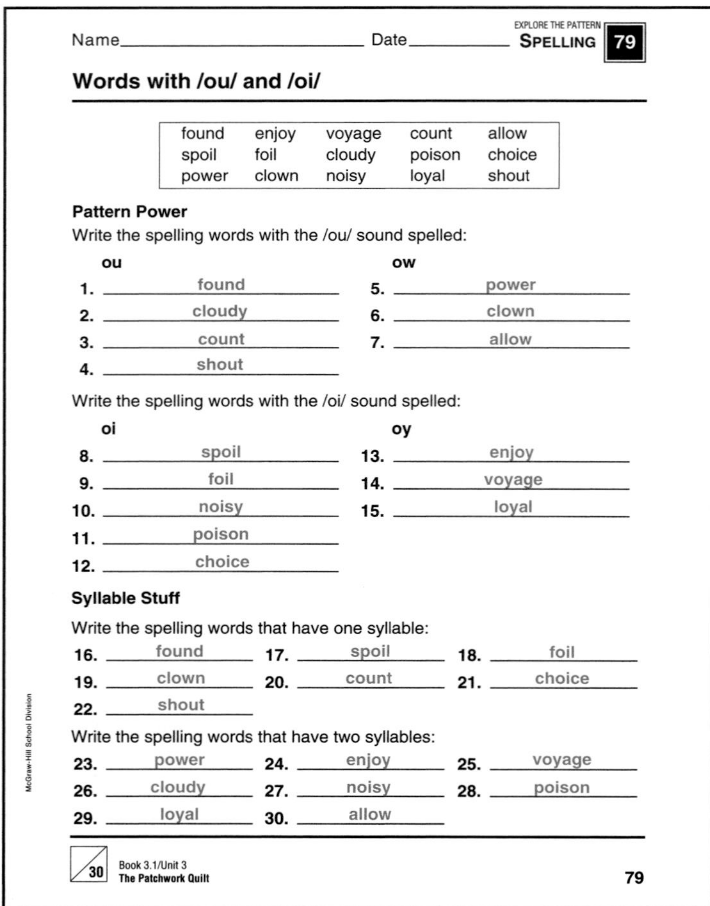

Name________________ Date________ EXPLORE THE PATTERN SPELLING **79**

Words with /ou/ and /oi/

found	enjoy	voyage	count	allow
spoil	foil	cloudy	poison	choice
power	clown	noisy	loyal	shout

Pattern Power

Write the spelling words with the /ou/ sound spelled:

ou
1. found
2. cloudy
3. count
4. shout

ow
5. power
6. clown
7. allow

Write the spelling words with the /oi/ sound spelled:

oi
8. spoil
9. foil
10. noisy
11. poison
12. choice

oy
13. enjoy
14. voyage
15. loyal

Syllable Stuff

Write the spelling words that have one syllable:

16. found 17. spoil 18. foil
19. clown 20. count 21. choice
22. shout

Write the spelling words that have two syllables:

23. power 24. enjoy 25. voyage
26. cloudy 27. noisy 28. poison
29. loyal 30. allow

30

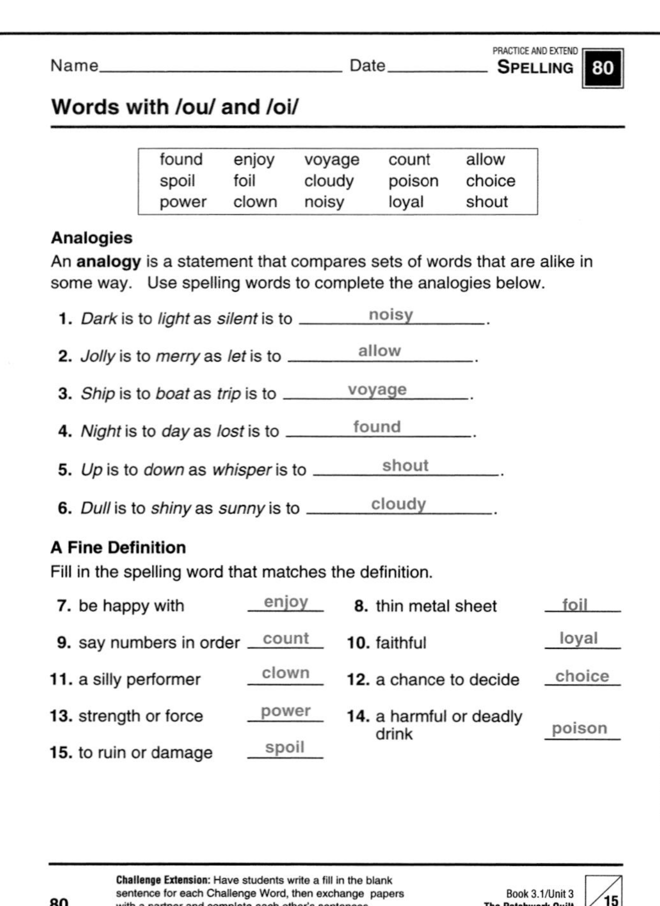

Name________________ Date________ PRACTICE AND EXTEND SPELLING **80**

Words with /ou/ and /oi/

found	enjoy	voyage	count	allow
spoil	foil	cloudy	poison	choice
power	clown	noisy	loyal	shout

Analogies

An **analogy** is a statement that compares sets of words that are alike in some way. Use spelling words to complete the analogies below.

1. *Dark* is to *light* as *silent* is to noisy.
2. *Jolly* is to *merry* as *let* is to allow.
3. *Ship* is to *boat* as *trip* is to voyage.
4. *Night* is to *day* as *lost* is to found.
5. *Up* is to *down* as *whisper* is to shout.
6. *Dull* is to *shiny* as *sunny* is to cloudy.

A Fine Definition

Fill in the spelling word that matches the definition.

7. be happy with enjoy
8. thin metal sheet foil
9. say numbers in order count
10. faithful loyal
11. a silly performer clown
12. a chance to decide choice
13. strength or force power
14. a harmful or deadly drink poison
15. to ruin or damage spoil

Challenge Extension: Have students write a fill in the blank sentence for each Challenge Word, then exchange papers with a partner and complete each other's sentences.

15

Name________________________ Date__________ PROOFREAD AND WRITE SPELLING 81

Words with /ou/ and /oi/

Proofreading Paragraph

There are six spelling mistakes in this letter. Circle the misspelled words. Write the words correctly on the lines below.

Dear President:

I am writing this letter to let you know about your toy cloun. I bought a Happy Face toy yesterday. But when I took the toy out of the box, I saw that it was broken. Boy, did it ever spoyle my day!

I used to be a loyle customer of Happy Face toys. However, now my Mom and Dad won't alow me to buy another one of your toys.

Now all I want is my money back. I hope I can counte on you to do the right thing. Since you are the president of the company, I know you have the powre to do it. Thank you.

Sincerely,
Marcy Shore

1. clown 2. spoil 3. loyal
4. allow 5. count 6. power

Writing Activity

Did you ever have a toy spoil your day? What went wrong? Write several sentences explaining what happened. Use six spelling words and circle them.

____

____

____

____

____

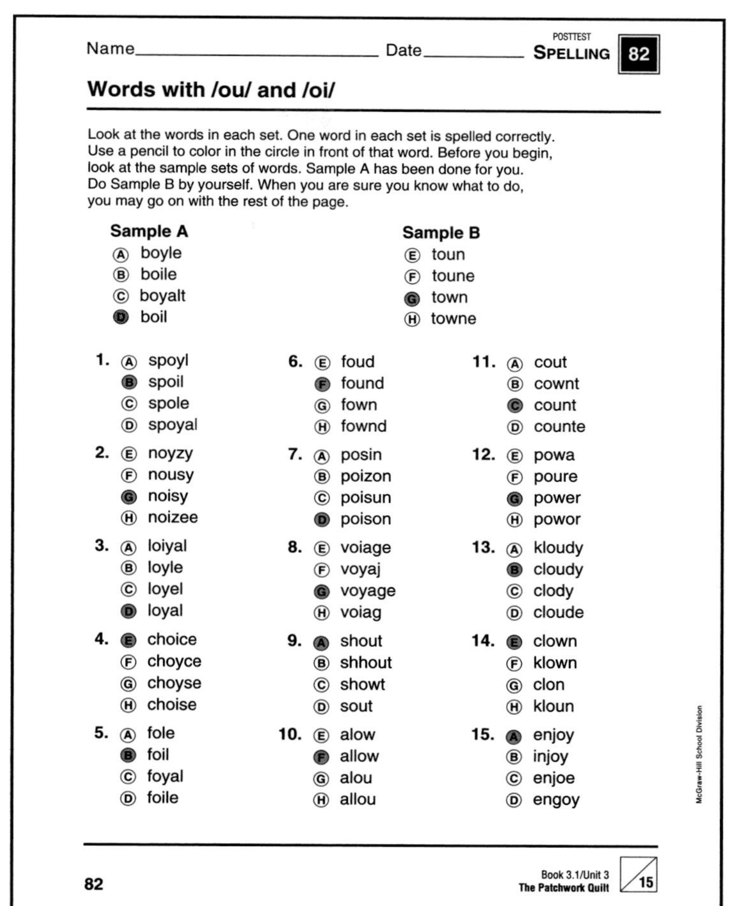

Name________________________ Date__________ POSTTEST SPELLING 82

Words with /ou/ and /oi/

Look at the words in each set. One word in each set is spelled correctly. Use a pencil to color in the circle in front of that word. Before you begin, look at the sample sets of words. Sample A has been done for you. Do Sample B by yourself. When you are sure you know what to do, you may go on with the rest of the page.

Sample A
Ⓐ boyle
Ⓑ boile
Ⓒ boyalt
● boil

Sample B
Ⓔ toun
Ⓕ toune
● town
Ⓗ towne

1. Ⓐ spoyl ● spoil Ⓒ spole Ⓓ spoyal
2. Ⓔ noyzy Ⓕ nousy ● noisy Ⓗ noizee
3. Ⓐ loiyal Ⓑ loyle Ⓒ loyel ● loyal
4. ● choice Ⓕ choyce Ⓖ choyse Ⓗ choise
5. Ⓐ fole ● foil Ⓒ foyal Ⓓ foile
6. Ⓔ foud ● found Ⓖ fown Ⓗ fownd
7. Ⓐ posin Ⓑ poizon Ⓒ poisun ● poison
8. Ⓔ voiage Ⓕ voyaj ● voyage Ⓗ voiag
9. ● shout Ⓑ shhout Ⓒ showt Ⓓ sout
10. Ⓔ alow ● allow Ⓖ alou Ⓗ allou
11. Ⓐ cout Ⓑ cownt ● count Ⓓ counte
12. Ⓔ powa Ⓕ poure ● power Ⓗ powor
13. Ⓐ kloudy ● cloudy Ⓒ clody Ⓓ cloude
14. ● clown Ⓕ klown Ⓖ clon Ⓗ kloun
15. ● enjoy Ⓑ injoy Ⓒ enjoe Ⓓ engoy

Name______________________ Date__________ **Practice 96**

Story Elements

Understanding the main **characters** and the **setting** can help you understand what happens in a story.

Read the story below. Then answer the questions.

Today in class, everyone was supposed to write a story. Jamar couldn't think of anything to write about, so he asked his friends for some ideas.

Erica said, "Write about horses."

Pedro said, "Write about a ship."

Bill suggested, "Write about a doctor."

He raised his hand. "Mr. Diaz, what should I do?" he said. "I'll never think of a story. I asked all my friends, but I don't want to write about the things they suggested."

Mr. Diaz said, "Usually, it's a good idea to write about things you like."

Jamar thought about it. "I like baseball. I know! I'll write a story about a baseball player who becomes an all-star!"

1. Where does the story take place? The story takes place in class.
2. Who is the main character? Jamar is the main character.
3. What is Jamar's problem? He can't think of anything to write about.
4. What does Jamar decide to do at the end of the story?
   He decides to write about something he likes—baseball.

At Home: Have students write a few sentences explaining how Jamar tries to solve his problem.

Name______________________ Date__________ **Practice 97**

Vocabulary

Write the vocabulary word that best fits in each of the sentences below.

combine invented located prairie stumbled wilderness

1. Let's ___combine___ your hard work with my good ideas. By joining together, we can do a much better job.
2. The scientist was well-known for thinking of useful new things. He ___invented___ egg timers and staplers, and he even made the first nonstick pan!
3. I live on Fire Street between the courthouse and the library. Where is your house ___located___?
4. I was camping in the forest. Crickets were singing, and frogs were croaking. It was so lovely being out there in the ___wilderness___.
5. The flat, grassy fields seemed like they would never end, and I hadn't seen a tree for miles. "This has to be the biggest ___prairie___ in the United States," I thought to myself.
6. My brother stepped on his shoelace, ___stumbled___, and then cried out as he fell down.

At Home: Have students think of other words that mean almost the same thing as the vocabulary words. Then have them use these words as clues for a vocabulary puzzle, crossword puzzle, or game.

Save the Animals!

Jed left his home on the *prairie*. He hoped to reach the edge of the *wilderness* before the sun set. He had something important to do.

Jed had *invented* a way to protect animals from floods. He wanted to show his invention to some of the animals along the way. The problem was, he couldn't find any animals! By late afternoon, Jed was about to give up. Suddenly he *stumbled* across a fox and her young. "Get away!" the fox shouted. "You will not hurt my babies and me!"

"I am here to help you," said Jed. "Let's *combine* what we know to save the animals. You tell me where the other animals are *located*, and I will share my invention with them."

The fox thought about it for a moment. Then she agreed. "I will show you," she said. "Follow me!"

1. Who *stumbled* across a fox?
   Jed
2. Where was Jed's home?
   on the prairie
3. What had Jed *invented*?
   a way to protect animals from floods
4. Where was Jed walking?
   to the edge of the wilderness
5. Why did Jed want to get to the animals?
   to share his invention

At Home: Encourage students to think of ways that animals might be protected from hunters.

Name______________________ Date__________ **Practice 98**

Story Comprehension

In "Pecos Bill," Cowboy Sam and Cowgirl Pam tell a story to Cookie and the ranch hands. "Pecos Bill" is a story within a story. Fill in the chart for each story.

	Main Story	Story Within a Story
Setting	cowboy camp in Texas	Texas
Characters	Cowboy Sam, Cowgirl Pam, Cookie, and the ranch hands	Pa, Ma, Pecos Bill, the other children, coyotes, Carl the Cowboy, Slue-Foot Sue, and the Judge
Beginning	They order pizza. Sam and Pam start telling a story.	Bill's family decides to go west.
Middle	The pizza comes.	Baby Bill falls out of the wagon. Coyotes raise him. Years later, Carl the Cowboy finds Bill and teaches him how to be a cowboy. Bill invents different things.
End	Everyone goes to sleep.	Bill meets and marries Slue-Foot Sue.

At Home: Ask students to circle the part of the chart that represents the plot.

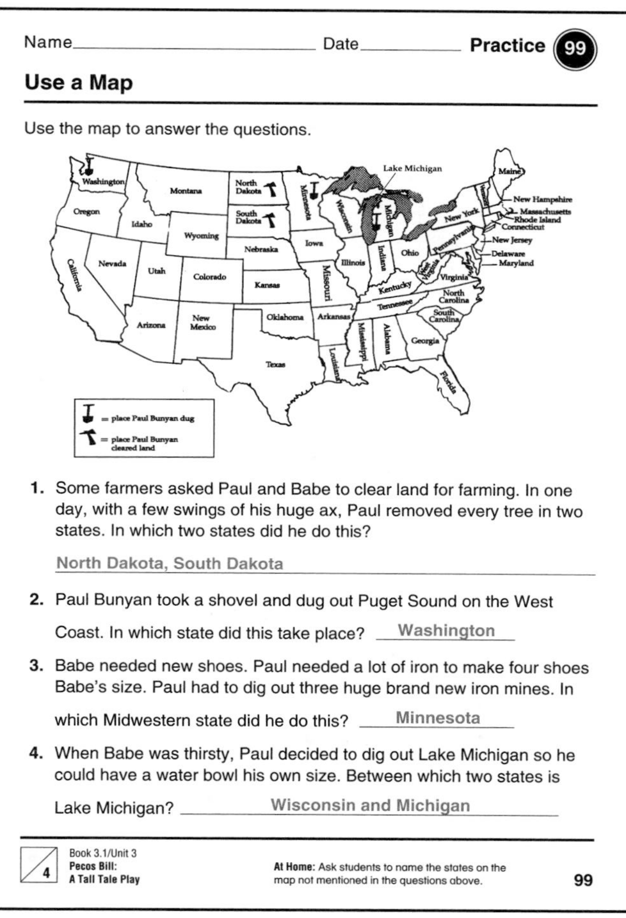

Name________________________ Date__________ **Practice 99**

Use a Map

Use the map to answer the questions.

1. Some farmers asked Paul and Babe to clear land for farming. In one day, with a few swings of his huge ax, Paul removed every tree in two states. In which two states did he do this?
   North Dakota, South Dakota
2. Paul Bunyan took a shovel and dug out Puget Sound on the West Coast. In which state did this take place? Washington
3. Babe needed new shoes. Paul needed a lot of iron to make four shoes Babe's size. Paul had to dig out three huge brand new iron mines. In which Midwestern state did he do this? Minnesota
4. When Babe was thirsty, Paul decided to dig out Lake Michigan so he could have a water bowl his own size. Between which two states is Lake Michigan? Wisconsin and Michigan

4 | Book 3.1/Unit 3 **Pecos Bill: A Tall Tale Play** | **At Home:** Ask students to name the states on the map not mentioned in the questions above. | 99

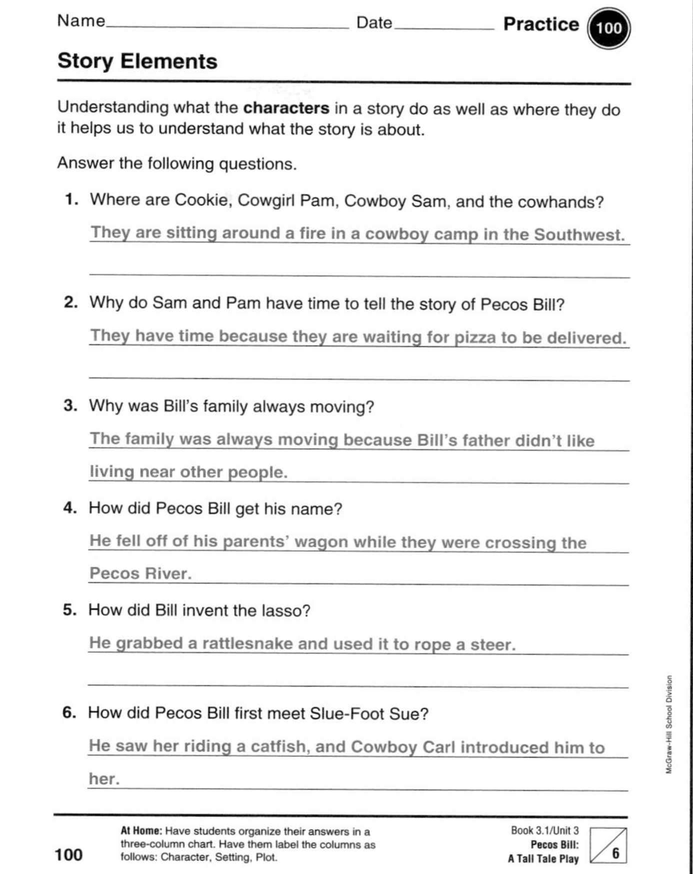

Name________________________ Date__________ **Practice 100**

Story Elements

Understanding what the **characters** in a story do as well as where they do it helps us to understand what the story is about.

Answer the following questions.

1. Where are Cookie, Cowgirl Pam, Cowboy Sam, and the cowhands?
   They are sitting around a fire in a cowboy camp in the Southwest.
2. Why do Sam and Pam have time to tell the story of Pecos Bill?
   They have time because they are waiting for pizza to be delivered.
3. Why was Bill's family always moving?
   The family was always moving because Bill's father didn't like living near other people.
4. How did Pecos Bill get his name?
   He fell off of his parents' wagon while they were crossing the Pecos River.
5. How did Bill invent the lasso?
   He grabbed a rattlesnake and used it to rope a steer.
6. How did Pecos Bill first meet Slue-Foot Sue?
   He saw her riding a catfish, and Cowboy Carl introduced him to her.

100 | **At Home:** Have students organize their answers in a three-column chart. Have them label the columns as follows: Character, Setting, Plot. | Book 3.1/Unit 3 **Pecos Bill: A Tall Tale Play** | 6

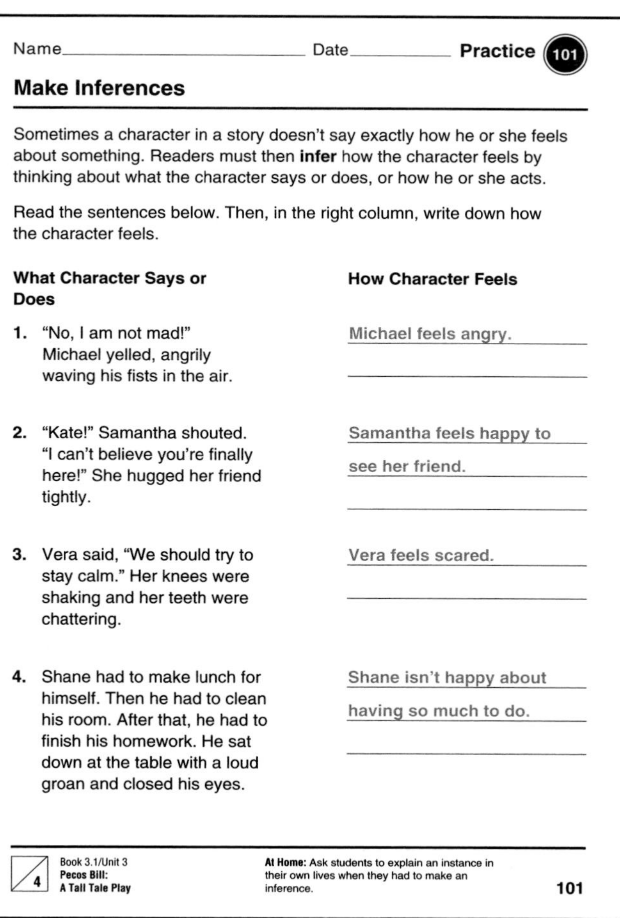

Name________________________ Date__________ **Practice 101**

Make Inferences

Sometimes a character in a story doesn't say exactly how he or she feels about something. Readers must then **infer** how the character feels by thinking about what the character says or does, or how he or she acts.

Read the sentences below. Then, in the right column, write down how the character feels.

What Character Says or Does	How Character Feels
1. "No, I am not mad!" Michael yelled, angrily waving his fists in the air.	Michael feels angry.
2. "Kate!" Samantha shouted. "I can't believe you're finally here!" She hugged her friend tightly.	Samantha feels happy to see her friend.
3. Vera said, "We should try to stay calm." Her knees were shaking and her teeth were chattering.	Vera feels scared.
4. Shane had to make lunch for himself. Then he had to clean his room. After that, he had to finish his homework. He sat down at the table with a loud groan and closed his eyes.	Shane isn't happy about having so much to do.

4 | Book 3.1/Unit 3 **Pecos Bill: A Tall Tale Play** | **At Home:** Ask students to explain an instance in their own lives when they had to make an inference. | 101

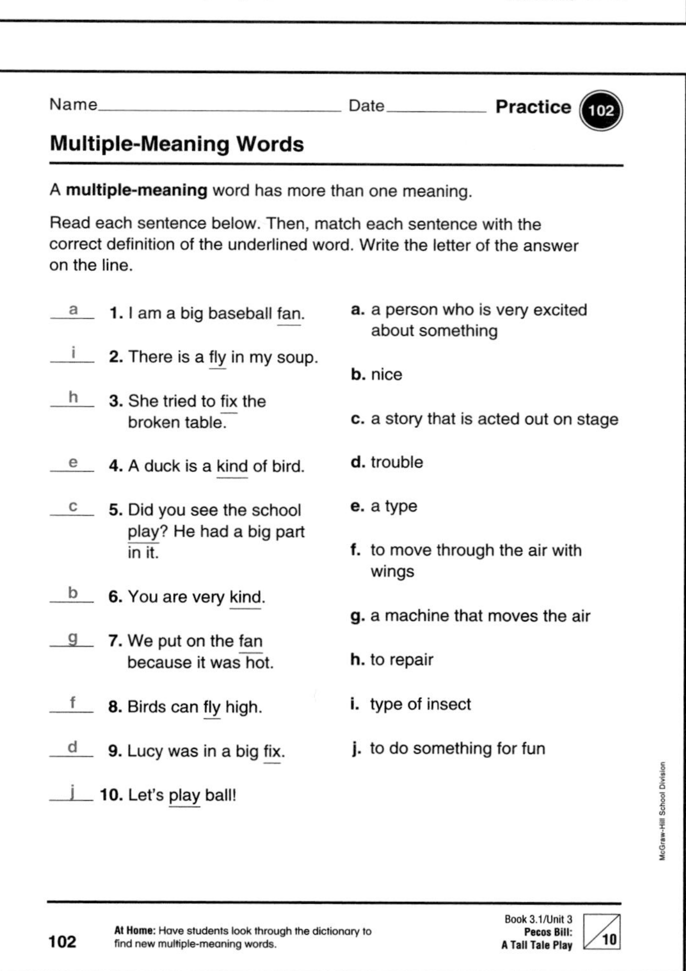

Name________________________ Date__________ **Practice 102**

Multiple-Meaning Words

A **multiple-meaning** word has more than one meaning.

Read each sentence below. Then, match each sentence with the correct definition of the underlined word. Write the letter of the answer on the line.

Answer	Sentence	Definition
a	1. I am a big baseball fan.	a. a person who is very excited about something
i	2. There is a fly in my soup.	b. nice
h	3. She tried to fix the broken table.	c. a story that is acted out on stage
e	4. A duck is a kind of bird.	d. trouble
c	5. Did you see the school play? He had a big part in it.	e. a type
b	6. You are very kind.	f. to move through the air with wings
g	7. We put on the fan because it was hot.	g. a machine that moves the air
f	8. Birds can fly high.	h. to repair
d	9. Lucy was in a big fix.	i. type of insect
j	10. Let's play ball!	j. to do something for fun

102 | **At Home:** Have students look through the dictionary to find new multiple-meaning words. | Book 3.1/Unit 3 **Pecos Bill: A Tall Tale Play** | 10

Name____________________ Date__________ **Reteach 96**

Story Elements

Characters are the people or the animals that are part of a story. The **setting** is when and where the story takes place. The **plot** tells about the events in a story.

Toshana, Tim, and their mom went into the city to see a movie called "Cooking Cowboys." It was about a group of cowboys who liked to cook together. At the end of the movie, the Cooking Cowboys won a cooking contest.

When they came out of the movie, Toshana said, "We should be like the cooking cowboys, too!"

"Yeah! Let's go buy some food and cook it, just like they did," said Tim.

Their mother said, "Cooking is a big job. Are you sure you want to do it?"

"We're sure," they both said. "We can do it!"

Circle the correct answer to the questions below.

1. Where does this story take place?
   a. on a boat (**b.**) in a city **c.** on a farm
2. Who are the main characters in the story?
   (**a.**) Toshana, Tim, and their mother **b.** Toshana, Tim, and their father **c.** Toshana and Tim
3. What movie did they see?
   a. "Cowboys" **b.** "Cowboys Who Care" (**c.**) "Cooking Cowboys"
4. What do Tim and Toshana decide to do at the end of the story?
   (**a.**) cook **b.** see another movie **c.** go to a museum

McGraw-Hill School Division

4 Book 3.1/Unit 3 **Pecos Bill: A Tall Tale Play**

At Home: Have students write two sentences about what might happen next in the story.

96

Name____________________ Date__________ **Reteach 97**

Vocabulary

Fill in the sentences with the words below.

combine invented located prairie stumbled wilderness

1. First you __combine__ sugar and butter.
2. I was lost deep in the __wilderness__.
3. We lived on a grassy __prairie__.
4. Who __invented__ the first car?
5. I was so tired that I __stumbled__ and almost fell down!
6. I finally __located__ my lost sweater.

6

Story Comprehension

Reteach 98

Answer the following questions.

1. What happened after Bill fell out of the wagon? __Some coyotes found him and raised him.__
2. What noisy thing did Bill and the coyotes do at night? __They all sang.__
3. What did Carl the Cowboy teach Bill? __Carl taught Bill how to be a cowboy.__
4. Name one thing that Bill invented. __Possible answers: the lasso, the guitar__

McGraw-Hill School Division

97–98 **At Home:** Have students think of a synonym for each vocabulary word.

Book 3.1/Unit 3 **Pecos Bill: A Tall Tale Play** 4

Name____________________ Date__________ **Reteach 99**

Use a Map

Some **maps** use symbols to show where certain products are made. For example, if you went to an area that was displayed on the map with oil symbols, you'd find oil rigs and other oil production equipment.

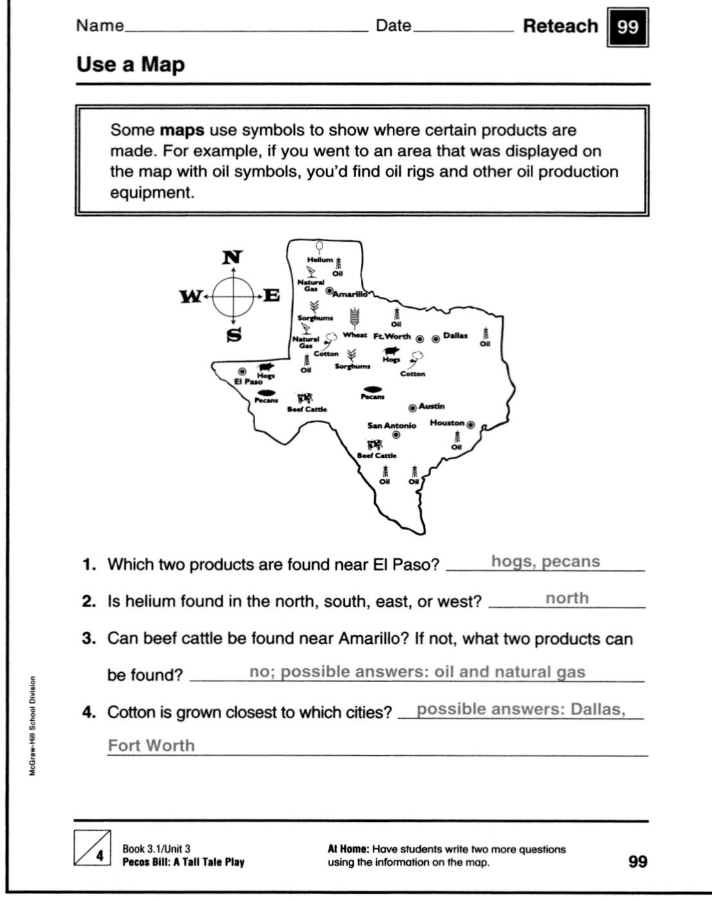

1. Which two products are found near El Paso? __hogs, pecans__
2. Is helium found in the north, south, east, or west? __north__
3. Can beef cattle be found near Amarillo? If not, what two products can be found? __no; possible answers: oil and natural gas__
4. Cotton is grown closest to which cities? __possible answers: Dallas, Fort Worth__

McGraw-Hill School Division

4 Book 3.1/Unit 3 **Pecos Bill: A Tall Tale Play**

At Home: Have students write two more questions using the information on the map.

99

Name____________________ Date__________ **Reteach 100**

Story Elements

Characters are *who* the story is about. **Setting** is *where* the story takes place. **Plot** is *what* the story is about.

Answer the questions.

1. **Character:** Who are the three main characters of the tall tale in "Pecos Bill"? __Pecos Bill, Carl the Cowboy, and Slue-foot Sue__
2. **Setting:** Where does the story of Pecos Bill take place? __The story takes place in Texas.__
3. **Setting:** Where does Bill fall out of his parents' wagon? __at the Pecos River__
4. **Plot:** Who finds baby Bill by the river and teaches him how to sing? __the coyotes__
5. **Plot:** Who finds Bill many years later and teaches him how to be a cowboy? __Carl the Cowboy__

McGraw-Hill School Division

100 **At Home:** Have students write sentences about how Bill invented bronco-busting, the guitar, cowboy songs, or the lasso.

Book 3.1/Unit 3 **Pecos Bill: A Tall Tale Play** 5

Pecos Bill • RETEACH

Name____________________ Date__________ **Reteach 101**

Make Inferences

You can make an **inference,** or a good guess, about how characters feel by noticing what they say and do.

Read each passage. Then choose the correct inference. Circle the correct answer.

1. Paul laughed and jumped up and down. "Is it eight o'clock yet?" he asked. His mother smiled and replied, "As I said before, the party will start in an hour."

- **a.** Paul felt sad about his mother.
- **b.** Paul felt scared about the party.
- **(c.)** Paul felt excited about the party.

2. When Dad asked Greg about losing Rashida's book, Greg frowned and hung his head.

- **(a.)** Greg felt sorry.
- **b.** Greg felt happy.
- **c.** Greg felt tired.

3. Tad yawned. He'd had a long day and couldn't keep his eyes open anymore. He lay back against the pillows.

- **a.** Tad felt awake.
- **(b.)** Tad felt sleepy.
- **c.** Tad felt happy.

4. The kitten ran back and forth across the room. Then she chewed on an old sock. After that, she played with a toy mouse.

- **(a.)** The kitten was playing.
- **b.** The kitten was tired.
- **c.** The kitten was sick.

At Home: Have students write a paragraph with a clear inference in it. Have them write the inference.

Name____________________ Date__________ **Reteach 102**

Multiple-Meaning Words

Some words have more than one meaning. For example, *cold* means both "not warm" and "a sickness that causes a stuffy nose." Reading the words around a **multiple-meaning word** can help you choose the correct meaning.

Use context clues to help you choose a word or phrase that has the same meaning as the word in dark type. Then put a check mark next to the word or phrase that you chose.

1. Every winter, the birds **fly** south.

____ a kind of insect _✓_ move through the air

2. The baseball game started. It was my turn at **bat**.

_✓_ a turn to hit the ball in baseball ____ a small, furry animal

3. My mother took us to the **fair**. We saw a huge cow there.

_✓_ a large show ____ going by the rules

4. The cake tasted very **sweet**.

____ nice _✓_ having a taste like sugar or honey

5. Our class will take a **trip** to the museum.

_✓_ a journey ____ to catch your foot and stumble

At Home: Have students write sentences using the meanings that they did not check.

Name________________________ Date__________ **Extend 96**

Story Elements

Complete the chart with information from your favorite fairy tale.

Title ______________________________

Author ______________________________

Setting ______________________________

Main Characters ______________________________

How did it begin? ______________________________

What happened in the middle? ______________________________

Answers will vary.

How did it end? ______________________________

At Home: Have students illustrate a cover for the story they described.

Name________________________ Date__________ **Extend 97**

Vocabulary

combine	invented	located	prairie	stumbled	wilderness

Write a paragraph on another piece of paper telling about an adventure, using as many vocabulary words from the box as you can. Then erase those vocabulary words or cover them with tape. Exchange paragraphs with a partner and fill in the blanks.

Extend 98

Story Comprehension

Work with a partner to make up your own tall tales. Think of situations that might be difficult to get out of. Write one of these below. Take turns giving a tall tale response. Make your tales as tall as can be! When you are finished, choose your favorite tall tale and tell it to the rest of the class.

Answers will vary.

At Home: Have students give a tall tale response to a question about why they were late for an imaginary appointment.

Name________________________ Date__________ **Extend 99**

Use a Map

Carl the Cowboy and Pecos Bill might have found a trail when they traveled home by using a map and map key. A map key has symbols to help you find things. Use the map and map key below to answer the questions.

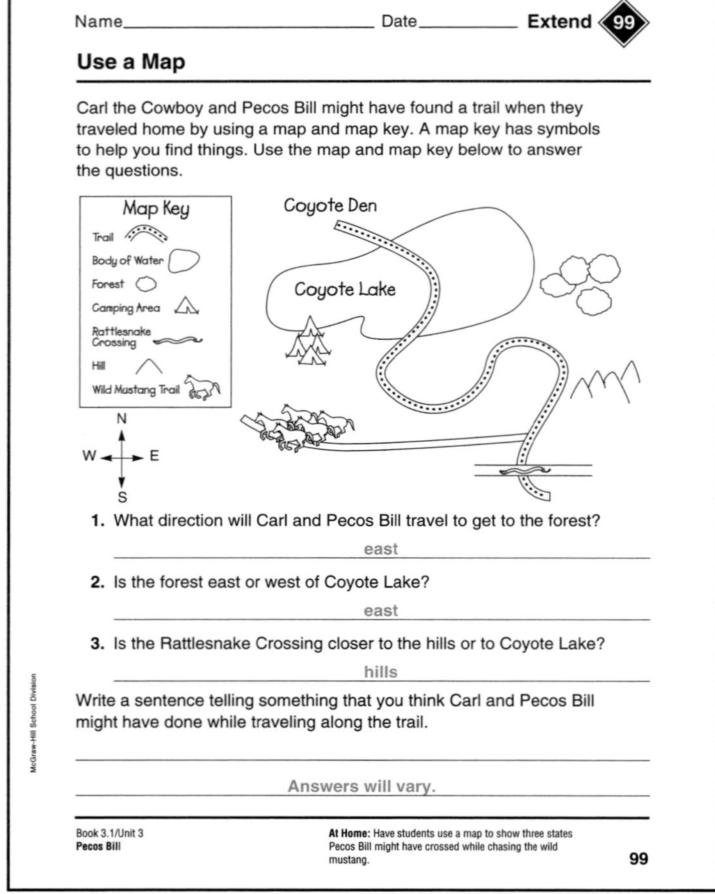

1. What direction will Carl and Pecos Bill travel to get to the forest?
   east
2. Is the forest east or west of Coyote Lake?
   east
3. Is the Rattlesnake Crossing closer to the hills or to Coyote Lake?
   hills

Write a sentence telling something that you think Carl and Pecos Bill might have done while traveling along the trail.

Answers will vary.

At Home: Have students use a map to show three states Pecos Bill might have crossed while chasing the wild mustang.

Name________________________ Date__________ **Extend 100**

Story Elements

Work with a group to present a "Pecos Bill" puppet show for your class. Decide which scene you will show. Fill out the chart.

Characters: ______________________________

Setting: ______________________________

What happens: ______________________________

Follow the directions below to make stick puppets of the characters. Practice moving your puppet as you read its part out loud. Cover the front of a table with a piece of cloth or cardboard to create a theater for your puppet show. Crouch behind the table with your puppets, and let the show go on!

How to Make Stick Puppets

Draw your character on poster board with crayons or markers. Cut out your character and paste it to a craft stick. Hold the stick at the end. Raise it, lower it, and wave it from side to side as the puppet speaks.

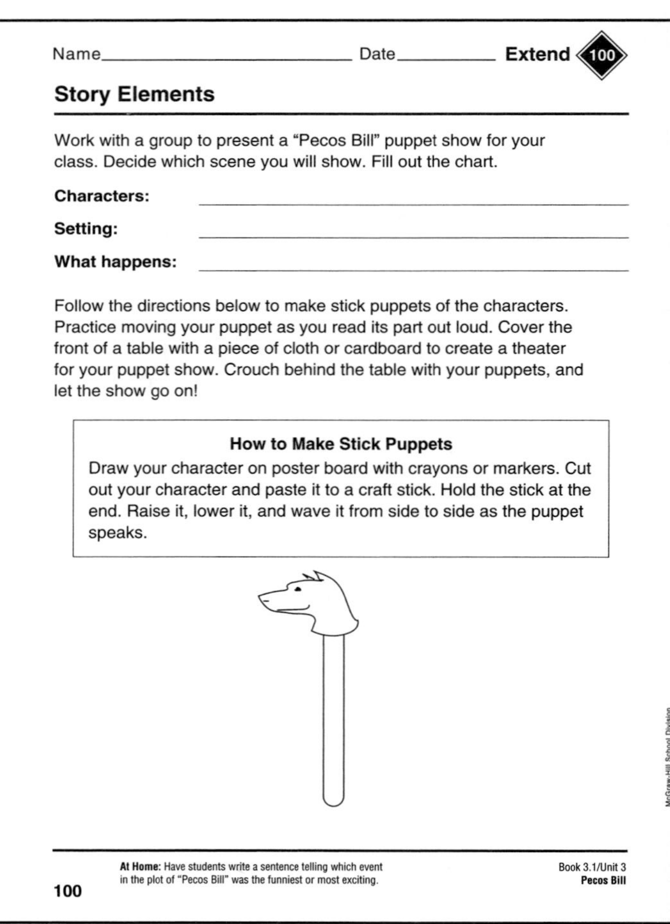

At Home: Have students write a sentence telling which event in the plot of "Pecos Bill" was the funniest or most exciting.

Name________________________ Date__________ **Extend 101**

Make Inferences

Play “Pass the Story” with a partner. Begin writing a story about anything you choose on the lines below.

Exchange pages with your partner. Finish the story you receive on the lines below. Use clues from the story and what you already know to make inferences about how it should end.

Exchange pages again. Read what your partner wrote. Did he or she end the story the way you would have?

At Home: Read the first paragraph from a news story and have students write an ending to it.

Name________________________ Date__________ **Extend 102**

Multiple-Meaning Words

fix	story	right	pack	den	close

Write a silly story with multiple-meaning words. Use each word from the word box twice. Be sure to use a different meaning of the word each time you use it. If you do not know multiple meanings for some of the words, you may use a dictionary for help. When you have finished, exchange stories with a partner. Tell the clues that helped you figure out the meaning of the multiple-meaning words used in your partner’s story.

At Home: Have students draw pictures to illustrate the multiple-meaning words *close* or *wind*. Challenge students to use them to create a tall tale.

Name_______________ Date_______ LEARN **Grammar** 83

Using Verb Tenses

- A **present-tense verb** tells what happens now.
  Cookie cooks beans every day.
- A **past-tense verb** tells about an action that already happened.
  Pecos Bill jumped on the mustang.

Circle the verb in each sentence. Decide whether it is in the present tense or the past tense. Write **present** or **past** on the line.

1. Cowboy Sam orders pizza for dinner. present
2. Cowgirl Pam and Cowboy Sam tell a story. present
3. The legend of Pecos Bill started in Texas. past
4. Pecos Bill's family moved west. past
5. Bill dropped out of the wagon. past
6. Ranch Hand #3 wonders about the pizza. present
7. Pecos Bill joined a family of coyotes. past
8. Years later, Bill learned human ways from his brother. past
9. The pizza finally arrives. present
10. Pecos Bill married Slue-Foot Sue. past

/10 Book 3.1/Unit 3 **Pecos Bill**

Extension: Have students work in small groups. Ask them to write short skits (five lines at most) using the same characters as those in *Pecos Bill*. They can write in either the present tense or the past tense. Later, they can act out their skits.

Name_______________ Date_______ LEARN AND PRACTICE **Grammar** 84

Future Tense

- A verb in the **future tense** tells about an action that is going to happen.
- To write about the future, use the special verb *will.*
  Cookie will cook lima bean pizza.

Find the future tense verb in each sentence. Underline your answer.

1. Pecos Bill will become a legendary cowboy.
2. He will meet his brother, Carl the Cowboy.
3. Carl will teach him in three days.
4. Bill will surprise Carl with his abilities.
5. He will chase Widow Maker across several states.
6. Pecos Bill will invent the lasso.
7. He will make the world's first guitar.
8. In the Rio Grande, he will find his future wife, Slue-Foot Sue.
9. The coyotes will attend the wedding, too.
10. All of them will live happily ever after.

Extension: Have each student write about what they think they will be in the future. They can start with "I think that I..." Encourage them to be fanciful if they wish. If time allows, they can illustrate their statements.

Book 3.1/Unit 3 **Pecos Bill** /10

Name_______________ Date_______ PRACTICE AND REVIEW **Grammar** 

Using Verb Tenses

- A **present-tense verb** tells what happens now.
- A **past-tense verb** tells about an action that already happened.
- A verb in the **future tense** tells about an action that is going to happen.
- To write about the future, use the special verb *will.*

Each sentence below has a time clue that tells if the action is happening now, in the past, or in the future. Choose the correct form of the verb to complete each sentence. Write your answer on the line.

1. Now the ranch hands (wait, waited) for dinner. wait
2. Tonight, Cowgirl Pam (will tell, tell) a story. will tell
3. In the early days of ranching, Pecos Bill (uses, used) a lasso. used
4. Today, Carl the Cowboy (stumbles, stumbled) upon Pecos Bill. stumbled
5. Years ago, the coyotes (treat, treated) Bill as their own student. treated
6. In the past, Bill (acts, acted) the same as a coyote. acted
7. Now he (discovers, discovered) his human nature. discovers
8. For many years, he (rushes, rushed) around the Southwest. rushed
9. Last night, Cowboy Sam (completes, completed) the story. completed
10. Tomorrow, the store (delivered, will deliver) the pizza. will deliver

/10 Book 3.1/Unit 3 **Pecos Bill**

Extension: Ask each student to describe one of the adventures of Pecos Bill using the present tense. They should record their sentences.

Name_______________ Date_______ MECHANICS **Grammar** 

Using Quotation Marks

- Use **quotation marks** at the beginning and end of a person's exact words.
  "Come and get it!" Cookie yelled.
- Use a **comma** after the name of a person being spoken to.
  "Cowboy Sam, will you help me?" she asked.

Correct each sentence. Add quotation marks at the beginning and end of the person's words. Put a comma after the name of any person being spoken to.

1. "Cookie, we're tired of eating beans!" yelled Cowgirl Pam.
2. "Cowgirl Pam, will you tell us a story?" pleaded Ranch Hand #3.
3. Pa called, "Ma, we've got new neighbors!"
4. "I'm Carl the Cowboy. What's your name?" asked Carl.
5. Carl insisted, "Son, you are not a coyote."
6. "I'm going to name this horse Widow Maker," Bill shouted.
7. "My pa was named Pa too," Bill said.
8. "The pizza is here! Yes!" said Ranch Hand #3.
9. "Sue, this is my long lost brother," said Carl.
10. The judge announced, "I now pronounce you Cowboy and Cowgirl!"

Extension: Students in small groups can write their own humorous dialogs. Have them work together to make sure the quotations are correctly punctuated.

Book 3.1/Unit 3 **Pecos Bill** /10

Name________________________ Date__________ TEST **Grammar** 87

Using Verb Tenses

A. Choose the correct form for each of the following verbs to go with the time clue in the sentence. Mark your answer.

1. Tomorrow, Sam ____ home.
ⓐ walks ⓑ walk ● will walk ⓓ walked

2. You ____ right now.
ⓐ steers ● will steer ⓒ steered ⓓ steer

3. They _____ last night.
● listened ⓑ listen ⓒ will listen ⓓ listens

4. In those days, he _____ behind.
ⓐ lag ⓑ lags ● lagged ⓓ will lag

B. Decide if the verb in each sentence should be past tense, present tense, or future tense. Find the verb that correctly completes the sentence. Mark your answer.

5. Long ago, Pecos Bill _____ with the other young coyotes.
● played ⓑ plays ⓒ will play ⓓ plaied

6. One day perhaps he _____ to the Southwest.
ⓐ return ● will return ⓒ returns ⓓ returned

7. In those days wild horses still _____ the Texas countryside.
ⓐ roam ● roamed ⓒ roams ⓓ will roam

8. Tall tales ____ popular today.
ⓐ remained ⓑ remains ⓒ will remain ● remain

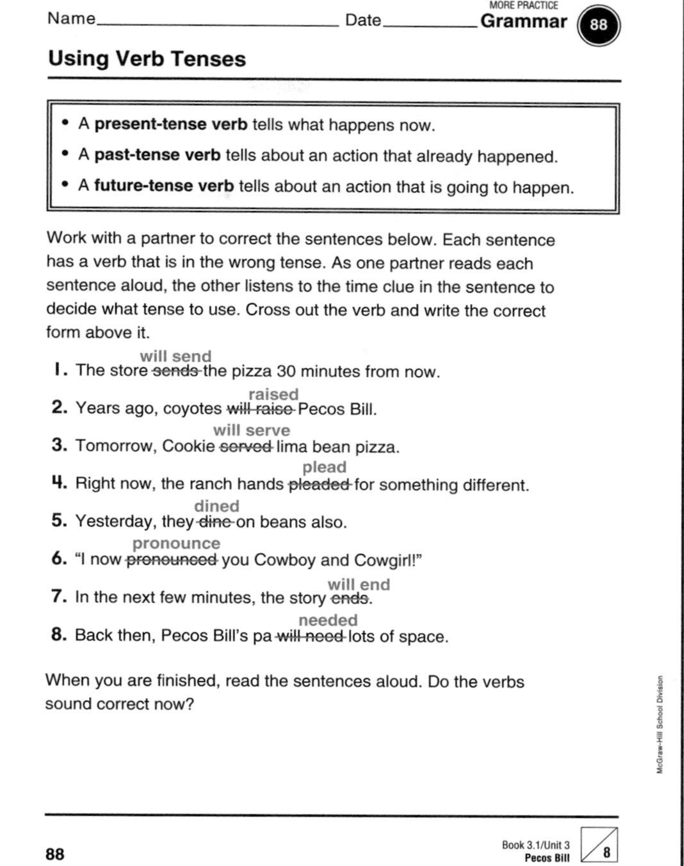

Name________________________ Date__________ MORE PRACTICE **Grammar** 88

Using Verb Tenses

- A **present-tense verb** tells what happens now.
- A **past-tense verb** tells about an action that already happened.
- A **future-tense verb** tells about an action that is going to happen.

Work with a partner to correct the sentences below. Each sentence has a verb that is in the wrong tense. As one partner reads each sentence aloud, the other listens to the time clue in the sentence to decide what tense to use. Cross out the verb and write the correct form above it.

1. The store ~~sends~~ will send the pizza 30 minutes from now.

2. Years ago, coyotes ~~will raise~~ raised Pecos Bill.

3. Tomorrow, Cookie ~~served~~ will serve lima bean pizza.

4. Right now, the ranch hands ~~pleaded~~ plead for something different.

5. Yesterday, they ~~dine~~ dined on beans also.

6. "I now ~~pronounced~~ pronounce you Cowboy and Cowgirl!"

7. In the next few minutes, the story ~~ends~~ will end.

8. Back then, Pecos Bill's pa ~~will need~~ needed lots of space.

When you are finished, read the sentences aloud. Do the verbs sound correct now?

Name________________ Date________ PRETEST SPELLING **83**

Adding *-ed* and *-ing*

Pretest Directions

Fold back the paper along the dotted line. Use the blanks to write each word as it is read aloud. When you finish the test, unfold the paper. Use the list at the right to correct any spelling mistakes. Practice the words you missed for the Posttest.

To Parents

Here are the results of your child's weekly spelling Pretest. You can help your child study for the Posttest by following these simple steps for each word on the word list:

1. Read the word to your child.
2. Have your child write the word, saying each letter as it is written.
3. Say each letter of the word as your child checks the spelling.
4. If a mistake has been made, have your child read each letter of the correctly spelled word aloud, and then repeat steps 1-3.

1. ________	1. spied
2. ________	2. moving
3. ________	3. robbed
4. ________	4. saving
5. ________	5. blamed
6. ________	6. beginning
7. ________	7. fried
8. ________	8. shaking
9. ________	9. supplied
10. ________	10. buried
11. ________	11. escaping
12. ________	12. hurried
13. ________	13. stirred
14. ________	14. splitting
15. ________	15. divided
Challenge Words	
________	combine
________	invented
________	located
________	prairie
________	wilderness

Name________________ Date________ AT-HOME WORD STUDY SPELLING **84**

Adding *-ed* and *-ing*

Using the Word Study Steps

1. LOOK at the word.
2. SAY the word aloud.
3. STUDY the letters in the word.
4. WRITE the word.
5. CHECK the word.
   Did you spell the word right?
   If not, go back to step 1.

Spelling Tip

- When words end in silent **e**, drop the **e** when adding an ending that begins with a vowel.
  save - **e** + **ing** = sav**ing**
- When a word ends with a consonant followed by **y**, change the **y** to **i** when adding any ending except endings that begin with **i**.
  spy + **es** = sp**ies**
- When a one-syllable word ends in one vowel followed by one consonant, double the consonant before adding an ending that begins with a vowel.
  begin + **ing** = begin**ning**

X the Word

Put an X on the word that does not fit the pattern in each row.

1.	rubbed	stirred	~~matched~~	grabbed
2.	moving	saving	shaking	~~playing~~
3.	~~lined~~	supplied	buried	spied
4.	beginning	splitting	running	~~counting~~
5.	~~hurried~~	blamed	decided	divided

To Parents or Helpers:

Using the Word Study Steps above as your child comes across any new words will help him or her spell well. Review the steps as you both go over this week's spelling words.

Go over each Spelling Tip with your child. Help your child find other spelling words that follow each rule. Help your child complete the spelling activity.

Name________________ Date________ EXPLORE THE PATTERN SPELLING **85**

Adding *-ed* and *-ing*

spied	saving	fried	buried	stirred
moving	blamed	shaking	escaping	splitting
robbed	beginning	supplied	hurried	divided

Pattern Power

Write the spelling words that show what you do before adding *-ed* or *-ing*.

double final consonant	drop e	change y to i
1. robbed	5. moving	11. spied
2. beginning	6. saving	12. fried
3. stirred	7. blamed	13. supplied
4. splitting	8. shaking	14. buried
	9. escaping	15. hurried
	10. divided	

Order, Please!

Write each group of spelling words in alphabetical order.

spied, saving, shaking, stirred

16. saving 17. shaking
18. spied 19. stirred

blamed, divided, escaping, beginning, buried

20. beginning 21. blamed
22. buried 23. divided
24. escaping

Name________________ Date________ PRACTICE AND EXTEND SPELLING **86**

Adding *-ed* and *-ing*

spied	saving	fried	buried	stirred
moving	blamed	shaking	escaping	splitting
robbed	beginning	supplied	hurried	divided

Finish the Sentence

Use a spelling word to complete each sentence.

1. The thief robbed me of my wallet!
2. The title page is at the beginning of a book.
3. We had fried chicken for dinner last night.
4. When Jay woke up late, he hurried to get to school on time.
5. My family and I are moving to a new home in Florida.
6. Our teacher supplied us with paints for the art project.
7. The prisoner was caught escaping from jail.
8. Alicia divided the ribbons into blue ones and red ones.

Find the Base Words

Write the base word of these *-ed* words:

9. spied spy 10. robbed rob
11. blamed blame 12. fried fry

Write the base word of these *-ing* words:

13. splitting split 14. shaking shake
15. beginning begin 16. escaping escape

Challenge Extension: Ask students to write a short paragraph that includes each Challenge Word.

Name________________________ Date__________ PROOFREAD AND WRITE **SPELLING** **87**

Adding *-ed* and *-ing*

Proofreading Paragraph

There are six spelling mistakes in this paragraph. Circle the misspelled words. Write the words correctly on the lines below.

Two men robed a bank. They berryed all but one of the sacks of money. They devided the rest of the money equally between the two of them.

When the two men reached the next town, they stopped. "I smell fryed chicken," said Luke. "Let's eat!" So the hungry men hurried into a small coffee shop and ordered everything on the menu. But when the time came to pay the bill, neither of the robbers wanted to pay.

"Come on, Luke, pay up!" said Bart. "What are you sayving it for?"

"Why should I pay?" asked Luke.

While the two men were busy arguing, the sheriff and his deputies walked in. Each blammed the other for their bad luck.

1. robbed 2. buried 3. divided

4. fried 5. saving 6. blamed

Writing Activity

Write a short story that takes place in the Old West. How does the story begin? What do the characters do? How does the story end? Use six spelling words.

____

____

____

____

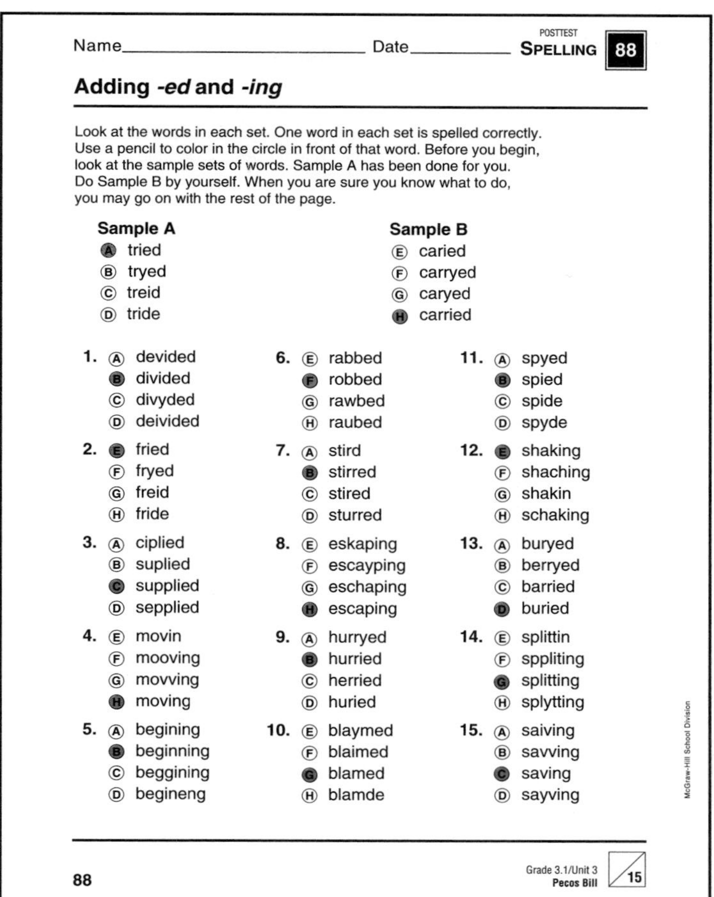

Name________________________ Date__________ POSTTEST **SPELLING** **88**

Adding *-ed* and *-ing*

Look at the words in each set. One word in each set is spelled correctly. Use a pencil to color in the circle in front of that word. Before you begin, look at the sample sets of words. Sample A has been done for you. Do Sample B by yourself. When you are sure you know what to do, you may go on with the rest of the page.

Sample A
- **(A) tried**
- (B) tryed
- (C) treid
- (D) tride

Sample B
- (E) caried
- (F) carryed
- (G) caryed
- **(H) carried**

1. (A) devided **(B) divided** (C) divyded (D) deivided
2. **(E) fried** (F) fryed (G) freid (H) fride
3. (A) ciplied (B) suplied **(C) supplied** (D) sepplied
4. (E) movin (F) mooving (G) movving **(H) moving**
5. (A) begining **(B) beginning** (C) beggining (D) begineng
6. (E) rabbed **(F) robbed** (G) rawbed (H) raubed
7. (A) stird **(B) stirred** (C) stired (D) sturred
8. (E) eskaping (F) escayping (G) eschaping **(H) escaping**
9. (A) hurryed **(B) hurried** (C) herried (D) huried
10. (E) blaymed (F) blaimed **(G) blamed** (H) blamde
11. (A) spyed **(B) spied** (C) spide (D) spyde
12. **(E) shaking** (F) shaching (G) shakin (H) schaking
13. (A) buryed (B) berryed (C) barried **(D) buried**
14. (E) splittin (F) sppliting **(G) splitting** (H) splytting
15. (A) saiving (B) savving **(C) saving** (D) sayving

A Very Cool Place to Visit • PRACTICE

Name________________________ Date__________ **Practice 103**

Main Idea

In a passage, the **main idea** is the most important point. **Supporting details** explain the main idea. Read the following story. Then write down the main idea and the supporting details.

> Winter is my favorite time of year. In winter, I spend my days playing outside in the cold. I love to build people out of snow. I also love to ice skate. At the end of each day, I love to come out of the cold and drink hot chocolate.

Main Idea:

1. Winter is my favorite time of year.

Supporting Details:

2. I love to build people out of snow.
3. I love to ice skate.
4. I love to drink hot chocolate.

At Home: Have students think of a main idea for a story and three supporting details. Encourage them to write a story using this information.

Name________________________ Date__________ **Practice 104**

Vocabulary

Write the vocabulary word that fits in each of the sentences below.

beauty creeps furniture palace pure visitors

1. The cat ___creeps___ quietly toward the old sock. Does the cat think the sock is a mouse?
2. Everyone was surprised when the king and queen sold the royal ___palace___. A week after that, they moved into a two-bedroom apartment.
3. My next-door neighbor had many friends. She always welcomed ___visitors___ into her home.
4. Mary bought the brown table. She thought it would look good with her other ___furniture___.
5. This water is very clean and ___pure___. It comes from a spring in the mountains.
6. The ugly duckling did not know that one day it would be a bird of great ___beauty___.

At Home: Have students write a story about a visit to an abandoned castle using the vocabulary words.

Chills and Thrills

Some people are not happy when winter comes. They do not like the way the cold *creeps* into their clothes. Eli, however, thinks winter is *pure* joy. He loves the *beauty* of the ice on the trees. He loves the limbs of the trees without their leaves.

Eli liked making a snow *palace* out of ice and snow. One day, he tried to bring a chair into his palace. The room needed *furniture*. It also needed some *visitors*. But neither things nor people fit in Eli's tiny snow cave.

Eli didn't mind too much. His dog could fit in the cave. And with that white fur, she looked like a big, warm polar bear! Eli's dog loved winter as much as Eli did.

1. How does the cold get into people's clothes?
   It creeps.
2. What kind of *furniture* did Eli try to bring to his cave?
   a chair
3. Who could not fit in Eli's cave?
   people
4. Which *visitor* could fit into Eli's cave?
   his dog
5. How does Eli feel about the winter time?
   It gives him pure joy because it is beautiful and he can build snow caves.

At Home: Have students discuss the different things they do in each of the four seasons. Then have them draw a picture showing one of the activities for each season.

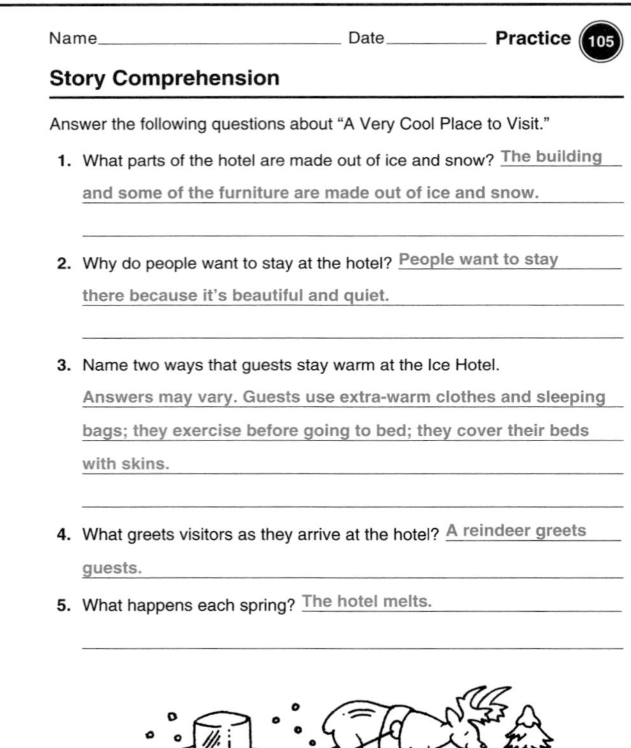

Name________________________ Date__________ **Practice 105**

Story Comprehension

Answer the following questions about "A Very Cool Place to Visit."

1. What parts of the hotel are made out of ice and snow? The building and some of the furniture are made out of ice and snow.
2. Why do people want to stay at the hotel? People want to stay there because it's beautiful and quiet.
3. Name two ways that guests stay warm at the Ice Hotel.
   Answers may vary. Guests use extra-warm clothes and sleeping bags; they exercise before going to bed; they cover their beds with skins.
4. What greets visitors as they arrive at the hotel? A reindeer greets guests.
5. What happens each spring? The hotel melts.

At Home: Have students imagine that they are visiting the Ice Hotel for a night, and have them write about their experiences.

Name____________________ Date__________ **Practice 106**

Use a Map

The map of Finland below is divided into four districts: the Upland District, the Lake District, the Coastal Lowlands, and the Coastal Islands.

Write the name of the district beside the description of it.

1. This district contains many lakes. Forests cover most of the land.
   Lake District
2. This district is found in the far north. It has the smallest population.
   Upland District
3. This district contains many small islands off the coast. Many Finns have summer cottages there. Coastal Islands
4. This district is found along the Gulf of Bothnia and the Gulf of Finland. Most of the farms and a milder climate can be found there.
   Coastal Lowlands
5. In which district can the capital, Helsinki, be found?
   Coastal Lowlands

At Home: Ask students to name the country that borders Finland to its west.

Name____________________ Date__________ **Practice 107**

Summarize

A **summary** tells the main ideas of a story.

Read the paragraphs about "A Very Cool Place to Visit." Then summarize each paragraph in one sentence.

1. At one place in Sweden, the cold is everywhere. Guests feel it in their toes, fingers, and noses. Welcome to the Ice Hotel, where the building and even some of the furniture are made of snow and ice.
   It is very cold at the Ice Hotel.
2. Why would people want to stay in a hotel that was cold and frozen? A worker at the hotel, says people love the hotel for its beauty. "The white fresh snow is pure winter." She also says that people want to see the northern lights.
   People stay at the hotel because it is beautiful.
3. Before you get into bed, you have to warm yourself up. Doing some push-ups at bedtime will help you feel warm even before you get into bed!
   Guests exercise to warm themselves up before bed.
4. In the springtime, when the weather gets warmer, the hotel melts. When winter returns, a new building is built from fresh snow and ice. And once again, the Ice Hotel welcomes everyone into its cold and wintry world.
   Every year, the hotel melts and a new hotel is built.

At Home: Have students summarize "A Very Cool Place to Visit."

Name____________________ Date__________ **Practice 108**

Multiple-Meaning Words

A word with **multiple meanings** has more than one meaning. Reading the words and sentences around a word can help you choose the correct meaning.

This list has two meanings for each underlined word in the sentences below. Look at the way each underlined word is used in the sentence. Then choose the right meaning for each word from the list.

between winter and summer	or	leap
not warm	or	sickness
move in a secret way	or	a dishonest person
pieces of something hard	or	gets in the way

1. At one hotel in Sweden, the cold doesn't have to sneak in.
   move in a secret way
2. The hotel's 100 beds are made from ice blocks covered with reindeer skins. pieces of something hard
3. Each spring, when the weather warms up, the hotel melts.
   between winter and summer
4. Once again, the Ice Hotel is ready to welcome people into the cold.
   not warm

At Home: Have students find a multiple-meaning word in a newspaper or magazine article.

Name____________________ Date__________ **Practice 109**

Context Clues

Context clues are words before or after an unfamiliar word that help us to understand its meaning.

Circle the context clues in each sentence that help you to figure out the meaning of the word in dark type. Then write a possible definition for the word. Answers may vary.

1. Nothing grew from this **barren** land.
   barren: where nothing grows
2. The girls ate the **entire** pie, and there wasn't even a crumb left.
   entire: the whole thing
3. He **improved** the garden when he made better paths through the roses.
   improved: made better
4. Grandma tells many tales and **legends** about our ancestors.
   legends: tales
5. The angry **scowl** on your face makes you look very unhappy.
   scowl: an angry expression
6. The **antique** clock was from a time long ago.
   antique: very old, from another time

At Home: Ask students to compare their definitions with the ones in the dictionary.

A Very Cool Place to Visit • RETEACH

Name____________________ Date__________ **Reteach 103**

Main Idea

Identifying the **main idea** and **supporting details** will help you to understand what you read. The main idea is the most important point. Supporting details are smaller points that help to explain the main idea.

Read each main idea below. Then look at the list of supporting details that follow. Mark an **X** next to each detail that supports the main idea.

Main Idea: Many types of clothing help you stay warm in the winter.

Supporting Details:

1. ____ You wear a bathing suit to go swimming.
2. __x__ Hats help your head stay warm.
3. __x__ A thick coat is good to wear on cold days.
4. __x__ Boots keep out the snow and rain.
5. ____ Brushes are used on tangled hair.

Main Idea: Some places look different in winter.

Supporting Details:

6. __x__ Trees lose their leaves.
7. ____ Many flowers grow.
8. __x__ Snow falls and covers the ground.
9. __x__ The lakes freeze over.
10. ____ It is very hot.

Name____________________ Date__________ **Reteach 104**

Vocabulary

Write the correct words from the list in the sentences.

beauty creeps furniture palace pure visitors

He opens the door and __creeps__ into the __palace__. He never imagined that a place could look so wonderful—its __beauty__ surprises him. All of the __furniture__ is special; each chair, table, and desk is like a work of art. "Why aren't there any other __visitors__?" He gets a glass, and pours himself some fresh, __pure__ water. 6

Story Comprehension **Reteach 105**

Think about what you learned in "A Very Cool Place to Visit." Then complete the summary below.

At the Ice Hotel, the __building__ and some of the furniture are made of ice and snow. People stay at the hotel because they love the __beauty__ and quiet there.

Visitors are given extra-warm snowsuits and sleeping bags. They are told to do some __push-ups__ to warm themselves before going to bed.

When visitors leave the hotel, they get a special __card__ that says they have stayed there.

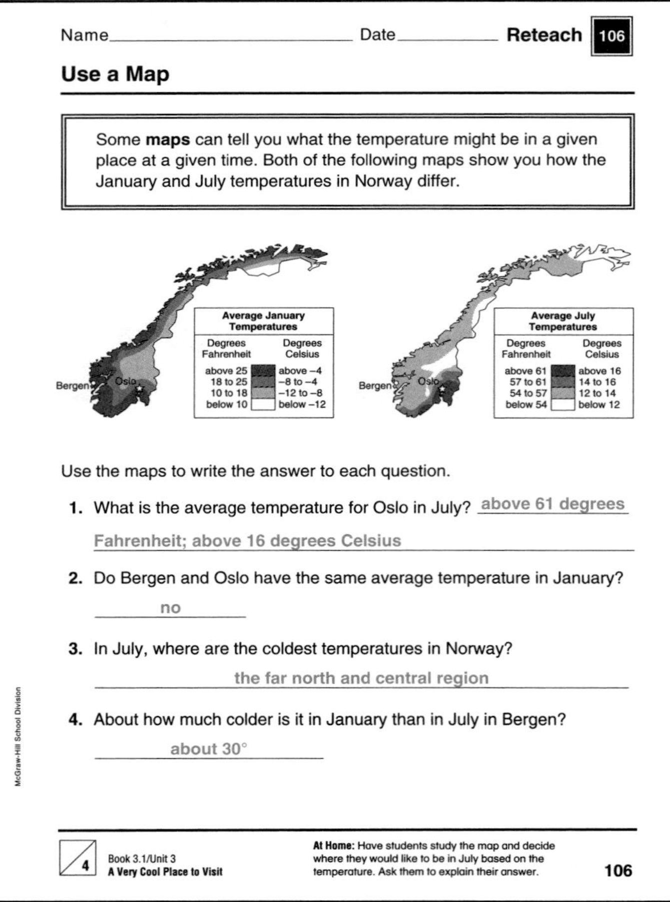

Name____________________ Date__________ **Reteach 106**

Use a Map

Some **maps** can tell you what the temperature might be in a given place at a given time. Both of the following maps show you how the January and July temperatures in Norway differ.

Use the maps to write the answer to each question.

1. What is the average temperature for Oslo in July? __above 61 degrees Fahrenheit; above 16 degrees Celsius__
2. Do Bergen and Oslo have the same average temperature in January? __no__
3. In July, where are the coldest temperatures in Norway? __the far north and central region__
4. About how much colder is it in January than in July in Bergen? __about 30°__

Name____________________ Date__________ **Reteach 107**

Summarize

A **summary** tells the important ideas of a selection.

Read the paragraphs about "A Very Cool Place to Visit." Then circle the sentence that best summarizes the paragraphs.

1. At one place in Sweden, the cold comes right in the door. Guests know it will nip at their entire bodies. The place is the Ice Hotel. Here, most of the furniture is made of snow and ice.
   - **(a.)** It is cold at the Ice Hotel.
   - **b.** Sometimes your toes, fingers, and nose can get cold.
   - **c.** Some of the furniture at the Ice Hotel is made out of ice.
2. Why would a person pay money to stay in a place like this? One worker at the hotel says people love the way the hotel looks.
   - **a.** There are lovely lights in the sky at night.
   - **b.** The Ice Hotel is in France.
   - **(c.)** People stay in the Ice Hotel because they love the look of the hotel.
3. When people check out of the hotel in the morning, they get a special card. The note proves that they beat the cold and slept in the hotel.
   - **a.** Visitors leave the hotel in the morning.
   - **b.** Some visitors think the hotel is too cold.
   - **(c.)** When visitors leave, they get a card.
4. Each spring, the weather gets warmer and the hotel melts. When winter comes, a new building is made from fresh ice and snow. And all over again, the Ice Hotel opens its chilly doors to fun-loving guests.
   - **(a.)** Every year, the hotel melts and a new hotel has to be built.
   - **b.** The hotel melts each spring.
   - **c.** People build a new hotel each winter.

A Very Cool Place to Visit • RETEACH

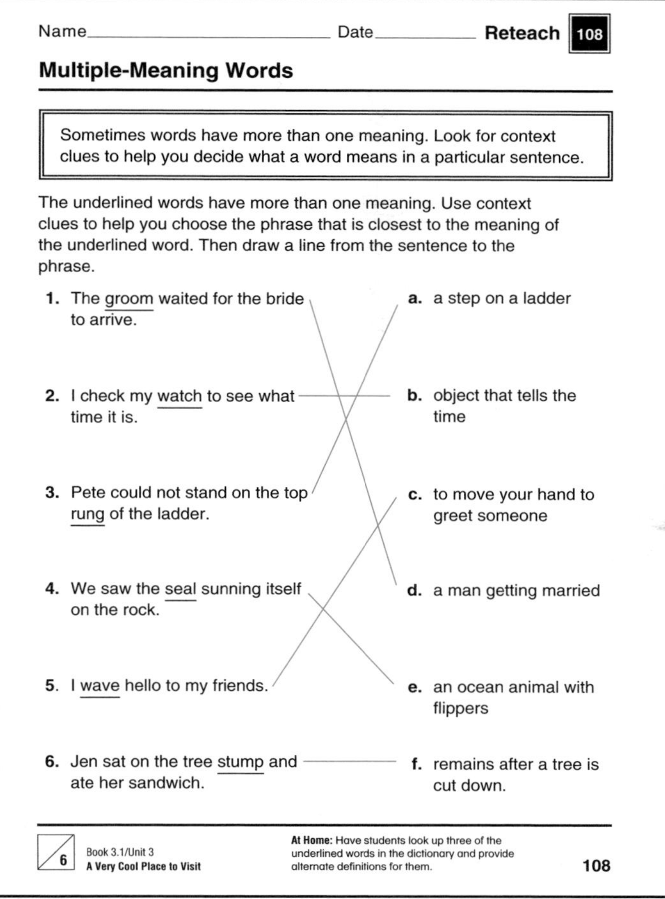

Name________________________ Date__________ **Reteach 108**

Multiple-Meaning Words

Sometimes words have more than one meaning. Look for context clues to help you decide what a word means in a particular sentence.

The underlined words have more than one meaning. Use context clues to help you choose the phrase that is closest to the meaning of the underlined word. Then draw a line from the sentence to the phrase.

1. The groom waited for the bride to arrive. — **d.** a man getting married
2. I check my watch to see what time it is. — **b.** object that tells the time
3. Pete could not stand on the top rung of the ladder. — **a.** a step on a ladder
4. We saw the seal sunning itself on the rock. — **e.** an ocean animal with flippers
5. I wave hello to my friends. — **c.** to move your hand to greet someone
6. Jen sat on the tree stump and ate her sandwich. — **f.** remains after a tree is cut down.

At Home: Have students look up three of the underlined words in the dictionary and provide alternate definitions for them.

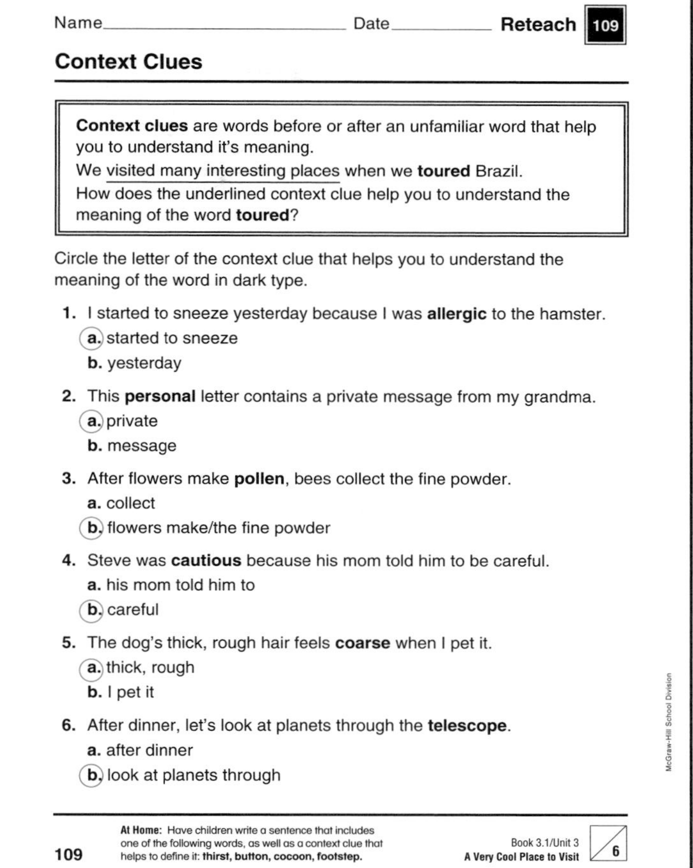

Name________________________ Date__________ **Reteach 109**

Context Clues

Context clues are words before or after an unfamiliar word that help you to understand it's meaning.
We visited many interesting places when we **toured** Brazil.
How does the underlined context clue help you to understand the meaning of the word **toured**?

Circle the letter of the context clue that helps you to understand the meaning of the word in dark type.

1. I started to sneeze yesterday because I was **allergic** to the hamster.
   (a.) started to sneeze
   b. yesterday
2. This **personal** letter contains a private message from my grandma.
   (a.) private
   b. message
3. After flowers make **pollen**, bees collect the fine powder.
   a. collect
   (b.) flowers make/the fine powder
4. Steve was **cautious** because his mom told him to be careful.
   a. his mom told him to
   (b.) careful
5. The dog's thick, rough hair feels **coarse** when I pet it.
   (a.) thick, rough
   b. I pet it
6. After dinner, let's look at planets through the **telescope**.
   a. after dinner
   (b.) look at planets through

At Home: Have children write a sentence that includes one of the following words, as well as a context clue that helps to define it: **thirst, button, cocoon, footstep.**

Name________________________ Date__________ **Extend 103**

Main Idea

Write a paragraph about an interesting animal. Include a main idea sentence and supporting details. Write one sentence in the paragraph that does not support the main idea. Exchange paragraphs with a partner. Have your partner find the sentence that does not belong. Then have your partner suggest one more supporting sentence for the paragraph.

Draw a picture that shows the main idea of your paragraph.

At Home: Ask students to create new titles for a favorite story. Have them write a main-idea sentence for the story using one of the new titles.

Name________________________ Date__________ **Extend 104**

Vocabulary

beauty	creeps	furniture	palace	pure	visitors

Write a paragraph about going to visit a castle. Use as many words from the box as you can to describe the people and the things that you see there.

Extend 105

Story Comprehension

Imagine that you are responsible for selling trips to the Ice Hotel. Work in a group to write advertisements and make posters for the Ice Hotel. Include information in your advertisements and posters that will make people want to visit. Write a slogan, or clever saying, about the Ice Hotel that you can use in your ads.

At Home: Have students write a sentence that might describe people who visit the Ice Hotel.

Name________________________ Date__________ **Extend 106**

Use a Map

Each spring, the Ice Hotel melts. When the winter comes, the building of the Ice Hotel begins again. If the owners of the Ice Hotel plan to begin building a new hotel when the temperature is below 25 degrees, the information on a climate map can help them. Use the climate map on page 384 in your pupil edition to help the owners at the Ice Hotel make their plans.

Write a sentence telling the owners where they could build a new hotel during the month of January.

They could build in any city with average January temperatures lower than 25 degrees.

Which city might be the best location for building an ice hotel? Why?

The city with the lowest temperature would be best because it would be the coldest.

At Home: Have students write a paragraph telling whether they would want to visit Sweden in January or July. Have them explain their answer.

Name________________________ Date__________ **Extend 107**

Summarize

Review "A Very Cool Place to Visit." Write a short summary of the article in the space below. Then use the summary to write a television commercial that you might make telling people what a great place the Ice Hotel is to visit on vacation. Present your commercial to your classmates.

"A Very Cool Place to Visit" tells about ________________

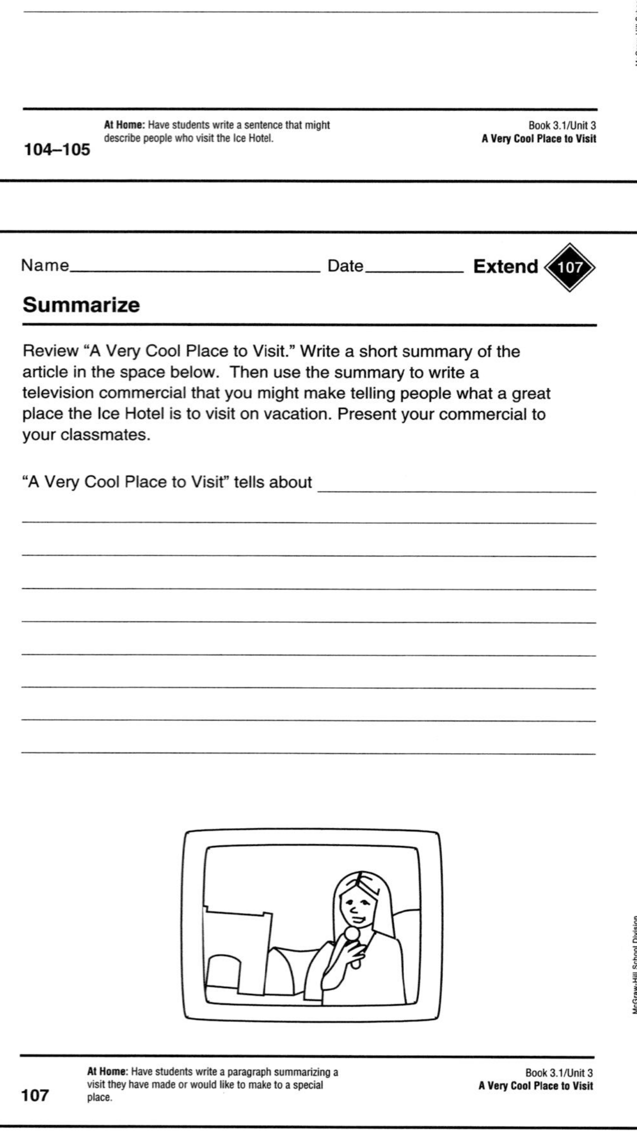

At Home: Have students write a paragraph summarizing a visit they have made or would like to make to a special place.

A Very Cool Place to Visit • EXTEND

Name________________________ Date__________ **Extend 108**

Multiple-Meaning Words

Read each sentence below. Use context clues in each sentence to define the meaning of each word in dark type. Circle the letter of the best meaning. Then, write sentences using the other meaning of each multiple-meaning word.

1. My friend lives on the same city **block** as I do.
   - (**a.**) an area surrounded by four streets
   - **b.** a piece of something hard
2. It is going to be a **cool** night at the park so Matt will bring a sweater.
   - **a.** fashionable and trendy
   - (**b.**) rather cold
3. The new student was given a **warm** welcome by the teacher and her classmates.
   - **a.** a bit hot
   - (**b.**) very friendly
4. When I stayed home from school with a **cold,** I sneezed and coughed all day.
   - (**a.**) a common mild illness
   - **b.** having a low temperature

1. ____

2. ____

3. ____

4. ____

At Home: Have students write a riddle for both meanings of the word bark.

Name________________________ Date__________ **Extend 109**

Context Clues

Use the words in the box to complete the sentences.

snowsuit	sleeping bag	push-ups	reindeer	cube	sprinkle

1. It is a good idea to put on a heavy ___snowsuit___ before going outside to play on a cold winter day.
2. ___Sprinkle___ a little brown sugar on your cereal to make it taste sweet.
3. There was plenty of room in the tent for me to roll out my ___sleeping bag___ at bedtime.
4. Sometimes I think I would like to drive a sled pulled by ___reindeer___ .
5. We warm up during gym class by doing sit-ups, ___push-ups___ , and other exercises.
6. The drink was so warm in the hot sun that the ___cube___ of ice melted right away.

Use all the words to write a paragraph telling what you might do on a visit to the Ice Hotel.

____

____

____

____

At Home: Have students draw picture clues for each word.

Name______________________ Date__________ LEARN **Grammar** 89

Sentence Combining with Verbs

> • Two sentences can be combined by joining the predicates with *and*.
> Two sentences: The guests smile. The guests talk.
> Combined sentence: The guests smile and talk.

The pairs of sentences below share the same subject. Make them into one sentence by using the word *and* to join the verbs. Write the new sentence on the line.

1. The hotel staff clean. The hotel staff sweep.
   The hotel staff clean and sweep.
2. The guests laugh. The guests talk.
   The guests laugh and talk.
3. The cold nips. The cold bites.
   The cold nips and bites.
4. The peace and quiet soothes. The peace and quiet relaxes.
   The peace and quiet soothes and relaxes.
5. The visitors chatter. The visitors shiver.
   The visitors chatter and shiver.
6. White, fresh snow glitters. White, fresh snow shines.
   White fresh snow glitters and shines.
7. The northern lights shimmer. The northern lights glow.
   The northern lights shimmer and glow.
8. The people gasp. The people stare.
   The people gasp and stare.
9. Every spring the hotel melts. Every spring the hotel disappears.
   Every spring the hotel melts and disappears.
10. Each winter, a new ice hotel rises. Each winter, a new ice hotel invites.
   Each winter, a new ice hotel rises and invites.

Extension: Have the students write three or four sentences describing a winter scene. Encourage them to share their descriptions with the class.

Name______________________ Date__________ LEARN AND PRACTICE **Grammar** 90

Sentence Combining with Verbs

> • Two sentences can be combined by joining the predicates with *and*.
> Two sentences: Guests wear snowsuits. Guests use sleeping bags.
> Combined sentence: Guests wear snowsuits and use sleeping bags.

Underline the predicate in each pair of sentences. Then combine the two sentences and write your one sentence on the line.

1. Guests visit Sweden. Guests stay at the Ice Hotel.
   Guests visit Sweden and stay at the Ice Hotel.
2. Johan helps the guests. Johan advises them.
   Johan helps the guests and advises them.
3. People love the beauty. People enjoy the quiet.
   People love the beauty and enjoy the quiet.
4. The northern lights astonish them. The northern lights delight them.
   The northern lights astonish and delight them.
5. Kerstin works at the hotel. Kerstin waits on the guests.
   Kerstin works at the hotel and waits on the guests.
6. Guests need snowsuits. Guests sleep on ice beds.
   Guests need snowsuits and sleep on ice beds.
7. Visitors conquer the cold. Visitors receive a special card.
   Visitors conquer the cold and receive a special card.
8. The ice melts from the salt. The ice freezes around the string.
   The ice melts from the salt and freezes around the string.

Extension: Have students work with partners. Each student writes pairs of sentences that have the same subject. The partners then join each other's sentences using *and*.

Name______________________ Date__________ PRACTICE AND REVIEW **Grammar** 91

Sentence Combining with Verbs

> • Two sentences can be combined by joining the predicates with *and*.

Read the sentences below. Rewrite them to join predicates that have the same subjects. Write the combined sentences as a paragraph on the lines.

1. The guests arrive slowly. The guests walk into the hotel.
2. These people like the cold. These people appreciate winter.
3. The staff offers warm snowsuits. The staff issues sleeping bags.
4. The hotel covers the ice beds. The hotel recommends exercises for warmth.
5. The next day, visitors accept special congratulations. The next day, visitors leave refreshed.

The guests arrive slowly and walk into the hotel. These people like the cold and appreciate winter. The staff offers warm snowsuits and issues sleeping bags. The hotel covers the ice beds and recommends exercises for warmth. The next day, visitors accept special congratulations and leave refreshed.

Extension: Encourage students to think of details they can add to the paragraph about the ice hotel. Have them write the new paragraph with their additions and if time permits, let them illustrate their work.

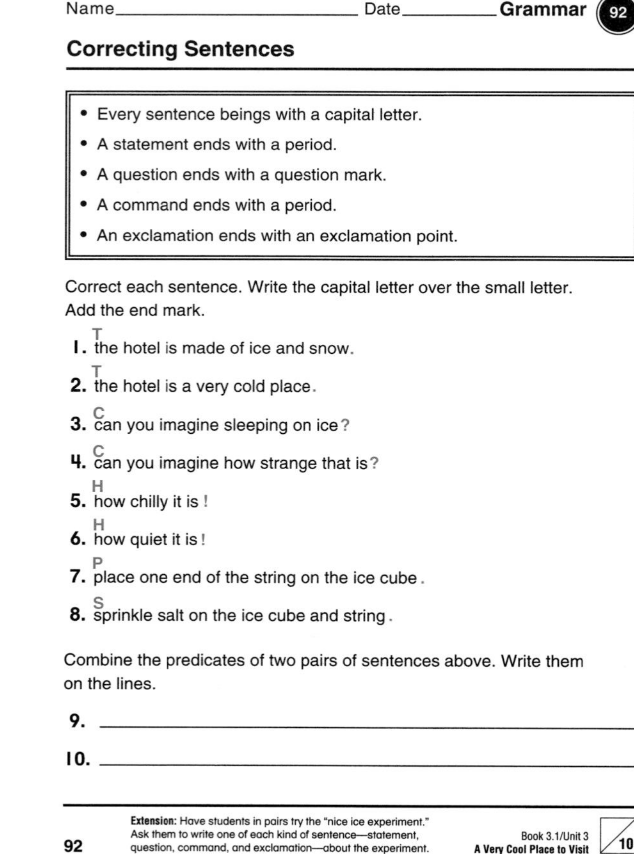

Name______________________ Date__________ MECHANICS **Grammar** 92

Correcting Sentences

> • Every sentence beings with a capital letter.
> • A statement ends with a period.
> • A question ends with a question mark.
> • A command ends with a period.
> • An exclamation ends with an exclamation point.

Correct each sentence. Write the capital letter over the small letter. Add the end mark.

1. [T] the hotel is made of ice and snow.
2. [T] the hotel is a very cold place.
3. [C] can you imagine sleeping on ice?
4. [C] can you imagine how strange that is?
5. [H] how chilly it is!
6. [H] how quiet it is!
7. [P] place one end of the string on the ice cube.
8. [S] sprinkle salt on the ice cube and string.

Combine the predicates of two pairs of sentences above. Write them on the lines.

9. ______________________
10. ______________________

Extension: Have students in pairs try the "nice ice experiment." Ask them to write one of each kind of sentence—statement, question, command, and exclamation—about the experiment.

Name_______________ Date_________ TEST Grammar 93

Sentence Combining with Verbs

Each pair of sentences below shares a subject. On the line, write the predicate of the first sentence. Then write the word *and* followed by the predicate of the second sentence.

1. The guests danced. The guests sang.
   danced and sang
2. The night sky sparkled. The night sky shone brightly.
   sparkled and shone
3. The staff announced dinner. The staff served the guests.
   announced and served
4. The cold air stung our faces. The cold air frosted our breath.
   stung and frosted

Join the sentence pairs below into single sentences. Write your answers.

5. A reindeer stands in front. A reindeer greets hotel visitors.
   A reindeer stands in front and greets hotel visitors.
6. Snow suits prevent chills. Snow suits allow guests to sleep.
   Snow suits prevent chills and allow guests to sleep.
7. Guests sleep soundly in their sleeping bags. Guests rise early.
   Guests sleep soundly in their sleeping bags and rise early.
8. The hotel boasts 100 ice beds. The hotel attracts many visitors.
   The hotel boasts 100 ice beds and attracts many visitors.
9. Winter pleases the guests. Winter makes the ice hotel possible.
   Winter pleases the guests and makes the ice hotel possible.
10. Warm weather ruins the ice hotel. Warm weather ends the season.
    Warm weather ruins the ice hotel and ends the season.

Name_______________ Date_________ MORE PRACTICE Grammar 94

Sentence Combining with Verbs

- Two sentences can be combined by joining the predicates with *and.*

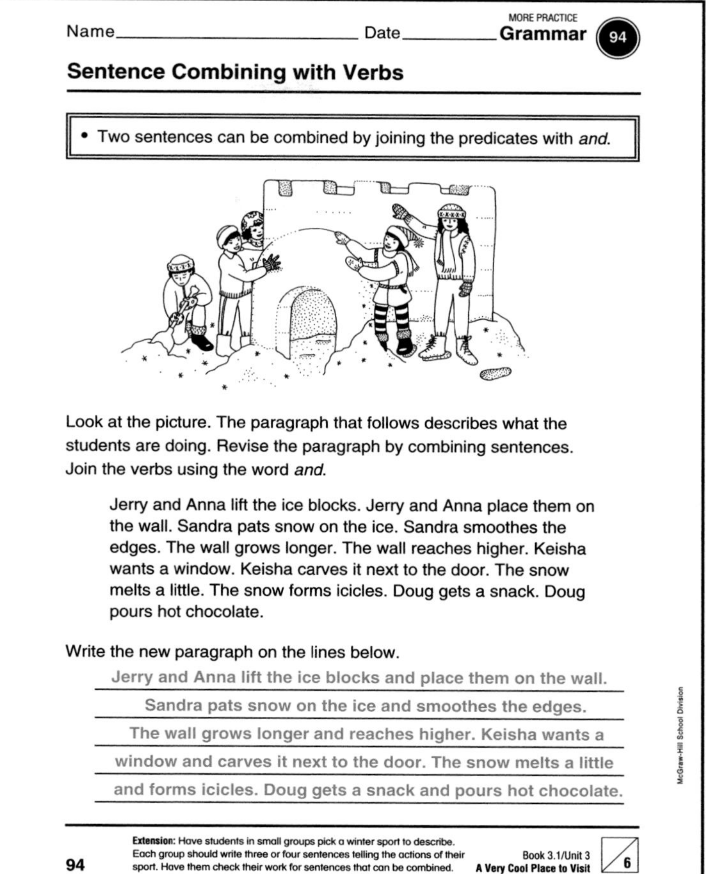

Look at the picture. The paragraph that follows describes what the students are doing. Revise the paragraph by combining sentences. Join the verbs using the word *and.*

Jerry and Anna lift the ice blocks. Jerry and Anna place them on the wall. Sandra pats snow on the ice. Sandra smoothes the edges. The wall grows longer. The wall reaches higher. Keisha wants a window. Keisha carves it next to the door. The snow melts a little. The snow forms icicles. Doug gets a snack. Doug pours hot chocolate.

Write the new paragraph on the lines below.

Jerry and Anna lift the ice blocks and place them on the wall. Sandra pats snow on the ice and smoothes the edges. The wall grows longer and reaches higher. Keisha wants a window and carves it next to the door. The snow melts a little and forms icicles. Doug gets a snack and pours hot chocolate.

Extension: Have students in small groups pick a winter sport to describe. Each group should write three or four sentences telling the actions of their sport. Have them check their work for sentences that can be combined.

Name__________ Date__________ PRETEST SPELLING 89

Words from Science

Pretest Directions

Fold back the paper along the dotted line. Use the blanks to write each word as it is read aloud. When you finish the test, unfold the paper. Use the list at the right to correct any spelling mistakes. Practice the words you missed for the Posttest.

1. ________	1. ice
2. ________	2. solid
3. ________	3. melt
4. ________	4. northern
5. ________	5. heat
6. ________	6. freezes
7. ________	7. matter
8. ________	8. frost
9. ________	9. snowflake
10. ________	10. thaw
11. ________	11. arctic
12. ________	12. dense
13. ________	13. degree
14. ________	14. chill
15. ________	15. igloo
Challenge Words	
________	beauty
________	furniture
________	palace
________	pure
________	visitors

To Parents

Here are the results of your child's weekly spelling Pretest. You can help your child study for the Posttest by following these simple steps for each word on the word list:

1. Read the word to your child.
2. Have your child write the word, saying each letter as it is written.
3. Say each letter of the word as your child checks the spelling.
4. If a mistake has been made, have your child read each letter of the correctly spelled word aloud, and then repeat steps 1-3.

Name__________ Date__________ AT-HOME WORD STUDY SPELLING 90

Words from Science

Using the Word Study Steps

1. LOOK at the word.
2. SAY the word aloud.
3. STUDY the letters in the word.
4. WRITE the word.
5. CHECK the word.
   Did you spell the word right?
   If not, go back to step 1.

Spelling Tip

Make up clues to help you remember the spelling.

It's c--**c**--cold in the arctic! (Don't forget the **c** in the middle of ar**c**tic.)

Find and Circle

Where are the spelling words?

s n o w f l a k e e n o r t h e r n
o m e l t c f r e e z e s l t h a w
l f r o s t r i c e x d e g r e e y
i g l o o q a r c t i c b d e n s e
d m a t t e r u c h i l l r h e a t

To Parents or Helpers:

Using the Word Study Steps above as your child comes across any new words will help him or her spell well. Review the steps as you both go over this week's spelling words.

Go over the Spelling Tip with your child. Help him or her think of other clues that will help to remember the spelling of new words.

Help your child find and circle the spelling words in the puzzle.

Name__________ Date__________ EXPLORE THE PATTERN SPELLING 91

Words from Science

ice	northern	matter	thaw	degree
solid	heat	frost	arctic	chill
melt	freezes	snowflake	dense	igloo

Pattern Power

Write the spelling words that have one syllable.

1. ice 2. melt 3. heat
4. frost 5. thaw 6. dense
7. chill

Write the spelling words that have two syllables.

8. solid 9. northern 10. freezes
11. matter 12. snowflake 13. arctic
14. degree 15. igloo

Rhyme Time

Write a spelling word that rhymes with each of these words.

16. fatter matter 17. claw thaw
18. sense dense 19. lost frost
20. seat heat 21. sneezes freezes

Word Scramble

Unscramble each spelling word.

22. nowesfakl s n o w f l a k e
23. ologi i g l o o
24. edgere d e g r e e
25. iec i c e

Name__________ Date__________ PRACTICE AND EXTEND SPELLING 92

Words from Science

ice	northern	matter	thaw	degree
solid	heat	frost	arctic	chill
melt	freezes	snowflake	dense	igloo

A Clue for You

Write the spelling word that fits the clue.

1. opposite of southern northern
2. a house made of ice igloo
3. if butter gets too warm it will do this melt
4. when cold water changes to a solid freezes
5. ice crystal in air snowflake
6. area at the top of the world arctic
7. before you cook frozen meat it must do this thaw
8. ice crystals that you can see on windows frost

Fill in the Blanks

Write the list word that completes each sentence.

9. Janice wore her sweater when she felt a chill in the air.
10. The car skidded on a patch of ice on the road.
11. It doesn't matter to me whether it rains or snows tomorrow.
12. The fog was so dense it was hard to see the road.
13. When water freezes it changes from a liquid to a solid.
14. A wood-burning fireplace provides heat.
15. The temperature today is only one degree warmer than yesterday.

Word Journal

One of your spelling words is *arctic*. Write about some things that happen in arctic weather.

____

____

____

Challenge Extension: Have students write each Challenge Word and then circle each syllable. Have them check their work in a dictionary.

Name______________________ Date__________ PROOFREAD AND WRITE **SPELLING** **93**

Words from Science

Proofreading Paragraph

There are six spelling mistakes in this weather report. Circle the misspelled words. Write the words correctly on the lines below.

In the northarn states, the weather will be quite cold tomorrow. The temperature may even reach one digre below zero. Now that's artic weather! This chill will last for several days. Anyone care to build an iglo?

Now, there's another mattir to report. Our friends down south, of course, have a different weather problem. They are complaining about the hete!

1. northern 2. degree 3. arctic

4. igloo 5. matter 6. heat

Writing Activity

What questions would you like to ask someone who lives in a very cold climate? Write your interview questions, using at least six spelling words.

____

____

____

____

____

McGraw-Hill School Division

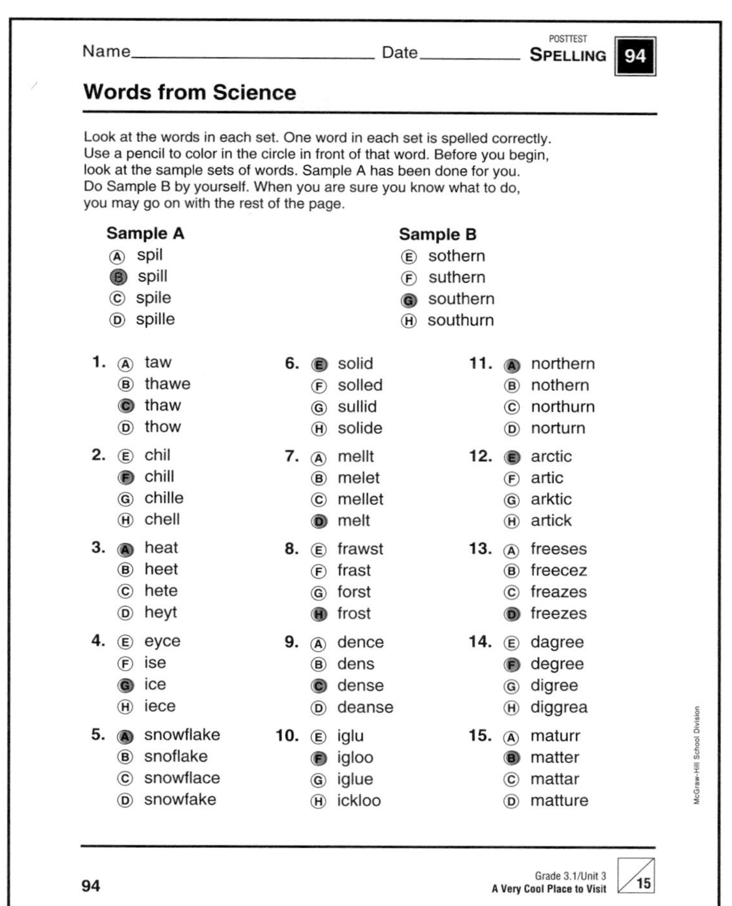

Name______________________ Date__________ POSTTEST **SPELLING** **94**

Words from Science

Look at the words in each set. One word in each set is spelled correctly. Use a pencil to color in the circle in front of that word. Before you begin, look at the sample sets of words. Sample A has been done for you. Do Sample B by yourself. When you are sure you know what to do, you may go on with the rest of the page.

Sample A
Ⓐ spil
Ⓑ spill
Ⓒ spile
Ⓓ spille

Sample B
Ⓔ sothern
Ⓕ suthern
Ⓖ southern
Ⓗ southurn

1. Ⓐ taw Ⓑ thawe Ⓒ thaw Ⓓ thow
2. Ⓔ chil Ⓕ chill Ⓖ chille Ⓗ chell
3. Ⓐ heat Ⓑ heet Ⓒ hete Ⓓ heyt
4. Ⓔ eyce Ⓕ ise Ⓖ ice Ⓗ iece
5. Ⓐ snowflake Ⓑ snoflake Ⓒ snowflace Ⓓ snowfake
6. Ⓔ solid Ⓕ solled Ⓖ sullid Ⓗ solide
7. Ⓐ mellt Ⓑ melet Ⓒ mellet Ⓓ melt
8. Ⓔ frawst Ⓕ frast Ⓖ forst Ⓗ frost
9. Ⓐ dence Ⓑ dens Ⓒ dense Ⓓ deanse
10. Ⓔ iglu Ⓕ igloo Ⓖ iglue Ⓗ ickloo
11. Ⓐ northern Ⓑ nothern Ⓒ northurn Ⓓ norturn
12. Ⓔ arctic Ⓕ artic Ⓖ arktic Ⓗ artick
13. Ⓐ freeses Ⓑ freecez Ⓒ freazes Ⓓ freezes
14. Ⓔ dagree Ⓕ degree Ⓖ digree Ⓗ diggrea
15. Ⓐ maturr Ⓑ matter Ⓒ mattar Ⓓ matture

McGraw-Hill School Division

Unit 3 Review • PRACTICE and RETEACH

Name__________ Date______ **Practice 110**

Unit 3 Vocabulary Review

A. Supply the correct word from the box.

orchestra	concert	imaginary	conductor	musician

Helen pretended she was the conductor of an orchestra. She could hear the imaginary music in her head. When she waved her arms, each musician played faster. The pretend audience clapped wildly. At the end of the concert, they threw her flowers.

B. Read each word in Column 1. Then find a word in Column 2 that means the opposite. Write the letter of the word on the line.

1. shallow c — **a.** bright
2. ill e — **b.** cellar
3. miserable f — **c.** deep
4. faded a — **d.** lost
5. attic b — **e.** well
6. stumbled g — **f.** happy
7. located d — **g.** leaped

At Home: Have students write a story that uses the vocabulary words in Part B.

Name__________ Date______ **Practice 111**

Unit 3 Vocabulary Review

A. Answer the questions. Then explain each answer by writing what the vocabulary word means.

1. Which is more likely to have a pattern on it, a star or a sweater? A sweater; pattern means "a design made of colors, shapes, or lines."
2. Would you find blossoms on a tree or on a bird? A tree; blossoms are flowers.
3. What would you do at dawn, wake up or eat lunch? Wake up; dawn means "first light of morning."
4. Which would you combine, a fried egg and milk or bread and butter? Bread and butter; combine means "to put together."
5. Which would you find in the wilderness, a deer or a grocery store? A deer; wilderness means "a place where no people live."

B. Label each column with a word from the box below.

costume	furniture	instrument

furniture	costume	instrument
bed	sailor	piano
chair	scarecrow	horn
table	magician	drum

At Home: Have students make lists like the ones in Part B that name things you could find in the wilderness.

Name__________ Date______ **Reteach 110**

Unit 3 Vocabulary Review

A. Find the word in the list that means the same or almost the same as the underlined word. Write it on the line.

ill	miserable	gazed	combine	visitors

1. Theo stayed home from school because he was sick. ill
2. Karen looked at the moon. gazed
3. Oscar said good-bye to the guests when they left. visitors
4. Shelley didn't know why Seth looked so sad. miserable
5. Dana had to mix many ingredients to make the bread. combine

B. Supply the correct word from the list.

palace	instrument	invented	stumbled	attic

1. Jose invented a new game.
2. Is the piano a hard instrument to play?
3. The old trunk was up in the attic.
4. Peter stumbled and almost fell down.
5. The prince lives in a palace.

At Home: Have students write a short story that contains the vocabulary words in Part A.

Name__________ Date______ **Reteach 111**

Unit 3 Vocabulary Review

A. Match each vocabulary word with its definition. Write the letter of the definition on the line.

1. faded c — **a.** not mixed with anything
2. examined b — **b.** looked at closely
3. prairie e — **c.** lost color
4. pure a — **d.** found where something was
5. located d — **e.** flat land covered with grass

B. Complete each sentence by writing a word from the list on the line.

beauty	concert	shallow	wilderness	anxious

1. If you could hardly wait for something to happen, you would feel anxious.
2. If you were sitting in the audience while people played music, you would be at a concert.
3. If the water in a stream didn't cover your feet, it would be shallow.
4. If something were very pretty, it would have beauty.
5. If you went someplace where no people lived, you would be in a wilderness.

At Home: Have students make flash cards with the words and definitions in Part A. Then practice reading each word and telling its definition.

Name________________________ Date__________ Extend 110

Vocabulary Review

Find each word in the box in the puzzle. Words may be written forward, backward, or down. Circle the words in the puzzle. Put the letters you did not circle in the spaces in the order you find them. Then answer the question.

anxious	invented	dawn	pattern	pure	prairie	gazed
palace	creeps	stumbled	ill	instrument	combine	blossom

p	r	a	i	r	i	e	s	w	i	p
a	n	x	i	o	u	s	t	l	d	a
l	c	r	e	e	p	s	u	e	r	t
a	i	n	s	t	r	u	m	e	n	t
c	l	n	e	c	o	m	b	i	n	e
e	l	m	o	s	s	o	l	b	s	r
p	u	r	e	g	a	z	e	d	s	n
i	n	v	e	n	t	e	d	a	w	n

Describe what you would do for a week in the

w i l d e r n e s s

Answers will vary

At Home: Have students write the words in the box on cards. Ask students to choose two cards and make up a sentence or riddle using the two words.

Name________________________ Date__________ Extend 111

Vocabulary Review

Read the sentences. Circle the word that completes each sentence. Use the pictures as clues.

1. We walk up the stairs to the ______________________.
   basement **attic**
2. When Max was sick, he had many ______________________ to keep him company.
   visitors **chairs**
3. The sun came up at ______________________.
   dusk **dawn**

Use each word below to write a sentence that tells about the picture.

Answers will vary. Possible answers are given.

4. **pattern**
   The dog has a pattern on his sweater.
5. **stumbled**
   The bear stumbled over a rock.
6. **palace**
   The Queen and King live in a palace.

At Home: Have students make up a fairy tale using the following words: **musician, imaginary, miserable, shallow, anxious, located, beauty, furniture, invented.** They can write and illustrate their story on paper folded in half to make a book to read to a younger child.

Name________________________ Date__________ REVIEW Grammar 95

Verbs

Read the passage and look at the underlined parts. Is there a better way to say each part? If there is, which is the better way? Mark your answer.

A summer storm.(1) Thunder rumbles overhead. Waves crashing on the shore.(2) Heavy rain is coming to the beach. Let's run for cover!

1. ⓐ Summer storm coming!
   ⓑ A summer storm passes by.
   ⓒ A summer storm pass.
   ⓓ No mistake.
2. ⓔ Waves on the shore.
   ⓕ Waves crashes on the shore.
   ⓖ Waves crash on the shore.
   ⓗ No mistake.

I didn't see the hailstorm. My sister told me that it is noisy.(3) Hail fell from the sky like rain. It dropped like stone. It hit glass windows. It crashed on the ground.(4) She said, "I heard a rumbling sound."

3. ⓐ My sister told me that it was noisy.
   ⓑ My sister it was noisy.
   ⓒ It is noisy my sister told me.
   ⓓ No mistake.
4. ⓔ It crashes on the ground.
   ⓕ It crash on the ground.
   ⓖ It's not on the ground.
   ⓗ No mistake.

Name________________________ Date__________ REVIEW Grammar 96

Yesterday morning, I gather dried leaves in the backyard.(5) By evening, I had finished my lessons. Today, I prepare for my tests. I will take them tomorrow. My mom bring me to school.(6)

5. ⓐ Yesterday morning, I gathered dried leaves in the backyard.
   ⓑ Yesterday morning, I will gather dried leaves in the backyard.
   ⓒ Yesterday morning, I gathers dried leaves in the backyard.
   ⓓ No mistake.
6. ⓔ My mom has brought me to school.
   ⓕ My mom was bringing me to school.
   ⓖ My mom will bring me to school.
   ⓗ No mistake.

Last summer we went on vacation. We camped in the mountains.(7) My grandmother came with us. She brought along her pet dog. It was a cute terrier. It had white fur.(8) When it heard a noise, it barked. We could not sleep from its barking.

7. ⓐ Last summer, we went camp on vacation in the mountains.
   ⓑ Last summer. We went on vacation in the mountains.
   ⓒ Last summer, we went on vacation and camped in the mountains.
   ⓓ No mistake.
8. ⓔ It was a cute terrier and had white fur.
   ⓕ It was a white fur cute terrier.
   ⓖ It was cute white fur.
   ⓗ No mistake.

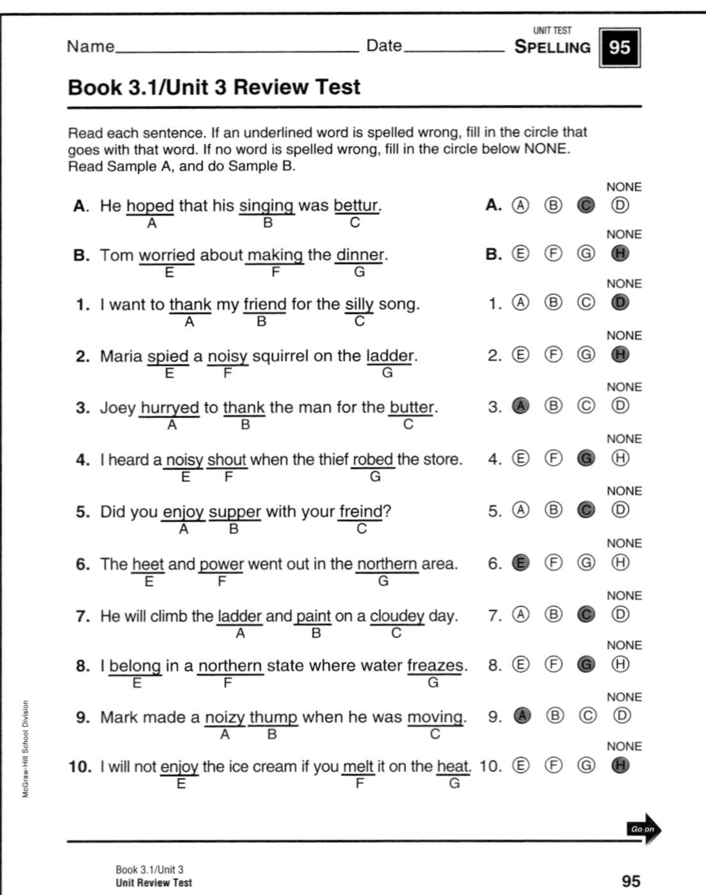

Name________________________ Date__________ UNIT TEST SPELLING 95

Book 3.1/Unit 3 Review Test

Read each sentence. If an underlined word is spelled wrong, fill in the circle that goes with that word. If no word is spelled wrong, fill in the circle below NONE. Read Sample A, and do Sample B.

A. He hoped that his singing was bettur. (A hoped, B singing, C bettur) — **A.** Ⓐ Ⓑ Ⓒ Ⓓ NONE

B. Tom worried about making the dinner. (E worried, F making, G dinner) — **B.** Ⓔ Ⓕ Ⓖ Ⓗ NONE

1. I want to thank my friend for the silly song. (A thank, B friend, C silly) — 1. Ⓐ Ⓑ Ⓒ Ⓓ NONE

2. Maria spied a noisy squirrel on the ladder. (E spied, F noisy, G ladder) — 2. Ⓔ Ⓕ Ⓖ Ⓗ NONE

3. Joey hurryed to thank the man for the butter. (A hurryed, B thank, C butter) — 3. Ⓐ Ⓑ Ⓒ Ⓓ NONE

4. I heard a noisy shout when the thief robed the store. (E noisy, F shout, G robed) — 4. Ⓔ Ⓕ Ⓖ Ⓗ NONE

5. Did you enjoy supper with your freind? (A enjoy, B supper, C freind) — 5. Ⓐ Ⓑ Ⓒ Ⓓ NONE

6. The heet and power went out in the northern area. (E heet, F power, G northern) — 6. Ⓔ Ⓕ Ⓖ Ⓗ NONE

7. He will climb the ladder and paint on a cloudey day. (A ladder, B paint, C cloudey) — 7. Ⓐ Ⓑ Ⓒ Ⓓ NONE

8. I belong in a northern state where water freazes. (E belong, F northern, G freazes) — 8. Ⓔ Ⓕ Ⓖ Ⓗ NONE

9. Mark made a noizy thump when he was moving. (A noizy, B thump, C moving) — 9. Ⓐ Ⓑ Ⓒ Ⓓ NONE

10. I will not enjoy the ice cream if you melt it on the heat. (E enjoy, F melt, G heat) — 10. Ⓔ Ⓕ Ⓖ Ⓗ NONE

Go on

Name________________________ Date__________ UNIT TEST SPELLING 96

11. Susan is moveing the paint and the ladder. (A moveing, B paint, C ladder) — 11. Ⓐ Ⓑ Ⓒ Ⓓ NONE

12. Will a snowflak melt if it's near heat? (E snowflak, F melt, G heat) — 12. Ⓔ Ⓕ Ⓖ Ⓗ NONE

13. Let's shout the silly, noisey song! (A shout, B silly, C noisey) — 13. Ⓐ Ⓑ Ⓒ Ⓓ NONE

14. Frank and Jim enjoy butter with their souper. (E enjoy, F butter, G souper) — 14. Ⓔ Ⓕ Ⓖ Ⓗ NONE

15. I engoy shaking the gift tied with a ribbon. (A engoy, B shaking, C ribbon) — 15. Ⓐ Ⓑ Ⓒ Ⓓ NONE

16. It was cloudy the day he spyed the silly goose. (E cloudy, F spyed, G silly) — 16. Ⓔ Ⓕ Ⓖ Ⓗ NONE

17. The electric power freezer freezes his butter. (A power, B freezes, C butter) — 17. Ⓐ Ⓑ Ⓒ Ⓓ NONE

18. Did you paint a silly ribban in her hair? (E paint, F silly, G ribban) — 18. Ⓔ Ⓕ Ⓖ Ⓗ NONE

19. We enjoy shakeing the apples because they thump. (A enjoy, B shakeing, C thump) — 19. Ⓐ Ⓑ Ⓒ Ⓓ NONE

20. Shout a noisy word when it's time for suppir. (E Shout, F noisy, G suppir) — 20. Ⓔ Ⓕ Ⓖ Ⓗ NONE

21. Steven spied a ribbun tied to the ladder. (A spied, B ribbun, C ladder) — 21. Ⓐ Ⓑ Ⓒ Ⓓ NONE

22. Who robbed my friend and took her paynt? (E robbed, F friend, G paynt) — 22. Ⓔ Ⓕ Ⓖ Ⓗ NONE

23. If the powur goes out the butter will melt. (A powur, B butter, C melt) — 23. Ⓐ Ⓑ Ⓒ Ⓓ NONE

24. If you belong to the Noisy Club you can shout! (E belong, F Noisy, G shout) — 24. Ⓔ Ⓕ Ⓖ Ⓗ NONE

25. Bob hurried up the latter and began to paint. (A hurried, B latter, C paint) — 25. Ⓐ Ⓑ Ⓒ Ⓓ NONE

Notes

Main Idea

TESTED OBJECTIVES **Students will identify main ideas and supporting details.**

Kinesthetic

TRUNKFUL OF IDEAS

Materials: small branches, heavy paper, tape, pencils, hole punch

Ask students to think about how the main idea and supporting details of a story are like the trunk of a tree and its branches. Guide them to understand that all the branches grow out of the trunk of the tree. In a similar way, supporting details are all related to the main idea of a piece of text.

- Give each student a small branch and a photocopy of a nonfiction paragraph.

WRITING Have students analyze the writing and write the main idea in their own words. Tell them to attach the main idea paper to the main part of the branch with glue.

- Have students write supporting details on separate pieces of paper and attach these to the smaller twigs of the branch with string.
  ▶Bodily/Kinesthetic

Visual

STAND BY ME

Materials: passages from a content area textbook

On different parts of the chalkboard, write two main idea statements on a related topic, using paragraphs from a science or social studies text.

- Read one supporting detail sentence at a time.
- Ask students to point to the main idea statement that each detail supports. Have students justify their choices.
- Continue with other details from the paragraphs.
  ▶Spatial

Auditory

LISTEN UP!

Ask students to listen carefully as you read the following paragraph, which is missing a topic sentence.

__________. First, run warm water in the bathtub. You can use shampoo for people or you can buy special pet shampoo. If your pet sheds, don't let its hair go down the drain. Dry the animal in an old towel. Make sure it is completely dry before it goes outside again, so it doesn't get chilled or dirty.

- Have students write the main idea in their own words.
- Then have students share their main idea statements and discuss which ones capture the main idea of the paragraph effectively. **▶Linguistic**

See Reteach 75, 79, 94, 103

Graphic Aids

TESTED OBJECTIVES **Students will construct and interpret diagrams and maps.**

Kinesthetic

DIAGRAM IT

PARTNERS **Materials:** tissue paper, newspaper, or origami paper; craft or activity books with diagrams for folded paper toys

Provide students with copies of a diagram for making a simple folded paper object such as a hat, a pinwheel, snowflake, or other simple object.

- Have students follow the diagram to make the object out of folded paper.
- They can then draw a diagram for another person to use. Have students work with a partner to make sure the steps are clear and complete. ▶**Interpersonal**

Visual

SCHOOL MAP

Materials: mural paper, pencils, markers, compass

Students will make a map for school visitors.

- Have students begin by identifying the north, east, south, and west sides of the school building.
- They can lay out a design and label classrooms, the office, and special areas, such as the gym, library/media center, lunchroom, and so on. Suggest they include a legend for areas with multiple locations such as restrooms and water fountains. ▶**Spatial**

Auditory

WHERE IN THE WORLD

Materials: photocopies of a section of a road map, pencils or thin markers

Provide students with copies of a road map section.

- Give students a series of directions to follow, pausing as they find the starting place on the map.
- Tell students to mark the route as they follow each direction. Check to make sure they "arrive" at the correct destination. ▶**Logical/Mathematical**

See Reteach 78, 85, 92, 99, 106

Summarize

OBJECTIVES **Students will create written and oral summaries of news reports, books, and stories.**

Alternate Activities

Auditory

TV TEASERS

Materials: tape-recorded television or radio news broadcast

Have students listen to a tape-recorded television or radio news report.

- Assign each student to one of the news stories. Have students make up "teasers," or headlines the announcer might use to introduce the story.
- Students can read their teasers in an announcer's voice—as if they were on radio or television. ▶**Musical**

Visual

BOOK JACKET BLURBS

Materials: heavy paper, markers or crayons, pencils

Display book jackets from children's picture books and chapter books.

- Tell students they will design a book jacket for a favorite book.
- Check students' choices to be sure they are appropriate for the activity.
- Students may begin by drawing a cover illustration that depicts an important scene from the story.

Have students write a book jacket summary and attach it to the cover illustration.

- Display the completed book jackets on the bulletin board or in the classroom reading corner. ▶**Linguistic**

Kinesthetic

SEND A TELEGRAM

ONE **Materials:** paper and pencil

Explain that, before the days of fax machines and e-mail, people often sent important messages in telegrams. Since people paid a charge based on the number of words, telegrams were usually short and to the point. Explain that telegrams were transmitted by Morse code, a series of long and short taps or beeps.

WRITING Tell students to prepare telegrams to summarize a story they have read. Limit the number of words used in the telegram.

- Have students review each other's telegrams to see if any important information is missing or whether they can omit any unnecessary words.
- Students can pretend to transmit their telegrams by Morse code, reading and tapping out words as a partner records them. ▶**Bodily/Kinesthetic**

See Reteach 80, 87, 107

Context Clues

OBJECTIVES Students will use context clues to recognize meanings of unfamiliar words.

Kinesthetic

HIGH AND LOW

Materials: prepared sentence strips as described below

Write sentences with context clues to the meanings of missing words. In place of each missing word, make boxes to show the shapes of the letters, with tall boxes for letters such as *f, t, l,* and *k*—and boxes that drop below the line for letters like *y, g,* and *j.* Write the correct answer on the back of the sentence strip.

- Have students use the context and shape clues to determine the missing words. Students can list missing words on a separate sheet of paper.
- Tell students to compare their answer to the correct response on the back of each sentence strip. ▶**Spatial**

Visual

A PICTURE'S WORTH

Materials: interesting and attractive posters or photographs

Display one or more posters or photographs. Make up a sentence about each picture that contains a word above grade level.

- Have students use the picture clues to figure out the meaning of the unfamiliar word.

Invite a volunteer to write a list of unfamiliar words on the chalkboard to create a word bank. Have students use words from the word bank to write a short story about one of the pictures. ▶**Spatial**

Auditory

NONSENSE!

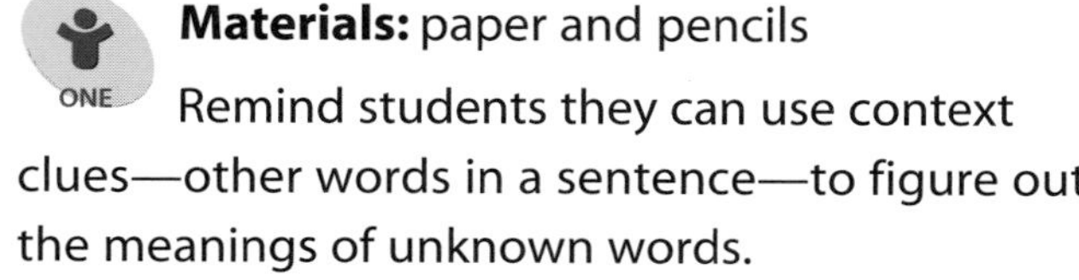

Materials: paper and pencils

Remind students they can use context clues—other words in a sentence—to figure out the meanings of unknown words.

- Write the following sentences on the chalkboard. Then provide context clues to help listeners understand the meanings of the nonsense words.

Have students write down what they think each nonsense word represents.

1. Quilt-making is fun and doesn't have to cost much *darmia.*
2. You can collect *sniggles* of fabric from sewing projects or old clothing.
3. Your friends will be *doppled* when they see your creation.

- Encourage students to share their meanings for the nonsense words. Discuss which would be correct in each sentence and why.
- Have students write their own sentences with new nonsense words.
- Ask them to read their sentences to a partner who will use context clues to determine the meanings of nonsense words. ▶**Linguistic**

See Reteach 81, 88, 109

Story Elements

OBJECTIVES (Tested) **Students will identify story elements, including characters, plot, and setting.**

Alternate Activities

Visual

SCENIC STORY ELEMENTS

PARTNERS **Materials:** magazine pictures

Review basic story elements with students: character, plot, and setting.

- Cut out magazine pictures of people in a variety of settings.

WRITING Distribute one picture to each pair of students. Ask pairs to create the following story elements based on information in the picture: *character* (physical description, personality, likes, dislikes); *setting* (time and place); *plot* (what happens in the story).

- Encourage students to add other details if they wish. ▶**Linguistic**

Kinesthetic

STORY SPINNER

GROUP **Materials:** spinner divided into three sections

Make a story spinner on which you write the words *character, plot,* and *setting.* Use a paper fastener to attach an arrow or a paper clip that students can spin.

- Identify the story you want students to discuss.
- Have students take turns spinning the wheel. Ask them to describe the element of the story the arrow points to.
- Students should play until all story elements have been discussed. ▶**Interpersonal**

Auditory

WHO WHAT WHERE WHEN

Have students recite Mother Goose rhymes.

- For each rhyme, ask students to name *who* (the characters), *what* (describe the plot), *where* and *when* (the setting).

WRITING Tell students to write a new story, using the same characters, plot, and setting. Collect the stories to make a class storybook. ▶**Musical**

See Reteach 82, 86, 96, 100

Multiple-Meaning Words

OBJECTIVES **Students will identify the appropriate meanings of multiple-meaning words.**

Kinesthetic

PICK A SLIP

GROUP **Materials:** list of multiple-meaning words

Write multiple-meaning words on separate slips of paper. Place the slips in a coffee can or basket.

- Have students form teams. One person from each team will pick a word from the container and give a clue for each of two different meanings for the word on the slip.
- Members of that student's team guess the multiple-meaning word that fits both clues. ▶**Linguistic**

Visual

MULTIPLE MEANING COLLAGES

Materials: magazines, scissors, drawing paper, glue, pencils

Through magazine pictures and interaction, students recognize and use multiple-meaning words.

- Have students use magazine pictures to make collages illustrating multiple-meaning words. They can add their own details to the pictures.
- For example, they might show a winged bat swinging a baseball bat or a dollar bill changing into some change.
- Have students share their collages with classmates and talk about the multiple-meaning words they have depicted. ▶**Spatial**

Auditory

RIDDLES

Materials: list of multiple-meaning words

Display a wall chart of multiple-meaning words for students' reference.

Have students write riddles using multiple-meaning words.

- Tell students to share clues with classmates. Invite classmates to guess the multiple-meaning words.
- Have students draw pictures that illustrate two of the riddles. ▶**Linguistic**

See Reteach 95, 102, 108

Make Inferences

OBJECTIVES Students will practice making inferences.

Kinesthetic

FOLLOW THE CLUES

GROUP **Materials:** construction paper footprints

Cut out several footprint shapes from construction paper. Write a number of inferences that students could make from everyday observations.

- Have a volunteer read one statement. Invite the class to brainstorm inferences that could lead to that conclusion. Example:

  Observation: It's raining outside.

  Inference: There could be muddy footprints inside the door.

  Inference: Wet umbrellas might be stacked inside the door.

- Use other observations such as: A pet broke a dish. Your favorite team won a game. ▶**Logical/Mathematical**

Visual

WHAT'S MY LINE?

GROUP **Materials:** magazine pictures

Show a series of pictures of people dressed for different kinds of work, such as a construction worker, a teacher, a firefighter, a doctor.

- Ask: "What do you think each person does for work?"
- Have students answer and explain which clues helped them decide.

WRITING Ask students to write short stories that include clues to help readers determine what kind of job a friend or family member has. Tell them not to mention the name of the job. Ask volunteers to read their stories aloud. Invite volunteers to guess what the job is. ▶**Logical/Mathematical**

Auditory

WHODUNIT

GROUP Have students work in groups to create minimysteries. They can add sound effects to provide clues to the mystery.

- Example: George lay helplessly wiggling on the ground in a tiny splash of water. He was unable to walk back home. He lay gasping for breath, hoping that his whiskered neighbor would not discover him. (Meow) (Inference: George is a fish out of his tank, hoping that the cat won't find him.)
- After each group reads its minimystery, others can discuss inferences they can make about the clues given.
- Have students discuss which clues helped them make inferences about the mystery. ▶**Interpersonal**

See Reteach 89, 93, 101

Notes

A Communication Tool

Although typewriters and computers are readily available, many situations continue to require handwriting. Tasks such as keeping journals, completing forms, taking notes, making shopping or organizational lists, and the ability to read handwritten manuscript or cursive writing are a few examples of practical application of this skill.

BEFORE YOU BEGIN

Before children begin to write, certain fine motor skills need to be developed. Examples of activities that can be used as warm-up activities are:

- **Simon Says** Play a game of Simon Says using just finger positions.
- **Finger Plays and Songs** Sing songs that use Signed English, American Sign Language or finger spelling.
- **Mazes** Mazes are available in a wide range of difficulty. You can also create mazes that allow children to move their writing instruments from left to right.

Determining Handedness

Keys to determining handedness in a child:

- Which hand does the child eat with? This is the hand that is likely to become the dominant hand.
- Does the child start coloring with one hand and then switch to the other? This may be due to fatigue rather than lack of hand preference.
- Does the child cross midline to pick things up or use the closest hand? Place items directly in front of the child to see if one hand is preferred.
- Does the child do better with one hand or the other?

The Mechanics of Writing

DESK AND CHAIR

- Chair height should allow for the feet to rest flat on the floor.
- Desk height should be two inches above the level of the elbows when the child is sitting.
- The chair should be pulled in allowing for an inch of space between the child's abdomen and the desk.
- Children sit erect with the elbows resting on the desk.
- Children should have models of letters on the desk or at eye level, not above their heads.

PAPER POSITION

- **Right-handed children** should turn the paper so that the lower left-hand corner of the paper points to the abdomen.
- **Left-handed children** should turn the paper so that the lower right-hand corner of the paper points to the abdomen.
- The nondominant hand should anchor the paper near the top so that the paper doesn't slide.
- The paper should be moved up as the child nears the bottom of the paper. Many children won't think of this and may let their arms hang off the desk when they reach the bottom of a page.

The Writing Instrument Grasp

For handwriting to be functional, the writing instrument must be held in a way that allows for fluid dynamic movement.

FUNCTIONAL GRASP PATTERNS

- **Tripod Grasp** With open web space, the writing instrument is held with the tip of the thumb and the index finger and rests against the side of the third finger. The thumb and index finger form a circle.
- **Quadrupod Grasp** With open web space, the writing instrument is held with the tip of the thumb and index finger and rests against the fourth finger. The thumb and index finger form a circle.

INCORRECT GRASP PATTERNS

- **Fisted Grasp** The writing instrument is held in a fisted hand.

- **Pronated Grasp** The writing instrument is held diagonally within the hand with the tips of the thumb and index finger on the writing instrument but with no support from other fingers.
- **Five-Finger Grasp** The writing instrument is held with the tips of all five fingers.

TO CORRECT WRITING INSTRUMENT GRASPS

- Have children play counting games with an eye dropper and water.
- Have children pick up small objects with a tweezer.
- Do counting games with children picking up small coins using just the thumb and index finger.

FLEXED OR HOOKED WRIST

- The writing instrument can be held in a variety of grasps with the wrist flexed or bent. This is typically seen with left-handed writers but is also present in some right-handed writers. To correct wrist position, have children check their writing posture and paper placement.

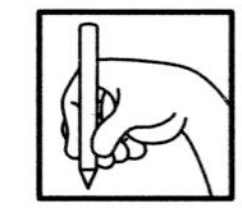

Evaluation Checklist

Functional writing is made up of two elements, legibility and functional speed.

LEGIBILITY

MANUSCRIPT

Formation and Strokes

- ☑ Does the child begin letters at the top?
- ☑ Do circles close?
- ☑ Are the horizontal lines straight?
- ☑ Do circular shapes and extender and descender lines touch?
- ☑ Are the heights of all upper-case letters equal?
- ☑ Are the heights of all lower-case letters equal?
- ☑ Are the lengths of the extenders and descenders the same for all letters?

Directionality

- ☑ Are letters and words formed from left to right?
- ☑ Are letters and words formed from top to bottom?

Spacing

- ☑ Are the spaces between letters equidistant?
- ☑ Are the spaces between words equidistant?
- ☑ Do the letters rest on the line?
- ☑ Are the top, bottom and side margins even?

CURSIVE

Formation and Strokes

- ☑ Do circular shapes close?
- ☑ Are the downstrokes parallel?
- ☑ Do circular shapes and downstroke lines touch?
- ☑ Are the heights of all upper-case letters equal?
- ☑ Are the heights of all lower-case letters equal?
- ☑ Are the lengths of the extenders and descenders the same for all letters?
- ☑ Do the letters which finish at the top join the next letter? (*b, o, v, w*)
- ☑ Do the letters which finish at the bottom join the next letter? (*a, c, d, h, i, k, l, m, n, r, s, t, u, x*)
- ☑ Do letters with descenders join the next letter? (*f, g, j, p, q, y, z*)
- ☑ Do all letters touch the line?
- ☑ Is the vertical slant of all letters consistent?

Directionality

- ☑ Are letters and words formed from left to right?
- ☑ Are letters and words formed from top to bottom?

Spacing

- ☑ Are the spaces between letters equidistant?
- ☑ Are the spaces between words equidistant?
- ☑ Do the letters rest on the line?
- ☑ Are the top, bottom and side margins even?

SPEED

The prettiest handwriting is not functional for classroom work if it takes the child three times longer than the rest of the class to complete work assignments. After the children have been introduced to writing individual letters, begin to add time limitations to the completion of copying or writing assignments. Then check the child's work for legibility.

Handwriting Models—Manuscript

Handwriting Models—Cursive

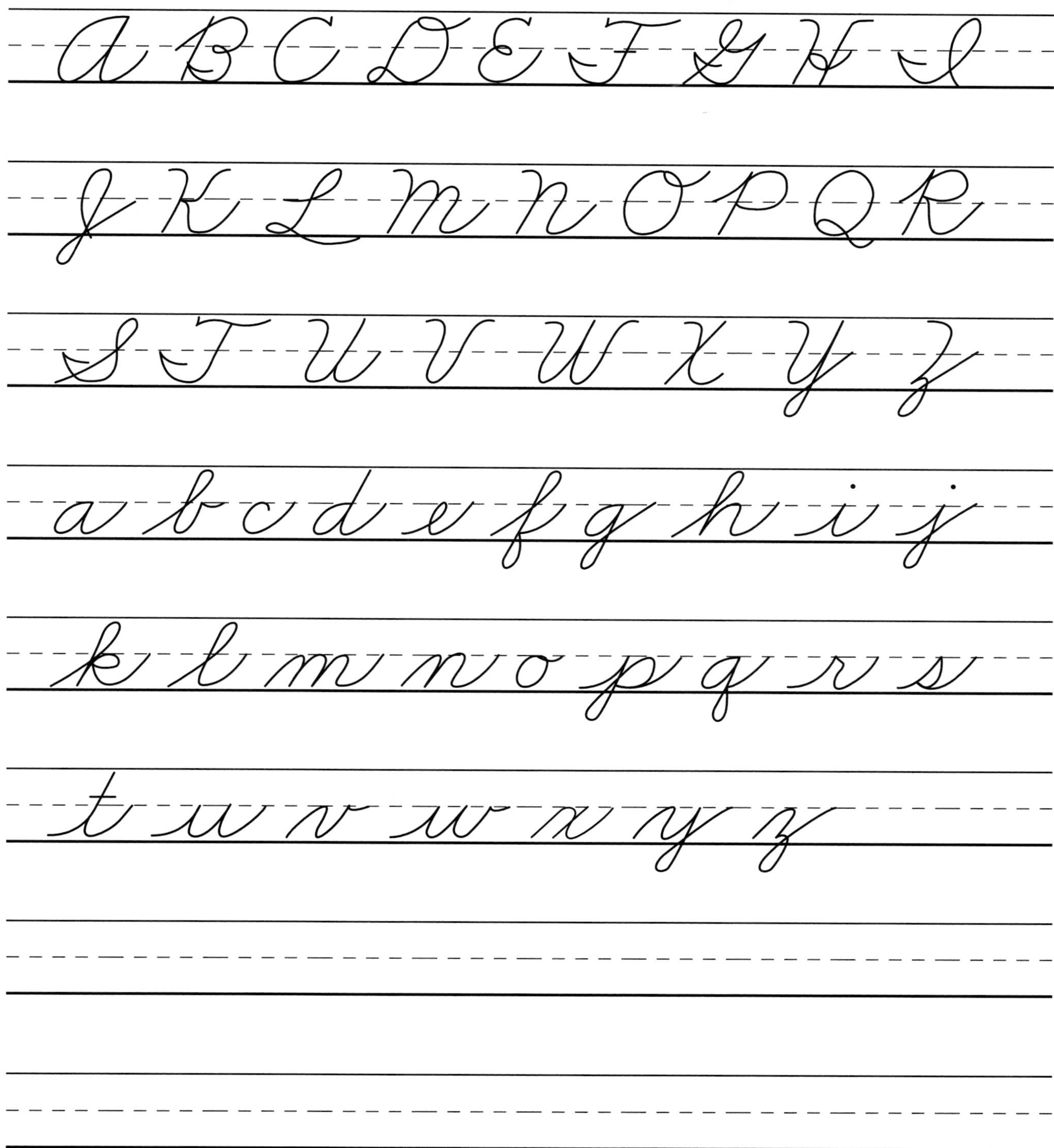

Selection Titles	Honors, Prizes, and Awards
CLOSED, I AM A MYSTERY Book 1, p.10 by ***Myra Cohn Livingston***	**Poet:** ***Myra Cohn Livingston,*** winner of National Council of Teachers of English Award for Excellence in Poetry for Children (1980); ALA Notable (1984) for *Christmas Poems;* ALA Notable (1987) for *Cat Poems;* ALA Notable (1992) for *Poem-Making: Ways to Learn Writing Poetry*
GRANDFATHER'S JOURNEY Book 1, p.14 by ***Allen Say***	**Caldecott Medal, Boston Globe-Horn Book Award, ALA Notable, Booklist Editor's Choice, Blue Ribbon,** ***New York Times*** **Best Illustrated, School Library Journal Best Books of the Year (1994)** **Author/Illustrator:** ***Allen Say,*** winner of Caldecott Honor, ALA Notable (1989), Boston Globe-Horn Book Award (1988) for *The Boy of the Three-Year Nap;* Christopher Award (1985) for *How My Parents Learned to Eat*
OPT: AN ILLUSIONARY TALE Book 1, p.80 by ***Arline and Joseph Baum***	**IRA-CBC Children's Choice (1988), National Science Teachers' Association Outstanding Science Trade Book for Children (1987)**
ABUELITA'S LAP Book 1, p.138 by ***Pat Mora***	**Author:** ***Pat Mora,*** winner of National Association for Chicano Studies Creative Writing Award (1983); New America: Women Artists and Writers of the Southwest Award (1984)
FOG Book 1, p.140 by ***Carl Sandburg***	**Poet:** ***Carl Sandburg,*** winner of Pulitzer Prize for history (1940); ALA Notable (1993) for *More Rootabagas*
CITY GREEN Book 1, p.144 by ***DyAnne DiSalvo***	**Author/Illustrator:** ***DyAnne DiSalvo,*** winner ALA Notable (1996) for *You Want to Vote, Lizzie Stanton?*
THE SUN, THE WIND AND THE RAIN Book 1, p.174 by ***Lisa Westberg Peters*** Illustrated by ***Ted Rand***	**Illustrator:** ***Ted Rand,*** winner of Christopher Award (1991) for *Paul Revere's Ride;* ALA Notable, National Council for Social Studies Notable Children's Book Award (1998) for *Mailing May;* National Council for Social Studies Notable Children's Book Award (1998) for *Storm in the Desert*

Selection Titles	Honors, Prizes, and Awards
DREAM WOLF Book 1, p.206 by ***Paul Goble***	**Author/Illustrator: *Paul Goble,*** winner of ALA Notable, Caldecott Medal (1979) for *The Girl Who Loved Wild Horses;* ALA Notable (1985) for *Buffalo Woman;* ALA Notable (1989), Aesop Accolade (1994) for *Iktomi and the Boulder: A Plains Indian Story;* ALA Notable (1993) for *Love Flute*
WHO AM I? Book 1, p.254 by ***Felice Holman***	**Poet: *Felice Holman,*** winner of Lewis Carroll Shelf Award, ALA Notable (1978) for *Slake's Limbo;* ALA Best Book for Young Adults (1985) for *The Wild Children;* Flora Steiglitz Straus Award (1990) for *Secret City, USA*
THE LITTLE PAINTER OF SABANA GRANDE Book 1, p.292 by ***Patricia Markun Maloney*** Illustrated by ***Robert Casilla***	**National Council for Social Studies Notable Children's Book Award (1994)**
THE PATCHWORK QUILT Book 1, p.320 by ***Valerie Flournoy*** Illustrated by ***Jerry Pinkney***	**Coretta Scott King Award, ALA Notable, Christopher Award, Reading Rainbow Book (1986)** **Illustrator: *Jerry Pinkney,*** winner of Newbery Medal, Boston Globe-Horn Book Honor (1977) for *Roll of Thunder, Hear My Cry;* Coretta Scott King Award (1987) for *Half a Moon and One Whole Star;* ALA Notable (1988) for *Tales of Uncle Remus;* ALA Notable, Caldecott Honor, Coretta Scott King Award (1989) for *Mirandy and Brother Wind;* ALA Notable, Caldecott Honor, Coretta Scott King Honor (1990) for *Talking Eggs;* Golden Kite Award Book (1990) for *Home Place;* ALA Notable (1991) for *Further Tales of Uncle Remus;* ALA Notable (1993) for *Back Home;* ALA Notable, Boston Globe-Horn Book Award, Caldecott Honor (1995) for *John Henry;* ALA Notable, Blue Ribbon (1997) for *Sam and the Tigers;* ALA Notable, Christopher Award, Coretta Scott King Award, Golden Kite Honor Book (1997) for *Minty;* Aesop Prize (1997) for *The Hired Hand;* NCSS Notable Children's Book Award (1998) for *The Hired Hand,* and *Rikki-Tikki-Tavi;* Rip Van Winkle Award (1998); 1998 Hans Christian Andersen nominee
PECOS BILL Book 1, p.352 by ***Angela Shelf Medearis***	**Author: *Angela Shelf Medearis,*** winner of IRA-Teacher's Choice Award Winner Primary Grades (1995) for *Our People*

Selection Titles	Honors, Prizes, and Awards
 IN MY FAMILY Book 2, p.40 by ***Carmen Lomas Garza***	**Texas Bluebonnet Master List (1998–99), Pura Belpré Illustration Honor Book (1998)** **Author/Illustrator: *Carmen Lomas Garza,*** winner of Pura Belpré Illustrator Honor (1996); ALA Notable, Pura Belpré Honor Book for Illustrations (1996) for *Family Pictures*
 CACTUS HOTEL Book 2, p.58 by ***Brenda Z. Guiberson*** Illustrated by ***Megan Lloyd***	**Parents' Choice Award, ALA Notable, NSTA Award for Outstanding Science Trade Book for Children (1991)** **Illustrator: *Megan Lloyd,*** winner of IRA-CBC Children's Choice (1997) for *Too Many Pumpkins;* ALA Notable (1985) for *Surprises*
 BIG BLUE WHALE Book 2, p.86 by ***Nicola Davies*** Illustrated by ***Nick Maland***	**IRA-Teacher's Choice (1998), Blue Ribbon (1997)**
 DO OYSTERS SNEEZE? Book 2, p.122 by ***Jack Prelutsky***	**Poet: *Jack Prelutsky*,** winner of SLJ Best Book (1979) for *Nightmares: Poems to Trouble Your Sleep; New York Times* Notable Book (1980) for *The Headless Horseman Rides Tonight;* ALA Notable (1993) for *Random House Book of Poetry for Young Children;* ALA Notable (1985) for *New Kid on the Block;* ALA Notable (1990) for *Poems of A. Nonny Mouse;* ALA Notable (1991) for *Something Big Has Been Here;* ALA Notable (1993) for *Talking Like the Rain*
 LON PO PO Book 2, p.128 by ***Ed Young***	**Caldecott Medal, Boston Globe-Horn Book Award, ALA Notable (1990), NCSS Notable Children's Book Award (1989)** **Author/Illustrator: *Ed Young,*** winner of Caldecott Honor (1968) for *The Emperor and the Kite;* Boston Globe-Horn Book Honor (1983) for *Yeh Shen;* ALA Notable, Boston Globe-Horn Book Honor (1984) for *The Double Life of Pocohontas;* ALA Notable (1986) for *Foolish Rabbit's Big Mistake;* ALA Notable (1989) for *Cats Are Cats;* ALA Notable (1989) for *China's Long March;* ALA Notable (1991) for *Mice Are Nice;* ALA Notable (1992) for *All Of You Was Singing;* ALA Notable, Boston Globe-Horn Book Award, Caldecott Honor (1993) for *Seven Blind Mice;* ALA Notable (1994) for *Sadako;* ALA Notable (1995) for *Ibis;* Aesop Accolade (1996) for *The Turkey Girl;* National Council for Social Studies Notable Children's Book Award (1998) for *Genesis* and *Voices of the Heart*

Selection Titles	Honors, Prizes, and Awards
ANIMAL FACT/ANIMAL FABLE Book 2, p.160 by ***Seymour Simon*** Illustrated by ***Diane de Groat***	**A Child Study Association Book of the Year (1979), Texas Blue Bonnet Master List (1982-83)** **Author: *Seymour Simon,*** winner of Texas Blue Bonnet Master List (1996–7) *Sharks;* NSTA Outstanding Science Tradebook for Children (1997) *The Heart;* ALA Notable (1985) *Moon,* (1986) *Saturn,* (1987) *Sun,* (1988) *Mars,* (1993) *Our Solar System* and *Snakes*
THE MANY LIVES OF BENJAMIN FRANKLIN Book 2, p.180 by ***Aliki***	**Author: *Aliki (Brandenberg),*** winner of NSTA Outstanding Science Tradebook for Children (1990) and Library of Congress Children's Book Award (1972) for *Fossils Tell of Long Ago*
CLOUDY WITH A CHANCE OF MEATBALLS Book 2, p.208 by ***Judi Barrett*** Illustrated by ***Ron Barrett***	***New York Times* Best Illustrated, IRA-CBC Children's Choice (1978)**
DREAMS Book 2, p.250 by ***Langston Hughes***	**Poet: *Langston Hughes,*** winner of ALA Notable (1995) for *Sweet and Sour Book*
THE BAT BOY AND HIS VIOLIN Book 2, p.254 by ***Gavin Curtis*** Illustrated by ***E. B. Lewis***	**The New York Public Library 100 Best Books for Reading and Sharing (1998); Coretta Scott King Honor for Illustration (1999)**
TWO BAD ANTS Book 2, p.284 by ***Chris Van Allsburg***	**NSTA Outstanding Science Trade Book for Children (1988), IRA-CBC Children's Choice (1989)** **Author/Illustrator: *Chris Van Allsburg,*** winner of ALA Notable, Caldecott Medal (1982), Boston Globe-Horn Book Honor, for *Jumanji;* ALA Notable (1984), for *The Wreck of the Zephyr;* ALA Notable, Boston Globe-Horn Book Honor (1985), for *The Mysteries of Harris Burdick;* ALA Notable, Boston Globe-Horn Book Honor, Caldecott Medal (1986) for *The Polar Express;* ALA Notable (1988) for *The Z Was Zapped,* (1993) for *Widow's Broom,* (1994) for *The Sweetest Fig*
CHARLOTTE'S WEB Book 2, p.332 by ***E. B. White*** Illustrated by ***Garth Williams***	***Newbery Honor (1953)*** ***Illustrator:* Garth Williams**, winner of Newbery Honor (1959) for *The Golden Name Day*; (1959) for *The Family Under the Bridge*; and (1961) for *The Cricket in Times Square*

Trade Books

Additional fiction and nonfiction trade books related to each selection can be shared with children throughout the unit.

Moses Goes to a Concert

Bravo, Minski!
Arthur Yorinks, illustrated by Richard Egielski (Farrar, Straus & Giroux, 1988)

Minski travels throughout Europe inventing wonderful things, but he does not feel happy until he becomes famous for his singing.

The Flute Player / La Flautista
Robyn Eversole, illustrated by G. Brian Karas, (Orchard Books, 1995)

An imaginative fantasy about a young girl who has an unusual way of repairing a flute for its owner.

Gabriella's Song
Candace Fleming, illustrated by Giselle Potter (Atheneum, 1998)

Travel through Venice and see how one girl's song spreads throughout the city and ends up inspiring a famous composer.

The Little Painter of Sabana Grande

Appelemando's Dreams
Patricia Polacco (Putnam Publishing Group, 1997)

A young boy uses his dreams to brighten the village around him and inspire the artist in everyone.

My Great Aunt Arizona
Gloria Houston, illustrated by Susan C. Lamb (HarperCollins, 1992)

A young girl living in the Appalachian Mountain region becomes a teacher who influences generations of children.

Family Farm
Thomas Locker, (Puffin Books, 1994)

The story of a family's struggle to save their farm, set in America's heartland.

Technology

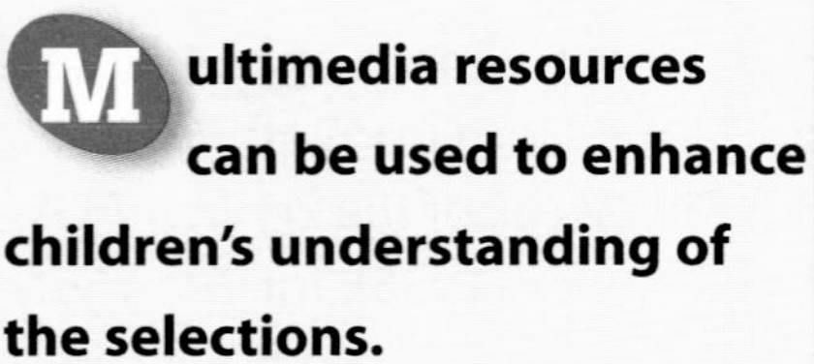

Multimedia resources can be used to enhance children's understanding of the selections.

Moses Goes to a Concert

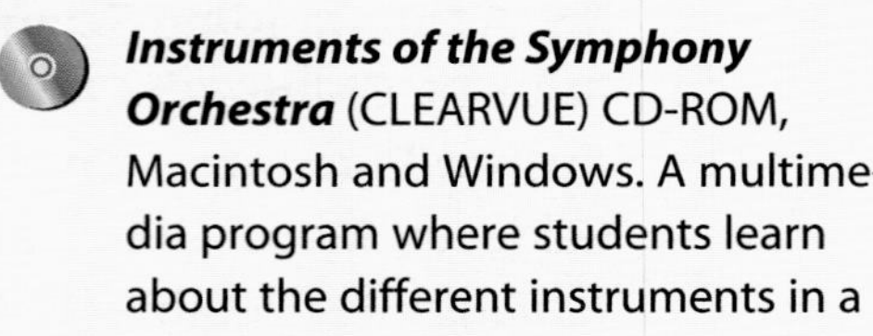

Instruments of the Symphony Orchestra (CLEARVUE) CD-ROM, Macintosh and Windows. A multimedia program where students learn about the different instruments in a symphony orchestra.

The Percussion Show (Musical Encounter Series) (GPN) Video, 30 min. A talented young musician shares his love of percussion and demonstrates his talents by playing several percussion instruments.

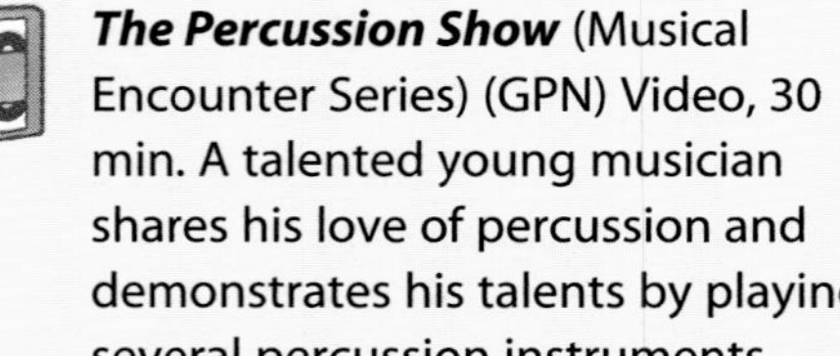

Silent Lotus (Reading Rainbow/GPN) Video, 30 min. A young deaf girl expresses herself and communicates with others through dance.

The Little Painter of Sabana Grande

Appelemando's Dream (Reading Rainbow/GPN) Video, 30 min. A young boy uses his dreams to brighten the world around him.

Diego (SRA/McGraw Hill) Video, 10 min. As an artist, Diego is inspired to paint by things that surround him.

Easy Color Paint (MECC) Computer software Macintosh. A program that encourages the artist in each student.

The Patchwork Quilt

The Lotus Seed
Sherry Garland, illustrated by Tatsuro Kiuchi (Harcourt Brace Jovanovich, 1993)

A young Vietnamese girl keeps a lotus seed with her when she comes to America to help her remember her homeland.

Your Dad Was Just Like You
Dolores Johnson (Macmillan, 1993)

While visiting his grandfather, Peter hears a story about his father's boyhood that brings him new insight.

Mrs. Katz and Tush
Patricia Polacco (Dell, 1994)

Mrs. Katz shares her Jewish heritage with her African American friend as their friendship grows.

The Patchwork Quilt (Reading Rainbow/GPN) Video, 30 min. A narration of the story and a visit to the Boston Children's Museum.

The Patchwork Quilt (Macmillan/McGraw-Hill) CD-ROM Macintosh. An interactive program based on the literature.

Annie and the Old One (Phoenix/BFA) Video, 15 min. A little girl and her grandmother weave a rug and share stories and lessons on life.

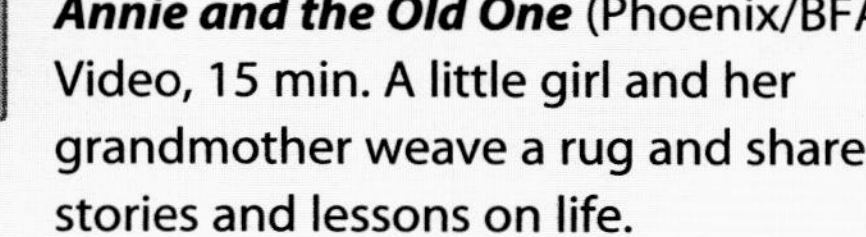

Pecos Bill: A Tall Tale

Reader's Theatre for Children
Mildred Knight Laughlin and Kathy Howard Latrobe (Teacher Ideas Press, 1990)

Well-known children's stories are presented in play form for reader's theatre.

The Bunyans
Audrey Wood, illustrated by David Shannon (Scholastic, 1996)

The classic folk hero, Paul Bunyan, is now with his family, larger than life, and causing many astounding events to occur.

McBroom and the Great Race
Sid Fleischman, illustrated by Walter Lorraine (Little, Brown, 1980)

McBroom has to race against Crafty Heck Jones in order to save his one-acre farm.

The Art of Storytelling: Tall Tales (SVE) Video, 29 min. Storytellers tell tall tales and demonstrate the art of storytelling.

Pecos Bill (AIMS Multimedia) Video, 30 min. Narrated by Robin Williams, this is the story of Pecos Bill. (Grammy, CINE Golden Eagle, Parents Choice, ALA Awards)

Storybook Weaver Deluxe (MECC) CD-ROM, Macintosh and Windows. A bilingual multimedia program where students use graphics, sound, music, and the folklore of many cultures to create their own stories. (Teachers Choice Winner)

TIME FOR KIDS: A Very Cool Place to Visit

Nessa's Fish
Nancy Luenn, illustrated by Neil Waldman (Atheneum, 1990)

Nessa is very brave as she watches over her sick grandmother on the tundra and protects her from wild animals.

Arctic Memories
Normee Ekoomiak (Owlet, 1992)

The author recalls many memories of his childhood in Arctic Quebec.

Marven of the Great North Woods
Kathryn Lasky, illustrated by Kevin Hawkes (Harcourt Brace Jovanovich, 1997)

When Marven is sent to a Minnesota logging camp to escape the influenza epidemic of 1918, his experience is very enlightening.

Arctic Borderlands in Winter (Coronet/MTI) Video or videodisc, 12 min. An introductory look at the people, plants, and animals who live in the Arctic regions.

Hello and Goodbye Mr. Winter (Pied Piper/AIMS Multimedia) Video, 9 min. Animation is used to introduce students to how animals and people prepare for winter.

Polar Regions: Hunters and Herders (BFA Educational Media) Video, 17 min. An exploration of the culture, customs, and survival skills of the Eskimos and Laplanders.

Publishers Directory

Abdo & Daughters
4940 Viking Drive, Suite 622
Edina, MN 55435
(800) 458-8399 • www.abdopub.com

Aladdin Paperbacks
(Imprint of Simon & Schuster Children's Publishing)

Atheneum
(Imprint of Simon & Schuster Children's Publishing)

Bantam Doubleday Dell Books for Young Readers
(Imprint of Random House)

Blackbirch Press
1 Bradley Road, Suite 205
Woodbridge, CT 06525
(203) 387-7525 • (800) 831-9183

Blue Sky Press
(Imprint of Scholastic)

Boyds Mills Press
815 Church Street
Honesdale, PA 18431
(570) 253-1164 • Fax (570) 251-0179 • (800) 949-7777

Bradbury Press
(Imprint of Simon & Schuster Children's Publishing)

BridgeWater Books
(Distributed by Penguin Putnam)

Candlewick Press
2067 Masssachusetts Avenue
Cambridge, MA 02140
(617) 661-3330 • Fax (617) 661-0565

Carolrhoda Books
(Division of Lerner Publications Co.)

Charles Scribners's Sons
(Imprint of Simon & Schuster Children's Publishing)

Children's Press (Division of Grolier, Inc.)
P.O. Box 1796
Danbury, CT 06813-1333
(800) 621-1115 • www.grolier.com

Child's World
P.O. Box 326
Chanhassen, MN 55317-0326
(612) 906-3939 • (800) 599-READ • www.childsworld.com

Chronicle Books
85 Second Street, Sixth Floor
San Francisco, CA 94105
(415) 537-3730 • (415) 537-4460 • (800) 722-6657 • www.chroniclebooks.com

Clarion Books
(Imprint of Houghton Mifflin, Inc.)
215 Park Avenue South
New York, NY 10003
(212) 420-5800 • (800) 726-0600 • www.hmco.com/trade/childrens/shelves.html

Crowell (Imprint of HarperCollins)

Crown Publishing Group
(Imprint of Random House)

Dial Books
(Imprint of Penguin Putnam Inc.)

Dorling Kindersley (DK Publishing)
95 Madison Avenue
New York, NY 10016
(212) 213-4800 • Fax (800) 774-6733 • (888) 342-5357 • www.dk.com

Doubleday (Imprint of Random House)

E. P. Dutton Children's Books
(Imprint of Penguin Putnam Inc.)

Farrar Straus & Giroux
19 Union Square West
New York, NY 10003
(212) 741-6900 • Fax (212) 633-2427 • (888) 330-8477

Four Winds Press
(Imprint of Macmillan, see Simon & Schuster Children's Publishing)

Greenwillow Books
(Imprint of William Morrow & Co, Inc.)

Grosset & Dunlap
(Imprint of Penguin Putnam, Inc.)

Harcourt Brace & Co.
525 "B" Street
San Diego, CA 92101
(619) 231-6616 • (800) 543-1918 • www.harcourtbooks.com

Harper & Row (Imprint of HarperCollins)

HarperCollins Children's Books
10 East 53rd Street
New York, NY 10022
(212) 207-7000 • Fax (212) 202-7044 • (800) 242-7737 • www.harperchildrens.com

Henry Holt and Company
115 West 18th Street
New York, NY 10011
(212) 886-9200 • (212) 633-0748 • (888) 330-8477 • www.henryholt.com/byr/

Holiday House
425 Madison Avenue
New York, NY 10017
(212) 688-0085 • Fax (212) 421-6134

Houghton Mifflin
222 Berkeley Street
Boston, MA 02116
(617) 351-5000 • Fax (617) 351-1125 • (800) 225-3362 • www.hmco.com/trade

Hyperion Books
(Imprint of Buena Vista Publishing Co.)
114 Fifth Avenue
New York, NY 10011
(212) 633-4400 • (800) 759-0190 • www.disney.com

Ideals Children's Books
(Imprint of Hambleton-Hill Publishing, Inc.)
1501 County Hospital Road
Nashville, TN 37218
(615) 254-2480 • (800) 336-6438

Joy Street Books
(Imprint of Little, Brown & Co.)

Just Us Books
356 Glenwood Avenue
E. Orange, NJ 07017
(973) 672-0304 • Fax (973) 677-7570

Alfred A. Knopf
(Imprint of Random House)

Lee & Low Books
95 Madison Avenue
New York, NY 10016
(212) 779-4400 • Fax (212) 683-1894

Lerner Publications Co.
241 First Avenue North
Minneapolis, MN 55401
(612) 332-3344 • Fax (612) 332-7615 • (800) 328-4929 • www.lernerbooks.com

Little, Brown & Co.
3 Center Plaza
Boston, MA 02108
(617) 227-0730 • Fax (617) 263-2864 • (800) 343-9204 • www.littlebrown.com

Lothrop Lee & Shepard
(Imprint of William Morrow & Co.)

Macmillan
(Imprint of Simon & Schuster Children's Publishing)

Marshall Cavendish
99 White Plains Road
Tarrytown, NY 10591
(914) 332-8888 • Fax (914) 332-1082 • (800) 821-9881 • www.marshallcavendish.com

William Morrow & Co.
1350 Avenue of the Americas
New York, NY 10019
(212) 261-6500 • Fax (212) 261-6619 • (800) 843-9389 • www.williammorrow.com

Morrow Junior Books
(Imprint of William Morrow & Co.)

Mulberry Books
(Imprint of William Morrow & Co.)

National Geographic Society
1145 17th Street, NW
Washington, DC 20036
(202) 828-5667 • (800) 368-2728 • www.nationalgeographic.com

Northland Publishing
(Division of Justin Industries)
P.O. Box 62
Flagstaff, AZ 86002
(520) 774-5251 • Fax (800) 257-9082 • (800) 346-3257 • www.northlandpub.com

North-South Books
1123 Broadway, Suite 800
New York, NY 10010
(212) 463-9736 • Fax (212) 633-1004 • (800) 722-6657 • www.northsouth.com

Orchard Books (A Grolier Company)
95 Madison Avenue
New York, NY 10016
(212) 951-2600 • Fax (212) 213-6435 • (800) 621-1115 • www.grolier.com

Owlet (Imprint of Henry Holt & Co.)

Willa Perlman Books
(Imprint of Simon & Schuster Children's Publishing)

Philomel Books
(Imprint of Putnam Penguin, Inc.)

Puffin Books
(Imprint of Penguin Putnam, Inc.)

G.P. Putnam's Sons Publishing
(Imprint of Penguin Putnam, Inc.)

Penguin Putnam, Inc.
345 Hudson Street
New York, NY 10014
(212) 366-2000 • Fax (212) 366-2666 • (800) 631-8571 • www.penguinputnam.com

Random House
201 East 50th Street
New York, NY 10022
(212) 751-2600 • Fax (212) 572-2593 • (800) 726-0600 • www.randomhouse/kids

Rourke Corporation
P.O. Box 3328
Vero Beach, FL 32964
(561) 234-6001 • (800) 394-7055 • www.rourkepublishing.com

Scholastic
555 Broadway
New York, NY 10012
(212) 343-6100 • Fax (212) 343-6930 • (800) SCHOLASTIC • www.scholastic.com

Sierra Junior Club
85 Second Street, Second Floor
San Francisco, CA 94105-3441
(415) 977-5500 • Fax (415) 977-5799 • (800) 935-1056 • www.sierraclub.org

Simon & Schuster Children's Books
1230 Avenue of the Americas
New York, NY 10020
(212) 698-7200 • (800) 223-2336 • www.simonsays.com/kidzone

Smith & Kraus
4 Lower Mill Road
N. Stratford, NH 03590
(603) 643-6431 • Fax (603) 643-1831 • (800) 895-4331 • www.smithkraus.com

Teacher Ideas Press
(Division of Libraries Unlimited)
P.O. Box 6633
Englewood, CO 80155-6633
(303) 770-1220 • Fax (303) 220-8843 • (800) 237-6124 • www.lu.com

Ticknor & Fields
(Imprint of Houghton Mifflin, Inc.)

Usborne (Imprint of EDC Publishing)
10302 E. 55th Place, Suite B
Tulsa, OK 74146-6515
(918) 622-4522 • (800) 475-4522 • www.edcpub.com

Viking Children's Books
(Imprint of Penguin Putnam Inc.)

Watts Publishing
(Imprint of Grolier Publishing; see Children's Press)

Walker & Co.
435 Hudson Street
New York, NY 10014
(212) 727-8300 • (212) 727-0984 • (800) AT-WALKER

Whispering Coyote Press
300 Crescent Court, Suite 860
Dallas, TX 75201
(800) 929-6104 • Fax (214) 319-7298

Albert Whitman
6340 Oakton Street
Morton Grove, IL 60053-2723
(847) 581-0033 • Fax (847) 581-0039 • (800) 255-7675 • www.awhitmanco.com

Workman Publishing Co., Inc.
708 Broadway
New York, NY 10003
(212) 254-5900 • Fax (800) 521-1832 • (800) 722-7202 • www.workman.com

Multimedia Resources

AGC/United Learning
6633 West Howard Street
Niles, IL 60714-3389
(800) 424-0362 • www.unitedlearning.com

AIMS Multimedia
9710 DeSoto Avenue
Chatsworth, CA 91311-4409
(800) 367-2467 •
www.AIMS-multimedia.com

BFA Educational Media
(see Phoenix Learning Group)

Broderbund
(Parsons Technology;
also see The Learning Company)
500 Redwood Blvd
Novato, CA 94997
(800) 521-6263 • Fax (800) 474-8840 •
www.broderbund.com

Carousel Film and Video
260 Fifth Avenue, Suite 705
New York, NY 10001
(212) 683-1660 • e-mail:
carousel@pipeline.com

Cloud 9 Interactive
(888) 662-5683 • www.cloud9int.com

Computer Plus (see ESI)

Coronet/MTI
(see Phoenix Learning Group)

Davidson (see Knowledge Adventure)

Direct Cinema, Ltd.
P.O. Box 10003
Santa Monica, CA 90410-1003
(800) 525-0000

Disney Interactive
(800) 900-9234 •
www.disneyinteractive.com

DK Multimedia (Dorling Kindersley)
95 Madison Avenue
New York, NY 10016
(212) 213-4800 • Fax: (800) 774-6733 •
(888) 342-5357 • www.dk.com

Edmark Corp.
P.O. Box 97021
Redmond, CA 98073-9721
(800) 362-2890 • www.edmark.com

Encyclopaedia Britannica Educational Corp.
310 South Michigan Avenue
Chicago, IL 60604
(800) 554-9862 • www.eb.com

ESI/Educational Software
4213 S. 94th Street
Omaha, NE 68127
(800) 955-5570 • www.edsoft.com

GPN/Reading Rainbow
University of Nebraska-Lincoln
P.O. Box 80669
Lincoln, NE 68501-0669
(800) 228-4630 • www.gpn.unl.edu

Hasbro Interactive
(800) 683-5847 • www.hasbro.com

Humongous
13110 NE 177th Pl., Suite B101, Box 180
Woodenville, WA 98072
(800) 499-8386 • www.humongous.com

IBM Corp.
1133 Westchester Ave.
White Plains, NY 10604
(770) 863-1234 • Fax (770) 863-3030 •
(888) 411-1932 •
www.pc.ibm.com/multimedia/crayola

ICE, Inc.
(Distributed by Arch Publishing)
12B W. Main St.
Elmsford, NY 10523
(914) 347-2464 • (800) 843-9497 •
www.educorp.com

Knowledge Adventure
19840 Pioneer Avenue
Torrence, CA 90503
(800) 542-4240 • (800) 545-7677 •
www.knowledgeadventure.com

The Learning Company
6160 Summit Drive North
Minneapolis, MN 55430
(800) 685-6322 • www.learningco.com

Listening Library
One Park Avenue
Greenwich, CT 06870-1727
(800) 243-4504 • www.listeninglib.com

Macmillan/McGraw-Hill
(see SRA/McGraw-Hill)

Maxis
2121 N. California Blvd
Walnut Creek, CA 94596-3572
(925) 933-5630 • Fax (925) 927-3736 •
(800) 245-4525 • www.maxis.com

MECC
(see the Learning Company)

Microsoft
One Microsoft Way
Redmond, WA 98052-6399
(800) 426-9400 • www.microsoft.com/kids

National Geographic Society Educational Services
P.O. Box 10597
Des Moines, IA 50340-0597
(800) 368-2728 •
www.nationalgeographic.com

National School Products
101 East Broadway
Maryville, TN 37804
(800) 251-9124 • www.ierc.com

PBS Video
1320 Braddock Place
Alexandria, VA 22314
(800) 344-3337 • www.pbs.org

Phoenix Films
(see Phoenix Learning Group)

The Phoenix Learning Group
2348 Chaffee Drive
St. Louis, MO 63146
(800) 221-1274 • e-mail:
phoenixfilms@worldnet.att.net

Pied Piper (see AIMS Multimedia)

Scholastic New Media
555 Broadway
New York, NY 10003
(800) 724-6527 • www.scholastic.com

Simon & Schuster Interactive
(see Knowledge Adventure)

SRA/McGraw-Hill
220 Daniel Dale Road
De Soto, TX 75115
(800) 843-8855 • www.sra4kids.com

SVE/Churchill Media
6677 North Northwest Highway
Chicago, IL 60631
(800) 829-1900 •www.svemedia.com

Tom Snyder Productions (also see ESI)
80 Coolidge Hill Rd.
Watertown, MA 02472
(800) 342-0236 • www.teachtsp.com

Troll Associates
100 Corporate Drive
Mahwah, NJ 07430
(800) 929-8765 • Fax (800) 979-8765 •
www.troll.com

Voyager (see ESI)

Weston Woods
12 Oakwood Avenue
Norwalk, CT 06850
(800) 243-5020 • Fax (203) 845-0498

Zenger Media
10200 Jefferson Blvd., Room 94,
P.O. Box 802
Culver City, CA 90232-0802
(800) 421-4246 • (800) 944-5432 •
www.Zengermedia.com

Word List

BOOK 1, UNIT 1

	Vocabulary	Spelling			
GRANDFATHER'S JOURNEY		Words with short vowels			
	astonished	bag	ever	mix	thing
	enormous	**black**	hid	**much**	van
	journey	body	**kept**	**rocks**	window
	scattered	buzz	leg	rub	
	surrounded				
	towering				
PHOEBE AND THE SPELLING BEE		Words with long *a* and long *e*			
	continue	awake	creek	**paper**	team
	correct	**breeze**	grade	plane	thief
	embarrass	carry	marry	**raise**	weigh
	groaning	**cream**	neighbor	sail	
	legend				
	unusual				
OPT		Words with long *i* and long *o*			
	gift	ago	lie	**own**	**tie**
	guard	bicycle	life	**rode**	toast
	royal	**find**	might	spoke	wipe
	within	flight	most	thrown	
	length				
	straighten				
MAX MALONE		/ū/ and /ü/			
	ceiling	broom	**excuse**	huge	produce
	cents	crew	fruit	juice	soup
	eager	dew	**goose**	music	truth
	including	drew	group	pool	
	scene				
	section				
TIME FOR KIDS: CHAMPIONS OF THE WORLD		Words from Physical Education			
	celebrated	action	crowd	mound	**record**
	cork	**baseball**	foul	outfield	**season**
	fans	bases	glove	**parade**	strike
	pitcher	batter	mitt	**player**	
	score				
	wrap				

Boldfaced words appear in the selection.

BOOK 1, UNIT 2

	Vocabulary	Spelling
City Green	**area** **excitement** **halfway** **heap** **schedule** **stems**	**Two-syllable words with accented first syllable** battle, bottle, candle, **carrots**, even, fellow, fifty, flavor, floppy, frozen, lazy, **lettuce**, maple, **open**, silent
The Sun, the Wind and the Rain	**canyons** **flowed** **grains** **handful** **peaks** **traded**	**Words with initial *bl, br, cr, fl, gr, pl*** blind, **blink**, block, brake, brisk, **broad**, crazy, **crumble**, flame, flash, flood, grab, grand, plate, plenty
Dream Wolf	**buffalo** **darkness** **echoes** **herds** **ripe** **shelter**	**Words with initial *sp, str, scr, spr, sk, sl*** scream, screen, scrub, skate, skin, sleeve, **slept**, slice, spend, spider, spring, sprinkle, **stream**, string, strong
Spiders at Work	**capture** **liquid** **ruin** **serious** **skills** **struggles**	**Plurals—add *s, es,* and change *y* to *i* add *es*** addresses, **blankets**, branches, bunches, companies, daisies, enemies, **flies**, inches, **jungles**, libraries, **mountains**, pairs, pockets, **states**
Time for Kids: Web Wonders	**crops** **earthquake** **hatch** **respect** **soldiers** **woven**	**Words from Science** bait, beetle, breathe, cell, fang, **fiber**, prey, science, **silk**, **sticky**, **strands**, taste, **thread**, **weave**, web

Boldfaced words appear in the selection.

BOOK 1, UNIT 3

	Vocabulary	Spelling			
Moses Goes to a Concert		Words with final *nk, mp, ng, nd, nt*			
	concert **conductor** **ill** **instrument** **musician** **orchestra**	behind belong faint friend	husband ink paint parent	stamp student swing **thank**	**thump** trunk young
The Little Painter of Sabana Grande		Words with *tt, ll, bb, dd, pp, ss*			
	blossoms **dawn** **faded** **imaginary** **miserable** **shallow**	butter **grass** happen hobby	ladder lesson **little** **middle**	possible ribbon rubber silly	**small** supper **unhappy**
The Patchwork Quilt		/ou/ spelled *ow, ou*; /oi/ spelled *oi, oy*			
	anxious **attic** **costume** **examined** **gazed** **pattern**	allow choice **cloudy** clown	count **enjoy** foil **found**	loyal noisy poison power	shout **spoil** voyage
Pecos Bill		adding *ed* and *ing*			
	combine **invented** **located** **prairie** **stumbled** **wilderness**	beginning blamed buried divided	escaping fried hurried moving	robbed **saving** shaking spied	splitting stirred supplied
Time for Kids: A Very Cool Place to Visit		Words from Science			
	beauty **creeps** **furniture** **palace** **pure** **visitors**	arctic chill degree dense	**freezes** frost heat **ice**	igloo matter **melt** **northern**	snowflake solid thaw

Boldfaced words appear in the selection.

BOOK 2, UNIT 1

	Vocabulary	Spelling			
The Terrible Eek		**Words with initial *ch, sh, th, wh***			
	completely **humans** **meal** **motion** **reply** **weight**	chain cheese cherry **chicken**	shadow shelf shock **shone**	thick **thirsty** thirty thousand	whether whip whisker
In My Family		**Words with final *ch, sh, tch, th***			
	comforting **designed** **dozens** **encouraging** **members** **relatives**	approach coach crash fetch	finish fourth itch peach	sketch splash **squash** stitch	teach tooth **underneath**
Cactus Hotel		**/ô/ spelled *a, o, au, ough;* /ù/ spelled *oo, u, o***			
	discovered **insects** **remains** **ribs** **tough** **treat**	**across** **always** bought cause	cookie footprint fought often	**pulls** saucer song sugar	**tall** wolf woman
Big Blue Whale		**Compound Words**			
	adult **calm** **feast** **mammal** **swallow** **vast**	afternoon anything barnyard basketball	cardboard everything **fingernails** newspaper	notebook outside playground sidewalk	someone **sometimes** without
Time for Kids: J.J.'s Big Day		**Words from Math**			
	clams **compared** **experts** **gain** **powdered** **switched**	data gallon gram **hour**	mass measure meter month	ounce pint **pounds** **problems**	scale second week

Boldfaced words appear in the selection.

BOOK 2, UNIT 2

	Vocabulary	Spelling			
Lon Po Po		**Soft *c* /s/ spelled *ss, ce, c, s* Soft *g* /j/ spelled *j, g, dge, ge***			
	claws **delighted** **disguised** **furious** **paced** **route**	circle city giant gym	**jewels** jolly judge ledge	message once rage **sisters**	stage **sunset** twice
Animal Fact/ Animal Fable		**/är/ spelled *ar;* /ûr/ spelled *ur, or, ir, er, ear***			
	attack **bother** **expects** **label** **rapidly** **temperature**	alarm curtain firm learn	market merchant **person** search	**sharp** skirt startle **turtle**	**words** world worth
The Many Lives of Benjamin Franklin		**/âr/ spelled *are, air;* /ôr/ spelled *or, ore;* /îr/ spelled *ear, eer***			
	advice **curious** **discuss** **experiment** **hero** **scientific**	beard dare deer engineer	fair **force** glare hair	**important** **near** sore stare	store storm **weary**
Cloudy with a Chance of Meatballs		**Contractions**			
	avoid **brief** **frequently** **gradual** **periods** **report**	**didn't** doesn't don't he's	I'll I'm it's she'll	shouldn't they've we're we've	won't you'll you're
Time for Kids: Pure Power		**Words from Social Studies**			
	energy **entire** **future** **model** **pollution** **produce**	climate **coal** **fossil** **fuels**	**gas** globe lumber **millions**	natural **planet** recycle save	**solar** **sunlight** windmills

Boldfaced words appear in the selection.

BOOK 2, UNIT 3

	Vocabulary	Spelling			
The Bat Boy and His Violin		*/ər/ er, ar, or; /əl/ le, el, al*			
	accept **equipment** **invisible** **mistake** **perform** **talented**	barrel cellar **center** collar	**dinner** favor **fiddle** **handle**	**metal** motor sailor signal	**stumble** **summer** travel
Two Bad Ants		**Silent letters *k, w, l, b, gh***			
	bitter **crystal** **gripped** **kingdom** **vanished** **whirling**	calf comb crumb **daylight**	folk **frightening** **height** knife	knock **known** limb palm	whole wrinkle wrong
Do Animals Think?		**Homophones**			
	brain **communicate** **crafty** **social** **solve** **subject**	**ant** ate aunt **do**	due eight meat meet	**one** sew **so** **to**	**too** two won
"Wilbur's Boast" from Charlotte's Web		**Suffixes *-ly, -ful, -able, -tion, -sion***			
	boasting **considering** **conversation** **hesitated** **interrupted** **seized**	**busily** collection **comfort-able** direction	discussion expression invention possession	powerful **quietly** **sadly** unbelievable	useful valuable **wonderful**
Time for Kids: Koala Catchers		**Words from Social Studies**			
	crate **loops** **rescuers** **snug** **starve** **strip**	bay coast continent country	**forests** gulf **harmed** **island**	mainland **migrate** outdoors port	**safe** valley **wildlife**

Boldfaced words appear in the selection.

Listening, Speaking, Viewing, Representing

☑ Tested Skill

Tinted panels show skills, strategies, and other teaching opportunities

	K	1	2	3	4	5	6
LISTENING							
Learn the vocabulary of school (numbers, shapes, colors, directions, and categories)							
Identify the musical elements of literary language, such as rhymes, repeated sounds, onomatopoeia							
Determine purposes for listening (get information, solve problems, enjoy and appreciate)							
Listen critically and responsively							
Ask and answer relevant questions							
Listen critically to interpret and evaluate							
Listen responsively to stories and other texts read aloud, including selections from classic and contemporary works							
Connect and compare own experiences, ideas, and traditions with those of others							
Apply comprehension strategies in listening activities							
Understand the major ideas and supporting evidence in spoken messages							
Participate in listening activities related to reading and writing (such as discussions, group activities, conferences)							
Listen to learn by taking notes, organizing, and summarizing spoken ideas							
SPEAKING							
Learn the vocabulary of school (numbers, shapes, colors, directions, and categories)							
Use appropriate language and vocabulary learned to describe ideas, feelings, and experiences							
Ask and answer relevant questions							
Communicate effectively in everyday situations (such as discussions, group activities, conferences)							
Demonstrate speaking skills (audience, purpose, occasion, volume, pitch, tone, rate, fluency)							
Clarify and support spoken messages and ideas with objects, charts, evidence, elaboration, examples							
Use verbal and nonverbal communication in effective ways when, for example, making announcements, giving directions, or making introductions							
Retell a spoken message by summarizing or clarifying							
Connect and compare own experiences, ideas, and traditions with those of others							
Determine purposes for speaking (inform, entertain, give directions, persuade, express personal feelings and opinions)							
Demonstrate skills of reporting and providing information							
Demonstrate skills of interviewing, requesting and providing information							
Apply composition strategies in speaking activities							
Monitor own understanding of spoken message and seek clarification as needed							
VIEWING							
Demonstrate viewing skills (focus attention, organize information)							
Respond to audiovisual media in a variety of ways							
Participate in viewing activities related to reading and writing							
Apply comprehension strategies in viewing activities							
Recognize artists' craft and techniques for conveying meaning							
Interpret information from various formats such as maps, charts, graphics, video segments, technology							
Evaluate purposes of various media (information, appreciation, entertainment, directions, persuasion)							
Use media to compare ideas and points of view							
REPRESENTING							
Select, organize, or produce visuals to complement or extend meanings							
Produce communication using appropriate media to develop a class paper, multimedia or video reports							
Show how language, medium, and presentation contribute to the message							

Reading: Alphabetic Principle, Sounds/Symbols

✓ Tested Skill

Tinted panels show skills, strategies, and other teaching opportunities

PRINT AWARENESS	K	1	2	3	4	5	6
Know the order of the alphabet							
Recognize that print represents spoken language and conveys meaning							
Understand directionality (tracking print from left to right; return sweep)							
Understand that written words are separated by spaces							
Know the difference between individual letters and printed words							
Understand that spoken words are represented in written language by specific sequence of letters							
Recognize that there are correct spellings for words							
Know the difference between capital and lowercase letters							
Recognize how readers use capitalization and punctuation to comprehend							
Recognize the distinguishing features of a paragraph							
Recognize that parts of a book (such as cover/title page and table of contents) offer information							
PHONOLOGICAL AWARENESS							
Identify letters, words, sentences							
Divide spoken sentence into individual words							
Produce rhyming words and distinguish rhyming words from nonrhyming words							
Identify, segment, and combine syllables within spoken words							
Identify and isolate the initial and final sound of a spoken word							
Add, delete, or change sounds to change words (such as *cow* to *how*, *pan* to *fan*)							
Blend sounds to make spoken words							
Segment one-syllable spoken words into individual phonemes							
PHONICS AND DECODING							
Alphabetic principle: Letter/sound correspondence	✓	✓	✓				
Blending CVC words	✓	✓					
Segmenting CVC words	✓						
Blending CVC, CVCe, CCVC, CVCC, CVVC words	✓	✓	✓				
Segmenting CVC, CVCe, CCVC, CVCC, CVVC words	✓	✓	✓				
Initial and final consonants: /n/n, /d/d, /s/s, /m/m, /t/t, /k/c, /f/f, /r/r, /p/p, /l/l, /k/k, /g/g, /b/b, /h/h, /w/w, /v/v, /ks/x, /kw/qu, /j/j, /y/y, /z/z	✓	✓					
Initial and medial short vowels: *a, i, u, o, e*	✓	✓	✓				
Long vowels: *a-e, i-e, o-e, u-e* (vowel-consonant-e)		✓	✓				
Long vowels, including *ay, ai; e, ee, ie, ea; o, oa, oe, ow; i, y, igh*		✓	✓				
Consonant Digraphs: *sh, th, ch, wh*		✓					
Consonant Blends: continuant/continuant, including *sl, sm, sn, fl, fr, ll, ss, ff*		✓					
Consonant Blends: continuant/stop, including *st, sk, sp, ng, nt, nd, mp, ft*		✓					
Consonant Blends: stop/continuant, including *tr, pr, pl, cr, tw*		✓					
Variant vowels: including /ü/*oo*; /ô/*a, aw, au*; /ü/*ue, ew*		✓	✓				
Diphthongs, including /ou/*ou, ow*; /oi/*oi, oy*		✓	✓				
r-controlled vowels, including /âr/*are*; /ôr/*or, ore*; /îr/*ear*			✓				
Soft *c* and soft *g*			✓				
nk		✓	✓				
Consonant Digraphs: *ck*	✓	✓					
Consonant Digraphs: *ph, tch, ch*			✓				
Short *e*: *ea*			✓				
Long *e*: *y, ey*			✓				
/ü/*oo*		✓	✓				
/är/*ar*; /ûr/*ir, ur, er*		✓	✓				
Silent letters: including *l, b, k, w, g, h, gh*			✓				
Schwa: /ər/*er*; /ən/*en*; /əl/*le*;			✓				
Reading/identifying multisyllabic words		✓	✓				

✓ Tested Skill

Tinted panels show skills, strategies, and other teaching opportunities

Reading: Vocabulary/Word Identification

WORD STRUCTURE	K	1	2	3	4	5	6
Common spelling patterns							
Syllable patterns							
Plurals		✓					
Possessives		✓					
Contractions		✓					
Root, or base, words and inflectional endings (*-s, -es, -ed, -ing*)		✓	✓	✓		✓	
Compound words			✓	✓	✓	✓	✓
Prefixes and suffixes (such as *un-, re-, dis-, non-; -ly, -y, -ful, -able, -tion*)				✓	✓	✓	✓
Root words and derivational endings				✓	✓	✓	✓
WORD MEANING							
Develop vocabulary through concrete experiences							
Develop vocabulary through selections read aloud							
Develop vocabulary through reading							
Cueing systems: syntactic, semantic, phonetic							
Context clues, including semantic clues (word meaning), syntactical clues (word order), and phonetic clues	✓	✓	✓	✓	✓	✓	✓
High-frequency words (such as *the, a, an, and, said, was, where, is*)							
Identify words that name persons, places, things, and actions							
Automatic reading of regular and irregular words							
Use resources and references (dictionary, glossary, thesaurus, synonym finder, technology and software, and context)							
Synonyms and antonyms			✓	✓	✓	✓	✓
Multiple-meaning words			✓	✓	✓	✓	✓
Figurative language			✓	✓	✓	✓	✓
Decode derivatives (root words, such as *like, pay, happy* with affixes, such as *dis-, pre-, un-*)							
Systematic study of words across content areas and in current events							
Locate meanings, pronunciations, and derivations (including dictionaries, glossaries, and other sources)							
Denotation and connotation							✓
Word origins as aid to understanding historical influences on English word meanings							
Homophones, homographs							
Analogies							✓
Idioms							

Reading: Comprehension

PREREADING STRATEGIES	K	1	2	3	4	5	6
Preview and predict							
Use prior knowledge							
Establish and adjust purposes for reading							
Build background							
MONITORING STRATEGIES							
Adjust reading rate							
Reread, search for clues, ask questions, ask for help							
Visualize							
Read a portion aloud, use reference aids							
Use decoding and vocabulary strategies							
Paraphrase							
Create story maps, diagrams, charts, story props to help comprehend, analyze, synthesize and evaluate texts							

(continued on next page)

✓ Tested Skill

Tinted panels show skills, strategies, and other teaching opportunities

(Reading: Comprehension continued)

SKILLS AND STRATEGIES	K	1	2	3	4	5	6
Recall story details	✓						
Use illustrations	✓	✓					
Distinguish reality and fantasy	✓	✓	✓				
Classify and categorize	✓						
Make predictions	✓	✓	✓	✓	✓	✓	✓
Recognize sequence of events (tell or act out)	✓	✓	✓	✓	✓	✓	✓
Recognize cause and effect		✓	✓	✓	✓	✓	✓
Compare and contrast	✓	✓	✓	✓	✓	✓	✓
Summarize	✓	✓	✓	✓	✓	✓	✓
Make and explain inferences		✓	✓	✓	✓	✓	✓
Draw conclusions		✓	✓	✓	✓	✓	✓
Distinguish important and unimportant information				✓	✓	✓	✓
Recognize main idea and supporting details	✓	✓	✓	✓	✓	✓	✓
Form conclusions or generalizations and support with evidence from text			✓	✓	✓	✓	✓
Distinguish fact and opinion (including news stories and advertisements)				✓	✓	✓	✓
Recognize problem and solution			✓	✓	✓	✓	✓
Recognize steps in a process		✓	✓	✓	✓	✓	✓
Make judgments and decisions				✓	✓	✓	✓
Distinguish fact and nonfact				✓	✓	✓	✓
Recognize techniques of persuasion and propaganda							✓
Evaluate evidence and sources of information							✓
Identify similarities and differences across texts (including topics, characters, problems, themes, treatment, scope, or organization)							
Practice various questions and tasks (test-like comprehension questions)							
Paraphrase and summarize to recall, inform, and organize							
Answer various types of questions (open-ended, literal, interpretative, test-like such as true-false, multiple choice, short-answer)							
Use study strategies to learn and recall (preview, question, reread, and record)							
LITERARY RESPONSE							
Listen to stories being read aloud							
React, speculate, join in, read along when predictable and patterned selections are read aloud							
Respond through talk, movement, music, art, drama, and writing to a variety of stories and poems							
Show understanding through writing, illustrating, developing demonstrations, and using technology							
Connect ideas and themes across texts							
Support responses by referring to relevant aspects of text and own experiences							
Offer observations, make connections, speculate, interpret, and raise questions in response to texts							
Interpret text ideas through journal writing, discussion, enactment, and media							
TEXT STRUCTURE/LITERARY CONCEPTS							
Distinguish forms of texts and the functions they serve (lists, newsletters, signs)							
Understand story structure							
Identify narrative (for entertainment) and expository (for information)							
Distinguish fiction from nonfiction, including fact and fantasy							
Understand literary forms (stories, poems, plays, and informational books)							
Understand literary terms by distinguishing between roles of author and illustrator							
Understand title, author, and illustrator across a variety of texts							
Analyze character, character's point of view, plot, setting, style, tone, mood		✓	✓	✓	✓	✓	✓
Compare communication in different forms							
Understand terms such as *title, author, illustrator, playwright, theater, stage, act, dialogue,* and *scene*							
Recognize stories, poems, myths, folktales, fables, tall tales, limericks, plays, biographies, and autobiographies							
Judge internal logic of story text							
Recognize that authors organize information in specific ways							
Identify texts to inform, influence, express, or entertain							
Describe how author's point of view affects text				✓	✓	✓	✓
Recognize biography, historical fiction, realistic fiction, modern fantasy, informational texts, and poetry							
Analyze ways authors present ideas (cause/effect, compare/contrast, inductively, deductively, chronologically)							
Recognize flashback, foreshadowing, symbolism							

(continued on next page)

☑ Tested Skill

Tinted panels show skills, strategies, and other teaching opportunities

(Reading: Comprehension continued)

VARIETY OF TEXT	K	1	2	3	4	5	6
Read a variety of genres							
Use informational texts to acquire information							
Read for a variety of purposes							
Select varied sources when reading for information or pleasure							
FLUENCY							
Read regularly in independent-level and instructional-level materials							
Read orally with fluency from familiar texts							
Self-select independent-level reading							
Read silently for increasing periods of time							
Demonstrate characteristics of fluent and effective reading							
Adjust reading rate to purpose							
Read aloud in selected texts, showing understanding of text and engaging the listener							
CULTURES							
Connect own experience with culture of others							
Compare experiences of characters across cultures							
Articulate and discuss themes and connections that cross cultures							
CRITICAL THINKING							
Experiences (comprehend, apply, analyze, synthesize, evaluate)							
Make connections (comprehend, apply, analyze, synthesize, evaluate)							
Expression (comprehend, apply, analyze, synthesize, evaluate)							
Inquiry (comprehend, apply, analyze, synthesize, evaluate)							
Problem solving (comprehend, apply, analyze, synthesize, evaluate)							
Making decisions (comprehend, apply, analyze, synthesize, evaluate)							

Study Skills

INQUIRY/RESEARCH	K	1	2	3	4	5	6
Follow directions							
Use alphabetical order							
Identify/frame questions for research							
Obtain, organize, and summarize information: classify, take notes, outline							
Evaluate research and raise new questions							
Use technology to present information in various formats							
Follow accepted formats for writing research, including documenting sources							
Use test-taking strategies							
Use text organizers (book cover; title page—title, author, illustrator; contents; headings; glossary; index)		☑	☑	☑	☑	☑	☑
Use graphic aids, including maps, diagrams, charts, graphs		☑	☑	☑	☑	☑	☑
Read and interpret varied texts including environmental print, signs, lists, encyclopedia, dictionary, glossary, newspaper, advertisement, magazine, calendar, directions, floor plans		☑	☑	☑	☑	☑	☑
Use reference sources, such as glossary, dictionary, encyclopedia, telephone directory, technology resources		☑	☑	☑	☑	☑	☑
Recognize Library/Media center resources, such as computerized references; catalog search—subject, author, title; encyclopedia index		☑	☑	☑	☑	☑	☑

Writing

☑ Tested Skill

Tinted panels show skills, strategies, and other teaching opportunities

MODES AND FORMS	K	1	2	3	4	5	6
Interactive writing							
Personal narrative (Expressive narrative)			✓	✓	✓	✓	✓
Writing that compares (Informative classificatory)			✓	✓	✓	✓	✓
Explanatory writing (Informative narrative)		✓	✓	✓	✓	✓	✓
Persuasive writing (Persuasive descriptive)			✓	✓	✓	✓	✓
Writing a story		✓	✓	✓	✓	✓	✓
Expository writing		✓	✓	✓	✓	✓	✓
Write using a variety of formats, such as advertisement, autobiography, biography, book report/report, comparison-contrast, critique/review/editorial, description, essay, how-to, interview, invitation, journal/log/notes, message/list, paragraph/multi-paragraph composition, picture book, play (scene), poem/rhyme, story, summary, note, letter							
PURPOSES/AUDIENCES							
Dictate messages such as news and stories for others to write							
Write labels, notes, and captions for illustrations, possessions, charts, and centers							
Write to record, to discover and develop ideas, to inform, to influence, to entertain							
Exhibit an identifiable voice in personal narratives and stories							
Use literary devices (suspense, dialogue, and figurative language)							
Produce written texts by organizing ideas, using effective transitions, and choosing precise wording							
PROCESSES							
Generate ideas for self-selected and assigned topics using prewriting strategies							
Develop drafts							
Revise drafts for varied purposes, elaborate ideas							
Edit for appropriate grammar, spelling, punctuation, and features of polished writings							
Proofread own writing and that of others							
Bring pieces to final form and "publish" them for audiences							
Use technology to compose text							
Select and use reference materials and resources for writing, revising, and editing final drafts							
SPELLING							
Spell own name and write high-frequency words							
Words with short vowels (including CVC and one-syllable words with blends CCVC, CVCC, CCVCC)							
Words with long vowels (including CVCe)							
Words with digraphs, blends, consonant clusters, double consonants							
Words with diphthongs							
Words with variant vowels							
Words with r-controlled vowels							
Words with /ər/, /əl/, and /ən/							
Words with silent letters							
Words with soft *c* and soft *g*							
Inflectional endings (including plurals and past tense and words that drop the final *e* when adding *-ing, -ed*)							
Compound words							
Contractions							
Homonyms							
Suffixes including *-able, -ly,* or *-less,* and prefixes including *dis-, re-, pre-,* or *un-*							
Spell words ending in *-tion* and *-sion*, such as *station* and *procession*							
Accurate spelling of root or base words							
Orthographic patterns and rules such as *keep/can; sack/book; out/now; oil/toy; match/speech; ledge/cage;* consonant doubling, dropping *e,* changing *y* to *i*							
Multisyllabic words using regularly spelled phonogram patterns							
Syllable patterns (including closed, open, syllable boundary patterns)							
Synonyms and antonyms							
Words from Social Studies, Science, Math, and Physical Education							
Words derived from other languages and cultures							
Use resources to find correct spellings, synonyms, and replacement words							
Use conventional spelling of familiar words in writing assignments							
Spell accurately in final drafts							

(continued on next page)

☑ Tested Skill

Tinted panels show skills, strategies, and other teaching opportunities

(Writing continued)

GRAMMAR AND USAGE	K	1	2	3	4	5	6
Understand sentence concepts (word order, statements, questions, exclamations, commands)							
Recognize complete and incomplete sentences							
Nouns (common; proper; singular; plural; irregular plural; possessives)							
Verbs (action; helping; linking; irregular)							
Verb tense (present, past, future, perfect, and progressive)							
Pronouns (possessive, subject and object, pronoun-verb agreement)							
Use objective case pronouns accurately							
Adjectives							
Adverbs that tell how, when, where							
Subjects, predicates							
Subject-verb agreement							
Sentence combining							
Recognize sentence structure (simple, compound, complex)							
Synonyms and antonyms							
Contractions							
Conjunctions							
Prepositions and prepositional phrases							
PENMANSHIP							
Write each letter of alphabet (capital and lowercase) using correct formation, appropriate size and spacing							
Write own name and other important words							
Use phonological knowledge to map sounds to letters to write messages							
Write messages that move left to right, top to bottom							
Gain increasing control of penmanship, pencil grip, paper position, beginning stroke							
Use word and letter spacing and margins to make messages readable							
Write legibly by selecting cursive or manuscript as appropriate							
MECHANICS							
Use capitalization in sentences, proper nouns, titles, abbreviations and the pronoun *I*							
Use end marks correctly (period, question mark, exclamation point)							
Use commas (in dates, in addresses, in a series, in letters, in direct address)							
Use apostrophes in contractions and possessives							
Use quotation marks							
Use hyphens, semicolons, colons							
EVALUATION							
Identify the most effective features of a piece of writing using class/teacher generated criteria							
Respond constructively to others' writing							
Determine how his/her own writing achieves its purpose							
Use published pieces as models for writing							
Review own written work to monitor growth as writer							

For more detailed scope and sequence including page numbers and additional phonics information, see McGraw-Hill Reading Program scope and sequence (K-6)

Index

Scoring Chart

The Scoring Chart is provided for your convenience in grading your students' work.

- Find the column that shows the total number of items.
- Find the row that matches the number of items answered correctly.
- The intersection of the two rows provides the percentage score.

TOTAL NUMBER OF ITEMS

NUMBER CORRECT	1	2	3	4	5	6	7	8	9	10	11	12	13	14	15	16	17	18	19	20	21	22	23	24	25	26	27	28	29	30
1	100	50	33	25	20	17	14	13	11	10	9	8	8	7	7	6	6	6	5	5	5	5	4	4	4	4	4	4	3	3
2		100	66	50	40	33	29	25	22	20	18	17	15	14	13	13	12	11	11	10	10	9	9	8	8	8	7	7	7	7
3			100	75	60	50	43	38	33	30	27	25	23	21	20	19	18	17	16	15	14	14	13	13	12	12	11	11	10	10
4				100	80	67	57	50	44	40	36	33	31	29	27	25	24	22	21	20	19	18	17	17	16	15	15	14	14	13
5					100	83	71	63	56	50	45	42	38	36	33	31	29	28	26	25	24	23	22	21	20	19	19	18	17	17
6						100	86	75	67	60	55	50	46	43	40	38	35	33	32	30	29	27	26	25	24	23	22	21	21	20
7							100	88	78	70	64	58	54	50	47	44	41	39	37	35	33	32	30	29	28	27	26	25	24	23
8								100	89	80	73	67	62	57	53	50	47	44	42	40	38	36	35	33	32	31	30	29	28	27
9									100	90	82	75	69	64	60	56	53	50	47	45	43	41	39	38	36	35	33	32	31	30
10										100	91	83	77	71	67	63	59	56	53	50	48	45	43	42	40	38	37	36	34	33
11											100	92	85	79	73	69	65	61	58	55	52	50	48	46	44	42	41	39	38	37
12												100	92	86	80	75	71	67	63	60	57	55	52	50	48	46	44	43	41	40
13													100	93	87	81	76	72	68	65	62	59	57	54	52	50	48	46	45	43
14														100	93	88	82	78	74	70	67	64	61	58	56	54	52	50	48	47
15															100	94	88	83	79	75	71	68	65	63	60	58	56	54	52	50
16																100	94	89	84	80	76	73	70	67	64	62	59	57	55	53
17																	100	94	89	85	81	77	74	71	68	65	63	61	59	57
18																		100	95	90	86	82	78	75	72	69	67	64	62	60
19																			100	95	90	86	83	79	76	73	70	68	66	63
20																				100	95	91	87	83	80	77	74	71	69	67
21																					100	95	91	88	84	81	78	75	72	70
22																						100	96	92	88	85	81	79	76	73
23																							100	96	92	88	85	82	79	77
24																								100	96	92	89	86	83	80
25																									100	96	93	89	86	83
26																										100	96	93	90	87
27																											100	96	93	90
28																												100	97	93
29																													100	97
30																														100

Persuasive Writing: Writing a Speech

Scoring Rubric: 6-Trait Writing

6. Exceptional	5. Excellent	4. Good	3. Fair	2. Poor	1. Unsatisfactory
• **Ideas & Content** crafts a strong persuasive argument that could affect a reader's opinion; thoughtful details sharpen the argument. • **Organization** thoughtfully-planned strategy moves a reader easily through clear stages of the argument; may have a pertinent conclusion. • **Voice** shows originality and deep involvement with the topic; matches an engaging personal style to the persuasive purpose. • **Word Choice** makes resourceful use of figurative and everyday language; sophisticated vocabulary conveys a forceful opinion. • **Sentence Fluency** crafts complex, effective sentences that flow naturally; writing is easy to follow and read aloud; fragments or other devices, if used, strengthen and add interest to the argument. • **Conventions** is skilled in a wide range of writing conventions; proper use of the rules of English enhances clarity, meaning, and style; editing is largely unnecessary.	• **Ideas & Content** crafts a cohesive, carefully-detailed argument that might affect a reader's opinion; makes some fresh observations. • **Organization** presents a well-planned strategy, in a sequence that helps the reader follow the argument's logic; may draw a conclusion. • **Voice** shows originality and strong involvement with the topic; matches a personal style to the task of persuading an audience. • **Word Choice** makes original use of accurate, specific language; experiments with new words, or uses everyday words in a new way; message is clear and interesting. • **Sentence Fluency** crafts well-paced simple and complex sentences that flow naturally; has a variety of lengths, beginnings, and patterns that fit together. • **Conventions** shows skills in a wide range of writing conventions; proper use of the rules of English enhances clarity, meaning, and style; editing is largely unnecessary.	• **Ideas & Content** presents a solid, clear argument, with details that help the reader understand the main idea. • **Organization** presents facts and ideas in a logical sequence; has a clear beginning and ending; reader can follow the writer's logic. • **Voice** attempts to convey an authentic personal touch to the reader; shows involvement with the topic; message matches the purpose and audience. • **Word Choice** uses a variety of words that fit the argument; experiments with some new words, or makes fresh use of everyday day words. • **Sentence Fluency** careful, easy-to-follow sentences vary in length, beginnings, and patterns; uses simple and complex constructions, with stronger control of simple sentences. • **Conventions** may make some errors in spelling, capitalization, punctuation or usage, but these do not interfere with understanding the text; some editing is needed.	• **Ideas & Content** attempts to argue a position; may include ideas or details which are not clear, or do not fit the topic. • **Organization** attempts to argue a position, but the logic is sometimes hard to follow; has a basic structure, but ideas, sentences, and paragraphs may need to be more connected. • **Voice** may not show involvement with the topic; opinion comes across, but may not be clearly connected to the purpose and audience, or show who is behind the writing. • **Word Choice** states the main argument in an ordinary way; may attempt to use a variety of words, but some do not fit; may overuse some words/expressions. • **Sentence Fluency** most sentences are readable, but may be limited in lengths and patterns; some rereading may be necessary to follow the meaning; some sentences may be choppy or overlong. • **Conventions** has basic control of conventions, but makes enough errors to interfere with a reading the text; significant editing is needed.	• **Ideas & Content** has little control of task of persuading, or seems unsure of the topic; ideas are vague; details are few, repeated, or inaccurate. • **Organization** has no clear structure; the order of ideas is hard to follow; few connections are made between facts and ideas; details don't fit where they are placed. • **Voice** is not involved in sharing ideas or opinions with a reader; writing may be lifeless, with no sense of who is behind the words. • **Word Choice** does not choose forceful words to convey an opinion; some words are overused , or may detract from the meaning or impact of the text. • **Sentence Fluency** sentences may be choppy or awkward; patterns are similar or monotonous; text may be hard to follow or read aloud. • **Conventions** makes frequent errors in spelling, word choice, punctuation and usage; sentence structures may be confused; paper is difficult to read, and requires extensive revision and editing.	• **Ideas & Content** does not state an opinion; writer is unsure of what s/he wants to say. • **Organization** has an extreme lack of organization; ideas and details are disconnected; details, if presented, are irrelevant or vague. • **Voice** does not address an audience at all; does not have a sense of sharing a personal message or style. • **Word Choice** uses words that do not fit, or are vague and confusing; no new words are attempted. • **Sentence Fluency** uses incomplete, rambling, or confusing sentences that make the text hard to follow and read aloud. • **Conventions** makes severe errors in most conventions; spelling errors may make it hard to guess what words are meant; some parts of the text may be impossible to follow or understand.

0: This piece is either blank, or fails to respond to the writing task. The topic is not addressed, or the student simply paraphrases the prompt. The response may be illegible or incoherent.

Persuasive Writing: Writing a Speech

8-Point Writing Rubric

8	7	6	5	4	3	2	1
The writer • has presented an unusually well-organized, insightful, and convincing argument for a specific position. • adeptly uses different forms of research to bolster the argument with interesting facts and details. • has used varied transitions to create a fluid structure for the argument. • demonstrates an exceptional grasp of persuasive language. • uses numerous details from personal experience to strengthen the persuasive position. • has offered an argument that is likely to change the mind of the listener. • demonstrates a strong sense of audience and purpose.	The writer • has presented a highly-convincing argument for a specific position. • uses many well-researched facts and thoughtful comments to elaborate on the main position. • uses many transition words to lead the reader from point to point. • employs some strong examples from personal experience to build a position. • demonstrates an excellent grasp of persuasive language. • offers an argument that could convince readers to change their minds on an issue. • shows a persistent awareness of audience and purpose.	The writer • has presented a convincing argument for a clearly-stated position. • uses interesting research to elaborate upon each idea in logical sequence, with a good use of transition words. • shows a capable overall structure, and good understanding of persuasive language. • has offered an argument that has the potential to change a reader's mind. • shows a good awareness of audience and purpose.	The writer • has presented a solid argument for a stated position. • has elaborated sufficiently on most points, using some facts from research. • shows an overall grasp of persuasive language. • exhibits minor organizational difficulties that do not distract from overall understanding. • demonstrates an awareness of audience and purpose.	The writer • has presented a somewhat convincing argument for a position. • states, but does not adequately explain, a position. • has elaborated on some points with basic facts from limited research. • uses some persuasive language. • may exhibit organizational difficulties that occasionally distract from readability. • sometimes demonstrates an awareness of audience.	The writer • has presented a minimally-successful argument for a position. • may not have sufficiently elaborated upon important points, and uses sketchy facts. • demonstrates limited control of persuasive language and writing conventions. • may lose the focus of an idea after stating an initial position, or may include digressions serious enough to impair readability. • demonstrates a vague sense of audience and purpose.	The writer • has made a disorganized, unclear attempt at arguing a poorly-stated position. • offers few supporting facts and details. • uses few examples of persuasive language. • exhibits problems connecting ideas meaningfully. • incorrectly uses or inconsistently applies writing conventions. • does not demonstrate a sense of audience awareness or purpose.	The writer • does not develop a clearly-stated position on an issue. • has not used supporting facts or details to elaborate an argument. • has not used persuasive language. • exhibits difficulties with language and organization that severely distract from understanding. • has not demonstrated a grasp of the criteria that comprise a persuasive argument.

0: This piece is either blank, or fails to respond to the writing task. The topic is not addressed, or the student simply paraphrases the prompt. The response may be illegible or incoherent.

Notes

Notes

Notes

Notes

Notes

Notes